A Companion to
Philosophy of Religion

Blackwell Companions to Philosophy

This outstanding student reference series offers a comprehensive and authoritative survey of philosophy as a whole. Written by today's leading philosophers, each volume provides lucid and engaging coverage of the key figures, terms, topics and problems of the field. Taken together, the volumes provide the ideal basis for course use, representing an unparalleled work of reference for students and specialists alike.

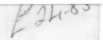

▣ BLACKWELL
Publishers

Copyright © Blackwell Publishers Ltd 1997, 1999

First published 1997

First published in paperback 1999

Reprinted 2000

Blackwell Publishers Inc
350 Main Street
Malden, Massachusetts 02148, USA

Blackwell Publishers Ltd
108 Cowley Road
Oxford OX4 1JF, UK

Library of Congress Cataloging in Publication Data has been applied for
ISBN 0–631–19153–4 (hbk) — ISBN 0–631–21328–7 (pbk)

British Library Cataloguing in Publication Data
A CIP catalogue record for this book is available from the British Library

Typeset in 10 ½ on 12 ½ pt Photina
by Wearset, Boldon, Tyne and Wear
Printed and bound in Great Britain
by T. J. International Limited, Padstow, Cornwall

This book is printed on acid-free paper

Contents

PART II: PHILOSOPHICAL THEOLOGY AND PHILOSOPHY OF RELIGION IN WESTERN HISTORY

PART III: SOME CURRENTS IN TWENTIETH CENTURY PHILOSOPHY OF RELIGION

PART IV: THEISM AND THE LINGUISTIC TURN

PART V: THE THEISTIC CONCEPTION OF GOD

PART VI: THE JUSTIFICATION OF THEISTIC BELIEF

PART VII: CHALLENGES TO THE RATIONALITY OF THEISTIC BELIEF

PART VIII: THEISM AND MODERN SCIENCE

PART IX: THEISM AND VALUES

PART X: PHILOSOPHICAL REFLECTION ON CHRISTIAN FAITH

PART XI: NEW DIRECTIONS IN PHILOSOPHY OF RELIGION

Acknowledgments

We are grateful to Dorothy Bolton at St Olaf College and the Arts and Letters Steno Pool at the University of Notre Dame for secretarial assistance. We are also grateful to Stephan Chambers and Steve Smith at Blackwell Publishers who encouraged us to undertake the project of editing this volume and supported us from the beginning. We owe special thanks to Pandora Kerr Frost and Valery Rose for doing an outstanding job of copy-editing.

Philip L. Quinn
Charles Taliaferro

List of Contributors

William J. Abraham, Albert Cook Outler Professor of Wesley Studies, Perkins School of Theology, Southern Methodist University, Dallas, Texas.

Robert Audi, Professor of Philosophy, University of Nebraska, Lincoln, Nebraska.

The Revd Canon David Brown, Van Mildert Professor of Divinity, University of Durham, Durham, UK.

David Burrell, CSC, Hesburgh Professor of Philosophy and Theology, University of Notre Dame, Indiana.

James F. Childress, Kyle Professor of Religious Studies and Professor of Medical Education, University of Virginia, Charlottesville, Virginia.

Sarah Coakley, Edward Mallinckrodt, Jr Professor of Divinity, Divinity School, Harvard University, Cambridge, Massachusetts.

Gary L. Comstock, Associate Professor of Religious Studies, Iowa State University, Ames, Iowa.

William Craig, Visiting Scholar, Brussels University, Belgium.

Richard E. Creel, Professor of Philosphy and Religion, Ithaca College, New York.

Stephen T. Davis, Professor of Philosophy, Claremont McKenna College, California.

Clement Dore, Professor Emeritus of Philosophy, Vanderbilt University, Nashville, Tennessee.

Aziz A. Esmail, Dean of the Institute of Ismaili Studies, London.

C. Stephen Evans, Professor of Philosophy, Calvin College, Grand Rapids, Michigan.

Ronald J. Feenstra, Heritage Professor of Systematic and Philosophical Theology, Calvin Theological Seminary, Grand Rapids, Michigan.

Frederick Ferré, Research Professor of Philosophy, University of Georgia, Athens, Georgia.

Kevin L. Flannery, SJ, Professore Straordinario, Pontificia Universitas Gregoriana, Rome.

Antony Flew, Professor Emeritus of Philosophy, University of Reading, Berks, UK.

Thomas P. Flint, Associate Professor of Philosophy, University of Notre Dame, Indiana.

Nancy Frankenberry, Stone Professor of Intellectual and Moral Philosophy, Dartmouth College, Hanover, New Hampshire.

Laura L. Garcia, Adjunct Professor of Philosophy, Rutgers University, New Jersey.

Robert P. George, Associate Professor of Politics, Princeton University, New Jersey.

Robert Gibbs, Associate Professor of Religion, Princeton University, New Jersey.

Lenn E. Goodman, Professor of Philosophy, University of Hawaii, Honolulu, Hawaii.

David Ray Griffin, Professor of Philosophy of Religion and Theology, School of Theology at Claremont, and Claremont Graduate School, California.

Paul J. Griffiths, Associate Professor of the Philosophy of Religions, Divinity School, University of Chicago, Illinois.

Chad Hansen, Professor of Philosophy, University of Hong Kong, Victoria, Hong Kong.

John E. Hare, Professor of Philosophy, Calvin College, Grand Rapids, Michigan.

William Hasker, Professor of Philosophy, Huntington College, Huntington, Indiana.

The Revd Canon Brian Hebblethwaite, Lecturer in Divinity, Queens' College, University of Cambridge, UK.

Paul Helm, Professor of the History and Philosophy of Religion, King's College, University of London, UK.

John Hick, Danforth Professor Emeritus of the Philosophy of Religion, Clairmont Graduate School, California, and Fellow of the Institute for Advanced Research in the Humanities, University of Birmingham, UK.

Joshua Hoffman, Professor of Philosophy, University of North Carolina at Greensboro, North Carolina.

John Hyman, Fellow of Queen's College, University of Oxford, UK.

Janine Marie Idziak, Professor of Philosophy, Loras College, Dubuque, Iowa.

Jeffrey Jordan, Assistant Professor of Philosophy, University of Delaware, Newark, Delaware.

Jonathan L. Kvanvig, Professor of Philosophy, Texas A & M University, College Station, Texas.

Edward Langerak, Professor of Philosophy, St Olaf College, Minnesota.

Brian Leftow, Associate Professor of Philosophy, Fordham University, New York.

Hugh J. McCann, Professor of Philosophy, Texas A & M University, College Station, Texas.

Scott MacDonald, Professor of Philosophy, Cornell University, New York.

Ralph McInerny, Michael P. Grace Professor of Philosophy, University of Notre Dame, Indiana.

William E. Mann, Professor of Philosophy, University of Vermont, Burlington, Vermont.

Michael Martin, Professor of Philosophy, Boston University, Massachusetts.

George I. Mavrodes, Professor Emeritus of Philosophy, University of Michigan, Ann Arbor, Michigan.

Basil Mitchell, Nolloth Professor Emeritus of Philosophy of the Christian Religion, Oriel College, University of Oxford, UK.

Azim A. Nanji, Professor of Religion, University of Florida, Gainesville, Florida.

Kai Nielsen, Professor Emeritus of Philosophy, University of Calgary, Calgary, Alberta.

Gene Outka, Dwight Professor of Philosophy and Christian Ethics, Yale University, New Haven, Connecticut.

Terence Penelhum, Professor Emeritus of Religious Studies, University of Calgary, Calgary, Alberta.

Derk Pereboom, Associate Professor of Philosophy, University of Vermont, Burlington, Vermont.

Michael L. Peterson, Professor of Philosophy, Asbury College, Wilmore, Kentucky.

Alvin Plantinga, John A. O'Brien Professor of Philosophy, University of Notre Dame, Indiana.

Jean Porter, Professor of Moral Theology, University of Notre Dame, Indiana.

Philip L. Quinn, John A. O'Brien Professor of Philosophy, University of Notre Dame, Indiana.

Robert C. Roberts, Professor of Philosophy and Psychological Studies, Wheaton College, Wheaton, Illinois.

Gary Rosenkrantz, Professor of Philosophy, University of North Carolina at Greensboro, North Carolina.

William L. Rowe, Professor of Philosophy, Purdue University, West Lafayette, Indiana.

Tamar Rudavsky, Associate Professor of Philosophy, and Jewish Studies, Ohio State University, Columbas, Ohio.

Patricia A. Sayre, Assistant Professor of Philosophy, Saint Mary's College, Notre Dame, Indiana.

George N. Schlesinger, Professor of Philosophy, University of North Carolina, Chapel Hill, North Carolina.

Patrick Sherry, Lancaster University, Lancaster, UK.

Ninian Smart, J. F. Rowny Professor of Comparative Religion, University of California at Santa Barbara, California.

Janet Soskice, University Lecturer and Fellow of Jesus College, University of Cambridge, Cambridge, UK.

Eleonore Stump, Robert J. Henle Professor of Philosophy, Saint Louis University, St Louis, Missouri.

Charles Taliaferro, Associate Professor of Philosophy, St Olaf College, Minnesota.

Thomas F. Tracy, Professor of Religion, Bates College, Lewiston, Massachusetts.

Roger Trigg, Professor of Philosophy, University of Warwick, Warwick, UK.

Paul Valliere, McGregor Professor in the Humanities, Butler University, Indiana.

William J. Wainwright, Professor of Philosophy, University of Wisconsin at Milwaukee, Wisconsin.

Paul J. Weithman, Assistant Professor of Philosophy, University of Notre Dame, Indiana.

Merold Westphal, Professor of Philosophy, Fordham University, New York.

Edward R. Wierenga, Professor of Religion, University of Rochester, New York.

C.J.F. Williams, Professor of Philosophy, University of Bristol, Bristol, UK.

Kwasi Wiredu, Professor of Philosophy, University of South Florida, Tampa, Florida.

Nicholas Wolterstorff, Noah Porter Professor of Philosophical Theology, Divinity School, Yale University, New Haven, Connecticut.

Keith E. Yandell, Professor of Philosophy and South Asian Studies, University of Wisconsin at Madison, Wisconsin.

Linda Zagzebski, Professor of Philosophy, Loyola Marymount University, Los Angeles, California.

Introduction

This *Companion* is a guide to philosophy of religion for nonspecialists, but it will also engage specialists. It aims to provide the reader with a fairly detailed map of the territory covered by philosophical thought about religion in the English-speaking world. All philosophical thought is shaped by its cultural context. The volume therefore begins with three parts that discuss the main contexts in which English-speaking philosophers do their thinking about religion.

The religions of the world are irreducibly diverse and likely to remain so. Part I surveys the plurality of philosophical issues to which this religious diversity gives rise. Much philosophical thought about religion in the English-speaking world focuses on problems specific to theism or distinctive of Christianity. However, it would be extremely parochial to suppose that these are the only problems of philosophical interest generated by religion. As cultural contacts among religions increase, philosophical thought about religion is acquiring a growing awareness of and sensitivity to both similarities and differences among the ways in which diverse religious traditions raise issues for philosophers to ponder.

The philosophy of religion of the English-speaking world is the product of a long history of Western philosophical thought. Part II retraces some of the historical developments in philosophy that led up to the emergence of modern philosophy of religion. This history displays both continuities and discontinuities. Throughout it, some philosophical thought about religion has taken the form of philosophical theology, which is the attempt to reflect philosophically within a theistic perspective and is often described as faith seeking understanding. From the Enlightenment on, however, philosophy of religion increasingly took the form of philosophical reflection on religion as a cultural phenomenon from an external and sometimes highly critical point of view.

In the twentieth century, philosophy of religion in the English-speaking world has been carried on in many different religious traditions and philosophical movements. Part III covers some of them. Philosophy of religion has been no exception to the general trend toward greater pluralism in philosophy. Rival traditions and movements in philosophy of religion have produced a rich array of approaches to the philosophical study of religion and of claims, sometimes complementary but often clashing, about religion.

In short, the first three parts of the volume make it clear that philosophy of religion in the English-speaking world is practiced under conditions that have been shaped by the history of Western philosophy and in circumstances in which both

1

religious diversity and philosophical pluralism are important factors. What do philosophers of religion actually accomplish under such conditions and in such circumstances? The remainder of the volume is devoted to answering this question.

One thing philosophers of religion do is discuss language. It is often said that the linguistic turn has been the single most important development in twentieth century philosophy. The rise to prominence in the English-speaking world of philosophy of language was accompanied by a great increase of interest in religious language on the part of philosophers of religion. In the 1950s and 1960s a controversy over whether theistic language was cognitively meaningful occupied center stage in philosophy of religion. Although discussions of theistic language are no longer dominant to the extent they once were, work on religious language continues to play an important role in the field. Part IV surveys some of the issues that arise in such work.

Philosophers of religion also reflect upon the theistic concept of God. They ask: what sort of being is God supposed to be? Attempts to answer this question frequently take the form of specifying a list of divine attributes, that is, properties theists have traditionally wanted to attribute to God. But puzzles arise almost as soon as one begins to think seriously about the traditional divine attributes. Can God make a stone so heavy that even God cannot lift it? Whichever way this question is answered, it seems that there is at least one thing that God cannot do. What sense, then, can be made of the claim that God is almighty or omnipotent? Philosophers of religion typically respond to such puzzles by proposing analyses of the concepts of divine attributes in terms of which the puzzles can be solved and the attributes can be seen to be internally coherent and mutually compatible. To the extent that such efforts succeed progress is made toward a consistent theistic conception of God. There has been much work along these lines recently. It is particularly noteworthy for the way in which philosophers of religion have made fruitful use of work in other areas of philosophy such as metaphysics, ethics, philosophy of mind and action theory to address problems in their own area. Part V contains discussions of the chief divine attributes on which attention has been focused in recent years.

Of course theists would not be content to know merely that a consistent conception of God exists. They also want to know whether such a conception applies to anything, whether the God whom they believe to exist actually does exist. Thus questions in religious epistemology naturally arise. Is theistic belief justified? Is it rational to believe that God exists? Part VI is devoted to considerations that have been taken to provide evidential support for theistic belief; they include arguments for the existence of God or for the rationality of belief in God, miracles and religious experience. It also discusses views according to which theistic belief does not need evidential support from such considerations.

If one is to arrive at a fair assessment of the epistemic status of theistic belief, both the considerations that count against it and those that count for it must be taken into account. So Part VII gives the case against the rationality of theistic belief its day in court.

As they have traditionally been understood, the theistic religions make claims about the way the world is, and such claims can apparently conflict with the claims of modern science. Cases of such conflict are to be found in the condemnation of Galileo's views by the Roman Catholic Church and the rejection of Darwin's views by some theists who hold that evolution is inconsistent with the biblical story of creation. Such conflicts have sometimes been described as episodes in the warfare of science with religion. Even if this description is somewhat exaggerated, there seems to be a certain amount of tension between some of the claims made on behalf of the world view of modern science and some varieties of theism. Hence it is not surprising that philosophers wonder whether traditional theistic belief can be reconciled with, or even derive some support from, the results of the scientific investigation of nature. Part VIII explores this issue. It also addresses the question of how theists should respond to the vast powers that have been placed in human hands by the technologies derived from modern science.

The theistic religions are not, however, merely bodies of doctrine, even though they do contain doctrines. They are also ways of life. They make claims about the nature of human flourishing and the ethical norms that should guide the conduct of life. They propose distinctively religious ethical theories and have implications for applied ethics and politics. Part IX provides an overview of theistic perspectives on several important topics involving human values.

Although problems that arise from generic theistic belief are often at the center of philosophical discussion, generic theism is not a living religion. Each of the major monotheisms – Judaism, Christianity, and Islam – has traditions and doctrines that the other two do not share. Christians alone, for example, believe that the one God consists of three distinct divine persons and that one of them, God the Son, became incarnate as the man, Jesus of Nazareth, who was therefore both fully human and fully divine. These doctrines are sources of much philosophical perplexity. One of the most dramatic developments in philosophy of religion since the 1970s has been the attention devoted to such doctrines in the work of Christian philosophers and others. Part X presents the results of recent work on distinctively Christian doctrines.

Philosophy of religion is not static. It will no doubt change in unpredictable ways in the coming years, but some promising new directions for growth can be identified without much difficulty. Part XI explores three of them. Feminism, religious pluralism, and comparative philosophy of religion offer strong prospects for new philosophical insights into religion and are also likely to spark the sort of controversy that is the lifeblood of philosophy.

To return to the cartographic metaphor, the many distinguished contributors to this volume have collectively drawn a better map of the territory of philosophy of religion in the English-speaking world than any single philosopher could produce on his or her own. But the map is not the country. We hope that reading the map will stimulate in many readers a desire to explore the country. The bibliographies appended to the articles should help such readers to get started. We have provided a brief discussion of resources for further study to give them additional help.

PHILIP L. QUINN
CHARLES TALIAFERRO

PART I

PHILOSOPHICAL ISSUES IN THE RELIGIONS OF THE WORLD

1

Hinduism

NINIAN SMART

The Hindu tradition is important for the philosophy of religion from a number of angles. First, there is the intrinsic interest of a non-Western tradition, given that the philosophy of religion is often treated in such a Western way. I shall therefore begin with a general introduction to the intellectual history of Hinduism. Second, there are interesting notions of God as refracted through so many gods and goddesses in Hindu mythology, ritual, and piety. Third, there are various notions such as karma and reincarnation, and concepts of the self, which differ from Western ones, together with the difference in epistemology, which can create interesting and fruitful areas of discussion. Fourth, there are debates with other schools, mainly the Buddhists, which are suggestive for Western scholars. Fifth, the modern Hindu philosophical revival, especially through Vivekananda and Radhakrishnan, and in its claim that all religions point to the same goal, meets with certain recent philosophers of religion, notably John Hick.

First, then, a brief history and description of the Hindu tradition. Hinduism is so to speak a tradition (or collection of them) by induction. It does not, like Islam, emanate from a single source, the Qur'an (see Article 7, ISLAM). Though it has admittedly ancient roots, such as the Indus Valley civilization, the Vedic hymns, ancient tribal myths, and so forth, it was only about the third century CE that it came together into anything like the shape which we identify as Hindu. For example there are key ideas and sources, and institutions, which come together thus relatively late: belief in reincarnation, karma, the great epics (the *Mahabharata* and the *Ramayana*), the vast expanse of the cosmos and its periodic sleep and recovery, devotion to such great gods as Siva and Vishnu, the emerging class and caste system, the aphoristic summaries or *sutras* relating to the beginnings of philosophical schools, temple worship, statues incarnating the gods, the worship of the Goddess, gurus, yoga, austerity, the practice of pilgrimage, sacred cows, the dominance of brahmins, and so on. This wonderful amalgam came to characterize Hinduism as a loosely knit system – mainly by contrast with contemporary Buddhism (see Article 2, BUDDHISM). From the eleventh century onwards the contrast was chiefly with Islam, with its relatively austere theism, while Buddhism, partly under pressure from Islam (for its monasteries were vulnerable to alien rule), faded away. Meanwhile various important philosophies or theologies were formulated, above all those of Sankara (8–9th century), Ramanuja (11th century) and Madhva (13th century). These were systems known as Vedanta (the End or Purport of the Vedas or Sacred Revelation). Other Hindu schools (as opposed to

Buddhist, Jain, Materialist, etc.) included Samkhya, Yoga, Nyaya, Vaisesika, and Mimamsa, and various Saiva schools (dedicated, that is, to the god Siva).

The oldest Hindu texts are the Vedic hymns. They center on various deities, such as Indra, Agni, Varuna, Dyauspitr, and so on. There is in the hymns a tendency to think of them essentially as the same – a theme also found in modern Hinduism. Also, a degree of henotheism is in evidence, namely, treating a god addressed in a given hymn as *the* god: this has its analogue in the later Hindu motif of treating Vishnu and Siva as alternative representations of the One. In the period of the main Upanisads, dating from about the fifth to the second century BCE, two main trends emerge. One is the search for the esoteric or true meaning of the Brahminical sacrifice. The second is a degree of influence from contemporary sramanic thinking, that is, the thinking of those like the Buddhists, Jains, and others who practiced a degree of austerity and withdrawal from the world in order to gain release from the round of rebirth. In connection with the first, the texts identify the one Reality as Brahman, a non-personal power on the whole, but sometimes seen as personal Lord and creator. The Reality is also identified with the *atman* or inner self. Later Vedanta discussed whether this means strict identity (so there is only one Self) or merely some kind of union or communion. The doctrine is expressed in a number of great sayings, notably in *Chandogya Upanisad*, VI.viii.7, *tat tvam asi* or "that art thou."

In the somewhat later *Bhagavadgita* (but note: early Indian dating is highly speculative), a more personal picture of God is presented, in the context of the warrior hero Arjuna's dilemma before battle of having his duty to fight, though in conflict with relatives. The notion is presented of the need to carry on with one's duty or dharma, despite its consequences: one will not reap the bad fruits of karma if one carries it out without selfishness and for the love of God. This more theistic picture came to be vital in later Vedanta. Meanwhile the six schools of orthodox Indian philosophy were forming. In some ways the most basic was Samkhya.

It saw the world as consisting on the one hand of *prakrti* or nature and innumerable souls or *purusas* which were, as it were, embedded in nature. Since the nature of reincarnated existence is basically painful, the aim of a soul is to attain liberation from rebirth and the world. The Samkhya system came to be conjoined to that of Yoga, and it is by practicing contemplation through various techniques that the individual soul comes to see that its essence is different from that of the subtle and gross matter that makes up the world and the psychophysical organism (often in Indian philosophy consciousness is thought of as transcending the biological and psychological factors which make up an individual human being). While the Samkhya and Yoga cosmologies are very similar, Yoga does posit a Lord or God, who is actually not so much creator as the one soul who has never been immersed in the round of rebirth, and so serves as an inspiration to the contemplative individual who is seeking liberation. The basic Samkhya cosmology was used by Vaishnava forms of theism for explicating the way God evolves the world. The system posits three *gunas* or ingredients in matter which in differing blends help to explain the nature of things and of individuals.

In Samkhya and Yoga, as with virtually all Indian systems of thought, the cosmos pulsates, that is, it evolves from a quiescent state before ultimately lapsing back into sleep. But the Mimamsa viewpoint holds rigidly to the idea that revelation is uncreated and eternal, and so denies both God and the pulsation of the universe. Its attention is fixed on ritual: and so the Vedic hymns are treated simply as a set of injunctions. Even the gods turn out to be mere mentions. Mimamsa is paired with Vedanta, though its presuppositions are so very different. We shall return to Vedanta later. Meanwhile the Logic School (Nyaya) is usually grouped with Vaisesika or atomism. Nyaya sets forth ancient Indian logic (later logic is known as Navya-Nyaya or new logic). Vaisesika exhibits an atomistic cosmology, with a presiding God. Nyaya was host to the most famous work on the proof of God's existence (the *Kusumanali* of Udayana, 10th century CE).

The schools known as Vedanta are in principle based on the *Brahmasutras* or Aphorisms on the Holy Power, assembled in the first or second century CE. These somewhat enigmatic utterances attracted major commentaries from the main figures of the Vedanta school, notably Sankara (8th century), Ramanuja (12th century), and Madhva (13th century). Sankara's rather rigorous Advaita Vedanta or Non-Dualistic Vedanta was influenced by the Buddhist Madhyamaka theory or viewpoint, which saw supposed reality at two levels: as it is, empty, at the "higher level," and at the empirical level. Sankara makes use of this differentiation, so that Brahman (divine reality) is truly non-personal, with no properties, though it is constituted by being, bliss and consciousness. At the lower level of illusion Brahman is the Lord (or personal God). It is by knowledge of the higher truth that a person is liberated, so that she or he is no longer reborn. This monism of Sankara's arose from his strong interpretation of "that art thou." All separate individuality is an illusion. At a lower level, however, a person can worship God and express devotion. Sankara thus accommodated the "ordinary" religious believer. But in the end God herself is an illusion, caught up in the very illusion she creates. Modern thinkers made use of an adaptation of this schema in formulating modern Hinduism and modern Hindu nationalism. Though Sankara has become highly influential in the modern formulation of the Indian tradition, his reinvigoration of the tradition in the latter part of the first millennium stirred resistance from those who took the personal side of theism more seriously, especially because in that era and after Buddhism faded from view, partly under Muslim onslaughts, Hindu controversy had its own traditions to turn against.

Ramanuja objected to Sankara both on religious and philosophical grounds. He considered that Sankara's non-personalism made nonsense of the very idea of grace, intrinsic to Ramanuja's strongly held theism. Ramanuja believed that the cosmos is God's body (see Article 34, INCORPOREALITY), by analogy with the way the soul controls the human or animal body. Ramanuja also objected to Sankara's theory of illusion or *maya*. He held to a realist theory of perception. Moreover, he thought that the notion that not only the cosmos can be God's body, but also souls, created a sufficiently intimate union between God and souls for the "that art thou" saying to be true. In his commentary on the *Bhagavadgita*, it would seem that Ramanuja was nearer to the original intent of the text than was Sankara. Madhva, on the other hand, went far in the other direction.

9

He argued, by a gerrymandering of language, that theoretically the great text read (with an inserted "non-" so to speak), "that thou art not." His position is known as Dvaita or Dualism, as against both Sankara's Non-Dualism and Ramanuja's Qualified Non-Dualism. Madhva emphasized the particularity of substances and souls, and affirmed God's difference from both. Later Vedantins tended toward forms of theism, as did the followers of Siva. Thus, in a way, Vedanta had as its core variations on theism and devotional religion.

However, during the British period new factors entered into Indian philosophical self-understanding. While some veered toward simplifying Hindu belief and reforming practice, others preferred a way of harnessing the classical tradition to the preservation and formulation of a new Hinduism intertwined with Indian nationalism. British institutions had unified India as never before, while English-speaking higher education gave Indian intellectuals a new entrée on to the world. It was above all the work of Sankara that some of the most influential drew upon to express the new outlook. This was a new pluralism, building on Sankara's notion of levels of truth and his idea of an ultimate reality (which all religions point to). We shall return to these developments later on.

Our next section concerns the sense in which (on the whole) Hinduism is theistic. At first sight (for the Westerner) there is a certain degree of bafflement: each goddess has a god, and vice versa. There are children, mythic beasts, lots of equivalents of the main god or goddess. Christian missionaries in nineteenth century India tended to look on the system as idolatrous. There were also features such as non-personal representations of the deity, above all the lingam. Hindus denied that they worshiped idols or that the lingam was a phallic symbol. I think that the best model of God (or Goddess) as conceived in modern Hinduism (and to some extent the ancient Hindu traditions) is as refracted. What Hindus tend to believe is a refracted theism. This is the thought that God and gods and goddesses are one, but, unlike the Semitic religions (see Article 5, JUDAISM; Article 6, CHRISTIANITY; and Article 7, ISLAM), Hinduism tends to see the gods and goddesses as offshoots of the one Great God (Siva, Vishnu, Devi). The deities are allowed a bit of individuality, for they figure in stories of various kinds. On the other hand, if you worship Ganesa too intensely you can fail to see the Divine Spirit behind his symbolic visage. This attitude to the gods lies behind the modern Hindu penchant both for tolerance and for philosophical pluralism (see Article 77, RELIGIOUS PLURALISM; and Article 65, THEISM AND TOLERATION). Another feature of Indian theism is Ramanuja's view that the cosmos is God's body. In our case the body is only imperfectly under our control: whereas in God's case the universe is wholly under her or his control. This analogy is haunting, because it means that we get a vivid sense of God's presence everywhere in his universe, as we are present in our fingertips, etc. Though Ramanuja did not think that the cosmos looks like a body, it is so. He also analogized the universe to an organic body: in other words here we are dealing with the relevant Sanskrit term standing for human or other animal body, as distinct from a physical body, such as a stone dropped from a height by Galileo. Another point worth mentioning is that through large parts of India God is the Goddess, Devi or Kali or Durga, and so on. Moreover every God has his consort, such as Vishnu and

Laksmi, and Siva and Minaksi in Madurai, etc. Hinduism does not emphasize the male in the way the Abrahamic religions do. Anyway, on these various issues there are grounds for debate with customary Western philosophical thinking. Finally it may be noted that Hindu theism has a place for the non-personal side of God: there is no unrelenting anthropomorphism or personalism (see Article 15, PERSONALISM). This is in part because the very notion of God is also a neuter noun, that of *brahman*.

Next, Hinduism inherits from the sramanic movements such as Jainism and Buddhism the prevalent belief in reincarnation or rebirth, though the Mimamsa school is an exception, since early Vedic hymns did not incorporate the belief, but rather forms of ancestor ritual. Generally, reincarnation exhibits various features: first, a human can be reborn in a variety of forms, whether in heaven as a god, in a hellish purgatory, as a ghost, or as another life form, from insect to elephant. At the end of the day, she might achieve *moksha* or liberation from the round of rebirth. In this case there are varying possibilities: it might be an isolated, suffering-less existence; or it might be in some degree of intimate closeness to God, in a heavenly realm. A person who is liberated may have done it on her own, as in Samkhya-Yoga (though in this case she will have gained help from God); or it may be due entirely to God's grace, especially in the Qualified Non-Dualistic school known as the Cat School, since God transports the soul to salvation as a cat transports her kitten from A to B, by the scruff of the neck. In the sramanic schools and in Samkhya, salvation is as it were dictated by the state of one's karma; while the theistic traditions treat karma as administered (so to speak) by God, and indeed it becomes itself an expression of God's grace. In Madhva's system karma is intrinsic to the life of the individual: God simply works out his destiny. This has an analogy to Calvinist predestination (see Article 72, PROVIDENCE AND PREDESTINATION). In some traditions "living liberation" is possible, in which a saint reaches a kind of perfection and complete serenity. Mostly theistic liberation is post mortem (see Article 70, SURVIVAL OF DEATH).

The typical assumption in the Hindu tradition is that every living body is matched by a soul (sometimes called *atman* and sometimes *purusa*, or else *cit* or consciousness). However, in Advaita Vedanta the identity between the Divine Being and the Self is taken strictly. Consequently we all, so to speak, share the same Self. It is our limited view or projection which causes us to see separate selves. It is like a light seen through a colander. It looks like many lights when it is in fact only one. Advaita in this way shows an affinity to Buddhism, in that the latter has many individual consciousnesses but none are permanent: so at the lower or empirical level of truth we have a host of transmigrating individuals, lacking permanence.

Apart from the karmic linkage between lives, it is assumed that yogis can by the process of purifying their consciousness remember previous lives. Spiritual leaders are held also to have other paranormal powers, such as telepathy and the ability to read others' minds. In regard to rebirth, arguments other than appeal to putative memory are used, mostly empirical – notably the occurrence of child geniuses, apparently paranormal recognitions, and so on.

The most important ontological divide in the Indian tradition is between the permanent and the impermanent. Advaitins interestingly define the illusory as that which is impermanent. But even the rest of the tradition which takes the impermanent to be real, sees the distinction to be vital. This introduces a difference from Western distinctions. It means that in the Hindu schools the consciousness or self, which is permanent, is sharply distinguished from the psychophysical organism. Consequently such entities as *buddhi* and the *ahamkara* or individuating factor, literally the "I-maker," are composed of subtle matter. In short, the mind–body distinction is drawn rather differently in the Hindu tradition. Moreover, the psychic geography differs: there is nothing corresponding to the will or to reason. (There is of course such a notion as reasoning or *tarka*.)

Indian epistemology plays a role in philosophy of religion, of course. The various systems have lists of *pramanas* or sources of knowledge, such as perception and inference. Though inference is conceived differently in relation to styles of syllogism used compared with the West, the basic notion of inference is similar. But perception is often taken to include yogic perception or (roughly) religious experience, or perhaps more narrowly contemplative or mystical experience (see Article 47, RELIGIOUS EXPERIENCE). A third source is acknowledged in most Hindu schools, namely testimony or *sabda*. This refers not just to empirical testimony but also transcendental testimony, i.e. revelation (see Article 74, REVELATION AND SCRIPTURE). Hindu schools are technically known as *astika*. Literally this means "there is –ish": this refers to the existence of revelation (conceived as a Brahminical oral tradition). The notion of testimony as a source of knowledge is an interesting one, little treated in the West.

Since Mimamsa wished to rest its case wholly upon testimony with regard to its injunctional view of revelation, and did not wish its authority to rest upon an omniscient God (see Article 29, OMNISCIENCE), it rejected both the existence of, and arguments for, God. Oddly, Ramanuja, the most fervent philosophical theologian, also rejected the arguments, because he wanted salvation to depend solely upon God and not at all upon reasoning (we can compare Karl Barth on this point). Ramanuja's subtle critique of traditional Indian versions of the teleological argument (comparing the cosmos to a thing made of parts and to an organism, needing a soul to keep it alive) anticipate some of David Hume's (see Article 43, TELEOLOGICAL AND DESIGN ARGUMENTS). Among his points: there might have been many creators, not one; they might recur at differing emerging world periods; the stronger the argument the more anthropomorphic its conclusion; and the cosmos does not resemble an organism. Among other arguments used on behalf of God's existence was a version of the ontological (see Article 41, ONTOLOGICAL ARGUMENTS), and the thought that the moral effects of karma need an intelligent director to organize them (see Article 44, MORAL ARGUMENTS).

Through much of Indian history Hinduism had an important rival in Buddhism, and to a lesser extent in Jainism, and Indian philosophy continuously nourished arguments between the main traditions. Generally, Indian theism made use of Samkhya categories in framing its cosmology, and an area of contention came to center on causation. The Buddhist schools had a non-identity theory, detaching events from one another somewhat in the manner of Hume. The Samkhya favored an identity or transformation theory in which substances change themselves (as milk into curds). Because Buddhism attacked the very notion of substance, breaking the world into short-lived events, the Samkhya thinkers were critical of the notion of an underlying Divine Being or *brahman*. This proved a major difference between Mahayana metaphysics and that of Sankara, despite the influence of Buddhism on him. The "absolute" in Buddhism is emptiness, not a Being. The Buddhists also criticized the Hindu reliance on testimony, and indeed their theory of the Sanskrit language as primordial with a natural fit to reality. The Buddhists were conventionalists. Among Jain critiques of Hindu thinking was the view that religious experience derives from prior belief and not vice versa.

The modern period saw the unification of the subcontinent under British rule, and with it the foundation of English-speaking colleges and universities. The new English-speaking elite were challenged by Christian and British criticisms of Hindu religion and society, as being idolatrous and backward. They acquired a new pan-Indian nationalism in the face of British imperialism. But it was in a new key, because they tended to draw on both traditions. We can pick out four movements in the modern period. One was the Brahmo Samaj founded by Ram Mohan Roy (1772–1833). It was strongly modernist in presenting the Upanisads as being unitarian, and in dismissing a great deal of actual Hinduism. Another was the Arja Samaj, created by Dayananda Sarasvati (1824–83) who reverted to the Veda as the true source of faith, but like Ram Mohan Roy dismissed, indeed strongly attacked, image worship. As a movement it has had good success overseas, among Hindus in Fiji, South Africa, and elsewhere. But these movements were too critical of the main, warm tradition of Hindu worship. It was left to Swami Vivekananda (1863–1902) – drawing on the inspiration of his charismatic teacher Ramakrishna (1834–86), a person of wide sympathies, intense spirituality, but ignorance of the English-speaking world – to formulate a position which was powerful in rolling back intellectual and Christian criticisms of the Hindu world, and in mobilizing Indian national sentiment. His position was based on an updated version of Sankara. It exploited the idea of levels of truth as well as the general idealism of the British philosophical tradition at the end of the nineteenth century. He was pluralist: all religions point to the same Reality. Hinduism has always had such a tolerant attitude. People are on differing stages of the upward spiritual path. His philosophy could underpin a pan-Indian patriotism: Muslims, Christians, and others could all take part, for they all had a view of the truth. Vivekananda was also a social reformer. Following indirectly in his footsteps was Mahatma Gandhi (1869–1948), whose pluralist attitude and conveniently vague appeal to Truth helped to cement Indian nationalism. Also important (though often despised by Western philosophers, who did not see the wider meaning of his ideology) was Sarvepalli Radhakrishnan (1888–1975), later president of India. Naturally, the idealism which had underpinned much of the Indian renaissance died in World War I, and Indian philosophy of religion came to be largely neglected in the period after World War II. However, the pluralist tradition was very important in the thinking behind the Indian constitution and the idea of India as a secular state (that is, pluralistic, not "secular" in the sense of non-religious). Naturally, the main consumption of Indian philosophy in relation to religion was in the business of worldview-reconstruction. In this it was successful, but in the early 1990s there is a turn away from the old pluralism, and among philosophers a more technical methodology.

Bibliography

The magisterial history of Indian philosophy is that of Surendranath Dasgupta in 5 vols. (London 1922–55). Important sources of information include the *Encyclopedia of Indian Philosophies* (Princeton 1970 and following) and Ninian Smart: *Doctrine and Argument in Indian Philosophy*, 2nd edn. (Leiden 1992). For an excellent survey, see J. L. Brockington: *The Sacred Thread: Hinduism in its Continuity and Diversity* (New York 1970 and following volumes). See also P. T. Raju: *Structural Depths of Indian Thought* (Albany 1985).

2

Buddhism

PAUL J. GRIFFITHS

This article will outline the philosophical problems that have seemed most urgent to Buddhist thinkers, together with the kinds of answers they have found persuasive.

Tradition and sources

Buddhism began in India with the birth of Gautama Sakyamuni, the Buddha, about 500 years before Christ. While it effectively ceased to exist in most of the Indian subcontinent by the twelfth century CE, it had by then spread through almost all of South, Central, and East Asia. It remains a significant presence in many parts of Asia (and has seen a revival in India since independence), though the effects of European colonialism since the sixteenth century, and of the Communist revolutions of the twentieth, have on the whole been negative.

Buddhist philosophers have therefore done their work in a wide variety of languages and cultural settings. There is a massive amount of material available in the imperial and canonical languages of Pali, Chinese, Tibetan, Korean, and Japanese; some literary remnants of a once-flourishing Sanskrit Buddhist philosophical tradition; and much work in a variety of South and Central Asian vernaculars. Only a tiny proportion of this body of work has been translated into European languages, and even less has been given serious study by European or American philosophers. This situation creates some difficulties. The first is that of fragmentary and partial knowledge: we do not know as much as we should in order to make responsible generalizations about Buddhist philosophical concerns. And the second is that of internal variety: the Buddhist tradition is, if anything, even more differentiated than the Christian; while it may be difficult to see what unites (or even connects) Origen and Jonathan Edwards, philosophically speaking, it is even more difficult to see what unites or connects Buddhaghosa (a philosopher working in Sri Lanka about 1,500 years ago) with Nichiren (a philosopher working in Japan about 700 years ago) – even though both are Buddhist. These difficulties should be borne in mind when reading what follows, and it should also be noted that what is said here is drawn more from Indo-Tibetan materials than from Sino-Japanese ones.

Ontology

Buddhist philosophers typically think of themselves as arguing for a middle way between extremes, whether of asceticism and indulgence in matters of the flesh, determinism and randomness in causal relations, or eternalism and nihilism in ontology. The necessity of steering a course between the members of this last pair – the view on the one hand that everything exists just as it seems, eternally and without change; and on the other that nothing at all exists – provides Buddhist philosophers with their main impulse toward systematic ontology. The rubric usually used to direct this enterprise is the claim that everything (or at least almost everything; there are some difficulties here) is impermanent, which is typically taken to mean that in so far as anything exists at all, it has both a beginning and an end in time, and that the amount of time separating these two events is very small. Ratnakirti, an eleventh century Indian Buddhist philosopher, provides a systematic and classical defense of one version of this basic insight (for a translation see McDermott 1970).

This claim as to impermanence is not of merely conceptual or academic interest to Buddhist philosophers. On it is thought to hang much of strictly religious significance, for if you get your ontology wrong, if you misconstrue the nature of what exists, you are very likely also to have improper emotional reactions to your misconstruals: to become excessively attached to what is (falsely) thought to be beginninglessly and endlessly desirable (God, perhaps; or other human persons), which is eternalism; or to despair at the (mistaken) judgment that there exists nothing at all, which is nihilism. One result of such conceptual mistakes will be continued rebirth and redeath in the cycle of Samsara, and a concomitant failure to reach Nirvana. The claim that everything is impermanent, then, is an initial step in the development of an ontology that will be accurate and that will as a result foster a properly dispassionate emotional condition. But it is a claim capable of numerous construals. Four have been influential among Buddhist philosophers, and to varying degrees they all remain so.

The first is an attempt to develop an atomistic ontology according to which every existent occupies the smallest amount of space possible and lasts for the shortest amount of time possible. These existents were called by the Sanskrit term *dharma* in India, where this ontology was first systematized; and both the theory and the texts in which it was expressed are often referred to by the name *abhidharma*. Its most influential exposition may be found in a work called *Abhidharmakosa* ("Treasury of Abhidharma"), probably composed in India in the fourth century CE by Vasubandhu (for a translation see Pruden 1988–90). According to this theory, objects that appear to be extended in space or to last longer than an instant are in fact composed of collocations of *dharmas*, either aggregated in space or strung together causally through time. Further, proponents of this ontology are typically interested in providing a catalogue or list of the kinds of *dharma* there are, and then of accounting for medium-sized physical objects – trees, say, or tables – in terms of the different kinds of *dharma* that may be found aggregated or connected causally in them. A typical list is fairly short, containing between 50 and 150 categories, including items such as tangibility, shape/color, perception, memory, and anger. Such lists are meant to be exhaustive, to provide a catalogue of every kind of existent, and as a result also to make it possible to account for everything ordinarily perceived and thought to exist – things such as human persons, stars, and holes in the ground. Both mental and physical phenomena are included in the *dharma* lists.

An ontology of this sort immediately suggests some problems. First, it requires a sophisticated causal theory, for if all ordinary objects of sensory perception are to be accounted for in terms of causal interaction among *dharmas*, a tremendously complex account of even the simplest of events will be needed. And Buddhist philosophers have in fact developed an appropriately nuanced and subtle (if unwieldy) causal theory, often using the ancient twelvefold formula of dependent co-origination (*pratitya-samutpada*) as a starting point (Lamotte 1958, pp. 23–53, provides the details). Second, there are difficulties with the idea of something that exists for an irreducibly small amount of time and takes up an irreducibly small amount of space. If a *dharma* takes up any space at all, or lasts for any time at all, why can it not be further subdivided into existents that take up less space and time? Third, how can disputes as to just which categories are needed to give the shortest possible comprehensive list of kinds of existents (are 50 categories needed? or 100? should memory be an item on the list or not?) be resolved? And fourth, might not the attribution of real (if transient) existence to the *dharmas* offend against the basic philosophico-religious insight that one's ontology should not foster improper attachments? These difficulties contributed to the development of other construals of the basic claim that everything is impermanent, for example the one discussed below.

The second influential construal is that associated with thinkers belonging to the Madhyamaka ("Middle") school of thought, among whom the Indian philosopher Nagarjuna, who may have lived in the first or second century CE, is considered the founder (for a translation of one of his works see Bhattacharya 1986). Nagarjuna, and his followers and commentators in India, Tibet, and China, argued that the pluralistic atomism of the defenders of *dharma* theory has internal problems of the kinds mentioned, and that the basic philosophical insight that everything is impermanent should be interpreted much more radically in order to avoid these difficulties. This Madhyamaka radicalization makes central use of the dialectical arguments associated with the idea of emptiness (*sunyata*). These arguments try to show that every version of realism, every view that assumes or tries to show that there are individuatable and describable entities possessed of defining characteristics that make them what they are and not something else, is either prima facie incoherent or can be shown by argument to issue in incoherence. This, it is said, is just as true of an ontology based upon *dharmas* as it is of one based upon the idea that there are enduring substances; and so all ontologies of these kinds had better be dropped. An added advantage, according to this way of thinking, is that such a radical rejection of realism will do even more than *dharma* theory to dispose of inappropriate emotional responses issuing from ontological misconceptions. This second ontological construal is not, according to its

understanding of itself, nihilism; it is, rather, an attempt at a principled rejection of the language of existence and non-existence. To say that everything is empty is not to deny that there is anything so much as to say that all attempts to catalogue and define what there is will necessarily issue in incoherence.

Yet a third ontological position agrees with the Madhyamaka rejection of the realistic pluralism of the *dharma* theorists, but differs from it in affirming the final reality of a single category: that of mind. So this broadly idealistic construal differs from that of the emptiness theorists principally in that it is willing to state a positive ontology. According to most defenders of the mind-only ontology there are two main reasons to prefer this construal. First, it is not subject to the internal difficulties of *dharma* theory; much emphasis is typically placed here upon the difficulty of coherently explaining the idea of a partless spatially or temporally extended object, which is what a *dharma* must be. And second – or so argue the defenders of the view – it is possible to give a coherent and complete account of human experience without being forced to appeal to external mind-independent objects. Much is made here of dream-experience: if it is characteristic of mind-independent objects that they appear to be located at particular places and times, that they are intersubjectively available, and that they have direct and apparently physical effects upon those who come into contact with them (for a classical statement of these points see Anacker 1984, pp. 161–75), then all these things can be true of objects that everyone agrees to be mental, such as dream-images. Why then, given the internal difficulties in doing so, postulate any mind-independent objects at all? The simplest coherent position, according to this construal, is the view that there is only mind. This position, or family of positions, also has its internal difficulties and tensions; but it has been and remains one of the more important construals of the basic ontological intuition.

There is yet a fourth ontological construal. It too, like the other three, claims to be founded upon the basic intuition, but it has a more difficult time than the others in showing this to be the case. This is because this view focuses upon a set of changeless facts about the cosmos, and as a result appears to run directly contrary to the claim that everything is impermanent. Adherents of this construal tend to say that everything that exists has the potential to become fully awakened, to become Buddha; or to say that there is some sense in which everything that exists already is awakened, already is Buddha (on which view see Ruegg 1989, and Griffiths 1994). It is likely that this ontological position grew out of, or is in some way significantly related to, speculation about the nature and properties of the Buddha. For if, as many Buddhist philosophers say, Buddha is strictly omniscient, and if this means that Buddha has directly present to its awareness all states of affairs, then there must be some sense in which this infinite set of states of affairs can be known atemporally. But it can also be shown that this fourth construal is not logically incompatible with the claim that everything is impermanent; for by applying a theory of types it is easy to show that the state of affairs picked out by the claim *everything is impermanent* is not itself impermanent, but rather permanent. And in similar fashion, the claim *everything is already and always Buddha*, it can be argued, is not obviously or directly incompatible with the claim that everything is impermanent, but is instead a restatement of the implications of that claim.

These four construals of the fundamental ontological intuition have provided, and continue to provide, the main options in Buddhist ontology. Their terms are the terms of most Buddhist philosophizing in this area, and it should be clear from what little has been said in this discussion that they provide much scope for fruitful and interesting philosophical debate: a strong proponent of the claim that everything is always already awakened is likely to have much to say in disagreement with a strong proponent of *dharma* theory.

Epistemology and philosophy of language

According to Buddhist ontology things are not as they seem. Any ontology whose upshot is such a view must work to develop an epistemology and a theory of language that cohere with it, for the ordinary commonsense versions of both these enterprises tend to assume, to the contrary, that things are pretty much as they seem, and that human languages as ordinarily used can get rather close to accurate and adequate description of the way things are. Buddhist philosophers, constrained by this necessity, put a lot of effort into elaborating epistemological and linguistic theories that will do the job they need done.

To take philosophy of language first, Buddhists tend to exhibit a deep suspicion of language, and its correlate, concept formation. One form of this suspicion – perhaps the most extreme form – is evident in the attempt by some (especially those versed in Madhyamaka modes of thought) to engage in philosophical argumentation without making any substantive claims, but rather only by laying bare the contradictions present in or entailed by those put forth by others. But this proved a controversial strategy even among Buddhists, and still more so among their non-Buddhist interlocutors and debaters in India and China. The chief issue here was whether the view, "I have no philosophical views," is itself a philosophical view, and, if it is, whether it does not fall victim to a common but damaging form of self-referential incoherence. This debate surfaces already in the work of Nagarjuna (Bhattacharya 1986, pp. 107–14), and thereafter becomes a standard part of philosophical debate in this tradition of reasoning.

But there are other ways to treat and elaborate this suspicion of language and concept. Some Buddhists deploy a distinction between two kinds of truth, one of which operates at the level of appearance and talks of such things as tables, chairs, and persons, and the other of which transcends language and conceptual distinctions altogether, and issues finally in silence. Others use a theory of the relations between words and things that makes such relations always indirect: using a term such as "cow," for instance, does not on this view involve any reference to a particular cow, nor to the presence of the universal "cowness" present in some particular. Instead it removes or excludes from consideration all non-cows (on this theory see Hayes 1988).

Epistemologically speaking, Buddhists had not only to develop a theory that would explain why the ordinary means of gaining knowledge are misleading, but also one that would explain how the errors produced by deployment of these ordinary means might be corrected. One important move here is the development of arguments against regarding certain common belief-forming practices as productive of knowledge. In India, epistemological debates centered around the enumeration and definition of the belief-forming practices that should be thought of as authoritative, as capable of producing knowledge. Many non-Buddhist philosophers in India recognize at least three of these: sensory perception, reasoning, and testimony. Buddhists typically allow only the first two, and even these they tend to redescribe in ways that radically limit their knowledge-producing capacity. Sensory perception, for instance, is separated definitionally from any connection with concept or language: the bare percept may indeed produce knowledge (better, it is an instance of the occurrence of knowledge, on which see Hattori 1968), but any attempt to classify or categorize its phenomenal properties, its qualia, will not be an instance of knowledge. And since perceptual acquaintance with medium-sized physical objects always involves such classificatory activity, it follows that such acquaintance is never knowledge – and this takes us back to the fundamental ontological intuition already noted.

Reasoning is thought of as a knowledge-producing instrument in two senses. First, under the rubric of "reasoning for others," it can demonstrate the fallacies in the arguments of others, and to this end Buddhist philosophers in India, Tibet, and China developed a complex system of analyzing and classifying logical fallacies (Randle 1930, pp. 147–303, provides some details). Their interests in doing this appear to have been in part formal and in part polemical, which is to say that they were interested both in the development of systems and in the sharpening of tools for winning arguments. But it is certainly true that the system thus developed rivals in complexity the systems of logic and argument developed in medieval Europe. The second major function of reasoning (called "reasoning for oneself") is to provide action-guides, whether in day-to-day interaction with the physical world, or in more abstruse matters of meditational practice or ethical decision-making. If, on seeing that there is smoke on the mountain, for instance, one wants to know whether there is also likely to be fire there (perhaps in order to guide one's decisions as to proper places for meditating or monastery-building) one will need to use an inference-schema (there is smoke on the mountain; wherever there's smoke there's fire; so there's fire on the mountain) in order to come to a decision. And so Buddhist philosophers have devoted a good deal of attention to the formal analysis of arguments of this sort, even though they typically do not judge that the objects with which such reasoning is concerned (mountains and the like) have any final reality.

Persons

The ontological intuition that everything is impermanent is taken by Buddhist philosophers to apply to human persons as much as to anything else. Indeed, they often present the claim *there are no enduring selves* as the philosophico-religious claim that is more distinctive of Buddhism than any other. The claim does not, of course, amount to a denial that there are persons, that part of the ordinary experience of us humans is a sense that we are subjects perceiving objects, that we endure through time, and that each of us is significantly different from other such centers of identity and action. But it does amount to a strong claim that some construals of these phenomenal facts are deeply mistaken; and, moreover, that giving one's assent to such a mistaken construal is a deeply damaging error, one that will likely prevent those who make it from acting properly, and will certainly prevent them from advancing toward Nirvana.

The usual construal of the phenomenal facts indicated is that each human person is an enduring entity: that my past and future are mine and not yours, that while I certainly seem to myself to have had a beginning in time (and may have an end in time), I none the less have had a continuous history since then, and as a result am justified in thinking of myself as an entity with both essential and accidental properties. But all, or almost all, of this is mistaken according to classical Buddhist philosophy. The truth, by contrast, is that what is picked out by my personal proper name (and yours, and everyone's) is only a collocation of events, connected causally but without any enduring or persisting entity of which these events may be predicated. Usually, the events that constitute a person are said to be of five kinds: physical events, and events of sensation, conceptualization, volition, and consciousness. An exhaustive analysis of what constitutes a person at a particular time can then be given by listing the events of these kinds that are occurring at that time. There is no further fact, no possessor of these events. The past and future of the person in question can be described by tracing the precursors of these events backward in time and by projecting them forward.

Arguments for this view usually proceed on two fronts. The first begins with phenomenology and ends with logic. It is said that the fivefold analysis of kinds of event mentioned above describes a set of facts open to discovery by dispassionate introspection: that close examination of what goes on in the continua of events that we call human persons will reveal events of these kinds, and will reveal nothing else. The introspection intended, naturally, is usually guided by instruction in meditational techniques that are precisely designed to reveal these kinds of events and no others, and this is a significant weakness in the argument, which requires for its full force that unmanipulated bare experience will reveal just and only these facts. Nevertheless, Buddhist arguments on this topic normally assert the phenomenological claim as if it were unproblematic. Coupled with the phenomenological claim is a set of logical arguments. These ask those who would wish to assert that there is more to human persons than the phenomenal facts mentioned to explain the relation between the postulated further fact – a soul, perhaps, or some other kind of nonphysical substance – and these phenomenal facts. Perhaps the soul is the possessor of these phenomena, or their controller, or the whole of which they are parts, or the like. In the classical texts devoted to this topic (see, for example, Huntington 1989, pp. 170–7), attempts are made to give an exhaustive list of the relations that could obtain between postulated soul and the phenomenal facts of personhood, and to show that no such relations either are or can be

21

coherently accounted for. The upshot of such arguments is taken to be that there are no enduring selves, though there are certainly phenomenal persons.

The second front upon which arguments for the non-existence of enduring selves proceed is a broadly ethical one. Having the view that there are enduring selves makes, it is said, the practice of the Buddhist path impossible. Briefly, the point is this: if you judge that you are an enduring entity, that you have a past and a future, you are very likely to be interested in that past and that future in ways that make it effectively impossible for you to be properly interested in the past and future of other sentient beings. You will be self-interested in ethically improper ways. If the goal is to have a compassionate attitude (and the actions that ought to accompany it) directed without distinction to all instances of suffering, then the view that sentient beings are genuinely (substantively) distinct from one another will make this difficult. The toothache that you think you are likely to have next week will be of greater concern to you than the toothache that your best friend will have, and of much greater concern than your enemies'. From this basic mistake about the nature of persons, it is argued, spring all the most damaging ethical offenses.

This view of persons creates some interesting difficulties of a strictly philosophical kind. The two most obvious are the difficulty of giving an account of the process of death and rebirth if there is not enduring self to die and be reborn. And the second is the difficulty of combining this view of persons with standard Asian views about karma, ideas that require, or seem to require, that the agent of a particular action be the same as the agent who experiences the results of that action at some time in the future. Dealing with these difficulties has given, and still gives, Buddhist philosophers much to do.

God

If God is thought of as Jews, Christians, Muslims, and some Hindus typically think of him – as the eternal, changeless, omniscient, omnipotent, unsurpassably benevolent creator of all that is – then most Buddhist philosophers have little time for him (see Article 28, OMNIPOTENCE; Article 29, OMNISCIENCE; and Article 30, GOODNESS). More precisely, the time they do have for him is mostly spent on developing arguments whose conclusion is that there can be no such being, and that it would be a bad thing if there were. Buddhist arguments against the coherence of the very idea of God will be largely familiar to philosophers of religion whose work has been within the ambit of the Abrahamic traditions. There are criticisms of the standard positive theistic arguments, notably of the argument from design; but there are also criticisms of the coherence of the claim, for example, that God knows events in time and acts in time, but is not himself subject to change (for a classical example see Jha 1986, pp. 68–100).

But there are equally deep and pressing ethical arguments on this question. If God is thought to be eternal and unchanging, as well as unsurpassably compassionate and loving toward human beings, and if, moreover, he is capable of delivering us from our miseries simply by his free choice so to do, then, in Buddhist eyes, we are unlikely to develop the mental and moral discipline we shall need in order to follow the Buddhist path to its end. God will become for us an object of such fascination that we are likely to spend all our time in contemplation of his glories, an activity that will foster in us emotional states of no help to us. Even if God could exist, then, we ought not to believe in him, much less worship him. None of this is to say that there are not many minor deities, beings who may be very powerful, almost unimaginably more powerful and knowledgeable than humans. Buddhist cosmology requires that there be many such; the standard stories about Sakyamuni's own awakening to Buddhahood involve the participation of at least two major deities. But these beings are not God in the Christian sense. They, like us, are subject to delusion and passion; and, so the argument goes, they must follow the same path that we must follow if they are ultimately to be liberated from their sufferings. Buddhism has been characterized quite aptly not as atheism but rather as trans-polytheism.

But there is a peculiar irony here. While on the one hand Buddhist philosophers are keen to reject the idea and the actuality of God, on the other they devote a great deal of intellectual energy to considering Buddha, to developing theories of what Buddha must really be like in order to have done the things the tradition claims him to have done. And as this intellectual tradition developed it came to look more and more like what Christians have called "theology" in the sense of reasoned discourse about God. Buddha came to be seen as omniscient, omnipotent, and even as coextensive with the limits of the cosmos. And the arguments in support of these views about the nature of Buddha often look very like Christian discussions of the attributes of God. Sometimes the tension between the rejection of theism and a strong view of the nature of Buddha is dramatic, as when a single thinker spends time demolishing arguments about God's omniscience, and then resurrects what look like very similar arguments whose conclusion is that Buddha is omniscient (for example, Jha 1986, pp. 68–100, 1391–579). Theology, understood as ordered and systematic reasoning about what a maximally significant being must be like, here makes a re-entry even when the door has apparently been firmly closed against it.

Bibliography

Anacker, S. (tr.): *Seven Works of Vasubandhu: The Buddhist Psychological Doctor* (Delhi: Banarsidass, 1984).

Bhattacharya, K. (tr.): *The Dialectical Method of Nagarjuna* (Delhi: Banarsidass, 1986).

Griffiths, P. J.: *On Being Buddha: The Classical Doctrine of Buddhahood* (Albany: State University of New York Press, 1994).

Hattori Masaaki (tr.): *Dignaga, On Perception* (Cambridge: Harvard University Press, 1968).

Hayes, R. P. (tr.): *Dignaga on the Interpretation of Signs* (Dordrecht: Kluwer, 1988).

Huntington, C. W., Jr (tr.): *The Emptiness of Emptiness* (Honolulu: University of Hawaii Press, 1989).

Jha, G. (tr.): *The Tattvasamgraha of Santaraksita*, 2 vols. (New Delhi: Munshiram Manoharlal, 1986).

Lamotte, E.: *History of Indian Buddhism from the Origins to the Saka Era* (1958), tr. S. Webb-Boin (Louvain-la-Neuve: Institut Orientaliste, 1988).

McDermott, A. C. S. (tr.): *An Eleventh-Century Buddhist Logic of "Exists"* (Dordrecht: Reidel, 1970).

Pruden, L. (tr.): *Abhidharmakosabhasyam*, 4 vols. (Berkeley: Asian Humanities Press, 1988–90).

Randle, H. N.: *Indian Logic in the Early Schools* (Oxford: Oxford University Press, 1930).

Ruegg, D. S.: *Buddha-Nature, Mind and the Problem of Gradualism in a Comparative Perspective* (London: School of Oriental and African Studies, 1989).

3

Chinese Confucianism and Daoism

CHAD HANSEN

One problem Chinese thought raises for philosophy of religion is that it raises so few problems clearly in philosophy of religion as usually understood. This is awkward because we class Confucianism and Daoism among the world's major religions and philosophies. Arguably, however, neither has a theology – a theory of the divine. They force us to reflect on how we define "religion." This article will first touch on the problem of definition, then outline the interpretative puzzles surrounding the chief candidates for the divine: $tian^{nature}$ and dao^{way}, and then undertake a narrative exploration of the practical analogues of some familiar issues in philosophy of religion: evil, fatalism, divine command morality, religiosity, and absolute simplicity.

The problem of definition

This problem arises because if we compare them with our conceptual stereotype religions, we will doubt that Daoism and Confucianism are religions. If we accept the present use of "religion" to include both, then we must revise our definition to accommodate what turns out to be true of them. The contrasts underscore the historical theory that Western religions flow from a common Indo-European origin. Our shared notion of religion emphasizes theology: we identify religions primarily with what they believe in.

A typical Indo-European theology has doctrines of pneumatology (theory of spirit), soteriology (theory of salvation), eschatology (theory of the beginning and end), and anthropology (theory of human nature). Western religious scholarship often treats these theological motivations as natural, universal reflective urges. The Chinese examples suggest that speculative religiosity is a learned cultural inheritance. Any universal religious questions may turn out to be highly nebulous.

Classical Chinese philosophy shows signs neither of creation myths, of attempts to explain "why we are here," of a mind/body (or spirit/body) dichotomy, nor of supernaturalism. Full-fledged creation stories seem not to have circulated until the end of the classical period of thought. The "spirits" of popular Chinese religion live after the body, but are not immortal. The same qi^{matter} that makes up the rest of the world is in spirit. Spirit qi dissipates over time. The world reabsorbs it. "Spirit" explains the energizing of the body, but not its thought or cognition. The philosophers dealt mostly with the problems of a naturalistic ethics (moral psychology and metaethics) and political theory. Their myths depicted mortal exemplars of moral wisdom who invented language, morality, and culture and transmitted them to us.

The division of religions into prophetic, ritualistic, and mystical helps justify the inclusion of Chinese schools among religions. Their non-theological character merely signals that the prophetic variety, which dominates Indo-European religions, is absent in China. Confucian religious content counts as "ritualist" and the usual place for Daoism (along with its Buddhist incarnation, Zen) is "mystical." Our problem recurs, though, if we then pose questions that put a prophetic frame around all religious types. "What do mystics believe?"

Popular Confucian and Daoist religious practice poses no special classification problems. Both have temples, priests, rituals, and scriptural texts. Interpreting the texts is what raises problems. Most scholars draw a sharp distinction between religious and philosophical Daoism and treat the former as bowdlerizing the philosophy. The religious form of Confucianism seems more integrated with the philosophy partly because most scholars accept that Confucianism developed from an early religion.

The teachings of Confucius (551–479 BCE) focused on its core religious feature – ritual. Some tenuously link Confucianism to the ancient religion of ancestor worship. They do share a familial focus. Classical texts, however, did not rationalize ancestor worship itself except for encouraging ritual practice in general. Confucius is famous for his pragmatically "agnostic" replies to questions about spirits and the afterlife (see Article 70, SURVIVAL OF DEATH). "Until you know about life, how can you know about death?"

Problems of interpretation

The problem of definition links up with the interpretative controversies. If we map Chinese ideographs on to Indo-European religious concepts, we will then find a familiar "implicit" theology. The controversy, of course, is whether to use that mapping. I am more interested in how Chinese thought forces us to broaden our conceptions of intellectual possibility. This article will, therefore, highlight the contrasts and challenge the missionary mappings.

Missionaries facilitated the Western introduction to Chinese thought. Convinced of their rationality, natural theology liberals charitably assumed the Chinese must have a concept of God – the problem was identifying it. (Conservatives simply declared the Chinese "atheists.") One liberal assumption was that $tian^{nature:sky}$ (typically translated "heaven") is the Confucian "God" while the Dao plays that role for the Daoists. The two mappings raise different but related difficulties. I will start with $tian^{nature}$ and use it to explain the development of a Daoist $dao^{guiding\ discourse}$.

Many historical scholars assume that $tian^{nature:sky}$ had been an anthropomorphic god prior to the philosophical period. It is clear that $tian$ was an authority and, in the official dynastic religion, an object of prayer and royal sacrifice. Ancients considered $tian$ a crucial ally in political rivalries. None of this entails that $tian^{nature:sky}$ is anthropomorphic or supernatural. Its use in other contexts marks it as sky in contrast to earth and natural in contrast to social or conventional. If we do not start with the assumption that the Chinese must have a God concept, the obvious alternative possibility is that they worshiped, obeyed, and were in awe of nature. Where this awe leads Indo-European theology to postulate and worship a transcendent cause of the natural world, Chinese "awe" arguably stays put.

Tian^(nature:sky) emerges into philosophy in the doctrine of the "mandate of Heaven" (*tian*^(nature:sky) *ming*^(name:command) see p. 31). The doctrine justified political legitimacy, military success, and revolution. The last element marks its most striking contrast with the divine right of kings. When the dynastic family loses its *de*^(virtuosity) (the normal eventuality), *tian-ming* justifies rebellion by someone with more *de*. Some signals of such a loss are that the people abandon the ruler; his soldiers defect rather than fight, and the weather, luck, choice of general strategy, and so forth bring about his defeat in battle.

The crucial evidence of the shift of the mandate to another family is, conversely, the new family's winning and effectively assuming authority. The detailed mechanism of transfer of the mandate is consistent with a secular notion of "natural" legitimacy – particularly so since it eschews a permanent, hereditary aristocracy. A peasant family can become a dynasty if they have sufficient *de*^(virtuosity).

A political *dao*^(guide) ties the mandate to the "natural" social order. It derives from actions that preserve it, and is lost by the opposite. The model ruler's way is the way societies work in the natural world. Later, more superstitious, versions suggested that being out of harmony with the natural order could trigger freak phenomena. Confucian advisors manipulated their rulers by identifying bizarre events (ducks flying backward, two-headed calves) as portents that the ruler's policies were alienating the mandate.

Nature and convention

The theoretical complement of *tian*^(nature:sky) was conventional society. Ancient thinkers contrasted the realms of *tian* and *ren*^(human) not supernatural–natural. Social conventions that were consistent with nature should be constant. Disputes raged over how much variation this left to social construction. Did nature dictate a single constant *dao*^(guide) or could we choose our guiding system from a range of workable alternatives for utilitarian or moral purposes?

Confucians, with their adoration of the traditional and partly mythical "sage kings" tended toward a more religious (authoritarian and revealed) answer. Morally motivated mortals created the original (and still correct) conventions (the *li*^(ritual)). For Confucians, the moral issue was how to recover and follow the guidance of these culture heroes.

Other schools, including Daoism, tended to be more skeptical of convention and more pluralistic. Gradually Daoism came to question even the authority of *tian*^(nature:sky) itself – a development marked in the claim that Daoism abandons *tian*^(nature:sky) as an authority in favor of *dao*. Exactly what that amounts to raises similar interpretative problems.

One of the tempting ways to understand the slogan was that Daoists came to regard the whole range of competing *dao*s as equally "natural." *Tian*^nature:sky has no preference among the competing *dao*s and, thus, offers no effective guidance separate from the *dao*s themselves. When we select among them, we must do so by reference to some prior guiding perspective (a *dao*) and its standards of right and wrong. We find no natural guidance apart from *dao*s.

The alternative (and dominant) view is the assumption that the word *dao* changed meaning when used by Daoists. Confucians referred thereby to moral systems, but Daoists used it as the name of the supernatural, divine, creator of the world – a mystical "God." The problem is that the claimed properties of the alleged transcendent object follow mainly from the interpretative hypothesis.

Transcendence

The debate often turns to the question of "transcendence." This formulation, however, adds little clarity. *Tian*^nature:sky is far from a clear case of something metaphysically separate from the natural world and, unless we accept the meaning-change assumption, neither is *dao*. Notoriously, Chinese thought avoids the metaphysical gulf between mind and body that informs one Indo-European conception of transcendence (non-location in time and space). Some cite the presence of moral doctrines as evidence of transcendence, but I know of no sound argument that morality must be non-natural – certainly none in early Chinese thought.

The case for a transcendent concept in *Dao*ism (the mystical *Dao*) comes from assorted "creation" passages. They say that *dao*s support, sustain, and even create things. Paradoxically, however, these passages explain that *dao*s give birth to "non-existence" which gives rise to "existence," or to "one" which creates "two," then "three!"

Obviously these passages do not force a transcendent Creator (see Article 39, CREATION AND CONSERVATION) interpretation of *dao*. If *dao*s are forms of guiding discourse, we can read the passages as linguistic idealism. Concepts (e.g. being and non-being) are conventionally "carved out" for practical purposes by our guiding discourse. We can view *dao*s creating and sustaining "things" as blending this idealism with the commonsense view that a natural "guide" nurtures and develops things.

The hypothesis would stumble if it relied on the claim that Daoists ground their religion on a mystical experience (see Article 47, RELIGIOUS EXPERIENCE). But there is little evidence of a concept of "experience" (which typically informs a mind/body distinction), let alone any clear reference to such experiences in the texts. An interesting view of language, however, fuels this interpretation.

Chinese thinkers, especially Daoists, viewed language as consisting of "names" which mark distinctions (is *x*/is not *x*). Linguistic idealists fallaciously conclude that since the distinctions are conventional, natural reality must lack distinctions. Hence, language distorts the way things are. This claimed consequence of linguistic idealism generates paradox, but we can explain its motivation without assuming it depended evidentially on some esoteric experience.

A cluster of thinkers (led by the Confucian idealist, Mencius, 371–285 BCE) also claim special access (intuition) to moral guidance. They are wary of appeals to convention or tradition and still accept the authority of *tian*^{nature}. Their view is that we have a natural inclination (if uncorrupted by linguistic guides) to select the situationally correct action for us. This could be a religious doctrine (divine conscience), but the Mencian form is naturalistic. The tendencies that are in our motivational organ (the *xin*^{heart-mind}) *tian*^{nature} produces in harmony with its moral *dao*. Paradoxically, the Daoist thinkers seem to have doubted these "religious" elaborations of the underlying linguistic insight.

Death and the afterlife

The absence of theology and pneumatology parallels a lack of soteriology and eschatology. The individual perspective (the conscious subject of experience) plays little role in classical Chinese moral theories. A social focus dominates Chinese philosophy. Their *dao*s do project utopian possibilities for society, but have little to do with individual "redemption" separate from social reform. In each utopia we all will lead more fulfilling natural lives. The cosmic feature is simply that the well-ordered society is one in harmony with the world (*tian–di*^{sky–earth}). Post-Buddhist Neo-Confucianism has a more individualistic content. It treats becoming a sage (being morally wise enough to succeed) as the counterpart to Buddhist enlightenment.

The popular Chinese religion of ancestor worship presupposes an afterlife "heaven." One reveres one's dead ancestors, but they lack supernatural or divine status. On the contrary, ancestors depend on their earthly progeny for basic support. The duties and obligations of natural social relationships thus extend beyond death. We support our ancestors in paradise by sacrifices – from food to "hell money," houses, and concubines. If the support ends, they are cast out of heaven (non-payment of rent?) to wander on earth causing trouble.

Religious readings project a "universal" fear of death on Chinese thinkers. Their ways of dealing with it, however, typically ranged from (1) Confucius' pragmatic agnosticism, to (2) seeking natural elixirs and practices for "long life," or (3) reinterpreting it as surviving through one's moral influence or offspring, or (4) understanding life and death as a continuous and natural process of change in which nothing is really gained or lost. Chinese thinkers hardly seemed to have drawn comfort from claims of the immortality of the spirit.

Problems of evil

Its theological character is controversial, but since Chinese thought treats nature as the source of ethics it generates approximations of some traditional religious puzzles. Confucianism faced two different versions of the problem of evil (see Article 50, THE PROBLEM OF EVIL). The first stems from Confucius' "one man" political theory. The premises are: (1) if a sage is in power, then all will develop their moral potential; (2) everyone has the moral potential to become a sage; (3) sage kings

29

(Yao and Shun) were in power in the past. Induction suggests that we are all still sages. We cannot explain the descent from the Confucian "golden age."

A metaphysical version plagues the Mencian and Neo-Confucian forms of Confucian idealism. Mencius' theory starts from the premise that human nature is instinctively good. Correct action requires no calculation or theory. Our innate intuition selects the situationally correct action. Neo-Confucians interpret this metaphysically. The stuff (qi^{matter}) of the universe has moral principle in it. Since the same qi^{matter} makes up our heart-mind, it is morally "tuned" to the universe and will respond to any concrete global situation with the single correct action for "me-here-now."

Parallels with Western puzzles in philosophy of religion emerge if we rephrase the problem of evil as "whatever I do must be God's will." In China the conclusion is whatever I do, I shall be following the natural *dao*. An early Daoist, Shen Dao, first exposed the problem. He observed that we will follow exactly one actual course (which he called the Great *Dao*). Nothing, not even a clod of earth, can "miss" it. Since everything will follow the Great *Dao*, there can be no practical point in learning the distinction between right and wrong. If correct action is following the natural *Dao*, then following the actual *Dao* is surely enough. He concludes (paradoxically) that we should abandon knowledge. To follow Shen Dao's teaching would be to violate it.

Laozi (4th century BCE) proffered a primitivist version of a similar theory. He viewed being wrong as being unnatural in the sense of being generated by learning, culture, language, distinctions, rules, and so forth. Natural action requires "forgetting." This also leads to paradox since a theory with distinctions (e.g. between natural and conventional) guides the forgetting.

Zhuangzi (369–286 BCE) points to another problem for idealist Confucians who advocate "cultivating" the heart-mind to achieve this action-selecting ability. Any cultivation presupposes a distinction between a sage's and a fool's heart. Some hearts must be naturally "bad" or out of tune with the universe and require calibration. In that case, one must abandon the intuitive criterion of action in favor of some (probably controversial) moral theory that grades "natural" hearts.

The Neo-Confucian metaphysics takes a dualistic form – $li^{principle}$ and qi^{matter}. Mencius' optimism translates to the slogan that there is no $qi^{matter\text{-}force}$ without $li^{principle}$. So everything in nature conforms to $li^{principle}$ and exists in a global harmony. The moral injunction thus becomes puzzling. Humans should act in the way that contributes to and sustains that metaphysical harmony, but as a part of nature, composed of qi^{matter} and infused with $li^{principle}$, it is not clear how we could fail. Why are humans, of all species, capable of departing from natural harmony? How can humans fail to be natural? Wang Yang-ming (1472–1529) appears to have toyed with abandoning the distinction between good and evil.

Fatalism and free will?

The problem of fatalism parallels the problem of evil. In both cases the contrast between the two traditions goes beyond mere lack of theology (see Article 37, FORE-

KNOWLEDGE AND HUMAN FREEDOM). Some theory of causation (creation) usually informs Western conceptions of fatalism. Chinese "fatalism" is an aspect of their normative theory. This makes translators use different terms in rendering the key term *ming*$^{\text{to name:command}}$ (used in "mandate of *tian*$^{\text{nature:sky}}$"). Usually they gloss it as "order" or "command," though most accept the theory that it is the verbal form of *ming*^{name}. When a text uses it to justify stoic attitudes, however, translators assume it changes meaning and becomes "fate."

What is missing is any analogue of argument from a creator's intent, divine foreknowledge, or a concept of deterministic laws. The arguments that usually accompany such uses of *ming* are typically moral nihilism arising from sardonic application of the ideal of "natural" morality. The normal accompaniment of accepting *ming* is that one ceases to make distinctions between *shi*$^{\text{this:right}}$ and *fei*$^{\text{not-this:wrong}}$. It is to accept that *tian*^{nature} or the Great *Dao* has produced this. A naturalist morality can but cease making judgments about it.

The only form of determinism required here is Shen Dao's logical determinism (there will be exactly one future course of events) and few philosophers take that line. Laozi follows Shen Dao in advocating that we abandon knowledge, but his apparent motivation is not resignation, but a desire for a different kind of freedom. Laozi focuses on how we free ourselves from social control or distortion of our natural action impulses. "Abandon knowledge" for him is a straightforward normative principle.

No notion in pre-Buddhist Chinese philosophy coincides closely with Indo-European freedom of the will. The closest "value" is that of spontaneous (nonguided, intuitive) action, which, most frequently, Chinese thinkers treat as following nature, not transcending it.

Divine command theory

Some religious puzzles related to morality do translate across the two traditions. The counterpart of a traditional puzzle for divine command morality is: "is there a natural inclination to morality because it is right or is it right because there is a natural inclination to it?" This becomes a puzzle for Chinese natural moralism which shares the " 'is' implies 'ought' " structure of divine command theory (see Article 57, DIVINE COMMAND ETHICS). Confucius started with an authority – tradition. It was religious in being "revealed" in texts surviving from the mythical sages. Their authority, however, rested on mainly epistemic grounds – their wisdom.

Mozi (ca. 470–390 BCE) reflected that Confucians were confusing what was traditional with what was right. His problem was justifying a standard to substitute for tradition. Mozi responded by drawing *tian*$^{\text{nature:sky}}$ more directly into the ethical project. He argued that *tian*^{nature} has a preference for benefit over harm (implicitly human benefit). The evidence, as Zhuangzi pointed out later, depended on taking a human point of view. Still, Mozi did note that a natural ethics was a "universal" one – utilitarianism. He contrasted Confucian traditional morality, with its preference for special relations, as "partial." The Confucian attitude, he admitted, was arguably also natural.

Mencius developed the idealist version of Confucianism in response to Mozi's challenge. We discover the preferences of *tian*^{nature} for humans in the innate structure of our moral psychology – the heart-mind that directs action. He argued that the seeds of compassion, shame, conformity, and judgment were "inborn." Their "unimpeded growth" (given concerned cultivation) would produce mature tendencies to moral action. It is not clear how Mencius responds to the puzzle. He seems sometimes to assume that an action is right because a (mature) sage's heart-mind would choose it. Other times his implicit criterion looks to be idealist utilitarianism.

Later thinkers (including Daoists) attacked that reliance on the authority of *tian*^{nature}. Mohists observed (along with Shen Dao) that anyone could claim that authority for anything they did. The text credited to Laozi suggested that natural (pre-learned) action would surely be a less elaborate morality than Mencius needed (though Laozi, too, favored "unlearning"). Zhuangzi argued that all actual characterizations of "right and wrong" are products of training and a learned perspective and, hence, all natural.

These attacks on the authority of nature prompted the third version of Confucian ethics. Xunzi (ca. 300–230 BCE) returned to relying on conventional authority but now with an implicit acceptance of the answer: "it is right because convention says it is right." Xunzi's apparent justification is philosophical despair. The discussion had settled that nature is not an authority because it gives no clear direction. The only alternative must be historical convention. Xunzi's conventionalism was influential as political authority swamped the classical period of philosophy under official "cosmic" superstition.

Religious attitudes flourished, but apart from the skeptical Wang Cong (CE 27–97), little philosophical reflection on religious issues ushered in Buddhism. His skepticism, typically, targeted the view that nature reflects human concerns and moral attitudes. Buddhism, with its own sets of issues, then dominated Chinese intellectual life for a millennium and the Confucianism that emerged was an intellectualized version of Mencius.

Piety and divine simplicity

If Daoism stands as a paradigm of Chinese mysticism, then the question is how to characterize Daoist mysticism. How can we recognize "religiosity" or "spirituality" in a non-theological Daoism? I noted above that no alleged "experience" of inexpressible "oneness" informs the view. Still, we find the familiar language of incommensurability.

The incommensurable subject (also found in the Zen focus on "practice") is pragmatic. The "mystical" attitude is not a belief content, but a non-propositional life-attitude. Paradigms of the attitude include the consummate artist, craftsman, lover, priest, sports competitor, etc., who "plays out of his mind." The activity so absorbs us that we "lose" our "ego" and become one with the art or activity. We cannot, however, directly teach this as we can the skill itself. The injunction to "do it spontaneously" hardly helps a person to learn.

So absorbed, we cannot distinguish acting from being "led" by the "spaces" and shape of the situation in which we act. A musician may describe himself as "being played by the instrument." A Daoist "mystic" lives her life with that immediacy, intensity, and focus.

On many modern interpretations, this characterization of the appropriate life attitude applies as well to Confucianism. They identify it as total involvement in ceremony, chanting, and ritual dance. Confucians celebrate the attitudinal rewards of total absorption in ceremony alongside Confucius' pragmatic agnosticism and the intellectualized Confucian refusal to accept the popular "theology" behind their ancient rituals. Conventions and ceremony are means of social cohesion and the healthy expression of human feelings. Practice and participation stand as an independently rewarding and wholly absorbing aesthetic value.

The Buddhist period in China is largely responsible for the theological reading of Daoism, which became common in the Neo-Confucian revival. It viewed Buddhism and Daoism as near theological twins with an all-encompassing (pantheistic) divine "stuff." The Buddhists called it Buddha-Nature and the Daoists called it *"Dao."* Such a reading of Daoism does provide some near parallels to Western puzzles and paradoxes of divine attributes such as perfect simplicity (see Article 31, SIMPLICITY). There were, however, only Neo-Confucian theologians expounding this allegedly Daoist theology as an interpretation of ancient texts – Daoist philosophy had disappeared.

Classical thinkers, however, may have confronted these puzzles in a purely metaphysical guise. An obscure dialogue seems to challenge the coherence of any reference to "everything." Zhuangzi most obviously picks up the theme when he shows that any claim that "all is one" must be wrong. Whenever we try to speak of the "everything" taken as a unity, there is the one and the saying which, he notes, makes two! He thus denied what Neo-Confucian interpretations took to be the central tenet of Daoism!

Bibliography

Chan, Wing tsit: *A Source Book in Chinese Philosophy* (Princeton: Princeton University Press, 1963).

Eno, R.: *The Confucian Creation of Heaven* (Buffalo: State University of New York Press, 1990).

Fingarette, H.: *Confucius: The Secular as Sacred* (New York: Harper & Row, 1972).

Fung, Yu lan: *The Spirit of Chinese Philosophy*, tr. E. R. Hughes (London: Routledge & Kegan Paul, 1947).

Gia-fu Feng and English, J.: *Lao Tsu: Tao Te Ching* (New York: Random House, 1972).

Graham, A.: *Chuang tzu: The Inner Chapters* (London: George Allen & Unwin, 1981).

——: *Disputers of the Tao* (La Salle: Open Court, 1989).

Hansen, C.: *A Daoist Theory of Chinese Thought* (New York: Oxford University Press, 1992).

Lau, D. C.: *The Mencius* (Harmondsworth, UK: Penguin, 1970).

—— (tr.): *Confucius: The Analects* (New York: Penguin, 1979).

Schwartz, B.: *The World of Thought in Ancient China* (Cambridge: Harvard University Press, 1985).

4

African religions from a philosophical point of view

KWASI WIREDU

If there is wisdom in starting with first things first, then a philosophical discussion of African religions should start with an inquiry into the applicability of the concept of religion to African life and thought. Not only is the word "religion" not an African word – this in itself is not necessarily a problem – but also, as Mbiti suggests, it is doubtful whether there is a single-word or even periphrastic translation of the word in any African language. This does not mean, of course, that the phenomenon itself does not exist among Africans. One may have something without being given to talking about it. Mbiti himself, for example, maintains in his *African Religions and Philosophy* that Africans are pre-eminently religious, not even knowing how to live without religion (Mbiti 1990, p. 2). Be that as it may, there is at this stage an assumption that we need to disavow, at least methodologically. We must not assume that having a religion is necessarily either a moral or an intellectual credit. Some of the early European visitors to Africa, going, it would seem, principally on a cheeky ignorance, freely opined that the African mind was in too rude a condition to be capable of a religious feeling or perception. By contrast, many African scholars have been keen to prove that Africans, by their own unsupplemented lights, were able to develop a belief in God and related matters before ever a European set foot in Africa. In either case there is the presupposition that having a religion is a kind of achievement. This assumption, unfortunately, is likely to handicap a dispassionate examination of the sense, if any, in which religion may be said to have a place in African culture.

Obviously, we need in this connection to be clear about what religion itself is. In this enterprise we need not be unduly intimidated by the well-known multiplicity of definitions of religion; for, when the willfully idiosyncratic ones are discounted, what this situation really presents is a legion of sufficient conditions. And if that is an embarrassment, it is only an embarrassment of riches. Moreover, there is a necessary distinction, not often enough drawn, which can gain us considerable simplification. It is the distinction between religion and *a* religion. Religion as such is, in essence, simply a metaphysic joined to a particular type of attitude. A religion, on the other hand, is, typically, all this plus an ethic, a system of ritual, and an officialdom (usually hierarchical) for exhorting, reinforcing or monitoring conformity to them. In the first sense, religion can be purely personal – one can be religious without having a religion; which, actually, is not at all uncommon. In the second, religion is both personal and institutional. One of the theses of the present discussion is going to be that, contrary to frequent suggestions, religion in Africa is predominantly of a personal rather than an institutional character. The claim, in other words, is that the concept of religion applies to African culture in most instances only in the minimal sense.

In this minimal sense to be religious is to entertain certain ontological and/or cosmological beliefs about the nature of the world and about human destiny and to have an attitude of trust, dependency, or unconditional reverence toward that which is taken to be the determiner of that destiny, whether it be an intelligent being or an aspect of reality. In terms of this characterization, it is not necessary for religion to include belief in a deity. In Africa, however, as in a great many areas of the world, that belief is the centerpiece of religion. But in Africa, unlike elsewhere, it also frequently more or less exhausts its scope. African world views usually, though not invariably, feature a supreme being who is regarded as responsible for the world order. Generally, that being is explicitly conceived to be omniscient, omnibenevolent and, subject to a rider to be entered in due course, omnipotent (see Article 29, OMNISCIENCE; Article 30, GOODNESS; and Article 28, OMNIPOTENCE). A sense of dependency, trust, and unconditional reverence is almost everywhere evident in African attitudes to the supreme being.

Strikingly, however, rituals of God-worship are often absent from African life. Mbiti (1970, p. 178) has observed that the word "worship" has no counterpart in many African languages. While this does not necessarily imply that the practice did not exist, it would explain it, if that were the case. In the particular case of the Akans, Abraham (1962, p. 52) has pointed out (correctly) not only that they "never had a word for worship" but also that "worship is a concept that had no place in Akan thought." Even when there is a simulacrum of worship among an African people, there is nothing comparable to the regular, rigorously organized and officer-led, group-praying and divine praise-singing characteristic of Christianity, for example. Nor is there an analogue to the weekly moral and metaphysical discourses from Christian pulpits. Many African peoples are, indeed, known to pray, and some to make offerings and sacrifices, to God. But these activities are often personal and informal or, when formal, as in some of the sacrifices, rather episodic; while some African groups, such as the Ankore and the Banyarwandas, are positive that an omnibenevolent being does not need or expect such things as sacrifices (see Mbiti 1970, p. 180 and on worship generally chs. 16–20). Indeed, it is difficult to see what use a perfect being could have for worship or how he could welcome it at all. But what, from a philosophical point of view, is of the utmost importance in all this is that Africans tend not to base their conceptions of the meaning of morality on their belief in God. And this must account largely for the non-institutional character of their religion. Given, however, the prevalence of the contrary impression in the literature, these claims require a lot of explaining.

Consider, then, the general idea of the dependency of morality on religion. If this relation is interpreted in a causal or genetic sense, there is an iota, though only an iota, of truth in it. Some people in Africa (and presumably outside Africa)

35

are discouraged from mischief by the fear of divine retribution. But freedom from this kind of reason for action or inaction is, in fact, one of the marks of moral maturity recognized among the wise folks of well-known traditional African societies. But even if this were not the case, it still would not follow that *evil* is understood to mean *that which will bring divine retribution*; for, in that case, to warn that evil will bring those consequences will amount to announcing that what will bring divine retribution will bring divine retribution – a splendid truth, regrettably lacking in moral information. The suggestion is not necessarily that traditional sages are known to have formulated this particular consideration, though the philosophic ones among them are capable of even more incisive argumentation; it is rather that the communalist ethic typical of many traditional African societies is just such as to inhibit trafficking in such tautologies. From the communalist standpoint, morality is the adjustment of the interests of the individual to the interests of the community on the principle of sympathetic impartiality. On this view, morality derives, rationally, from the desiderata of social existence, not from any transcendent source. In the African example this is easily inferred from the corpus of moral maxims commonplace among the people (see, for example, Gyekye 1987, chs. 8–10). Given some such conception of morality and an unqualified belief in the justice of God, there is no reason why a flagging virtue may not be bolstered up by thoughts of divine sanctions even if good and evil are conceived in a manner logically independent of the will of God (see Article 57, DIVINE COMMAND ETHICS). Again, although it is true to say that most Africans believe that it is God who, as Idowu (1962, p. 145) puts it, implanted in human beings the sense of right and wrong, it does not follow that we should expect them to hold for this reason that "right," for example, means "approved by God"; just as it would not occur to anyone to suppose that if people believe that the sense of beauty and ugliness was implanted in us by God, then they will take "beautiful" to mean something like "appreciated by God."

One reason why morality has so often been thought to be closely connected with religion in Africa is because the scope of African religion has been routinely enlarged to include the beliefs and procedures relating to the great assortment of extra-human beings that is a component of various African worldviews. There is, indeed, no doubt that these worldviews usually postulate a hierarchy of beings. At the top is God; and, in the middle, various kinds of "spirits," some supposed to be resident in certain remarkable trees, mountains, and rivers, together with the departed ancestors. Below these are the human species, the lower animals, vegetation, and the realm of inanimate objects, in descending order. The "spirits" are credited with the ability to help or harm human beings in ways that surpass the causes and effects familiar in everyday life. For this reason people are careful to try to establish good relations with the more susceptible ones, and this often involves "rituals" replete with supplications sweetened with flattery. Among these extra-human beings the ancestors occupy a special position. They are not the most powerful, but they are, in the great majority of African societies, the best loved and respected. The world of the ancestors is conceived to be continuous and analogous to that of the living, and the interactions between the two realms are, by common reckoning, regular and on a day-to-day basis. In this setup the ancestors may be called the extra-mundane guardians of morality; their entire concern is to watch over the affairs of the living members of their families, rewarding right conduct and punishing its opposite, with unquestioned justice, while, at all times, working for their well-being. It is on this ground that the ancestors are so highly venerated. Notice that, on this showing, the orientation of the afterlife in the African "eschatology" is thoroughly this-worldly (see Wiredu 1992, ch. 7). Not surprisingly, many African customs and institutions have some connection with the belief in the ancestors in particular and the world of spirits at large.

What, however, is the justification for calling the attitude to the ancestors and the other "spirits" religious? It is apparent that this is based on certain ways of ontologically compartmentalizing the worldview just adumbrated. The orders of existence above the human sphere are categorized as supernatural, spiritual, and, in some connections, transcendent, while the rest is designated as natural, material, and temporal. If to this is added the characterization of the activities dedicated to establishing useful relations with the extra-human powers and forces as worship, then the stage is set for attributing to Africans not only an intense religious sense but also a particularly pervasive institutional religion with unmistakable imprints on all major aspects of life (see Mbiti 1990, Introduction and *passim*). In this perception of African religion it is not even necessary to bring God into the picture. It seems sufficient, under some available definition of religion, that Africans be seen to believe in, and worship, a great many "supernatural" and "spiritual" entities who are credited with power over the life and fate of human beings and in some cases invested with a moral authority. This, actually, is how Christian missionaries saw African religion, which they called paganism. Missionary semantics in Ghana offer an almost picturesque illustration of this fact. In vernacular communication in the Akan area of Ghana the missionaries called the indigenous religion *Abosomsom* which means "stone-service" (*Abo* means "stones" and *som* means "service," which, in the evangelical translation, is a forced approximation to the concept of worship). Their own religion they called *Nyamesom*, meaning the service of God (*Nyame* means "God" and *som*, as we have seen, means "service"). Interestingly, what many Akan Christians, sincere in the faith and, at the same time, proud of the indigenous religion – conceptual incompatibilities notwithstanding – have done about this linguistic anomaly is merely to insist that the indigenous religion includes, in addition to the business about the "spirits," recognition of the existence of the Almighty God.

The incompatibilities, however, cut too deep to be so cheerfully skated over. Not only are there radical disparities between the Christian worldview and its African counterparts with respect to specific ontological issues, but also the categories of thought underpinning the concept of religion which has just been used have a questionable coherence in the relevant African contexts. A most fundamental pair of such categories is the natural/supernatural distinction. In describing the "spirits" in question as supernatural, it is assumed that this distinction is intelligible within the conceptual framework of the African peoples concerned. Yet one who consults any average text on African religion will be readily furnished with stories of spirits not only living in material circumstances but also indulging in physical ventures, gyrating upon the head not excluded. Moreover, spirits are not spoken of in any other terms. The conceptual implications of this have rarely been seriously explored *from the point of view of the African worldviews themselves.* Occasionally, though, a foreign researcher into African thought has come close to the beginnings of wisdom in this matter. Thus, Kenneth Little (1954, p. 113), in a study of the Mende of Sierra Leone, notes that "the situation seems to be that they regard 'supernatural' phenomena in much the same kind of way and frame of mind as they regard the material circumstances of their environment and the motives and actions of human beings .... Such an attitude is [also], within the bounds of Mende knowledge, quite empirical." The quotes around the word "supernatural" do not betray any uneasiness regarding the intelligibility of the metaphysical dichotomy of the natural and the supernatural in the abstract; they are merely indicative of Little's suspicion that the Mende do not employ it in their thinking. His explanation is that "they have an essentially 'practical' attitude to life" which manifests itself as a "lack of interest in metaphysics." It is arguable, however, that they don't use that dichotomy because it is fundamentally incompatible with their metaphysic. At all events, in the conceptual framework of the African group to which the present writer belongs, namely, that of the Akans of Ghana, which, on the evidence of various studies (e.g. Sawyer 1970), is very similar to that of the Mende in many important respects, it makes scant sense to divide the world order into two, calling one nature and the other supernature.

Within the system of thought just alluded to, the world (*wiase*) is a unified order of created things (*abode*). (*Bo* means "to make" and *(a)de* means "thing(s)." But see the comment on creation in our final paragraph.) The so-called spirits are as creaturely as the humblest animal. The world order operates in every detail according to laws, some commonplace, others more recondite; but the latter do not contradict or abrogate the former, and interactions between the realms predominantly governed by these kinds of laws are perfectly regular in a cosmological sense. Accordingly, explanations of some puzzling phenomena in common experience in terms of the activities of "spirits," for example, do not generate the sense of "going out of this world" which the ascent, in another worldview, from the natural to the supernatural would seem to suggest. Certainly, "spirits" are regarded as being out of the ordinary, but they are not felt to be out of this world. Moreover – so the belief goes – they can actually be seen and communicated with by those who have medicinally reinforced eyes and appropriate resources of communication. And there is no lack of such "specialists" in many African societies. Significantly, when descriptions are given of what is thus seen, they are positively material in imagery. It is apparent, on these considerations, that calling the "spirits" supernatural represents a substantial misunderstanding. The same considerations must give pause to those who would speak of the "spirits" as spiritual. But there is a very much more fundamental objection. The word "spiritual" has a neo-Cartesian sense; it connotes non-spatiality. But – to turn to the African language that I know from the inside – in the Akan language the concept of existence, as Gyekye (1987, pp. 179–81) rightly insists, is intrinsically spatial: to exist (*wo ho*) is to be somewhere. Consequently, in the Akan understanding, if "spirits" exist, they must be spatial and cannot be spiritual in a neo-Cartesian sense (see

Article 34, INCORPOREALITY). They are not, on that account, fully material; for to be such it is necessary to be not just spatial but also subject to the causal laws of common experience. By all indications, however, the extra-human beings in question are supposed to be exempt, for example, from some of the dynamical laws that constrain the motion and efficiency of ordinary objects. Thus they are thought to be capable of affecting human beings without, *normally*, being seen, and the action can be at a great distance. Such entities may, for convenience, be called quasi-material or quasi-physical. It is because they are quasi-material rather than spiritual that I have so far used the word "spirits" with quotational reservations. The aim has been to forestall the common fallacy of supposing that spirits must be necessarily spiritual. In fact, it is not only with respect to Akan discourse that this is not the case; Western spiritualist literature also is full of stories of quasi-material apparitions. The difference is that Western metaphysics additionally harbors schools of thought dedicated to the propagation of notions of spiritual entities in the Cartesian sense, and Akan traditional thought is devoid of such an inclination for the deep semantical reason already adduced. It is probably unnecessary at this stage to belabor the point that in being quasi-material, the spirits of the Akan worldview are quasi-empirical and therefore not transcendent in any useful sense. The decidedly empirical bent of discourse about spirits among various African peoples suggests that the Akan language is not unique in the present respect.

Revisiting now the question of the worship of the ancestors and certain other spirits, it emerges that if the attitude involved is that of worship, then it is not the worship of anything that may appropriately be called supernatural or spiritual or transcendent. But is it really worship, religious worship, that is? The following considerations do not encourage an affirmative answer. Leaving the ancestors out of account for a moment, it is a commonplace of African studies that the African attitude to the spirits, often hyperbolically called "lesser gods," is purely utilitarian. Ritualized praise is rendered unto them only because of expected benefits. As Busia (1954, p. 205) remarks: "the gods are treated with respect if they deliver the goods, and with contempt if they fail." Or worse: if devotees develop a confirmed impression of futility, attention is withdrawn, and the "god" concerned is left in fatal solitude. The reference to fatality is intended with all seriousness. In 1975 the African Nobel laureate Wole Soyinka startled an audience of African scholars at the University of Ghana when, in remarks enthusiastic of the Yoruba "gods," he pointed out quite serenely that the Yorubas create their own "gods" (such as the god of electricity) and can on occasion kill them. Yet the idea that an inefficient "god" can be denuded of all vital power through an enforced shortage of attention or other, more technical, means is widely received among traditional folks.

Allied to the last reflection is the consideration that the "gods," not unlike the Greek varieties of old, are not of a uniform moral standing: some are good, some bad, others nondescript; from which it is apparent that the devotee reserves the right of periodic review of their moral credentials. It follows, in turn, that the wishes of the "gods" – of even the moral elite among them – do not define moral goodness, notwithstanding the fact that the reactions of some of them may have a policing influence on conduct. The same is true of the ancestors, although, except in a few cases in Africa, such as among the Nuer and the Dinka (see, for example, Lienhardt 1961, p. 129) they are held in higher and warmer esteem and are more irreversibly credited with immortality (see Article 70, SURVIVAL OF DEATH). The ancestors are frequently so important in African life that something called ancestor worship is sometimes elevated into the veritable essence of African religion. But, in truth, the veneration of the ancestors is only an accentuated form of the respect given to the living elders of the group, and their moral authority is exerted only in the enforcement of morals established on pre-mortem criteria. These criteria of good conduct, as noted earlier, are founded on the quest for the impartial harmonization of human interests. It might be said, on this ground, by the way, that the ethic in question is a rational, humanistic one (see Gyekye 1987, ch. 8; Wiredu 1983). It should be noted, furthermore, that in most traditional African societies the average individual hopes eventually to gain a place in the community of the honored ancestors. If the ancestors were standardly worshiped and thought of as a species of gods, this would mean that a hankering after self-apotheosis is routine in those societies, suggesting a generalized megalomania quite frightening to contemplate. As it happens, the truth is less frightening. "Worship" is an elastic word, but it is stretching it rather far to call the attitude to the ancestors worship in any strict religious sense. And if this is so with respect to the ancestors, it is even more evident with respect to the assortment of spirits mentioned above.

If we now compare African attitudes to God with their attitudes to the spirits as just characterized, the contrast is tremendous. True, the will of God also does not define goodness, but, on the other hand, goodness (along with other qualities) does define God. And this is unique to God. Not even the ancestors are considered good by definition. In consequence, the reverence accorded to God is, as previously noted, unconditional, which is what the object of a genuinely religious attitude must evoke. The ancestors and "lesser gods" certainly fail to elicit this kind of respect. If, in spite of all this, one insists – as many do – on including the doctrines and doings regarding the spirits in the scope of African religions, this can only be by dint of a considerable extension of the concept of religion. Aside from the gratuitous assumption that, of religion, the more the better, it is not clear what the point of it is. But it is clear what some of its negative consequences are. One such consequence is that skepticism, on the part of contemporary Africans, regarding the spirits and their capabilities tends to be perceived by them (and others as well) as disenchantment with the traditional religion. Adherence to a foreign religion, say ISLAM (see Article 7) or CHRISTIANITY (see Article 6), is then seen as a desirable substitution. If it had been realized that the beliefs and practices revolving round the spirits do not really constitute a part of the religion, conversion might still conceivably have taken place, but it might perhaps have been for weightier reasons. A reverse side of this phenomenon is that other Africans, wishing to demonstrate their indigenous authenticity in the matter of religion, are apt to engage in proud exhibitions of spirit-oriented rituals with calls on their compatriots to join in the preservation of our religious heritage. But the beliefs involved will probably not survive the advance of modern knowledge. One cannot, of course, be dogmatic in this, for in the West progress in scientific knowledge has not, by any stretch of the imagination, wiped out the belief in all kinds of spirits and related practices. Still, a properly discriminating understanding of the nature of African religions is likely to promote more pertinent programs for their preservation, if preserved they must be.

Philosophically speaking, whether a religion is worthy of preservation should depend on the validity of its metaphysic. In Africa, however, a judicious metaphysical evaluation is impeded by conceptual distortions resulting from the fact that the reigning traditions of scholarship in African religions, for reasons connected with colonialism, were established by foreign scholars who, naturally enough, articulated their accounts in terms of the intellectual categories of their own culture. Among the most basic of these are the dualisms of the natural and the supernatural, the material and the spiritual and the transcendent and the empirical. I have argued that these categorial distinctions are not coherent within typical African conceptual frameworks. Whether this incoherence is due to a defect in those schemes of thought or in the dualisms themselves is a cross-cultural issue, which, *pace* relativism, can be fruitfully investigated. In the present connection, however, it only needs to be noted that, on account, partly, of this contextual incoherence, the concept of religion itself applies to African thinking (in at least many cases) only in the most minimal sense. It should be clear from the above discussion that we can speak of religion in African life only because of the widespread belief and trust in a supreme being who is the author of the world order. Incidentally, although the belief is widespread in Africa, it is not universal. If p'Bitek (1970, chs 8 and 9) is right, the central Luo, for instance, do not even operate with the concept of a supreme being. Besides, individual traditional skeptics are not unknown even in the God-believing societies. In any case, because of the non-transcendental cast of much African thought, even when the belief is entertained its meaning is usually more radically different from Christian conceptions, for instance, than it has been orthodox to suppose. Thus the supreme being is conceived to be the author of the world in the sense of a cosmic designer or architect rather than a creator *ex nihilo* (from nothing; see Article 39, CREATION AND CONSERVATION), and his omnipotence is understood to mean that he can accomplish any well-defined project, not that he can do absolutely everything, including, for example, abrogating the world order or even aspects of it. Taken together with the independence of morality from this belief, both conceptually and institutionally, the frequent absence or marginality of the worship of God, and the this-worldliness of the afterlife, a distinctive picture of African religions emerges that will have to be deeply pondered in any study of the religions of the world.

References

Abraham, W. E.: *The Mind of Africa* (Chicago: University of Chicago Press, 1962).

Busia, K.A.: "The Ashanti." In Daryll Forde (ed.), *African Worlds: Studies in the Cosmological Ideas and Social Values of African Peoples* (Oxford: Oxford University Press, 1954).

Gyekye, K.: *An Essay on African Philosophical Thought* (New York: Cambridge University Press, 1987).

Idowu, E. B.: *Olodumare: God in Yoruba Belief* (London: Longman, 1962).

Lienhardt, G.: *Divinity and Experience: The Religion of the Dinka* (Oxford: Oxford University Press, 1961).

Little, K.: "The Mende in Sierra Leone." In Daryll Forde (ed.), *African Worlds: Studies in the Cosmological Ideas and Social Values of African Peoples* (Oxford: Oxford University Press, 1954).

Mbiti, J. S.: *Concepts of God in Africa* (London: SPCK, 1970).

——: *African Religions and Philosophy* (London: Heinemann, 1969; 2nd ed., 1990).

p'Bitek, O.: *African Religions in Western Scholarship* (Nairobi, Kenya: East African Literature Bureau, 1970).

Sawyer, H.: *God: Ancestor or Creator?* (London: Longman, 1970).

Wiredu, K.: "Morality and religion in Akan thought." In H. Odera Oruka and D. A. Masolo (eds), *Philosophy and Cultures* (Nairobi, Kenya: Bookwise, 1983). (Repr. in N. R. Allen, Jr.: *African-American Humanism: An Anthology*, New York: Prometheus Books, 1991.)

——: "Death and the afterlife in African culture." In K. Wiredu and K. Gyekye (eds), *Person and Community: Ghanaian Philosophical Studies, I* (Washington, DC: Council for Research in Values and Philosophy, 1992).

Further reading

Appiah, K. A.: "Old gods, new worlds." In *In My Father's House*, ch. 6 (New York: Oxford University Press, 1992).

Danquah, J. B.: *The Akan Doctrine of God: A Fragment of Gold Coast Ethics and Religion* (London: Frank Cass, 1944; 2nd edn with introduction by K. A. Dickson, 1968).

Oladipo, O.: "Metaphysics, religion and Yoruba traditional thought: an essay on the status of the belief in non-human agencies in an African belief-system," *Journal of the Indian Council of Philosophical Research*, 7 (1990).

Shaw, R.: "The invention of 'African traditional religion'," *Religion*, 20 (1990).

5

Judaism

LENN E. GOODMAN

In the heyday of positivism philosophy was often a kind of metadiscourse. There were philosophy of science, philosophy of law, philosophy of language, and, of course, philosophy of religion. These metadisciplines sought to clarify the various modes of discourse and untangle the conceptual confusions that might arise within them. Sometimes the function was propaedeutic, sometimes apologetic, but the bracketing of the object language was decisive: philosophers of science were not doing science when they put on their philosophical hats, but clarifying conceptual foundations, justifying, sometimes, almost, acting as cheerleaders. Philosophy of law or ethics did not indulge in normative discourse but explained it, or exposed its pretensions. Philosophy of religion was not about the sacred but about the modes of speech and judgment that religious persons might use (see Article 24, RELIGIOUS LANGUAGE). Users of the "object language" were thought of as somewhat unselfconscious naifs or naturals. Philosophy might awaken them to the inner problems of the language they were using, and then, it was assumed, they would no longer speak or act in the same way. Philosophy would make them cautious or skeptical or tolerant. Perhaps it would teach them the deep inner truth of relativism, symbolism, or positivism itself. Certainly their thinking would never be the same. Philosophy of Judaism was about the problems of being Jewish – just as philosophy of religion was about the problems of being religious, or metaethics was about the problems of speaking or thinking ethically.

Today, happily, the tide has come in, or the catwalk has collapsed, and philosophers now find themselves swimming in the same water as those other human beings whose thoughts they seek to understand. We have religious and ethical philosophy, rather than just philosophy *of* . . .; normative ethics has resumed with gusto, and religious philosophy can speak of God, or ritual, or the nexus between divinity and obligation, and not just about the problems of religious discourse. The quest for a peculiar mode of religious speech or thought has all but ended, except in some rather projectively romantic forms of armchair anthropology. We can speak of Jewish philosophy rather than just philosophy of Judaism. The change is liberating, not least because it returns this ancient discipline to its roots and broadens its scope to match its widest historical range. Jewish philosophy will include a universe of problems that have exercised thoughtful exponents of the Jewish tradition – problems of cosmology and theology, social history, hermeneutics, philosophical anthropology, jurisprudence, and indeed aesthetics.

If philosophy is an open inquiry that seeks critical scrutiny of its own assumptions, Jewish philosophy will involve the informing of that inquiry by the resources of the Jewish tradition. Jewish philosophy so defined subsumes the narrower question, "what does it mean to be a Jew?" in the larger universe of Jewish concerns – from the problem of evil to divine transcendence, immortality, human freedom, justice, history and destiny, nature and economy, the value and meaning of life, and of human life in particular.

What unites practitioners of Jewish philosophy is not some exotic logic that we can label chauvinistically or patronizingly as "Talmudic," nor a common store of doctrines, but a chain of discourse and problematics, an ongoing conversation that is jarred but not halted by shifts of language, external culture, or epistemic background. What makes this conversation distinctive is no unique flavor or accent, no values or concerns that are unshared by others, but a respect for prior Jewish efforts found worthy as points of reference or departure as the conversation continues.

The unity and distinctiveness of Jewish philosophy, then, are both conceptual and historical. There is a historical continuity from one participant to the next – as there is in general philosophy. And there is a critical reappropriation and redefinition of the elements of the tradition in each generation – as there must be in any religious or cultural transmission.

The first major Jewish philosopher was Philo (ca. 20 BCE–ca. CE 50), a cultured Alexandrian whose commitments to his people were evident in his embassy to Caligula in their behalf, but also in his creative synthesis of Platonic, Stoic, and Biblical ideas (see Article 8, ANCIENT PHILOSOPHICAL THEOLOGY). Adapting the Stoic technique of allegory, Philo presented the Torah as a paradigm of the rational legislation Plato had called for, a law that grounds its commands in reasons, not sheer sanctions or obscure mysteries. Underlying the Law's authority was God's role as the Creator, not as arbitrary lord but as source of the wisdom manifest in nature and echoed in the Mosaic norms pursuing human harmony, creativity, and charity. It was by wisdom that God made his love manifest. For the plan of nature, the Logos (a concept appropriated by Jewish, Christian, and Muslim thinkers) was at once nature's immanent archetype and God's transcendent attribute. In nature and in the Law we grasp, as it were, God's idea.

Philo spoke of philosophy as the handmaiden of theology. But it was to philosophy, not astrology or textual stratigraphy, that he entrusted theology. Through his eyes we see the Torah as a philosophical text – Genesis, not just as a creation myth but as a self-conscious effort to fathom the natural world, by reference to the act of an utterly transcendent – yet not inscrutable – God (see Article 39, CREATION AND CONSERVATION). Just as modern Bible scholars assay the poetic chastity of Genesis against the theomachies and theogonies of ancient Near Eastern myths, Philo assays Mosaic naturalism and rationalism against the Hellenistic mystery cults. He finds in Moses the philosophical lawgiver for whom Plato had hoped. But reliance on a single individual's discretion is gone, displaced by a calm confidence in the norms of the Law; and philosophy guides the reading of those norms. For human wisdom reflects the wisdom that founded the Law.

The first systematic Jewish philosopher was Saadiah Gaon (882–942), a pioneer exegete, grammarian, liturgist, and lexicographer. Born in Egypt, Saadiah studied in Tiberias and led the ancient Talmudic academy of Pumpedita, by now located in Baghdad. His *Book of Critically Selected Beliefs and Convictions* surveys the views on major issues and defends those judged best-founded in reason and scripture – creation, providence, and accountability, but also moral and epistemic objectivism (see Article 72, PROVIDENCE AND PREDESTINATION). Saadiah rebuts skepticism and moral/aesthetic monism, favoring a humanizing pluralism over the Neoplatonic, mystical, or ascetic appetite for simplicity or austerity. Maimonides speaks of Saadiah as a practitioner of *kalam*, an apologetic, dialectical theology rooted in authority. But Saadiah's Biblical hermeneutics are as informed by philosophy as his philosophical views are by scripture. Convinced of the Torah's veracity, he insists that Biblical expressions be taken as familiarly understood only if logic and science, sound tradition and other texts permit. Otherwise we must read figuratively, forestalling capricious readings by citing textual parallels to warrant each departure from familiar Hebrew usage.

The Hebrew poet Ibn Gabirol, as discovered only in 1845, was the philosopher Avicebrol, author of the *Fons Vitae* ("The Fountain of Life"), which survives intact only in Latin, although passages quoted in Hebrew point us toward the lost Arabic original. Written as a dialogue between teacher and disciple, it addresses the ontology of the One and the many, relying on "intellectual matter," and a primal Will to mediate divine simplicity (see Article 31, SIMPLICITY). Among its most endearing exchanges: "*Disciple*: 'The resolution of all things to these two (universal matter and form), is this fact or opinion?' *Master*: 'It is not a fact but an opinion.' "

Ibn Gabirol's *On the Improvement of the Moral Qualities* examines moral psychology in a physiological vein. While upholding the soul's immortality (see Article 70, SURVIVAL OF DEATH) and the mind's affinity with the divine Intellect, Ibn Gabirol links human emotions with the bodily senses – hauteur, humility, shame, and shamelessness with seeing; love, hate, pity, and hardheartedness with hearing; ire, complaisance, jealousy, and spunk with smelling; joy, anxiety, serenity, and regret with tasting; free-spending, tightfistedness, boldness, and timidity with touching. The virtues, of course, are means between extremes. But, since each disposition represents a specific "temperament," or blending of the bodily humors, Ibn Gabirol can discuss and "treat" the dispositions by reference not only to social norms but also to our embodiment, laying the groundwork for Maimonides' treatment of virtues and vices as habits which our choices overlay upon our inborn propensities.

Judah Halevi (before 1075–1141), perhaps the greatest post-Biblical Hebrew poet, was another medically-minded thinker who grounded a theology in nature and looked to nature as the realm in which understanding would bear fruit. His philosophical dialogue the *Kuzari* imagines the encounter with Judaism of the King of the Khazars, a people of the far off Volga, who had adopted Judaism in the eighth century. As Halevi sets the scene, the king has dreamed that his intentions please God, but not his actions. He summons a spokesman of the "despised religion" only after hearing from a Neoplatonist, a Christian, and a Muslim. The philosopher's ideas are attractive. But, as the king explains, it is his way of life, not his mind, that needs improvement. He worries that sectarians who share the philosopher's ideas all seem sincerely bent on one another's murder. The problem is no mere abstraction. Halevi's poems reflect the mayhem he had seen in Spain, the Bosnia or Guernica of his time, where Jews were caught between the hammer and anvil of Reconquista and *jihad*. The philosopher's attempt to set the life of the mind above such conflicts vividly reveals the poverty of the prevailing intellectualism that passed for philosophy. Halevi's own response is to pursue a way of life and thought firmly rooted in practice and community with his people, in the past and future as well as the present.

Because Halevi places culture (including material culture), imagination, and history where more conventional philosophers had placed logic, reason, and cosmology, moderns of romantic bent see in him an adversary of philosophy. But closer study shows him as a skilled philosopher committed to a profound critique of established philosophical notions. His ontology is deeply rooted in Ibn Gabirol, as Marx is in Hegel. But Halevi banishes the stream of emanating celestial intellects that had entranced earlier thinkers. Seizing on Ibn Gabirol's idea of a union of will and wisdom and brilliantly transforming his spiritual matter, Halevi returns to the divine word, now called *'Amr*, Arabic for God's word of command, embodying the imperative force of archetypal and normative wisdom. Like Philo and the prophets in their way, he finds God's word immanent and accessible, in nature and the Law.

Halevi's Khazar responds thoughtfully to the Christian and Muslim spokespersons: not having been reared among them, he does not long to make sense of Christian mysteries or warmly resonate to the Arabic of the Qur'an. Naturalists always try to rationalize what they observe. But without direct experience or the heart's consent that is won in early childhood, Christian and Muslim traditions do not compel. The roots of commitment, Halevi finds, lie not in the momentary ecstasies of an isolated anchorite or the abstract ruminations of intellectualist philosophers but in the transgenerational life of a people.

Touched by the yearnings of the Hebrew liturgy (to which he, like Ibn Gabirol, contributed), Halevi demands to know how one can weep for Zion and not go there, where God's Presence is clearest and the life God commanded is most fully lived. Acting on this yearning, Halevi left Spain and journeyed to his people's ancient home, where he died, as legend has it, kissing the soil of Zion, run through by an Arab horseman's spear. But, even had he lived, his yearnings would not have ended with arrival in the holy city. For his famous lines, "My heart is in the East, but I am in the utmost West," voice spiritual as well as earthly longing, not to be sated by mere presence in the Land.

In the *Book of Guidance to the Duties of the Heart* Bahya Ibn Pakuda (mid-11th to mid-12th century) made philosophic understanding a spiritual obligation, involving study of nature, probing of God's Law, and internalization of its commands. Following the ancient pietist tradition, Bahya finds a kernel of self-serving in typical worries about free will, which neither reason nor texts can resolve. Wisdom urges us to accept maximal responsibility for our own acts and to accept all that befalls us as God's work (see Article 37, FOREKNOWLEDGE AND HUMAN FREEDOM). Humanism, we note, often does just the opposite, blaming fate, or God (as in the Epicurean dilemma) over what we do not control, even in ourselves, but indulging in self-congratulation, anxiety, or remorse over what we deem our own domain. Bahya's approach, like that of the Stoics, is rhetorical, a tactic for coping, not a metaphysical solution. But in voicing an outlook we can never wholly share, he offers us a kind of reality check: our own excuses and castigations are equally rhetorical, as we notice when they assign credit or blame, shoulder or shirk responsibility, otherwise than Bahya does.

Maimonides, called the Rambam, an acronym of the Hebrew, Rabbi Moses ben Maimon (1135?–1204), was born in Cordova but exiled with his family in 1148, when the Almohad invaders imposed conversion on non-Muslims. Living first in North Africa, then briefly in Palestine, he settled in Cairo and took up medicine to support his family after his brother's death in a shipwreck. His medical service to Saladin's *wazir* was complemented by a busy private practice, and he authored ten medical treatises.

Maimonides wrote three major juridical works: (1) *The Book of the Commandments* schematized the traditional 613 *mitzvot* or divine commands of the Pentateuch, notably including "I am the Lord thy God . . ." and "Thou shalt have no other gods before me . . ." as the first of the positive and negative commandments, arguing, with rabbinic precedent (*Makkot*, near the end) that these two precepts, addressed directly by God to human understanding, are the axioms grounding all the rest. (2) His Arabic commentary on the Mishnah, the ancient legal code that forms the backbone of the Talmud, interprets the "oral law" by which the Rabbis elaborated Biblical legislation as containing the rational principles of that law. Maimonides structures the commandments in terms of Aristotelian VIRTUE ETHICS (see Article 59), arguing that they seek human moral and intellectual perfection, the virtues that enable us to know God and realize our likeness to Him. Commenting on the promise to all Israel of "a portion in the world to come," Maimonides lays out thirteen credal articles that assure even non-philosophers a share in immortality, since beliefs are practical surrogates for the ideas that render the intellect immortal. (3) His major and still authoritative 14-volume codification of Talmudic law, the *Mishneh Torah*, or Law in Review, was written in Mishnaic Hebrew. Familiarly cited as the *Yad Hazakah*, "The Strong Hand," because the word *Yad*, hand, has the numerical value of 14, it takes as its motto the verse "Then shall I be unabashed to scrutinize all Thy commandments" (Psalm 119:6). It systematizes all of Talmudic law, omitting rabbinic citations (although faithfully respecting rabbinic authority and precedent) and cutting clear of the often digressive Talmudic discussions, organizing the laws according to their purposes: a few brief commandments ground a moral code, the laws of torts and the penal code pursue peace and justice, those of the Sabbath or the elaborate Temple ritual draw the mind to the idea of a transcendent God and wean it from all that is even reminiscent of pagan beliefs and practices. Strikingly, Maimonides elaborates a rabbinic political ideal, with the Torah as its constitution, a strong central ruler, "to fight the battles of the Lord," but under the authority of the Law and the wisdom of its interpreters (see Article 62, THEISM, LAW, AND POLITICS).

Maimonides' crowning philosophical achievement was the *Guide to the Perplexed*, which examines theological problems under the rabbinic rubrics of "the act of creation" and "the act of the chariot" – the Biblical accounts of Genesis and the vision of Ezekiel (see Article 11, THE JEWISH CONTRIBUTION TO MEDIEVAL PHILOSOPHICAL THEOLOGY). The Rabbis permitted explication of these passages only one-on-one and only for the best-prepared students, who need no more than hints to provoke their understanding. The problems, as Maimonides understood them, were those of cosmology and metaphysics, centered on the accommodation of the infinitely transcendent God to the finitude of creation. For Ezekiel seems to suggest, with much periphrasis, that he saw God in human form; and Genesis clearly proposes a causal relation between God's timeless perfection (see Article 32, ETERNITY) and our changeable world.

To keep faith with the Talmudic injunction, lest unprepared readers face problems they cannot resolve, Maimonides couches his *Guide* as a letter to a single disciple with specific capabilities and needs. He never calls the *Guide* a book; and, more tellingly, does not state the problems it addresses, leaving readers in the dark about its subject matter, unless they have grappled with these problems. So effective is this approach that even careful readers often imagine the *Guide* opens by refuting anthropomorphism, when in fact its first 70 chapters *assume* that all ordinary predicates and relations are inapplicable to God and address the question how it is possible for us to speak of God at all, a problematic voiced in the Midrashic remark: "How great is the boldness of the prophets, who liken the creature to its Creator!" Maimonides deconstructs prophetic anthropomorphism, carefully avoiding the "onion peeling" that was the bugbear of his predecessor al-Ghazali (1058–1111), who feared that de-anthropomorphizing, carried too far, might leave one with nothing (see Article 10, THE ISLAMIC CONTRIBUTION TO MEDIEVAL PHILOSOPHICAL THEOLOGY). Maimonides shows how all Biblical anthropomorphisms aim to communicate some (human) idea of perfection, while excluding the limitations that human ideas typically entail. The God that emerges from this analysis is no ordinary being (Maimonides urges that even little children should be taught that God is not a person) but a being of sheer perfection whose absolute and necessary existence (see Article 33, NECESSITY) is made explicit when God reveals Himself to Moses as "I AM THAT I AM," an All-sufficiency encapsulated in the Tetragrammaton, whose letters are those of the verb to be (see Article 27, BEING).

Maimonides, like Saadiah, defends creation, but he warns against assuming that either creation or eternity can be proved. Aristotle, who taught us the difference between apodictic and dialectical arguments, reveals by his resort to persuasive language that he knew his own arguments for the eternity of the natural order were not rigorous proofs. They were in fact projections of an eternalism already implicit in the Aristotelian analysis of time and change, matter and potentiality. But the defenses of creation proposed in the *kalam* proved too much, making continuous creation a necessity by dissolving the continuities of nature, splintering time, and making science impossible, freedom inconceivable, and the idea of creation itself incoherent.

In place of the certitude sought by the polemical exponents and adversaries of creation, Maimonides proposes only that creation is more probable conceptually and preferable theologically to eternalism. For the eternalist scheme of emanation without volition cannot explain how complexity emerged (by some automatism) from divine simplicity. And the Aristotelian claim that nature has always been as it is does not leave room for God's determination to have made a difference – as the voluntarism of Ibn Gabirol, Halevi, and al-Ghazali, suggested that it should. Indeed, if Aristotelian essentialism and Neoplatonic emanationism are taken strictly, change would not seem possible at all.

Pondering the problems of evil, of providence, and of revelation – all questions which involve the limits in God's creative manifestation – Maimonides finds precious hints in the book of Job (1:6), where Satan, the adversary, is said to have come "along with" the children of God (see Article 50, THE PROBLEM OF EVIL). Satan, according to one rabbinic gloss, is simply sin, or death. But the book of Job (which Maimonides reads as a fictional allegory of the problem of evil) tells us that Job was innocent. Satan, whom he identifies with metaphysical "otherness," alienation from God's absolute perfection, is matter; and Maimonides chides the Neoplatonists for not recognizing in their own idea of matter a solution to the problem of evil. For matter is a concomitant of creation. It is not a positive reality, a principle like the divine ideas, the forms and forces that give reality to natural beings, but it "comes along with them," in the sense that there will be no gift of existence without alienation, no creation without separation. Matter is thus the basis of evil, including human differences and vulnerabilities. It is not evil in itself, and indeed is not real, as the Neoplatonic forms are. At once the heroic wife of Proverbs 31 and the married harlot of Proverbs 7, never content with just one form, matter in our own body is a receptivity that can be turned upward or downward, since the soul has her own power to govern it.

We are, then, neither as abandoned to circumstance as, say, Alexander of Aphrodisias suggests, nor as smothered by attentiveness as the *kalam* might have it in assigning God to superintend the fall of every leaf. Providence comes to nature through the forms, perfection scaled to the capacities of finitude; but providence does reach individuals and is not confined to species (see Article 30, GOODNESS). For Aristotle himself taught us that universals exist only in their particulars. And the human form is not just a pattern of life but a substantial entity, a rational soul, whose guidance is the providence of the wise and whose fulfillment, in knowledge of God, is immortality. This ultimate goal of the philosopher is visited on others by prophets, those rare philosophers who are graced with clarity of imagination to translate pure concepts into images and institutions, laws and symbols, beliefs and practices, that allow all humanity to share in the fruits of philosophy.

Space permits only brief mention of a few post-Maimonidean philosophers: Levi ben Gershom (Gersonides, 1288–1344), astronomer, mathematician, and exegete, sought in his *Wars of the Lord* to mediate between naturalism and theism, even compromising God's OMNISCIENCE (see Article 29) in the interest of human freedom. Hasdai Crescas (1340–1410), born in Barcelona, imprisoned for "desecrating the host" but later, as a courtier, charged by the Crown with rehabilitating Spanish Jewry after the terrible anti-Jewish riots of 1391, addressed his task, on its intellectual level, through his *Light of the Lord*, a stunning critique of Aristotelian cosmology. In arguments that inspired Spinoza (who cites him as Rab Jasdaj), Crescas rejects Aristotle's abhorrence for the void and for "actual infinity" and anticipates the ideas of gravity and multiple worlds, each with its own gravitational center. His student Joseph Albo (ca. 1360–?1444) defended Judaism in the Tortosa Disputation of 1413–14 and sought to forge a philosophically defensible creed based on God, revelation and requital, de-emphasizing messianism, the sore point of Christian–Jewish polemics, but using the idea of natural law, gleaned from the writings of Thomas Aquinas (see Article 9, THE CHRISTIAN CONTRIBUTION TO MEDIEVAL PHILOSOPHICAL THEOLOGY; Article 58, NATURAL LAW ETHICS; and Article 74, REVELATION AND SCRIPTURE). Isaac Abravanel (1437–1508), leader of the Jews expelled from Spain in 1492, described the ideal government of the Messianic age not as a monarchy – which is not at all the image of God's rule – but as a mixed constitution, Mosaic in model, with "lower courts" chosen by the people to govern local matters and a high court, appointed by the ruler, to institute the overarching legal structure. Abravanel's son Judah, known as Leone Ebreo (ca. 1460–ca. 1521), in his *Dialoghi d'amore*, celebrates love as a cosmic and spiritual force that pervades nature, from the mutual attraction of the elements to the divine love that unites the cosmos and draws the mind toward God. Judah Messer Leon (ca. 1425–ca. 1495) in his *Book of the Honeycomb's Flow*, draws on Aristotle, Cicero, and Quintilian to analyze the poetics of the Hebrew Bible, finding in its appeals to human sensibilities no detriments to the text but marks of divine artistry, to be emulated by human orators and authors. Ibn Gabirol took his title *Fons Vitae* ("The Fountain of Life") from the Psalms (36:9), to show the affinity between Biblical and Neoplatonic ideas. Messer Leon, similarly, chose a title from the Psalms (19:10), calling scripture to support his humanist thesis in a Biblical metaphor that makes God's law a work of natural artistry and praises it not only for truth and justice but for beauty and delight (see Article 35, BEAUTY).

Among the modern exponents of Jewish philosophy, few rank with those already mentioned. Moses Mendelssohn (1729–86), grandfather of the composer, is one. He was called the German Socrates, in part for his original arguments for immortality in his *Phaedo* or *Phaidon*. Academic entrée was out of the question for a Jew in Mendelssohn's time, and his outpouring of important publications was produced while he earned his living as managing director of a silk factory. Imbued with traditional and philosophical Jewish learning, he mastered independently Wolff and Leibniz, the culture and literary language of modern Europe, and won fame by taking the prize in the Berlin Academy competition of 1763, in which Kant won honorable mention (see Article 12, EARLY MODERN PHILOSOPHICAL THEOLOGY). Mendelssohn was the first Jew to be accepted among modern European intellectuals, he inspired his friend Gotthold Lessing's play *Nathan the Wise*, and his idea of immortality as unending moral progress became that of Kant. Pressed by critics to justify his loyalty to his ancient faith, Mendelssohn responded in *Jerusalem* with a comprehensive philosophy of Judaism, arguing that it was not their religious beliefs that Israel had acquired at Sinai, since these were simply the natural religion they had already discovered by reason. What was revealed, and eternally valid, was a system of practices designed to sustain Israel's loyalty to that faith, making them "a light unto the nations." Enforcement of these ceremonial symbols had passed, with the destruction of the ancient Hebrew commonwealth, from that state to the hearts of individuals, where providence decreed it should forever abide. Mendelssohn thus blunted accusations of illiberality and the somewhat inconsistent charges of dual loyalties that were already becoming cliches of anti-Semitic modernism, but only by forswearing the social authority of Judaic institutions and forestalling the first modern glimmerings of Zionism. A founder of the Jewish Enlightenment, the *Haskalah*, he worked to elevate his fellow Jews by championing German-Jewish education, translating the Pentateuch, Psalms, and Song of Songs, and effectively combating such civil disabilities as the infamous oath *more Judaico*.

Hermann Cohen (1842–1918) was the son of a cantor and son-in-law of the splendid Hebrew liturgical composer Lewandowski. He became a major Kantian, an early critic of the *Ding an sich*, and supplemented Kantian ethics with Aristotelian and Biblical ideas of virtue and justice. Cohen championed the loyalty and authentic Germanness of German Jews against attacks from the anti-Semitic historian Heinrich von Treitschke, by marking the affinities of Jewish values with Kantian ethics. In *Religion of Reason out of the Sources of Judaism*, he made God the moral standard and guarantor of justice and charity that seek to create a community of free individuals, a kingdom of ends that philosophy cannot prove to be inevitable but that personal conviction must somehow uphold (see Article 22, THE JEWISH TRADITION).

Franz Rosenzweig (1886–1929) nearly abandoned Judaism but discovered its inner spirituality at the Yom Kippur services he attended in 1913, out of a desire to enter Christianity not as a pagan but as a Jew. An important Hegel scholar, Rosenzweig uncovered a more liberal, less Machiavellian Hegel than was familiar in his time. His *Star of Redemption*, written largely in postcards home from the German trenches during World War I is a manifesto of spiritual existentialism that breaks with the classic primacy of the (intellectualist) Logos and foregrounds the immediacy of creation, encountered, rather than understood, more mythic than rational. We escape mythic atemporality, Cohen urges, not through reason but through revelation, which speaks to us, primordially, in a command, to love God; and, therefore, our fellow humans (see Article 61, AGAPEISTIC ETHICS). Revelation creates community, and community creates the individual, capable of dialogue with God. Thus the birth of the I–Thou relationship, crucial to several philosophers of the day, including Buber.

The star of David, signified in Rosenzweig's title, is his emblem of the dynamic relations of creation, revelation, and redemption that link God, man, and the universe. Like Mendelssohn, Rosenzweig translated much of the Bible into German, collaborating with Buber, who completed the work on his death. He helped found the Free Jewish House of Learning in Frankfurt and translated Halevi's liturgical poetry. But, unlike Halevi, Rosenzweig saw Israel's intimacy with God as a contact with eternity that somehow draws Jews out of history, living redemption while the world prepares for it in more material ways. He thus opposed Zionism, and, perhaps as tellingly, told an inquirer who asked whether he prayed with *tefillin*, "Not yet."

Martin Buber (1878–1965) was raised in the home of his grandfather Solomon Buber, a well-known scholar of Midrash. He studied with Dilthey and Simmel, became a youthful Zionist leader, and was drawn to the tales of the Hasidic Master Nahman of Bratslav, which he adapted into German. His novels gave modern Jews friendly access to the Hasidic world, and his Zionism proposed a Jewish–Arab community in Palestine, where he settled in 1938. His *I and Thou* (1922) foregrounds the relationality of human with human or of human with God. We constitute both self and other in radically different ways when we use an *it* or confront a *thou*. Authenticity, freedom, even genuine presentness depend on the I–Thou relation. God is the eternal Thou, never made an it by spiritual fatigue, but glimpsed through human encounters with others, and with art. When we speak to God, not about Him, we encounter the living presence. Revelation is humanity's continuing response to that presence, epitomized in Israel's covenant with God.

Emil Fackenheim is best known perhaps (although his career began with studies of Avicenna's doctrine of love and Hegel's religious dimensions) for the prominence he gives the Holocaust. His conclusions are not intellectual but existential. Their core, like the determination of the protagonist in Bernard Malamud's *The Fixer*, is a determination "not to give Hitler a posthumous victory" – to find some mode of action or expression that will affirm Jewish vitality and strengthen the commitment of Jews.

Emmanuel Levinas is a Midrashic thinker, a master of aspects, and thus a phenomenologist, much admired by postmodernists, perhaps in part because he shuns sustained argument and system with the same discomfort that post-Holocaust musicians may show for melody, harmony, or symmetry. But Levinas is an avowedly ethical and indeed a constructive thinker. In speaking of the claims made upon us by the face of the other, he speaks, in his own way, of the same person whose cloak and millstone the Torah commands us not to take in pledge, the stranger whom we are commanded to love and told that God loves, the same thou that Buber and Rosenzweig find at the roots of our humanity and God's commanding word – although Levinas quarrels with Buber's somewhat romantic, non-intellectual construal of the I–Thou relation. In the dialectic of rabbinic thought Levinas finds a very Hebrew awareness of the everpresent face of the other. But he admires Rosenzweig for refusing to subjectivize nature in the post-Kantian mode, and thus for respecting the inalienable otherness of the other. Cautious of the mere posit of God as the parent who authorizes or commands our respect for one another, Levinas sees a trace of divine transcendence in the sheer alterity of the other, a trace that he connects with the Biblical dictum that one cannot see God's face and with the Maimonidean gloss that when Moses was allowed to see God's "back," it was a "trace" of God – here understood as the ethical demand of alterity – that he was vouchsafed to know, and thus to enshrine in the Law.

Pausing now to sum up what it is that the philosophers we have considered have in common – since I think it best to ask the question empirically here, rather than to beg it prescriptively – we find that the exponents of Jewish philosophy in every period share the prophetic concern. That is, they continue to interpret the ethical socially and the social ethically. They share the Mosaic interest in cosmology and in the metaphysics of divinity, even when they fight shy (as Moses did) of efforts to bring God to terms in fanciful narratives or bring him to his knees in the graven images of theory. They remain sensitive to the absoluteness of the Mosaic I AM, which contrasts vividly against the ground of Parmenides' sheer affirmation of being (*esti*). For in the I AM, which will become the one item of the Decalogue that all Israel must hear for themselves, God speaks to us in the first person and in a language that does not negate appearances but invites our humanity, our acceptance of creation and of one another. Objectivity does not exclude but presupposes subjecthood, and subjecthood does not entail but excludes the mere subjectivity of self or other.

All of the philosophers we have considered are in touch with their surroundings. None speaks a language too remote to be translated or uses an idiom that the others cannot catch, or trusts in categories incommensurate with those of humanity at large. Their philosophies are neither the symptoms of a *Zeitgeist* nor apologetics for a *Volksgeist* but products of reflection, enlivened by a tradition of critical thought and discourse. That reflection is made critical in part by its openness to the larger philosophical world, the world of Plato, Aristotle, the Stoics and Epicureans, the Neoplatonists and Muslim philosophers and theologians, the work of Thomas or the Renaissance humanists, of Leibniz, Kant and Hegel, the phenomenologists, existentialists, and postmodernists. Among these voices, the exponents of Jewish philosophy have been prominent and original participants, just as Josephus is among historians, or Saul Bellow among novelists. Their stance is creative, not merely (as Hitler thought) "parasitic" or reactive. Their creativity is fostered by the wealth of their own traditions and by the crosstalk of their philosophical milieu.

In every period there are certain Jewish thinkers, or thinkers of Jewish origin, whose work cannot be classed as a contribution to Jewish philosophy. One thinks of those who succumbed to conversionary pressures in the medieval or the modern age and of those who internalized the anti-Jewish hostilities they felt. More broadly, certain major thinkers, whose ideas are inspired by Jewish sources, are not participants in the conversation of Jewish philosophy. Marx and Freud must be numbered among these. They paid a price for their cosmopolitanism, in terms of the free or forced abandonment of orientation toward their Jewish roots when they entered the mainstream of Western culture. Spinoza is a crucial case. His philosophy is deeply immersed in the great problematics of the Western tradition but also in the specific issues by which Jewish philosophers sought to address those problematics. What makes it hard to count Spinoza as a contributor to

Jewish philosophy is not that he did not confine himself to a philosophy of Judaism – for no major Jewish philosopher did that – but that the circumstances of his life and epoch turned him decisively away from the methods of accommodation and critical appropriation that other Jewish philosophers had found. The result, as with Marx or Freud, was a rupture that led to greater radicalism – both creativity and hostility – than is found in those who were able, or enabled, to keep faith with the generations of their Jewish predecessors and contemporaries.

The outcome of such radicalism is striking: for such thinkers, in their moment, like any alienated person, become isolated both from some of the constraints and from some of the resources of a human community that might have been of help to them. Later Jewish thinkers can still profit from what Spinoza, Marx, or Freud achieved. Parts of their thought become dated and provincialized by the very topicality that once made them the matter of the moment or the century. Other elements are reabsorbed into the continuing conversation of philosophy at large or the particular foci of Jewish philosophical conversation. One cannot say, moralistically, that such thinkers, who are alienated to one degree or another, by choice or exclusion or force of circumstance, have thereby lost more than they have gained. For there is a deep potential for conceptual value to be gleaned in radicalism. But radicalism, like heresy, limits catholicity, blunts synthesis, focuses attention sharply on a single issue or nexus, and may overstress it or press it to the breaking point. Just as there is balance in community and value in synthesis, there is philosophical and not just practical wisdom in an irenic posture towards the philosophical past. Thus, when the prophets reflect on the future of human thinking, they envision all nations turning to a purer language (Zephaniah 3:9), and part of the means by which they expect this to be achieved is the reconciling of the fathers to the sons (Malachi 3:24).

Bibliography

The JPS Torah Commentary: The Traditional Hebrew Text with the New JPS Translation, ed. N. Sarna, 5 vols. (Philadelphia: Jewish Publication Society, 1989–   ).

Bahya ibn Pakuda: The Book of Direction to the Duties of the Heart, tr. Menachem Mansoor (London: Routledge & Kegan Paul, 1973).

Cohen, H.: Religion of Reason out of the Sources of Judaism, tr. Simon Kaplan (New York: Ungar, 1972).

Goodman, L. E.: On Justice: An Essay in Jewish Philosophy (New Haven: Yale University Press, 1991).

——: God of Abraham (New York: Oxford University Press, 1996).

Halevi, Judah: The Kuzari, tr. H. Hirschfeld, 1905 (New York: Schocken, 1964). [A new and more adequate translation is in preparation by Barry Kogan.]

Levi ben Gershom (Gersonides): Wars of the Lord, tr. Seymour Feldman, 3 vols. (Philadelphia: Jewish Publication Society, 1984–   ).

Maimonides, Moses: The Guide of the Perplexed, tr. Shlomo Pines (Chicago: University of Chicago Press, 1963). [I find this translation, although accurate, to be somewhat wooden. Some readers may prefer the earlier version by M. Friedlander (London, 1904; reprinted by Dover since 1956). Fairly extensive selections of my own translation with commentary, along with most of the "Eight Chapters" are also available in my *Rambam: Readings in the Philosophy of Moses Maimonides* (New York: Viking, 1976; reissued by Gee Tee Bee, 1984).]

Philo: *Works*, ed. and tr. F. H. Colson and G. H. Whitaker, 12 vols. (Cambridge: Harvard University Press, 1929–).

Rosenzweig, F.: *The Star of Redemption*, tr. William Hallo (Boston: Beacon Press, 1964).

Saadiah Gaon: *The Book of Beliefs and Opinions*, tr. Samuel Rosenblatt (New Haven: Yale University Press, 1948). [This translation of the *Book of Critically Selected Beliefs and Convictions* needs reworking.]

6

Christianity

WILLIAM J. WAINWRIGHT

Christianity's complex relations with philosophy can be approached from three angles – by surveying the problems which Christian philosophy of religion must address, by examining Christian theism's impact on Western philosophy and the resources it provides for solving problems arising within that tradition, and by considering Christianity's ambivalent attitudes towards philosophy.

Philosophical problems associated with Christianity

Christian theism is a specification of more generic religious conceptions. At the most general level, it is an instance of William James's "religious hypothesis":

1 There is a higher universe.
2 We are better off if we believe this and act accordingly.
3 Communion with the higher universe "is a process wherein work is really done," and effects produced in the visible world.

James's "higher universe" can be interpreted in a number of ways, however – as an impersonal power or force, as "emptiness," as cosmic law, and so on. Theists construe it as God – an omniscient mind, an omnipotent will, an unlimited love. Christians are distinguished from other theists by their understanding of the Godhead as both one and three, and by their belief that God has redeemed the world through Jesus of Nazareth.

Many philosophical difficulties which the literature associates with Christianity are problems for any religious worldview. Whether religious hypotheses are metaphysically otiose, for example, and naturalism sufficient. Or whether religious language is cognitively meaningful and (if it is) what kind of meaning it has (see Article 24, RELIGIOUS LANGUAGE). Or whether experience of the "higher universe" is genuinely possible. Of the remaining difficulties, most are problems for any standard form of theism – whether God's existence can be proved, whether and how OMNIPOTENCE (see Article 28) and other divine attributes can be defined, whether such properties as timelessness (see Article 32, ETERNITY) and providential activity are consistent, whether MIRACLES (see Article 46) are possible or likely, whether God's FOREKNOWLEDGE AND HUMAN FREEDOM (see Article 37) are compatible, and so on. The problem of evil is particularly acute for theists since they believe that an omnipotent and morally perfect God knowingly permits it (see Article 50, THE PROBLEM OF EVIL). (However, some form of the difficulty besets any religious worldview which maintains, as most do, that reality is fundamentally good.) Other problems are common to Christianity and to some but not all non-Christian forms of theism. An example is the tension between strong doctrines of grace such as those found in Christianity and (for example) Sri Vaisnavism or Siva Siddhanta, and human responsibility. Another is the "scandal of particularity" – the potential conflict between doctrines of God's justice and love, and the belief that salvation depends on a conscious relation to historical persons or events that are unknown (and thus, on the face of it, inaccessible) to large numbers of people. Thus, most of the philosophical problems associated with Christian theism are not peculiar to Christianity. But some are. Obvious examples are difficulties associated with the Trinity, the Incarnation or atonement, and original sin (see Article 66, TRINITY; Article 67, INCARNATION; Article 69, ATONEMENT, JUSTIFICATION, AND SANCTIFICATION; and Article 68, SIN AND ORIGINAL SIN).

Christian theism may also provide unique resources for dealing with problems common to other theistic or religious systems. Marilyn Adams, for example, has recently argued that Christian theism furnishes materials for handling the problem of evil. Discussions of the issue typically assume that the system of rights and obligations connects all rational agents, and that a satisfactory solution of the problem must show that evils are logically necessary conditions or consequences of "religiously neutral" goods like pleasure, knowledge, or friendship. Both assumptions are suspect. God escapes the network of rights and obligations in virtue of His transcendence. Furthermore, God and communion with Him don't just surpass temporal goods; they are incommensurable with them. The beatific vision will therefore "engulf" any finite evils one has suffered. Adams also suggests that Christian theodicists should explore the implications of such goods as Christian martyrdom and Christ's passion. Suffering may be a means of participating in Christ, thereby providing the sufferer with insight into, and communion with, God's inner life. Adams's first suggestion is available to other theists, but her second is not.

Christian philosophers in the Middle Ages addressed all of these issues. Since Descartes, they have largely confined themselves to discussing generic questions. There are two exceptions, however. Since the early 1980s, Christian analytic philosophers have turned their attention to uniquely Christian issues. Richard Swinburne's work on the atonement, Thomas Morris's book on the Incarnation, and the essays collected in *Philosophy and the Christian Faith* are important examples. The other notable exception is Immanuel Kant's and G. W. F. Hegel's philosophical reconstructions of such peculiarly Christian doctrines as original sin and the Trinity.

Christian theism and Western philosophy

Some intellectual historians have claimed that Christian theism's encounter with Greek thought profoundly altered the course of Western philosophy. For example, Etienne Gilson has argued that the Christian notion of God as a self-existent act of existence that freely bestows actuality on created beings had revolutionary consequences. The basic ontological dividing line was no longer between unity and multiplicity, or between the immaterial and material, as it was in Plato, Aristotle, and Plotinus, but between a God who exists necessarily, on the one hand, and created (and therefore contingent) being, on the other (see Article 39, CREATION AND CONSERVATION). As a result, philosophy was forced to draw a sharp distinction between a thing's being and its being a certain kind of thing, i.e. between its existence and its essence. Philosophy no longer confined itself to asking, with the Greeks, "how is the world ordered, and what accounts for its order?" (see Article 8, ANCIENT PHILOSOPHICAL THEOLOGY). It also asked, "why does any world exist and not nothing?" The being of things as well as their order was problematized. Others contend that these themes had further consequences. Pursuing suggestions of M. B. Foster and A. N. Whitehead, Eric Mascall has maintained that Christian theism cleared a metaphysical space within which modern science became possible. Since the Christian God is a God of reason and order, any world He creates will exhibit pattern and regularity. But because He *freely* creates the world, its order will be contingent. The world's structures cannot be deduced a priori, then, but must be discovered by observation and experiment. Others have claimed that Christian theism's desacralization of nature also helps explain why modern science arose in the West and not elsewhere. Christian theism maintains that nothing contingent is inherently holy. Places (Sinai, Jerusalem), persons (prophets, priests, divinely anointed kings), artifacts (the ark), and so on, aren't intrinsically holy; any holiness they possess is extrinsic – conferred upon them by God from without. Nature is no longer regarded as divine and therefore becomes an appropriate object for manipulation and detached observation.

However, while these claims may point to important truths, they are overstated. The conception of God in question is not peculiarly Christian, for Muslims and Jews share it. Nor is the desacralization of nature a uniquely Western phenomenon. (It occurs in Hinayana Buddhism.) Furthermore, that the created order is contingent is a consequence of at least one major form of Indian theism – Ramanuja's (1017–1137) Visistadvaita Vedanta. The world's "material" ("prakritic") substrate necessarily exists (for the world in either its latent or manifest form is God's body), but the phenomenal world or manifest universe does not. God is free to create it or not (i.e. He is free either to bring the world from an unmanifest to a manifest state or not to do so), and to give it any order He pleases.

Christian theism does appear to be largely responsible for the importance of the free will problem in Western philosophy. Neither Plato's nor Aristotle's philosophical psychology contains anything that precisely corresponds to the will. Augustine is the first to clearly recognize that some moral failures cannot be plausibly ascribed to imperfections of reason or desire, and to attribute them to a misuse of will. Again, while Aristotle's discussion of voluntary and involuntary action is quite sophisticated, he does not clearly ask whether human freedom and moral responsibility are compatible with universal causal determination. Christian theism's emphasis on the will, heightened sense of humanity's moral responsibility, and vivid awareness of God's sovereignty and causal universality, made this problem acute. Works like Augustine's *On Free Choice of the Will* and his anti-Pelagian writings, Anselm's *On Freedom of Choice* and *The Fall of Satan*, and Jonathan Edwards's *Freedom of the Will* raise issues which aren't squarely addressed in ancient philosophy, and discuss them with a sophistication and thoroughness which are absent in their Indian counterparts. (Indian philosophy examines these issues in connection with the doctrines of karma and God's sovereign causal activity. But the discussions are brief and comparatively unsophisticated. Ramanuja, for example, argues that God's causal sovereignty is preserved because God is the free agent's existential support and because He "consents" to their free actions, i.e. allows them to be actualized. Ramanuja thus resolves the tension between human freedom and God's causal sovereignty by restricting the latter's range. This is to dissolve the problem, not solve it.) Arguably, both the distinctions drawn and moves made in secular discussions of the free will problem, and the importance ascribed to it, have their ultimate roots in these theological discussions.

Some Christian philosophers believe that the resources of Christian philosophy can be used to "solve" or illuminate philosophical problems arising independently of theism. Two examples will suffice. First, if natural laws are no more than constant conjunctions (as David Hume thought), they will not support counterfactuals. That striking a match is always followed by its bursting into flame does not imply that if a match were struck in certain counterfactual situations, it would burst into flame. For the conjunction could be accidental. Of course, if laws of nature were necessary truths, they would support counterfactuals. But they aren't. What is needed is an account of natural laws that respects both their subjunctive character and their contingency. Jonathan Edwards regarded them as expressions of God's settled intentions with respect to the natural world, descriptions of His habitual manner of acting. Del Ratzsch has recently argued that views of this sort can provide a more adequate account of the subjunctive character of natural laws than non-theistic alternatives. Second, other philosophers have claimed that theism alone can adequately account for the objectivity and inescapability of moral value (see Article 44, MORAL ARGUMENTS; and Article 57, DIVINE COMMAND ETHICS). Suppose that God Himself is the standard of moral goodness, or that moral values are necessary contents of the divine intellectual activity, or that an action's obligatory character consists in God's having commanded it. Moral facts will then be objective in the sense that they are not human constructs. If God exists necessarily, then (on the first two views), moral truths are necessary. If God necessarily exists and necessarily commands that (for example) we tell the truth, then truth telling is necessarily obligatory on the third view as well. Views of this sort can also do a better job of accommodating two apparently conflicting intuitions: that moral values exist in minds, and that morality cannot command our allegiance unless it expresses a deep fact about reality. But whatever merit these solutions to wider philosophical problems have, they are not specifically Christian. For they are also available to other theists.

Christianity's attitude towards philosophy

Christianity's attitude towards philosophy has been ambivalent. One strand of the tradition is openly hostile. Its seminal figure is Tertullian (155–222).

Tertullian does not deny that the writings of the philosophers contain truths. Nor does he deny that God can be (imperfectly) grasped without the aid of revelation. For He can be known from His works and by the interior witness of our souls. Philosophy is none the less repudiated. "What indeed has Athens to do with Jerusalem? the Academy and the Church? What concord is there between heretics and Christians? Our instruction comes from the porch of Solomon, who had himself taught that the Lord should be sought in simplicity of heart. Away with all attempts to produce a mottled Christianity of Stoic, Platonic, and dialectic composition. We want no curious disputation after possessing Christ, no inquisition after enjoying the Gospel" (Roberts and Donaldson 1950, vol. 3, p. 246). Tertullian's objection is threefold. First the introduction of philosophy among Christians has resulted in heresy. Second, whereas schools of philosophy have human founders, the school of the Gospel is founded by God. Christianity is a *revealed* doctrine that demands obedience and submission. Philosophy, by contrast, relies on *human* wisdom, and is an expression of self-seeking and of a fallible and corrupt reason. Finally (and most profoundly), the mysteries of faith *repel* reason. "The Son of God died; it is by all means to be believed because it is absurd. And he was buried, and rose again; the fact is certain because it is impossible" (Roberts and Donaldson 1950, vol. 3, p. 535). Christian philosophy is a contradiction in terms because Christianity's truths are impenetrable to reason.

Tertullian is by no means alone. In the Christian Middle Ages, Bernard of Clairvaux (1090–1153) claimed that those who "called themselves philosophers should rather be called the slaves of curiosity and pride." The true teacher is the Holy Spirit, and those who have been instructed by Him can "say with the Psalmist (Psalm 119:99) *I have understood more than all my teachers.*" Commenting on this text, Bernard exclaims: "Wherefore, O my brother, does thou make such a boast? Is it because . . . thou has understood or hast endeavored to understand the reasonings of Plato and the subtleties of Aristotle? God forbid! thou answerest. It is because I have sought Thy commandments, O Lord" (Gilson 1938, pp. 12–13).

This attitude persists and is especially prominent in the Protestant reformers and among the skeptical fideists of the sixteenth and seventeenth centuries (see Article 48, FIDEISM).

An equally important, and ultimately more widespread, attitude towards philosophy was expressed by Justin Martyr (105–65), Clement of Alexandria (150–215), and Origen (185–254). Philosophy is a preparation for the gospel. According to Clement, for example, it was "a schoolmaster to bring the Hellenic mind, as the Law, the Hebrews, to Christ" (Roberts and Donaldson 1950, vol. 2, p. 305). This positive attitude towards philosophy was supported in two ways. The first was the "loan" hypothesis: the truths in Greek philosophy were ultimately plagiarized from Moses and the prophets. The second was the Logos theory: all human beings participate in the Logos – God's eternal word or wisdom who became incarnate in Jesus Christ. The Greek writers were thus, as Justin says, "able to see realities darkly through the sowing of the implanted word that was in them." Since "Christ . . . is the Word of whom every race of men were partakers, . . . those who lived reasonably are Christians, even though they have been thought atheists; as, among the Greeks, Socrates and Heraclitus, and men like them" (Roberts and Donaldson 1950, vol. 1, pp. 193, 178). And both Clement and Origen believe that the Logos is the archetype of which human reason is the copy.

It is important to notice, however, that while these doctrines make a positive evaluation of Greek philosophy possible, they also imply philosophy's inferiority to revelation. The loan hypothesis implies that the truths found in philosophy are fragmented and mixed with error. Whatever authority they have depends on their origin. Only in scripture can truth be found whole and undistorted. The Logos theory implies that Christians are better off than the philosophers. For, as Justin says, Christians "live not according to a part only of the word diffused [among men] but by the knowledge and contemplation of the whole Word, which is Christ" (Roberts and Donaldson 1950, vol. 1, p. 191).

Even so, philosophy isn't *just* a preparation for the Gospel. Both Clement and Origen believe that our blessedness consists in knowing or understanding the Good, and that philosophy can be employed to deepen our understanding of the truths of scripture in which that Good reveals itself. The seminal treatment of this theme is Augustine's.

Revelation is a safer and surer guide to truth than philosophy. Any truths about God taught by the philosophers can be found in scripture as well, but unmixed with error and enriched by other truths. Reason and philosophy aren't to be despised, however. Reason is needed to understand what is proposed for belief and to make the divine speaker's claims to authority credible. Nor should reason be discarded once faith has been achieved. "God forbid that He should hate in us that faculty by which He has made us superior to all other living beings. Therefore, we must refuse so to believe as not to receive or seek a reason for our belief . . ." (Augustine 1953, p. 302). The mature Christian will therefore use reason and the insights of philosophy to understand (to the extent possible) what he already believes. But faith remains a precondition of the success of this enterprise. For some things must first be believed to be understood. "Therefore the prophet said with reason: 'If you will not believe, you will not understand' " (Augustine 1953, p. 302). Augustine is principally thinking, in this passage, of the Christian "mysteries" (the Trinity, Incarnation, and so on). Yet he clearly believes that sound faith is needed for *any* adequate understanding of God. (But it is not needed for grasping some truths about Him. The "Platonists" lacked faith yet not only affirmed God's existence and the immortality of the soul but also that the Logos or Word was born of God and that all things were made by Him.)

Augustine's attitudes towards philosophy are echoed by Anselm and dominate the Christian Middle Ages. Modern Christian attitudes towards philosophy are, on the whole, variants of those seminally expressed by Tertullian and Augustine.

Closer inspection reveals that the two views are not always as sharply opposed as at first appears. Consider, for example, the attitudes towards reason expressed by Puritan divines, on the one hand, and by the Cambridge Platonists who opposed their so-called "dogmatism" and "narrow sectarianism," on the other.

As good Calvinists, Puritans believed that while reason was competent in "civill and humane things," it was not competent in divine things. Because of the fall, "the whole speculative power of the higher and nobler part of the Soule, which wee call the Understanding . . . is naturally and originally corrupted, and utterly destitute of all Divine Light" (Robert Bolton, quoted in Morgan 1986, p. 47). Francis Quarles therefore recommends: "In the Meditation of divine Mysteries, keep thy heart humble, and thy thoughts holy: Let Philosophy not be asham'd to be confuted, nor Logic blush to be confounded . . . The best way to see day-light is to put out thy Candle [reason]" (Patrides 1970, p. 9). The Cambridge Platonists sounded a very different note. "Reason is the Divine governor of man's life; it is the very voice of God" (Benjamin Whichcote, quoted in Powicke 1970 [1926], p. 23). According to John Smith, it is "a Light flowing from the Foundation and Father of Lights." Reason was given "to enable Man to work out of himself all those Notions of God which are the true Ground-work of Love and Obedience to God, and conformity to him . . ." (Smith 1978 [1660], p. 382). Scripture simply reinforces and clarifies what a properly functioning reason discerns.

Neither position, however, is as extreme as this suggests. Many Puritan diatribes against reason are expressions of Puritanism's emphasis on experience and not of a belief that reason's "notional" understanding of religion is invariably false. As Arthur Dent says, "The knowledge of the reprobate is like the knowledge which a mathematicall geographer hath of the earth and all the places in it, which is but a generall notion, and a speculative comprehension of them. But the knowledge of the elect is like the knowledge of a traveller which can speake of experience and feeling, and hath beene there and seene . . ." (Morgan 1986, p. 59).

Puritans also insisted that God's word is *intrinsically* rational. "The Sunne is ever cleere" although we are prevented from seeing it because "wee want eyes to behold it" or because it is "so be-clowded, that our sight is thereby hindered . . ." (Richard Bernard, quoted in Morgan 1986, p. 55). Furthermore, grace can cure our blindness and remove the clouds. *Regenerate* reason can unfold scripture and defend the faith. Puritan divines were therefore prepared, in practice, to ascribe a high instrumental value to reason and humane learning. As John Rainolds said, "It may be lawfull for Christians to use Philosophers, and books of Secular Learning . . . with this condition, that whatsoever they finde in them, that is profitable and usefull, they convert it to Christian doctrine and do, as it were, shave off . . . all superfluous stuffe" (Morgan 1986, p. 113). Even a radical Puritan like John Penry could insist that "the Lord doth not ordinarily bestowe [full comprehension of the Word] . . . without the knowledge of the artes," especially rhetoric and logic, Hebrew and Greek (Morgan 1986, p. 106). Logic, indeed, was so important that the missionary John Eliot translated a treatise on it into Algonquin "to initiate the Indians in the knowledge of the Rule of Reason" (Miller 1961 [1939], p. 114).

The Cambridge Platonists' exaltation of reason must be similarly qualified. Because of the fall, reason is "but an old MS., with some broken periods, some letters worn out," it is a picture which has "lost its gloss and beauty, the oriency of its colours . . . the comeliness of its proportions . . ." (Powicke 1970 [1926], p. 30). As a consequence, divine assistance is now necessary. And God has provided it. Not only is there "an Outward revelation of God's will to men [scripture], there is also an Inward impression of it on their Minds and Spirits . . . We cannot see divine things but in a divine light . . ." (Smith 1978 [1660], p. 384). "Right reason" is indeed sufficient to discern the things of God, but right reason is sanctified reason. Henry More speaks for all the Cambridge Platonists when he says, "The oracle of God [reason] is not be heard but in his Holy Temple – that is to say in a good and holy man, thoroughly sanctified in Spirit, Soul and body" (More 1978 [1662], vol. 1, p. viii).

The dispute between the Puritans and Cambridge Platonists is typical of similar disputes in the history of traditional Christianity. Attacks on the use of reason and philosophy are seldom unqualified. (Tertullian himself was strongly influenced by Stoicism.) The reason which is commended, on the other hand, is what the seventeenth century called "right reason" – a reason that is informed by the divine light, and is an expression of a properly disposed heart. Conflicting views on the relation between faith and reason or philosophy within traditional Christianity are, for the most part, less a matter of outright opposition than of difference in emphasis.

Bibliography

Augustine: *Letters*, 5 vols., tr. Sister Wilfred Parsons, SND: vol. 2, *Letters, 83–130* (*The Fathers of the Church*, vol. 18) (Washington, DC: Catholic University of America Press, 1953).

Gilson, E.: *Reason and Revelation in the Middle Ages* (New York: Charles Scribner's Sons, 1938).

James, W.: *The Varieties of Religious Experience* (New York: The Modern Library, 1902).

Kretzmann, N.: "Faith seeks, understanding finds: Augustine's charter for Christian Philosophy." In *Christian Philosophy*, ed. Thomas P. Flint (Notre Dame: University of Notre Dame Press, 1990), pp. 1–36.

Mascall, E.: *Christian Theology and Natural Science* (London: Longmans, Green, 1956).

Miller, P.: *The New England Mind: The Seventeenth Century* (New York, 1939) (Boston: Beacon Press, 1961).

More, H.: *A Collection of Several Philosophical Writings*, 2nd edn, 2 vols. (London, 1662) (New York: Garland Publishing, 1978).

Morgan, J.: *Godly Learning: Puritan Attitudes towards Reason, Learning and Education, 1560–1640* (Cambridge: Cambridge University Press, 1986).

Norris, R. A.: *God and the World in Early Christian Theology: A Study in Justin Martyr, Irenaeus, Tertullian and Origen* (London: Adam & Charles Black, 1966).

Patrides, C. A. (ed.): *The Cambridge Platonists* (Cambridge: Harvard University Press, 1970).

Powicke, F. J.: *The Cambridge Platonists: A Study* (London, 1926) (Westport: Greenwood Press, 1970).

Roberts, A., and Donaldson, J. (eds): *The Ante-Nicene Fathers*, 10 vols. (Edinburgh and London, 1867–72) (Grand Rapids: Eerdmans, 1950).

Smith, J.: *Select Discourses* (London, 1660) (New York: Garland Publishing, 1978).

Tulloch, J.: *Rational Theology and Christian Philosophy in England in the Seventeenth Century*, 2nd edn, 2 vols.; vol. 2, *The Cambridge Platonists* (Edinburgh and London, 1874) (Hildesheim: George Olms, 1966).

7

Islam

AZIM A. NANJI AND AZIZ A. ESMAIL

Islam belongs to the family of monotheistic faiths that also includes JUDAISM (see Article 5) and CHRISTIANITY (see Article 6). Its history began in the seventh century in what is modern-day Saudi Arabia, but its larger cultural and social context included the ancient civilizations of the Middle East and the Mediterranean. The norms and assumptions that have characterized belief and action in Islam are based on the message revealed to the Prophet Muhammad (d. 632) and recorded in the Qur'an. While Muslims regard the Qur'an as the closure in a series of revelations to humankind, they have also sought to understand this religious history in its relation to the intellectual environment in which they found themselves.

Philosophical thought in Islam (*falsafa*, in Arabic) emerged as one product of this new intellectual climate and grew out of attempts at discursive reflection on truths believed to be grounded in revelation but intelligible to the disciplined use of human reason. While the methods and tools of *falsafa* were inspired primarily by the heritage of classical antiquity mediated by its Christian students, its fullest expressions were not restricted by either classical antecedents or the constraints of religious dogma.

The historical origins of this intellectual tradition are to be found in the encounter of scholars in the Muslim world of the time with translations of Greek, Pahlavi, and Sanskrit (but principally Greek) philosophical texts.

The ethic of reverence for knowledge, prompted among Muslims by the Qur'anic appeal to reasoning and the Prophetic traditions that challenged Muslims to pursue learning ("even as far as China" according to one saying), was one among several factors that provided the impetus for the appropriation of new learning. Thus, in the translation movement that followed, a large portion of the scientific and philosophical legacy of Ancient Greece was made available in Arabic. Patronage by ruling Caliphs and the establishment of endowed institutions to promote translation and learning (such as the *Bayt al-Hikma* (House of Wisdom) and al-Azhar established in Baghdad and Cairo respectively, during the ninth and tenth centuries) further stimulated interest in philosophical and scientific work. From the very first, the scholars who studied these materials seem to have been aware of them as a whole tradition of thought – of observation, argument, and deduction. They dedicated themselves to its mastery, and not least, to its augmentation through their own interpretation and commentary.

There were two broad circumstances affecting philosophy in the early Muslim environment. It had its own identity, an inner independence from theology, which was referred to as *kalam*. But it was dependent on a polity for its own existence, and that polity was founded on religion. The philosophers had to reckon with this dual circumstance. They did so, and it was at this task that they may be said to have made their best contribution to the pluralistic environment of medieval Muslim culture and thought. The foremost exponents of *kalam* were the Mutazila, who emerged during the later part of the ninth and the early tenth centuries as a distinctive school of thought. Logic, epistemology, cosmology, politics, and ethics constituted the content of their theology while their emphasis on reason and method of argument drew on the resources of philosophy. Other schools of thought that emerged at this time and which were deeply committed to a type of religious philosophy were the Shia, and, in particular, the Ismaili branch of the Shia who developed an extensive intellectual tradition during the period of Fatimid Ismaili rule based in Cairo in the tenth through twelfth centuries. Philosophy, as conceived in the thought of major Ismaili writers of the period, had as its goal the enlarging of the meaning of religion and revelation through the application of a hermeneutics based on *tawil*, a Qur'anic term exemplifying the disclosure of the inner meaning of revelation and religious language. Among the Shia in general, such a hermeneutic task was guided by the *Imam*, the designated successor of the Prophet, whose authority in intellectual as well as spiritual matters served to consolidate and contextualize the faith in changing environments.

While law and theology provided the moral and conceptual foundation of society, philosophy reflected a universalism, and a relative indifference to parochial or denominational interests. It recognized no theoretical restraints on its own scope and capacity other than that of reason. (That it did allow practical restraints was a sign partly of political expedience, and partly of a genuine recognition of the foundational value of religion.) Philosophy developed in the Islamic cultural context, and was written in Arabic and much later in Persian. Some of the earliest translators of Greek texts into Arabic were Christians. The first major philosophers to work from the translated texts and write commentaries on them were Muslims. But they were soon followed by Jewish and Christian authors. In the twelfth and thirteenth centuries, much of the Arabic heritage was translated into Latin and to an extent into Hebrew, so that a continual negotiation went on between these traditions. The role of philosophy in these three faith communities represents one perspective through which the whole history of medieval philosophy linking Muslim, Christian, and Jewish thought, may be seen (see Article 9, THE CHRISTIAN CONTRIBUTION TO MEDIEVAL PHILOSOPHICAL THEOLOGY; Article 10, THE ISLAMIC CONTRIBUTION TO MEDIEVAL PHILOSOPHICAL THEOLOGY; and Article 11, THE JEWISH CONTRIBUTION TO MEDIEVAL PHILOSOPHICAL THEOLOGY).

The first Muslim to be regarded as a philosopher in the formal sense, is al-Kindi (d. 870), who was closely associated with the Mutazila, and was a keen student of Greek philosophy as well as Indian arithmetic. His exposure to these subjects gave him an appreciation of the possibility of human knowledge. While Neoplatonic ideas exercised a strong influence on his thought, he also departed from some of their assumptions. Where Neoplatonism looks at the universe as a series of emanations from The One, al-Kindi proposed a theory more congenial to the Qur'anic (and Biblical) doctrine of temporal creation (see Article 39, CREATION AND CONSERVATION). In this theory, as also in his avowal of the immortality of the soul (see Article 70, SURVIVAL OF DEATH), al-Kindi laid some of the first planks in a bridge between the doctrinal content of Islam and classical learning.

Among those philosophers who followed al-Kindi, the only one who chose to break with religion altogether was Abu Bakr al-Razi (d. 925), who opposed all authority in matters intellectual, asserting the sufficiency of human reason. Declaring prophecy to be superfluous, he denounced religion as a ruse, feeding on the gullibility of the masses, and responsible for sowing discord and division in the world. The Ismaili philosopher Abu Hatim al-Razi fought back against this attack on religion and vigorously defended the principles of revealed faith and prophetic authority against his (partial) namesake. Abu Bakr obviously stood in the tradition of the ancient materialists. It is scarcely surprising that in the context of his times he was an isolated figure, remarkable for his courage, but marginal to both the philosophical and theological traditions of the age.

Far more influential and positive towards religion was the philosopher al-Farabi (d. 950). He was the first major philosopher, in the Islamic context, to study the materials before him systematically, and to proceed to give his own commentary on them. These materials were varied. They included tracts on Aristotle, the works of Plato, the texts of Neoplatonism, of other ancient writers like Porphyry, and commentaries written on Aristotle by Christian scholars of late antiquity. Even more importantly, he was an early representative, at least in its incipient form, of what we now call philosophy of religion. The term "philosophy of religion" should be understood in its precise sense: not religious thought, but thought that seeks to make sense of religion. For al-Farabi, philosophy of religion in this sense was also linked to political philosophy. He saw that Qur'anic exegesis, prophetic tradition, and ancillary religious subjects were but functions of the law revealed through Muhammad. Hence, to understand the character and objective of prophetic revelation and of the community founded on it has to be a cardinal task of philosophy. But this was not all. The relation of philosophy to religion in al-Farabi went further. Not only did philosophy seek to understand religion: the two shared a basic kinship. Thus, for instance, the philosopher-king of Plato and the prophets, such as the Prophet Muhammad, draw on the same cosmological sources of knowledge. Religion, properly understood, and philosophy are not opposed to each other. In this way, there is an organic quality in al-Farabi's philosophical handling of religion which is absent in al-Kindi. Al-Kindi's perspective is limited and raw: essentially, he juxtaposes the two traditions. Al-Farabi seeks to integrate them, though not to identify them. His is therefore an achievement at a more mature stage of the tradition.

By proposing Muhammad (among the others acknowledged in the Qur'an as prophets) as analogous to Plato's philosopher-king, al-Farabi was able to propose a relationship between the universal and the particular. The prophet's unique skill is to render philosophical truth into symbols. This is a function of creative imagination, and its audience is the masses (whereas philosophy and science are accessible only to an intellectual elite). According to al-Farabi, the reason why philosophy is universal is because it is theoretical or general, while religion is political (in the serious, moral sense of the word in classical thought, where the true end of politics is virtuous life in the City.) Al-Farabi's thought is an attempt at a harmonization – an "analogization," really – of the Hellenistic and Islamic traditions.

In the hands of the great Abu Ali ibn Sina (980–1037), or Avicenna, as he became known in the West, this process was taken considerably further. Ibn Sina describes in his autobiography his upbringing as a child prodigy and his vast reading and erudition in philosophy and the sciences as a youth. As a 17-year-old, he had already acquired a reputation as an excellent physician and treated rulers, thereby gaining access to their well-endowed libraries where he mined ancient knowledge. His chief aim was to harness philosophical thought to the principles of religion. This meant the incorporation of an independent rationality into foundational interests. This ambition was reflected in several features of his philosophy. One of these was a philosophical proof showing God as the creator of the world (see Article 42, COSMOLOGICAL ARGUMENTS). This proof rested on a famous and widely influential distinction between "essence" and "existence." Existence, Ibn Sina showed, cannot be inferred from essence. For an object to come to be, it requires the addition of existence to an essence. This assumes an existing cause. He imagined the universe as a hierarchy of beings, each of whom bestows existence on the one below. As such, a chain, in his view, cannot be infinite, it must terminate in a being whose very essence is to exist, and hence needs no cause outside itself. Such a being is God.

Ibn Sina's conclusions were not, from a religious point of view, orthodox. While insisting that everything is eternally dependent on God – a major departure from Aristotle in the direction of religious doctrine – he also ascribed eternity to many other things besides, such as intellects, souls, and the sublunary spheres. This was in keeping with the Aristotelian view of the eternity of the world (see Article 32, ETERNITY). This view was to create immense controversy, and to give the Sunni theologian, al-Ghazali (d. 1111), cause to declare Avicennan philosophy un-Islamic. But Islamic orthodoxy itself was a product of circumstances, and a relatively late one at that. Ibn Sina's doctrine of the eternity of the world is in part a reflection of the openness of Muslim thought as late as his time, before the crystallization of "orthodoxy."

The second religious issue which Ibn Sina examined philosophically was the fate of the individual self. The Qur'an speaks of reward and punishment in the hereafter. This implies a re-creation (or continuation) of individual identity after death. (Whether it is re-created at the moment of judgment, or sustained after the individual's death, and if so, in what form and what states, is a question which was endlessly debated by theologians, and not surprisingly, without agreement.) Ibn Sina took a major step away from Hellenistic thought by arguing for individual immortality. In the process, he proposed what he thought was a proof for the existence of the soul. If a person were to imagine himself as "suspended" in space, i.e. without dimensions, weight, and organs or limbs, he would still retain a sense of "I." This proved that there is an individual soul, and that it does not have to perish with the body.

67

Another religious principle to which Ibn Sina gave a rational formulation was that of revelation (see Article 74, REVELATION AND SCRIPTURE). On this issue he followed the view of earlier thinkers, namely that revelation is a symbolization, for the benefit of the masses, of philosophical knowledge. Ibn Sina was inclined to see religious rites, such as prayer or fasting, in terms of what we would today call their practical utility or function. This interpretation was logically related to the theory of allegorical meaning. If a principle of belief or practice is said to have a meaning other than what is explicitly stated in it, it follows that it must be encoded; and that the code must be deciphered. His work is noteworthy for its symbolic exegeses of the Qur'an and the beliefs and practices of Islam. This is something that al-Farabi never did. Al-Farabi had offered a philosophy of religion. Ibn Sina narrowed – but at the same time deepened – the focus. His was a theory not just of religion but of Islam and its larger context, knowledge and philosophy. In the process, philosophical reason was domesticated and brought into the framework of Islam. Al-Farabi had spoken of the particularity of the community. He had theorized about the symbolic character of prophetic language. Ibn Sina spoke from within a particularity. And he not only spoke about allegory but practiced allegorical interpretation. There is a dual dynamic within his thought. There is, on one hand, a rationalization of faith through allegorical and functionalist exegesis. On the other hand, there is an assimilation of philosophy into religious experience.

Ibn Sina's influence was considerable. Thomas Aquinas adopted his distinction between essence and existence, as part of an argument for the existence of God. The Jewish philosopher of Spain, Abraham ibn Daud, followed him closely, with minor adaptations. Some of his works were translated into Latin and Hebrew. In the Islamic world, he was revered especially in the Persian-speaking East, where, however, his ideas were so thoroughly absorbed into mysticism that their intellectual edge, it has been said, was largely blunted. Apart from philosophy, he was widely admired for his vast medical knowledge and his work on the natural sciences.

Muslim Spain in the twelfth century was also a significant center of philosophical activity. Ibn Bajja (d. 1139) commented extensively on al-Farabi's works on logic and also argued against Ibn Sina's view of the immortality of the soul. His student, Ibn Tufayl (d. 1186) is best known as the author of *Hayy ibn Yaqzan*, a philosophical narrative that explores the divide between philosophical understanding and the literalist approaches to religion. The narrative tells the story of Hayy (lit. the living one) ibn Yaqzan, a child born without parents out of the ferment of natural materials, who grows up alone on an island and infers philosophical truths through observation and reflection. When he eventually comes into contact with people practicing revealed religion, he is unable to reconcile them to the validity of his own unaided spiritual development and concludes that philosophy and literally-understood revealed religion must go their separate paths and satisfy the needs of separate constituencies.

In Ibn Tufayl's student, Ibn Rushd (1126–98), or Averroës as he came to be known in the West, philosophy found a gifted spokesman, theology a stern critic, and the law an eloquent defender. He served as a judge in Seville, and later as

Chief Judge of Cordoba. His commentaries on Aristotle were translated into Latin and transmitted to Europe, where Dante referred to him as "the great Commentator." His best-known works on the relation between philosophy and religion are *On the Harmony Between Religion and Philosophy* and his defense of philosophy against the attack on it by al-Ghazali, the Sunni theologian and Professor of Law at the Nizamiyya College in Baghdad.

Ibn Rushd was stirred into a defense of philosophy by the gauntlet that al-Ghazali had flung at it. He was quick to perceive the intellectual power in al-Ghazali's attack, and the need to ensure that it did not go unchallenged. In repelling al-Ghazali's assault, Ibn Rushd voiced severe criticism of both al-Farabi and Ibn Sina. He disliked their concessions to theology. His position may be interpreted as a desire to save philosophical reason from being swallowed by a hybrid intellectualism. He wished to restore to philosophy its essence and its independence. As a judge, well versed in Islamic law, he also had a deep interest in practical religion and wished to demonstrate a basic harmony between reason and religious tradition.

Ibn Rushd believed strongly in the unity of truth, and rejected the theory that it had a twofold – intellectual and imaginative (or symbolic) – representation. The difference between intellectuals and the masses was real enough. But it was a difference of approach, not of representation. If al-Farabi had established an analogy between philosophy and religion, Ibn Rushd thought in analogous terms about philosophy and (divinely revealed) law. The philosophical attention he paid to law distinguishes him from the others. His reflections on the place of philosophy in society were as much a contribution to jurisprudence as to philosophy. While allowing that philosophy must follow its own rigorous methods, he insisted that the masses ought not to be exposed to it, nor to allegorical interpretation, lest they lose the assurance of faith without gaining the refined consolations of science or philosophy. Theologians, in particular, need to be especially wary. For theology occupies a middle ground between philosophy and religious law (to whose literal meaning ordinary people must adhere for their own good). Ibn Rushd would seem not to have been too fond of intellectual hybrids. And in his attack on the blunders of theology – to which he attributed misconceptions about philosophy – he tried, in one stroke, to defend philosophy from al-Ghazali's attack, and to attack al-Ghazali the theologian.

Another towering figure, born in Muslim Spain, who had enormous influence on the subsequent development of Muslim intellectual and mystical thought (Sufism), is Ibn Arabi (d. 1240). Among the major doctrines that represent a key strand in his multifaceted works, are the concepts of the "Oneness of Being" (*wahdat al-wujud*), the "Perfect Man" (*al-insan al-kamil*) and the "world of analogical imagination" (*alam al-mithal*). Ibn Arabi's work, according to the late Henri Corbin, the noted French scholar of his thought, links philosophy and mysticism into a profoundly original wisdom tradition, that he calls a visionary theosophy (Corbin 1993), and it is developed into a complex series of syntheses.

Towards the eastern part of the Muslim world in Iran, the philosophical heritage of Ibn Sina and others took a different direction. It coalesced with

Sufism–Muslim mysticism and produced an intellectual school that included such creative figures as Shihab al-din Shurawardi (d. 1191), the founder of Illuminationist (*ishraqi*) philosophy. Some scholars have referred to this tradition as "theosophy," reflecting a harmonization of spirituality and philosophy. It represents a synthesis of the tools of Muslim peripatetic philosophy, ascribed to Ibn Sina, with the wisdom traditions associated with Gnosticism, ancient Hermetic and Persian wisdom, and Sufism. At the heart of its cosmology lies the symbolism of illumination – light – and its epistemology synthesizes intellectual as well as mystical forms of knowing. The tradition flourished and received new impetus after a relatively long dormant period, with the establishment of the Shia Safavid state in Iran (1501–1722). The intellectual and philosophical developments of the period are marked by the emergence of the "School of Isfahan" that produced thinkers like Mir Damad (d. 1630) and Mulla Sadra (d. 1640). They developed further the tradition of Shia intellectual thought, drawing upon the contributions of al-Shurawardi, Ibn Arabi and their successors and also the intellectual foundations laid down in the work of Nasir al-din Tusi (d. 1273).

This short survey illustrates the influence of major Muslim philosophers on Muslim thought and religious education, an influence that has persisted in parts of the Muslim world until modern times. It also highlights the impact of Muslim philosophers on intellectual developments in medieval European and even Renaissance thought. Its universalism and cosmopolitanism remain a source of inspiration for the development of philosophical inquiry among contemporary Muslim thinkers.

Bibliography

Averroës: *On the Harmony of Religions and Philosophy*, tr. George Hourani (London: Luzac & Co., 1967).

Corbin, H.: *History of Islamic Philosophy*, tr. L. Sherrard (London: Kegan Paul International, 1993).

Dhanani, A.: "Muslim philosophy and the sciences." In Azim A. Nanji (ed.), *The Muslim Almanac*, pp. 189–204 (Detroit: Gale Research, 1996).

Fakhry, M.: *A History of Islamic Philosophy* (New York: Columbia University Press, 1983).

Farabi, al-: *On the Perfect State*, tr. R. Walzer (Oxford: Clarendon Press, 1985).

Gutas, D.: *Avicenna and the Aristotelian Tradition* (Leiden: E. J. Brill, 1988).

Mahdi, M.: *Alfarabi's Philosophy of Plato and Aristotle. Translated with an Introduction* (Ithaca: Cornell University Press, 1969).

Mulla Sadra: *The Wisdom of the Throne*, tr. J. W. Morris (Princeton: Princeton University Press, 1981).

Nasr, S. H., and Leaman, O. (eds): *The Routledge History of Islamic Philosophy* (London: Routledge, 1996).

——: *Three Muslim Sages: Avicenna, Suharawardi, Ibn Arabi* (Cambridge: Harvard University Press, 1964).

Netton, I. R.: *Allah Transcendent: Studies in the Structure and Semiotics of Islamic Philosophy, Theology and Cosmology* (London: Routledge, 1989).

Walker, P.: *Early Philosophical Shiism* (Cambridge: Cambridge University Press, 1993).

PART II

PHILOSOPHICAL THEOLOGY AND PHILOSOPHY OF RELIGION IN WESTERN HISTORY

8

Ancient philosophical theology

KEVIN L. FLANNERY SJ

Presocratics

Aristotle's terminology tells us much about how the Presocratics' philosophical project was perceived in the ancient world and probably, therefore, also by the Presocratics themselves. He never calls a Presocratic (that is, a presocratic philosopher) "theologian," preferring the word "physicist," at least for those among them who agreed that motion is possible (*Physics* i,1,184b25ff). The word "theologian" (or *theologos*) has for him, in fact, a derogatory sense and is often translated "mythologist" (e.g. *Metaphysics* iii,4,1000a9; xii,6,1071b27) and includes such figures as Hesiod and the Orphic poets. (He does, however, speak of "first philosophy" or "the science of being *qua* being" which he develops in his own *Metaphysics* as "theology": vi,1,1026a13–32.) The Presocratics who are interested in theology are interested in it in a philosophical way. "Theologians" like Hesiod are not bothered by the implausibility of their gods, says Aristotle – we need not waste our time on them; but philosophers like Empedocles and the Pythagoreans "use the language of proof" and therefore merit our attention (*Metaphysics* iii,4,1000a18–20).

Earlier in the present century, the most influential approach to such issues was that of John Burnet who held that the Presocratics employ terms like "God" (*ho theos*) and "the divine" (*to theion*), which they do often, in a totally non-religious way (Burnet 1920, pp. 14, 80). Werner Jaeger's authoritative Gifford Lectures demonstrated, however, the impossibility of Burnet's thesis. Speaking of Aristotle's association of Anaximander's "the boundless" (*to apeiron*) with "the divine" (*Physics* iii,4,203b13–15), Jaeger says, "[t]he phrase 'the Divine,' does not appear merely as one more predicate applied to the first principle; on the contrary, the substantivization of the adjective with the definite article shows rather that this is introduced as an independent concept, essentially religious in character, and now identified with the rational principle, the Boundless" (Jaeger 1947, p. 31).

Still, the Presocratics are for the most part not interested in cultic religion as such. They believe in "God" or "the gods," but this divine element is meant primarily to provide a relatively simple explanation of the order found in the universe (or *kosmos* – which word can mean both "universe" and "order"). The Presocratics are thus "rationalizers" of the divine. The theologians (in Aristotle's sense) are quite happy to multiply gods as surprising or significant events present themselves; but inventions of this sort do no more than attach names to the events

73

themselves (*Metaphysics* xii,10,1075b26–7). The Presocratic philosophical theologians want to get behind the events to their principles (or *archai*) which, according to their very nature as explanations, need to be different from that which they explain: they need, that is, to be cleaner, less particular. Such an approach bears with it a certain ontological austerity, presupposing as it does that an explanation is better the more diverse the things it explains.

As early as Xenophanes (ca. 565–470 BCE), therefore, we find at least a tendency toward monotheism: "One god, greatest among gods and men, in no way similar to mortals either in body or in thought" (Diels and Kranz 1951, 21B23; see also Aristotle's *Metaphysics* i,5,986b24–5). Xenophanes comes out against the anthropomorphism of Homer and Hesiod, who "attributed to the gods everything that is a shame and a reproach among men, stealing and committing adultery and deceiving each other" (1951, 21B11). This leads him to posit a god who is the cause of all: "Always he remains in the same place, moving not at all; nor is it fitting for him to go to different places at different times" (1951, 21B26), "but without toil he shakes all things by the thought of his mind" (1951, 21B25). We see, however, even in the fragments here quoted (especially 1951, 21B23: "greatest among gods") that this god who causes all things is not incompatible with the existence of other divine beings – any more than Christian monotheism is incompatible with the existence of angels.

Nor should we presume that Xenophanes' anti-anthropomorphism implies that his God is impersonal, if "impersonal" is meant to deny God a mind. For, although Xenophanes holds that the one God's thought is unlike mortal thought (Diels and Kranz 1951, 21B23), he also says that mind (or *nous*) is God's most important attribute (1951, 21B25). This notion is even more prominent in Anaxagoras, whose conception of the first cause as Mind (1951, 59B12) becomes very influential in subsequent Greek thought, as we shall see.

Although the greatest of the Presocratics, Parmenides, does not explicitly refer to his monolithic "being" as God or as divine, his notion of being as utterly independent of contingency – uncreated, imperishable, one, continuous, unchangeable, and perfect (1951, 28Bb8.1–49) – establishes the problematic for subsequent philosophical theology at least until Plotinus. It ought also to be noted that the prologue to Parmenides' sole work *On Nature* is, in effect, an invocation of "the goddess," who will guide him to the realm of being, otherwise inaccessible to mere mortals. This gives us some indication of how Parmenides regards being. With Parmenides the question becomes, not how best to describe the relationship of the originating principle (*archē*), unchanging being, to those things dependent on it, but whether anything besides the *archē* exists at all. To say the least, for Parmenides, all else pales in the face of the transcendent, whatever we are to call it.

Plato

Like many of the Presocratics, Plato often speaks unfavorably of cultic worship and of the gods of the mythologists. In *Euthyphro*, one of the early Socratic dialogues, he lampoons as "bartering" sacrificial offerings to the gods. In the *Republic* (in which the Socratic traces are fewer), Plato puts into the mouth of Adeimantus a very persuasive indictment of the gods of Hesiod and Homer, which focuses on their licentiousness and willingness to accept bribes from the unjust. Later in the same book (that is, in book 2), the works of Hesiod and Homer are subjected to censorship in the scheme of the ideal city; and in book 10 poets and other artists are banned from the city on the grounds that they distort reality and pander to human weaknesses.

The general tendency to prefer an image of the divine as less "human" and arbitrary is much in evidence in Plato's one strictly cosmological work, *Timaeus*. (One needs to be wary when citing *Timaeus*, since Plato explicitly says that he is presenting there a "likely myth" (29d2); but it is unlikely that he would present even as myth something that is very different from his own considered opinion, so we can ignore this complication for the time being). In *Timaeus*, Plato portrays God as a Divine Craftsman or Demiurge who brings order to formlessness or "the Receptacle" (50d). (Thus, he is not a creator god; but cp. Aristotle, *De Caelo* i,10,280a28–32 and Long and Sedley 1987, 13G1,4.) It is striking that he should use precisely this image of God since Plato was no exalter of craftsmen – they are not even citizens of the ideal city of the *Republic*. The point of the image is to insist that God's activity is rule-governed and rational, like the activity of a craftsman who creates products according to set procedures and models.

The type of rationality that the Demiurge brings to the universe is mathematical: the four elements are actually, in their indiscernible deeper-structure, geometrical figures. Fire is pyramidal, earth cubical, air octahedral, and water icosahedral. Each of the geometrical figures is resolvable into right triangles, which allows the elements to change into each other. Or at least three of them can do so – air, fire, and water – which are all resolvable into scalene right triangles. Earth, whose cubes are resolvable only into isosceles right triangles, resists such intermingling. Plato appears to have made earth cubical for theoretical reasons and was criticized for this by Aristotle on the grounds that the theory did not correspond to the facts. Aristotle says of the Platonists, "they had predetermined views, and were resolved to bring everything into line with them" (*De Caelo* 360a8–9). Whether Aristotle was being fair to Plato and his schools is questionable; but he is certainly correct in discerning the predominance of theory in the *Timaeus* at the expense of particularity. This is all part of Plato's project, shared with the Presocratics, of rationalizing the divine. "For while Plato's cosmology makes fulsome acknowledgment of supernatural power in the universe, it does so with a built-in guarantee that such power will never be exercised to disturb the regularities of nature" (Vlastos 1975, p. 61).

Nothing, however, is simple in the study of Plato, and there are passages which pull us in the opposite direction. The most important of these are in the tenth book of *Laws*, where Plato discusses theological issues quite straightforwardly – that is, for the most part, without the use of myth. His spokesman, the Athenian Stranger, is primarily concerned about religious impiety which, he is sure, undermines the constitution of a city. At the end of the book, he imposes penalties – including the death penalty (908e1) – on the various classes of "atheist." He disparages the doctrines of certain unnamed physicists who say that the four elements exist "by nature and by chance" (889b1–2). The position attacked is a type of materialistic evolutionism (Solmsen 1942, pp. 137, 145–6), quite within the genius of Presocratic rationalism. The position advocated is teleological and anticipates in places (893bff) Aristotle's causal argument for the existence of God in *Physics* vii–viii. Although here in the *Laws* the Divine Craftsman makes an appearance (under the cloak of myth – 903b1–2), God is depicted primarily as the World Soul (896a5–b1; also *Phaedrus* 244c5–246a2; but cp. *Laws* xii,967d6–7), even more intimately bound up in the universe than in *Timaeus*. This close relationship in either case is also in deliberate contrast to Anaxagoras' Mind, criticized at *Phaedo* 98cd for not being sufficiently involved in the universe. Plato also mounts in *Laws* x a defense of the idea – called into question, for instance, in Euripides (see Plutarch, *Moralia* 464A) – that the gods concern themselves with the details of personal lives.

Is there a way to reconcile these two strands of Platonic doctrine, the one depicting a "rational," the other a more "interventionist" God? There is, by taking into consideration the way in which Plato argues for the latter. In *Laws* x Plato argues that for the gods *not* to concern themselves with the details of personal lives would be incompatible with their nature. If human craftsmen know to attend to the details of their own business, so much more do the gods, who "being good, possess every virtue proper to themselves for care of all things" (900d1–2). Once this point is established, it is an easy thing to justify cultic practices, provided they do not involve the gods in things incompatible with their divine nature, such as injustice (905d8–906d6). In this way, the gods' concern for mankind becomes part of their very rationalization or intelligibility. Arguments of this type based on God's natural characteristics will, of course, come to play a huge role in subsequent philosophical theology. The most important of the characteristics isolated by Plato is God's goodness (see, for example, *Timaeus* 29e1–3, *Phaedrus* 247a4–7; *Republic* ii,381b1–5,382e8–11). With that established, he is free philosophically to argue also that we ought all to seek likeness to God (*homoiōsis theōi* – *Theaetetus* 176b1–3), a sort of divine intervention in reverse.

Aristotle

Aristotle's philosophical theology has much in common with Plato's. His teleological approach to physics and cosmology is similarly incompatible with the materialistic evolutionism that Plato criticizes in *Laws* x (see *Physics* viii,1 and *Metaphysics* i,8,988b22–8); and he favors a demythologizing of theology (*Metaphysics* xii,8,1074a38–b14; *Politics* i,2,1252b26–7) without denying that the lower gods exist (*Metaphysics* xii,8).

He also suggests in a number of places that he is not entirely opposed to the idea of God as the World Soul (although he has no time for a Divine Craftsman). For instance, in *Metaphysics* xii,8, at the end of his explanation of how the unmoved mover works through the planets and stars, influencing also human events

(1074a25–31), he says that the ancients had an inkling of this – i.e. that the heavenly bodies "are divine and that the divine embraces the whole of nature" (1074b2–3). In *Metaphysics* xii (especially 7 and 9), he identifies God, "a living being" (1072b29), with *nous* (mind), a component of course also of the human soul (see also *Metaphysics* xii,9,1075a6–10 and *De Anima* iii,5). And in *Nicomachean Ethics* x,8, he uses, as the basis of an argument that philosophical contemplation is the highest vocation, the idea that the gods have care for human affairs (1179a24–5). So, although it appears that Aristotle never speaks of God as the World Soul (see, however, Clement of Alexandria, *Protrepticus* v,66,4), he is certainly in favor of a God who is intimately bound up in the world.

In *Physics* viii,5, however, he also speaks favorably of Anaxagoras' Mind in so far as it is "impassive and unmixed [with the world]" (256b24–7; cp. *Metaphysics* i,4,985a18). The former word especially ("impassive" or *apathēs*) turns up in a number of other passages crucial to the present consideration (e.g. *Metaphysics* xii,7,1073a11; *De Anima* iii,5,430a24, i,4,408b27–31), so we can be sure that Aristotle's praise of Anaxagoras is no stray remark. How can Aristotle have held both that God is immanent and also "impassive and unmixed?" Much of his argument depends on an analogy drawn from geometry. Just as the primary locus of power and influence in a rotating sphere is its central axis, which, although it moves (transitively) the other parts of the sphere, remains quite still, so also the unmoved mover remains majestically impassive even while being the very source of the activity of the universe (*Physics* viii,9,265b7–8; see also *Movement of Animals* iii). Aristotle combines this idea of immanent power with the idea that God is a final cause such as are "the object of desire and the object of thought" since they "move but are not moved" (*Metaphysics* xii,7,1072a26–7). The end result is a conception of God as both an impelling force within the universe and an object of desire drawing man beyond it.

Aristotle also speaks of the unmoved mover as "thought thinking itself" (*Metaphysics* xii,9,1074b33–5) and has been criticized for thereby positing a self-absorbed, distant God. But this is quite irreconcilable with his overall theory and should be resisted as a possible interpretation. Aristotle rejects the notion that God might think of something other than himself precisely because this would be to diminish his power (*Metaphysics* xii,9,1074b34). The power that Aristotle is concerned about is the power whereby God has an effect in the world (*Metaphysics* xii,6,1071b12–32). (In *Physics* viii,5, Aristotle also says of Anaxagoras' Mind that "it could only cause motion the way it does being unmoved, and it can only *rule* being unmixed" – 256b26–7; emphasis added.) So, we must conceive of God's thoughts about himself as bound up with his immanency (*Metaphysics* i,2,983a8–10; iii,4,1000b3–6). Aristotle offers an explanation of how this works: just as our (internal) intentions *are* their external objects less their matter, so God thinks himself in the things that depend on him (*Metaphysics* xii,9,1047b38–a5; also *De Anima* iii,5,430a19–20). The interpretation of Thomas Aquinas would appear then to be correct, that it is precisely in thinking of himself that God knows – and controls – all other things (in *Metaphysics* §§2614–16).

Hellenistic and later philosophy

Two new major schools of thought arise in Athens shortly after the death of Aristotle in 322 BCE: Stoicism, founded by Zeno of Citium in about 300, and Epicureanism, founded by Epicurus in about 307. Varieties of skepticism are also important during this time and after, some of the most important philosophical skeptics setting themselves up in Plato's own Academy. Platonism also gives rise to Middle Platonism and then Neoplatonism, which itself went through a number of phases and is hardly identifiable as a "school" due to its often syncretistic nature and the true originality of some of its major figures – notably Plotinus (CE 205–70). From the Aristotelian Lyceum emerge a number of philosophers called Peripatetics, the last of whom was Alexander of Aphrodisias (fl. early 3rd century CE). It is impossible in the present context to treat at all adequately such a vast and complicated philosophical legacy as followed the classical period. A few comments about Stoicism, Epicureanism and Plotinus and how these relate to ideas already discussed will have to suffice.

The God of Stoicism is an immortal and rational animal, perfectly blessed, good, and provident (Long and Sedley 1987, 54A,K). The Stoics hold that these and other characteristics of God – including, according to Diogenes of Babylon, his existence (1987, 54D3) – are self-evident in our "preconceptions" (1987, 54K: also pp. 249–53). They provide a number of proofs for God's existence (1987, 54C–E). They are interested in assimilating into their theology the traditional gods of the pantheon, although they insist too that God is not anthropomorphic (1987, 54A). (As often occurs in Greek writings, they go back and forth easily between speaking of the divine in the singular and in the plural: see, for example, 1987, 54E.) God pervades all the world by bringing reason (*logos*) or cause to shapeless and inert matter (1987, 44B–E,46A–B,55E); and the traditional gods represent this immanent, active presence of God in the universe (1987, 54I). This divine causation, although rational, is not conceived of as Aristotelian final causation since cause, according to the Stoics, is simply "that because of which" and is associated with bodies (1987, 55A–C). God in fact is bodily (46H), the "designing fire" or rational "seed" that pervades the universe (46A1, B2). Accordingly, God does not stand apart as a craftsman planning; what plan there is resides in the causal structure of the world. Sometimes God is referred to as the World Soul (44C, 46E,F). Divine providence is evident in this teleologically ordered world (54H); another name for providence is "fate" – meaning, however, "not the 'fate' of superstition, but that of physics" (55L, also 54U). One lives virtuously by living in accordance with reason, which is to live in accordance with divine causation (60H4, 63C). (The Stoic conception of fate, however, is an extremely complex subject: see pp. 342–3, 392–4.)

Epicureanism explicitly contests a number of Platonic and Stoic ideas. Notably, as part of a general anti-teleologism (1987, 13E, F5), it rejects both the notion of a Divine Craftsman (13F4, G2) and the notion of a reasonable nature to which we might conform ourselves (13E,I,J, 21F2). It does not explicitly consider Aristotelian teleology, Alexander of Aphrodisias suggesting that it simply neglects

Aristotle in this respect (13J2). Epicureanism is not atheistic, encouraging even worship of the gods (23D, E5,I) who are of human form (23E6); but the worshiper is not to expect the gods' intervention. The two self-evident characteristics of the gods are blessedness and immortality (23E2–3): involvement in a world so full of savage beasts and wailing babies (13F6–7) would tarnish the former (13D3). Long and Sedley argue that Epicurus himself was an atheist – at least in the sense that the gods were for him merely psychological projections of man's ethical ideas (1987, v.1,pp. 147–9); but this theory founders on Epicurus' statement that the gods are immortal (23B1; see also 23B2, E2, 54J5). Epicureanism also puts forward a type of materialistic evolutionism (13E,I,15J1–2) very much like that which Plato rejects in *Laws* x.

Plotinus' attitude toward traditional pagan religion is ambivalent if not hostile (*Life* 10.35–6; but see *Enneads* III.5.2–3). For him God is the ineffable One, below whom are ranged divine Mind (which is not just "a god" but divinity in its entirety – *Enneads* V.5.3.1–3) and Soul. The One is simple, different from all that comes after it; it exists by itself, unmixed with the beings that depend on it, capable none the less of being present, in its own way, in all beings (*Enneads* V.4.1.5–10). Mind, on the other hand, is complex (*Enneads* V.4.2, 6.6) in so far as, in thinking of itself (as in Aristotle), it thinks of the Platonic Forms and functions thereby as Craftsman (*Enneads* V.9.3, 5). Soul has direct contact with the material world: it is in fact a World Soul (*Enneads* IV.8.1–3, V.9.14). The causal relationship of the One (also called the Good) to the rest of the universe is, as in Aristotle, one of attraction and finality (*Enneads* VI.7.16–20, 42). Mind exists in so far as it contemplates the One; Soul exists in so far as it looks to the Forms in the Mind; nature, which is not really separate from Soul, produces the world by a sort of accident, due to its orientation toward the divine and its distance from it. Plotinus compares nature to a weak contemplator who eventually resorts to a physical device in order to understand (*Enneads* III.8.4). His last words were, "Seek to lead the god in you up to the divine in the universe" (*Life* 2.26–7).

Bibliography

Aquinas, Thomas: *In Metaphysicam Aristotelis Commentaria*, ed. M.-R. Cathala (Turin: Marietti, 1926).

Barnes, J. (ed.): *The Complete Works of Aristotle: The Revised Oxford Translation*, 2 vols. (Princeton: Princeton University Press, 1984).

Burnet, J.: *Early Greek Philosophy*, 3rd edn (London: A. & C. Black, 1920).

Clemens Alexandrinus (Clement of Alexandria): *Protrepticus und Paedagogus*, ed. O. Stählin (Leipzig: J. C. Hinrichs'sche Buchhandlung, 1905).

Cooper, J. (ed.): *The Complete Works of Plato* (Indianapolis: Hackettt, 1996).

Diels, H., and Kranz, W. (eds): *Die Fragmente der Vorsokratiker*, 6th edn 3 vols. (Dublin/Zurich: Weidmann, 1951).

Jaeger, W.: *The Theology of the Early Greek Philosophers* (Oxford: Clarendon Press, 1947).

Long, A., and Sedley, D.: *The Hellenistic Philosophers*, 2 vols. (Cambridge: Cambridge University Press, 1987).

Solmsen, F.: *Plato's Theology* (Ithaca, NY: Cornell University Press, 1942).

Vlastos, G.: *Plato's Universe* (Seattle: University of Washington Press, 1975).

9

The Christian contribution to medieval philosophical theology

SCOTT MacDONALD

Medieval philosophy in Europe and the Mediterranean world is shaped by the confluence of two traditions: the ancient Greek philosophical tradition and the Judeo-Christian religious tradition. Christianity is the single most important extra-philosophical contributor to medieval philosophy. Indeed it would be no exaggeration to say that from the time of Augustine (CE 354–430) until the rise of Renaissance humanism in the fourteenth century, philosophy in those areas is dominated by Christianity. Christianity's influence on medieval philosophy comes both from within philosophy itself and from outside it. On the one hand, Christian texts and doctrine provide rich subject matter for philosophical reflection, and the nature and central claims of Christianity force its reflective adherents to work out a systematic account of reality and to deal explicitly and theoretically with deep issues about the aims and methods of the philosophical enterprise. In these ways Christianity is taken up into philosophy, adding to its content and altering its structure and methods. On the other hand, Christianity imposes external constraints on medieval philosophy. At various times these constraints take institutional form: the official proscription of texts, condemnation of philosophical positions, and censure of individuals. Institutional constraints of this sort are manifestations of a more general, sometimes latent hostility toward philosophy that is deeply rooted in the Christian tradition.

Christianity's influence on the aims and methods of medieval philosophy

It is natural that early intellectual converts to Christianity, many of whom were philosophers prior to their conversions, should have been led to think reflectively about the Christian faith not only by their own curiosity but also by the need to defend the new religion before other intellectuals and to spread its message to them. Apologists and evangelists alike needed philosophical resources to perform their tasks, and they helped themselves to philosophical ideas and devices that were ready to hand. But it is unlikely that Christianity could have so thoroughly permeated medieval philosophy were it not for the explicit theoretical rapprochement provided by Augustine.

Christianity placed three significant obstacles in the path of the development of

Christian philosophy in the Middle Ages. First, philosophy, and in particular the pagan philosophy of late antiquity, offered accounts of the nature of reality and human beings' place in it that conflicted with the Christian account in important ways. Pagan philosophy, therefore, not only competed with Christianity for converts but also threatened to subvert Christianity from the inside, tempting Christian thinkers who used its methods and resources into error and heresy. Second, philosophy claimed to have arrived at the truth by human reason alone, eschewing (and in some cases openly despising) reliance on the authority of special persons or sacred texts, authority of just the sorts that are essential to Christianity. Third, by virtue of its intellectualist methods philosophy appealed to and promised to benefit only the intellectual elite of the late ancient world, in contrast to Christianity which claimed to bring salvation to all. According to Christianity, God's salvation comes to all people, by faith rather than intellectual achievement, through persons and events attested to in a sacred text, and in accordance with a plan that is unintelligible to those who are wise in this world. These features of the relation between Christianity and philosophy ground a kind of Christian anti-intellectualism that is expressed early and famously in Christian history by Tertullian (ca. CE 160–230) who excoriated philosophy in the name of the Gospel.

Augustine articulated a theoretical basis for Christian philosophy that was to undermine Christian anti-intellectualism and undergird the huge edifice of medieval Christian philosophical theology. He assigned priority to the revealed truths that are expressed in Christian doctrine and known through the Bible. With respect to the *content* of pagan philosophy, revealed truth serves as the kind of rule the Christian philosopher uses to measure philosophical claims and arguments. With revealed truth in hand the Christian philosopher is in a position to salvage what is true and useful in pagan philosophy while repudiating what is false. With respect to philosophical *method* – the use of human reason – revealed truth serves as a kind of starting point and guide. The Christian philosopher starts by *believing* revealed truth and seeks, by the use of reason and with God's help, to acquire *understanding* of what he formerly merely believed. Augustine argues that when philosophical reflection begins from revealed truth and seeks to understand, it will strengthen Christianity while avoiding the dangers identified by the Christian anti-intellectualists. Moreover, he argues not only that it is legitimate and useful to bring philosophical method to bear on Christianity, but that doing so is a Christian's positive duty in so far as he or she is able. Reason is created by God and is that in virtue of which human beings are most like God. To repudiate reason, then, would be to despise God's image in human beings.

Augustine's position is based on a distinction between the epistemic propositional attitudes *belief* and *understanding*. To believe a given proposition p is to assent to p on the basis of authority. To understand p is to assent to it on the basis of reason, by virtue of seeing for oneself the reason for its truth. For example, at the beginning of *De Libero Arbitrio*, book 2, Augustine and his interlocutor claim to believe on the basis of authority that God exists – because it is attested by historical accounts reliably handed down through the Church and in the Bible. But they

81

go on in that book to seek understanding of the proposition that God exists: Augustine constructs a rational proof that manifests God's existence and explains God's place in reality. This Augustinian distinction and the Augustinian method of belief seeking understanding is taken for granted by the vast majority of Christian philosophers in the Middle Ages, including Anselm (1033–1109) who tells us that the original title of his *Proslogion* (the work containing his famous ontological argument, see Article 41, ONTOLOGICAL ARGUMENTS) was "Faith Seeking Understanding" (*fides quaerens intellectum*).

Later medieval philosophers such as Thomas Aquinas (1225–74), who conceives of theological inquiry primarily as conforming to the model of an Aristotelian science, nevertheless makes room for the Augustinian method within his system. Acknowledging that certain matters of faith – such as the belief that God is triune – cannot be established by human reason and must be accepted on authority, Aquinas claims that there is still important philosophical work to be done with respect to those matters. He calls work of that sort *clarification*, and he takes it to involve the analysis of concepts and doctrines central to Christianity, the investigation of Christianity's internal coherence and external consistency, the drawing of explanatory conceptual connections, and the development of illuminating analogies. When he describes this sort of enterprise near the beginning of a lengthy discussion of the doctrine of the Trinity, Aquinas seems clearly to have in mind and to be advocating the sort of philosophical project he knew from Augustine's *De Trinitate* (*Summa Theologiae* Ia q. 32, a. 1, ad2).

Christianity's influence on the content of medieval philosophy

In articulating a rationale and method for Christian philosophy Augustine clears the way for medieval philosophers to bring philosophical tools and skills to bear on Christianity. Moreover, his writings provide a wealth of rich and compelling examples of philosophical reflection on topics ranging from the nature of sin to the nature of the Trinity. Boethius (ca. 480–524) stands with Augustine in this respect as an important model for medieval philosophical theologians. He composed several short theological treatises, two of which (*De Trinitate* and *Contra Eutychen et Nestorium*) consciously attempt to bring the tools of Aristotelian logic to bear on issues associated with doctrines central to the Christian creed, namely, the Trinity and the two natures of Christ (see Article 66, TRINITY; and Article 67, INCARNATION). The sort of philosophical theology prominent in these writings of Augustine and Boethius and in similar works by philosophically minded patristic and late antique writers – namely, the discussion of specifically Christian topics by means of rigorous philosophical analysis and argumentation – constitutes a substantial part of the philosophical heritage of medieval philosophy.

It is no surprise, then, that medieval philosophers should take up, develop, and extend the enterprise of philosophical theology. Much of Anselm's work, including *Cur Deus Homo*, *De Casu Diaboli*, and *De Conceptu Virginali et de Peccato Originali*, falls squarely in this tradition, as does Peter Abelard's (1079–1142) *Theologia*

Summi Boni, Hugh of St Victor's (1096–1141) *De Sacramentis*, the commentaries on Boethius' theological treatises by Thierry of Chartres (d. 1154) and Gilbert of Poitiers (1085–1154), and Richard of St Victor's (d. 1173) *De Trinitate*. It would be a mistake to think of these treatises as theological in a narrow sense that distinguishes theology sharply from philosophy. As their titles suggest, they deal explicitly and primarily with topics in Christian theology, but the sorts of questions they raise and attempt to illuminate and the kinds of analysis and argumentation they employ are in many cases paradigmatically philosophical. They exemplify the way in which Christianity and philosophical method merge to constitute medieval philosophical theology.

With the emergence of academic faculties of theology in the new European schools and universities of the twelfth and thirteenth centuries, theology becomes the paramount academic discipline in a formal curriculum of higher education. The academic study of theology presupposed advanced formal training in philosophy and its main component apart from the study of the Bible was the study of theological texts and issues drawn from the Church Fathers and Doctors and from early medieval philosophical theologians. By the mid-thirteenth century, Peter Lombard's *Sentences* (composed ca. 1158) had become the standard textbook for the study of theology. The *Sentences* is a systematic topical presentation of Christian doctrine rich in quotation and paraphrase from authoritative theological sources and heavily weighted toward Augustine. It consists of four books devoted, respectively, to the Trinity, creation (see Article 39, CREATION AND CONSERVATION), the Incarnation, and the sacraments. Since most of the greatest philosophical theologians from the period 1240–1350 (including Albert the Great [d. 1280], Thomas Aquinas, Bonaventure [1221–74], John Duns Scotus [1265/66–1308], and William of Ockham [d. 1349]) studied and wrote commentaries on the *Sentences* as the final stage of their formal training, Lombard's text to a significant extent provides the framework within which Christian philosophical theology was to develop in the thirteenth and fourteenth centuries. During these years the vast majority of the best minds in the Latin West and those with the highest level of philosophical training and sophistication were devoting the major part of their intellectual attention to philosophical theology.

Christianity's influence on medieval philosophy extends beyond the addition of specifically Christian ideas and doctrines such as Trinity, Incarnation, and atonement (see Article 69, ATONEMENT, JUSTIFICATION, AND SANCTIFICATION) to the subject matter of philosophical investigation. Medieval philosophers' reflections on Christianity also affected their philosophical work on non-theological topics. This sort of influence takes several different forms. In some cases, medieval philosophers modify or extend a philosophical theory in order to adapt it to or make it adequate for a Christian understanding of reality. Aquinas, for example, takes over the basic structure of Aristotle's ethical theory but in doing so molds it to the shape of Christianity. He elaborates Aristotle's claims (in *Nicomachean Ethics* x) about the life of *theoria* being the best life for a human being in an explicitly theological direction: intellectual vision of the divine essence in the next life is a human being's supernatural ultimate end. Moreover, in order to enable human beings to attain

83

that end, God infuses them supernaturally with certain theological virtues – including faith, hope, and charity – over and above the acquired moral and intellectual virtues identified by Aristotle (see Article 59, VIRTUE ETHICS). These infused virtues are modeled on and play a role in the economy of redemption and salvation analogous to that played by the Aristotelian virtues in the attainment of *eudaimonia*. Like his modified Aristotelian moral philosophy, Aquinas's theory of knowledge reflects the conviction that a complete theory must extend to all of reality. Accordingly, he develops a unified epistemology that explains the nature, mechanisms, and scope not only of ordinary human cognition but also of angelic and divine cognition and the cognition characteristic of humans before their fall (see Article 68, SIN AND ORIGINAL SIN) and after their union with God in the next life (see Article 71, HEAVEN AND HELL).

In other cases, important developments in medieval philosophy are motivated or guided by concerns about theological issues even when those developments themselves have no theological component. For example, Henry of Ghent's (d. 1293) development of a sophisticated argument for rejecting one of the central principles of Aristotelian natural philosophy – Aristotle's denial of the possibility of instantaneous change – is motivated by his perception that the Aristotelian principle is incompatible with the correct understanding of the immaculate conception of the Virgin Mary. (He believes that the only acceptable account of the immaculate conception requires that Mary undergo an instantaneous change at the moment of her conception from being stained by original sin to being cleansed of it.) Henry intends the results of his anti-Aristotelian argument to have theological applications, but he defends them exclusively on grounds appropriate to natural philosophy and takes them to be compelling quite apart from whatever theological applications they may have. In similar fashion, the Christian doctrine of the creation of the universe in time generates a large and sophisticated body of literature in the later Middle Ages surrounding the issue of whether the universe does (or must) have a beginning. Despite having been occasioned by theological concerns, that literature focuses largely on non-theological questions about the nature of time, change, and infinity.

Christianity as an external constraint on medieval philosophy

Christianity permeates medieval philosophy, giving rise to philosophical reflection on specifically theological matters, occasioning the extension of philosophical theory in new directions, and spurring philosophical investigation of a broad range of basic issues in metaphysics, epistemology, natural philosophy, and ethics. In many of these ways Christianity is a source of energy and movement in medieval philosophy. But Christianity sometimes motivated efforts aimed at retarding the development of the philosophical enterprise in the Middle Ages. Religiously or theologically motivated resistance to philosophy in general and to the use of philosophical tools and methods for understanding Christianity in particular emerges in different forms throughout the period.

Virulent, institutionally supported forms of resistance appear at three particular times in the later Middle Ages, apparently in reaction to major philosophical trends. The first appears in the first half of the twelfth century when the recovery of what became known as the new logic (including Aristotle's *Analytics, Topics*, and *Sophistical Refutations*) and activities associated with the growing schools at Paris focused attention on and invigorated the study of dialectic and the application of its methods to theological problems. Influential clerics, Bernard of Clairvaux (1090–1153) prominent among them, saw these developments as a threat to Christianity, leading to heresy and the corruption of doctrine. Attempting to use ecclesiastical authority as a means of suppression, they brought charges against leading philosophical theologians such as Peter Abelard and Gilbert of Poitiers. In the former case Bernard succeeded in obtaining the condemnation of Abelard's Trinitarian views in 1141 and Abelard was forbidden to teach.

The late twelfth and early thirteenth century recovery of large portions of the Aristotelian corpus of natural philosophy, metaphysics, and ethics together with associated philosophical texts by Muslim philosophers such as Avicenna and Averroës prompted a second period of sustained ecclesiastical reaction to new philosophical developments (see Article 10, THE ISLAMIC CONTRIBUTION TO MEDIEVAL PHILOSOPHICAL THEOLOGY). In this case the reaction was motivated not only by a general worry about the harm the new methods and interests might do to theology but also by the fact that the new philosophical material explicitly and directly contradicted the teachings of Christianity. Aristotle had argued in the *Physics* that the universe is beginningless, contradicting the Christian view that it has existed for a finite length of time. Moreover, Averroës' development of themes from Aristotle's *De Anima* contradicted the Christian view of the human soul, its relation to God, and the possibility of personal immortality (see Article 70, SURVIVAL OF DEATH). In 1210 and again in 1215 ecclesiastical authorities issued edicts proscribing the teaching of Aristotle's natural philosophy at Paris. In 1231 the ban was reaffirmed by the pope, who appointed a commission to examine the works of natural philosophy and purge them of error. The commission seems never to have discharged its task and the ban was eventually forgotten (by the 1250s the entire Aristotelian corpus, including the books of natural philosophy, was part of the curriculum at Paris). It is important, however, not to exaggerate the influence of the proscriptions of 1210 and 1215. Their authority extended only to Paris and not to Oxford or other major European universities, and it seems to have affected only formal teaching at Paris. We have evidence in the writings of important philosophical theologians at Paris during this time that the proscribed works of Aristotle were being read and used.

A similar ecclesiastical reaction occurs in the 1270s, this time largely in response to the radical Averroistic interpreters of Aristotle's philosophy. In 1277 Etienne Tempier, bishop of Paris, issued a condemnation of 219 articles covering a wide range of theological and philosophical topics. The condemnation seems to have been in force at Paris throughout the fourteenth century. It condemns, among other things, the view that the universe is beginningless, that God creates out of necessity, and that there is a single intellect for all human beings. But among its most significant features is the condemnation of views that suggest in various ways that God's power is circumscribed or limited by principles of natural philosophy – for example, that God cannot move the world rectilinearly since a vacuum would thereby be created. The general force of these condemnations is to affirm God's power to do anything that does not involve a contradiction – God's so-called "absolute power." Regardless of whether the principles of natural philosophy permit the existence of a vacuum, God's acting in such a way that a vacuum is created seems to involve no contradiction, and so is possible by God's absolute power (see Article 28, OMNIPOTENCE). Affirming God's absolute power no doubt seemed to the bishop of Paris the appropriate way to remind over-zealous philosophers of the deepest truths about reality already possessed through revelation. References by fourteenth century writers to the condemnation of 1277 suggest that it was to a significant extent successful in silencing the views it targeted.

The condemnation's emphasis on God's absolute power highlights a broadly logical notion of possibility, distinguishing that notion from a notion of what we might call natural or physical possibility. As a result, the principle that God can do whatever does not involve a contradiction becomes an important tool of philosophical analysis and criticism. On the one hand, asking whether a certain proposed analysis or hypothetical state of affairs involves a contradiction (or is the sort of thing God could bring about by his absolute power) leads to interesting and useful investigation and thought experiment. On the other hand, pointing out that God could bring about a certain result by his absolute power becomes an effective refutation of philosophical claims and analyses. This is an important tool in William of Ockham's critical arsenal. He allows, for example, that as far as *natural* causes are concerned intuitive cognition can be caused or preserved only by an existing object of cognition. He denies, however, that an intuitive cognition unqualifiedly requires the existence of its object, for God's producing an intuitive cognition where there is no object of cognition involves no contradiction. Similarly, Ockham denies the metaphysical doctrine that essence and existence are really distinct on the grounds that if they were, then (contrary to fact) no contradiction would be involved in God's preserving a thing's essence in the world without the thing's existence, and vice versa. In this way, the condemnation of 1277 – itself a kind of external constraint on medieval philosophy – provides late medieval philosophers with new tools and new direction and is thereby taken up into the philosophy of the fourteenth century.

Bibliography

Anselm: *Monologion* and *Proslogion*, tr. J. Hopkins, *A New Interpretive Translation of St. Anselm's Monologion and Proslogion* (Minneapolis: Banning Press, 1986).

Augustine: *De libero arbitrio*, tr. T. Williams, *On Free Choice of the Will* (Indianapolis: Hackett, 1993).

——: *De utilitate credendi*, tr. J. H. S. Burleigh, *Augustine: Earlier Writings* (Philadelphia: Westminster Press, 1953), pp. 291–323.

Aquinas, Thomas: *Summa Theologiae*, tr. Fathers of the English Dominican Province, *The*

Summa Theologica of St. Thomas Aquinas (Westminster: Christian Classics, 1981).

Boethius: *De Trinitate* and *Contra Eutychen et Nestorium*, ed. and tr. H. F. Stewart, E. K. Rand, and S. J. Tester, *Boethius: The Theological Tractates and the Consolation of Philosophy* (Cambridge: Harvard University Press, 1973).

Gilson, E.: *Reason and Revelation in the Middle Ages* (New York: Charles Scribner's Sons, 1938).

Grant, E.: "The condemnation of 1277, God's absolute power, and physical thought in the late Middle Ages," *Viator: Medieval and Renaissance Studies*, 10 (1979), pp. 211–44.

Kretzmann, N.: "Faith seeks, understanding finds: Augustine's charter for Christian philosophy." In T. P. Flint (ed.), *Christian Philosophy* (Notre Dame: University of Notre Dame Press, 1990), pp. 1–36.

Pelikan, J.: *Christianity and Classical Culture* (New Haven: Yale University Press, 1993).

Steenberghen, F. Van: *Aristotle in the West: The Origins of Latin Aristotelianism*, tr. L. Johnston (Louvain: E. Nauwelaerts, 1955).

10

The Islamic contribution to medieval philosophical theology

DAVID BURRELL, CSC

If we wish to gain perspective on the medieval world of reflection we must replace our Eurocentric image with that of a Mediterranean basin, with a great deal of commerce across this interior lake, with that commerce including warfare and hostilities, yet with scholars profiting from the consequent exchange. We must also remind ourselves that if that basin was partitioned into Muslim and Christian sectors, then Christian communities continued to function (and sometimes even thrive) within the Islamic world, and Jews were tolerated in both, often serving as *port-parleurs* (intermediaries). So while the spirit of this basin could hardly be described as "ecumenical" in current terms, for religious differences seemed always to trump commonalities, the convictions they shared become evident to readers today across the debates which those differences engendered. For Jews, Christians, and Muslims avow the free creation of the universe – that is, all-that-is – by the one God whose action in doing so epitomizes graciousness (see Article 39, CREATION AND CONSERVATION). That is a startling avowal at any time, yet these traditions had to make it in the early medieval period in the face of a picture of the universe and its origins that was seamless and quite intellectually satisfying. So the story of Islamic contributions to medieval philosophical theology will largely recount the ways in which a common Hellenic heritage was challenged to accommodate so startling a faith-assertion as that of free creation. As a matter of historical record, the sharp debates within the Muslim context were not that well known to their Christian interlocutors, but the initial reworking of al-Farabi and Ibn Sina (Avicenna) certainly were, and the ways in which Christian thinkers adapted those schemes make a fascinating tale. Again, for the historical record, Ibn Rushd (Averroës) made far more impact among thinkers in the West (Jewish as well as Christian) than he did in the Islamic world, largely as a result of al-Ghazali's polemical treatise on "deconstructing the philosophers" (*Tahafut al-Falasifa*). Yet his part in the story needs to be told more sympathetically than it has in the past, for many of his objections were also registered by Western thinkers, albeit in a less contentious key.

Initial Islamic forays into philosophical theology – "the philosophers"

When Islam entered the sophisticated world of the Byzantine empire, the works of Plato and of Aristotle were made available to them by virtue of Syriac translators from Greek into Arabic (Walzer 1962). Of the works of Plato it was the *Republic* which offered a model for the role of reason in the formation of a new society, and al-Farabi (875–950) articulated that model in his ground-breaking essay on the "ideas of the inhabitants of the virtuous city" (Walzer 1985). In that work of distinctly Neoplatonic cast the One is deemed to emanate all-that-is according to an order perfect in conception, an order to be emulated by those responsible for ordering the perfect society. A distinctively Islamic note was struck when the author insisted that those responsible will be required to be prophets as well as philosophers, since the proper place in the divine ordering needs to be able to be communicated to each person in the society, and few of them will be able to follow the pattern of deductive reasoning which comprises the original emanation. It is the Qur'an, after all, which offers the paradigm of a text divinely revealed and hence impeccably wise, yet cast in a language accessible to all, replete with images and examples. None but prophets are able so to order metaphor and image as to communicate the results of philosophical reasoning, however; indeed, it is Muhammad who offers the paradigm for a responsible and wise ruler.

It was Aristotle's *Metaphysics*, however, which offered the paradigm for doing philosophy to al-Farabi's successor, Ibn Sina (Avicenna, 980–1037). In his *al-Shifa*, he adapted the cosmological scheme of al-Farabi, whereby the planetary spheres transmit the primary causal influence of the One successively to the earth. So this One provides far more than Aristotle's prime mover, for in the spirit of Plotinus and of Proclus, the movement from unity to multiplicity is at once one of logic and of vitality: what is communicated is a participation in what the One possesses by nature, existence and all that flows from it. What Avicenna added to al-Farabi was an all-important distinction between the ordering and the activity which suffused it. Things are what they are by virtue of their inherent natures; their actual existence they owe directly to the One as the source of all activity. This distinction between *what* something is and the *fact* that it is had been suggested in Aristotle but was never exploited by the Greeks. Its presence in a thinker as preoccupied with essences as Ibn Sina leads one to ask why he deemed it so central to his effort to articulate the movement from the One to the many. The most plausible response is to see it as a philosophical residue of the Qur'anic teaching that the universe was freely created by the one God. It is little more than a residue, however, since the entire process of emanation flows ineluctably from the One; yet it stands none the less, and will be exploited by Thomas Aquinas as the keystone in his attempt to articulate "the distinction" of the creator from creation.

God alone, as both al-Farabi and Ibn Sina had averred, is understood to be One whose very nature is to exist; everything else must have existence bestowed upon it by the One to whom everything that is traces its origination. In this way the distinction of *essence* from *existence* offered Ibn Sina a handy way of articulating what he had already recognized to be the fundamental division in being: between that One which exists of itself, and everything else which may or may not exist. Aristotle had defined contingency in terms of some things being able to be other than they are; Ibn Sina found a yet deeper understanding: everything other than the One source of all might never have been at all! By focusing in this fashion on *existing* as something which "comes to" an essence, he was able in one formula to distinguish necessary from contingent beings as well as to limit necessary being to the One, so offering a philosophical analogue to the Qur'an's insistence that all-that-is derives from a single creator. Furthermore, the formula that God is that very one whose essence is to exist provides a formulation of "necessary being" which corresponds to the deeper understanding of contingency just noted. It is this formulation which Aquinas will exploit to offer a way of uniquely characterizing God as well as signaling "the distinction" of creatures from the creator (*Summa Theologiae* 1.3.4). So the distinction which Ibn Sina remarked could be touted as the primary contribution of Islamic thought to medieval philosophical theology. His unfortunate identification of *existing* as an "accident," however, following the etymology of the Arabic (and Latin) expression of its "*coming to* the essence," left him vulnerable to the trenchant critique of Ibn Rushd, in his *Tahafut al-Falasifa*. It also betrayed his own predilection for essences, a tendency which Aquinas sought to correct in his early opusculum, *On Being and Essence*, by reshaping the basic categorial structure of *being*, as received from Aristotle, to make *existing* the activity most reflective of creation, and so to place essences in potency to this creative influence of God (Burrell 1986).

Averroës' return to Aristotle and al-Ghazali's critique of these initiatives

Both al-Farabi and Ibn Sina had based their speculation on a work transmitted as the "Theology of Aristotle," but which in fact represented a selection from the *Enneads* of Plotinus. This happenstance allowed them to bring these two classical thinkers into closer rapport than the texts proper to each would have permitted, but the results offended two later Islamic thinkers, Averroës (Ibn Rushd) and al-Ghazali, though for very different reasons. Ibn Rushd resented the way in which Aristotle's pristine reasoning had been transmuted into a quasi-mystical ascent to the One, thereby pre-empting something of the proper role of the Qur'an as well as injecting foreign elements into the philosophy associated with the "master of those who know" (Dante). Indeed, Averroës can easily be read as one convinced that Aristotle exhibited the paradigm of human reasoning, so that attempts to know the truth will succeed only in the measure that they follow his teaching and resolve to his proper methods. For al-Ghazali, on the other hand, Ibn Sina's teaching offended against the received doctrine of the Qur'an, notably in its conclusions regarding the necessary emanation of the universe from the One (God), as well as its Neoplatonic insistence on the immortality of the soul to the exclusion of bodily resurrection (Gardet 1951).

Ibn Rushd's celebrated response to al-Ghazali's objections to "the philosophers" exhibits both sets of objections: al-Ghazali's refutation of the inherited emanation scheme as an adequate formulation of "the distinction" of creator from creatures, as well as Averroës' dual response to al-Ghazali and to Ibn Sina. Entitled *Tahafut al-Tahafut* (or "Deconstruction of the Deconstruction"), Averroës' text contains the body of the original work by al-Ghazali which he sets out to refute: *Tahafut al-Falasifa*, or "Deconstruction of the Philosophers" (Van den Bergh 1954). The results of this exchange, however, far exceeded the reasoning proper to the respective texts. Al-Ghazali was perceived to have the better of the debate in the Muslim intellectual world, with the result that Ibn Rushd virtually disappeared from their map, and while a select band of Western thinkers did not hesitate to identify themselves as "Averroists," the subsequent work of al-Ghazali never crossed the linguistic barrier to become accessible to Western medievals (Van Steenberghen 1977, Vajda 1960). In fact, the only work of his which was known to them was the introduction to the *Tahafut*, separately published as the *Maqasid al-falasifa* (or "Aims of the Philosophers"), where he surveyed the systems of al-Farabi and Ibn Sina so sympathetically that Western medievals identified him as one of them, as one of the *falasifa*.

So it can fairly be said that this debate in the Islamic world had very little direct resonance in the West, although the concerns of the three faith traditions which avowed the free creation of the universe intersected in various ways. The most central of these had to do with the manner in which one could amend philosophic reason as transmitted to the faith traditions of the early Middle Ages to accommodate divine freedom, especially when the Plotinian emanation scheme presented itself as the most elegant alternative to philosophers, though it seemed to exclude origination as an intentional act (Burrell 1986, Gerson 1990). To mention divine freedom, however, immediately raises the question of human freedom as well: an issue which preoccupied Islamic thought early on, as it would bring Christian theology to a deadlock much later in the *de auxiliis* controversy. The Islamic controversy is telling for its methodological implications, even though Western medievals were not party to its specific terms. The Qur'an left an equivocal legacy respecting the relation between divine and human freedom: on the one hand, the response to God's call must be a free one, susceptible of praise or blame; on the other, God's sovereignty is complete. The initial response to this dilemma turned on a decidedly univocal meaning for "act," namely "originate," which made God and human beings competitors for the origination of human actions.

Given that initial univocal understanding of *acting* as *creating*, the argumentation is direct and emphatic: human beings and *not* God must be the cause of human actions, especially since God can never be convicted of performing evil actions. This school became known as Mutazilite, and our best source is the *al-Mughni* of 'Abd al-Jabbar (d. 978) (Frank 1982, Burrell 1993). Their understanding of human freedom as autonomy, however, coupled as it was with their univocal notion of *agency*, effectively removed the entire domain of human acts from the creator's sovereignty. Such a move could not long be compatible with an Islam which so emphasized Allah as Lord. So it was a Mutazilite thinker, al-Ashari (d. 935), who began the search for an alternative rendering of the agency proper to human freedom. That teaching, which was dubbed Asharite and soon became the accepted strategy among Muslim theologians, held that "God creates the act while human beings *acquire* it"; in other words, "the act is the act of God in so far as God creates it [*halaqahu*] and is the act of a human being in so far as one acquires it [*iktisabahu*]" (Gimaret 1980, pp. 67–8). This notion of *appropriation*, carried by the Qur'anic terms *kasb* and *iktisab*, attempts to introduce a contrast term to "create" and so break the prevailing univocal understanding of "act" which identified "acting" with "creating," yet the history of its use has never clarified *in what* that contrast consists. Richard Frank proposes to translate it as "performance," which offers a fascinating optic on the earlier discussion (Frank 1983; Gimaret 1990, p. 371).

What we may discern, however, is the way in which this controversy must needs attempt to articulate what defies clarification: the "distinction" of creator from creatures. It is that very relationship which becomes dramatized in the interaction of divine with human freedom, and so is perhaps better understood in the doing than in attempting to articulate it. Such is at least the mature position of al-Ghazali in his magnum opus, *Ihya Ulum ad-Din*. Yet it is fair to say that the Islamic tradition has not succeeded in articulating coherently the relation of primary to secondary causality in the context of a created universe. It is worth contrasting this tortuous path with Aquinas's deft observation that while "the very meaning of voluntary activity denotes an internal principle within the subject, this . . . does not have to be the utterly first principle, moving yet unmoved by all else. The proximate principle is internal, but the ultimately first moving principle is external, as indeed it is for natural movement, this being the cause setting nature in motion" (*Summa Theologiae* 1–2.9.4.1). Roger Arnaldez (1977) pinpoints this issue of secondary causality as a neuralgic point in Islamic thought more generally; what remain to be explored are the comparative reasons for this telling difference.

The lasting contribution of Islamic thought to philosophical theology

Philosophical theology inevitably walks a tightrope between two sets of criteria: those belonging to rational inquiry as such, and those inherited from a faith tradition. Yet we have come to see that such a way of putting the question hardly poses a dilemma, but rather offers the sort of fruitful tension which should animate any sustained inquiry. For we never encounter rational inquiry *as such*; we always find ourselves reasoning from presuppositions held in various ways and reflecting dimensions of our personal and communal history not fully open to scrutiny. In short, all inquiry is "tradition-directed." Traditions which last must themselves be open to criticism from within, a large part of which will itself be directed to clarifying unexamined presumptions or exploring cultural accretions in the ongoing inquiry. So the key to a fruitful philosophical theology will lie in the manner in which its practitioners execute this maneuver of reconciling these two sets of criteria, continually examining each set for internal consistency. Islamic thought has held tenaciously to the premise that the universe is freely created and continuously sustained by a sovereign God. The Asharite response to the Mutazilite formulation of the structure of human freedom and the relation between our freedom and the creator's effectively illustrated this penchant in Islamic thought.

Yet what Islam, notably in the works of al-Ghazali, never quite succeeded in articulating, namely a coherent account of primary and secondary causality in a created universe, continues to stand as the challenge to philosophical theology today. What is needed is a set of philosophical tools which can be shaped and adapted to do the work required once one acknowledges the presence of a creator to everything that is. And while Islamic thought may have failed to craft those tools, it never shirked from presenting us with the challenge to do so. That challenge may be its most telling contribution to the current enterprise of philosophical theology. Even if the task can be seen a priori to be an impossible one, given the intractability of "the distinction" of creator from creatures, it must none the less be undertaken, for that is the nature of philosophical theology: to attempt to formulate what we know must escape formulation. At least such is the task of philosophical theology as seen from the vantage point of one accustomed to the acute reasoning and astute formulations of medieval thought, be it Jewish, Christian, or Muslim (see Article 9, THE CHRISTIAN CONTRIBUTION TO MEDIEVAL PHILOSOPHICAL THEOLOGY; and Article 11, THE JEWISH CONTRIBUTION TO MEDIEVAL PHILOSOPHICAL THEOLOGY). For these thinkers, beginning as they all did with the postulation of a universe freely created, were forced to find a way of articulating divinity which assured its uniqueness, and then a manner of conceiving the universe so related to that divinity as to depend upon it in everything. It is fair to say that philosophy of religion in its Western Christian form has not always observed those strictures, so that difficult issues attending the relation of primary to secondary causality have often simply been ignored. Perhaps one of the fruits of the inescapably interfaith context of our life and inquiry today will be to recall Western thinkers to the intellectual exigencies of faith in "one God, creator of heaven and earth." If so, the contribution of Islam to the discussion will prove telling, as this brief sketch of the history has tried to show.

Bibliography

Arnaldez, R.: "Intellectualisme et voluntarisme dans la pensée musulmane." In *1274 – Année charnière – Mutation et continuité* (Paris: Editions du centre nationale de la recherche scientifique, 1977), pp. 121–9.

Avicenna: *La Métaphysique du Shifa'*. tr. G. C. Anawati (Paris: Vrin, 1978, 1985).

Burrell, D.: *Knowing the Unknowable God: Ibn Sina, Maimonides, Aquinas* (Notre Dame: University of Notre Dame Press, 1986).

——: *Freedom and Creation in Three Traditions* (Notre Dame: University of Notre Dame Press, 1993).

Frank, R.: "The autonomy of the human agent in the teaching of 'Abd al-Jabbar," *Le Museon* (Louvain-la Neuve), 95 (1982), pp. 232–55.

——: "Moral obligation in classical Muslim theology," *Journal of Religious Ethics*, 11 (1983), pp. 204–23, esp. p. 218 n. 19.

Gardet, L.: *La Pensée religieuse d'Avicenne* (Paris: Vrin, 1951).

Gerson, L. P.: *God and Greek Philosophy* (London and New York: Routledge, 1990).

Ghazali: *Ihya' Ulum ad-Din*, Book 35: *Book of Faith in Divine Unity [tawhid] and Trust in Divine Providence [tawakkull]*, tr. D. Burrell (Cambridge: Islamic Texts Society, 1966).

Gimaret, D.: *Théories de l'acte humain* (Paris: Vrin, 1980).

——: *La Doctrine d'al-Ash'ari* (Paris: Cerf, 1990).

Vajda, G.: *Isaac Albalag: Averroïste Juif, traducteur et annotateur d'al-Ghazali* (Paris: Vrin, 1960).

Van den Bergh, S.: *Averroës' Tahafut al-Tahafut* (Cambridge: Cambridge University Press, 1954).

Van Steenberghen, F.: *Maître Siger de Brabant* (Louvain: Publications Universitaires, 1977).

Walzer, R.: *Greek into Arabic: Essays in Islamic Philosophy* (Columbia: University of South Carolina Press, 1962).

——: *Al-Farabi on the Perfect State* (Oxford: Clarendon Press, 1985).

11

The Jewish contribution to medieval philosophical theology

TAMAR RUDAVSKY

Introduction

The fundamental problem of Jewish philosophy, like that of Islamic and Christian philosophy, is summed up in the formula "faith and reason." Arising as an effort toward harmonizing the tenets of Judaism with philosophic teachings that held sway at successive periods of Jewish history, medieval Jewish philosophy dealt with problems in which there seemed to be a conflict between philosophical speculation (*iyyun*) and acceptance of dogmas of the Judaic faith (*emunah*). The goal of the Jewish philosopher was not so much to buttress faith with understanding, but rather to reconcile two distinct bodies of knowledge. In this article we shall examine the attempts of Maimonides (1135–1204) and Gersonides (1288–1344) to reconcile the strictures of faith and reason in the context of the following issues: the doctrine of creation, negative theology, and doctrines of divine omniscience. Before turning to these topics, however, let us examine briefly the underlying theological epistemology employed by both thinkers.

The nature of belief in Jewish thought

Maimonides' *Guide of the Perplexed* is the most important work of medieval Jewish philosophy and exercised a profound influence upon all subsequent Jewish thought, as well as upon Christian scholasticism (see Article 9, THE CHRISTIAN CONTRIBUTION TO MEDIEVAL PHILOSOPHICAL THEOLOGY; and Article 22, THE JEWISH TRADITION). However, the ostensibly orthodox views espoused in the *Guide of the Perplexed* are not necessarily Maimonides' own. He characterizes belief (*emunah*) as follows: "belief is the affirmation that what has been represented is outside the mind just as it has been represented in the mind" (*Guide* I.50, p. 111). But how is the reader to approach beliefs espoused in the *Guide*? In the Introduction Maimonides distinguishes two levels of interpretation, exoteric and esoteric, and suggests that it is sometimes incumbent upon a philosopher to conceal his own esoteric position behind the veil of exoteric doctrine: "For my purpose is that the truths be glimpsed and then again be concealed, so as not to oppose that divine purpose which one cannot possibly oppose and which has concealed from the vulgar among the people those truths especially requisite for His apprehension" (*Guide*, Intro., pp. 6–7).

95

Maimonides further describes seven sorts of contradictions commonly found in philosophical works and suggests that two of these (numbers 5 and 7) may be used specifically to conceal potentially controversial or even heretical doctrines from the masses. The seventh is the most important for our purposes, and is used, Maimonides notes, when "speaking about very obscure matters . . . to conceal some parts and to disclose others. . . . In such cases the vulgar must in no way be aware of the contradiction; the author accordingly uses some device to conceal it by all means" (*Guide*, Intro., p. 18). He then states that any contradictions found in the *Guide* itself are intentional (*Guide*, Intro., p. 20). In light of these cautionary comments, generations of scholars have devoted their lives to unpacking the underlying esoteric meaning of the *Guide*.

Perhaps unwisely, Gersonides did not create around his works such an aura of intrigue and his philosophical corpus was largely ignored until the present century. Writing in fourteenth century France, Gersonides spent several years in the papal court in Avignon, and may at that time have come into contact with the views of William of Ockham and other fourteenth century scholastics. His major work *The Wars of the Lord* is a sustained examination of the major philosophical issues of the day. In his Introduction to *Wars* Gersonides emphasizes that he will not adopt esotericism in his own work. While he is sensitive to the problem in revealing philosophical theories to a traditional audience, he does not resort to obfuscation. Suggesting that those who "increase obscurity either because of poor organization or opacity of language, so that the easy becomes difficult, defeat the purpose for which they have written their books" (*Wars*, Intro., p. 100), he proclaims his intention to use clear, straightforward language, and to avoid obscurity (*Wars*, Intro., p. 101).

But is reason the final arbiter for Gersonides? In the Introduction to *Wars*, he stressed that "if the literal sense of the Torah differs from reason, it is necessary to interpret those passages in accordance with the demands of reason" (*Wars*, Intro., p. 98). However, in other passages Gersonides appears to acknowledge the supremacy of scripture over reason. For example, in *Wars* I. ch. 14, he suggests that ". . . adherence to reason is not permitted if it contradicts religious faith. This is incumbent upon all the faithful; . . . if there appears to be a problem concerning which our view differs from the accepted view of religion, philosophy should be abandoned and religion followed" (*Wars* I. ch. 14, p. 226). Recent scholars have disagreed over how to read Gersonides on this issue. Following Eisen's recent argument, let us suggest that Gersonides be read politically: for individuals who have not progressed philosophically, it is better that *they* remain committed to religious faith and ignore the philosophical doctrines of *Wars*. Concerned not to disrupt the beliefs of the traditionalists, Gersonides politely suggests that they desist from reading his work. Unlike Maimonides, however, he does not resort to esotericism to hide his intentions.

Divine attributes

Do the different attributes of God constitute many distinct aspects or persons in the Divine essence? Jewish philosophers were divided on this question, as were medieval thinkers in general. Saadyah Gaon, a tenth century Jewish philosopher whose works reflected the influence of the Islamic Mutazila (see Article 10, THE ISLAMIC CONTRIBUTION TO MEDIEVAL PHILOSOPHICAL THEOLOGY), followed the tradition of Philo and the *kalam* thinkers in denying multiplicity to God: the three attributes of Life, Power, and Wisdom are implied in the very notion of God. It is due to the deficiency of human language that they cannot be expressed in one single term.

Maimonides' theory of divine predication followed the Neoplatonic tradition and was built primarily upon al-Farabi's and Avicenna's distinction between essence and existence: this distinction implied that in the case of contingent beings existence was accidental to essence, whereas in God essence and existence were one (see Article 31, SIMPLICITY). Hence God's nature is totally unlike ours, and terms used to describe God must be used either in a homonymous way or as negative predicates. The four essential attributes of God – life, power, wisdom, and will – are of one simple essence; all other attributes are to be conceived either as descriptive of divine action, or as negative attributes. However, even these four attributes, when predicated of God, are used in a homonymous, or equivocal, sense (*Guide* I.56, p. 131). The difference between human and divine predicates is qualitative: since the terms are applied by way of perfect homonymity, they admit of no comparison between God and His creatures.

Gersonides, on the other hand, disagreed with Maimonides' celebrated theory of negative theology and sided with Averroës who, rejecting the Avicennan distinction between essence and existence, argued that existence is not an accident of Being. In following Averroës, Gersonides paves the way for a positive theology which permits of positive attributive ascription. Gersonides disagrees with Maimonides, claiming that divine predicates are to be understood as *pros hen* equivocals, or derivative equivocals, rather than absolute equivocals (as Maimonides had argued). That is, according to Gersonides, predicates applied to God represent the prime instance or meaning of the term, whereas human predicates are derivative or inferior instances. So, for example, knowledge when applied to God is perfect knowledge and constitutes the standard for human knowledge, which is less perfect than divine knowledge (*Wars* III.4107–15). The implications of this discussion will become apparent when we turn shortly to the predicate of divine omniscience.

Creation

The problem of creation is a good example of the attempted synthesis between philosophy and Jewish tenets (see Article 39, CREATION AND CONSERVATION). Working within a framework which upheld the infinity of time, Aristotle posited an eternal universe which had no temporal beginning. Jewish thinkers as far back as Philo had already grappled with reconciling this framework with the Biblical account of creation. Saadyah, for example, argued that both Platonic and Aristotelian theories of eternity and uncreatedness of the universe are incompatible with the Jewish view of creation *ex nihilo* (from nothing). After examining and rejecting the current philosophical views of creation, he stressed the philosophical significance of the Biblical viewpoint. Gersonides and Maimonides are equally committed to a cosmology in which the Deity willed the universe to exist. Unwilling to reject Aristotle's ontology of time altogether, both philosophers posit a resolution which can be construed as a version of eternal creation.

It is in the topic of creation that Maimonides' esotericism is most cogently revealed, warning as he does that the dangers of expounding upon creation are intimated in the Introduction, where he asserts that this topic must not be taught even to one individual. In *Guide* II.13 Maimonides summarizes what he considers to be the three standard views on creation as the Scriptural, Platonic, and Aristotelian views. The main elements of each theory, as depicted by Maimonides, can be summarized briefly as follows:

1   The Scriptural view: that the universe was brought into existence by God after "having been purely and absolutely non-existent;" through His will and His volition, God brought into "existence out of nothing all the beings as they are, time itself being one of the created things." (*Guide* II.13, p. 281)

2   The Platonic view: that inasmuch as even God cannot create matter and form out of absolute non-existence, there "exists a certain matter that is eternal as the deity is eternal . . . He is the cause of its existence . . . and that He creates in it whatever He wishes." (*Guide* II.13, p. 283)

3   The Aristotelian view: agrees with (2) in that matter cannot be created from absolute non-existence, but concludes that the heaven is not subject to generation/corruption; that "time and motion are perpetual and everlasting and not subject to generation and passing-away." (*Guide* II.13, p. 284)

Which of these three views is espoused by Maimonides himself? Ostensibly, at least, Maimonides supports (1). Having dismissed (2) as a weaker version of (3), he argues that (1) is no more flawed than is (3). Then, pointing to the possibility of (1), coupled with its Mosaic (and Abrahamic) sanction, Maimonides argues that the very plausibility of (1) suggests the non-necessity of (3). Why does Maimonides not accept (2)? The main reason, as he tells us, is that the Platonic view has not been demonstrated (*Guide* II.25, p. 329).

If we take Maimonides at his word, then, it is clear that (1), creation in time of the universe out of absolute non-existence, is his view. If, however, we are inclined to take seriously his original demarcation between an exoteric and esoteric reading of controversial issues, then it is tempting to dismiss his espousal of (1) as an exoteric position and to search for the underlying, or concealed, interpretation which is Maimonides' real view of creation. And as commentators working through the text have demonstrated, there is certainly ample evidence to support either (2) or (3) as his esoteric view. In fact, there is so much conflicting evidence, all of which can be supported with plausible argument, that recent scholars have suggested that ultimately Maimonides upheld a skeptical stance in light of the evidence and did not take to heart any of the three positions. Although such a skeptical view would not be quite as heretical as espousing either (2) or (3), it still constitutes a provisional rejection of (1), which is tantamount to a rejection of the Mosaic theory.

Gersonides' discussion of time and creation is contained primarily in *Milhamot* VI.1. Like Maimonides, he is concerned with whether time is finite or infinite, as well as with whether the creation of the world can be said to have occurred at an instant. In order to uphold the finitude of time, Gersonides refutes the Aristotelian arguments by attempting to demonstrate that time must have been generated. He will argue that just as quantity is finite, so too is time, since time is contained in the category of quantity (*Milhamot* VI.1.10, pp. 329ff).

Having posited that the world was created at an initial instant of time by a freely willing agent, Gersonides must decide whether the world was engendered out of absolute nothing or out of a pre-existent matter. Arguing that creation out of nothing is incompatible with the facts of physical reality, he adopts a Platonic model of matter drawn ultimately from the *Timaeus* (see Article 8, ANCIENT PHILOSOPH-ICAL THEOLOGY). The opening verses of Genesis 1 are used to distinguish two types of material reality: *geshem* and *homer rishon* (*Milhamot* VI.I, ch. 17, pp. 267–71). In *Milhamot* (V.2, ch. 2, pp. 193–4) Gersonides argues that this formless matter accounts for various astronomical phenomena. Totally devoid of form, *geshem* is the primordial matter out of which the universe was created. Since it is not informed, it is not capable of motion or rest; and since it is characterized by nega-tion, *geshem* is inert and chaotic (*Milhamot* VI.1, ch. 17, pp. 367–8; 374). This pri-mordial matter is identified with the "primeval waters" described in Genesis 1:2 (*tohu, tehom,* and *mayim*). However, Gersonides points out that *geshem* does not itself exemplify absolute non-being, but rather is an intermediary between being and non-being (*Milhamot* VI.1, ch. 18, p. 372).

In contrast to *geshem, homer rishon* is the second type of reality. It is understood in the Aristotelian sense as a substratum which is allied to form. *Homer rishon,* or matter, is inferior to form and hence cannot be known in itself. It contains within itself the potentiality to receive forms, yet has no actuality of its own (*Milhamot* VI.1, ch. 17, p. 367). Inasmuch as it does not contain its own actuality, *homer ris-hon* is not an ontologically independent entity. Rather, Gersonides is wont to refer to it as "the matter that does not keep its shape" (*Milhamot* V.2, ch. 1; VI.6, pt 2, ch. 4). In *Milhamot* (VI, pt 2, ch. 7), Gersonides compares this matter to darkness, for just as darkness is the absence of light, so too this matter represents the absence of form or shape. For Gersonides, therefore, creation means that the plu-rality of forms contained in God is released and imparted to the *prima materia,* the substratum of being. In this way he upholds creation in time, but sacrifices cre-ation *ex nihilo.*

Divine providence

We turn now to one of the most intractable problems in medieval Jewish thought, namely that of divine omniscience (see Article 29, OMNISCIENCE). Medieval philoso-phers, concerned with safeguarding the freedom of human action, worried whether God's foreknowledge of future contingent events entailed the necessary occurrence of these events (see Article 37, FOREKNOWLEDGE AND HUMAN FREEDOM). That the force of God's knowledge need not be causal was already claimed by Saadyah

Gaon. In answer to the apparent paradox that God's foreknowledge necessitates the objects of his knowledge, Saadyah's response is that "he who makes this assertion has no proof that the knowledge of the Creator concerning things is the cause of their existence" (*Book of Beliefs and Opinions*, p. 186). What concerned medieval philosophers in general, and Jewish philosophers in particular, was the fact that if God is infallible, then the objects of his knowledge *can not fail to be* what God already knows them to be. How to account for the ability of humans to contravene the prior infallible knowledge which God has of their actions became of paramount importance to Maimonides, Gersonides, and later Jewish philosophers.

Under what conditions does God know unactualized particulars? Maimonides emphasizes that the term knowledge is predicated equivocally of God and humans, maintaining that God is in no way affected by what He knows. God remains one even though His objects constitute a plurality, and He remains unchanged even though the objects of His knowledge are mutable (see Article 40, IMMUTABILITY AND IMPASSIBILITY). These points are reflected in two brief assertions: first, that God's knowledge does not contain plurality, and second, that God cannot acquire at a certain time knowledge He did not possess previously. Since the divine knowledge is a priori, it is not affected by the ontological status of objects which result from this knowledge. Hence Maimonides argues that since the objects of God's knowledge do not causally act upon His knowledge, His essence is unaffected by their multiplicity. The second claim, that God's knowledge is unaffected by any change in its objects, is supported in the context of a distinction between absolute and relative non-existence. Absolute non-existence is never an object of God's knowledge (*Guide* III.20, p. 480). Relative non-existents, or future contingents, are possible objects of God's knowledge. It is not impossible, Maimonides claims, that God's knowledge has as its object those "non-existent things about whose being brought into existence we knew beforehand" (*Guide* III.20, p. 481). Like Averroës, Maimonides asserts that God's knowledge of future possibles does not change their nature; neither is His nature altered by a change in the objects of His knowledge.

Gersonides is the only Jewish philosopher, with the exception of Ibn Daud, who presented a tentative indeterminist theory, to uphold a form of indeterminism as a solution to the paradox of divine omniscience. Although intimated in a number of texts, this position is developed most fully in treatise III of *Wars*, wherein he develops his main argument that an omniscient, immutable deity cannot know changing particulars. The underlying premise in this argument is that all future particular objects are in fact mutable: that is, they change from a state of non-existence to one of existence. Gersonides claims that an immutable deity cannot be omniscient, if omniscience entails knowing objects which undergo change. But does it follow from God's knowing a future contingent that it is necessary? In contradistinction to Maimonides, who claims that God's knowledge does not render the objects of his knowledge necessary, Gersonides will want to maintain that divine foreknowledge and contingency are incompatible.

Arguing that divine omniscience severely compromises the contingency of the objects of God's knowledge, Gersonides dismisses Maimonides' form of compatibilism. Having rejected Maimonides' attempts to harmonize foreknowledge and contingency, and having upheld the existence of contingency in the universe, Gersonides adopts the one option left to him, namely that God does not know future contingents. According to Gersonides, God knows that certain states of affairs may or may not be actualized. But in so far as they are contingent states, he does not know which of the two alternatives will in fact be actualized. For if God did know future contingents prior to their actualization, there could be no contingency in the world (*Wars* III.4, pp. 116ff). Echoing Ibn Daud, Gersonides claims that God's inability to foreknow future contingents is not a defect in his knowledge (*Wars* III.4, pp. 235–6).

In this fashion, Gersonides concludes, the problem of divine omniscience has been resolved in favor of indeterminism. With respect to future contingents, God knows their ordered nature or essence, and he knows that they are contingent, but he does not know which alternative will become actualized. But has Gersonides in fact solved the problem of divine omniscience? Despite his admonition to the contrary, I have argued in other works that ultimately Gersonides' theory of divine omniscience does not fully account for other theological concerns, for example prophecy (Rudavsky 1985).

Conclusion

We have seen that Jewish philosophy arises out of a clash of two worldviews: the tenets of Jewish faith and belief on the one hand, and the strictures of philosophy on the other. This clash permeated much of Jewish philosophical debate in the Middle Ages. With respect to method, we have seen that Maimonides adopts an esoteric method in order to safeguard the philosophically unsophisticated masses from the potentially threatening implications of philosophical truth; Gersonides, on the other hand, eschews esotericism in favor of leading the masses gradually toward a more sophisticated level of philosophical understanding. Both philosophers agree that philosophical truths can harm the untrained, traditionally-rooted reader, and both believe that reason and faith are mutually complementary. But Gersonides disagrees with Maimonides over the method to be employed, believing that the masses can ultimately be taught. Discussions pertaining to divine predication, creation, divine omniscience have reflected this tension as well. In short, both Maimonides and Gersonides reflect the medieval Jewish attempt to reconcile traditional Jewish beliefs with what they feel are the strongest points in Greek philosophy, be it Plato, Aristotle, or Neoplatonism; although a synthesis of these systems is their ultimate goal, the strictures of philosophy often win out at the expense of theology.

Bibliography

Eisen, R.: *Gersonides on Providence, Covenant and the Chosen People* (Albany: State University of New York Press, 1995).
Levi ben Gerson (Gersonides): *Sefer Milhamot Adonai* (Leipzig, 1866); tr. S. Feldman, *The*

Wars of the Lord, 2 vols. (3rd vol. forthcoming) (Philadelphia: Jewish Publication Society, 1984–7). [Reference to untranslated Hebrew text will be to *Milhamot*; reference to English translation will be to *Wars*.]

Moses ben Maimon (Maimonides): *Moreh ha-Nevukhim*, tr. into Hebrew by Samuel ibn Tibbon, standard ed.; tr. Shlomo Pines, *The Guide of the Perplexed* (Chicago: University of Chicago Press, 1963).

Rudavsky, T. M.: "Divine omniscience, contingency and prophecy in Gersonides." In *Divine Omniscience and Omnipotence in Medieval Philosophy*, ed. T. Rudavsky, pp. 161–81 (Dordrecht: Reidel, 1985).

Saadyah Gaon: *Al-Mukhtar fi'l Amanat wa-'l-I'taquadat* (Arabic text with Hebrew translation by Yosef Karih, Jerusalem, n.d.); tr. Samuel Rosenblatt, *The Book of Beliefs and Opinions* (New Haven: Yale University Press, 1948).

Sirat, C.: *A History of Jewish Philosophy in the Middle Ages* (Paris: Cambridge University Press, 1985).

Touati, C.: *La Pensée philosophique et théologique de Gersonide* (Paris: Editions de Minuit, 1973).

12

Early modern philosophical theology

DERK PEREBOOM

The legacy of seventeenth and eighteenth century philosophical theology is very substantial. René Descartes's contributions include a reconstruction of Anselm's ontological argument (see Article 41, ONTOLOGICAL ARGUMENTS), development of a theology in which radical conceptions of divine power and sovereignty play a central role (see Article 28, OMNIPOTENCE), and a reworking of Stoic and Augustinian themes in theodicy (see Article 50, THE PROBLEM OF EVIL). Descartes's ontological argument, first presented in the Fifth Meditation, aims to prove the existence of God from the idea of the divine essence alone (Descartes 1964–76 [1641], AT VII 63–71):

(1) When I have an idea of an object, whatever characteristics I clearly and distinctly understand the object of the idea to have, it really has. (*premise*)
(2) I have a clear and distinct idea of God, as the maximally perfect being. (*premise*)
(3) God has all perfections. (1, 2)
(4) Everlasting existence is a perfection. (*premise*)
(5) God has everlasting existence. (3, 4)
(6) Therefore God exists. (5)

Caterus objects that by similar reasoning one can prove the real existence of the object of my idea of the existent lion (AT VII 99). Gaunilo's reply to Anselm's version is similar: by analogous reasoning one can prove the existence of the maximally perfect island. A second objection, anticipated by Descartes in the Fifth Meditation, is that if we are speaking accurately, predicating a property of something without any conditions presumes that the thing exists. So if "Clinton is president of the USA" is true, it follows that Clinton exists. "Pegasus is a winged horse" is strictly speaking false, whereas "In the myth, Pegasus is a winged horse" is true. Premise 3 thus begs the question. Descartes can legitimately claim only something like "In the concept of God, God has all perfections" (or "If God exists, then God has all perfections"). But then all that follows is "In the concept of God, God has existence" (or "If God exists, then he exists"), which falls short of the conclusion Descartes desires. A third problem, raised in the Second Objections, is that the argument is sound only if a most perfect being is possible, or equivalently (on some views), if there is a divine essence (AT VII 127), and this has not been established.

Descartes's reply to the first two objections involves the notion of a true and immutable nature (TIN), a descendant of Plato's notion of a Form (AT VII 101ff).

Descartes maintains that TINs exist in some sense, although they need not be exemplified as really existent things. But the kind of existence TINs have is, on Descartes's view, sufficient to undermine the second objection above: one need not prefix anything like the phrase "in the concept of God" to premise (3) if God is a TIN. One challenge for Descartes is to show that God is a TIN but that the existent lion and the maximally perfect island are not. In the Fifth Meditation Descartes maintains that TINs are different from fictitious objects of ideas in that TINs are independent of the thought of their conceivers. For example, a triangle is a TIN because it has properties that I don't realize it has when I first form the idea of a triangle. God also has this feature – I don't grasp all of the properties of the maximally perfect being when I first form the idea. The most perfect island, however, is also a TIN by this criterion. Later Descartes (AT VII 83–4) characterizes a TIN as having a unity such that it cannot be split up by the intellect. He thinks that having this feature shows that it hasn't been put together by the intellect. Accordingly, an existent lion is not a TIN because I can conceive of a lion that doesn't exist. But I can also conceive of an omnipotent being lacking maximal benevolence, and so by this standard God would not be a TIN. To the third problem, concerning the possibility of God, Descartes replies that at least as far as our concepts are concerned, there is no contradiction in the nature of God, and that the denial that the nature of God is a possible one is on equal footing with the denial that the angles of a triangle are equal to two right angles (AT VII 150–1).

On the divine attributes, Descartes argues that God's perfection entails that for everything that happens or exists, God is the first and immutable cause of it. This in turn entails that everything that happens, even human decisions and actions, is entirely caused by God (Descartes 1964–76 [1645], AT IV 313–14). In particular, it is the infinitude of divine power that requires God to be the cause of everything. If, for example, human actions did not depend on God's will, his power would be finite (AT IV 332). For Descartes this conception of divine power also has the consequence that the eternal (necessary) truths are created by God.

Descartes's theodicy focuses on the problem of intellectual error. How can God be supremely perfect and yet create us with the capacity to make errors in judgment? In his Fourth Meditation reply, Descartes revives the Stoic theory of judgment, in which judgment is a two-stage process. In the first, an idea is presented to the mind, and in the second, the will is engaged, and it has the ability to affirm, deny, or suspend judgment with respect to the idea. If the idea is affirmed or denied, a judgment is formed. Error is threatened when an idea that is not clear and distinct is affirmed or denied. We can avoid error if we suspend judgment whenever an idea is not clear or distinct. God has given us the capacity to suspend judgment in such situations, and this is indeed what we should do. We err only because we fail to follow this recommendation. A problem arises for this strategy because, as we have seen, Descartes affirms that "the least thought cannot enter the mind of man if God had not wished and willed from all eternity that it enter therein." Perhaps this explains why Descartes asserts that he "cannot therefore deny that there may in some way be more perfection in the universe as a whole because some of its parts are in error, while others are immune, than there would be if all the parts were alike" (AT VII 63). Descartes advocates a version of the Stoic theodicy that apparent imperfections are required for the good of the whole, and that if one were to take a broader view, one would no longer see reason to believe that if God existed he would be morally imperfect. Gottfried Leibniz advocates a similar theodicy by claiming that considered as a whole, this is the best of all possible worlds, since it is the "simplest in its hypotheses and the richest in phenomena" (Leibniz 1969 [1686], p. 306).

In his *Ethics* Baruch Spinoza introduces a revolutionary conception of God, which is accompanied by a theodicy unavailable to adherents of a more traditional notion. According to Spinoza there is only one substance, and that is God, and there is nothing outside this substance. Accordingly, Spinoza believes that God does not transcend creation, but creation is part of God – a view which is at odds with traditional Judeo-Christian theology (see Article 39, CREATION AND CONSERVATION). Another radical view of Spinoza's is that God has no plans or purposes. This is so, first, for the reason that God's intellect does not precede his will, and therefore God does not think about what he does before he does it, and second, that if God were to act with an end in view, there would be something he lacks, which is not the case. Instead, everything that happens follows without design or purpose from the divine nature (see Article 43, TELEOLOGICAL AND DESIGN ARGUMENTS). Furthermore, from the divine perspective, there is nothing in the universe that is bad. We have the habit of calling things good or bad relative to our own needs and wants. But for Spinoza, the perfection of a thing is measured not by the needs and wants of some other being, but by its own nature. Spinoza's conception of God is a component of a neo-Stoic vision of the universe, according to which we can come to accept with equanimity anything that happens if we identify intellectually with the divine perspective. We will then understand and accept everything as following necessarily from the divine nature, and we will regard nothing as bad or evil.

Another innovative conception of God's relation to the universe is developed by George Berkeley. In his view, physical objects do not exist independently of minds, but consist solely of ideas. The source of these ideas is God, and God produces them in us in accord with lawlike regularities – the laws of nature. God's existence can be demonstrated from the involuntariness of the greater part of our ideas in conjunction with the harmony, regularity, and beauty they display (a teleological argument) (Berkeley 1982 [1710], §146). Since according to Berkeley our ordinary experience is a type of direct divine communication, our relationship with God is in this respect especially intimate. As Berkeley frequently remarks, quoting scripture, "in God we live and move and have our being" (Acts 17:28).

Among Leibniz's contributions to philosophical theology are his development of the ontological and cosmological arguments, and his introduction of a theistic argument from the existence of eternal truths (see Article 42, COSMOLOGICAL ARGUMENTS). He takes on several difficulties for Descartes's ontological argument: first, that the claim that the essence of a most perfect being includes its existence – that existence is a perfection – requires argument; second, that all this argument can demonstrate is the conditional "if God exists, then he exists," and third, that the possibility of a most perfect being needs substantiation (e.g. Leibniz 1969 [1676], pp. 167–8; [1677], pp. 177–80; [1684], pp. 292–3; [1692], p. 386; Adams 1994, pp. 135–56). In several places Leibniz addresses the first of these problems by arguing that by our conception of God we understand a necessary being, and from this it follows that the essence of God involves his existence (see Article 33, NECESSITY). In this way one can avoid altogether the premise that existence is a perfection. In some writings Leibniz bypasses the second of these problems by formulating the argument modally. In his view, a successful ontological argument must show that there is such a thing as the essence of God, and this is the same task as showing that God is a possible being. If it can be shown that God is a possible being, one can conclude that there is a divine essence, and because this divine essence involves necessary existence, it will follow that God exists. Such a modal argument might be formulated in this way:

(1)   If there is a divine essence, then the divine essence involves necessary existence.   (*premise*)
(2)   If God is a possible being, then there is a divine essence.   (*premise*)
(3)   If God is a possible being, then the divine essence involves necessary existence.   (1, 2)
(4)   If God is a possible being, then God necessarily exists.   (3)
(5)   Therefore, if God is a possible being, then God actually exists.   (4)

What has yet to be demonstrated, then, is that God is a possible being. Leibniz offers several types of argument for this premise. One sort relies on the cosmological argument, according to which only a necessary God could provide a satisfactory explanation for the existence of the aggregate of all the contingent beings. So on the assumption that these contingent beings possibly exist, it must be possible for a necessary God to exist. A second type of argument for God's possibility returns to the thesis that God is the most perfect being, and adds that perfections are positive and simple, unanalyzable qualities. In outline, Leibniz's reasoning has the following form. Consider any proposition of the form "A and B are incompatible," where A and B are any two perfections. Two properties are incompatible only if they are logically incompatible. Thus "A and B are incompatible" will be true only if one of these perfections turns out to be the negation of the other, as in *omniscient* and *non-omniscient*, or if their analyses reveal simpler properties one of which is a negation of another. But since all the perfections are positive and simple and thus unanalyzable, this cannot be the case. Consequently, "A and B are incompatible" will be false, "A and B are compatible" will be true, and a being with all perfections will be possible (Adams 1994, pp. 142–8).

Leibniz's argument from the eternal truths involves the premises that truths must be true in virtue of something distinct from them, and that certain propositions would be necessarily true even if there were no finite minds. It follows that these necessary truths could not be true in virtue of facts about human psychology alone. Against the Platonist conception, that these truths are true in virtue of Forms existing outside of any mind whatsoever, Leibniz argues that abstract entities are not the kinds of things that could have mind-independent existence. The contending view that remains is that these truths are true by virtue of the divine nature, in particular, by ideas in God's mind (Leibniz 1969 [1714], p. 647; Adams 1994, pp. 177ff).

Leibniz's cosmological argument aims to demonstrate the existence of God from the need to explain certain facts about the world. For Leibniz the world is the complete aggregate of actual *merely hypothetically necessary* beings, i.e. actual beings that are necessary consequent on the existence of some other being(s) (Leibniz 1969 [1697], pp. 486–91), or the complete aggregate of actual *contingent* beings (Leibniz 1969 [1714], p. 646). His cosmological argument overcomes an important objection to earlier versions, since Leibniz's does not assume that the world has a beginning in time. Suppose that in fact the world has no beginning in time, and that each being in the world has an explanation in some previously existing being(s). Then two demands for explanation yet arise: why is there a world at all rather than none? and: why does this world exist and not some other world? Neither explanation can be provided on the basis of entities within the world. Leibniz's conclusion is that there must be a being that is not merely hypothetically, but *absolutely* necessary, on the basis of which the requisite explanations can be provided, and whose own explanation is contained within itself. This being is God. (A similar argument is advanced around the same time by Samuel Clarke.)

David Hume's endowment to philosophical theology, contained mainly within his *Dialogues Concerning Natural Religion*, includes several powerful challenges to the cosmological and teleological arguments. Hume advances three objections to the type of cosmological argument advanced by Leibniz and Clarke (Hume 1980 [1779], Part IX). The first is that the notion of (absolutely) necessary existence is problematic. Suppose that if a being is necessary, its non-existence will be inconceivable. But for any being whose existence we can conceive, we can also conceive of its non-existence, and thus there couldn't be a necessary being. Hume anticipates the objection that if we genuinely understood the divine nature, we would be unable to conceive God's non-existence. He replies that an analogous point can be made about matter: perhaps, if we really understood the nature of matter, we would be unable to conceive its non-existence. And therefore the argument cannot establish that God is the necessary being.

Hume's second objection is that God cannot be the causal explanation for the existence of a series of contingent beings that has no temporal beginning, since the causal relation "implies a priority in time and a beginning of existence." One might reply, with Immanuel Kant, that we can in some sense conceive of a non-temporal causal relation, and that God, from outside of time, causes a series of contingent beings that has always existed. The third objection is that in a causal series of contingent beings without a temporal beginning, each being will have a causal explanation by virtue of its predecessors. Since there is no first being, there will be a causal explanation for every contingent being on the basis of previously existing contingent beings. But if each individual contingent being has a causal explanation, the entire series has an explanation. For wholes are nothing over and above their parts: "did I show you the particular causes of each individual in a collection of twenty particles of matter, I should think it very unreasonable should you afterwards ask me what was the cause of the whole twenty." Replies to this objection include the claim that even if one has explained in this way the existence of each individual in this contingent series, one still has not answered the questions: why is there a world at all rather than none? and: why does this world exist and not some other world?

Hume presents an especially elegant version of the teleological argument (Part II), which can be formulated as follows:

(1) Nature is a great machine, composed of lesser machines, all of which exhibit order (especially adaptation of means to ends).   (*premise*)
(2) Machines caused by human minds exhibit order (especially adaptation of means to ends).   (*premise*)
(3) Nature resembles machines caused by human minds.   (1, 2)
(4) If effects resemble each other, their causes do as well.   (*premise*)
(5) The cause of nature resembles human minds.   (3, 4)
(6) Greater effects demand greater causes (causes adequate to the effects).   (*premise*)
(7) Nature is much greater than machines caused by human minds.   (*premise*)
(8) The cause of nature resembles but is much greater than human minds.   (5, 6, 7)
(9) The cause of nature is God.   (8)
(10) Therefore, God exists.   (9)

Hume's objections to this argument include the claims that the analogies on which it is dependent are not strict, and that there are alternative explanations for order and apparent design in the universe. The contemporary reply to these objections is that the teleological argument should be conceived as an argument to the best explanation, on the model of most scientific arguments. For then the analogy need not be exact, and it will be useful if it helps show that the theistic explanation is indeed the best one. In addition, on this model one can allow alternative explanations, as long as the theistic one is best. Hume, or at least his character Philo, concedes "that the works of nature bear a great analogy to the productions of art is evident; and according to all the rules of good reasoning, we ought to infer, if we argue at all concerning them, that their causes have a proportional analogy" (Part XII). But Philo also affirms that we cannot infer any important similarities between humans and the author of nature beyond intelligence, and in particular we cannot infer some of the divine attributes that are most important for sustaining traditional theistic religion (Part V). Most significantly, given the evil that there is in the universe, we cannot conclude that its designer has the moral qualities traditional religion requires God to have (Part X).

One of Hume's most interesting objections to the teleological argument is that it generates an absurd infinite regress (Part IV). If order and apparent design in the material universe are explained by divine intelligence, a further demand for explanation is thereby generated. What explains the order and apparent design that give rise to intelligence in the divine mind? By reasoning of the sort employed in the teleological argument, it would have to be a super-divine intelligence. But what explains the order and apparent design that give rise to super-divine intelligence? An absurd infinite regress results, and to avoid it, one might simply suppose the material world to "contain the principle of order within itself." To this Hume has Cleanthes reply that "even in common life, if I assign a cause for any event, is it any objection that I cannot assign the cause of that cause, and answer every new question which may incessantly be started?" In scientific theorizing it is no decisive objection against an explanation that it contains entities that are themselves not adequately explained. Crucial to the value of scientific explanations is that they supply an explanatory advance, and we can reasonably believe that a theory does so without our having in hand adequate explanations for all of the entities it posits.

Among Kant's contributions to philosophical theology are his criticisms of the ontological argument and his introduction of a moral proof for belief in God (see Article 44, MORAL ARGUMENTS). Kant's first criticism of the ontological argument is encapsulated in his claim that existence is not a perfection, and indeed, not even a predicate (Kant 1929 [1781/1787], A592/B619ff). Difficult issues in philosophy of logic beset this objection. but it can be sidestepped by proposing that necessary existence is a perfection or by presenting a modal version of the argument. Perhaps Kant's more telling criticism is that given what we can know, we cannot determine whether God is a *really* possible being. He grants that the notion of a most perfect being may not involve a logical contradiction, but he argues that this is not enough to show that it is really possible (A602/B630). For example, we cannot know whether it is causally possible for certain of the perfections to be coexemplified, "for how can my reason presume to know how the highest realities operate, what effects would arise from them, and what sort of relation all these realities would have to each other?" (Kant 1978 [1830], p. 57).

Central to the theistic argument of Kant's critical period is the claim that belief that God exists is required for the moral life. In the *Critique of Practical Reason*, Kant argues that the *end* of the moral life is the highest good – that rational beings be virtuous and that they be happy in accord with their virtue (Kant 1993 [1788], Ak V, 106ff). Furthermore, rationality demands that we promote the highest good, and by the principle that *ought* implies *can*, it follows that it is possible for us to bring it about. But there is nothing in the world of experience that makes for a necessary connection between virtue and happiness. We must therefore assume the existence of a non-empirical being, God, who can bring this connection about. In his *Religion Within the Bounds of Reason Alone*, Kant no longer argues on the basis of the premise that we ought to promote the highest good (Kant 1960 [1793], pp. 3–7). Rather he claims that given how human beings are psychologically constituted, we must view our actions as aiming at an end, although this end need not function as a reason for action. So although for us moral action does not require an end as reason for action, we must have a conception of an end towards which our moral action is directed. This end is the highest good, and for the possibility of the realization of this end, "we must postulate a higher, moral, most holy, and omnipotent being. . . ." Kant also intimates that failure to believe that the highest good is an end that can be realized would constitute "a hindrance to moral decision." Perhaps he believes that if the virtuous lived miserable lives without any hope of happiness, and if they believed that their efforts could not help realize a moral universe, then a sense of sadness or frustration would undermine their moral motivation. Whether Kant holds that such an argument secures only the rationality of the belief that God exists or that it in addition undergirds a type of knowledge of the existence of God is a difficult matter for interpretation (Kant 1993 [1788], Ak V, 134–6).

Bibliography

Adams, R. M.: *Leibniz: Determinist, Theist, Idealist* (Oxford: Oxford University Press, 1994).

Berkeley, G.: *A Treatise Concerning the Principles of Human Knowledge* (Indianapolis: Hackett, 1982).

Descartes, R.: *Oeuvres de Descartes*, ed. Ch. Adam and P. Tannery (rev. edn, Paris: Vrin/CNRS, 1964–76).

Hume, D.: *Dialogues Concerning Natural Religion* (Indianapolis: Hackett, 1980).

Kant, I.: *Critique of Pure Reason*, tr. N. K. Smith (London: Macmillan, 1929).

——: *Religion within the Bounds of Reason Alone*, tr. T. M. Greene and H. H. Hudson (New York: Harper & Row, 1960).

——: *Lectures on Philosophical Theology*, tr. A. W. Wood and G. M. Clark (Ithaca: Cornell University Press, 1978).

——: *Critique of Practical Reason*, tr. L. W. Beck (New York: Macmillan, 1993).

Leibniz, G. W.: *Philosophical Papers and Letters*, tr. and ed. L. E. Loemker (Dordrecht: Reidel, 1969).

Spinoza, B.: *The Collected Works of Spinoza*, 2 vols., tr. and ed. E. M. Curley (Princeton: Princeton University Press, 1985).

13

The emergence of modern philosophy of religion

MEROLD WESTPHAL

There seems to be no clear and consistent distinction between philosophical theology and the philosophy of religion. Yet, on purely linguistic grounds one would seem to have God and the other religion as its primary subject matter. I think it is not an accident that the editors of this volume used the term "philosophical theology" in the titles of the preceding five articles, but switched to "philosophy of religion" for the present one. For during the time from David Hume and Immanuel Kant to Friedrich Nietzsche the focus shifted from philosophizing about God to philosophizing about religion.

Thus G. W. F. Hegel complains bitterly about the prevailing assumption that we do not know God, which, therefore, "permits us to speak merely of our relation to Him, to speak of religion and not of God Himself." The result is that "we at least hear much talk . . . about religion, and therefore all the less about God Himself" (1962 [1832], pp. 191–2).

The matter is not that simple, for talking about religion cannot so easily be separated from talking about God. Still, Hegel calls our attention to what amounts to a sea change in modern philosophy, the transition from philosophical theology to philosophy of religion in the narrower sense of philosophizing about religion. In light of his intended resistance to this feature of post-Kantian modernity, it is ironic that we owe to him more than to anyone else the notion that there is a subdivision of philosophy called the philosophy of *religion*, that he develops this in his *Lectures on the Philosophy of Religion*, and that the three parts of these lectures are "The Concept of *Religion*," "Determinate *Religion*," and "Consummate *Religion*." When philosophical theology will return in our own time, often as if nothing had happened in the meanwhile, it will call itself the philosophy of religion.

Pre-Kantian philosophical theology

Two species of philosophical theology form the background for the movement Hegel deplores. I shall call them, rather loosely, scholastic and deistic. Both are concerned to explore what can be established about the existence and nature of God by means of human reason unaided by revelation. But the scholastic versions of this enterprise share the Augustinian assumption that pure reason, on the one hand, and faith, revelation, and authority, on the other, are harmonious and should be seen as working together. The deistic versions by contrast, are concerned not merely to distinguish but also to separate the two. They wish to bring religion, in Kant's phrase, "within the limits of reason alone." To that end they seek to separate the rational kernel of religion from the irrational husk that exceeds those limits in the direction of faith, revelation, and authority. Typical examples of the kernel are God as creator and God as author and enforcer of the moral law, not only in this life but in the life to come. Typical examples of the husk are anything miraculous or supernatural and the tendency to give essential significance to anything historically particular such as the life and death of Jesus. These general strategies are worked out in a variety of ways in the English deism of Lord Herbert of Cherbury (1583–1648), John Toland (1670–1722), and Matthew Tindal (1657–1733); in the French deism of Voltaire (1694–1788) and Jean-Jacques Rousseau (1712–78); and in the German deism of Moses Mendelssohn (1729–86), Gotthold Lessing (1729–81), and Kant (1724–1804).

Deism rather than scholasticism is the immediate precursor and even the beginning of the emergence here to be narrated. It can be called the religion of the Enlightenment. The horror of religious warfare and persecution hung heavy over European history, and when Enlightenment thinkers did not espouse an entirely anti-religious materialism, they sought above all to define a religion that would foster moral unity rather than immoral hostility within and among human societies.

This political agenda had both epistemological and ecclesiastical ramifications. For it was believed that a non-violent religion could only rest on the universality of reason and not on the particularity of any special revelation; nor could it reside in any church or sect which claimed authority in matters of faith and practice on the basis of such a revelation. In this context, Enlightenment rationalism (or the autonomy of reason) does not signify a rejection of the empiricist appeal to experience in favor of a purely a priori mode of thought; it rather signifies an appeal made by rationalists and empiricists alike to limit religion to those grounds, whether a priori or experiential, which are available to all people, at all times, and in all places. The contrast is not between reason and experience but between reason and faith, in so far as the latter is tied to special revelation and a particular "church."

Thus the deist project is motivated by three powerful, interlocking Enlightenment motifs: an epistemic concern for the autonomy of a universal human reason, a political concern for religious tolerance, and an anti-clericalism designed to deny to the church both epistemic and political authority. This project clearly antedates the prevalence of the assumption, bemoaned by Hegel, that we do not know God and must therefore talk about religion. It is confident that, in one way or another, unaided human reason can know all we need to know about God. Still, in seeking to distinguish good religion (morally and politically speaking) from bad religion it begins the shift to philosophizing about religion. It is unembarrassed by talk about God, but it spends more of its energy talking about religion as a human, all too human social reality that is, for better and often for worse, a player on the stage we call history. The problem is less to prove God's existence than to make religion the ally rather than the enemy of morality.

Enter Hume and Kant. Their combined critique of the ontological, cosmological, and teleological proofs of the existence of God was a devastating blow to the many forms of both the scholastic and the deistic projects that built on the foundation of those proofs (see Article 41, ONTOLOGICAL ARGUMENTS; Article 42, COSMOLOGICAL ARGUMENTS; and Article 43, TELEOLOGICAL AND DESIGN ARGUMENTS). The widespread (if temporary) belief that Hume and especially Kant had said the last word on the subject is what Hegel referred to as the assumption that we cannot know God and must therefore only talk about religion. The pressing issue became: what can philosophy say about the religious dimension of human life now that the metaphysical proofs of God's existence have been taken away?

Enter Hume and Kant, again. It is not surprising that two thinkers who were as concerned as they were about the religious dimension of human life and who were as convinced as they were that the metaphysical foundations of scholastic and deistic philosophical theology had crumbled should point in new directions. But how different are those directions!

Post-Kantian reconstructions of the deist project

Kant is the deist who, having undermined the metaphysical foundations of many forms of deism, sought to provide the project with alternative foundations. Since this alternative comes in the *Critique of Practical Reason* (1788) and *Religion within the Limits of Reason Alone* (1793), which follow Kant's demolition of the theistic proofs in *Critique of Pure Reason* (1781; 2nd ed. 1787), we can speak of Kant as the first post-Kantian to try to rescue the deist project.

Kant's (re)formulation is distinctive in two ways. First, he claims that if there is no knowledge of God by means of pure (a priori) theoretical reason, we can have such knowledge by means of pure practical reason. Thus the *Critique of Practical Reason* develops moral arguments for God and immortality to take the place of the arguments discredited in the *Critique of Pure Reason*. Second, Kant's account of *Religion within the Limits of Reason Alone* begins with an account of radical evil in human nature that departs drastically from the more typically optimistic view whose fullest expression is to be found in Rousseau (see Article 68, SIN AND ORIGINAL SIN).

In the final three books of *Religion*, Kant gives a classical account of the kind of religion that could be acceptable in the Age of Reason. It is grounded in universal reason and in the service of universal morality. Kant is especially concerned to clarify the relation between religion and morality, and he does so in three basic principles. First, "morality does not need religion at all" – either in the discovery of what our duty is or in the motivation for doing it (1960 [1793], p. 3). Second, "morality leads inevitably to religion" (p. 7n.). This is a reminder of the moral arguments for God and immortality given in the *Critique of Practical Reason*. Finally, "religion is (subjectively regarded) the recognition of all duties as divine commands" (p. 142). As such it is an aid, useful if unnecessary, to the moral life.

But there can be "no special duties to God in a universal religion, for God can receive nothing from us" (p. 142n.). It follows that such "means of grace" as

113

prayer, church attendance, baptism, and communion are illusions that belong to "fetish-faith" if they are conceived as anything but means to the ends of moral living. A charitable interpretation would have Kant saying that there can be no love of God separate from the love of fellow humans, but the text seems to make the stronger claim that religion is exclusively concerned with our duty toward one another, that even God is nothing but a means toward human morality.

Kant continues his attempt to bring the Christian religion within the limits of reason alone by drawing corollaries concerning Christ and the church. The true church can only be the ethical commonwealth created on earth by the moral self-improvement of human persons. The "Augustinian" overtones of Kant's account of radical evil are here replaced by a fully "Pelagian" soteriology and ecclesiology. Christ, in turn, can be of significance only as an archetypal ideal of moral perfection. Any "Christology" within the limits of reason would be a construction of pure reason, independent of historical fact and historical knowledge. Here Lessing's principle (1957 [1777], pp. 51–6) that rational knowledge of God must depend on nothing historically contingent is employed, not to reject traditional Christian themes but to reinterpret (or, perhaps, "demythologize") them radically.

Unlike Kant, the Romantic Friedrich Schleiermacher and the anti-Romantic Hegel are not properly described as deists. But with Kant they are major figures in the post-Kantian effort to reformulate the deist project. Schleiermacher addresses an audience unsympathetic not only to the metaphysical quarrels of scholastic and deistic philosophical theologies, whose claims about providence and immortality he dismisses as "externals" (1958 [1799], p. 14), but also to the moral rigorism of a Kantian alternative. Both metaphysics and morality belong to the husk of religion; its kernel is to be found in feeling, in "the immediate consciousness of the universal existence of all finite things, in and through the Infinite, and of all temporal things in and through the Eternal" (p. 36).

Schleiermacher's explicit enthusiasm for Spinoza, whom he describes as "full of the Holy Spirit" (1958 [1799], p. 40), suggests a pantheistic move away from the deistic and theistic notions of God as a personal being distinct from the created world. Thus he writes: "The sum total of religion is to feel that, in its highest unity, all that moves us in feeling is one; to feel that aught single and particular is only possible by means of this unity; to feel, that is to say, that our being and living is a being and living in and through God. But it is not necessary that the Deity should be presented as also one distinct object." Such a representation would be "vain mythology" (p. 50).

Schleiermacher's "church" would be the communion of all who recognize the feeling or immediate contemplation of the unity of all in the Infinite and Eternal as the only true religion. But this does not mean the simple rejection of the churches committed to some specific system of metaphysical beliefs and moral or liturgical practices. Such a church is only "an association of persons who are but seeking religion . . . the counterpart of the true church" (p. 157). But "I would have you discover religion in the religions. Though they are always earthly and impure, the same form of heavenly beauty that I have tried to depict is to be sought in them" (p. 211).

This advice is possible because Schleiermacher believes that the universal ker-nel must clothe itself in particular ideas and practices. The immediacy of religious feeling needs to be mediated in some concrete form, however contingent. The important thing is to remember that such ideas and practices are neither neces-sary nor sufficient for true piety. With reference to any particular beliefs and prac-tices, their absence is no barrier to true religion, while their presence is no guarantee of it.

Hegel is too much the speculative thinker to be satisfied with either Kant's reduction of religion to morality or Schleiermacher's reduction to feeling. Religion must be the knowledge of God, and while Hegel finds Kant's theology unconvinc-ing, he finds Schleiermacher's, to which he is more sympathetic, simply confused. He rejects all Romantic claims to immediacy on the grounds that they are either empty of all conceptual content whatever and thus compatible with every absurd belief and every immoral practice, or they have a content that needs to be articu-lated and defended. The appeal to immediacy is merely dogmatism in disguise. Schleiermacher is just kidding himself when he thinks his own talk about the Infinite and Eternal is not already a conceptual mediation that requires analysis and argument as much as more traditional talk about Trinity, Incarnation, Atonement, and so forth.

Hegel thus assigns to himself the twin tasks of defending metaphysical theoriz-ing in the aftermath of Kant and of developing a religiously significant meta-physics. He undertakes these tasks primarily in his *Phenomenology of Spirit* (1807), his *Science of Logic* (1812–16), and his *Encyclopedia of the Philosophical Sciences* (1817, 1827, and 1830). His central thesis is that the content of religion and philosophy are the same but that they differ in form, with only philosophy having the conceptual form adequate to true knowledge. The religious form is too tightly tied to sensory images and historical narratives. Even the scholastic and deistic philosophical theologies, whose speculative instinct is to move beyond popular forms of religious representation, fail to free themselves sufficiently, for the con-cepts they employ are only suitable for a finite subject matter and not adequate to the Infinite and Eternal. Only a thoroughgoing reinterpretation of the philosophi-cal concepts of Idea and Spirit can (1) justify philosophical speculation itself, and (2) provide us with concepts suitable for doing philosophical theology.

Hegelian idealism is a philosophy of the Idea much closer to Aristotle and Plotinus than to George Berkeley and Kant. But it is perhaps best understood as a form of Spinozism. It is unlike that of Lessing (whose sympathy for Spinoza distin-guishes him from typical deists) in that it becomes the basis for the radical reinter-pretation (demythologizing) rather than the rejection of traditional theistic and Christian themes; and it is unlike the Spinozism of Schleiermacher in that it will not hide in claims to immediate feeling but will seek to articulate and defend itself in philosophical argument.

Finally, it is unlike Spinoza himself, but not because Hegel takes God to be a per-sonal being distinct from the created world. Only the understanding, which Kant rightly found incapable of knowing God, takes God and the world, or finite spirit and infinite spirit to be distinct beings; reason understands that they "are no

115

longer two" (1984–7 [the 1827 lectures], I, 425). Hegel's only defense against the charge that this is pantheism is that, unlike Spinoza, his highest category is spirit rather than nature or substance. When Spinoza says *Deus sive Natura* (God or Nature), Hegel replies *Gott oder Geist* (God or Spirit).

Religion is the elevation of finite spirit to absolute or infinite spirit. In its religious form, this is (mis)understood as encounter with Someone Other. In its philosophical form it is the discovery that the highest form of human self-awareness is the sole locus in which the infinite totality, which is the only reality, comes to self-knowledge and is spirit rather than just nature, subject rather than merely substance.

Religion as this elevation of the human spirit occurs in all the religions, but most fully and adequately in Christianity as the consummate religion. However, Christianity can play this role only when it takes on philosophical form and systematically reinterprets its basic themes. For example, it is the revealed religion, not because in Jesus and the prophets, the Bible, and the church God has come to the aid of a human reason limited by finitude and wounded by sin, but because in its philosophical form human reason makes the true nature of God fully manifest. Or again, Incarnation is the central Christian truth. Jesus is not, however, to be seen as the unique locus of the identity of the human and divine; rather, he is the embodiment of the universal truth that the human as such is divine.

Hume and the hermeneutics of suspicion

Modern philosophy of religion grew out of a deep dissatisfaction with historic Christianity. But the response of Hume and his followers was very different from that of Kant and his followers. Instead of seeking an alternative religion, inoffensive to modernity, they looked to see whether the problem might not lie at the very heart of religion and not in the disposable husks.

Suspicion, rather than skepticism, arises when instead of asking about the evidence for or against religious beliefs one asks what motives underlie religious beliefs and practices, and what functions they play in the lives of believers. In *The Natural History of Religion* Hume develops a notion of instrumental religion according to which piety is primarily a flattering of the gods grounded in selfish hopes and fears. The piety of self-interest immediately gives rise to self-deception, since the pious soul cannot acknowledge that it has reduced the sacred to nothing but a means to its own ends.

Self-interest and self-deception are basic themes in the hermeneutics of suspicion in Karl Marx and Nietzsche. With Marx the question shifts from motive to function, and thus from psychology to sociology. He asks what function religion plays in society and answers that it serves to legitimize structures of social domination. His theory of religion thus belongs to his theory of ideology. Every historical society involves economic and political exploitation, whether the victims are slaves, serfs, or wage laborers. Ideas that represent such an order as natural or rational are needed both to salve the consciences of the beneficiaries and to encourage cooperation by the victims, since violent repression by itself is never sufficient. Nothing does the job quite as well as religious ideas, for what higher justification could a social order receive than to be divinely ordained. For Marx, then, religion is primarily a matter of social privilege seeking legitimation and of the oppressed seeking consolation.

For Nietzsche religion is rooted in the slave revolt in morals, but given his postulation of the will to power as universal, his slaves are less concerned with consolation than with revenge. Unable to give vent to their resentment physically, they join forces with the priests who help them to designate their dominators as evil. This gives them the satisfaction of moral superiority and, to the degree that it permeates the social order, it makes the strong feel guilty. Divine perfection is defined as the one who will punish our enemies.

This kind of suspicion is not the monopoly of secular thought. It is the key to the attack on Christendom that is the heart of Søren Kierkegaard's writings. Their critique of bourgeois Christianity is not directed toward its theology, which Kierkegaard largely shares, but toward its double ideological function. By equating the present social order with the kingdom of God it not only confuses something finite and unfinished with something absolute and ultimate; it also tells the individual that God asks nothing more than that I be a respectable member of this society. The biblical tension between Jesus and every established order is lost.

Bibliography

Collins, J.: *The Emergence of Philosophy of Religion* (New Haven: Yale University Press, 1967). [On Hume, Kant, and Hegel.]

Hegel, G. W. F.: *Lectures on the Philosophy of Religion* (1832) tr. P. C. Hodgson et al., 3 vols (Berkeley: University of California Press, 1984–7).

——: *Lectures on the Proofs of the Existence of God*, tr. E. B. Speirs and J. B. Sanderson, in vol. 3 of *Lectures on the Philosophy of Religion* (New York: Humanities Press, 1962).

Hume, D.: *The Natural History of Religion* (1757) (Stanford, CA: Stanford University Press, 1957).

——: *Dialogues Concerning Natural Religion* (1779) (Indianapolis: Hackett, 1980).

Kant, I.: *Critique of Practical Reason* (1788), tr. L. W. Beck (New York: Macmillan, 1956).

——: *Religion within the Limits of Reason Alone* (1793), tr. T. M. Greene and H. H. Hudson (New York: Harper & Brothers, 1960).

Kierkegaard, S.: *Practice in Christianity* (1850), tr. H. V. and E. H. Hong (Princeton: Princeton University Press, 1991).

Lessing, G.: *Nathan the Wise* (1779), tr. B. Q. Morgan (New York: Ungar, 1955).

——: *Lessing's Theological Writings* (1777) tr. H. Chadwick (Stanford: Stanford University Press, 1957).

Schleiermacher, F.: *On Religion: Speeches to its Cultured Despisers* (1799) tr. J. Oman (New York: Harper & Brothers, 1958).

Westphal, M.: *Suspicion and Faith: The Religious Uses of Modern Atheism* (Grand Rapids: Eerdmans, 1993). [On Feuerbach, Marx, Nietzsche, and Freud.]

PART III

SOME CURRENTS IN TWENTIETH CENTURY PHILOSOPHY OF RELIGION

14

American pragmatism

NANCY FRANKENBERRY

The most important intellectual movement produced in the United States, pragmatism embraces the writings of Charles Sanders Peirce, Josiah Royce, William James, George Santayana, John Dewey, and George Herbert Mead in the first half of the twentieth century, and of Wilfrid Sellars, W. V. O. Quine, Hilary Putnam, Nelson Goodman, and Richard Rorty in the second half. The various forms of pragmatism are distinguishable one from the other mainly in terms of the degree of dependence on the primacy either of experience or of language, and the degree of paradigmatic status accorded to natural science.

The American philosophers who dealt with religion in the period from the 1870s to the 1930s brought both naturalism and pragmatism to bear on such topics as religious experience, the meaning and reference of "God," the nature of religious truth, and the community of interpreters (see Article 24, RELIGIOUS LANGUAGE; and Article 47, RELIGIOUS EXPERIENCE). Beginning with Charles Sanders Peirce's claim that any difference in meaning, however fine, must make some sensible difference in the course of experience, pragmatism wielded a two-edged sword in relation to religious beliefs. Peirce and James thought the religious hypothesis (variously defined) could make an enormous positive difference in experience, but later pragmatists, cutting in the opposite direction, viewed religion as making a difference for the worse and as destined to be superseded.

Charles Sanders Peirce

Considered the founder of pragmatism, Peirce (1839–1914) worked as a logician, an experimental scientist, and a mathematician. His pragmatism, theory of signs, phenomenology, and theory of continuity were governed by a conception of evolutionary change according to which the universe manifested a developmental teleology. From 1880 on, Peirce was committed to the view of nature as pervaded by chance or spontaneity, creatures as partially free, and the future as partly indeterminate. Beliefs were treated as habits of action and truth defined as inquiry.

Two seminal essays, "The fixation of belief" (1877) and "How to make our ideas clear" (1878), suggested important new ways of treating truth and meaning, respectively. The pragmatic maxim of meaning was "to consider what effects, that might conceivably have practical bearings, we conceive the object of our conception to have. Then, our conception of the effects is the whole of our conception of the object" (*Collected Papers* 5.402). The proper method to fix beliefs relied on a process of inquiry in which a community of investigators would eventually converge on truth, in the infinite long run. In the meantime, all beliefs, whether scientific or religious, were fallible and criticizable. The superiority of science over other methods was due to its corrigibility.

In his metaphysical investigations Peirce was an early antifoundationalist, abandoning the Cartesian quest for incorrigible grounds for knowledge claims. The process metaphysics he developed defended the threefold claim that there is a connectedness or continuity between and among elements in the world (synechism); the role of chance in the universe is real and ineradicable (tychism); and a principle of cosmic convergence and love is fundamental to the continuous cosmos (agapeism). Out of three simple categories of possibility ("firstness"), actuality ("secondness"), and necessity or law ("thirdness"), Peirce developed a complex and intricate system. All sign-functioning was also understood in terms of a triadic relation of sign, object, and interpretant.

For philosophy of religion, Peirce's most intriguing contribution concerns the Humble Argument found in his 1908 essay "A neglected argument for the reality of God." The Humble Argument concluded that God (signifying *ens necessarium*) is real (see Article 33, NECESSITY). The neglected defense of that argument showed that this conclusion is instinctive; rational belief in God was universally accessible. More notable for making explicit the stages Peirce considered common to any scientific or religious inquiry, than for its conclusion, the argument highlighted musement and abduction. As an "argument," it was a process of thought reasonably tending to produce a definite belief, rather than an "argumentation" proceeding upon definitely formulated premises. It was rooted in musement, or pure play and free flow of ideas, intimations, apprehensions, or speculations. Musement moved from vague apprehension through imagination toward hypothesis, that is, to a belief that could be made the subject of inquiry. The vague sense of a whole within which all things relate is one example and the idea of God is another. Although not knowledge, musement could yield a possible subject matter for inquiry.

The vague hypothesis of God was an "abduction," a generative process neither deduced from evidential premises nor inductively generalized from them. Now known as "inference to the best explanation," abduction was an important branch of logic for Peirce, along with deduction and induction which comprised the next two steps in the neglected argument. Deduction or explication of the God-hypothesis was to proceed in two stages of inquiry, according to analogies and further guesses, as well as logical deductions or predictions from the hypothesis that would make a pragmatic difference in experience. Finally, the inductive step would test the validity of the hypothesis. To render the vagueness of the God-hypothesis more precise, however, was to make it vulnerable to falsification.

Religion as much as science was in principle oriented to objective truth and must, like science, subject its doctrines to the test of experience. Peirce thought religion was a universal sentiment, more a way of living than a way of believing. Critical of the unqualified description of God as eternal or immutable (see Article 32, ETERNITY; and Article 40, IMMUTABILITY AND IMPASSIBILITY), his theism was left somewhat vague, functioning as a kind of regulative hope of the possibility of inquiry. Commentators are divided on whether Peirce's theism should be interpreted according to process philosophy in a panentheistic way (Donna Orange) or in a more traditional Thomistic direction (Michael Raposa) (see Article 16, PROCESS THEOLOGY; and Article 19, THOMISM). Peirce's injunction, "do not block the way of inquiry," and his vision of an endlessly self-correcting community of inquiry was to form a basis for Royce's recommendation that the Christian church model itself on the scientific community.

William James

William James's (1842–1910) chief contributions to philosophy of religion are often mistakenly associated only with his arguments in *The Will to Believe* (1897) and his conclusions in *The Varieties of Religious Experience* (1902). In the first, he argued that in the presence of "genuine" options that are "momentous, forced, and lively," an individual has a right to believe a hypothesis that cannot be proved by direct evidence (see Article 45, PRAGMATIC ARGUMENTS). But here he overinflated the distinction between intellectual and passional interests, and problematically defined the religious hypothesis to mean "perfection is eternal." In the second, he argued that indirect verification of the religious hypothesis could be conducted by careful psychological studies, which showed that the conscious mind was "continuous with a wider self through which saving experiences come," and that powers were at work in the world that might help to save people from various forms of shipwreck when they could not save themselves.

But too much has been made of James's assertion of "piecemeal supernaturalism" in *The Varieties* and not enough attention devoted to the "pluralistic pantheism" he espoused in his last published lectures on *A Pluralistic Universe* (1910). James became too good a historicist over the course of his career to remain content with stale dualisms between nature and supernature, the temporal and the eternal, the physical and the mental. The overbeliefs he expressed tended to defend a species of justified hope more than to warrant propositional belief. The radical empiricism which complemented his pragmatism provided a notion of "experience" that could bear the weight of a naturalized theory of religious experience while avoiding the charge of subjectivism invited by *The Varieties*. "Pure experience" and "reality" came to the same thing for James, but radical empiricism described the reality of experience as relational, as broader than sensation, and as giving rise to artificially carved-out distinctions, such as that between subject and object, or mind and matter, that are purely functional and contextual, rather than ontological. Radical empiricism was distinguished from other, disjunctive empiricisms by virtue of its insistence that conjunctive relations were a vital feature of experience, and were felt as directly given in experience. On this basis, the "More" that James associated with religious experience in *The Varieties* can be understood as referring not to *another* world but to a *wider* world.

Impressed by the facts of struggle and pluralism, James formulated his pluralistic pantheism to allow for the likelihood that "the absolute sum-total of things

123

may never be actually experienced or realized in that shape at all, and that a dis-seminated, distributed, or incompletely unified appearance is the only form that reality may yet have achieved" (*A Pluralistic Universe*, p. 25). This was a rejection of the monistic view which held that the divine exists authentically only when the world is experienced all at once in its absolute totality. Rejecting both extreme monism as well as extreme pluralism, James's final vision was of a single universe of nature in which "the whole" is neither absolutely one, nor absolutely many, and both human and non-human powers cooperate together. The whole exhibits "concatenated unity" or a multiplicity of irreducibly particular events in the midst of intricate patterns of relatedness. Unlike Royce and F. H. Bradley, James found himself "willing to believe that there may ultimately never be all-form at all, that the substance of reality may never get totally collected, that some of it may remain outside of the largest combination of it ever made." Like recent postmodernists who resist totalizing intellectual gestures, James was clear that "ever not quite has to be said of the best attempts anywhere in the universe at attaining all-inclusive-ness. The pluralistic world is thus more like a federal republic than like an empire or a kingdom" (*A Pluralistic Universe*, p. 145). While conceding that monism, like pluralism, could also stimulate strenuous moods, James noted that "[P]luralism actually demands them, since it makes the world's salvation depend upon the energizing of its several parts, among which we are." To the end, James himself was haunted by the possibility that "[T]he world *may* be saved, *on condition that its parts shall do their best*. But shipwreck in detail, or even on the whole, is among the open possibilities" (*Some Problems in Philosophy*, p. 73). As a lifelong sick-souled type, he complicated the healthy-mindedness of his pragmatism with the sense that humans are not finally captains of their ships, masters of their fate, or con-trollers of their ultimate destiny, that voluntarism could sometimes lead to virtue, but that willpower would only go so far in the face of evil, suffering, failure, and the inevitability of death.

John Dewey

In *A Common Faith* (1934) Dewey (1859–1952) aimed to divorce the meaning of the adjective "religious" from the traditional sense of the noun "religion." He could then define the religious as "any activity pursued in behalf of an ideal end against obstacles and in spite of threats of personal loss because of conviction of its general and enduring value." Life was lived with a religious quality whenever and wherever anyone experienced "a sense of human nature as a cooperating part of a larger whole." This pragmatist spirituality could be achieved in a variety of ways, "sometimes brought about by devotion to a cause; sometimes by a passage of poetry that opens a new perspective; sometimes as was the case with Spinoza . . . through philosophical reflection." In all cases, the religious dimension or function was felt as having the force of bringing about a better, deeper, and enduring adjustment to life. The adjustment or harmony of self with environment was attended by a calm resulting less from particular causes than from life changes that "pertain to our being in its entirety."

124

On the problem of how the self is integrated as a whole, Dewey made three proposals. First, the religious aspect of experience pointed to some complex of conditions that operated to effect a significant adjustment in life, a reorientation that was transformative and integrative in effect. Second, imagination played a key role in the unification of the self in harmony with its surroundings. Both the ideal of the whole self and of the totality of the world were held as imaginative projections, although the work of self-integration, far from being a matter of willpower simply projected by the self, was itself dependent upon "an influx from sources beyond conscious deliberation and purpose." Third, insisting that "we are in the presence neither of ideals completely embodied in existence nor yet of ideals that are mere rootless ideals, fantasies, utopias," Dewey proposed that the real object of faith and source of spiritual regeneration was nothing supernatural but rather "the unity of all ideal ends arousing us to desire and action," or, alternatively, "the active relation between the ideal and the actual." The distinctive values that Dewey himself wanted to uphold against what Walter Lippman would call "the acids of modernity" were identical with the democratic life of inclusiveness, openness, and growth.

This was the naturalistic meaning of God consistent with a common faith. As such, the divine was rooted in the natural conditions of history and the material world while transcending any single time and place. Unlike the Hegelian idea of God as the unity of the ideal and the real, Dewey's pragmatic naturalism captured the evolutionary, processive-relational sense of "uniting" as an ongoing activity. Impressed early in his career with the neo-Hegelian notion of a cosmic organic unity in which the ideal and the real are one, Dewey's struggle to slough off the vestiges of idealism was solved by affirming the "continuity" of the many with each other as many, but not their literal oneness.

Criticized for offering only a form of secular humanism, excessive optimism, and little sense of sin or tragedy, Dewey's philosophy of religion had considerably more resonance and breadth than *A Common Faith* alone reveals. In addition, readers should consult two other sources: *Art as Experience* (1934), which Dewey worked on at the same time as *A Common Faith* and in which the aesthetic character of his thought is more apparent; and *Experience and Nature* (1925), in which the attitude of natural piety is evident. (These richer aspects of Dewey's philosophy of religion are brought out well in Steven Rockefeller's 1991 study.) In brief, consummatory experiences of quality or value were for Dewey the very aim of human praxis. In aesthetic experience the continuities of form and matter appeared directly and with consummatory power that was a good in itself. Works of art created a sense of communion which could in turn generate or shade off into religious quality. The sense of belonging to a whole which accompanied intense aesthetic perception also explained the religious feeling. "We are, as it were, introduced into a world beyond this world which is nevertheless the deeper reality of the world in which we live in ordinary experience. We are carried beyond ourselves to find ourselves."

Nature in turn was understood as both thwarting and supporting human efforts. Humankind was continuous with and dependent upon an environing world which, however imperfect or riddled with ambiguity, should evoke "heart-felt piety as the source of ideals, of possibilities, of aspirations" (*The Quest for Certainty*, p. 244). This made natural piety a genuine and valuable part of human life in the world, needing more careful cultivation and expression in order to play a positive role in the development of society and culture. Although no antecedent being could be presumed in whom an integration or unification of all ideal ends was already accomplished, Dewey repeatedly appealed to "a sense of the whole," "the sense of an enveloping whole," "the sense of this effortless and unfathomable whole" that is experienced as a natural response of the human organism to its environment. In *Reconstruction in Philosophy* (1920) he described "the miracle of shared life and shared experience" as bound up with a vital feeling of unity with the universe. In *Human Nature and Conduct* (1922) the enveloping world of nature was identified as "the totality of natural events" and described as vague, unde-fined, and undiscriminated, hardly capable of objective presentation. Present emo-tionally in "appreciations and intimations" that yield feelings of freedom and peace, the sense of an enveloping whole could sustain and expand selves in feeble-ness and failure.

Amplifying the status of "wholes" and the close relation between the aesthetic and the religious in Dewey's thought, we might say that "the religious," recon-structed naturalistically, represented an intensification and broadening of the aes-thetic quality of experience, having to do with what Dewey called "consummatory moments," involving "fulfillments" and "immediately enjoyed meanings." Wholeness was the quality that linked aesthetic experiences, ordinary secular experiences, and religious ones. Every experience, according to Dewey, possessed a peculiar "dim and vague" quality, of "margins" or "bounding horizon." It was a sense of an "enveloping undefined whole." Any work of art could be described as a whole which elicited and accentuated a sense of "belonging to the larger, all-inclusive whole which is the universe in which we live." The difference between aesthetic and religious experiences was one of degree, not of kind. Natural piety, in contrast to aesthetic experience, sought an unrestricted field of value whose har-mony involved an ever-enlarging synthesis of the widest range and deepest con-trasts of relational data.

However, the all-inclusive whole of nature was not a unitary subject or a single, complex, organic individual. Dewey's final verdict was that the conditions and forces in nature and culture that promote human well-being were plural. In contrast to H. N. Wieman's thesis, he found no inherent unity to the forces and factors which made for good. The organizing and integrating of these forces or factors was the work of human imagination and human action.

Contemporary directions

Currently, pragmatism's agenda is being set by a variety of American philosophers of religion who elaborate a conceptual basis for antifoundationalism without sheer fideism, for pluralism without radical relativism, and for secular forms of "transcendence" without otherworldliness. These include: Jeffrey Stout's "modest pragmatism," influenced by Richard Rorty's neopragmatism; H. S. Levinson's "festive Jewish American" pragmatic naturalism, which draws inspiration from George Santayana; Cornel West's "prophetic pragmatism," which harks back to the Jewish and Christian tradition of prophets; and William Dean's "naturalistic historicism," derived from the Chicago school of religious empiricism. These authors typically emphasize that beliefs are tools for dealing with reality, not representations, and they attend to historically contingent forms of consensus, not correspondence to the intrinsic nature of things. Following out the Peircean line of pragmatism's development, Robert Neville's speculative philosophy and Robert Corrington's "ecstatic naturalism" build upon the metaphysical insights of the classical tradition.

At least two characteristic features of pragmatism have yet to be fully exploited in philosophy of religion. First, pragmatism entails a rigorous challenge to the use of such distinctions as cognitive–noncognitive, scheme–content, object–subject, intellectual–emotive. To the extent that debates in philosophy of religion are still riddled with these invidious contrasts, pragmatism stands for purging them on the grounds that the same events are needlessly hypostatized into two descriptions, one propositional and one not. Second, pragmatist philosophy of religion has yet to pursue the implications of what James meant when, following Peirce's plea, he called for "the reinstatement of the vague to its proper place in our mental life." To take pragmatism as a method of inquiry into that which is *vague* in human understanding, located on the fringes, not at the focal region of awareness, requires exploration of the transitions, felt qualities, and indeterminacies of experience – the very data that figure in a pragmatist account of the causes, consequences, and reference range of religious phenomena.

Bibliography

Collected Papers of Charles S. Peirce, vols. 1–6 ed. C. Hartshorne and P. Weiss; vols. 7–8 ed. A. W. Burks (Cambridge: Harvard University Press, 1931–58).

Corrington, R.: *Ecstatic Naturalism: Signs of the World* (Bloomington: Indiana University Press, 1994).

Dewey, J.: *A Common Faith* (New Haven: Yale University Press, 1934).

——: *Art as Experience* (New York: G. P. Putnam's Sons, 1934).

——: *Experience and Nature* (Chicago: Open Court, 1925).

——: *Human Nature and Conduct* (New York: Henry Holt, 1922).

Frankenberry, N.: *Religion and Radical Empiricism* (Albany: State University of New York Press, 1987).

James, W.: *Pragmatism* (1907) (Cambridge: Harvard University Press, 1975).

——: *The Varieties of Religious Experience* (1902) (Cambridge: Harvard University Press, 1985).

——: *Essays in Radical Empiricism* (1912) (Cambridge: Harvard University Press, 1976).

——: *A Pluralistic Universe* (1910) (Cambridge: Harvard University Press, 1977).

Levinson, H. S.: *Santayana, Pragmatism, and the Spiritual Life* (Chapel Hill: University of North Carolina Press, 1992).

Neville, R. C.: *The Highroad Around Modernism* (Albany: State University of New York Press, 1992).

Rockefeller, S. C.: *John Dewey: Religious Faith and Democratic Humanism* (New York: Columbia University Press, 1991).

Stout, J.: *Ethics after Babel: The Languages of Morals and Their Discontents* (Boston: Beacon Press, 1989).

West, C.: *The American Evasion of Philosophy: A Genealogy of Pragmatism* (Madison: University of Wisconsin Press, 1989).

15

Personalism

PATRICIA A. SAYRE

Introduction

Personalism, in its broadest sense, is a philosophical stance that takes the concept of personhood to be indispensable and central to a proper understanding of reality. As a self-conscious movement, or more accurately, family of movements, personalism flourished in the first half of the twentieth century with distinct but related branches in Europe and the United States. Both branches of personalism share a commitment to Christian theism and are motivated by practical as well as philosophical concerns.

European personalism

In the period between the two world wars, European thought was characterized by a number of movements responsive in one way or another to a growing sense of crisis in human affairs. Among these movements were an array of philosophies sometimes described as personalisms, but more commonly known by other names. These included the theistic existentialism of Karl Jaspers, Gabriel Marcel, Martin Buber, and Nikolai Berdyaev, and the neo-Thomism of Jacques Maritain and Étienne Gilson (see Article 17, PHENOMENOLOGY AND EXISTENTIALISM, and Article 19, THOMISM). European personalism as a movement in its own right centered around the work of the French philosopher Emmanuel Mounier. Mounier was founder and guiding spirit of *Esprit*, a journal committed to promoting dialogue between representatives of divergent points of view, but especially to encouraging exchange between Marxists and Christians. The Christian community, Mounier believed, needed to pay more attention to the social and economic conditions in which human life is embedded, while the Marxists needed to realize that these conditions do not constitute the whole human story.

Personalism on Mounier's reading is not, however, a political program. And, in so far as the central affirmation of personalism is the existence of free and creative persons, it is less a philosophical system than a method for drawing us into the thick of things by alerting us to the conflicting processes of personalization and depersonalization at play in human history. To be a person is to be in the process of becoming a person and hence to be contributing to the process of personalization. We become persons through the activity of choosing, and with each choice we make we transcend and hence must sacrifice our former selves. This transcendence, Mounier is quick to add, is not in the direction of detachment from the material conditions of human life. Mounier wants to avoid not only mind–body dualisms but all dualisms of the material and the spiritual order. To be a person is to live an embodied existence, and, precisely because we are embodied, we are situated from the start in a world that extends beyond our own immediate selves. Mounier's transcendence is thus an inherently generous "overflow of personal being" that moves us in the direction of ever deeper communion with others. This communion respects the integrity of the other while at the same time recognizing the mutuality of endeavor required if the process of personalization is to continue. Fear, egotism, and a distaste for sacrifice can keep us from realizing ourselves as persons, but so too can social and political structures that impose repetition and sameness on human life. Hence, while personalism is not in itself a political platform, personalist convictions are bound to have political implications. For Mounier they implied a pacifist socialism that he hoped would gradually transform capitalist technology into an ally rather than an enemy of human creativity. In other historical circumstances, personalist convictions might point in quite different political directions.

At the same time that it leads to a proliferation of forms of human life, Mounier claims, the process of personalization brings us ever closer to an ultimate unity of humankind that recognizes each person as significant and irreplaceable in the position he or she occupies in the world of persons. The progressive realization of this unity is what Christians call the coming of the "Kingdom of God." Mounier believes that Christianity in its original conception has much to contribute to the fuller realization of the personal, affirming as it does the incarnational unity of matter and spirit in a multiplicity of unique, whole, and free individuals. Christianity also shares with personalism an outlook of "tragic optimism" in which commitment to the process of personalization must be total at the same time that it can never be more than conditional. We must, Mounier insists, throw ourselves wholeheartedly and hopefully into the project of becoming persons despite our awareness that our own particular versions of this project will almost certainly prove inadequate and need to be transcended.

In sum, Mounier offers us a philosophical vision in which the primacy given to the personal provides the catalyst for transforming depersonalizing economic, political, social, and religious structures so as to make possible lives that are lived freely and creatively as "open adventures." Such lives are the only "proof" that can be offered for Christianity and the existence of a personal God.

American personalism

More systematic in their approach than Mounier, the American personalists are equally suspicious of abstractions that divorce philosophy from the concrete experiences that constitute our lives. American personalism was hence from the start associated with a series of social reform movements responding to the needs of the day. Its founder, Borden Parker Bowne, was an outspoken defender of women's suffrage; over the years, Bowne's philosophical heirs at Boston University applied personalist principles in defense of socialism, pacifism, and, perhaps most famously, racial equality. Personalism had a significant impact on the American civil rights movement through the activities of Martin Luther King, Jr., who as a graduate student at Boston University studied under Bowne's immediate successor, Edgar Sheffield Brightman.

Bowne's 1908 publication of *Personalism* came at a time when the partnership between religion and intellectual life that had led to the founding of so many American institutions of higher education was beginning to show signs of strain. The shift from theological to mechanistic explanation effected by modern science, combined with the additional boost Darwinism had given to philosophical naturalism, raised serious doubts about the intellectual respectability of religious belief. Bowne attempts to lay these doubts to rest by arguing that philosophical naturalism is beset by insuperable difficulties, offering instead a theistic version of personal idealism that he claims is more consistent with our lived experience. In his concern to make lived experience the ultimate arbiter in philosophical debates, Bowne reflects his ties to his pragmatist cousins (see Article 14, AMERICAN PRAGMATISM).

Bowne willingly acknowledges the value of naturalistic descriptions in ordering certain aspects of our experience. The philosophical naturalist, however, moves beyond description to explanation, asserting that all of reality can be understood in terms of mechanical interactions between material objects. Forgetting that the impersonal terms in which we couch our scientific descriptions are the product of personal activity, the philosophical naturalist reverses the proper order of explanation and insists that personal activity (like everything else) is the product of impersonal forces. Consequently, philosophical naturalism encounters a number of seemingly intractable problems generated by its own procedures. How, for example, can naturalism give an adequate account of the qualitative feel of things using only the quantitative language of force and motion? Or, how can naturalism render comprehensible those of our physical attitudes and movements – kissing a loved one, or kneeling in prayer – that appear so inexplicable when abstracted from the context of persons acting with their purposes?

Even beyond the difficulties attending the reduction of personal activities to impersonal happenings, it remains a serious question whether philosophical naturalism accomplishes anything useful. The claim that we can describe all phenomena in terms of matter in motion is so general "as to include all things at the expense of meaning practically nothing. . . . [T]o be of any use to us, it must go beyond these superficial generalities of classification, and must descend into the realm of causation, and also give account of the specific peculiarities or differentia of concrete things" (Bowne 1908, p. 228). Yet when offered as an account of the way in which specific things arrived at the typically complex states in which we find them, naturalism founders on a contradiction. If the natural order is all there is, whatever led to these states being as they are must be immanent in that order; thus whatever happens now or in the future has been potentially present all along. Potentiality, however, has to be something other than the actual arrangements of material masses if is to explain such arrangements – but naturalism is committed to there being nothing over and above these arrangements.

To make matters worse, the philosophical naturalist typically assumes space and time to exist independently of experience as containers for arrangements of physical matter. Bowne argues that neither space nor time can be conceived as independently real without generating a whole host of contradictions involving the conflicting demands of unity and infinite divisibility; he thus concludes that space and time function as forms structuring our experience. Following Kant, Bowne insists that these forms are not arbitrary: "there must be something in the dynamic relations of the system which demands just this order and no other" (Bowne 1908, p. 139). But to look for this "something" as Kant did in a realm of unknowable things-in-themselves only introduces further mysteries; explanation by appeal to that which cannot be known is no explanation at all, while any claim to know something about these hidden objects merely presumes further structuring and hence requires further explanation.

The solution to these difficulties is to assume the existence of a dynamic power behind knowable objects which is not another object, known or unknown, but a center of active knowing. For Bowne, to be a dynamic center of active knowing is just what it is to be a person. Thus the ultimate explanation of the order we discern in nature is found in persons and their activities. That there are persons in the plural and that they are capable of communication Bowne takes to be a given supplied by lived experience; it is impossible, he claims, to maintain serious doubts that we are sharing our experience with others. When we consider the matter carefully, he adds, the most effective explanation for the high degree of coincidence among our individual experiences is to "plant behind the phenomenal system . . . a Supreme Intelligence which manifests his thought through it and thus founds [its] objective unity" (Bowne, 1908, p. 78). Bowne makes no claims to have thus proven the existence of God; he claims merely to have identified the hypothesis making most consistent sense of our experience.

Bowne's critique of philosophical naturalism thus leads directly to a theistic personal idealism reminiscent of George Berkeley but responsive to Kant (see Article 12, EARLY MODERN PHILOSOPHICAL THEOLOGY; and Article 13, THE EMERGENCE OF MODERN PHILOSOPHY OF RELIGION). It was left to Bowne's student, Edgar Sheffield Brightman, to explore systematically the implications of personal idealism for our conception of God. Brightman adopts what he describes as an "empirical approach to God," proposing likely characteristics of the divine person based on our experience of ourselves as persons. For example, if God is a person and persons are centers of activity, then, Brightman reasons, God must be a temporal being, for activity implies process and process implies temporality. Arguments for an atemporal God that appeal to the apparently atemporal contents of our experience when we think about logic, mathematics, or morals are, Brightman claims, based on a misunderstanding of that experience. If we take seriously the claim that personal activity is the fundamental reality, the contents of our thoughts in such cases must be construed as permanently recurring patterns that exist only through our thinking, rather than atemporal realities existing independently of thought. A properly temporalist analysis of our experience is particularly important in the case of our thinking about morals, for were moral experience construed as a passive encounter with values as independently existing objects, rather than an active striving to body forth value, we would cease to view ourselves as responsible moral agents. This line of reasoning implies that if God as a personal being is also a moral agent, then God too is engaged in a temporally structured process of moral striving.

To understand how this divine striving is possible, Brightman claims, we need to conceive of God not merely as temporal but also as limited. This is not to say that God is limited in the sense of having a beginning or end in time. God's limitations, rather, are of the following two sorts. First, limitations are placed on God's will and intellect by the activities of other persons. These limitations are freely chosen by God as part of an ongoing decision to share the activity of creation by stepping aside to allow for the free play of other wills. The outcome of this free play, on Brightman's account, can come as a genuine and not always pleasant surprise to God. Hence God's striving must be in part redemptive – a struggle to use outcomes otherwise evil in themselves to create something good. By conceiving of a personal God as limited in this way, Brightman argues, we not only build on what we know experientially about the limitations that one person's activities can place on another person's activities, but we are also able to make some sense of the existence of moral evil without compromising God's goodness.

To account for natural evil, Brightman assumes a second, internal, set of limitations on God. We best understand these limitations by returning once again to our own experience. Human experience, on Brightman's analysis, involves at any given moment the following three factors: an activity of willing, a rational structure displayed by this activity, and an element of "brute fact" that gives this activity its content. Creation as an activity of the will thus presumes the unwilled elements of rational structure and brute fact as internal to the experience of that activity. In the case of divine creativity, Brightman calls these uncreated parts of God's experience the "Given." He writes that "the Given is, on the one hand, God's instrument for the expression of aesthetic and moral purposes and, on the other, an obstacle to their complete and perfect expression" (Brightman 1958, p. 342). That God's will is at times at least partially thwarted by the internal obstacles supplied by the Given is evidenced by the occurrence of natural evils. And yet, while God's will may be limited, God's goodness is not, and thus "no defeat or frustration is final." God's unlimited love is forever finding "new avenues of advance" (Brightman 1958, p. 342).

As we have just seen, Brightman wants to offer an account of divine activity grounded in what we know about human activity. Exploring the relationship between these two forms of personal activity is the central task in the work of Peter Bertocci, Brightman's student and successor at Boston University. Less interested than his predecessors in defending a metaphysic of personal idealism, Bertocci is primarily concerned with exploring the implications of the personalist notion that human persons function as co-creators with the divine person. Arguing in the same vein as Brightman for a finite and temporal God, Bertocci suggests that we think of God as both conductor and composer of a symphony in which human persons are the players. The players respond creatively in their

133

interpretive interactions with the created score, while the Composer-Conductor also responds creatively to the performance of each player. The metaphysics of creation, on this model, involve "Creator and co-creators in the ebb and flow of a responsive-responsible cosmic community in which the sensitivity of free spirits to each other and to their Creator is reflected in every moment of human and divine history" (Bertocci 1970, p. 222).

In a world where persons are co-creators with God, surprising felicities as well as unfortunate tragedies are bound to arise when the freely chosen activities of one person intersect with those of another. The felicities are easier to accept as signs of grace than the tragedies. We may try to buy security from tragedy by curtailing the freedom of others, but this is to deny ourselves the highest form of loving. If we are to move beyond prudential to creative love, we must risk letting others be the persons they are. This is the risk God takes in creating human persons, and what distinguishes God most crucially from us, Bertocci claims, is God's greater capacity to suffer for the sake of this creative love. Creative love is given its ultimate expression in forgiveness – a form of loving that refuses to give up on other persons but continues the effort to work creatively with them whatever harm they may have done. As co-creators with God we too have a responsibility to practice forgiving love: "[T]o be able to forgive is to reach perhaps the highest peak of moral creativity in human experience. The person who can forgive is not only proving that he is a creative person, he is increasing the power and quality of his creativity" (Bertocci 1958, p. 86).

Bertocci thus presents religious life as a willingness to live with the creative insecurity that comes from loving other persons. This creative insecurity has much in common with Mounier's vision of human life as an open adventure. In both cases we become persons through the free and creative choices we make as members of a community of other persons, and in both cases, although these choices can at times be unfortunate, even the most tragic can be redeemed as part of the progressive realization of the Kingdom of God.

Conclusion

Although interest in personalism and personalist themes has persisted, personalism itself as a cohesive philosophical movement with a distinctive metaphysic and social program, is on the wane. In Europe, social and economic changes have robbed Mounier's particular version of personalism of some of its political urgency. In America, changes in philosophical fashion have shifted many philosophers' interests away from systematic accounts of reality and toward more specialized pursuits within the philosophical subdisciplines. The philosophy of religion, for example, is often approached as one specialty among others rather than as one thread in the weave of an overall perspective on the world. Shifting fashions and politics notwithstanding, there is much to be learned from personalism with its emphasis on the personal as being of prime importance in a world assumed to have been created by a personal God. Philosophers of religion, in particular, would do well to heed the personalist call to take seriously the personal character of the

God most theists worship – a God who often gets displaced by a more abstract and impersonal "God of the Philosophers."

While the personal idealism that Bowne and Brightman put at the center of their philosophy may strike some as excessive in the priority it gives to the personal, the real difficulty may be their failure to give enough weight to the personal. Although they assert that the rational principles structuring our experience have no reality independently of personal activity, both Bowne and Brightman seem to treat these principles as curiously unconditioned by that activity. Principles of reason, argues Brightman, must be the condition of, rather than being conditioned by, even divine creative activity; were it not the case, this activity would be fundamentally nonrational and all communication between the divine person and human persons would break down. This argument, however, presumes a rather narrow conception of the possible forms of communication between persons. While it certainly is true that a good deal of our communication is discursive, and hence reliant on some rational principle or other, persons can also communicate with one another in a variety of nondiscursive modes. The notion that the structure of discursive communication might grow out of these nondiscursive modes need not, as Brightman assumes, mean an end to rationality and communication. Personalist arguments regarding the nature of God based on this assumption may thus need rethinking.

This need is, of course, entirely consistent with personalism as a philosophical outlook. At the very core of personalism, in both its American and European versions, is a commitment to ongoing revision that undermines any attempt at final systematization. This aspect of its method works against personalism ever succeeding as a rigidly defined philosophical movement. Indeed, as Mounier wrote, "the best future one could wish for Personalism is that it should awaken in every man the sense of the whole meaning of man, so that it could disappear without trace, having become the general climate of our days" (Mounier 1962, pp. 111–12).

Bibliography

Bertocci, P. A.: *Religion as Creative Insecurity* (New York: Association Press, 1958).
——: *The Person God Is* (New York: Humanities Press, 1970).
Bowne, B. P.: *Personalism* (Boston: Houghton, Mifflin, 1908).
Brightman, E. S.: *The Problem of God* (New York: Abingdon Press, 1930).
——: *Person and Reality: An Introduction to Metaphysics*, ed. P. A. Bertocci, J. E. Newhall, and R. S. Brightman (New York: Ronald Press, 1958).
Mounier, E.: *Personalism* (1950), tr. P. Mairet (Notre Dame: University of Notre Dame Press, 1952).
——: *Be Not Afraid: A Denunciation of Despair* (1946 and 1948), tr. C. Rowland (New York: Sheed & Ward, 1962).

16

Process theology

DAVID RAY GRIFFIN

The term "process theology" usually, as here, refers to the theological movement inspired primarily by Alfred North Whitehead (1861–1947) and secondarily by Charles Hartshorne (b. 1897). Whitehead, after having devoted most of his professional life to mathematics and natural philosophy, turned to metaphysical philosophy at the age of 62, upon being invited to teach in the Philosophy Department at Harvard in 1924. Although he had long been agnostic, perhaps atheistic, his turn to metaphysics quickly led to a type of theism. Whereas his Lowell Lectures delivered in February 1925 contained no positive reference to God, their publication later that same year as *Science and the Modern World* contained an affirmation of God as the "principle of limitation" (or "concretion"). In *Religion in the Making* the following year and even more clearly in *Process and Reality* in 1929, this impersonal principle is expanded into an actuality responsive to the world. Hartshorne, who had already developed similar ideas about both God and the world, incorporated much of Whitehead's thought, while differing on some points.

In Whitehead's usage, "metaphysics" is the attempt not to describe things that are beyond the possibility of experience but to explain the coherence of *all* things that *are* experienced. Whitehead's shift from the philosophy of nature to metaphysics meant the inclusion of the human perceiver, which raises the mind–body problem (see Article 55, THEISM AND THE SCIENTIFIC UNDERSTANDING OF THE MIND). Whitehead's approach led to "a recurrence to that phase of philosophic thought which began with Descartes and ended with Hume" (Whitehead 1978 [1929], p. xi) to overcome errors that led to the Kantian turn to idealism. As "a recurrence to pre-Kantian modes of thought" (p. xi), process theology is a form of realism, with regard to both God and the world (see Article 26, THEOLOGICAL REALISM AND ANTI-REALISM).

The chief error of René Descartes was the conception of matter as "vacuous actuality," as wholly devoid of experience, which makes the body's ability to interact with the mind utterly mysterious. One solution was to explain their interaction – whether thought to be real or merely apparent – by appeal to divine omnipotence. Alternatively, George Berkeley's idealism denied the actuality of matter, explaining our sensory perceptions as God's direct impressions on our minds. Both approaches involved "an appeal to a *deus ex machina* who was capable of rising superior to the difficulties of metaphysics" (Whitehead 1967 [1925], p. 156), which is "a device repugnant to a consistent rationality" (Whitehead 1978, p. 190). Although Whitehead himself assigns an explanatory role to God, he rejects that supernaturalistic type of theism. He also rejects, due to its inability to explain the unity of our experience and its self-determining freedom, the materialistic denial of the mind as an actuality distinct from the brain.

The key is to realize that the notion of matter as vacuous actuality arises from "the fallacy of misplaced concreteness," in which abstractions, useful for certain purposes, are equated with concrete actualities. We can understand what other actual entities are in themselves only by analogy with the part of nature known most directly, our own experience. Whitehead hence agrees with Berkeley that we can think meaningfully about *actual* entities only as *perceiving* things. He disagrees, however, with Berkeley's conclusion that the world of nature must be *merely perceived* and thereby non-actual. While avoiding the fallacy of misplaced concreteness with regard to matter, Berkeley, like Descartes, committed it with regard to mind, by identifying mind with *conscious* perceptions and thoughts. Whitehead here follows Gottfried Leibniz, who said that subjectivity, experience, or perception can be generalized all the way down, so that even the lowliest individuals bear some analogy with the human mind. Given this non-dualism. the interaction of mind and body can be understood naturalistically (see Article 12, EARLY MODERN PHILOSOPHICAL THEOLOGY).

Leibniz himself did not achieve this naturalism, because his monads were "windowless," having no openings to be influenced by each other. Their apparent interaction had to be explained as a harmony pre-established by God. Whitehead modified the Leibnizian structure by installing windows. Evidently influenced by BUDDHISM (see Article 2), quantum physics, and William James (who said that our experience comes in "drops"), Whitehead portrayed each enduring individual, from a human mind to an electron, as a rapidly repeating series of "occasions of experience," each of which begins as an open window, into which rush influences from the past world (see Article 14, AMERICAN PRAGMATISM). Once this efficient causation has constituted the occasion's "physical pole," the occasion makes its own self-determining response, which is its "mental pole." When the occasion's self-determination is completed, it becomes an object for subsequent occasions, exerting efficient causation on them. Through this perpetual oscillation between efficient and final causation, there is a mixture of real influence and freedom.

Positing an iota of self-determination at the subatomic level is a necessary but not sufficient condition for human freedom. The conventional view is that any indeterminacy at the quantum level is eliminated in perceptible things by the "law of large numbers." Things such as sticks and stones are "confused aggregates," in which all individual spontaneities are mutually thwarting, so that the things as such have no freedom (Whitehead 1967 [1925], p. 110). However, some larger things are not mere "aggregational societies" but "organisms of organisms," in which a higher-level series of occasions of experience, with greater mentality, arises. Atoms, cells, and animals are examples. In societies of this type, the higher-level occasions of experience, with their greater capacity for self-determinism, are "regnant" or "dominant" occasions, because they exert a guiding influence over the society as a whole, giving it a unity of partly self-determining action.

This same distinction between aggregational societies and what Hartshorne

137

(1972) dubs "compound individuals" (the distinction that is, according to Hartshorne, the greatest discovery of Leibniz) also answers the most common objection to this type of philosophy, which is traditionally called "panpsychism" but better named "panexperientialism" (although Whitehead used neither term and Hartshorne prefers "psychicalism"). This objection is that such philosophies imply that rocks have feelings. The "pan-" in panexperientialism, however, does not mean that literally *all* things, including aggregational societies such as rocks, have experience, but only that all genuine *individuals* do.

Another error of the pre-Kantian period, perpetuated by Kant himself, is the doctrine that all perception is by means of our physical sensory organs. Whitehead's rejection of this sensationist doctrine is implicit in the fact that, having agreed with the Berkelean view that to be an actual individual is to perceive, he assigns perception to cells, atoms, and electrons (as well as, to be mentioned later, God). He uses "prehension" for the non-sensory form of perception shared by all individuals. Sensory perception, if it occurs, is a derivative mode, which is illustrated by the fact that, when we see a tree, we see it *by means of our eyes*. The sensory image of the tree presupposes that I – as the series of dominant occasions of experience – have prehended my brain cells, through which the information from the eye is derived. Memory provides another example of this non-sensory perception, as a present occasion of experience directly prehends earlier occasions.

This distinction between prehension and sensory perception is central to overcoming another problem of modern philosophy: the distinction between theory and (the presuppositions of) practice. The classic example – alongside that of presupposing freedom while espousing determinism – is provided by David Hume, who said that we have no empirical knowledge of either causality (as real influence) or the existence of an "external world." We must, accordingly, espouse solipsism and define causation as mere "constant conjunction," even though in practice we cannot help presupposing a world of causally efficacious actualities. Whitehead rejects this antirational disjunction:

Whatever is found in "practice" must lie within the scope of the metaphysical description. When the description fails to include the "practice" the metaphysics is inadequate and requires revision.   (Whitehead 1978 [1929], p. 13)

Lying behind this statement is a more rigorous version of the "commonsense" criterion that Thomas Reid had employed against Hume: "[T]he metaphysical rule of evidence [is] that we must bow to those presumptions, which, in despite of criticism, we still employ for the regulation of our lives" (1978, p. 252). This version includes only those notions that are truly common to all people because they are *inevitably* presupposed in practice. Also, whereas Reid explained these commonsense notions as supernatural implantations, Whitehead accounts for them naturalistically. (These two differences also distinguish Whiteheadian "commonsense beliefs" from the "basic beliefs" of REFORMED EPISTEMOLOGY, see Article 49.) Most of them, including causation and an actual world, are accounted for by our non-sensory prehensions.

Sensory perception as usually understood, which Whitehead calls "perception in the mode of presentational immediacy," indeed gives no knowledge of either causal efficacy or other actualities. In this mode, one is aware of, say, a green shape, which in itself tells no tales of its origins. Hume concludes that it arises from "unknown causes." But we usually *do* know where visual data come from – namely, the eyes – thanks to our non-sensory "prehension," which Whitehead also calls "perception in the mode of causal efficacy." In this mode, we directly prehend other *actualities* beyond our own conscious experience – most directly our bodily members – which is why none of us are solipsists in practice; and we prehend these other actualities *as causally efficacious* for our own experience, which gives us the notion of causation as real influence.

Two other commonsense notions explained by this non-sensory mode of perception involve values and a Holy Reality. Most modern philosophies cannot account for our presuppositions about values because, not being physical things, they are not perceivable through our senses. Whitehead's philosophy, while allowing for enough free construction to account for cultural differences, avoids complete relativism by portraying our notions of truth, beauty, and goodness as rooted in non-sensory prehensions of a realm of values.

The other prevalent reason for denying objectivity to values, stressed by Martin Heidegger, is the inability to conceive how a realm of values could exist, given the "death of God." While rejecting traditional theism, Whitehead did develop a concept of God in which eternal possibilities, including values, subsist. Our prehension of this aspect of God, which Whitehead calls God's "primordial nature" and from which each experience receives an "ideal aim," lies behind our awareness of values. We can also experience God as fully actual, which Whitehead calls God's "consequent nature" because it is responsive to the happenings in the world. Far from being characterized by impassibility, God is "the great companion – the fellow-sufferer who understands" (Whitehead 1978 [1929], p. 351). If our prehension of God, which occurs at the unconscious level all the time, rises to consciousness, we speak of a RELIGIOUS EXPERIENCE (see Article 47) or the experience of the "holy."

Because prehension and causal influence are two sides of the same relation, our prehension of God's ideal aims is God's action on our experience. This idea, in conjunction with panexperientialism, allows process theologians to speak of DIVINE ACTION (see Article 38) in nature: the cells, molecules, and still lower-level individuals making up the "physical world" differ only in degree from our own experience. The way that God influences us, by means of an aim towards the best values possible in a given situation, can therefore be generalized to God's influence on all individuals. Process theologians have been able, accordingly, to speak rather straightforwardly of God as creator (see Article 39, CREATION AND CONSERVATION), in the sense that God accounts for the directionality of the evolutionary process (Birch and Cobb 1981; see Article 54, THEISM AND EVOLUTIONARY BIOLOGY).

Speaking of divine activity does not raise an insuperable problem of evil, because divine influence is exclusively persuasive (see Article 50, THE PROBLEM OF EVIL). Whitehead considers the idea, enunciated (if inconsistently) by Plato, that "the divine element in the world is to be conceived as a persuasive agency and not as a coercive agency," as "one of the greatest intellectual discoveries in the history of religion" (Whitehead 1933, p. 213). He also suggests that "the power of Christianity lies in its revelation in act, of that which Plato divined in theory" (1933, p. 214). Evil can occur in the world because God, while influencing all events, fully determines no events. Each event is necessarily influenced by its past world as well as by God, and each actual entity is partly self-determining, even vis-à-vis divine agency. This position differs from most "free will defenses" by applying to all, not only human, events, and also by saying that creaturely freedom is rooted not in a *voluntary* self-limitation by God but in the very nature of things: "[T]he relationships of God to the World should lie beyond the accidents of will," being founded instead "upon the necessities of the nature of God and the nature of the World" (1933, p. 215). This naturalistic theism entails that God cannot occasionally violate the normal causal relationships.

Lying behind this denial is the rejection of creation *ex nihilo* (from nothing), in the absolute sense (Whitehead 1978 [1929], pp. 95–6). What exists necessarily is not simply God alone but God-and-a-world – not our particular world, with its contingent forms of order, but some world or other. This point can be expressed in terms of "creativity," which is the ultimate reality embodied in all actualities (see Article 23, THE ORTHODOX TRADITION). Whereas traditional theism said that the power of creativity exists necessarily only as instantiated in God, for process theology it is necessarily instantiated in both God and a plurality of finite actualities. Creativity, in its two forms of self-determination and efficient causation, belongs as much to finitude as it does to God. This is why God cannot cancel out, or override, either the efficient causation or the freedom of the creatures. In traditional theism, by contrast, because any creative power possessed by the creatures was theirs purely by divine volition, it could be freely revoked. It was this supernaturalistic doctrine of OMNIPOTENCE (see Article 28) that created an insoluble problem of evil. A process theodicy, by contrast, can fully accept the reality of genuine evil (which is one of our inevitable presuppositions) without implying the existence of evil urges in God, e.g. as E. S. Brightman does (see Article 15, PERSONALISM), or appealing to inscrutable "mystery" (Griffin 1991).

This replacement of a supernaturalistic with a naturalistic theism also allows for a reassessment of the widespread assumption that Hume and Kant have demonstrated the invalidity of all natural theology. Whitehead describes his own discussion of God as "merely an attempt to add another speaker to that masterpiece, Hume's *Dialogues Concerning Natural Religion*" (Whitehead 1978 [1929], p. 343). Hume's major argument, directed against both deism and traditional theism, presupposed the notion of divine omnipotence. Another argument depended on Hume's understanding of causation as "constant conjunction," which Whitehead has provided good reason to reject. Still another argument is that the notion of (efficient) causation is used equivocally in COSMOLOGICAL ARGUMENTS (see Article 42), because the alleged creation of the world out of nothing is different in kind from the causation we experience in the world, from which we derive the very notion of causation. But Whitehead's naturalistic theism does not suffer from that problem either (1978, p. 93). Kant also provided no refutation of Whitehead's type of natural theology, because Kant agreed that the order of the world provides evidence of an Orderer, denying only that it provides evidence for the omnipotent deity of classical theism (see Article 43, TELEOLOGICAL AND DESIGN ARGU-MENTS). Kant is, accordingly, a witness for, not against, the kind of natural theology offered by process theology. Its version of this argument is that, given a vast plu-rality of finite actual entities with spontaneity, the order of the world betokens an Orderer. Another argument is from novelty: the emergence of novel forms in the evolutionary process implies an actuality in which previously unrealized possibili-ties subsist and by which they become effective. An argument from the human experience of values (see Article 44, MORAL ARGUMENTS) can be regarded as a special version of the argument from novelty. Unlike Whitehead, Hartshorne (1941) defends a version of the ontological argument, but many process theologians do not accept its validity (see Article 41, ONTOLOGICAL ARGUMENTS).

With regard to the nature of God: process theology rejects divine SIMPLICITY (see Article 31) in favor of a "dipolar theism." Whitehead's version, which distin-guishes between the primordial and consequent natures, is modified by Hartshorne (1941, 1948), who distinguishes between the "abstract essence" and the "concrete states" of God. Many of the traditional attributes of God, such as impassibility, immutability (see Article 40, IMMUTABILITY AND IMPASSIBILITY), NECESSITY (see Article 33), and ETERNITY (see Article 32), apply to the abstract essence (which includes the divine existence), while the concrete states involve possibility (suffer-ing with our sufferings and rejoicing with our joys), change, and contingency. For example, OMNISCIENCE (see Article 29) belongs to the abstract essence of God, because God in every moment knows everything that is then knowable. Future events, not yet being actual, are not yet knowable, except as more or less probable. (There is no problem, accordingly, of FOREKNOWLEDGE AND HUMAN FREEDOM, see Article 37.) This abstract attribute of omniscience is eternal, necessary, immutable, and impassible. God's *concrete knowing*, by contrast, changes in every moment, because there are always new things to know. It is contingent, because it depends on contingent happenings; it is perfectly passible, because it involves perfect sym-pathy with the feelings of all the creatures.

Hartshorne also calls his doctrine "panentheism," which means that all things are *in* God. The relation between soul and body is used as an analogue for the God–world relation, which means regarding God as the soul of the universe. On the basis of the hierarchy of compound individuals, Hartshorne (1972) takes the idea of divine OMNIPRESENCE (see Article 36) literally: just as the soul literally encom-passes the region occupied by the brain, so God encompasses the world. The way in which the mind or soul prehends and is prehended by the brain cells provides the basis for understanding how God is affected by and influences the creatures. In one sense, the doctrine of divine INCORPOREALITY (see Article 34) is denied, in that the world can be considered the body of God. In another sense, however, incorporeal-ity is affirmed, in that there is no divine body *between* God and the world through which God could act coercively upon the world (Hartshorne 1941; Griffin 1991).

Although this article has focused on Whitehead and Hartshorne as its founders, "process theology" is a movement involving a diverse group of theolo-gians dealing with a wide range of issues. For example, because of its panentheism and panexperientialism, process theology has been employed as the basis for an ecological ethic (see Article 64, THEISM AND ENVIRONMENTAL ETHICS), as exemplified by Birch and Cobb (1981) and McDaniel (1989). Thanks to these emphases and others, such as internal relatedness and a non-coercive deity, process theology has also been closely intertwined with FEMINISM (see Article 76) in theology, as exemplified by Keller (1986). It has also proved fruitful with regard to the relation between science and religion (Barbour 1966) and in the area of interreligious dialogue (see Article 77, RELIGIOUS PLURALISM; and Article 78, COMPARATIVE PHILOSOPHY OF RELIGION), as exemplified by Cobb (1982). These recent developments follow upon several decades in which Christian process theologians have used the philosophies of Whitehead and Hartshorne to understand traditional Christian doctrines, such as Christology (Cobb 1975, Ogden 1961), eschatology, and immortality (Suchocki 1988). Although most process theologians have followed Hartshorne in speaking only of "objective immortality," others, following up Whitehead's observation that his philosophy is neutral on the question of life after death (see Article 70, SURVIVAL OF DEATH) so that it is to be settled on the basis of empirical evidence, have affirmed this notion as well (Cobb 1965, Griffin 1989).

Bibliography

Barbour, I. G.: *Issues in Science and Religion* (Englewood Cliffs: Prentice-Hall, 1966).
Birch, C., and Cobb, J. B., Jr.: *The Liberation of Life: From the Cell to the Community* (Cambridge: Cambridge University Press, 1981).
Cobb, J. B., Jr.: *A Christian Natural Theology: Based on the Thought of Alfred North Whitehead* (Philadelphia: Westminster, 1965).
——: *Christ in a Pluralistic Age* (Philadelphia: Westminster, 1975).
——: *Beyond Dialogue: Toward a Mutual Transformation of Christianity and Buddhism* (Philadelphia: Fortress, 1982).
Griffin, D. R.: *God and Religion in the Postmodern World* (Albany: State University of New York Press, 1989).
——: *Evil Revisited: Responses and Reconsiderations* (Albany: State University of New York Press, 1991).
Hartshorne, C.: *Man's Vision of God and the Logic of Theism* (New York: Harper & Row, 1941).
——: *The Divine Relativity: A Social Conception of God* (New Haven: Yale University Press, 1948).
——: *Whitehead's Philosophy: Selected Essays* (Lincoln: University of Nebraska Press, 1972).
Keller, C.: *From a Broken Web: Separation, Sexism, and Self* (Boston: Beacon Press, 1986).
McDaniel, J. B.: *Of God and Pelicans: A Theology of Reverence for Life* (Louisville: Westminster/John Knox, 1989).
Ogden, S. M.: *Christ without Myth: A Study Based on the Theology of Rudolf Bultmann* (New York: Harper & Brothers, 1961).
Suchocki, M. H.: *The End of Evil: Process Eschatology in Historical Context* (Albany: State University of New York Press, 1988).
Whitehead, A. N.: *Adventures of Ideas* (New York: Macmillan, 1933).
——: *Science and the Modern World* (1925) (New York: Free Press, 1967).
——: *Process and Reality* (1929), corrected edn, ed. D. R. Griffin and D. W. Sherburne (New York: Free Press, 1978).

17

Phenomenology and existentialism

MEROLD WESTPHAL

Phenomenology, with its roots in Edmund Husserl, and existentialism, with its roots in Søren Kierkegaard and Friedrich Nietzsche, are two major traditions of twentieth century philosophy. Husserl almost never philosophizes about religion; by contrast, Kierkegaard and Nietzsche are incessantly preoccupied with questions of religion in general and Christianity in particular. Not surprisingly, when phenomenology and existentialism flow together in works like Martin Heidegger's *Being and Time* and Jean-Paul Sartre's *Being and Nothingness*, there is more of interest to the philosophy of religion than is found in Husserl, if less than in Kierkegaard and Nietzsche. This article will concern itself with the import of these two traditions for the philosophy of religion, but not with the explicitly theological appropriation of existential phenomenology in the work of thinkers like Rudolf Bultmann, Paul Tillich, and Karl Rahner.

Phenomenology

Husserl's phenomenological project is the attempt to continue and to combine the projects of David Hume and René Descartes. Its Humean heritage, which we might call its experientialism, is the attempt to get back "to the things themselves," to allow things to show themselves to us directly and without the mediations and distortions of the pre-interpretations we bring with us from various theories and from common sense. The categorical imperative of phenomenology is, "Shed your pre-judices (pre-judgments); be attentive. Look, listen, . . ."

The Cartesian element is the quest for absolute clarity and certainty. Philosophy must be the one completely rigorous science and, as such, the foundation of all the other sciences. Its cognitions must be absolute in the sense of not being relative to either natural or historical determinants. (My) consciousness must be the absolute point of reference for the world both as nature and as history. Thus the first beatitude of Husserlian phenomenology joins promise to command, "Blessed are the attentive, for they shall achieve absolute clarity and certainty."

There are two distinct ways in which phenomenology has become significant for the philosophy of religion. In the first place, it has contributed significantly to a way of doing philosophy of religion, often called phenomenology of religion, that is quite different from the normative philosophical theology and philosophy of religion that have their roots in scholasticism and deism (see Article 13, THE EMERGENCE OF MODERN PHILOSOPHY OF RELIGION). It is a descriptive approach that brackets the

143

interrelated projects of evaluating and explaining religious beliefs and practices in order to attend as carefully as possible to ways in which the religious "object" (often generalized as the Sacred or the Holy) is given to the religious subject, sometimes designated "the believing soul," but often recognized to be as much communal as personal. The goal is to understand what it means to be religious, where such understanding is viewed both as an end in itself and as a necessary prerequisite to any critical or evaluative philosophy of religion that would not lose touch with its subject matter (see Westphal, forthcoming).

The Cartesian element of the Husserlian project is present when the phenomenology of religion is motivated by the sense that reflection on religion can be "scientific" only if it abstracts from questions of truth and value and restricts itself to pure description. But even when the notion that description can be "pure" or "scientific" is rejected in terms of a more hermeneutical understanding of understanding, the Humean element is strongly present. Whether or not the phenomenology of religion aspires to be rigorous science, it seeks, without presupposing faith, to be faithfully attentive to the actual experience of the religious life. Just as it is a major task of the philosophies of science and of art to get clear, respectively, about what science and art are, so the phenomenology of religion seeks to show what religion is as human experience and practice.

The nineteenth century roots of existentialism

The second way in which phenomenology has become involved in the philosophy of religion is through its confluence with existentialism, especially in the work of Heidegger and Sartre. Their accounts of human existence draw methodologically on the work of Husserl (whose Cartesianism they significantly modify in the service of his Humeanism); but in terms of substance it is Kierkegaard and Nietzsche who are the crucial background. Their contributions might be summed up this way: in reflecting on the meaning of human existence, Kierkegaard demands that we take the reality of God more seriously than Christendom does, while Nietzsche demands that we take the unreality of God more seriously than secular modernity does. In its nineteenth century origins, existentialism is already postmodern by its refusal to accept any of the standard interpretations of the conflict between faith and reason, theism and atheism, whether offered by religious orthodoxy, by militant atheism, or by the deisms and idealisms that sought a middle ground.

For Kierkegaard (by which is meant the flow of his writings, pseudonymous and otherwise, toward a religious interpretation of existence) this means in the first instance the teleological suspension of the ethical. This is the refusal to allow the laws or the customs of one's people, along with the theories that legitimize such practices, to be the highest norm for life. When God is taken seriously neither the individual (the aesthetic stage) nor society (the ethical stage) is taken to be absolute, but both are seen in their finitude and sinfulness to stand before the judgment of God. The individualism that emerges is not an intensification of modernity's atomistic quest for autonomy but just the opposite. The self is essentially relational, and yet because the social order in which it is naturally immersed is not fit to be the mediator of its relation to God, each self must be awakened from the complacent slumber of that immersion (the relative relation) so as to stand alone before God (the absolute relation).

That slumber turns out to be dogmatic as well as complacent because it involves the tendency to absolutize not only the practices of one's social order but the ideologies that legitimate both them and it. Kierkegaard's assault on speculative philosophy (in the person of Hegel) is but the extension of the teleological suspension of the ethical into the realm of epistemology. Human finitude and sinfulness together combine to make the project of absolute knowledge at once comic and tragic. In short, if God is real the divine absoluteness renders everything human relative at best; every attempt to make human existence, whether individual or collective, practical or theoretical, its own foundation and norm is at once foolish and arrogant. The securities offered to the self by socialization and legitimation are radically put in question as being human, all too human.

Nietzsche's point of departure is that God is not real and that when religion is examined apart from the ontological support that theism would provide for it, it turns out to be the ideological support for a moral order that does not deserve our support. When secular modernity recognizes the full implications of its atheistic posture, it will see that it has lost its moral compass and has become human existence at sea, a freedom at once exhilarating and terrifying. New values will have to be created to replace the old, discredited ones.

What is wrong with the old values of ascetic and altruistic morality, according to Nietzsche, is that they are rooted in the resentment of the weak against the strong. As such they are expressions of the will to power of the weak; "good" and "evil" are the only weapons they have in the life and death struggle with those who would otherwise take ruthless advantage of them. Nietzsche is not offended by the will to power as such, but by the lack of honesty involved. For this reactive expression of the will to power vehemently denies that it is a clever form of egoism. Religions like Christianity and Buddhism, and philosophies like Platonism are merely the metaphysical ideologies with whose help the weak seek to make themselves strong, the masters of society. Moral domination replaces military domination.

As the repeated use of the term "ideology" suggests, Kierkegaard and Nietzsche are closer to Marx than to Hume and Kant. They are more concerned with the social function of religion than with debates about proving the existence and nature of God and worrying about the problem of evil in that connection. They represent a philosophizing about religion that is neither dispassionate description (phenomenology of religion) nor passionate debate over the truth of various religious beliefs (philosophical theology).

Jean-Paul Sartre

The existential phenomenologies of Heidegger and Sartre do not simply continue the work of Kierkegaard and Nietzsche; but that work is never very far beneath the surface of their thought. This is perhaps most obvious in the work of Sartre. In

145

his famous essay, "Existentialism is a humanism" (Sartre 1947, and various anthologies), he acknowledges the existence of a Christian existentialism, but defines his own as the attempt to work out the implications of atheism. In the absence of a creator God we cannot construe ourselves to be like artifacts, having a nature that stems from the prior design of the maker. Sartre's slogan "existence precedes essence" means that we define ourselves, giving meaning and guidance to our lives only after finding ourselves already on the scene. Nothing in the nature of things either determines or justifies our self-definitions or the values they entail.

To put this point more concretely, Sartre borrows the saying of Dostoevsky's Ivan Karamazov, "If God did not exist, everything would be permitted." For Sartre this loses its subjunctive character; God is dead and everything is permitted. This means both that morality has no foundation in either divine or human nature, and that the creation-talk at the heart of theistic religion (as Nietzsche and Ludwig Feuerbach have already said) is projection, attributing the definitions we give to our own life to someone else, God, rather than taking responsibility for them ourselves. Religion is essentially bad faith or self-deception.

Sartre emphasizes the terrifying rather than the exhilarating aspect of this freedom. He describes humans as "condemned to be free" and as those who experience their freedom in anxiety, abandonment, and despair. Over against the bourgeois complacency of secular modernity, he emphasizes the dark side of human experience and relates it to the most fundamental religious concern. On his interpretation of existence, the absence of God is the most fundamental fact about the world; just for this reason Kierkegaard is right in treating anxiety and despair as modes of relating to the human condition and not just as reactions to occasional unwelcome circumstances.

The literary existentialism of Franz Kafka and Albert Camus, as indeed Sartre's own literary works, can be read as working out in a different genre the same essentially Nietzschean project of trying to think through the death of God.

Sartre's *magnum opus*, *Being and Nothingness*, is less explicitly oriented to Nietzsche's death of God theme. Still, it can be read as an extended meditation on human existence in a world whose two most basic facts are the absence of God and the presence of the will to power. Sartre's individualism, like Kierkegaard's, presupposes that the self is essentially relational. It is the Other who teaches me who I am. But this Other, before whose look I experience fear, shame, and pride, is triply problematic. First, as an embodied self I am afraid of what the other self can do to me. Second, two of the three basic responses to the Other's look, shame and pride, concern my worthiness to be happy and not just my ability to be happy. Moreover, of these two, Sartre devotes considerably more attention to shame, suggesting that the Other is more conspicuous in judgment than in affirmation. This is not an empirical claim about the frequency with which I get praised; it is a phenomenological claim about the structure of my perception of the Other. Finally, even when the Other's look gives rise to pride, I am dependent on the Other for the meaning of my being. Nietzsche's will to power theme is interpreted in the light of

Hegel's master–slave dialectic, and I perceive myself to be slave rather than master even when the Other is proud of me.

But I want to be the master, the absolute end to which others are the means, the absolute value by which others are judged. Accordingly I adopt one of two strategies before the look of the Other, or alternate between them. Either I seek to deny and eliminate the freedom and subjectivity of the Other by making the Other the object of my look, or I seek to possess and appropriate that freedom and subjectivity by manipulating it to my own ends. In both cases I seek to be master, reducing the Other to my slave. In the sexual sphere sadism and masochism are the enactments of these strategies, but in this context they become metaphors for the entirety of human relations. It is not just that the world is filled with hate and indifference; love itself is nothing more than the demand to be loved. As each will to power struggles to be master rather than slave, it seeks to be God, the absolute source of all judgments of worth and, as such, the justification of itself. Of course, this project cannot be realized and "Man is a useless passion" (Sartre, 1992, p. 784).

In a footnote to this bleak account, Sartre adds, "These considerations do not exclude the possibility of an ethics of deliverance and salvation. But this can be achieved only after a radical conversion which we cannot discuss here" (1992, p. 534). It becomes clear that Sartre is a secular theologian of original sin (see Article 68, SIN AND ORIGINAL SIN). The will to power and the master–slave struggle that Sartre weaves together in his account are what Augustine calls pride as the darkness of the human heart. On Sartre's account, as on Augustine's, our freedom is so enthralled by this primordial self-assertion that short of a radical conversion we are neither able to love God, since we wish to be God ourselves, nor to love our neighbor as ourselves, since even our love is but the demand to be loved.

Although Sartre speaks of the Other as my "original fall" (1992, p. 352), he mostly portrays the deep egocentrism of human existence in secular language; and the evidence to which he appeals is consistently phenomenological rather than theological. He is, then, a secular Augustinian, living in a world filled with sin but devoid of grace. His work represents two challenging questions addressed to the philosophy of religion. Isn't the question of God fundamental to human existence in ways that philosophical theology (including atheology – the presentation of arguments against belief in God) often loses sight of? Isn't the tendency to radical self-assertion, by whatever name it is called, so deeply ingrained in our lives and so destructive in its effects that it deserves more attention from the philosophy of religion than it usually receives?

Martin Heidegger

While Heidegger explicitly adopts the phenomenological posture, he resists the existentialist label because, he insists, his fundamental question is about the meaning of being rather than human existence. Nevertheless, his approach to the question of being is by means of an analysis of *Dasein*, the name he gives to human being in the attempt to free thinking from the presuppositions built into such notions as self, soul, person, and so forth. *Dasein* is normally translated as being-there, or left untranslated, but it is an ordinary German word for existence. When Heidegger then restricts the term "existence" (*Existenz*) to *Dasein* and writes, *"The essence of Dasein lies in its existence"* (1962, p. 67), he guarantees that an existentialist reading of *Being and Time* will never be entirely eclipsed by other readings.

Whereas Sartre is overtly atheistic Heidegger is methodologically agnostic. He wishes to pose the question of the meaning of being, which he takes to be prior to discussing the existence and nature of any being, including God. The critique of Western metaphysics that begins in *Being and Time* is thus not a contribution to the debate over the reality of God. But in the tradition of Martin Luther and Blaise Pascal it argues against trying to talk about God with categories that have not arisen "from an inquiry in which faith is primary'" (1962, p. 30). Interpreting reality in terms of mere presence or thereness, as presence-at-hand rather than readiness-to-hand, is a fallacy of misplaced concreteness that distorts beings of all sorts, including God. We have here the seeds of Heidegger's later critique of onto-theology as the reduction of God to a means toward the human end of making the whole of reality intelligible by our standards.

Like Sartre's interpretation of human existence, Heidegger's has religious over-tones. He complains that the interpretation of human finitude in terms of being created or being produced leaves *Dasein* at the mercy of categories as inappropriate to it as to God, the philosophical discourse of substance and the common sense discourses of thing and object. He proposes an alternative, phenomenological (and thus pre-theological) interpretation of human finitude in terms of its temporality, spelled out in such notions as thrownness and being-toward-death. Human existence is much more open and much less stable or secure than substance-talk, whether dualistic or not, suggests.

It is on the theme of human fault, however, that comparison with Sartre invites itself. Heidegger gives detailed descriptions of *Dasein* as falling, of the call of conscience, and of the experience of guilt. But while the language is more nearly Augustinian than Sartre's, the substance is far less so. For at this stage Heidegger has not taken his cue from either Nietzsche, or Hegel, or any other secular phenomenology of self-assertion. The result is an analysis so formal that Heidegger can deny, even if not entirely convincingly, that it has normative significance. If *Being and Nothingness* has no ethics because Sartre is an Augustinian who recognizes that conversion must precede ethics, *Being and Time* has no ethics because Heidegger's phenomenology operates at a pre-ethical as well as pre-theological level of abstraction.

Other existentialists

Without denying the reality of the dark intersubjectivity Sartre portrays, Martin Buber (see Article 22, THE JEWISH TRADITION) and Gabriel Marcel (see Article 15, PER-SONALISM) point to the possibility of an open, vulnerable, and giving relation to the Other, a posture that seeks to preserve the subjectivity of the Other without manipulating it. Then they point to this region as the horizon within which it makes sense to talk about God. In the objective world of subject and object, the I–it world, God and faith are at best square pegs in a round hole. Only in the intersubjective world of dialogue, belonging, availability, and being at another's disposal can philosophical reflection be faithful to religious experience. Heidegger is right to question the adequacy of certain metaphysical discourses to religious subject matter.

By juxtaposing courage to contemporary modes of anxiety, Paul Tillich seeks to articulate a kind of Stoicism for the modern world, an ethic inspired by both the ancient Stoics and their modern disciples, Spinoza and Nietzsche. But when he speaks of the courage to accept acceptance he moves in biblical directions. On the other hand, Nikolai Berdyaev (in *The Destiny of Man*) develops an ethics of redemption and eschatological hope whose inspiration is consistently biblical. Berdyaev's work can be read as seeking to provide what Sartre, in the footnote mentioned above, did not have time to discuss.

Lev Shestov (in *Athens and Jerusalem*) and Karl Jaspers (in *Reason and Existenz*, among other works) emphasize, with Kierkegaard and Nietzsche, the ways in which human existence transcends human reason, at least when the latter is interpreted as the project of conceptual mastery that renders everything clear and distinct. For Shestov this involves an explicit attempt to justify the appeal to revelation. Like Kierkegaard's Johannes Climacus, he thinks it is the height of arrogance for speculative metaphysics to require God and human existence to conform to its theoretical prejudices. For Jaspers, by contrast, the challenge to reason involves distancing reflection from such isms as theism, atheism, and pantheism on the grounds that each puts too much faith in its own conceptual account of the world. The Encompassing, his name for the sacred, is the unthinkable, something we are never out of touch with but which we can never get in our sights, something which always exceeds our conceptual telescopes and microscopes.

Bibliography

Buber, M.: *I and Thou*, tr. W. Kaufmann (New York: Charles Scribner's Sons, 1970).

Heidegger, M.: *Being and Time*, tr. J. Macquarrie and E. Robinson (New York: Harper & Row, 1962).

Kierkegaard, S.: *A Kierkegaard Anthology*, ed. R. Bretall (New York: Random House, 1946).

Marcel, G.: *Creative Fidelity*, tr. R. Rosthal (New York: Farrar, Straus & Giroux, 1964).

Nietzsche, F.: *The Portable Nietzsche*, tr. W. Kaufmann (New York: Viking, 1954).

Sartre, J.-P.: *Existentialism*, tr. B. Frechtman (New York: Philosophical Library, 1947).

——: *Being and Nothingness: A Phenomenological Essay on Ontology*, tr. H. Barnes (New York: Washington Square Press, 1992).

Tillich, P.: *The Courage to Be* (New Haven: Yale University Press, 1952).

Westphal, M.: "Phenomenology of religion," *Routledge Encyclopedia of Philosophy*, ed. E. Craig (London: Routledge, forthcoming in 1998).

18

Wittgensteinianism

JOHN HYMAN

The best introduction to Wittgensteinianism is Wittgenstein. The bibliography appended to this article includes some books and articles by philosophers who have sought to develop, defend, or criticize Wittgenstein's ideas in the philosophy of religion. However, I shall confine my discussion to Wittgenstein himself.

Wittgenstein's early philosophy was worked out in the six years or so following his arrival in Cambridge, and published in the *Tractatus Logico-Philosophicus* in 1922. After a long hiatus, he took up philosophy again in 1929, and soon began to develop the ideas which were published after his death – first in the *Philosophical Investigations*, the masterpiece of his mature philosophy, and then in editions of various notebooks, drafts, and collections of philosophical remarks. I shall discuss these two philosophies in turn.

Wittgenstein said that the fundamental idea of the *Tractatus* is "that the 'logical constants' are not representatives; that there can be no representatives of the *logic* of facts" (*TLP*, 4.0312). Perhaps a simpler way of expressing this thought is to say that the *propositions* of logic are not descriptions. Gottlob Frege had thought that the propositions of logic describe timeless relations between abstract objects; Bertrand Russell had thought that they describe the most general features of the world. We arrive at the propositions of logic, according to Russell, by abstracting from the content of empirical propositions, and so the propositions of logic themselves describe the world we encounter in experience, but they do so in the most abstract and general terms.

Wittgenstein argued that Frege and Russell underestimated the difference between the propositions of logic and empirical propositions, because according to Frege and Russell, however different these kinds of propositions may be, however different the kinds of things they say *are*, they still have this much in common, that they say *something*. Wittgenstein's own view was that the propositions of logic say nothing; they give no information whatsoever about the world; they are simply *tautologies*. "For example," Wittgenstein says, "I know nothing about the weather when I know that it is either raining or not raining." ". . . all the propositions of logic say the same thing, to wit nothing" (*TLP*, 4.461, 5.43).

If logical propositions say nothing, what is it for a proposition to say *something*? The answer that Wittgenstein gave in the *Tractatus* is one that he later summarized as follows: "The individual words of language name objects – sentences are combinations of such names" (*PI*, §1). Accordingly, the sense of a sentence will depend on the meanings of the words which are combined in it, and the *way in which* they are combined. Just as the objects to which the individual words correspond can be combined or arranged in different ways, so can the words in a sentence; and the sense of the sentence will depend on what arrangement of objects it presents to us. Hence, if a proposition says anything at all, it says that such-and-such objects are arranged in such-and-such a way. The only thing we can do with words is to describe, or misdescribe, the facts.

Thus, according to the *Tractatus*, "One name stands for one thing, another for another thing, and they are combined with one another. In this way the whole group – like a *tableau vivant* – presents a state of affairs" (*TLP*, 4.0311). This is the *picture theory of meaning*. Words are combined in sentences to form a *picture* or *model* of a possible state of affairs in the world. If the way that things are arranged corresponds to the way the words are combined, then the sentence is true; and if not, then it is false.

In his own preface to the *Tractatus*, Wittgenstein said that "the whole sense of the book might be summed up in the following words: what can be said at all can be said clearly, and what we cannot talk about we must pass over in silence" (*TLP*. p. 3). So far, I have commented on "what can be said," as Wittgenstein himself did, in the larger part of the *Tractatus*. But by doing so, I have broken the very rules which fix the limits of what can be said. For as soon as I try to explain how a sentence must be related to the state of affairs it represents, I try to do more with words than merely describe the facts (4.12).

This implication of Wittgenstein's doctrine, that philosophical propositions are themselves nonsensical, did not escape him. He states it explicitly at the end of the *Tractatus* (6.53):

The correct method in philosophy would really be the following: to say nothing except what can be said ... and then, whenever someone else wanted to say something metaphysical, to demonstrate to him that he had failed to give a meaning to certain signs in his propositions ... // My propositions serve as elucidations in the following way: anyone who understands me eventually recognizes them as nonsensical, when he has used them – as steps – to climb up beyond them. (He must, so to speak, throw away the ladder after he has climbed up it.)

But it is not just philosophy that lies beyond the reach of language. Ethics, aesthetics, and whatever thoughts we might aspire to have about the meaning of life, or about God, all belong to what Wittgenstein calls "the mystical"; and they are alike incapable of being put into words. Nothing which touches on matters of value can be captured in words. Every human effort to address or even to articulate what Wittgenstein called "the problems of life" must be in vain: "When the answer cannot be put into words," he said, "neither can the question be put into words" (*TLP*, 6.5).

If we accept Wittgenstein's austere conception of language, and its consequence that the ethical, aesthetic, and religious aspects of human life – the mystical – cannot be put into words, we may feel tempted to conclude that the importance we attach to aesthetic experience, to ethics, and to religion is the result of an illusion. Alternatively, we may conclude that what can be put into words is paltry by comparison with what cannot. There is no doubt at all that Wittgenstein intends us to draw the latter conclusion. In fact, in a letter written in 1919, Wittgenstein says that the *Tractatus* "consists of two parts: of that which is under consideration here and of all that I have *not* written. And it is precisely this second part that is the important one" (Luckhardt 1979, p. 94).

Still, it is difficult to know what place, if any, God and faith have in the system of the *Tractatus*. God is mentioned four times, but only the last of these comments has anything to do with religion. It is this (6.432):

How things are in the world is of complete indifference for what is higher. God does not reveal himself *in* the world.

The emphasis on the word "in" is Wittgenstein's; and I think its significance is explained in the next remark but one: "It is not *how things are in the world* that is mystical, but *that it exists*" (*TLP*, 6.44). Thus, Wittgenstein may have wanted to intimate that God reveals himself in the fact that the world exists, the fact that "there is what there is" (*NB*, p. 86) – which is not strictly speaking a fact at all, and is therefore impossible to state.

We should not imagine that this is meant to be an argument for God's existence – one with a nonsensical premise and a nonsensical conclusion. What may be intended, however, is that a religious attitude is an attitude towards the world *as a whole*, an attitude in which it isn't *how things happen to be in the world* that absorbs our attention, but *that it exists* (see Article 42, COSMOLOGICAL ARGUMENTS). And a religious attitude can also be described as an acknowledgment of God, although of course it is an attitude which we must never attempt to articulate by *saying* that God exists: "What we cannot speak about we must pass over in silence" (*TLP*, 7).

If this is what the *Tractatus* hints at, some remarks in Wittgenstein's notebooks, which he wrote in July 1916, when his life was in constant danger, are more explicit. They identify God with "the meaning of life, i.e. the meaning of the world," with fate and with the world itself (*NB*, pp. 73f). However, the impression they convey most forcibly is that faith consists in the ability to see that life has a meaning; that this in turn consists in living in such a way "that life stops being problematic," for "the solution to the problem of life is to be seen in the disappearance of this problem" (*NB*, p. 74; cf. *TLP*, 6.521); and that living thus will enable one to achieve a sort of happiness – a Stoic calm – by detaching oneself from the uncontrollable contingencies of the world, and accepting it without fear. Wittgenstein incorporated some of these remarks into the *Tractatus*; and it seems that the rest continued to exert an influence on his thought, and remain, albeit with an altered emphasis, in the background of the *Tractatus*.

The *Tractatus* presents an austere view of human language, perhaps a repressive one. It denies the intelligibility of much of what we say, including everything which mattered most to Wittgenstein himself. However, the doctrine that religious truths are ineffable has an important place in the history of religious thought, and is likely to appear plausible if one thinks that language cannot capture our profoundest feelings. Wittgenstein's upbringing led him to revere musical creativity, and it is possible that his love of music made him receptive to this thought. Be that as it may, the achievement of his early philosophy, so far as the philosophy of religion is concerned, was to have formulated the doctrine that religious truths are ineffable in terms which are clear and explicit precisely because they are founded on a theory of language (see Article 24, RELIGIOUS LANGUAGE).

In the 1930s, Wittgenstein's philosophy of language was dramatically transformed, and his earlier view of religion could not survive the transformation. He abandoned the doctrines that a proposition is a logical picture compounded out of names whose meanings are the things they stand for, and that the intelligible use of language always serves a single purpose – to describe the facts. He came to believe – on the contrary – that the meaning of a word is its use in the language; that words can be used for an indefinitely broad and heterogeneous range of purposes; and hence that the task of philosophy is not logical analysis but the description of our various "language-games." Since speech and writing are part and parcel of human activities which take place and have significance only in the context of human forms of life and culture, the question of what an expression in a language means can only be answered by considering it in its context, and by asking how it is used.

When the later Wittgenstein writes about religious belief, he continues to argue that the use of language to express religious beliefs is quite unlike the use of language to state facts; but he no longer infers that it must therefore be a *mis*use of language. His principal aim is to explain how concepts such as sin, redemption, judgment, grace, and atonement can have an indispensable place in an individual's or a community's way of life, and to show how we can resist assimilating the use of these concepts to hypotheses, predictions, and theoretical explanations.

For example, he talks at length about the belief that there will be a last judgment. His stated intention is to show that "in religious discourse we use such expressions as: 'I believe that so and so will happen,' . . . differently to the way in which we use them in science" (*LC*, p. 57). However, he argues in favor of a far more radical doctrine, namely, that believing in a last judgment does not mean thinking it certain or probable that a certain kind of event will occur sometime in the future. This does not merely distance the use of an expression like "I believe that so and so will happen" in religious discourse from its use in science, but from any kind of prediction at all.

So, if the expression "I believe that there will be a last judgment" is not used to make a prediction, how is it used? This is Wittgenstein's answer (*LC*, p. 56):

Here believing obviously plays much more this role: suppose we said that a certain picture might play the role of constantly admonishing me, or I always think of it. Here there would be an enormous difference between those people for whom the picture is constantly in the foreground, and others who just didn't use it at all.

This example is not atypical. Wittgenstein equates having religious beliefs with using religious concepts and having the attitudes and emotions that their use implies. He says this most explicitly as follows: "It strikes me that a religious belief could only be something like a passionate commitment to a system of reference" (*CV*, p. 64). And he says this about coming to believe in God (p. 86):

Life can educate one to a belief in God. And *experiences* too are what bring this about; but I don't mean visions and other forms of sense experience which show us "the existence of this being," but, e.g., sufferings of various sorts. These neither show us God in the way a sense-impression shows us an object, nor do they give rise to *conjectures* about him. Experiences, thoughts, – life can force this concept on us.

Now, it was one of the fundamental themes of Wittgenstein's later philosophy that the concepts we use cannot be justified by reference to reality. Some philosophers have argued that our concepts, or at any rate the concepts of science, are correct, that they conform to the nature of the things we use them to describe. Wittgenstein argues that our network of concepts, which he calls *grammar*, cannot either conflict or accord with the facts. For what one says conflicts with the facts if it is false and accords with the facts if it is true. The concepts we use determine what it makes sense to say; and only what it makes sense to say is capable of being either true or false. Grammar itself is therefore *arbitrary*, i.e. not accountable to any reality. (This does not mean unimportant, capricious, or readily alterable.) A system of measurement for example, is not correct or incorrect in the way that a statement of length is; although of course some systems are more useful, convenient, and easy to take in and apply than others.

So, if Wittgenstein is right, religious beliefs are not *true* or *false*; and they are not *reasonable* or *unreasonable* either, if that means that they can or cannot be justified:

I would say, they are certainly not reasonable, that's obvious. "Unreasonable" implies, with everyone, rebuke. I want to say: they don't treat this as a matter of reasonability. Anyone who reads the Epistles will find it said: not only that it is not reasonable, but that it is folly. Not only is it not reasonable, but it doesn't pretend to be.   (*LC*, p. 58).

The people Wittgenstein regards as *un*reasonable are apologists for, or against, religion who make the assumption – Wittgenstein calls it "ludicrous" – that religious beliefs can be corroborated or falsified by evidence. But unless religion is confused in this way with something quite different, it is not *un*reasonable. "Why shouldn't one form of life culminate in an utterance of belief in a Last Judgement?" Wittgenstein asks rhetorically (*LC*, p. 58). And this immunity from rational criticism extends even to Christian beliefs about Jesus:

The historical accounts in the Gospels might, historically speaking, be demonstrably false and yet belief would lose nothing by this . . . because historical proof (the historical proof-game) is irrelevant to belief.   (*CV*, p. 32)

In sum, Wittgenstein defends two principal doctrines: first, a doctrine about the meaning of religious discourse, and second, a doctrine about the epistemology of religious beliefs. The first is that the expression of a religious belief in words is not a prediction or a hypothesis, but "something like a passionate commitment to a system of reference"; the second is that religious beliefs are therefore equally immune from falsification and from verification (see Article 25, THE VERIFICATIONIST CHALLENGE). Critics and apologists who mistake religious beliefs for hypotheses and muster evidence in their favor or against them confuse religious faith and superstition, Wittgenstein says (*CV*, p. 72).

Is Wittgenstein's account of religious belief convincing? I doubt it. Admittedly, belief in the existence of God is very unlike a hypothesis in history or in science. But it does not follow that it is *nothing but* "a passionate commitment to a system of reference" – i.e. a commitment to leading a life in which questions will be asked, obligations will be acknowledged, decisions taken and actions performed, which can only be explained or understood by the use of religious concepts. And surely, if I had and retained that commitment, my belief that God exists would typically be part of my reason for doing so.

Perhaps one can defend Wittgenstein on this point: as he says, "where that practice and these views go together, the practice does not spring from the view, but both of them are there" (*GB*, p. 2). But even if this is often true, it does not follow that the "view" *is* the commitment to the "practice." No doubt the expression of a religious belief can often convey a passionate commitment to a way of life; but we should not infer that this is all it signifies, any more than we should infer from the fact that a moral judgment may convey admiration or disgust that this is all *it* signifies.

Wittgenstein is also right to insist that there are many different kinds of existential propositions. Belief in God's existence is *not* the same sort of existential belief as the belief that there are infinitely many primes or the belief that there is a planet between Neptune and Pluto. But one good way of seeing the differences between these propositions is to consider the different ways in which they are proved or supported. And since evidence and argument are not the exclusive property of science, Wittgenstein cannot be right to insist that if we try to prove or support the proposition that God exists we are already trapped in confusion, because we are treating religion as if it were science. It would, I think, be foolish to maintain that Anselm and Aquinas were peddling superstitions, or that apostasy cannot be based on reasons. It is certainly impossible to insulate religion entirely from rational criticism: "If Christ be not risen, our faith is vain" implies "Either Christ is risen or our faith is vain" for exactly the same reason as "If the weather is not fine, our picnic is ruined" implies "Either the weather is fine or our picnic is ruined." But if religious beliefs and systems of religious beliefs are not invulnerable to logic, why should they be cocooned from other sorts of rational scrutiny? (see Article 48, FIDEISM).

Finally, Wittgenstein may be right to insist that religious faith is not so much a matter of assenting to a series of doctrines as cleaving to a form of life. But nothing in his later philosophy of language, and in particular no part of his doctrine about the relation between language and forms of life, implies that a form of life cannot involve historical or metaphysical beliefs (such as that Jesus rose from the dead or that the soul is immortal) as well as concepts and attitudes: all of them – beliefs, concepts, and attitudes – in a mutually supporting relation. Nor does it imply that the beliefs which form part of the core of a form of life cannot include false or incoherent ones.

Christians have traditionally believed a number of well-defined historical propositions and rather ill-defined metaphysical ones, which Christian philosophers have sought to formulate precisely. This is not to say that these formulations (such as Aquinas' teaching on the soul or the Eucharist) tell us *exactly* what Christians have traditionally believed: on the contrary, a precise formulation cannot exactly capture something imprecise, precisely because of its precision. However, it can help us to settle whether the ill-defined belief is paradoxical or implicitly contradictory (*PG*, p. 76).

Are history and philosophy therefore capable of demonstrating that traditional Christianity is worthless, or that "people do all of this out of sheer stupidity" (*GB*, p. 1)? Not at all; for if the gospels are demonstrably false and no coherent formulation of the central Christian doctrines is possible, it does not follow that Christianity is either stupid or worthless. The Stoic doctrine of preferred indifferents may be incoherent; the doctrine that forms are material certainly is. It would be a gross mistake to infer that Stoicism was a stupid or worthless system. Incoherence is a defect in a system of religious beliefs, because if one can *see* that a doctrine is incoherent, that is a compelling reason to disbelieve it. But philosophers, who have a professional interest in coherence and consistency, are prone to exaggerate their importance.

Wittgenstein's influence in the philosophy of religion is due to scattered remarks, marginalia, and students' notes. He never intended to publish any material on the subject, and never wrote about it systematically. Nevertheless, it is possible to glean a moderately clear picture of his views about the nature and justification of religious belief.

His semantic doctrine is an ingenious application of a powerful strategy, which consists in making "a radical break with the idea [which lay at the heart of the *Tractatus*] that language always functions in one way, always serves the same purpose: to convey thoughts – which may be about houses, pains, good and evil, or anything else you please" (*PI*, §304). This strategy produced radical and fruitful ideas in the philosophy of mind and the philosophy of mathematics. Its application in the philosophy of religion has a kinship with both, but is less successful than either.

The epistemological corollary, that religious beliefs are immune from rational criticism and incapable of receiving rational support, has the interesting consequence that, as Wittgenstein said, "if Christianity is the truth then all the philosophy that is written about it is false" (*CV*, p. 83), but it has little else to recommend it.

Bibliography

Works by Wittgenstein

NB   *Notebooks 1914–1916*, ed. G. H. von Wright and G. E. M. Anscombe, tr. G. E. M. Anscombe (Oxford: Blackwell, 1961).

TLP   *Tractatus Logico-Philosophicus*, tr. D. F. Pears and B. F. McGuinness (London: Routledge & Kegan Paul, 1961).

PG   *Philosophical Grammar*, ed. R. Rhees, tr. A. J. P. Kenny (Oxford: Blackwell, 1974).

GB   *Remarks on Frazer's "Golden Bough"*, ed. R. Rhees, tr. A. C. Miles and R. Rhees (Retford: Brynmill, 1979).

LC   *Lectures and Conversations on Aesthetics, Psychology and Religious Belief*, ed. C. Barrett (Oxford: Blackwell, 1970).

CV   *Culture and Value*, ed. G. H. von Wright and H. Nyman, tr. P. Winch (Oxford: Blackwell, 1980).

PI   *Philosophical Investigations*, ed. G. E. M. Anscombe and R. Rhees, tr. G. E. M. Anscombe, 2nd ed. (Oxford: Blackwell, 1958).

Other works

Hick, J. (ed.): *Faith and the Philosophers* (London: Macmillan, 1964).

Luckhardt, C. G.: *Wittgenstein: Sources and Perspectives* (Hassocks: Harvester, 1979).

Nielsen, K.: "Wittgensteinian fideism," *Philosophy*, 42 (1967), pp. 191–209.

Phillips, D. Z.: *The Concept of Prayer* (London: Routledge & Kegan Paul, 1965).

——: *Faith and Philosophical Enquiry* (London: Routledge & Kegan Paul, 1970).

Rhees, R.: *Recollections of Wittgenstein* (Oxford: Oxford University Press, 1984).

Winch, P.: "Meaning and religious language." In *Trying to Make Sense* (Oxford: Blackwell, 1987).

19

Thomism

RALPH McINERNY

The Leonine revival

The modern history of Thomism may be said to begin with the appearance of Leo
XIII's encyclical *Aeterni Patris* in August 1879. Thomas Aquinas, who was not
mentioned until the midpoint of the papal document, was taken to be representative of a style of philosophy – an alternate title of the encyclical was *On Christian
Philosophy* – and not the unique instance of that style. But if Albert the Great and
Bonaventure, as well as many of the Fathers, were cited, the thought of Thomas
was said to epitomize the best of the best, such that in studying him one received
the benefit of all the others (see Article 9, THE CHRISTIAN CONTRIBUTION TO MEDIEVAL PHILO-
SOPHICAL THEOLOGY). Leo clearly regarded Thomas himself as a veritable Summa of
the perennial philosophy, a phrase appropriated by the Thomistic revival. And
Leo's successors, notably Pius X, Pius XI, and Pius XII, lent their authority to
Thomas almost to the exclusion of other Christian teachers.

During his lifetime (1225–74), immediately after his death, and throughout
the intervening centuries, Thomas Aquinas had as many opponents as he had followers. As a newly installed Dominican Master of Theology, he found himself in a
fierce battle at the University of Paris, defending the propriety of mendicant monks
holding university professorships. His appropriation of Aristotle was to make him
a target of Franciscan criticism, including that of Bonaventure, when the controversy over Latin Averroism heated up. And, among the 219 propositions condemned in 1277, three years after the death of Thomas, by a commission
appointed by the bishop of Paris, are to be found a number of Thomistic tenets.
The dispute over Aristotle, actually a dispute over Avicennian and Averroistic
interpretations of Aristotle, dominated Thomas's second regency at Paris
(1269–72). Its lasting effect was to establish a rivalry between the Dominicans
and Franciscans, with Thomas functioning as the paladin of his order, and John
Duns Scotus (and other Franciscans) opposing him. During what has been called
Second Scholasticism, which took place after the Reformation and was largely an
Iberian phenomenon, the Jesuits became the preferred opponents of Thomists,
who were usually Dominicans. It would be quite wrong, accordingly, to imagine
that Thomas enjoyed an intellectual hegemony in European universities prior to
the Reform, or indeed after it among Catholics. The Thomistic Revival initiated by
Leo XIII was thus in many ways a genuine innovation, according Thomas a status
he had not hitherto enjoyed.

What was the motivation for *Aeterni Patris*? The underlying assumption of the encyclical was that dominant philosophical positions of the day were false and pernicious. Errors about human nature and destiny, about the criteria for moral evaluation, and about the ontological status of the physical world, might seem to be matters best left to the interchange among professional philosophers. And it is well known that wherever two philosophers are gathered together, there are at least three different views. Leo's sense of urgency is explained as much by the practical, social, and political, as by the theoretical effects of the philosophical positions to which he objects. On the level of theory, if certain dominant philosophical positions were true, then Christianity is false, an inconceivable upshot for a rational believer. The papal presupposition is a straightforward instance of a simple argument: if Christianity is true, modern views of man, morals, and the universe are false; but Christianity is true; therefore those positions of modern philosophy are false. Leo was writing at a time when the agnostic, even atheist, philosopher was no longer a rarity, and he could not expect his argument to carry weight with the non-believer. Nor, however impeccably logical, would a believing philosopher call Leo's argument a philosophical one. That is why Leo appealed to Christian philosophers to confront the offending doctrines on a philosophical basis. Proving them false would not, of course, establish the truth of Christianity, but it would remove an impediment to seeing acceptance of the faith as reasonable.

While such philosophers as Josiah Royce welcomed *Aeterni Patris*, the papal recommendation of the thought of Thomas Aquinas had a largely intramural effect, certainly during what might be called the first phase of the Thomist Revival. This was the period extending from the late nineteenth century to World War I, during which new colleges and institutes, new associations and academies, as well as new journals and publications proliferated throughout the world. First order scholarship was soon translated into digests and manuals, so that the thought of Thomas could be taught in seminaries and colleges. L'Institut Supérieur de Philosophie at historic Louvain, founded by the eventual Cardinal Mercier, was one of the most noteworthy factors in this first phase. The religious orders, the Dominicans and the Jesuits, even the Franciscans, responded with enthusiasm to *Aeterni Patris*. There was an unsurprising symbiosis between the rise of medieval studies and the Thomistic Revival. The task Leo assigned his reader was twofold. First, to assimilate what Thomas had taught, and this entailed placing him within intellectual history, and, second, to show the relevance of his thought to the modern problematic.

Jacques Maritain and Etienne Gilson

If there was an undeniably clerical cast to the first phase of the Thomistic Revival, its second phase – from World War I to the Second Vatican Council, which opened in 1962 – was defined by laymen, most notably Jacques Maritain (1882–1973) and Etienne Gilson (1884–1978). Both men were French, both attended the famous Lycée Henri IV in Paris, both were prolific writers whose influence in

North America was solidified by long sojourns in the New World, and both lived into their nineties. In their published correspondence is included a letter from Gilson written late in life, after the death of Maritain, in which he said that he had finally grasped the difference between Maritain and himself. I, Gilson said, have spent my life seeking as accurate a knowledge as possible of what Thomas Aquinas actually taught. Maritain, on the other hand, sought to replicate in the twentieth century what Thomas had done in the thirteenth (Gilson/Maritain 1991, pp. 275–6).

Catchy as this comparison is, it is not fair to either man. Some of Gilson's most influential books were philosophical rather than historical, and Maritain was a close and careful reader of the text of Thomas. But Gilson's remark indicates the dual character of Thomism – and perhaps of any philosophical school. There must be the painstaking assimilation of the texts of the master, followed by the addressing of current issues in the light of the doctrine learned. Kantians, Platonists, Hegelians, have similarly double tasks. It is the rare thinker who achieves excellence in both.

Maritain, after completing his university studies in Paris, where he followed Henri Bergson's lectures avidly, went on to study biology for two years at Heidelberg. His conversion to Catholicism in 1906 led to an interest in the thought of Aquinas, whom he studied alone and with a Dominican tutor. Enthralled by the *Summa Theologiae*, he devoured the writings of Thomas as well as those of the great Thomistic commentators, Cajetan, John of St Thomas, the Salmanticenses. His first philosophical paper was "Reason and modern science" (1910). In 1913 he became a professor of philosophy at the Lycée Stanislas, wrote a book on Bergson's philosophy, then joined the faculty of the Institut Catholique in Paris and, with *Art and Scholasticism* (1920), began a series of books which conveyed a Thomist philosophical perspective. In 1932 he published both *The Dream of Descartes* and his masterpiece *The Degrees of Knowledge*. The latter was the most influential twentieth century rethinking of the thought of Aquinas, extended into areas and problems undreamt of by Thomas himself.

The first part deals with philosophy and experimental science, critical realism, philosophy of nature, and metaphysics. The second treats of "suprarational knowledge," and begins with a distinction between three wisdoms, metaphysics, theology, and mysticism, and then, after a discussion of grace, turns to Augustine and John of the Cross. While developing and defending the distinction between philosophy and theology, the *Degrees* makes it clear that Thomism in the full sense of the term comprises both. Not until the posthumous publication of Edith Stein's *Endliches und Ewiges Sein* in 1962 did Maritain's comprehensive effort to rethink Thomism have a counterpart. While in good measure an autodidact as a Thomist, Maritain was considerably more comfortable in the philosophical movement of which he was a leader than was Gilson.

Etienne Gilson studied under Emile Durkheim and Lucien Lévy-Bruhl, as well as Bergson, and wrote two dissertations on Descartes that were fateful for his future work. The investigation of the relation between Descartes and the scholasticism he professed to have put behind him, and a compilation of medieval texts which

160

clarified the Cartesian, ignited Gilson's interest in the Middle Ages. When, after teaching in various lycées, he became a university professor, first at Lille, then Strasbourg, and finally the Sorbonne, he offered a course in Thomas Aquinas which would become *Le thomisme*, first published in 1920. The subsequent editions of this work provide the best record of the development of Gilson's thought. Books on Bonaventure, Scotus and Augustine followed. Far more of a university man than Maritain, eventually a member of the French Academy, Gifford lecturer, wooed by Harvard where he briefly taught, founder of the prestigious series Etudes de Philosophie Médiévale, Gilson was oddly unclubbable. He was a severe critic of his fellow Thomists, as his letters to Henri de Lubac reveal, and far less amenable to the Magisterium of the Church than was Maritain. Pius X, who condemned modernism, made Gilson feel downright unorthodox, though he was always a fervent Catholic (Shook 1984, pp. 66–7).

Realism

The fundamental issue of the Thomism of Gilson and Maritain, as indeed it had been of the first phase of the Thomist Revival, was epistemological. Is the human mind capable of knowing things as they are? Modern philosophy is rightly thought to begin when Descartes gave primacy to the question of the objective reference of ideas and judgments. All judgments about the sensible world as well as about mathematicals were susceptible of a doubt that is only removed by the conjunction of the *Cogito* and a proof for the existence of God, the latter based on the claim that only the idea of God *requires* an extra-mental counterpart. Modern philosophy is in many ways the story of variations on the theme of the justification of knowledge. Increasingly, what is known came to be seen as a product of the knower, bearing on phenomena not noumena, until, with Hegel, the noumenal is seen to be idle and discarded: the dichotomy of thought and being thereby disappears. When the theistic context of modern philosophy fades away, a Protagorean epistemology begins to emerge: the human mind is the measure. This is a rough sketch of what Leo wished to counter by a renewal of the kind of philosophy represented by Thomas.

Thomism as a realism – that is the central claim. At the University of Louvain, Cardinal Mercier seemed to accept the claim that the justification of knowledge is the first philosophical question, and the critical realism of M. Noel and others continued that. This became the target of Gilson's attack. Gilson rejected the suggestion that Realism had to be established critically, since he took this to concede the point contested. Maritain sided with Gilson, but was less critical of the Louvain school, as is clear from his treatment of the matter in his *chef d'oeuvre*, *The Degrees of Knowledge*.

During the first phase of the Thomist Revival, there was much talk of Aristotelico-Thomism. The suggestion was that, on the philosophical plane, Thomism was equivalent to Aristotelianism, and vice versa. In the 1930s, the work of C. Fabro and L. M. Geiger called attention to the overlooked Platonic elements in Thomas, citing the pervasiveness of the concept of participation in

161

Thomas's writings. At much the same time, a holograph of Thomas's commentary of Boethius' *De Trinitate*, drew renewed attention to Thomas's doctrine that, while essence and existence are of course distinct in creatures, in God, and in God alone, they are identical. This "sublime teaching" (*haec sublimis veritas*) conveyed by God's self-description in Genesis as "He Who Is," became for Gilson the *clef de voûte* of Thomas's thought. Under his influence, Thomists spoke of the differences between Aristotle and Thomas Aquinas. Gilson's strongest statement of the antipathy between Thomas and Aristotle is found in *Being and Some Philosophers* (1949).

During World War II, the Pontifical Institute of Medieval Studies at Toronto, which had been founded by Gilson and included Maritain on its visiting staff, as well as the Faculté de Philosophie at Laval in Quebec, attracted many North American students. The School of Philosophy at the Catholic University of America, as well as some graduate programs at Jesuit universities, contributed to the emergence of a Thomism that was more historically sophisticated and engaged in contemporary philosophical discussions. The schizophrenia endemic to any philosophical school – accurate assimilation of texts, application to contemporary problems – brought about changes. For example, after World War II, Louvain became the repository of the Edmund Husserl papers; there was also great interest in such contemporaries as Maurice Merleau-Ponty. More and more courses were offered in Thomistic interpretations of contemporary philosophy and with correspondingly less emphasis on courses aimed at the foundational texts of the tradition. Eventually, the study of Husserl and Merleau-Ponty would lose all pretense of a Thomistic critique and/or assimilation.

Philosophy and science

The issue which rivaled epistemology in importance during the second phase of the Thomist revival was philosophy of science. Thomas's thought is unintelligible apart from the Aristotelian hylomorphic analysis of natural things: the products of change – *ta physika, naturalia* – are compounds of matter and form. Chief among the Aristotelian causes is the end or *telos*, and for Thomas too the final cause is *causa causarum*: the cause of the other causes. Thomas's whole philosophy reposes on the validity of this analysis of change. But has not all that been rendered obsolete by modern science? Theories were developed to show the compatibility of Thomism and modern science. At Louvain, the tendency was to say that natural philosophy (the locus of hylomorphism) was a branch of metaphysics, the product of a different kind of knowing than the scientific. Other Thomists objected that hylomorphism was presupposed by, not a product of, metaphysics. Their question was: what is the relationship between a philosophy of nature and mathematical physics? Maritain's theory dominated and was either accepted or modified by most Thomists, with significant criticisms of it coming from Charles De Koninck at Laval and the Dominicans of the Albertus Magnus Lyceum at River Forest. Most Thomists agreed that the very possibility of the continued relevance of Thomas's philosophy depended upon the successful resolution of the problem posed by modern physics.

Vatican II

In 1960 a new Pope, John XXIII, decided to convene an ecumenical council, the twentieth in the history of the church. Vatican II, as it was called, met in four sessions from 1962 to 1965. It was the central event for Roman Catholicism in the twentieth century. Mention of it is relevant here, because Vatican II was widely taken to be the end of the Thomist Revival and the embrace of philosophical pluralism. Philosophers who had been Thomists now declared themselves to be something else, usually phenomenologists, more rarely analytic philosophers. The thought behind this pluralism was that, just as Thomas had assimilated the dominant Aristotelianism of his time, so contemporary Catholics were to put to the service of the faith the dominant philosophy of the day. Since there was no such dominant philosophy, a pluralism resulted with a somewhat relativistic meta-theory which held that Christians could come to terms with any philosophy.

As a result, for a quarter of a century, only a minority of Catholic intellectuals devoted themselves to a study of Thomas Aquinas. The sense that one who was both Catholic and a philosopher should know Thomas well became attenuated. Issues and arguments that had reached the peak of interest, suddenly seemed to drop off the radar screen. Those who said that Thomas had been dethroned were able to marshal a good deal of evidence for their claim.

What could not be maintained, however, was that the Council itself had dethroned Thomas. His role as principal philosophical and theological mentor of Catholics was in fact reiterated and ever since papal recommendations on the order of *Aeterni Patris* have continued unabated. Moreover, consultation of the international bibliographies of scholarly work on the thought of Aquinas reveals an unbroken flood of entries. The observance of the 700th anniversary of the death of Thomas in 1974 inspired interest in the history of the Thomist Revival. The Pontifical Academy of St Thomas Aquinas publishes several series of such historical studies. None the less, it is undeniable that Thomas ceased to function in the curricula of Catholic colleges and universities as he had before Vatican II. This has had the interesting consequence of releasing Thomas into the wider philosophical world. Once Mortimer Adler had to explain that his interest in Aquinas was not a prelude to conversion. Now work in Thomas goes on in secular as well as Catholic universities, underscoring the truth of one of Leo XIII's fundamental assumptions, namely that Thomism can compete well as a philosophy. The works of such giants of the golden years of the Thomist Revival as Maritain and Gilson continue to exert their influence; there are many national as well as two international Maritain associations and several editions of collected works. The *Index Thomisticus* and the *PastMaster* album have made the writings of Thomas himself available on compact disk in Latin and English, respectively. Whatever form the Thomism of the future takes it will doubtless differ from the Leonine Revival, while owing much to its achievements.

Bibliography

Gilson, E., and J. Maritain: *Correspondance, 1923–1971*, ed. Gery Prouvoust (Paris: J. Vrin, 1991).

Gilson, E.: *The Christian Philosophy of St. Thomas Aquinas* (Notre Dame: University of Notre Dame Press, 1994).

——: *Being and Some Philosophers*, 2nd ed. (Toronto: Pontifical Institute of Medieval Studies, 1952).

Maritain, J.: *The Angelic Doctor*, contains *Aeterni Patris* (New York: Meridian Books, 1958).

——: *The Degrees of Knowledge*, vol. 7, *Collected Works* (Notre Dame: University of Notre Dame Press, 1995).

McInerny, R.: *Thomism in an Age of Renewal* (Notre Dame: University of Notre Dame Press, 1968).

Shook, L. K.: *Etienne Gilson* (Toronto: Pontifical Institute of Medical Studies, 1984).

20

The reformed tradition

NICHOLAS WOLTERSTORFF

One of the most salient features of contemporary philosophy of religion in the Reformed tradition of Christianity is its negative attitude toward natural theology – this negative attitude ranging all the way from indifference to hostility. In this regard, the philosophers of the tradition reflect the dominant attitude of the theologians of the tradition, going all the way back to its most influential founder, John Calvin.

Calvin was of the view that religion is not the invention of religious thinkers or powerful figures, but that the "seed of religion" (*semen religionis*) is located in human nature. He was not entirely consistent in his view as to the structure of that indigenous seed of religion: sometimes he thought of it as the innate belief in the existence of a creating and obligating God; rather more often he thought of it as the innate disposition to believe in the existence of such a God, this disposition being activated especially, though not only, by awareness of design. Calvin was equally convinced, however, that to account for the religious attitudes, beliefs, and practices of human beings, one had to consider more than this theistic component in human nature. One had to consider as well the affections of human beings, along with the beliefs they have acquired by induction into some tradition. And here one finds a truly appalling state of affairs. As a consequence, in some individuals and societies the *semen religionis* becomes what Calvin called "a factory of idols." In some, it yields a non-theistic form of religiosity. And in some, the workings of the *semen religionis* are suppressed to the extent that overt manifestations of religiosity are entirely absent.

The point is that the actual religious beliefs, attitudes, and practices of human beings are the result of the indigenous *semen religionis* working in conjunction with defective contingencies of attitude and belief. To use theological language: the actual religions and irreligions of human beings are the result of the interplay of our *created* nature with our *fallen* nature. Thus a theology based entirely on the theistic deliverances of our indigenous human nature is an impossibility. We need some criterion for sorting through the confusions, and some cure for our disordered affections. Reason will not do the work; it too is fallen, as intertwined, in its workings, with defects in attitude and conviction as is the *semen religionis*. Only God's revelation in Jesus Christ and in the Bible, and faith in that revealing God, can save and guide us.

Belief in God does have a "foundation" in human nature; Calvin developed the rudiments of what some contemporary Roman Catholics call "foundational theology." But it was a foundational theology developed from an explicitly Christian perspective. Calvin thought there was no hope whatsoever of all of us together developing theology just *qua* human beings, no hope of developing a common "natural theology," thus understood.

That has remained the dominant – though not indeed the exclusive – attitude within the Reformed tradition. The Princeton theologians of the nineteenth century, inspired by "Common Sense" philosophy – itself a product of Scottish Presbyterianism – held out some bit of hope for natural theology. But Karl Barth, the most influential Reformed theologian of the twentieth century, went beyond Calvin by not only insisting on the impossibility of natural theology, but also insisting that there is not even so much as a "contact point" in our human nature for the Christian gospel – nothing in our nature to which the gospel "answers." Christian belief is a creation of the Spirit. A famous and rather acrimonious dispute erupted between Barth and Emil Brunner on the issue – Brunner being another important contemporary theologian in the Reformed tradition.

Barth had little direct influence on philosophy. There is, in that, a certain historical justice: Barth made clear that in his theology he had little use for philosophy. He regarded philosophical theology as idolatrous; and as to philosophy of religion, he insisted that Christianity is not a religion. None the less, two important theologians of Barthian orientation have produced reflections which, if not strictly philosophical, are certainly on the borderline between theology and philosophy of religion. Thomas F. Torrance, working in Edinburgh, has explored the "interface" between theology and natural science in a good many substantial books. And Hans Frei at Yale, along with his associate, George Lindbeck, has explored hermeneutical issues in some depth.

On the surface, the rejection by the bulk of Reformed theologians of the possibility of natural theology has simply been a discussion among theologians as to how their discipline ought to be practiced: no natural theology, just scriptural theology. But as Alvin Plantinga observed in his "Reason and Belief in God" (Plantinga and Wolterstorff 1983), there's something else, of great importance, going on beneath the surface of these discussions. It was characteristic of the Enlightenment to insist that no one is entitled to beliefs about God unless she holds those beliefs for reasons consisting of other, immediately formed, beliefs which are *epistemically certain* for her – or at least, *more certain* than any of her beliefs about God could ever be. The position has come to be called *evidentialism* concerning theistic beliefs. The Reformed theologians who rejected natural theology were also implicitly rejecting evidentialism of this sort; in doing so, they were both forming the Reformed tradition on this matter and expressing it.

Not until this century, however, has that rejection moved significantly beyond the status of an intuitively felt conviction to become a philosophically articulate position. It was first articulated in more or less Wittgensteinian fashion in a number of essays by O. K. Bouwsma (Bouwsma 1984). More recently it has been articulated by Alvin Plantinga, Nicholas Wolterstorff, and a number of others (Plantinga and Wolterstorff 1983), into an account of the epistemology of religious belief which Plantinga has dubbed "Reformed epistemology." The theory consists of the double thesis, that many people hold many of their beliefs about God basically (that is, immediately, not on the basis of other beliefs), and that often they are *entitled* thus to hold them. Such beliefs are, in Plantinga's terminology, "properly basic." It's important to be clear that the claim is not that anybody in any circumstance who holds any belief about God is entitled to do so; the claim is rather the much more nuanced claim that a good many of the beliefs about God that people hold basically are entitled beliefs (see Article 49, REFORMED EPISTEMOLOGY).

Even that cautious claim is sufficient, however, to contradict such Enlightenment figures as John Locke, who held it to be a matter of fundamental human responsibility that no normal adult ever holds any beliefs about God basically. Ever since the heyday of the Enlightenment there has been a great deal of scurrying, by Christians and other believers, both to provide the evidence called for by Locke and his cohorts, and to reduce or modify their religious convictions until the point is reached where the evidence available supposedly supports whatever belief remains. Plantinga, Wolterstorff, and their allies, have called that whole endeavor into question. Rather than trying to meet the demands of evidentialism, those demands ought to be rejected. At bottom, Christian belief neither is nor ought to be an inference from more fundamental beliefs, nor an explanatory theory. What led Locke and the other Enlightenment figures to espouse evidentialism concerning theistic belief was their adherence to classically modern foundationalism; accordingly, much of the discussion surrounding Reformed epistemology has focused on the tenability of that general epistemology.

If one is fully to understand contemporary philosophy of religion in the Reformed tradition one must be aware of a second line of thought, in addition to the rejection of natural theology and evidentialism; namely, the vision of Christian learning characteristic of the neo-Calvinist movement. The movement's principal founder was Abraham Kuyper, turn of the century Dutch theologian, journalist, university-founder, and politician.

We have seen it to be characteristic of theologians in the Reformed tradition to deny the possibility of theology as a generically human enterprise. Theology is unavoidably "perspectival," shaped by the particularities of attitude and conviction that one brings to the enterprise. Kuyper argued that the same is true for learning in general. Not each and every part thereof; significant portions of natural science may well have good claim to being generically human enterprises. But the humanities and the social sciences are clearly perspectival. What Kuyper especially emphasized is that the *religious* attitudes and convictions that we as human beings bring to the humanities and social sciences unavoidably shape our positions in those disciplines (Kuyper 1980). He urged that we forthrightly acknowledge this fact, surrender the pretense that academic learning is or can be a neutral enterprise, and allow the academy as a whole to be pluralized, so that Christians can practice forthrightly Christian learning, naturalists can practice forthrightly naturalistic learning, and so forth.

Of course there was wide recognition among Christian scholars in the nineteenth century that not only in theology, but in other fields as well, a good deal of the scholarship being produced was inimical to Christianity. In the Anglo-

American tradition, Hume functioned as the great *bête noire* (see Article 12, EARLY MODERN PHILOSOPHICAL THEOLOGY). But such tension was explained as the result of scholars not acting with due objectivity and impartiality; competent and responsible scholarship, so it was assumed, would always be compatible with Christianity. Kuyper's suggestion was profoundly different. By any reasonable test of academic competence and responsibility, at least some of the scholarship inimical to Christianity is competent and responsible. But scholarship yielding the opposite conclusions may also be that. The test of competence and responsibility does not weed significant diversity out of the academy. The academy is unavoidably pluralistic. Kuyper was attacking the fundamentals of the Enlightenment theory of the academy, espousing in its place what would now be called a "postmodern" theory of the academy.

Kuyper's influence within the field of philosophy divided into three major strands. In the Netherlands itself there emerged the so-called "Philosophy of the Law-Idea," developed especially by Herman Dooyeweerd and his close associate, Dirk Vollenhoven. Dooyeweerd taught for many years in the law faculty of the university founded by Kuyper, the Free University of Amsterdam, and Vollenhoven, for many years in its philosophy faculty. In South Africa, the main figure was H. G. Stoker, himself influenced by Dooyeweerd, who taught in the philosophy faculty at the University of Potchefstroom. In North America, the main figure was William Harry Jellema, who taught for many years at Calvin College. Jellema was joined in the 1940s by a former student, Henry Stob; and in the early 1950s they were joined by Evan Runner, a disciple of Dooyeweerd and Vollenhoven. Plantinga, Wolterstorff, and a large number of other philosophers, were in turn students of these three.

The philosophical differences among these three strands was and is considerable; they are united, however, in the conviction that scholarship is unavoidably perspectival with respect to humanity's religions; and that the Christian ought to conduct his or her learning in fidelity to the Christian gospel. Wolterstorff's booklet, *Reason within the Bounds of Religion* (Wolterstorff 1976) and Plantinga's Notre Dame inaugural address, "Advice to Christian philosophers" (Plantinga 1984) are attempts to articulate that central conviction within the conceptuality of Anglo-American philosophy, with Wolterstorff speaking about Christian learning in general, and Plantinga, about Christian philosophy.

Though a sizable body of philosophical scholarship emerged within each of these three strands, it is only within the American strand that philosophy of religion, and more specifically philosophical theology, has flourished. Its failure to flourish in the Dutch and South African strands is probably to be attributed to the neo-Kantian cast of Dooyeweerd's thought. Dooyeweerd held that our concepts lack applicability beyond the "temporal horizon," as he called it. We can talk about human religion, and we can talk about revelation; but about the God revealed we can say nothing beyond how God is revealed within the temporal horizon. Philosophical theology, understood as philosophers speaking about God, was thus ruled out of court. That left room, in principle, for philosophy of religion proper; in fact, however, very little of that emerged (see Article 13, THE EMERGENCE OF MODERN PHILOSOPHY OF RELIGION).

The attitude of Jellema, profoundly influenced by Kuyper but scarcely at all by Dooyeweerd, was very different. Jellema's philosophical affinities were not at all with Kant but with the Christian philosophers and theologians of the Middle Ages; that led him to encourage rather than proscribe philosophical theology. As with philosophy in general, he understood philosophical theology to be inevitably perspectival in character; he himself practiced and encouraged *Christian* philosophical reflections on God. But he did not doubt that we could genuinely speak of God.

Thus it is that a good deal of the philosophy of religion that has emerged in recent years from American representatives of the Reformed tradition has been philosophical theology. No consensus has yet developed: there is no such thing as a new Reformed philosophical theology. Members of the tradition have lively disagreements with each other on almost all of the important issues – with the signal exception of the fact that all of them adopt a realist interpretation of theistic language and belief (see Article 26, THEOLOGICAL REALISM AND ANTIREALISM).

There is a shared ethos, however. It is typical of these philosophers both to take the whole tradition of Christian philosophy and theology with great seriousness, and to feel free to rethink elements of the tradition, sometimes coming out in defense of the tradition, sometimes in disagreement. In this rethinking, Scripture is always treated as speaking with authority; and recent developments in general philosophy are used whenever appropriate. Sometimes the Reformed philosophers of religion have themselves played a prominent role in those recent developments. It is in this spirit that Plantinga has argued against the medieval doctrine of divine simplicity (Plantinga 1980), and has developed a now-classic formulation of the free-will defense in which he espouses an incompatibilist account of the relation between God and human freedom which would hardly have pleased Calvin (Plantinga 1974). It is also in this spirit that Wolterstorff has argued against the traditional doctrines of the eternity and the impassibility of God (Wolterstorff 1988), and has developed a philosophical articulation and defense of the traditional claim that God speaks (Wolterstorff 1995). No doubt this freedom that contemporary philosophers of the Reformed tradition feel, to rethink elements of the classical theory of God in the light of Scripture and with the aid of recent philosophy, is a manifestation of the fact, mentioned earlier, that they do not regard Christian belief itself as in any way a theory.

Bibliography

Barth, K.: *Church Dogmatics*, vol. II, tr. T. H. L. Parker et al. (Edinburgh: T & T Clark, 1955).

Bouwsma, O. K.: *Without Proof or Evidence* (Lincoln: University of Nebraska Press, 1984).

Calvin, J.: *Institutes of the Christian Religion*, tr. F. L. Battles (Philadelphia: Westminster Press, 1960). [Especially Book One is relevant.]

Dooyeweerd, H.: *A New Critique of Theoretical Thought*, 4 vols. (Philadelphia: Presbyterian and Reformed Publishing, 1969).

Frei, H.: *The Eclipse of Biblical Narrative* (New Haven: Yale University Press, 1974).

Kuyper, A.: *Principles of Sacred Theology* (Grand Rapids: Baker Book House, 1980). [Reprint of *Encyclopedia of Sacred Theology: Its Principles*, pub. by Charles Scribner's Son, New York, 1898.]

Plantinga, A.: *God, Freedom, and Evil* (New York: Harper & Row, 1974).

——: *Does God Have a Nature?* (Milwaukee: Marquette University Press, 1980).

——: "Advice to Christian philosophers." *Faith and Philosophy*, vol. I (July 1984), pp. 253–71.

—— and Wolterstorff, N. (eds): *Faith and Rationality* (Notre Dame: University of Notre Dame Press, 1983).

Torrance, T. F.: *Transformation and Convergence in the Frame of Knowledge: Explorations in the Interrelations of Scientific and Theological Enterprise* (Grand Rapids: Eerdmans Publishing, 1984).

Wolterstorff, N.: *Reason within the Bounds of Religion* (Grand Rapids: Eerdmans, 1976).

——: "Suffering love." In *Philosophy and the Christian Faith*, ed. T. V. Morris (Notre Dame: University of Notre Dame Press, 1988), pp. 196–237.

——: *Divine Discourse: Philosophical Reflections on the Claim that God Speaks* (Cambridge: Cambridge University Press, 1995).

21

The Anglican tradition

BRIAN HEBBLETHWAITE

It can hardly be claimed that philosophy of religion, as undertaken by twentieth century Anglicans, both clerical and lay, constitutes a particular identifiable school. Many and various are the contributions of Anglican philosophers from the turn of the century to the 1990s. But we may discern a number of common threads running through these diverse approaches – a persistent sympathy for natural theology, a willingness to engage the dominant secular philosophy of the day (whether in quest of metaphysical support or in response to attacks on religion and metaphysics) and a determination to explore philosophically not only the *praeambula fidei* (preambles of faith) but also the central doctrines of the Christian faith.

Personal idealism

At the turn of the century, the leading Anglican philosophers of religion *could* be described as belonging to a somewhat loose-knit school, namely, that of "personal idealism." This theologically motivated reaction to the "absolute idealism" of F. H. Bradley and Bernard Bosanquet included, of course, many non-Anglicans and thus can hardly be identified as an element in an Anglican tradition as such. But the names of J. R. Illingworth, Hastings Rashdall, and C. C. J. Webb stand out as powerful representatives of the attempt to make personality the key concept for an understanding of reality.

The main influences behind this school were the nineteenth century figures of T. H. Green in England and R. H. Lotze in Germany. Illingworth (1848–1915) remained a country clergyman until his death. He was more a philosophical theologian than a philosopher of religion, appealing to Christian revelation as supplying the necessary qualifications and supplements to philosophical idealism. His best-known work, *Personality, Human and Divine* (1894) was a product of the late nineteenth century, but right at the beginning of the twentieth he published *Reason and Revelation* (1902), a paradigm example of Anglican apologetics, spelling out the reasonableness of Christianity, and indicating, in a way that foreshadows later developments, the cumulative force of the evidences for Christianity, including its central doctrine of the Incarnation.

Much the most significant member of this group was Rashdall (1858–1924), fellow of New College, Oxford, and later dean of Carlisle. Rashdall was primarily a moral philosopher and moral theologian. His two main works, *The Theory of Good*

171

and Evil (1907) and *The Idea of Atonement in Christian Theology* (1919), present, respectively, a thoroughly worked out version of ideal utilitarianism, including an admirable treatment of the ethics of punishment, and an exemplarist view of the salvific significance of the life and death of Jesus Christ. But the theistic philosophy underlying and informing these positions is best discerned from Rashdall's contributions to two symposia, *Contentio Veritatis* (1902) and *Personal Idealism* (ed. H. Sturt, 1902). In the former, "The ultimate basis of theism," he advances a characteristically idealist proof of God's existence (along the lines of Bishop Berkeley's arguments), and in the latter, "Personality, human and divine," he suggests that it is God alone who satisfies, without qualification, the criteria of personality: consciousness, unity, self-identity, and individual agency. This emphasis on the distinctiveness of persons made Rashdall willing to question the idea of divine omnipotence and incline towards what many would describe as a virtually unitarian doctrine of God and a non-incarnational Christology. This last was adumbrated – though not in so many words – at the notorious 1921 Girton Conference of the Modern Churchmen's Union and clouded Rashdall's final years with much intemperate criticism. Another highly accessible presentation of the metaphysics underlying Rashdall's understanding of morality and religion (including the Christian revelation) is to be found in the six lectures delivered in Cambridge in 1908 and published the following year as *Philosophy and Religion*.

Rashdall's hostility to mysticism, understandable in the light of his highly individualist conception of personality was by no means shared by his one-time Oxford colleague, W. R. Inge (1860–1954), whose name may be inserted here as that of an outspoken opponent of personal idealism. His Bampton Lectures, *Christian Mysticism* (1899) and his later volume, *Personal Idealism and Mysticism* (1907), articulate a trenchant critique of the spiritual atomism of the personal idealists and a conviction of the centrality for Christianity of the idea of mystical union with the triune God. Inge became a national figure when he moved to London as dean of St Paul's in 1911. Thereafter much of his writing was high-class journalism, but, among his many subsequent books, there stands out his Gifford Lectures, *The Philosophy of Plotinus* (1918), a magisterial presentation of the perennial spiritual and mystical philosophy which Inge held to underlie the Christian religion. "The goal of philosophy," wrote Inge in a much quoted passage, "is the same as the goal of religion – perfect knowledge of the Perfect."

The most professional philosopher of religion among the personal idealists was C. C. J. Webb, fellow of Magdalen College, Oxford, and later of Oriel College to which he moved after becoming the first Oriel (subsequently Nolloth) professor of the Philosophy of the Christian Religion, a chair established very much with Webb in mind. Webb, the first Anglican layman to be named in this article, was in some ways a transitional figure. He was at once closer to Absolute Idealism than, say, his friend Rashdall – as is clear from his Gifford Lectures, published as *God and Personality* (1918) and *Divine Personality and Human Life* (1920), and at the same time strongly influenced by John Cook Wilson, with whose growing realism, it may be said, the future lay. Webb's historical studies, medieval and modern – for example, his *Studies in the History of Natural Theology* (1915) and his *Religious*

Thought in England from 1850 (1933) – illustrate his attention to detail and to what he finds in history and experience, while his more theoretical works are informed by a profound conviction of the reality of God, of personality in God, and, unlike Rashdall, of personal relation in God. This last consideration is another pointer to the future: as we shall see, recognition of the compatibility of inclusiveness and distinction in God is a salient characteristic of the most recent writings of the holder of the Nolloth Chair in 1995.

Natural theology

Anglican commitment to the possibility and importance of natural theology has already been mentioned – and exemplified, within the school of personal idealism, by Illingworth and Rashdall. We now turn to a group of three, very different, Anglican philosophers, all of whom had roots in the idealist tradition but who moved further away from it than anyone so far mentioned: A. E. Taylor, F. R. Tennant, and William Temple. It is their contributions to natural theology that provide the thread linking them together.

Taylor (1869–1945), professor of Moral Philosophy at Edinburgh, is best known for his Gifford Lectures, *The Faith of a Moralist* (1930), in which he argues that morality points beyond itself to an eternal good – to God, to divine grace, and to immortality. But Taylor had already provided a wider defense of theistic metaphysics in the article "Theism" which he contributed to the *Hastings Encyclopaedia of Religion and Ethics* in 1921; and later he was to offer a version of the teleological argument in *Does God Exist?* (1945). So, in Taylor's case, the moral argument is embedded in a wider natural theology.

Tennant (1866–1957), fellow of Trinity College, Cambridge, and at times a country clergyman, was perhaps the most distinguished Anglican philosopher of religion between the wars. His major work, the two-volume *Philosophical Theology* (1928 and 1930), is still read as a fine example of cumulative reasoning in defense of a teleological view of the world. Its chapter on the problem of evil is a classic of theodicy, and its treatment of the relation between religion and science foreshadows much later Anglican apologetics. In Tennant's case, the moral argument for God is only the culmination of the cumulative case, which proceeds by reflection both on nature's capacity for evolution and on *what* has evolved over time. Tennant also wrote on *Philosophy and the Sciences* (1932) and *The Nature of Belief* (1943). Earlier he had applied his understanding of ethical theism to *The Concept of Sin* (1912), again exemplifying a recurring Anglican concern with what came to be known as "doctrinal criticism."

William Temple (1881–1944), archbishop of Canterbury for the last two years of his life, was the century's paradigm of a scholarly Anglican bishop. In *Mens Creatrix* (1917) and in his Gifford Lectures, *Nature, Man and God* (1934), he developed a powerful evolutionary natural theology, arguing that the process that has led to the emergence of mind and spirit here on earth should be evaluated in terms of its highest product. This "dialectical realism," as Temple calls it, suggests a transcendent God as its source and principle of unity – a transcendence that

173

requires at the same time divine immanence throughout the whole world. Indeed, Temple urges a sacramental view of the universe, which a revealed theology complements with the emphasis on the Incarnation. Here too Temple manifests a quintessentially Anglican position.

The response to positivism

By the time of Temple's Gifford Lectures, secular philosophy in Britain had moved in quite a different direction. The repudiation of idealism by Bertrand Russell and G. E. Moore and the popularization of logical positivism by A. J. Ayer led to widespread questioning not only of the truth but also of the meaningfulness of religious statements, especially those concerning God. The chief preoccupation of mid-twentieth century philosophy of religion, including that of its Anglican representatives, was to respond to this hostile philosophical environment.

I. T. Ramsey (1915–72), the third holder of the Nolloth Chair at Oxford and later bishop of Durham, was indefatigable in his attempt to defend and explain the meaningfulness of religious language in face of the challenges of hard-line empiricism. In books such as *Religious Language* (1957), *Models and Mystery* (1964), *Christian Discourse* (1965), and *Models for Divine Activity* (1973), Ramsey endeavored to show how talk of God was rooted in experience of the world of science and of human life, yet went beyond it as dimensions of depth and transcendence in that world are revealed to the believer. Ramsey elaborated countless examples of such "disclosure situations," where models drawn from the empirical world are qualified in such a way as to open up these dimensions. For Ramsey, the traditional proofs of the existence of God are not so much arguments as techniques for evoking disclosures of God. This approach, while highly fruitful as a way of articulating insights already shared, is open to the criticisms that empiricism is perhaps not best challenged from an empirical starting point and that more attention should be given, in philosophical theology, to the logic of *what* is disclosed.

No such criticism can be leveled at the work of E. L. Mascall (1905–93), lecturer in the Philosophy of Religion at Christ Church, Oxford, and subsequently professor at King's College, London. Mascall was the most traditionalist of the writers mentioned in this article. Indeed much of his work was doctrinal, in the school of St Thomas Aquinas (see Article 19, THOMISM), rather than philosophical. But Mascall, like Ramsey, was a trained mathematician, and in a number of books, he applied his considerable logical and philosophical skills to the epistemology of theism, to the relation between theology and science, and to the possibility of natural theology. Thus in *Words and Images* (1957) he tackles robustly the issues of verification and falsification and outlines a realist epistemology and theory of religious language. In *Christian Theology and Natural Science* (1956) he deals expertly with the key problems of creation, cosmology and evolution, free will and determinism, and mind and brain. Although inevitably somewhat outdated, this remains a useful introduction to the religion and science debate. In his Gifford Lectures, *The Openness of Being* (1971), Mascall returned to the theme of his earlier works, *He Who Is* (1943) and *Existence and Analogy* (1949), namely, the question of metaphysical approaches to natural theology. Surveying recent work in this field, Mascall took the opportunity to introduce to British readers the so-called "transcendental Thomism" of K. Rahner, E. Coreth and B. Lonergan, as well as defending again his own realist metaphysic and objective doctrine of truth. The book concludes with a persuasive account of the "openness" of finite being and especially of human nature to the new creative activity of God, but at the same time with a highly traditional defense of God's changelessness and non-temporality.

The most substantial figure in this group was undoubtedly Austin Farrer (1904–68), for many years fellow and chaplain of Trinity College, Oxford, and subsequently warden of Keble College. His first main work, *Finite and Infinite* (1943), was a fresh and sustained presentation of theistic metaphysics, worked out in explicit response to positivist criticism, using as its starting point a detailed analysis of human subjectivity and human agency. There is a comparable concern in Farrer to evoke a cosmic disclosure as there is in Ramsey but the systematic contextualization and development of the resultant metaphysics is vastly more impressive. Farrer came to think, however, that his characterization of the infinite pole of the finite/infinite relation had been too traditional, too absolutist, in the Aristotelian manner of the Thomists; and in later works he moved much further away from this tradition than Mascall ever did. The analogical base for this process of rethinking theistic metaphysics remained human agency and free will. In his Gifford Lectures, *The Freedom of the Will* (1958), he mounted a strong defense of freedom against determinism. (The book won high praise from the Oxford philosopher, P. F. Strawson.) In a number of much shorter books, written in the last decade of his life, *Love Almighty and Ills Unlimited* (1961), *Saving Belief* (1964), *A Science of God?* (1966 – American title, *God is Not Dead*), and *Faith and Speculation* (1967), he developed a persuasive theodicy and theory of divine special providence, based on his analysis of the nature of creaturely energies and agencies, which themselves become the natural vehicles or instruments of divine agency. This theory of "double agency," whereby God "makes the creature make itself" is illustrated most tellingly with reference to the paradox of grace, where the believer is most conscious of God's act precisely in his own willing response. Farrer's religious epistemology emerges at this point. Again with empiricist criticism in view he allows that "to know real beings we must exercise our actual relation with them." But, unlike the scientific case where we can set up objective and repeatable experiments, we can only know the will of God through actively embracing it ourselves. Farrer's theology of God is now thought through wholly in voluntarist terms. God exists as the supreme agent and will, actively engaged in providence and grace, entering into creaturely temporality – but without being subsumed within creaturely categories themselves. Farrer insisted to the end, against A. N. Whitehead and the PROCESS THEOLOGY (see Article 16) derived from him, on the "prior actuality of God," and, indeed, was prepared to spell this out in trinitarian terms. In sum, it may be said that Austin Farrer provides the best example in this century of the Anglican tradition's ability to marry natural theology, rational theology, and the theology of revelation.

The Nolloth Chair

The contribution of the Nolloth (formerly Oriel) Chair at Oxford to twentieth century philosophy of religion has been very great. Its first and third holders, C. C. J. Webb and I. T. Ramsey, have already been mentioned. (The second, L. W. Grensted, who held the chair for 20 years, was a psychologist rather than a philosopher of religion.) The fourth Nolloth Professor, Basil Mitchell, and the fifth holder of the chair, Richard Swinburne, both of them Anglican laymen, have, in their different ways, raised the standard and increased the plausibility of natural theology to new levels. Swinburne, in addition, is advancing the cause of rational theology – the philosophical articulation and defense of the main articles of Christian doctrine – with a high degree of professional expertise.

Mitchell (b. 1917) held the Nolloth Chair from 1969 to 1984. He is best known for his book, *The Justification of Religious Belief* (1973), in which he developed and popularized the notion of a cumulative case for a theistic interpretation of the world – that is to say, the patient building up of considerations which, together, may be seen to support the conclusion like the four legs of a chair. Mitchell, unlike his successor, sees this as an informal kind of probabilistic reasoning, comparable to the kind of argumentation one finds in law or history, much depending on the skill and judiciousness of the reasoner. Mitchell is himself the most balanced and judicious of Anglican philosophers of religion. He is also a moral philosopher and his Gifford Lectures, *Morality: Religious and Secular* (1980), provide a wise assessment of the weaknesses of modern moral philosophy and of the relative strength of a religious ethic. In his retirement, Mitchell has written much on faith and reason, taking account of "Reformed epistemology" without being seduced by it, and showing how the commitments of religious faith are not opposed to the requirements of critical self-scrutiny. On these topics we may refer to the rather curiously entitled collection, *How to Play Theological Ping-Pong* (1990), and *Faith and Criticism* (1994).

Swinburne (b. 1934) moved from the professorship of philosophy at Keele University to the Nolloth Chair in 1985. His output has been immense. He had already completed the philosophy of religion trilogy, *The Coherence of Theism* (1977), *The Existence of God* (1979), and *Faith and Reason* (1981), which dealt, respectively, with the concept of God and its intelligibility, with the theistic arguments and their cumulative force, and with religious epistemology. The natural theology exemplified by the second of these volumes is comparable to that of Mitchell, but is much more formal, employing a technical theorem in modern probability theory to work out the degree of confirmation given to theistic belief by the theistic arguments taken separately and together. Interestingly, he concludes that only when taken together and in connection with the appeal to religious experience do the arguments render it more probable than not that God exists.

There followed Swinburne's Gifford Lectures, *The Evolution of the Soul* (1986) – a rigorous defense of mind/body dualism, after which he embarked upon a tetralogy of philosophical theology books, the first three of which have now appeared, *Responsibility and Atonement* (1989), *Revelation* (1992), and *The Christian God*

(1994). In each case the philosophical groundwork is meticulously prepared and then applied to the areas of Christian doctrine in question. The result is a defense of the coherence of Christian theism in a much fuller sense than that of his first philosophy of religion book. Indeed *The Christian God* contains the most unqualified defense of social trinitarianism to have appeared in the West since Richard of St Victor in the twelfth century. It has to be admitted that professional theologians remain uneasy about Swinburne's work. They accuse him of working with too anthropomorphic an idea of God and too literalist an understanding of religious language. There is a gap here between the theologians and the philosophers that is found in the American context as well. But the theologians can hardly afford to ignore the kind of philosophical defense of Christian doctrine with the degree of professional skill that Swinburne shows.

Other voices

Space prevents more than a mention of some other Anglican philosophers who have contributed significantly to twentieth century philosophy of religion. G. F. Woods (1907–66), dean of Downing College, Cambridge, and for a short time professor at King's College, London, in an unjustly neglected work, *Theological Explanation* (1958), expounded with great care the case for personal explanation as the most far-reaching kind of explanation available in any sphere, and in his inaugural lecture at London made the case for the necessity of "doctrinal criticism," such as was in fact already being attempted by Farrer, and would later be developed, in another key, by Swinburne.

John Macquarrie (b. 1919), Lady Margaret professor of Divinity at Oxford from 1970 to 1986, a most prolific author, has made a distinctive contribution in his use of existentialist philosophy in the articulation of Christian doctrine – a resource otherwise foreign to the Anglican temperament and mind. *An Existentialist Theology* (1955) and his Gifford Lectures, *In Search of Deity* (1984), are but two of some twenty books that have flowed from his pen.

Two Anglican laymen, Ninian Smart (b. 1927) and Donald MacKinnon (1913–94) have perhaps, in their different ways, had greater influence than any in the postwar period. Smart, whose early books, *Reasons and Faiths* (1958) and *Doctrine and Argument in Indian Philosophy* (1964), showed considerable philosophical expertise, has helped to make the study of comparative religion and the phenomenology of religion central not only to religious studies in general but to the philosophy of religion in particular. It is no longer possible, even for Anglicans, to pursue the subject in the context of the Christian tradition alone. MacKinnon, despite the tortuous nature of his verbal and written style, combined a polymathic knowledge of philosophy, literature, politics, and theology with a depth of insight and a dogged persistence in wrestling with the most intractable of human themes; and his pupils and audiences worldwide will never forget the way in which they were made to face up to the fundamental problems of existence, metaphysics, and tragedy. Something, but only something, of this emerged in his Gifford Lectures, *The Problem of Metaphysics* (1974).

The Anglican tradition worldwide

Inevitably this article has restricted itself to British philosophy of religion. It is hard enough to identify an Anglican tradition as such in that restricted context. Philosophers of religion in other countries who happen to be Anglicans are even less susceptible to classification within a distinctive tradition. But it may be mentioned, in conclusion, that within the remarkable Society of Christian Philosophers in the United States, who, together with Swinburne in England, have brought such high standards of philosophical competence to the analysis of Christian theism and Christian doctrine, there are to be found a number of Episcopalians, some of whose names will feature elsewhere in this volume, most notably that of William Alston (b. 1921), whose major study in the epistemology of religion, *Perceiving God* (1991), exemplifies a quintessentially Anglican penchant for unashamed natural theology.

Bibliography

Farrer, A. M.: *Faith and Speculation* (London: Adam & Charles Black, 1967).

MacKinnon, D. M.: *The Problem of Metaphysics* (Cambridge: Cambridge University Press, 1974).

Mitchell, B. G.: *The Justification of Religious Belief* (London: Macmillan, 1973).

Ramsey, I. T.: *Religious Language* (London: SCM Press, 1957).

Rashdall, H.: *The Theory of Good and Evil*, 2 vols. (Oxford: Oxford University Press, 1907).

Swinburne, R. G.: *The Existence of God* (Oxford: Clarendon Press, 1979).

——: *The Christian God* (Oxford: Clarendon Press, 1994).

Tennant, F. R.: *Philosophical Theology*, 2 vols. (Cambridge: Cambridge University Press, 1928 and 1930).

Webb, C. C. J.: *God and Personality* (London: Allen and Unwin, 1919).

22

The Jewish tradition

ROBERT GIBBS

Introduction

Jewish philosophy in the twentieth century has been led by a series of thinkers who emphasize a radical ethics. As philosophers, the group has made a continuing argument that ethics is first philosophy, and that social relations are the primary concern of ethics. They have translated theological concepts into ethical responsibilities. And in translating, they follow in a long tradition of Jewish thought. This article will first introduce this set of philosophers, then discuss the relationship of idealism and empiricism in their work. The third section will present their best-known emphasis: the dialogic nature of experience and thought. The fourth section will examine its implications for theology, and finally the conclusion will discuss these philosophers' interests in Jewish texts.

While Jewish philosophy has a long history, the key figure for its contemporary emergence is Hermann Cohen (1842–1918). Cohen was the leader of the Marburg school, the great re-discovering of Kant in the late nineteenth century. While all of Cohen's system addressed Jewish themes directly, and indeed conformed to an idealist concept of ethical monotheism, only later in his life did Cohen devote his philosophical energies to extensive direct examination of Jewish thought. The culmination was his final work *Religion of Reason out of the Sources of Judaism* (1919). Cohen argued that there is rational religion, religion produced by reason alone, but that Jewish sources provided key insight for constructing that religion. Particularly important were the insights into the re-creation of the individual in repentance and atonement, the messianic hope for a peaceful world, and the suffering of the Jewish people for the sins of the world. Cohen dominated the Jewish intellectual world during his life, and his account of these various themes has formed part of the agenda of Jewish philosophy throughout this century.

One of Cohen's students was Franz Rosenzweig (1886–1929). Rosenzweig was raised in a largely assimilated family, and eventually came to study Jewish thought philosophically. He wrote a dissertation with Meinecke on *Hegel and the State*, but opted not to pursue an academic career. Instead, he began an adult education school in Frankfurt (Freies Jüdisches Lehrhaus), where the German-Jewish community could learn more about Jewish tradition not only from Rosenzweig, but also from Martin Buber, Gershom Scholen, S. Y. Agnon, Nahum Glatzer, and others. Rosenzweig wrote only one other book, *The Star of Redemption*. After completing that book at the conclusion of the war, he lectured and wrote various smaller essays, and devoted his productive time to translation of, and commentary on, traditional texts. *The Star*, however is one of the grandest, most profound, and most challenging works in the whole of philosophical literature. Constructed with a rigorous and somewhat obscure architectonic, it has three tiers of eternities, each of which has its own methodology, and its own social reality. In this article, it would be impossible to give a fair sense of how the book works, but it directly transforms and challenges the work of his teacher, Cohen. Moreover, within this set of thinkers, Rosenzweig emerges as the intellectual leader. He not only transformed Cohen's thought, but he also directly challenged and aided Buber, particularly throughout the 1920s. And Emmanuel Levinas frankly admits in various places his great debt to Rosenzweig, and to *The Star* in particular.

Rosenzweig cooperated with Martin Buber (1878–1965) in a translation of the Bible into German during his last years. Rosenzweig was stricken with amyotrophic lateral sclerosis (ALS) and died at the age of 43. Buber, however, had a long and influential life, contributing to various intellectual movements, including the reception of Hasidic thought in the West, the emergence of Zionism, dialogical philosophy, and a humanist recovery of the Bible. The single most influential work from this group of writers, *I and You*, explored the relations between a speaker and others, displaying the key ethical responsibility in using language. The essays collected in the volume, *Between Man and Man*, develop this theme further, and also situate it in relation to existentialism (see Article 17, PHENOMENOLOGY AND EXISTENTIALISM).

The fourth and final member of this group is Emmanuel Levinas (1906–95). Levinas was raised in Lithuania and Russia, but moved to France in 1926. He was a student of Edmund Husserl and Martin Heidegger and the first translator of Husserl into French. He was an instructor and then principal of a Jewish school for training teachers, and only received an academic position in 1961, coinciding with the publication of his most important work, *Totality and Infinity*. This was followed in 1974 by a more dense and difficult work, *Otherwise than Being or Beyond Essence*. Levinas's work has transformed the phenomenological idiom into service for an ethics. His most famous concept is that of the face, as the address of another person to me that occurs when I am seen by another. Levinas's own writings, moreover, include a variety of essays on Jewish themes, including a set of Talmudic readings. His influence has extended throughout postmodern thought.

Epistemology converted to ethics

The initial step in this Jewish ethics is a critique of epistemology, and most of all, of an idealist epistemology. This step is largely against Cohen's system, but it is also against Hegel's. Interestingly, Cohen's argument for a thoroughgoing idealism itself has a Jewish analogue in creation *ex nihilo* (from nothing). Cohen argues that all knowledge and all experience must be produced through pure reasoning, admitting no contribution from passive sensation. He produces an idealist account of sensation by use of infinitesimal calculus, insisting that all knowledge about sensation must be based on the rational generation of sensation. To admit that there is passive reception in sensation is to limit God's freedom in relation to the world and to deny God's radical transcendence. Cohen, like the transcendental school before him, argues that all experience – of objects, of people, of culture – is produced in reason, indeed in pure reason. Hence he represents one of the high points of the idealistic account of the autonomous subject, transcendentally authorizing everything which is.

For his students and followers (including Rosenzweig, Buber, and also Mikhail Bakhtin and his circle) the problem that breaks this idealistic theory is the interruption by another person. When I hold that another person can appear to me only through my generation of the representation of that other, I compromise the other person's freedom. The discontinuity between me and an other, the imprevisibility of the other's freedom, indeed the contingency of the other's character and address to me – all break up the unifying integrity that a transcendental ego can give to experience. Cohen stretched both in his system and in his *Religion* to reach towards the particularity of the self. He discussed the creation of the I–you, focusing on sympathy for the other person, but the independence of the other person from my cognition was unassimilable in his thought. For each of the other thinkers the key moment for ethics is the inaccessibility of the other person to my thought, whatever I think, however I represent or intend others. The excess beyond my anticipation that another person bears reverses the epistemological authority of the self. Instead of acting as a clearing house or gatekeeper for what will be experienced, I become the object of experience, or become subjected to whatever the other chooses to do or say. Thought will have to take second place to another's address, appearing as a response to other people, and not as an a priori construction of what is possible.

But, despite this irruption, this ethics is not itself independent of thought's earlier idealism. Instead, it operates by inverting or reversing the system that enthrones the ego. Thus in the three "dialogic" members, there is a retention of a place for knowledge, indeed, for objectifying knowledge. This is clearest in Buber. who divides the world into I–you and I–it relations. In the I–you, I am open in a reciprocal dialogue with another person. I address that person directly, saying "you" to her. In the I–it relation, I regard or represent something else as an "it," as an object. Even people can be experienced in the I–it. For Buber, the I–it is not evil, not intrinsically a bad way to deal with things, or people. Rather, the stability and consistency of the I–it facilitates the knowledge and preservation of the possibilities for I–you dialogue. The two cycle through each other, in the best situation, and in no situation can an I–you last and endure. The relationship to an other requires moments of latency, where the possibility for I–you continues, but where the I–it appears.

Rosenzweig also required a place for cognition. Indeed, his argument in *The Star* requires a relation to pure cognition in order to interpret linguistic experience. Thus the linguistic turn cannot afford to dismiss reason. Instead, in Part I of *The Star*, Rosenzweig uses reason to construct three elements (God, World, and the Human). These elements are rational reconstructions of irrational objects, or of the unknowable God (or world, or human nature). The turn to language, in Part

II, requires an extraversion of the elements in pairwise fashion, as language is interpreted as the experience of limited two-term relations between pairs of elements. The resources for his theological interpretation of relations depend on having already secured independent terms. Only because God can be unknowable does revelation have the freedom and import that it has. Only because a person can withdraw from the world is moral action joining and trying to fix the world. Rosenzweig allows pure reason a place in his thought – as the concepts for interpreting the experiential relations of speech.

Levinas, too, despite his emphasis on the infinite in relation to another person, and the primacy of that ethical relation, preserves a place for idealism and its knowledge, under the rubric The Same. The title of his major work is not *Totality or Infinity*, but *Totality and Infinity*. When the transcendental ego intends its object of representation, it assimilates what is other to its own intentionality, and totalizes over its world. Since ethics is about the breaking up of that totality, it is all too easy to say that Levinas's egological reading of Husserl is a foil, a prime example of what is bad about the philosophical tradition. However, Levinas begins essay after essay by retelling the tale of philosophy as a totalizing idealism. The interruption by the face, the approach of the other, the wound of the naked skin – these various images of ethical assignment – are all situated after an often lengthy discussion of how consciousness works to unify and assimilate the world. For readers who want only to find out about responsibility, this detour through phenomenological idealism is often confusing and frustrating. But Levinas argues insistently that only as an extraverted idealist self can I become responsible for others, can I become ethical. The totality constructs a person who is able to not give to others, and so is commanded to give precisely what the person has hoarded. Idealism is not merely a prior historical moment, but is intrinsic in the emergence of this radical ethics. And in a similar vein, the postmodernism of this ethics is not a dismissal of the modern, but is rather a particular kind of transformation and retention of it.

Dialogues and others

The focus for this group is not, however, that idealism serves a key role, but rather that something happens in using language that breaks with what has been available to reason alone. The linguistic turn for Jewish thought is not so much a discovery of language as an inescapable medium for thought and for experience, but rather a discovery of a kind of pragmatics where relations between people are produced and lived in the act of speaking. The performance of speaking produces ethical relations not by subordinating desires to some general principles, but by offering signs and standing surety for the other person's words.

If we start with Buber, we can see that to say "you" to someone is to address that person directly, expecting to be spoken to in response. A "you" has a voice. To address someone as "you" is already to be in some sort of relation with the other person. Buber emphasizes a kind of cooperation between us, and demands that to say "you" is also to be addressable as a "you." The I–you is a reciprocal relation – but not one of simple unanimity or agreement. I can argue with you vociferously, but so long as I regard you or address you as "you," I am still in an I–you relation. From a pragmatics vocabulary, we see a variety of key concepts at play, most of all the indexicality of the terms "I" and "you": they do not name general characters or speakers, but indicate the specificity of speaker and listener positions – specificity not reducible to a rational deduction.

The issue for Rosenzweig and Levinas is still more complex: for both emphasize the asymmetries in speaking and listening. My role as listener is not the inverse of my role as speaker. First I must listen, and then respond. The responsiveness makes my own address (from my point of view) quite different than the address to which I attend. Moreover, in the first address to me both thinkers hear a command. The indicative develops only in response. I am obliged before I know, and also before I choose. This responsibility (re-sponse-ability) rests with me, but it is not symmetrically required of the person to whom I respond. For Rosenzweig, the key to interpreting the dialogue is to note that I cannot tell what the other person will say to me, and I might not even know what I will say. The need for time, the discontinuity in the conversation, makes listening and waiting for the other to take a turn central to the experience. Reason can deduce its principles and its conclusions in a timeless present, but speaking takes time. In Rosenzweig's work, moreover, communities form by saying "we," and not only "I" and "you." But even those groups are locked in dialogue with other groups ("ye") and achieve their own cooperative discourse in relation to further asymmetrical responsibilities. Using language, both as individuals and as communities, implicates both speakers and listeners in a wide range of responsibilities, and so orients ethics towards other people prior to justifying principles with recourse to reason.

God

There is also the possibility of a dialogue with God. One can say that prayer is a dialogue with God, an address to a "You." In Buber's work, we find this account of address to God to be the one I–you that cannot slip into an I–it, because God can be addressed only as "You." Buber also claims that God speaks to us in all I–you relations, that God is revealed in every moment when I am addressed as "you." That revelation is not revelation of God's properties, even of transcendental qualities. Rather, the revelation is instantaneous, but I do not learn anything about God. Indeed, the temporary quality of I–you relations accentuates how God is absent, or better, eclipsed, most of the time.

But when we shift to Rosenzweig, we find that room is made for transforming the instants of revelation into certain kinds of relational knowledge – knowledge garnered in linguistic relations, and knowledge that refers to those relations. For Rosenzweig, the traditional claim that God speaks in human language becomes literally true. Because revelation is a two-party relation, between God and people, God requires a medium that is accessible to the recipients of revelation. Language serves because it is the medium in which people form relations. Rosenzweig interprets the grammar of speaking as an organon for relations between God, human beings, and the world. Significantly, much of human speech about the world can be linked to a recognition that God has created the world – and in such a case God is not addressed directly, and so does not appear as "You." Human response to the irruptions of direct address serves to transform God from a "You" to a "He." (Rosenzweig does not examine the gender issues with great care.) But, in contrast to Buber, such address about God, in the context of address towards God and response to God, now appears as vital to the relation. Rosenzweig, unlike Buber, can redeem knowledge of God within the linguistic relations of human speech.

But for Levinas, the switch from "You" to "Ruler of the Universe" marks not the emergence of knowledge, but the measure of excessive objectivity. Indeed, the excess, the infinity of God, passes beyond presence. For Levinas, God cannot simply appear or join in a relation with a human. Instead, what we do encounter or experience is only a trace of God who has passed by. God's absence or presence is enigmatic: it can neither be converted into evidence, nor is it a simple absence. Rather, it is a trace that appears but cannot be resolved as a presence. The ethical import of traces is that responsibility commands but cannot compel. Moreover, God transcends the role of interlocutor. Yet the name, God, itself appears. Indeed, this austere theology appears in every good-bye (God be with you: *à-dieu*). It also appears in Jewish texts, and in the processes of reading those texts.

Reading Jewish texts

This set of Jewish thinkers inherits from Cohen an attention to traditional Jewish texts. They do not simply seek philosophical concepts in the Bible or the Talmud, but rather engage texts as sources for their philosophy, sources not only of concepts, but also of ways of interpreting. Most obvious is the joint translation of the Bible by Buber and Rosenzweig. Although Buber had to finish the translation alone, and although Rosenzweig was paralyzed during much of his life, the two engaged in the most important collaboration in modern Jewish thought. The translation attempted to disrupt the target language, to make German seem strange and new, by carrying over many Hebrew characteristics. The result is a deeply Jewish German Bible, in marked distinction from Luther's Bible. The commitment to displaying the difference of the earlier text to its new context reflects the way that dialogue is not about shared experiences, but about the risky bridges that do not reduce difference. The volume of essays that address this translation project stands as one of the most challenging accounts of translation, made richer by its concrete engagement with the Bible.

But Buber, Rosenzweig, and Levinas (as well as Cohen and others) are also readers. They participate in a hermeneutic version of the linguistic turn: that is, they think by interpreting Jewish texts, as well as philosophical texts. Unlike natural theology, their thought is situated within streams of interpreters, streams which have cut strata of interpretations: Bible, Midrash, Mishnah and Talmud, Commentaries and Codes, and so on. These thinkers are not merely adding a new shelf in the library of philosophy of religion, but rather a different tradition of reading – a way of reading that offers an alternative model for philosophical thought.

Characteristic of this reading is the attempt to solicit meaning in the text. An active trust animates the readers in the tradition when reading the earlier strata. This yields what Levinas will call the inspired nature of a text: that it bears more meaning than the author intends. The attempt to identify a singular historical intended meaning of a text is replaced with an ongoing solicitation of new meanings in new contexts. Rabbinic texts make this plurality of meanings explicit, often juxtaposing contrary readings and retaining even those opinions which are deemed inadequate. For philosophy, this introduces a sense that thought is located within a field of legitimate but contrary thoughts. Such openness is in contrast to a modern effort to fix meaning univocally.

This open field is not unbounded, not open to just any reading. Instead, the texts construct webs of opinions which are bounded by actions of the community. The social construction of rabbinic texts (Midrash and Talmud), for example, honors the memory of various sages, but obscures the identity of the editor, leaving the authority for the text in the community. Moreover, in Levinas's reading of Talmudic texts, he emphasizes that rabbinic reading emerges out of a concern for ethics and for others' suffering. While Rosenzweig interprets the Midrash as helping to form the Jewish community, Levinas interrogates Talmudic discourse to see the conflicts of responsibilities in play in making the weave of relations that is a community. These thinkers find the texts addressing contemporary communities and make the practices of reading accessible as a way of opening to the ethics that transpires between people engaged in conversation. The recourse to these reading and writing practices is the privileged way to discover the ethical address that forms the religious community. Jewish philosophy occurs at an intersection of reading Jewish texts and dialogic thought.

Bibliography

Buber, M.: *Between Man and Man*, tr. R. G. Smith (1939) (New York: Macmillan, 1965).

——: *I and You*, tr. W. Kaufmann (1923) (New York: Scribners, 1970).

Buber, M. and Rosenzweig, F.: *Scripture and Translation*, tr. L. Rosenwald (1936) (Bloomington: Indiana University Press, 1994).

Cohen, H.: *Religion of Reason Out of the Sources of Judaism*, tr. S. Kaplan (New York: Frederick Ungar, 1971).

Levinas, E.: *Totality and Infinity*, tr. A. Lingis (1961) (Pittsburgh: Duquesne University Press, 1969).

——: *Otherwise than Being or Beyond Essence*, tr. A. Lingis (1974) (The Hague: Martinus Nijhoff, 1981).

——: *Beyond the Verse: Talmudic Readings and Lectures*, tr. G. Mole (1982) (Bloomington: Indiana University Press, 1994).

Rosenzweig, F.: *The Star of Redemption*, tr. W. Hallo (1921) (Boston: Beacon Press, 1971).

23

The Orthodox tradition

PAUL VALLIERE

Philosophical and theological reflection in the modern Orthodox tradition has been both closely linked with Western thought and sharply divided from it. Most of the divisions can be traced to the separate historical evolution of the peoples and cultures of the Christian East.

The Orthodox peoples are heirs to the rich intellectual and spiritual patrimony of Byzantine civilization. Loyalty to this heritage steered the East clear of the most distinctive developments shaping philosophy and theology in the West, namely, scholasticism, the Renaissance and the Reformation. The decisive differentiator was probably scholasticism; at least this is how most Orthodox thinkers have tended to regard the matter. According to this view the schoolmen developed a methodology for abstract rational analysis which, while originally intended as a means of justifying faith claims, led to the cultivation of autonomous reason, i.e. reason methodologically independent of the dogmatic tradition and the lived (ethical, liturgical, mystical) experience of faith. The this-worldly sensibility of the Renaissance was one outcome of the exercise of autonomous reason; Protestantism, which employed scholastic methods to justify radically non-traditional interpretations of faith, was another.

To be sure, the Christian East did not "miss" the Renaissance and the Reformation out of theoretical considerations. The forcible incorporation of most of the Orthodox peoples into the Islamic Ottoman empire in the fourteenth and fifteenth centuries put a cruel end to intellectual pursuits and led to a steep decline in teaching and learning throughout the Christian East. The cultivation of secular erudition in particular was affected. Byzantium had known several periods of "humanism" in its long history, i.e. moments when the Greek literary, philosophical, and scientific tradition, which had never been lost, was renewed for a variety of useful purposes in church and state. But Hellenism was limited to the governing elite of the Byzantine empire, and with the destruction of the state it lost its *raison d'être*. The oppressed Christians of the East did not preserve their identity during centuries of Islamic hegemony by studying Plato but by clinging to their church.

The only sizable Orthodox country to escape the imposition of heterodox rule in early modern times was Russia. There, with its capital at Moscow, a mighty state arose to revitalize the Byzantine tradition. But this renewal did not extend to Byzantine "humanism" and could not have done so because of the nature of the cultural product exported to Russia by Byzantium. Unlike the Romans, the Byzantine missionaries carried the Gospel to the pagans of Northern Europe in the vernacular; the Greek language and the traditions of learning uniquely connected with it were not exported. While this approach to enculturating the Gospel has been much admired in modern times by missionary theorists and Slav philologists, it probably retarded the development of learning in the Christian East. Thus the culture of Muscovy shone with uncommon brightness in iconography, church architecture, asceticism, mysticism, and other pursuits closely connected with the practice of Orthodoxy, but one looks in vain for glimmers of the humane learning that was part of Byzantine culture. There were no schools or colleges, not even for training clergy. Theology as a formal discipline did not exist any more than philosophy did.

The academic study of theology and philosophy began to be cultivated in the Russian lands in the seventeenth century. Kiev Academy, which for nearly 200 years would rank as the premier theological institution in the Christian East, was founded in 1632 by Metropolitan Petro Mohyla. From the start the school had an apologetic vocation. Ukraine had long been under Polish rule, and the Roman Catholic authorities were making considerable progress in promoting a form of church union whereby Orthodox communities accepted papal authority while preserving their own liturgical and canonical traditions. The defense of Orthodox independence in the face of this threat was the main order of business at Kiev Academy. As so often happens, however, apologetics prompted the adoption of the opponent's methods, which in Ukraine meant the scholasticism of the Roman Catholic Counter-Reformation. The curriculum of Kiev Academy was patterned on that of a Jesuit college, most textbooks were of Western provenance, and Latin was the language of instruction.

In a famous study Father Georges Florovsky (1937) construed the history of modern Russian theology as a story of alienation from the Greek patristic tradition. Naturally he saw Kiev Academy as one of the culprits in the case. In its time, however, the Academy and other schools founded on its example fostered a significant religious and cultural revival, a Ukrainian Enlightenment which extended beyond the ecclesiastical sphere to include arts, letters, statecraft, and, finally, religious philosophy. The first original religious philosopher in the modern Orthodox tradition, Hryhory Savych Skovoroda (1722–94), was a product of this milieu.

After graduating from Kiev Academy Skovoroda eschewed priestly ordination. He taught poetics and classical languages in church colleges for a number of years before abandoning formal employment for a peripatetic lifestyle. His literary output, in a Russian idiom colored by Church Slavonic, includes poems, fables, an introduction to Christian morality, numerous essays in the allegorical interpretation of Scripture, and dialogues on classical philosophical themes such as self-knowledge and love of wisdom. The main sources on which he drew were ancient Latin authors, the Bible, and the Orthodox liturgical tradition. A God-intoxicated yet eminently sociable mystic, Skovoroda wrote exclusively for his friends, publishing nothing during his lifetime. Living dialogue was the medium of his philosophical *eros*.

Peter the Great relied heavily on the expertise of Ukrainian scholars and churchmen when he launched the titanic project of modernizing the Russian

187

empire in the eighteenth century. The methods of theological and philosophical study practiced at Kiev were adopted by the schools and seminaries set up by the Orthodox Church as part of the modernization program. Protestant and Enlightenment influences also began to be felt in Russia at this time, adding to the complexity of the theological scene.

In spite of powerful Western models, theological studies in Russia did not follow the European pattern in all respects. When the first Russian university was founded at Moscow in 1755, a theological faculty was not created for it; nor did theology figure in subsequent foundations. Early in the nineteenth century the Russian Orthodox Church established three graduate schools of theology, called academies, in association with the seminaries at St Petersburg, Sergiev Posad, and Kiev. A fourth academy was created at Kazan in 1842. The four theological academies, while administered exclusively by the Church, played an important role in the development of philosophy as well as theology in Russia.

The theological academies promoted the indigenization of theology in Russia. At all of them Russian was the language of instruction. Historical theologians – then as now more influential than Biblical or philosophical theologians in shaping Orthodox thought – began to direct attention to the patristic sources of Orthodox tradition. The academies also played a role in mediating the revival of contemplative monasticism to the Orthodox public.

The revival began in the eighteenth century in Greek and Romanian monasteries. Its vehicle was the *Philokalia*, a collection of patristic ascetical and mystical writings from various hands which the monk Paisy Velichkovsky and his disciples translated into Slavonic, Romanian, and eventually Russian. Because Paisy's movement propagated not just a monastic discipline but a body of texts, the way lay open for scholars and other consumers of theological literature who were not monks to appropriate the revival for their own purposes.

The spirituality associated with the *Philokalia* is usually called hesychasm, from Greek *hesychia* "quietude." At its core is the "prayer of the mind," a meditative discipline aimed at purifying the mind to such a degree that it can literally see the uncreated divine *energeiai* "energies" that pervade creation (but not the divine *ousia* "essence," which is unknowable). The ethical content of the vocation is supplied by mantra-like repetition of what came to be called the "prayer of the heart" or Jesus-Prayer: "Lord Jesus Christ, Son of God, have mercy on me, a sinner."

In terms of philosophical theology the most important feature of hesychast spirituality is its metaphysical optimism about the degree to which the "image and likeness" of God can be activated in human beings, both now and in the age to come. Western Christian theologians, at least since Augustine, have tended to emphasize the impairment of humankind's original God-like nature in consequence of the Fall, a view which the Reformation carried to an extreme in the theory of the radical depravity of human nature (see Article 68, SIN AND ORIGINAL SIN). Orthodox thinkers, by contrast, have held that the divine image can be obscured but not destroyed by sin. The dignity and beauty of human beings can be perceived (by those with eyes to see) in the most depraved of human beings. As for the saintliest, the divine image shines in them so brightly as to offer a glimpse of the eschatological goal of holiness: *theosis* "divinization," i.e. transfiguration in the divine glory (see Article 69, ATONEMENT, JUSTIFICATION, AND SANCTIFICATION). The saints validate the words of the Psalmist: "You are gods, sons of the Most High, all of you" (Psalm 82:6; cf. John 10:34).

The theology of *theosis* has been articulated with clarity and cogency by twentieth century Orthodox theologians of the neopatristic school, as it is called. John Meyendorff's pivotal study (1959) of Gregory Palamas, the fourteenth century Greek apologist of hesychasm, opened up the world of Byzantine theology to a wide theological public, East and West. Other medieval theologians prized by the hesychasts, such as Pseudo-Dionysius, Maximus the Confessor and Symeon the New Theologian, also received attention. In a stunning essay Vladimir Lossky (1944) developed the systematic aspects of the subject. Mystical theology, Lossky argued, is not cataphatic (positive) but apophatic (negative); it proceeds by saying what God is not as opposed to what God is. While this might sound like a recipe for skepticism, it is actually an ascetical discipline aimed at quieting and purifying the mind in preparation for transfiguration by the uncreated "energies." Apophasis is the methodological equivalent of *hesychia*.

Late twentieth century Orthodox theologians so admire the virtues of neopatristic theology that they tend to overlook its difficulties. One problem is the extent to which a theology fashioned to justify a rather extreme form of ascetical and mystical practice can serve as a comprehensive account of the meaning of the Gospel. Another problem concerns the content of the spirituality, specifically the role of neoplatonic concepts in it. The notion of a "prayer of the mind" leading to *theosis*, especially when combined with the concept of the metaphysical indestructibility of the divine image in human beings, could be interpreted as an application of the neoplatonic idea that the mind (*nous*) is inherently divine, albeit temporarily obscured by its envelopment in the material world. We know, for example, that the neoplatonizing theology of Origen and his monastic disciples gave the original impetus to intellectual monasticism in the East. Neopatristic scholars deal with this problem by distinguishing between two monotheisms: the impersonalist intellectual monotheism of Neoplatonism, and the personalist, biblically and liturgically shaped monotheism of the Orthodox Church. Naturally hesychasm is seen as an instance of the latter.

The two monotheisms hypothesis is more convincing as a historical observation than as a philosophical distinction. Clearly, the practice of contemplation was profoundly affected by the Bible, the liturgy and other Christian institutions during the thousand years of Byzantine history. The philosophical issue is whether the mystical theology of which neopatristic thinkers are justly proud is conceivable without the neoplatonic component. If not, then one should probably not speak of two monotheisms but seek the higher monotheism that accommodates the partial varieties; or abandon "monotheism" in favor of a more adequate concept.

Dominant since the mid-twentieth century, neopatristic theology is not the only force at work in modern Orthodox thought. Of equal importance, but quite different in its methods and concerns, is the tradition of religious philosophy

189

which originated in Russia in the nineteenth century. It arose in the generation following the Napoleonic wars when young Russian noblemen who had studied in European universities sought to interpret Russian reality, including Orthodoxy, using concepts drawn mainly from German idealism. The most notable thinkers of the first generation were Aleksei Stepanovich Khomiakov, whose work focused on church and society, and Ivan Vasilievich Kireevsky, who had a gift for speculative philosophy. Both were Orthodox renewalists dedicated to reinvigorating the sense of community and responsibility in their church. Khomiakov's term for these values, *sobornost'* "togetherness," became a staple of modern Orthodox ethics and ecclesiology. *Sobornost'* signifies the reconciliation of freedom with fellowship in the dynamic communion of the church.

Nineteenth century literary artists contributed to the rise of Russian religious philosophy, especially Nikolai Vasilievich Gogol, the metaphysical poet Fyodor Ivanovich Tiuchev and the novelists Fyodor Mikhailovich Dostoevsky and Lev Nikolaevich Tolstoy. Of these only Tolstoy elaborated a religious philosophy in discursive terms. His theological views, which owed much to nineteenth century liberal interpretations of Christianity, proved sufficiently heterodox to earn him excommunication from the Orthodox Church. The other writers, all deeply loyal to Orthodoxy, spoke chiefly through their art. Dostoevsky's works were especially prized by later Russian philosophers.

From a systematic point of view Dostoevsky's greatest achievement was his theological anthropology. By Dostoevsky's time the doctrines of Ludwig Feuerbach and other anti-idealist thinkers had reached Russia. Russian radicals enthusiastically embraced the thesis that theology was misplaced anthropology. Dostoevsky responded in a characteristically Orthodox fashion, the distinctiveness of which may be illustrated by contrasting it with the response to the same challenge made famous by Karl Barth.

As Barth saw it, philosophical radicalism was not the problem; it had merely exposed the original flaw of all idealist and liberal theology, which was the assumption that anthropology could serve as a starting point for theology. The theologians were hoist with their own petard; the solution was to return theology to its proper starting point: the revelation of the Word of God. Dostoevsky, by contrast, regarded anthropology as a natural starting point for theology. To his mind the radicals erred theologically because they had already erred anthropologically. Their "species being," while it posed as an empirical datum, was a sheer abstraction refuted daily by the way human beings actually behave. Every living human being is a numinous abyss, a pulsating matrix of motives from which transcendental ideals and religious promptings can never be expelled. "Broad, yes too broad, is man," Dmitry tells Alyosha in *The Brothers Karamazov* (1.3.3), "I would narrow him! What the mind sees as a disgrace is beauty to the heart. Is there beauty in Sodom? Believe me, that's just where it is for the vast majority of people – did you know that secret? What's terrible is that beauty is not just a frightening thing but a mysterious thing. There the devil fights with God, and the field of battle is the human heart." Dostoevsky rested his case on the metaphysical optimism of Orthodoxy: anthropology can be a starting point for theology because every human being bears the actual image of God in his or her being. Nikolai Berdyaev (1931), inspired by Kierkegaard and Nietzsche as well as by Dostoevsky, elaborated the proposition in a system of ethics.

The pivotal figure in the history of Russian religious philosophy was a young friend of Dostoevsky's, Vladimir Sergeevich Solovyev (1853–1900). Solovyev owed his influence not just to intellectual brilliance but to his genius for linking conventionally separated worlds: amateur wisdom-loving with professional philosophy, secular thought with Orthodox dogmatics, rational discourse with mystical contemplation. Methodologically Solovyev's philosophy was a form of idealism in the tradition of Schelling, especially the Schelling of the 1841 Berlin lectures and "positive philosophy" (concrete idealism). Solovyev's *Critique of Abstract Ideals* is one of the best cases for concrete idealism in all of philosophy.

The substantive ideal of Solovyev's thought was the grand union of opposites which he called *bogochelovechestvo* "Godmanhood," the divine–human union toward which he saw the entire world-process moving. Solovyev believed that Orthodox Christianity had an indispensable role to play in the historical realization of Godmanhood. He believed the same about other religious traditions, particularly Roman Catholicism and Judaism. Solovyev was a tireless prophet of ecumenism in Christianity and one of the most trenchant Russian critics of anti-Semitism.

Like the great German idealists, Solovyev cast his philosophical net wide, setting the agenda for Russian thought for years to come in several fields. His concept of *vseedinstvo* "the unity of all things" – which despite its name is not a formula for monism but for a metaphysics of relatedness that invites analogy with Anglo-American process philosophy (see Article 16, PROCESS THEOLOGY) – became the leitmotif of the twentieth century Russian school of metaphysics elaborated by Father Pavel Aleksandrovich Florensky, Lev Platonovich Karsavin and Semyon Liudvigovich Frank. Solovyev's writings on ethics and law, notably *The Justification of the Good*, contributed to the renewal of liberalism in early twentieth century Russia. His aesthetics figured in the rise of the Symbolist movement in Russian literature and oriented the work of the leading Russian aesthetician of the twentieth century, Aleksei Fyodorovich Losev. In *The Meaning of Love* Solovyev put the erotic on the agenda of theological debate, a subject developed by Vasily Vasilievich Rozanov, Karsavin and others. Finally, Solovyev's lifelong interest in the theosophic and kabbalistic underworld of speculative philosophy – another mark of his Schellingian affiliation – bequeathed the theologoumenon Sophia to Russian religious philosophy, inspiring Florensky and Sergei Nikolaevich Bulgakov to devise a discipline they called sophiology, i.e. the study of Divine Wisdom in the cosmic (and cosmogonic) process.

The overarching theological question about the Solovyevian stream in modern Russian thought is the extent to which it can be reconciled with Orthodox dogmatics. Neopatristic scholarship, providing far more precise knowledge of the dogmatic tradition than was available to Orthodox thinkers in Solovyev's day, has exposed the significant intellectual distance separating much modern Russian religious thought from the ways of patristic theology. The theoretical issue is compounded by the practical concern with rebuilding Orthodox church institutions following the ravages of the Communist period. Neopatristic theology with its explicit ecclesiastical commitments appears to pertain more directly to the task at hand than the speculative tradition of Solovyev.

Yet one should not jump to the conclusion that modern Orthodox thought has reached a fork in the road. The important attempts at reconciling speculative and dogmatic traditions made by Florensky (Slesinski 1984) and Bulgakov (1933–45) merit closer attention than they have received. Moreover, neopatristic thought remains unelucidated in philosophical-theological as distinct from historical-theological terms. The personalist ontology sketched by the modern Greek theologian John D. Zizioulas (1985) is a promising contribution in this regard but not a sufficient basis on which to judge the philosophical destiny of neopatristic thought (see Article 15, PERSONALISM) Meanwhile, the indigenous tradition of Russian religious philosophy, re-emerging in its homeland following the collapse of Communism, can be expected to renew its dynamic role in modern Orthodox thought. In the recent call for "synergistic" philosophy by a leading scholar of Russian religious thought (Khoruzhii 1994, pp. 7–12) one hears not just echoes of the Palamite theology explicated by neopatristic scholars but the exuberant strains of Solovyevian idealism. Orthodox thought seems poised for a remarkable career in the twenty-first century.

Bibliography

Berdyaev, N.: *The Destiny of Man*, tr. N. Duddington (1931) (New York: Harper & Row, 1960).

Bulgakov, Prot. S.: *O bogochelovechestve*, 3 vols. (Paris: YMCA Press, 1933–45). [Volume 1 is available in French: Serge Boulgakof, *Du Verbe incarné (Agnus Dei)*, tr. Constantin Andronikof (Paris: Aubier, Editions Montaigne, 1943).]

Florovsky, G.: *Ways of Russian Theology*, tr. R. L. Nichols (1937), Parts 1–2, *The Collected Works of Georges Florovsky*, ed. R. S. Haugh, 14 vols. (Belmont, MA: Nordland; Vaduz, Europa: Büchervertriebsanstalt, 1972–89), vols. 5–6.

Khoruzhii, S. S.: *Posle pereryva: puti russkoi filosofii* (St Petersburg: Izdatel'stvo "Aleteiia," 1994).

Lossky, V.: *The Mystical Theology of the Eastern Church*, tr. Fellowship of St Alban and St Sergius (1944) (Cambridge and London: James Clarke & Co, 1957).

Meyendorff, J.: *A Study of Gregory Palamas*, tr. G. Lawrence (1959) (London: Faith Press, 1964).

Philokalia, The: the complete text compiled by St Nikodimos of the Holy Mountain and St Makarios of Corinth, tr. G. E. H. Palmer, P. Sherrard and K. Ware, 3 vols. (London and Boston: Faber, 1979–84).

Slesinski, R.: *Pavel Florensky: A Metaphysics of Love* (Crestwood, NY: St Vladimir's Seminary Press, 1984).

Solov'ev, V. S.: *Sobranie sochinenii Vladimira Sergeevicha Solov'eva*, ed. S. M. Solov'ev and E. L. Radlov, 2nd ed., 10 vols. (St Petersburg, 1911; reprint, Brussels: Foyer Oriental Chrétien, 1966). [A new Russian edition of Solovyev's works is being published in twenty volumes by the Institute of Philosophy of the Russian Academy of Sciences,

Moscow. There is a German edition: *Deutsche Gesamtausgabe der Werke von Wladimir Solowjew*, ed. Wladimir Szylkarski, Wilhelm Lettenbauer and Ludolf Müller. 8 vols. (Freiburg im Breisgau and Munich: Erich Wewel Verlag, 1953–79).]

Zizioulas, J. D.: *Being as Communion: Studies in Personhood and the Church* (Crestwood, NY: St Vladimir's Seminary Press, 1985).

PART IV
THEISM AND THE LINGUISTIC TURN

24

Religious Language

JANET SOSKICE

The young Pip, hero of Charles Dickens's *Great Expectations*, had some trouble with religious language. He was fond of reading the family tombstones, he tells us, and

At the time when I stood there in the churchyard . . . I had just enough learning to be able to spell them out. My construction of their simple meaning was not very correct, for I read 'wife of the Above' as a complimentary reference to my father's exaltation to a better world; and if any one of my deceased relations had been referred to as 'Below', I have no doubt I should have formed the worst opinions of that member of the family. Neither were my notions of the theological position to which my Catechism bound me at all accurate; for I have a lively remembrance that I supposed my declaration that I was to 'walk in the same all the days of my life, ' laid me under an obligation always to go through the village from our house in one particular direction, and never to vary it by turning down by the wheel-wright's or up by the mill.

Pip reads the literal language of the inscriptions as figurative, and understands the figurative language of his catechism as literal. But no wonder the child is confused. No wonder well-educated adults are sometimes confused by religious language, for what is required is far more than an ability to "spell out the words." Pip's confusion is not so unlike that of the theology student who falls silent at that part of the Creed where he is meant to confess that Christ "descended into hell." He cannot, he feels, believe in a three-tiered universe where the damned live in fire beneath the earth's crust. He may be put at rest by the suggestion that the creedal intention was probably not so much geological as soteriological, drawing attention to ancient Christian beliefs that the salvation effected by Christ extends throughout time (past, present, and future), and that this is tied up with the notion of the "harrowing of hell" where Christ saves the faithful women and men from the Old Testament. (Christian iconography frequently showed Christ leading Adam and Eve, on either hand, out of hell.) The theological student might, of course, want to reject as meaningless this more historically nuanced construal of the Creed, along with his first, literal, one – he might wonder how it can make sense to speak of Christ being "present" to the past, or question the meaningfulness of the language of "salvation" altogether, but in doing so he is doing something rather different than rejecting a three-tier universe (see Article 71, HEAVEN AND HELL).

While "descended into hell" holds different difficulties than Pip's "wife of the Above," both illustrate that religious language is above all placed language. The contemporary analysis of religious language is above all aware that its construal requires some understanding of life and practice (Alston 1989), and above all location within the religious traditions and symbolisms of which it is part (1989, p. 8). This being said, amongst the "places" or "practices" must also be the language of theological abstraction (as in mystical and negative theology) and of more purely philosophical discussions of the existence and nature of God. Thomas Aquinas makes a distinction in the *Summa Theologiae* between the claims of *sacra doctrina* – revealed and to his mind privileged Christian teaching, especially in the Bible – and *theologia*, the speaking about God in which "pagan" philosophers such as Plato and Aristotle, as well as Christian writers, engaged. Yet the religious language of both poses philosophical problems; the language of Scripture is replete with metaphors, for instance, whose construals are not obvious. And the language of philosophical abstraction, while apparently more straightforward, contains its own layered complexity. If we say "God made the world" or even "God caused the world to come into being," we clearly speak of a "making" or "causing" quite different from that proper to human agents (see Article 39, CREATION AND CONSERVATION). Yet it is difficult to see what features these divine and human "makings" share. To say that God "caused" the world to come into being *except that*, since time and space are both features of the world God "caused," God "caused" the world to come into being "outside of" space and time, is scarcely to make a slight qualification. What can our language of causation mean when applied to one who is creator of space and time? Aquinas resolved some of these difficulties by means of his theory of analogy which he believed allowed us to say, for example, that God is "good" and the cause of goodness in creatures, without implying that we can comprehend what "goodness" fully means when predicated of God (see Article 30, GOODNESS). " 'God is good' therefore does not mean the same as 'God is the cause of goodness' . . . it means what we call 'goodness' in creatures pre-exists in God in a higher way" (*Summa* Ia.13.2). Aquinas's theory of meaning may no longer convince, but he can at least be credited with seeing the difficulties of God-talk, whether it be in the language of faith or of philosophical abstraction.

From the outset Jewish and Christian texts (those most influential for Western philosophy) concerned themselves with the words. God is represented in Genesis as "speaking" the world into being, and, in the already Platonized prologue to John's gospel, Christ is said to be the incarnate Word (Logos) through whom all is made. In Genesis again, the arrogance of the citizens of Babel is punished by destruction of their tower and confusion of their tongues. The idea of a lost original grammar where words faultlessly matched "things" was to have a long fascination for European philosophers and linguists.

The inadequacy of human speech to speak of God was a concomitant of Judaism's radical monotheism – God is too holy even to be named. Within Christianity, from its earliest centuries, God's self-disclosure to Moses from the burning bush (Exodus 3) as "I AM WHO I AM" was held to have the greatest religious and philosophical significance. While modern Biblical scholarship would caution against reading this kind of metaphysical ultimacy into the Hebrew text, theologians like Pseudo-Dionysius (5th–6th century CE) made much of the idea that God is too holy, too "other" to be named or captured adequately by any predicates applicable to creatures. God can only be named by what God is not, and in every case speech must be guided by what is revealed by scripture,

the inscrutable One is out of reach of every rational process. Nor can any words come up to the inexpressible Good, this One, this Source of all unity, this supra-existent Being. Mind beyond mind, word beyond speech, it is gathered up by no discourse, by no intuition, by no name. (*The Divine Names*, pp. 49–50)

This kind of meditation is by no means restricted to a mystical fringe. Augustine in *The Confessions* is equally mindful of the inexpressibility of the God who is everywhere present to him.

Anselm's famous argument in the *Proslogion*, if not successful as a "proof" for the existence of God, none the less provides a highwater-mark for religious language within this apophatic tradition. By his invocation of God as "that than which nothing greater can be conceived" Anselm speaks of God but avoids suggesting that God can be conceived. God can at best be invoked in prayer as that beyond naming and knowing. Anselm's Jewish near-contemporary, Moses Maimonides (1135–1204) writes similarly of the Tetragrammaton (the divine name) that "the majesty of the name and the dread of uttering it, are connected with the fact that it denotes God Himself." Thomas Aquinas distanced himself from any attempts to define God into existence, but believed that God's existence could be known by natural reason from God's effects. The names or attributes of God (simplicity, impassibility, limitlessness, and so on) are derived from these; yet, while these predicates have an initial substantive appearance, in reality they are negative and amount to glosses on what it might be to be "the Uncaused Cause" (see Article 31, SIMPLICITY; and Article 40, IMMUTABILITY AND IMPASSIBILITY). To say that God is eternal is to say that God is not a "creature" of space and time, and so on (see Article 32, ETERNITY).

Such strategies of reverent agnosticism were employed by the early theologians as a corrective against the human presumption to speak about that which cannot be named, but also to complement the positive and revealed knowledge of God they took as given in Scripture. In later centuries this "knowing ignorance" could be given more skeptical twists.

The modern English debate on religious language begins effectively with David Hume. Between the thirteenth and the eighteenth centuries much had taken place to affect European religious thought – the collapse of scholasticism, the rise of humanism and attendant suspicion, from both philosophical and theological quarters, of argumentation that was perceived to be speculative or metaphysical. Newton's new science disclosed a cosmos so apparently well-ordered as to evoke the lyric arguments from design which Hume was to dispatch in his *Dialogues Concerning Natural Religion*. Cleanthes in the *Dialogues* represents the Newtonesque apologist for design. It is less often remarked that Demea represents not just the orthodox faithful, but the "mystical" or apophatic strand of Christian thought mentioned above – all human language falls short of the glory of God. Hume is quick to suggest this pious agnosticism has little to differentiate it from a more open skepticism. If so little can be said positively of God, then perhaps nothing should be? Hume's *Natural History of Religion*, with its mock-historical account of the "origins" of religious belief, proposes that the divine names arose quite naturally as servile worshipers, fearful for their own security, sought more and more exalted titles with which to flatter their gods (see Article 12, EARLY MODERN PHILOSOPHICAL THEOLOGY). Within Hume's work it is possible to detect the seeds of two of the most devastating critiques of religious language in the modern period: first, that religious language is vapid or meaningless; and second, that, if one can speak of meaning, then certainly it is not the "meaning" religious people naively take it to be. Talk about God, on this argument, is quite literally talk about man writ large (Ludwig Feuerbach), or is the sigh of an oppressed creature (Karl Marx), or an indication of a disposition to behave in certain ways (R. B. Braithwaite).

Philosophy in the twentieth century has been preoccupied with questions of language. If Kant set out to sketch the bounds of what we might reasonably claim to know, then twentieth century philosophy has been concerned with what we might reasonably and meaningfully say. In the 1930s A. J. Ayer's *Language, Truth and Logic* popularized logical positivism in the English-speaking philosophical world and, in doing so, set a tone of philosophical hostility towards all attempts to articulate religious thought which would last for a generation. The positivists sought to weed out from scientific and philosophical assertions claims that were not so much false as, quite literally, meaningless. Ayer proposed a "verification principle" which, in its earliest formulation, suggested that in order for a statement to have factual significance one must be able to say what empirical observations would count decisively for or against its truth. Although Ayer's gunsights when framing his "verification principle" were not aimed only at religion, religious claims were amongst those least likely to be judged meaningful by its standards. The verification principle subsequently dissolved in its own acids, but for religious language the challenge stood (see Article 25, THE VERIFICATIONIST CHALLENGE). Are religious claims, if not verifiable, then at least in principle open to falsification, and if not, how can they claim to be meaningful? John Wisdom's parable of the "invisible gardener" (a clearing in the jungle appears to have benefited from a gardener's touch, yet no gardener has been seen near it) launched a debate on theology and falsification in which the participants debated what might have to happen to cause one to abandon an assertion such as "God loves us." In a related article, but within the same "spirit of empiricism," Braithwaite floated the substantially non-cognitivist thesis that religious assertions should be understood "as being primarily . . . declarations of commitment to a way of life" (Mitchell 1971, p. 80).

Of inestimable influence during the second part of the twentieth century was the work of Ludwig Wittgenstein (see Article 18, WITTGENSTEINIANISM). After an early positivist phase, Wittgenstein distanced himself from Bertrand Russell's insistence that ordinary language embodied the metaphysics of the Stone Age. The *Philosophical Investigations* make evident Wittgenstein's conviction that ordinary language is fine as it stands, and that most philosophical problems arise when philosophers ask inappropriate questions of a language "on idle." Wittgenstein's dictum, "don't ask for meaning, ask for use," encouraged movement away from the rather sterile ground mapped, to their own advantage, by "verificationists" and "falsificationists" on to consideration of the specificities of actual religious language. They include the varied contexts of the language of prayer, praise, moral injunction, and so on, but also of the rhetorical and textual structures found in religious writings.

Ian Ramsey's *Religious Language*, though admittedly more in the "empiricist" camp than displaying evident influence of Wittgenstein, was a pioneering book in the consideration of "ordinary" religious language. Religious claims, according to Ramsey, should properly be considered as qualified models, or stories, which under the right circumstances can bring about religious discernment ("the penny drops"). Ramsey was at pains to insist that this language, though "logically odd" was in some sense genuinely descriptive ("about God") and not in some merely Braithwaitean sense about moral commitment to pursue a way of life.

While the invocation of models goes a good way towards showing how one might find religious language "meaningful," it was not evident from Ramsey's "Christian empiricism" how these disclosure situations might claim to be more than emotive response. Neo-Feuerbachians and antirealists, such as Don Cupitt, are content to find religious language "meaningful," without committing themselves to belief in some absolute being who transcends the world. Some consideration of the issue of reference seems still to be required (see Article 26, THEOLOGICAL REALISM AND ANTIREALISM).

One great beneficiary of the new willingness to consider ordinary language was metaphor. That religious texts are highly metaphorical was disputed by no one. What was in question was what, if anything, might be the cognitive status of ineliminably metaphorical language. Earlier empiricists had dismissed metaphor as rhetorical ornamentation, part and parcel of the sophistries which true philosophers should "consign to the flames." But if we can only speak figuratively of God, where is the bedrock of speech? Closer attention reveals metaphor to be an important constituent of all language, and as a kind of language use, not a type of truth ("merely metaphorical"). Nor does the fact that an expression is metaphorical mean that it is not referential. Metaphors are particularly useful in areas where we need to be descriptively tentative but wish none the less to say something. One such area is the language of scientific theory construction, and the work of philosophers of science such as Mary Hesse has been drawn on by philosophers of religion in developing their discussion of the models and metaphors in religious language as "reality depicting" (Soskice 1984).

From an interest in metaphor must soon follow interest in the interpretation of texts. Metaphors can be construed as metaphors only within contexts (if I say "here comes the sun" you will need to know whether I'm referring to a colleague or to the no longer overcast sky to know what I'm saying), and for religious language the "context" of metaphor frequently is that of foundational texts (i.e. the Bible). The construal of complex religious metaphors (consider "the marriage of the Lamb has come, and his bride has made herself ready": (Revelation 19:7) requires of the reader some considerable acquaintance with Jewish and Christian uses of texts and symbols. Inevitably interest in actual religious language and philosophical problems of construal as they arise within religious texts and practice has meant a welcome convergence for philosophical, doctrinal, and Biblical studies in religion, and also between concerns of analytic philosophy of religion and of philosophical hermeneutics. This is most evident in debates like those surrounding "narrative theology."

Paul Ricoeur has shown a sustained interest in religious language throughout an impressively broad philosophical career. Beginning with studies in existentialism and phenomenology, Ricoeur became interested in the role of myth, symbolism, and interpretation (his is the much-used phrase "hermeneutics of suspicion"). *The Rule of Metaphor* is concerned both with exploring the creative and world-creating powers of figurative language, but also with preserving the "ontological vehemence" involved in metaphorical speech. Intentionality (the "aboutness" of language) has since his early studies in phenomenology remained one of Ricoeur's preoccupations. The work on metaphor and subsequently on narrative and time reflect his concern with questions of reference in the face of structuralist and later poststructuralist accounts of language which seem to cut language free from any questions of "aboutness" into a free play of signs.

Since religions are often such very *wordy* enterprises, almost anything within the remit of theology or philosophy of religion may provoke questions for the student of religious language. Let me here mention only two areas of contemporary interest, one (to return to a distinction made early on in this article) involving the "placed" language of a religion and the other the language of philosophical abstraction.

The first arises from feminist theology (see Article 76, FEMINISM). One of the strongest weapons in the arsenal of post-Christian feminists is substantially an argument about religious language – it is to say that the language of Christian scripture is ineradicably male-biased. In Christian (and other) religious texts we have a language and a symbolic system which privileges fathers and sons, and not mothers and daughters. No matter how much historical distance between reader and text, women immersing themselves in this tradition and its literature (so the post-Christian arguments go) are drinking an ideologically poisoned draft, in which male privilege and female subordination are ineluctably present. For the student of religious language the questions which arise are "how much can the symbolic language of a religion be revised or abandoned, without parting company from the religion itself? How do religious adherents read their texts as normative? What do we change if we change fundamental metaphors within a faith?"

The second example comes from "postmodern" philosophy, which, despite differences of emphasis, shares more concerns with analytic philosophy than is sometimes acknowledged. Recognition that we stand, as "knowers," already placed within languages, histories, and traditions (and in that sense not as atomistic Cartesian or Kantian agents) is an insight as familiar to English-language philosophers from the writings of Wittgenstein, Iris Murdoch, Alasdair MacIntyre, and Charles Taylor (to name but a few), as from Martin Heidegger, Michel Foucault, Jacques Derrida, and Luce Irigaray. How then do we do philosophy from within our own skins, within the "skin" of language? How can we proceed from the recognition that even our most seemingly straightforward claims are placed (consider "Columbus was the man who discovered America" in light of heightened "first nation" awareness) without collapsing into nihilism or despair? If Nietzsche was not wrong in thinking the death of God (and transcendental value) might in the long run mean the death of Man, then could the process be reversed? If not, how is speaking possible "under the emptiness of heaven?" Theological texts are once again attracting the attention from philosophers (and not just philosophers of religion) that they deserve. Derrida has noted that for the mystic (Pseudo-Dionsysius in this case) the "power of speaking and of speaking *well* of God already proceeds from God." God cannot be addressed as an object, but only, for the mystic, invoked in prayer. "This is why apophatic discourse must also open with a prayer that recognizes . . . its destination: the Other . . . which is none other than its Cause" (Coward and Forshay 1992, p. 98). Derrida – agnostic – even goes so far as to consider the possibility that not only talk of God, but all "speaking" must have its assumed origin in God. We are back to Anselm. It seems that some of the most ancient ruminations about religious language will continue to have a vitality for the foreseeable future.

Bibliography

Alston, W. P.: *Divine Nature and Human Language* (Ithaca: Cornell University Press, 1989).

Burrell, D. B.: *Knowing the Unknowable God: Ibn-Sina, Maimonides, Aquinas* (Notre Dame: University of Notre Dame Press, 1986).

Coward, H., and Forshay, T. (eds): *Derrida and Negative Theology* (Albany: State University of New York Press, 1992).

Fodor, J.: *Christian Hermeneutics: Paul Ricoeur and the Refiguring of Theology* (Oxford: Oxford University Press, 1995).

Mitchell, B. (ed.): *The Philosophy of Religion* (Oxford: Oxford University Press, 1971).

Pseudo-Dionysius: *The Complete Works*, tr. Colm Lubheid (London: SPCK, 1987).

Ramsey, I. T.: *Religious Language* (London: SCM Press, 1957).

Ross, J. F.: *Portraying Analogy* (Cambridge: Cambridge University Press, 1981).

Soskice, J. M.: *Metaphor and Religious Language* (Oxford: Oxford University Press, 1984).

25

The verificationist challenge

MICHAEL MARTIN

Background

The view that the meaningfulness of God-talk is problematic is not new. David Hume maintained that the only legitimate propositions are those of matters of fact and those of the relations of ideas. In a well-known passage in *An Enquiry Concerning Human Understanding*, he argued that, since sentences about God express neither statements of experimental reasoning concerning matters of fact and existence nor statements about the relations of ideas, any volume that contains them should be committed to the flames since it can contain "nothing but sophistry and illusion" (Hume 1955 [1748], p. 173). Moreover, many atheists of the past, for example Charles Bradlaugh (Stein 1980, p. 10), a well-known nineteenth century atheistic orator and writer, have denied that the concept of God has any meaning.

The positivist verifiability theory of meaning

The most sustained attack on the meaningfulness of religious language came in the twentieth century with the rise of logical positivism (Diamond and Litzenburg 1975, pp. 1–22). Wanting to eliminate what they considered to be meaningless discourse from philosophy and to establish philosophy on a sound empirical and logical basis, the logical positivists proposed the following theory of meaning:

1 A statement has factual meaning if and only if it is empirically verifiable.
2 A statement has formal meaning if and only if it is analytic or self-contradictory.
3 A statement has cognitive or literal meaning if and only if it has either formal meaning or factual meaning.
4 A statement has cognitive or literal meaning if and only if it is either true or false.

Since statements about God were believed to be unverifiable in principle and not considered to be analytic or self-contradictory, they were declared factually meaningless.

Three typical responses

There were three typical responses to the positivistic attack on the factual meaningfulness of religious language. Philosophers such as John Hick took it very seriously and attempted to meet it head on by arguing that religious statements are in principle capable of empirical verification. Hick argued that religious statements could be verified by postmortem experiences; that is, by experiences that take place in what he called a resurrected world – a world not in physical space – to "resurrected beings" (Diamond and Litzenburg 1975, pp. 181–208). But, as Hick's critics pointed out, it is not clear that his resurrected world is itself verifiable. Moreover, it is doubtful that the experiences of resurrected beings could confirm that an all-good, all-powerful, all-knowing being exists (Diamond and Litzenburg 1975, pp. 209–22).

Other philosophers, for example Richard Braithwaite (Diamond and Litzenburg 1975, pp. 127–47), maintained that the logical positivists were correct that religious discourse is not factually meaningful since it is not capable of empirical verification and proceeded to give non-cognitive interpretations of it. They argued that although religious language cannot be used to assert or deny the existence of any transcendent Being, it plays other roles in our language; for example, it expresses some moral point of view by means of parables. However, critics of the non-cognitive approach argued that this view of religious language completely distorts its meaning.

The most common reaction to the logical positivists' attack was to reject the verifiability theory of meaning. Thus, for example, Alvin Plantinga (1967, pp. 156–68) argued that the fact that religious statements do not meet the logical positivist criterion of verifiability, does not show that religious statements are factually meaningless; rather, the problem is with the verifiability theory.

Three standard criticisms of the theory and its present standing

There are three standard criticisms of the verifiability theory of meaning. One is that the positivist analysis of meaning seems arbitrary. It is held that there is no good reason why anyone should accept this theory, and that without adequate justification, the theory cannot be used to eliminate religious or metaphysical discourse. Another criticism is that the verifiability theory is self-refuting; that it is a meaningless theory in its own terms. Finally, critics hold that the positivists were unable to formulate a criterion of empirical verifiability precise enough to do the job expected of it, namely to eliminate metaphysical and theological statements as factually meaningless while showing the statements of science to be factually meaningful. They say that as it was presented in various positivistic writings, the criterion was either so broad that any sentence at all – even some clearly nonsensical ones – would be factually meaningful, or else it was so restrictive that it eliminated as "meaningless" the quite legitimate statements of theoretical science.

It is at least in part for these reasons that the verifiability theory is presently out of favor with philosophers of religion. Most leading theistic philosophers of religion believe that the theory has been shown to be inadequate and even leading atheists no longer take it seriously. Thus, the late J. L. Mackie in *The Miracle of Theism* assumed that any verifiability theory of meaning that entails that statements about the existence of God are literally meaningless would itself be highly implausible.

A few philosophers of religion do, however, still take the theory seriously. Kai Nielsen (1971, 1982), an atheist and perhaps the best known contemporary defender of the verifiability theory, has devoted several books to defending the thesis that religious language is factually meaningless because it is not verifiable in principle. Richard Swinburne (1977), a theist, has attempted to give a detailed refutation of the verifiability theory of meaning. More recently, Michael Martin (1990, ch. 2) has defended the verifiability theory of meaning in the context of justifying negative atheism – the view that one should not hold a belief in God.

Can the standard criticisms be answered?

The strongest available response to these criticisms can be found in the work of Nielsen. Although Nielsen was strongly influenced by the logical positivist verifiability theory of meaning, his argument is much more sophisticated and far more in tune with the subtleties of religious discourse. He does not maintain that all religious discourse is factually meaningless; on the contrary, he says that the unsophisticated discourse of believers in an anthropomorphic God is not meaningless, but false. He asks us to consider the view that God is a large and powerful spatial-temporal entity that resides somewhere high in the sky. A sentence expressing this is not factually meaningless, he says. We understand what it means and know in the light of the evidence that the statement it expresses is false. Nielsen is troubled, however, by the discourse of the sophisticated believer who says, for example, that God transcends space and time, has no body, and yet performs actions that affect things in space and time. He maintains that this sort of discourse is factually meaningless and therefore neither true nor false.

Nielsen does not claim that religious discourse is meaningless in all senses of "meaningless." In particular, he does not deny that religious expressions have a use in our language or that one can make inferences on the basis of them. He would hold, for instance, that the sentence:

(1)   God has no body and yet acts in the world

is clearly not meaningless in the sense that

(2)   God is gluberfied

or

(3)   God big impossible

or

(4)   Goo Foo is gluberfied

is meaningless. Terms such as "God," "has a body," "acts," "in the world," unlike "Goo Foo," and "is gluberfied," have uses in our language. Furthermore, (1) has no syntactical irregularities. In addition, "God" has a fixed syntax making possible certain logical inferences from (1). For example, from (1) it follows that

(1')   It is possible for God to act without a body

and

(1")   God does not have eyes and ears.

Nielsen insists, however, that none of this shows that statements like (1) are factually meaningful; that is, that they are either true or false. In the first place, he maintains that the mere fact that one can make an inference from some sentence does not show that it is factually meaningful. For example, from

(5)   Box sleeps more rapidly than Cox

it follows that

(6)   Cox sleeps more slowly than Box.

But it is generally agreed that (5) and (6) are meaningless sentences. Further, (5) illustrates that a sentence that has an unproblematic syntax is not necessarily factually meaningful.

Moreover, according to Nielsen, it does not follow that just because an expression has a use in our language it has factual meaning. He vigorously attacks the view he calls Wittgensteinian fideism that every so-called form of life has its own "language-game" with its own rules and logic and that one cannot critically evaluate a language-game from the outside. According to Wittgensteinian fideism, it is a serious mistake for a philosopher of religion to impose some external standard of meaning on religious discourse, for such discourse is acceptable as it stands. The job of a philosopher of religion is not to evaluate the discourse of a form of life but to clarify its logic and eliminate the confusions caused by the misuse of language in this form of life. Wittgensteinian fideism, Nielsen maintains, is committed to an absurd form of relativism, namely that every form of life is autonomous and can be evaluated on its own terms and cannot be criticized from the outside (see Article 18, WITTGENSTEINIANISM; and Article 48, FIDEISM). But this relativism, he argues, has absurd consequences. For example, it entails that the forms of life associated with belief in magic and fairies cannot be criticized from the outside.

How then would Nielsen respond to the three standard criticisms of the verifiability theory of meaning? He would maintain that the theory is not arbitrary. In order to understand a factual statement one must have some idea of what counts for or against it; indeed, he would maintain that it is simply part of what it means to understand a statement. That understanding what counts for or against a statement is part of what it means to understand a factual statement can, he thinks, be shown by actual examples. Consider clear cases of sentences that do not express statements, for example, "Colors speak faster than the speed of light," "Physics is more mobile than chemistry," "Close the door!," "I promise to pay you ten dollars." In contrast to clear cases of statements, we have no idea what evidence would in principle count for or against these. Nielsen has challenged critics of the verifiability theory of meaning to come up with one example of "an utterance that would quite unequivocally be generally accepted as a statement of fact that is not so confirmable or infirmable" (Nielsen 1971, p. 67). The verifiability theory matches our intuitions in clear cases of what is factually meaningful and what is not.

But why should we suppose that religious utterances are not cases of meaningful utterances? Nielsen maintains that we can legitimately suppose that there is something amiss in religious language because many religious practitioners suppose there is. Often, he says, religious believers themselves have doubts about whether they are believing anything that is true or false. This is not because of some externally imposed theory of factual meaning that they have accepted. He urges that the difficulty is intrinsic to sophisticated non-anthropomorphic God-talk with its references to "an infinite and non-spatial entity," "a disembodied spirit that acts in the world," and the like. Ordinary thoughtful religious people are puzzled to know what to make of this talk.

Nielsen can be understood to be approaching the problem as follows. Let us call the clear cases of factually meaningful and factually meaningless utterances, linguistic data E. According to Nielsen, the verifiability theory matches our intuitions with respect to E. Thus, the theory can be understood to be providing a clear criterion of factual meaningfulness. Once this criterion has gained support from E, it can be used to decide the more controversial cases. Given the fact, acknowledged even by many religious believers, that it is unclear if in speaking of God one is asserting any statements at all, one may wish a clear criterion of factual significance. The verifiability theory provides this criterion.

Nielsen's approach also provides an answer to the criticism that the verifiability theory of meaning is self-refuting. The criticism would be valid only if the theory is interpreted to be a statement. But on Nielsen's approach it should not be so interpreted. The theory is a proposal about how to separate factually meaningless sentences from factually meaningful ones and is to be judged in terms of how well it does this job. It provides a criterion for separating clear cases of factually meaningful statements such as "The cat is on the mat" from clear cases of factually meaningless statements such as "Close the door!" and it also provides a definite criterion in more problematic cases such as the sentence "God exists."

With respect to the third standard criticism of the verifiability theory of meaning that the criterion is either too narrow or else too broad, Nielsen argues that once one is clear about how in general the verifiability criterion is to be understood, the problems of particular formulations of the criterion can be ignored. Using a formulation of the verifiability theory based on Antony Flew's well-known paper "Theology and falsification" (Diamond and Litzenburg 1975, pp. 257–9), Nielsen maintains that in order to be factually meaningful, religious propositions must be confirmable or disconfirmable in principle by non-religious, straightforward, empirical statements.

Nielsen's formulation of the criterion can be explicated as follows:

(P_1) For any statement S, S is factually meaningful if and only if there is at least some observational statement O that could count for or against S.

(P$_2$) For any statement S$_1$ and any statement S$_2$, S$_1$ has the same factual meaning as S$_2$ if and only if the same observational sentences which count for or against S$_1$ count for or against S$_2$ and conversely and to the same degree.

Using this formulation Nielsen can show how some standard criticisms of the principle, for example those of Alvin Plantinga, fail. Plantinga had argued that

(7)   There is a pink unicorn

and

(8)   All crows are black

and

(9)   Every democracy has some Fascists

are ruled out as meaningless by various formulations of the verifiability principle although they are factually meaningful. For example, (7) is ruled out by formulations that require the possibility of decisive falsifiability; (8) is ruled out by formulations that require the possibility of decisive confirmability; and (9) is ruled out by formulations that require the possibility of either decisive falsifiability or decisive confirmability. However, on Nielsen's (P$_1$) none of the statements is ruled out since there are some observational statements that would count for or against them. Thus, he can maintain that the verifiability criterion of meaning, correctly understood, is not too restrictive.

Does the principle permit more than its followers would wish, however? Consider:

(10) It is not the case that all crows are black.

This statement is factually meaningful by (P$_1$). But it may be argued that if (10) is factually meaningful by (P$_1$), then so is

(11) Either it is not the case that all crows are black or God is gluberfied

which follows deductively from (10). Indeed, it may be said that it is plausible to suppose that any logical consequence of a confirmable statement is itself confirmable. But if this is allowed, then given (11) and

(12) All crows are black

we can deductively infer:

(13) God is gluberfied.

But since (13) deductively follows from confirmable statements – hence, from factually meaningful statements – it will be argued that (13) is confirmable and factually meaningful. However, since for (13) one could substitute any statement at all in the above argument, one could show that any sentence is meaningful. But this is absurd.

Although Nielsen does not explicitly consider this sort of problem, others have suggested ways to handle it. Thus, for example, Wesley Salmon (Diamond and Litzenburg 1975, pp. 456–80) in a general defense of the verifiability theory of meaning has argued that one may admit that a factually meaningful sentence can have factually meaningless components. Hence, he sees no problem in allowing that (11) is factually meaningful. Of course, as Salmon points out, such a view conflicts with the standard interpretation of the propositional calculus in which compound sentences must have component sentences that are true or false. But, he maintains, the propositional calculus view of this matter lacks intuitive support. Salmon goes on to show how it is possible to construct rules for eliminating factually meaningless components of compound sentences in ordinary language. Given these rules, one could say that (11) has the same meaning as (10). Consequently, one of the arguments given above:

(A)   It is not the case that all crows are black

Therefore, either it is not the case that all crows are black or God is gluberfied

is reduced to

(B)   It is not the case that all crows are black

Therefore, it is not the case that all crows are black

where the factually meaningless component of the conclusion is eliminated. The intuitive validity of (A) is thus preserved in the reduced version (B). The rule used to eliminate one component of the conclusion in (A) has its justification in terms of (P_2) since, according to (P_2), the sentence "Either it is not the case that all crows are black or God is gluberfied" has the same factual meaning as "It is not the case that all crows are black." However, in the second argument it is not possible to preserve validity since the conclusion is factually meaningless. In this way Salmon demonstrates the failure of one common attempt to show that the verifiability theory of meaning is too liberal.

But there is another way that one might attempt to show that (P_1) is too liberal. Consider the sentence:

(14) God is gluberfied and (if God is gluberfied, then this rose is red).

It may be argued that since (14) entails

(15) This rose is red

and (15) is confirmed by the direct observation of this rose, (14) is indirectly confirmed. Furthermore, since (14) entails

(2)   God is gluberfied

and whatever follows from a confirmed statement is confirmed, one would have to say that (2) is confirmed and, hence, is factually meaningful.

Since there are no redundant components in (14) and (14) is involved in the derivation of (15), (14) as a whole seems to be confirmed and hence meaningful by the confirmation of (15). Salmon argues, however, that this supposition is based on a widely held but incorrect view of inductive inference according to which induction is the converse of deduction. The thesis that the confirmation of (15) confirms (14) is based on the mistaken view that if *H* deductively implies *C*, then the confirmation of *C* inductively supports *H*. Salmon shows that many of the problems concerning the verifiability theory of meaning that have been noted in the philosophical literature, including Alonzo Church's widely cited critique (Church 1949) of A. J. Ayer's formulation, depend on this mistaken view of induction. And he goes on to show how a more adequate specification of induction and confirmation relations can eliminate the sort of examples typically brought up by critics.

Salmon's efforts at meeting the problems raised by the critics are only a beginning since at the present time we do not have a sufficiently worked out theory of confirmation to determine when one sentence confirms another. Salmon argues that it is important to realize that many of the problems raised against the verifiability theory of meaning are *not* with the inadequacy of the verifiability theory of meaning explicated in terms of confirmation and disconfirmation relations but with the inadequacy of the confirmation theory used to explicate these relations.

It is because of these uncertainties that Martin (1990, p. 77) has concluded that the case for the factual meaninglessness of God-talk is only prima facie justified and that it would be a mistake for atheists to rest their case completely on the verifiability theory of meaning.

Conclusion

Although attempts to meet the verificationist challenge either by showing that religious discourse is verifiable or by arguing that an adequate non-cognitive account of such discourse is possible seem unpromising, a rejection of the challenge seems premature. Despite the rejection of the verifiability theory of meaning by most contemporary philosophers of religion, it has the capacity to meet to a large extent the standard criticisms raised against it as well as to provide an important tool for philosophical criticism. The work of Nielsen shows that it can be developed in a sophisticated manner and Salmon's work demonstrates that many of its alleged problems might be overcome by a more adequate theory of confirmation.

Bibliography

Church, A.: "Review of Ayer's *Language, Truth, and Logic*," *Journal of Symbolic Logic*, 14 (1949), pp. 52–3.

Diamond, M. L., and Litzenburg, T. V. Jr. (eds): *The Logic of God* (Indianapolis: Bobbs-Merrill, 1975).

Hume, D.: *An Inquiry Concerning Human Understanding* (1748) (New York: Liberal Arts Press, 1955).

Martin, M.: *Atheism: A Philosophical Justification* (Philadelphia: Temple University Press, 1990).

Nielsen, K.: *An Introduction to the Philosophy of Religion* (New York: St Martin's Press, 1982).

——: *Contemporary Critiques of Religion* (New York: Herder & Herder, 1971).

Plantinga, A.: *God and Other Minds* (Ithaca: Cornell University Press, 1967).

Stein, G. (ed.): *An Anthology of Atheism and Rationalism* (Buffalo: Prometheus Press, 1980).

Swinburne, R.: *The Coherence of Theism* (Oxford: Clarendon Press, 1977).

26

Theological realism and antirealism

ROGER TRIGG

Understanding and reality

What reality is like and how we conceive it are always separate questions (Trigg 1989). What is real is independent of our conceptions of it. This, at least, is what the realist would maintain. The antirealist would wish to tie our conceptions of truth and reality to the way human language is integrated with particular ways of acting. This latter point is often linked with the later Wittgenstein's ideas of forms of life and language-games (see Article 18, WITTGENSTEINIANISM). The antirealist will always therefore tend to make a reference to human capabilities and limitations, and to connect our ideas of reality to the particular circumstances in which they can be formed.

Realism and its opponent involve the most basic of all philosophical disputes. How can we characterize the nature of reality, and what is its connection with our understanding? Verificationists typically linked such a question to a scientific world-conception, so that what cannot be verified scientifically is not real (see Article 25, THE VERIFICATIONIST CHALLENGE). This ignores any need for a metaphysical basis for science, and assumes that we do not need to justify the practice of science (Trigg 1993). It then just appears self-evident that scientific method provides the only way to truth. Yet such an approach immediately rules out the possibility of access to anything which is beyond our understanding (or "transcendent"). Indeed it runs into problems with science since physics, for example, does not seem afraid of dealing with entities which are in principle inaccessible to human beings. What of the other side of the universe or the interior of a black hole, let alone the many micro-entities continually being claimed by physics, even though they are unobservable?

If the notion of entities beyond our experience can be argued to be a necessary presumption in contemporary science, it hardly seems an objection to religion that it wishes to refer to the transcendent. Yet the debate between realists and antirealists has become as fierce in philosophy of religion as it has been within the philosophy of science. This emphasizes how realism and antirealism can appear in many guises. One could for instance be an antirealist about morality and a realist about tables and chairs, or an antirealist about the latter but a realist about sub-atomic particles. There would certainly be no contradiction about being a realist in science and an antirealist in religion. John Hick, himself a realist, makes this point when he says: "There are in fact probably no pan-realists who believe in the

213

reality of fairies and snarks as well as of tables and electrons; and likewise few if any omni-non realists, denying the objective reality of a material world and of other people as well as of gravity and God" (Runzo 1993, p. 4). In fact solipsism is the limiting case of antirealism, just as an emphasis on objective reality totally unrelated to our understanding can lead to skepticism. Nevertheless, although Hick is right about the varieties of realism and antirealism, what he says betrays a common confusion about the status of realism. Realists do not necessarily claim the existence of something. They are saying that it is the kind of thing that could exist. In other words a realist about fairies could deny there are any with perfect consistency, but would hold that their existence is a possibility. This would be in distinction to the person who claims that talk of fairies is in the same class as talk of heffalumps. We could not know one even if we saw one, and it is not even a possibility that such beings exist.

Realists about the existence of God will typically regard the question of whether God exists as genuine and would assert that such existence is in no way logically dependent on our understanding. Indeed, they would claim, God's existence must be wholly independent of the nature of contingent beings like ourselves. Atheists, however, would also agree with this. They might accept that there could be a God, but hold that there is not. This is an argument about what is in fact the case. Atheism holds that reality does not in fact include God, but its readiness to talk of falsity suggests that it concedes the possibility of truth in this area. Such an understanding of fact certainly goes far from a crude empiricist understanding of factuality, and one of the motives for antirealism about God comes from an unwillingness to think in any way of God as part of the "furniture" of reality, as somehow a mere ingredient in any objective state of affairs. Yet it is only a short step from this to conceiving of God as not objective at all.

Antirealism implicitly rules out atheism in the sense of a denial of the existence of a Being. Many antirealists would recoil in horror from the idea that God is a Being, one amongst many, who may or may not exist. Religion, they would claim, is not in the business of speculating about facts. What difference would it make to our lives if we accept that it is possible or even probable that fairies – quarks, or God – exist? The mere acknowledgment of the existence of an entity is surely, they would argue, not what true religion is about. Wittgenstein (1966, p. 59) says: "If the question arises as to the existence of a god or God, it plays an entirely different role to that of the existence of any person or object I ever heard of." The role of concepts in people's lives is the focus of Wittgenstein's interest. Having abandoned his earlier picture theory of meaning, he emphasizes instead the importance of how people use words (and hence concepts), and the part they play in their wider life. This means that he stresses the public and social role of concepts, so that what is important is the life we share with others, and the system of thought to which we happen to belong. It is what people collectively do with their concepts, and not what entity a concept purports to refer to or name, which gives them their meaning. A corollary of this approach is a challenge to the very idea of religious claims resting on evidence. Instead of being understood as making claims about the possible existence of anything, which might in turn be doubted, theists have to be seen as reaffirming their commitment to a way of life. All religious assertions have then to be reinterpreted in a manner which assumes that they are not claiming truth about an objective state of affairs. This not only applies to the question of God's existence. It also covers all religious claims which might appear to justify faith on rational grounds. Wittgenstein, for example, questions (1966, p. 57) the way in which Christianity rests on a historical basis. Even if the historical facts are indubitable (as of course they are not), Wittgenstein feels that that is not enough. He says: "The understanding wouldn't be enough to make me change my whole life." His conclusion therefore is that Christianity cannot rely on history in the sense that an ordinary belief in historic facts provides evidence for Napoleon. An acceptance of historical probability in a spirit of rational detachment seems, he believes, far removed from a genuine faith which animates one's whole life. The question to be addressed then becomes not "What is faith in?" or "Is it reasonable or justifiable?" It is "What does it mean for one's life?" There is, he thinks, no room in faith "for the doubt," as he puts it, "that would ordinarily apply to any historical propositions." Beliefs about Jesus have a different function from beliefs about ordinary historical figures.

Wittgenstein does not consider that language-games or forms of life are the kind of thing that could be justified. Both concepts, peculiar to him, are intended to underline the way in which our speaking of a language is interwoven with our social practices. Thus he is able to say of a language-game that "it is not based on grounds. It is not reasonable (or unreasonable). It is there − like our life" (Wittgenstein 1969). There is no possibility of standing outside such an activity and criticizing it or even giving it external support. One is either a participant, living the life and using the language, or one is going to be unable properly to understand what is going on or being said. There can be no room for making claims which purport to be true for everyone, whether they recognize it or not. As a result the very idea of an objective reality confronting us all makes no sense.

As a follower of Wittgenstein, D. Z. Phillips (1970a) goes so far as to claim that if a people lost their belief in God, "belief in God is not intelligible but false for them, but unintelligible." Believers and non-believers thus live in different worlds, and there is no neutral or detached position where anyone can stand to criticize the other. As Wittgenstein says (1969, p. 611): "Where two principles really do meet which cannot be reconciled with one another, then each man declares the other a fool and heretic." Wittgenstein explicitly rules out the possibility of giving reasons, because he believes that "at the end of reasons comes persuasion." In a dark aside, he remarks: "Think what happens when missionaries convert natives." Rationality is ruled out, together with any possibility of metaphysics, and any understanding of a reality which confronts us all whether we recognize it or not. Changes of way of life cannot thus be motivated by reason, precisely because what counts as a reason can only be recognized within a particular tradition or community which already possesses some shared understanding (see Article 75, TRADITION).

215

Tradition and interpretation

We all need a tradition to provide us with a platform from which to deal with reality. Everyone depends on some particular background of concepts and beliefs.
One cannot meet reality in the raw, devoid of any preconceptions. The antirealists,
however, are saying much more than this, by denying that there is anything real
beyond the tradition which could ground or justify it. It would be possible to speak
of what is judged correct or incorrect within, say, Catholicism, or indeed
Christianity, but not of whether either as a whole is misguided. It is hardly surprising that antirealists seem to be on the slippery slope which leads to relativism (see
Trigg 1973). Indeed, according to Don Cupitt, a philosopher of religion strongly
influenced by postmodernist understandings, "reality has now become a mere
bunch of disparate and changing interpretations" (Runzo 1993, p. 46). He dismisses a "realistic ontology, the notion that there is something out there prior to
and independent of our language and theories, and against which they can be
checked" (Cupitt 1991, p. 82). Yet the question remains as to what is left. For
Cupitt, once realism is jettisoned, we have to return "science into its own theories,
religion into its own stories and rituals – and history into its own varied narratives." There is no possibility of metaphysics to provide an ontological grounding
for our practices. Indeed Cupitt emphasizes the anthropocentric character of antirealism (and glories in it), when he says: "Metaphysics is anti-human" (1991,
p. 130). Why, though, should we then continue to perform rituals and tell stories?
Cupitt reinforces his emphasis on the human world, describing it as "a world
bounded by language, time and narrativity and radically outsideless." He
announces: "All this is all there is" (1994, p. 17). This seems indistinguishable
from an atheist denial of any transcendent reality (although Cupitt claims to be
talking from the position of contemporary understandings of Christianity). In fact
Cupitt claims: "In post-Christianity there are no longer two worlds but only one –
this world, and there is no longer an objective God" (1994, p. 23). This must refer
to changes in belief rather than in the nature of reality, but it is part of the character of antirealism to fail to distinguish the two. The absolute denial of objectivity
certainly is very dogmatic and goes far beyond the kind of relativism which refers
to the construction of different worlds by different societies. It poses the question
as to where Cupitt is himself standing to be so sure of what does not and cannot
exist. At best, on his own assumptions, his account is a story which we are at liberty to reject because we find it unpalatable. It cannot make claim to truth, since
that would import realist presuppositions. This also highlights a general problem
with relativism. When it denies any idea of reality and talks of the construction of
worlds by different societies rather than their discovery, it appears to be putting all
this forward as itself a fact about the world. Once relativists are seen as also in the
business of construction, they have no claim to be listened to by anyone else.

A much more subtle form of antirealism is one that does not make blanket
denials of what can exist, but which reinterprets what we mean when we use religious language. This can involve just a stipulative definition, so that "God" is not
to be used to refer to a supernatural Being, but the sum of all one's values and

ideals. This is bound to lead to some changes of use and for that reason will immediately provoke resistance from ordinary believers. More challenging is the view that the proper meaning of our language already implies an antirealism. The issue is then not whether there is or is not a transcendent reality, or whether God is a Being. It is what is the true meaning of such assertions. This form of antirealism is not going to stop us talking of God's reality, but rather will interpret what most of us mean in an unfamiliar way. This is the approach of D. Z. Phillips, who insists that our beliefs cannot be divorced "from the situations in human life in which they have their sense" (Runzo 1993, p. 89). The problem is that what he considers gives concepts sense may be very divergent from the understanding the holders of those concepts think they possess. "What," Phillips asks, "is involved in believing something to be true?" (1993, p. 92). He alleges that the realist can give no intelligible answer to this question, because what we apparently have beliefs about is so sundered from our beliefs and practices that our beliefs can no longer be understood. The realist, he claims, "severs belief from its object" (1993, p. 107). This is hardly surprising because this is the whole point of realism. What we have beliefs about is not meant to be logically related to them. Phillips, however, considers that our beliefs should be so anchored in our practices that they cannot be understood as projections on to something inaccessible. It is perhaps significant that the article in which he makes these claims is entitled "On really believing." The realist will insist that whether we really believe or not is a different issue from the connection of our beliefs to reality. The test of our sincerity lies in our actions. The test of truth, of having beliefs about what is actually real, must be different. This presupposes the intelligibility of the notion of what is actually real or "out there." It assumes the very split between the subject and object of belief which is challenged by antirealists. Thus while Phillips, unlike Cupitt, is happy to claim that God is a spiritual reality, he will still resist realist assumptions. Following Wittgenstein, he will insist that what matters is the "grammar" of spiritual reality. In other words, although we may still go on using the same language, to understand what is meant we have to relate it to the rest of our lives. This brings us back to Wittgenstein's ideas of forms of life.

In a similar manner there can be agreement that God is "independent" of us, but the disagreement between realist and antirealist about the meaning of "independent" may mean that nothing has been resolved. Phillips's view is that when people claim that they wish to hold on to traditional religious beliefs, what they are really doing is insisting on a traditional philosophical account of their meaning. Wittgenstein felt that we can be misled by our own language, and Phillips similarly claims that religious concepts can be systematically misunderstood. Thus he can claim (1970b, p. 49) about life after death: "Eternity is not an extension of this present life, but a mode of judging it. Eternity is not more life, but this life seen under certain moral and religious modes of thought." Even given such a radical reinterpretation, he holds that everyone can still go on using religious language as before. We may see that there is not some kind of continuation of life but can still continue using the language of eternity just the same, even if it is now recognized to have an exclusively ethical sense. In one way there is here an emphatic denial of "life after death," but Phillips considers that a view of that kind was a superstitious understanding of the idea of immortality. He feels that there never was a possibility of some such non-empirical reality, and language was never able to accomplish what the realist expected of it. Yet the result of this is that people do not in fact believe what they thought they did. They cannot be held to be making the ordinary factual claims they see themselves as making. From the realist point of view, it seems as if Phillips is actually subverting language. He uses familiar language but gives it an interpretation which completely changes its force. Certainly the analysis of concepts is hardly a neutral matter, when it restrains us from making claims to truth, as we would wish. Many of Phillips's complaints are about the way people are prone to understand the language of religion as if it is "factual" or "empirical." Certainly realists will be reluctant to restrict reality to what is observable. The objectively real can never be understood in physics or anywhere else as merely what is empirically accessible. Phillips's reluctance to see reality as anything other than what can be experienced suggests that he himself is still far too influenced by empiricist assumptions. It is perhaps noteworthy that these can continue to provide strong motivation for the espousal of antirealism.

Forms of realism

A distinction is sometimes made between various forms of realism, such as naive and critical realism. The terms are typically used in connection with perception, but John Hick, for example, talks of naive religious realism "which assumes that divine reality is just as spoken of in the language of some tradition" (Runzo 1993). He contrasts it with the kind of critical realism which refers to a transcendent divine reality, but "is conscious that this reality is always thought and experienced by us in ways which are shaped and colored by human concepts and images." Hick is himself deeply opposed (Runzo 1993, p. 12) to what he terms "non-realism," because it stops us maintaining that there is any benign reality beyond this universe, or any way in which what he terms "the spiritual project of our existence" can continue beyond this life. The result must, he thinks, be a profound "cosmic pessimism." Theism has to be realist to provide for the grounding of any hope.

Anyone confronted by religious disagreement may be tempted to make the kind of distinctions used by Hick. Unless we wish to claim finality for our understanding of God (whoever "we" may be), we are bound to recognize a gap between our limited understanding and the infinity of God. No tradition is likely to possess the whole truth. Christianity has always recognized the partial nature of our knowledge, and St Paul contrasts it with the full knowledge that we will obtain in the presence of God. A simple naive realism can hardly be held by any religion that takes the transcendence of God seriously. Yet Hick risks making the whole content of our beliefs relative to the concepts provided by our culture. He refers (1989, p. 15) to "the different ways of thinking-and-experiencing the Real." In this he is deliberately following Kant in distinguishing, as he puts it, "different phenomenal awarenesses of the same noumenal reality." It seems that because there can be no independent access to the so-called Real except through one tradition or another, there can be no clear way of adjudicating between them. The danger is that a noumenal reality drops out as irrelevant just because it is unknowable. Then we are merely left with the cultural fact of different religions.

Realism gives point to our search for truth, by sundering the subject and object of knowledge. There is something to know. Yet skepticism can arise because of the problem of how we can gain knowledge. The alternative, however, should not be an unthinking "fundamentalism" depending on an uncritical allegiance to particular tradition. It should be a metaphysical thesis about the character of reality. Epistemological questions about how (or whether) we can know that reality raise different issues. In fact the term "critical realism" appears to run together epistemological questions about us and our capabilities with metaphysical ones about the status of objective reality. Whatever is real is so whether we use our critical faculties or not. How naive we are says nothing about what may exist. We can recognize our own fallibility, but without the prior conception of an objective reality even the idea of fallibility does not have much sense. There is then nothing to be wrong about. Hick makes reality so inaccessible that nothing can be said about it and the whole emphasis may seem to move to our conceptual schemes and their revisability. There could then, however, be no rational grounds for revising our views since the acquisition of genuine knowledge is prohibited. Contact between conceptual schemes, such as different religions, can then only be a matter of political negotiation rather than a search for truth.

Metaphysical realism in religion upholds the "otherness" of God. This, however, brings us, as Hick's views show, to the question of how knowledge of such a Reality could ever be possible. A major function of any religion should be to give an answer to that question. What realism must maintain in a theological context is that religion is not in the business of constructing reality, but of responding to something that is totally apart from us. Gordon Kaufman (1993) puts forward a "constructive theology" which risks being a contradiction in terms. He considers that our idea of mystery must be traced back to a human origin. Yet the more he tries to examine the way the word "God" works as a human symbol, the less room he gives for any understanding of anything transcendent. The notion of an "ultimate mystery" (1993, p. 357) does little more than point to an ultimate void. The danger, too, is that the more we emphasize our own role in the construction of symbols, the more difficult it is to continue to be gripped by them. Realism in theology, like realism elsewhere, attempts to ground our knowledge. Indeed, in pointing to a transcendent God, it hopes to point to the source and guarantee of all knowledge.

Bibliography

Cupitt, D.: *What Is a Story?* (London: SCM Press, 1991).
——: *After All* (London: SCM Press, 1994).
Hick, J.: *An Interpretation of Religion* (London: Macmillan, 1989).

Kaufman, G.: *In Face of Mystery* (Cambridge: Harvard University Press, 1993).

Phillips, D. Z.: *Faith and Philosophical Enquiry* (London: Routledge, 1970a).

——: *Death and Immortality* (London: Macmillan, 1970b).

Runzo, J. (ed.): *Is God Real?* (New York: St Martin's Press, 1993).

Trigg, R.: *Reason and Commitment* (Cambridge: Cambridge University Press, 1973).

——: *Reality at Risk: A Defence of Realism in Philosophy and the Sciences*, 2nd edn (London: Harvester Wheatsheaf, 1989).

——: *Rationality and Science: Can Science Explain Everything?* (Oxford: Basil Blackwell, 1993).

Wittgenstein, L.: *Lectures and Conversations on Aesthetics, Psychology and Religious Belief*, ed. C. Barrett (Oxford: Basil Blackwell, 1966).

——: *On Certainty* (Oxford: Basil Blackwell, 1969).

PART V

THE THEISTIC CONCEPTION OF GOD

27

Being

C. J. F. WILLIAMS

God, in St Thomas Aquinas's view, is subsistent being itself (*Summa Theologiae*, I,11,4). What can he mean by this? What, if anything, do philosophers and theologians have in mind when they talk about "being"?

Some time ago, having written a book about Being (together with Identity and Truth), I was using my computer to compile the index. I instructed it to index every occurrence of the word "being." The result was disastrous. Twenty or thirty occurrences were listed on every page, including contexts like "If we are being strict about this, . . ." and "Being uncertain how to proceed at this point, . . .".

"Being" may be used either as the participle or as the verbal noun from the verb "be," and this verb itself may be used in any of a number of senses. How many senses is a disputed issue. Bertrand Russell, who counted four, described it as "a disgrace to the human race" that so much ambiguity should be tolerated (Russell 1919, p. 172). Two senses at least are unavoidable: the use of "is" as copula, as in "John is a teacher" (i.e. "John teaches"), and the existential use of "is," as in "There is an even prime number" (i.e. "An even prime number exists").

One reason for Aquinas's identification of Being with God may have been the account in the Book of Exodus of God's reply to Moses in the incident of the Burning Bush. Moses had inquired what he should say to the Children of Israel if they should ask for the name of the god who had sent him to them. God replied with words which could be translated as "I am what I am" (two occurrences of "am" in the copulative sense) or as "I am that which is" (one occurrence of "am" in the copulative sense and one of "is" in the existential sense). It is not impossible that the ambiguity is intended – that God is represented as making a pun. That it cannot simply be intended in the first sense is shown by the words which follow: "Tell them 'I am has sent me to you' " (Exodus 3:13–15).

If what God meant to say was "I am what I am," his remark must be construed as a "brush off" for Moses – as if he had said "Never you mind! That's nothing to do with you." Two occurrences of "am," both in the copulative sense would have no great metaphysical significance. It would indeed be difficult ever to find metaphysical profundity in this sense of the verb "be." It is noteworthy that many languages, Latin, Greek, and Hebrew, for instance, frequently do without it. "God is a just judge, strong and patient" the Psalmist tells us in the English version (Psalm 7:12). In the Latin version there is no word corresponding to "is" here: "*Deus judex justus, fortis et patiens.*" And the Hebrew is the same. English cannot, as these ancient languages could, and as Russian and Japanese amongst others still can,

223

form a sentence by simply juxtaposing a name and a common noun or adjective. But even in English there are other possibilities. As well as placing "is" between "Charles" and "a smoker" we can say "Charles smokes," substituting a verb for the combination of "is" with the noun phrase. The function of the copula is to convert a common noun or an adjective into a verb phrase for those languages which do not allow these parts of speech to perform this function as they stand. Its function is purely syntactic.

Amongst philosophers of religion the existential use of the verb "be" has been overwhelmingly the more popular. St Anselm's famous argument against the fool who says in his heart "There is no God" turns on the proposition that something is greater if it exists in reality as well as in the understanding than if it exists in the understanding alone (1965, 2). (That, at all events, is how his argument has most often been interpreted.) This relies on the view that real existence is a great-making characteristic of something, a view not dissimilar to René Descartes's view that existence is a perfection (*Meditations* V). Descartes argues that since God is by definition the being who possesses all perfections, and existence is a perfection, it is as certain that God exists as that a triangle has three angles. Immanuel Kant challenges this line of reasoning. Being, he says, is not a real predicate (1963, B 626). When I say that something is wise, I posit the thing and go on to say of it that it is wise; but when I say that it is, I simply posit it without saying anything about it. Existence in reality is not something that can be a component of the concept of a thing. As Kant says, "a hundred real thalers contain no more thalers than a hundred possible ones" (1963, B 627).

It was Gottlob Frege, a hundred years after Kant, who finally diagnosed the error of those who tried to treat being as a property of things (Frege 1950 [1884], pp. 58–67). He was primarily interested in the logic of our talk about numbers, and he began with statements which provide answers to questions introduced by "How many . . . ?" "How many planets are there? There are nine planets." "How many epistles are there written by St John? There are three epistles written by St John." Clearly being nine or being three is not the property of any single planet or epistle. Nor can answers to "how many . . . ?" questions be seen as assigning numbers to collections of things: nine to the collection consisting of the sun's planets and three to the collection consisting of the epistles of St John. For to what collection of things do the statements "Venus has no moons" and "There are no epistles written by St Andrew" assign a number? And yet these are perfectly good answers to the questions "How many moons has Venus?" and "How many epistles did St Andrew write?" Frege's view is that such statements do not ascribe properties to objects or collections of objects. "Mercury is a planet of the sun" tells us something about Mercury; it tells us, in Frege's terminology, that it falls under the concept *planet of the sun*, the concept which the predicate "is a planet of the sun" may be said to stand for. But "There are nine planets of the sun" does not tell us that some particular thing or things fall under this concept *planet of the sun*: rather, it says of this concept that nine objects fall under it. The concept for which the predicate "is a planet of the sun" stands is here having something predicated of *it*. The words "There are nine" which do this predicating may be called, therefore, a second-order or second-level predicate. It is, as it were, a predicate of a predicate.

"There is no epistle written by St James" assigns the number nought to the concept *epistle written by St James*. I might quite properly wish to deny this proposition. I could do so by saying "It is not the case that there is no epistle written by St James," or, equivalently, by saying "There *is* an epistle written by St James" or "An epistle written by St James exists." Frege summarized this by saying "Affirmation of existence is nothing other than denial of the number nought" (1950 [1884], p. 65). If "There are nine" is a second-level predicate which I can use to say something about the concept *planet of the sun*, "There is no" must similarly be saying something about the concept *epistle written by St James* and "There is no" accordingly be a second-level predicate; and to contradict what is thus said we can attach the contradictory of this second-level predicate to an expression which stands for the same concept, which we do when we say "There is an epistle written by St James." The contradictory of a predicate must surely be an expression of the same logical level as the predicate it contradicts. "There is" must therefore be just as much a second-level predicate as "There is no." But "is" here can be replaced without change of sense by "exists," and if we say "An epistle of St James exists" we say exactly what we have said by "There is an epistle of St James." The verb "exists," then, as well as the verb "be" in its existential sense, must be a second-level predicate, something we can use to say things, not about objects, but about concepts. It belongs to a class of expressions which includes not only expressions of the form "There are *n*," for each of the infinitely many whole numbers which may be substituted for *n*, but also expressions which we use to give less precise answers to the question "How many *as* are there?" such as "many," "few," "numerous," "scarce." We should now be in a position to see what is wrong with listing existence along with wisdom, power, and benevolence among the divine attributes or perfections: it is as nonsensical to say of someone that she is powerful and existent as to say that she is wise and numerous. The mistake of those who advance the ontological argument (see Article 41, ONTOLOGICAL ARGUMENTS) is not that they treat *being* as a real predicate but that they treat it as a first-level, when it is in fact a second-level predicate.

Not only does the recognition that "be" or "exist" cannot be a first-level predicate, a predicate of objects, show us where the fallacy lies in the ontological argument, but it also helps us solve a puzzle which goes back to Parmenides in the fifth century BCE. If I say that black-backed wrens don't build nests, I am asserting something about black-backed wrens, and may be presumed to have inspected some black-backed wrens before pronouncing on the subject. But if I tell you that black-backed wrens do not exist, I do not first have to research into the behavior of black-backed wrens to find evidence for my claim. If what I say is true, it is because there are no black-backed wrens for me to investigate. The predicate "do not exist" is not something that can be true of any object or objects. What I am claiming, of course, is that nothing at all falls under the concept *black-backed wren*, that the concept is not instantiated. Negative existential propositions are capable of being true, so long as they are regarded as using "do not exist" as a second-level, not a first-level, predicate.

Nor, of course, can we make sense of the doctrine that God is being itself: what God is can hardly be indicated by saying that the number of gods is not nought. But there is another theological view which may seem to be endangered by this account of being or existence. If theology can afford to give up the doctrine that God is being itself, it can hardly jettison the doctrine that God is the creator. Creation, however, has been explained as causing to exist. Not only did God cause me to begin to exist, but he causes me to go on existing for as long as I do (see Article 39, CREATION AND CONSERVATION). Secondary causes may be responsible for the color of my eyes or the length of my legs, but the fact that I exist must be due to the first cause alone (Davies 1992, pp. 33–5). Moreover, the fact that I was created by God and am sustained in existence by him is a fact about me: "God brought it about that I exist" predicates something of me; and I am an object, not a concept. Does not this suggest that "exist" is a predicate, not only of concepts, but sometimes also of objects?

Answering this objection involves complication. (For a slightly fuller discussion, see Williams 1989, pp. 35–8). The surface structure of "God brought it about that I exist" suggests that this proposition is formed by inserting the proposition "I exist" into the context "God brought it about that . . ." which, like "It is possible that . . .," is used to form a proposition from a proposition. "God brought it about that the Israelites escaped from Egypt" can indeed be seen in this way. "The Israelites escaped from Egypt" is a proposition to which can be prefixed the words "God brought it about that . . ." to form this other, relatively complex, proposition. Just so, "This house has dry rot" can have "It is possible that . . ." prefixed to it to form "It is possible that this house has dry rot." But in the case of "God brought it about that I exist" the corresponding suggestion is misleading. The deep structure of "God brought it about that I exist" is this: "For some f, I am f and God brought it about that there is something which is f," where f stands for a predicate which necessarily applies to me and only to me. (One such predicate would be a predicate specifying my origin, presumably the union of a particular sperm and a particular ovum.) Again, "It is due to God that I exist now" is not formed by making the proposition "I exist now" subject to the phrase "It is due to God that . . . ." For a start what is meant by calling God my sustainer, as well as my creator, is that it is due to God that I still exist; and the fact that I still exist is not on a par with the fact that I still smoke. My continued smoking is a matter simply of my having smoked in the past and smoking now, but my still existing is a matter of my having had a property, p^1 in the past and there being someone who has a property p^2 now, such that whoever had p^1 in the past is the same person as the one who has p^2 now. So although the proposition as a whole ascribes a predicate, a complex though first-level predicate, to me, "there is" occurs in it only as a second-level predicate, one which ascribes a property to a concept, not an object. And it is the fact stated by this complex proposition that is said to be due to God. The doctrine of creation, it seems, can be expressed without having to accept being as a property of individuals.

226

Those English-speaking Christians who are used to reciting the Nicene Creed as part of their regular act of worship on Sundays have for some years now been familiar with another use of the word "being." Their faith in "one Lord Jesus Christ" is amplified by the description of him as "one in being with the Father." These words replace an earlier translation which many will remember: "of one substance with the Father," a more or less literal translation of the Latin *consubstantialem Patri*. The Latin in its turn represented the Greek original, over which much blood was spilt: *homoousion tōi Patri*.

Whether the average churchgoer is provided with anything she can find easier to understand by the substitution of "of one being" for "of one substance" may be doubted. But one can see the rationale of it. *Homoousios* means "of the same *ousia*." The Greek word *ousia* was used as a technical term by Plato and Aristotle, but in both cases their choice of the word was determined by its connection with the Greek equivalent of the verb "be." It is a verbal noun from that word, corresponding to "be" as "laughter" corresponds to "laugh." It is Aristotle's use that is relevant to its use in Christology. Aristotle was interested in answers to questions of the form "What is it for *x* to be?" He says, for example, that for living things to be is to be alive, and a definition of "living," if available, would give the answer to the question "What is it for a living thing to be?" What such an answer would supply would be the being, or *ousia*, of the thing in question. Cicero invented a Latin equivalent for the word *ousia*, used in this sense: *essentia*.

No doubt the question "What is it for *x* to be?" is, by Frege's standards, and they are the right standards, ill-formed. *To be* cannot for anything be the same as *to be alive*, since the latter is something that can be said of objects, while the former is used to say something of concepts. But we know how Aristotle used the question, namely, to elicit definitions of words. What it is for a circle to be is to be the locus of points equidistant from a given point. This is the essence of *circle* and a definition of the word "circle."

Ousia is used in another sense in Aristotle, roughly to mean that which exists in its own right, neither in something else nor as something said of something else. Thus I am an *ousia* but my baldness is not. The Latin word which came to be used as the equivalent of *ousia* in this sense is *substantia*, and it is this word which is incorporated in the Latin equivalent of *homoousios*, namely *consubstantialis*.

To say that Christ is consubstantial, or *homoousios*, with the Father is to say that they are one substance, or have a single essence. No doubt this Aristotelian term had developed extra senses that were important in the thought of the theologians whose meditations on the Incarnation provided the context in which the Conciliar definitions were produced, but the Aristotelian usage is an important part of its history. The Son is being said to be God as the Father is God, so that what it is for God to be is truly said of them both. And it is not just that one thing is said of both of them, but that they are one God, since the very reasons we have for asserting that there is a God are reasons for asserting that there is only one God. It would have been better had the English translators left the obviously technical word "substance" in place than to have used the speciously intelligible "being."

Less easy to pardon is the English translators' insertion a little earlier in the

227

Creed of the words "all that is" which correspond to nothing at all in the original. "Maker of all things, visible and invisible" was doing no harm to anyone. "Maker of all that is, seen and unseen" suggests that being is a genus of which being seen and being unseen are species. That requires that we take "is," like "is seen" or "is unseen," as a predicate of objects. Frege has taught us that we cannot do that. But even without Frege's help Aristotle and Aquinas had maintained that being is not a genus – *things that are* is not the name of a class, not even of the universal class. If, *per impossibile*, it were, God would not be the Creator of all its members, since he is not the Creator of himself. But God is not the member of any class, nor is there such a class as the class of all that is. Alas, one fears that the recent translators of the Creed into English were as ignorant of the works of Aquinas as they were of the works of Frege.

I pass over in silence works of other philosophers entitled *Being and Time* (Martin Heidegger) and *Being and Nothingness* (Jean-Paul Sartre). Of them, and of the whole tribe of existentialists, the less said the better. Those who have understood what I have said of Frege will understand why.

Bibliography

Anselm, St: *Proslogion*, ed. M. Charlesworth (Oxford: Clarendon Press, 1965).

Aquinas, St Thomas: *Summa Theologiae*, New Blackfriars edn, vol. 2 (London: Eyre & Spottiswood, 1965).

Davies, OP, B.: *The Thought of Thomas Aquinas* (Oxford: Clarendon Press, 1992).

Frege, G.: *The Foundations of Arithmetic*, tr. J. L. Austin (1884) (Oxford: Basil Blackwell, 1950).

Kant, I.: *The Critique of Pure Reason*, tr. N. Kemp Smith (London: Macmillan, 1963).

Russell, B.: *An Introduction to Mathematical Philosophy* (London: George Allen & Unwin, 1919).

Williams, C. J. F.: *What is Existence?* (Oxford: Clarendon Press, 1981).

——: *Being, Identity, and Truth* (Oxford: Clarendon Press, 1989).

28

Omnipotence

JOSHUA HOFFMAN AND GARY ROSENKRANTZ

According to the traditional idea of God, God is the greatest being possible. Traditional theism, as formulated in the Middle Ages by such philosophers as Anselm, Maimonides, and Thomas Aquinas (see Article 9, THE CHRISTIAN CONTRIBUTION TO MEDIEVAL PHILOSOPHICAL THEOLOGY; and Article 11, THE JEWISH CONTRIBUTION TO MEDIEVAL PHILOSOPHICAL THEOLOGY), maintains that God possesses certain great-making properties, such as omnipotence, omniscience, omnibenevolence, and necessary existence (see Article 29, OMNISCIENCE; Article 30, GOODNESS; and Article 33, NECESSITY). In the case of omnipotence, at least, there is biblical authority for including it among the divine attributes. Yet, reflection on the concept of omnipotence raises puzzling questions which concern whether or not a consistent notion of omnipotence implies limitations on the power of an omnipotent agent. Our goal here is to provide an analysis of the concept of omnipotence which resolves all of the puzzles surrounding this concept.

What omnipotence signifies

One of the concerns of recent philosophy of religion is to investigate the coherence of the divine attributes, considered individually and in combination. Of course, omnipotence is one of these attributes.

According to some philosophers, omnipotence should be understood in terms of the power to perform *tasks*, for instance, to kill oneself, to make $2 + 2 = 5$, or to make oneself non-omniscient (see Article 38, DIVINE ACTION). Philosophical discussion has brought out that this approach to the analysis of omnipotence is fruitless. More successful is that of philosophers such as Rosenkrantz and Hoffman (1980), Flint and Freddoso (1983), and Wierenga (1989) to analyze omnipotence in terms of the power to bring about certain *states of affairs*, or propositional entities, which either obtain or fail to obtain.

One sense of "omnipotence" is that of having the power to bring about *any* state of affairs whatsoever, including necessary and impossible states of affairs. René Descartes in the *Meditations* seems to have had such a notion. But, as Aquinas in his *Summa Theologiae* and Maimonides in his *Guide of the Perplexed* recognized, it is *not* possible for an agent to bring about an *impossible* state of affairs (e.g. that there is a shapeless cube), since if it were, it would be possible for an impossible state of affairs to obtain, which is a contradiction. Nor is it possible for an agent to bring about a *necessary* state of affairs (e.g. that all cubes are shaped).

229

It is possible for an agent, *a*, to bring about a necessary state of affairs, *s*, only if possibly: (1) *a* brings about *s*; and (2) if *a* had not acted, then *s* would have failed to obtain. Because a necessary state of affairs obtains whether or not anyone acts, (2) is false. As a consequence, it is impossible for an agent to bring about a necessary state of affairs, and the first sense of omnipotence is incoherent.

A second sense is that of *maximal power*, meaning just that the overall power of an omnipotent being could not be exceeded by any being. It does not follow that a maximally powerful being can bring about any state of affairs, since bringing about some such states of affairs is impossible. Nor does it follow that a being with maximal power can bring about whatever any other agent can bring about. If *a* can bring about *s*, and *b* cannot, it does not follow that *a* is *overall* more powerful than *b*, since it could be that *b* can bring about some other state or states of affairs which *a* cannot. This *comparative* sense of omnipotence as maximal power is the only sense which has a chance of being intelligible.

Power should be distinguished from *ability*. Power is ability plus opportunity: a being having maximal ability who is prevented by circumstances from exercising those abilities would not be omnipotent. Nothing could prevent an omnipotent agent from exercising its powers, were it to decide to do so.

In the light of the foregoing, could there be two omnipotent agents, Dick and Jane, at the same time? If this were possible, then it could happen that at some time, *t*, Dick, while retaining his omnipotence, attempts to move a feather, and at *t*, Jane, while retaining her omnipotence, attempts to keep that feather motionless. Intuitively, in this case, the feather would not be affected (as to its motion or rest) by either Dick or Jane. Thus, in this case, at *t*, Dick would be powerless to move the feather, and at *t*, Jane would be powerless to keep the feather motionless! But it is absurd to suppose that an omnipotent agent lacks the power to move a feather or the power to keep it motionless. Therefore, neither Dick nor Jane is omnipotent. As a consequence, the simultaneous existence of two omnipotent agents is impossible.

Could an agent have the attribute of omnipotence contingently? At first glance, this appears possible, but there is the following argument for the opposite view.

Given the truth of traditional theism, God has necessary existence and is essentially omnipotent. Because there could not be more than one omnipotent being, there could not exist a being which had the attribute of omnipotence contingently.

This argument against the possibility of contingent omnipotence presupposes traditional theism. But it is preferable to remain neutral about whether theism is true or false. Thus, omnipotence will not be assumed to be attributable only to the God of traditional theism or only to an essentially omnipotent being.

The riddle of the stone

The intelligibility of the notion of omnipotence has been challenged by the so-called paradox or riddle of the stone. Can an omnipotent agent, Jane, bring it about that there is a stone of some mass, *m*, which Jane cannot move? If the answer is "yes," then there is a state of affairs that Jane cannot bring about, namely, (S1) that a stone of mass m moves. On the other hand, if the answer is "no," then there is another state of affairs that Jane cannot bring about, namely (S2) that there is a stone of mass m which Jane cannot move. Thus, it seems that whether or not Jane can make the stone in question, there is some possible state of affairs which an omnipotent agent cannot bring about. And this appears to be paradoxical.

A first resolution of the paradox comes into play when there is an *essentially* omnipotent agent, Jane. In that case, the state of affairs of Jane's being non-omnipotent is impossible. Therefore, Jane cannot bring it about that she is not omnipotent. Since, necessarily, an omnipotent agent can move any stone, no matter how massive, (S2) is impossible. But as we have seen, an omnipotent agent is not required to be able to bring about an impossible state of affairs.

If, on the other hand, both (S1) and (S2) *are* possible, then it *is* possible for some omnipotent agent to bring it about that (S1) obtains at some time, *and* that (S2) obtains at a different time. Thus, there is a second solution to the paradox. This solution has a different presupposition than the first solution, namely, that there is a *contingently* omnipotent agent. In this case, Jane's being non-omnipotent is a possible state of affairs; and we may assume that it *is* possible for Jane to bring it about that she is non-omnipotent. So, Jane can create and move a stone of mass m while omnipotent, and *subsequently* bring it about that she is not omnipotent and powerless to move that stone of mass m. As a consequence, Jane can bring about both (S1) and (S2), but only if they obtain at different times.

Further limitations on the power of an omnipotent agent

It might now be conjectured that omnipotence can be analyzed simply as the power to bring it about that any contingent state of affairs obtains. However, the following list of contingent states of affairs demonstrates that this simple analysis is inadequate.

(a) A raindrop fell.
(b) A raindrop falls at t (where t is a past time).
(c) Parmenides lectures for the first time.
(d) The Amazon floods an odd number of times less than four.
(e) A snowflake falls and no omnipotent agent ever exists.
(f) Plato freely decides to write a dialogue.

The first state of affairs (a) is in the past. As the "necessity of the past" implies, it is impossible for any agent to have power over the past. Hence, no agent, not even an omnipotent one, can bring it about that (a) obtains. Likewise, despite the fact that (b) can be brought about prior to t, the necessity of the past implies that even an omnipotent agent cannot bring it about that (b) obtains after t. In the case of (c), prior to Parmenides' first lecture, an omnipotent agent can bring about (c). But once he has lectured, even an omnipotent agent cannot bring it about that (c) obtains. As for (d), prior to the Amazon's third flooding, an omnipotent agent can bring it about that (d) obtains, while after the Amazon's third flooding, even an omnipotent agent cannot bring it about that (d) obtains. A special difficulty is introduced by (e). Although it is obvious that (e) could not be brought about by an omnipotent agent, it can be argued plausibly, as by Hoffman and Rosenkrantz (1988), that it is possible for a non-omnipotent agent to bring about (e) by causing a snowflake to fall when no omnipotent agent ever exists. As we argued earlier, a maximally powerful being need not have the power to bring about every state of affairs that any other being can. Lastly, an omnipotent agent *other than Plato* cannot bring about (f) if the libertarian theory of free will is correct, but apparently a non-omnipotent agent, namely, Plato, can bring it about that (f) obtains (see Article 72, PROVIDENCE AND PREDESTINATION).

Consequently, a satisfactory analysis of omnipotence ought not to require that an omnipotent agent have the power to bring about (a), (b), (c), (d), (e), or (f), if it is assumed, *arguendo*, in the case of (f) that libertarianism is true.

Because of the wide disparity among the contingent states of affairs (a) to (f), one might despair of finding an analysis of omnipotence that deals satisfactorily with all of these states of affairs and implies that an omnipotent being has, intuitively speaking, sufficient power. Yet, the following reflections show that such pessimism can be overcome.

By identifying certain features of (a) to (f), we will be able to find a factor in terms of which an analysis of omnipotence can be stated. To begin, an omnipotent agent ought not to be required to be able to bring about a state of affairs unless it is possible for some agent to bring about that state of affairs. But (a) is not possibly brought about by any agent. Second, (b) and (c) are possibly brought about by some agent. Yet they are not *repeatable*: it is not possible for either one of them to obtain, then fail to obtain, and then obtain again. Note that if an omnipotent agent is not required to be able to bring about (a), because it is not possibly brought about by someone, then that agent is not required to be able to bring about impossible or necessary states of affairs either. Moreover, if an omnipotent agent is not required to bring about (b) or (c) because they are not repeatable, then that agent is not required to be able to bring about impossible or necessary states of affairs, since they are not repeatable. Third, (d) is repeatable, but it is not *unrestrictedly* repeatable, that is, it cannot obtain, then fail to obtain, then obtain again, and so on, eternally. Fourth, (e) is unrestrictedly repeatable. Yet it is a complex state of affairs: a conjunctive state of affairs whose second conjunct is *not* repeatable. A reasonable hypothesis about repeatability and its relation to power is that an omnipotent agent should not be required to have the power to bring about either a state of affairs which is not unrestrictedly repeatable or a conjunctive state of affairs one of whose conjuncts is not unrestrictedly repeatable. Lastly, (f) is unrestrictedly repeatable. But (f) is identifiable with or analyzable as a conjunctive state of affairs. This state of affairs has three conjuncts, the second of which is not possibly brought about by anyone. The conjunctive state of affairs in question can be informally expressed as follows: Plato decides to write a dialogue; and there is no *antecedent* sufficient causal condition of Plato's deciding to write a dialogue; and there is no concurrent sufficient causal condition of Plato's deciding to write a dialogue. Because an agent could not have power over *the past*, the second conjunct of this state of affairs is not possibly brought about by anyone. Thus, an omnipotent agent ought not to be required to have the power to bring about a state of affairs which is identifiable with or analyzable as a conjunctive state of affairs one of whose conjuncts is not possibly brought about by anyone.

Omnipotence analyzed

In the light of the foregoing discussion, omnipotence can now be analyzed in terms of the following three definitions.

(D1) The period of time t is a sufficient interval for $s =$ *df.* s is a state of affairs such that: it is possible that s obtains at a time-period which has the duration of t.

(D2) A state of affairs, s, is unrestrictedly repeatable $=$ *df.* s is possibly such that: $(n) (\exists t_1) (\exists t_2) (\exists t_3) \ldots (\exists t_n) (t_1 < t_2 < t_3 < \ldots t_n$ are periods of time which are sufficient intervals for s & s obtains at t_1, s doesn't obtain at t_2, s obtains at t_3, $\ldots s$ obtains at $t_n \equiv n$ is odd).

In (D2), n ranges over all natural numbers, and $t_1 \ldots t_n$ are non-overlapping. In addition, it is assumed for the purposes of (D2) that either it is possible for time to have no beginning, or it is possible for time to have no end (or both).

(D3) x is omnipotent at $t =$ *df.* (s) (it is possible for some agent to bring about $s \rightarrow$ at t, x has it within his power to bring about s).

In (D3), x ranges over agents, and s over states of affairs which satisfy the following condition:

(C) (i) s is unrestrictedly repeatable, and of the form "in n minutes, p," & (p is a complex state of affairs $\rightarrow$ each of the parts of p is unrestrictedly repeatable & possibly brought about by someone), or (ii) s is of the form "q forever after," where q is a state of affairs which satisfies (i).

In (C), "n" ranges over real numbers, and p is not itself equivalent to a state of affairs of the form "in n minutes, r," where n is not equal to zero. Additionally, a *complex* state of affairs is one which is either constructible out of other states of affairs by use of the logical apparatus of first-order logic enriched with whatever modalities one chooses to employ, or else analyzable (in the sense of a philosophical analysis) into a state of affairs which is so constructible. Therefore, a *part* of a complex state of affairs, s, is one of those states of affairs out of which s, or an analysis of s, is constructed.

As intended, (D3) does not require an omnipotent agent to have the power to bring about either impossible or necessary states of affairs, or states of affairs such as (a) to (f). Furthermore, (D3) does not unduly limit the power of an omnipotent agent, since an agent's bringing about a state of affairs can always be "cashed out" in terms of that agent's bringing about an unrestrictedly repeatable state of affairs satisfying the antecedent of the definiens of (D3). That is, necessarily, for any state of affairs, *s*, if an agent, *a*, brings about *s*, then either *s* is an unrestrictedly repeatable state of affairs which satisfies the antecedent of the definiens of (D3), or else *a* brings about *s* by bringing about *q*, where *q* is an unrestrictedly repeatable state of affairs which satisfies the antecedent of the definiens of (D3). For instance, an omnipotent agent can bring about the state of affairs, *that in one hour, Parmenides lectures for the first time*, by bringing about the state of affairs, *that in one hour, Parmenides lectures*, when this lecture is Parmenides' first. And although the former state of affairs is a non-repeatable one which (D3) does *not* require an omnipotent agent to be able to bring about, the latter state of affairs is an unrestrictedly repeatable state of affairs which (D3) *does* require an omnipotent agent to be able to bring about.

Are divine omnipotence and omnibenevolence compatible?

It has been argued that the traditional deity has incompatible attributes, namely, necessary existence, essential omnipotence, essential omniscience, and essential omnibenevolence. The contention has been that God lacks the power to bring about evil, while non-omnipotent (and non-omnibenevolent) beings may have this power. The precise form of this argument varies depending on what precisely the relation between God and evil is assumed to be. Assume that if God exists, then this is a best possible world. In that case, if God exists, there could not be an evil unless it were necessary for some greater good, and any state of affairs containing evil incompatible with there being a maximally good world is impossible. A state of affairs of this kind could not be brought about by *any* agent. In this event, any moral evil, that is, any evil brought about by anyone, and any natural evil, or any evil which occurs in nature, must be necessary for some greater good. Suppose that God exists and that some other person, for example Cain, brings it about that an evil, *e*, exists. Then, given our assumptions, since Cain's bringing it about that *e* exists is necessary for some greater good, it is consistent with God's omnibenevolence that God brings it about that Cain brings it about that *e* exists. Alternatively, if God exists and some or all evil is impossible, given that this is a maximally good world, then neither God nor anyone else has the power to bring about that evil. If God's attributes impose moral restrictions on the nature of the universe and on what God can bring about, then they impose parallel restrictions on what any other agents can bring about. So, for instance, if there being misery in the universe is required for this being a maximally good world (for example, if [the evil of] misery is required for building good character or for the existence of happiness, and if these are in turn required for a maximally good world), then God cannot create a (maximally good) world without the presence of misery of the appropriate kind.

On the other hand, theists such as Alvin Plantinga (1974) do not hold that God's existence implies the existence of a maximally good world, but do hold that God seeks to create as good a world as God can. They allow for there to be evil that is unnecessary for any greater good that outweighs it. An evil of this kind involves free decisions of non-divine agents, which God does not prevent, but which these other agents can prevent. Plantinga contends that God is not wrong to permit an evil of this kind, since God cannot bring about a vital good – the existence of free human agents – without there being such an evil. Alternatively, it might be argued that God does no wrong in this sort of case, because God does not know how to do better (such knowledge being impossible). However, as an omnipotent God is *not* required to have power over free decisions of non-divine agents, it follows that on these views, God's omnipotence and omnibenevolence are more or less compatible to the extent indicated earlier in our discussion of the view that God's existence implies a maximally good world. Of course, nothing that has been said here answers the question of how much, if any, evil is compatible with the existence of the traditional God (see Article 50, THE PROBLEM OF EVIL).

Bibliography

Flint, T., and Freddoso, A.: "Maximal power." In *The Existence and Nature of God*, ed. Alfred Freddoso (Notre Dame: University of Notre Dame Press, 1983), pp. 81–113. [A recent attempt to analyze omnipotence.]

Hoffman, J.: "Can God do evil?," *Southern Journal of Philosophy*, 17 (1979), pp. 213–20. [Discusses the question of the compatibility of divine omnipotence and omnibenevolence.]

Hoffman, J., and Rosenkrantz, G.: "Omnipotence redux," *Philosophy and Phenomenological Research*, 49 (1988), pp. 283–301. [Critically reviews several analyses of omnipotence in the recent literature.]

Pike, N.: "Omnipotence and God's ability to sin," *American Philosophical Quarterly*, 6 (1969), pp. 208–16. [Argues that divine omnipotence and omnibenevolence are incompatible.]

Plantinga, A.: *God, Freedom, and Evil* (New York: Harper & Row, 1974). [Influential recent free will defense of theism against the problem of evil.]

Rosenkrantz, G., and Hoffman, J.: "The omnipotence paradox, modality, and time," *Southern Journal of Philosophy*, 18 (1980), pp. 473–9. [Discusses the paradox of the stone; contains a useful bibliography concerning this issue.]

Rosenkrantz, G., and Hoffman, J.: "What an omnipotent agent can do," *International Journal for Philosophy of Religion*, 11 (1980), pp. 1–19. [The original version of the analysis of omnipotence presented in the text above.]

Wierenga, E.: *The Nature of God* (Ithaca: Cornell University Press, 1989), pp. 12–35. [Extensive discussion of recent work on omnipotence with a defense of the author's analysis.]

29

Omniscience

GEORGE I. MAVRODES

The doctrine that God is omniscient is an element in most orthodox Christian theologies. One source for the doctrine consists of Biblical statements – e.g. Psalm 139, Hebrews 4:13 – which suggest a very wide scope for the divine knowledge. Perhaps another source is the conviction that without an appeal to omniscience one could not maintain a full confidence in God's ability to achieve His purposes in the world, including His purpose of redeeming and blessing His people. Probably the source which is most important philosophically, however, is that of "perfect-being" theology.

One begins, that is, with some "high" concept of God – perhaps Anselm's idea that God is that being than whom no greater can be conceived, or René Descartes's suggestion that God is a being who has all of the perfections, or the claim that God is the being who is worthy of whole-hearted worship. One then goes on to speculate about what properties a being must have in order to satisfy the high conception. Many philosophers have supposed that knowledge is a good thing, an intellectual perfection, and the more knowledge the better. It seems attractive, then, to infer that a perfect being, the greatest conceivable being, etc., will have perfect knowledge. And perfect knowledge must be full knowledge, with nothing left out. And so one concludes that God must have an all-encompassing knowledge, a knowledge of every truth, of every fact.

In its categorical form, in which it is linked with the conviction that there actually exists a being who satisfies the high concept, this line of argument yields the conclusion that there is a being – God – who knows every truth. In its hypothetical form – independent, that is, of any assumption about the actual existence of a greatest conceivable being – the argument generates a hypothetical conclusion. It concludes, that is, that *if* there is a greatest conceivable being, then that being knows every truth.

The doctrine is usually formulated, as above, in terms of a knowledge of truths or facts – what is often called "propositional knowledge," or "knowledge that. . ." I have such knowledge when, for example, I know that today is Monday, that I grew up in Albuquerque, that the earth is larger than the moon, etc. In these cases the verb "to know" takes a "that-clause" as its object, where the clause which follows the word "that" is an expression which could stand alone as a complete indicative sentence, expressing a proposition with a truth value. There are, however, other uses of "know" in which it takes other kinds of objects. One can speak of "knowing how . . .," knowing how to ride a bicycle, for example. This kind of

236

knowledge is not exhausted by knowing any set of facts, even a full set, about the activity in question. It requires that the knower have a certain skill – in the bicycle case, a neuromuscular disposition – which enables him or her to achieve a reasonable degree of success in the activity. One might also say of a destitute child, "She has known hunger throughout her life." In that case we would probably mean that the child had often been hungry, had experienced hunger, throughout her life. And there may be still other senses for "know."

Most theologians who accept the doctrine of the omniscience of God would probably not think themselves committed to the claim that God – a non-embodied being – has the neuromuscular skill of riding a bicycle, nor that He knows hunger in the sense of being hungry Himself (see Article 34, INCORPOREALITY). They would think that God knows every fact there is to know about bicycle riding and about hunger, all the truths about those subjects, but not necessarily that He has these other sorts of knowledge. The doctrine of the divine omniscience, that is, is a doctrine about "knowledge that . . .," a doctrine about propositional knowledge.

Perfect-being theology, though a rich and powerful source of speculation about the divine nature, has its limitations. In particular, there is the difficulty of determining just which properties are perfections or "great-making" properties. Aristotle, for example, argued that there are some things – vile and despicable things – which it is better not to know than to know. He presumably would have thought it a defect in God, rather than a perfection, if He were to know all about my sins, etc. (Thomas Aquinas provided a special argument to circumvent this Aristotelian suggestion.)

In recent philosophical discussions three lines of argument have been advanced against the claim that God is omniscient. Two of these are of recent origin, and are rather technical. The third goes back at least to medieval times, and depends less on technicalities.

One of these arguments depends on the claim that there are some propositions whose expression involves the first-person pronoun "I," and which cannot be expressed without that pronoun. It is argued, for example, that an accident victim suffering from temporary amnesia may know something which he can express by saying "I am in a hospital." But, for instance, he may not know that Mr Jones is in the hospital, even if in fact he is Mr Jones. For he may not know that he is Mr Jones. If there are truths of that sort, truths which can be expressed only as first-person propositions, then there are things which a person might know about himself or herself, but which it is logically impossible for anyone else – even God – to know. And if that is so, then God does not know every truth.

Not everyone, however, agrees that there are any such essentially first-person propositions. And if there are not, then of course this line of objection to the divine omniscience fails. For a further discussion of this argument see Swinburne (1977).

The second technical line of objection appeals to mathematical principles of the sort which Georg Cantor introduced in his discussion of the transfinite numbers. It is argued that if God knows every truth then there is a set of truths which God knows. But to every set of items there corresponds a "power set," and the power set contains more members than the original set (even if the original set is infinite). Furthermore, every member of the power set must have at least one distinctive truth associated with it. Consequently, there must be more truths than are included in any set of truths. And therefore no matter what set of truths a being knows, there is some truth which lies outside that set. The conclusion is that it is logically impossible that there exists an omniscient being. For a penetrating discussion of this line of argument, pro and con, see Grim and Plantinga (1993).

More generally, however, in connection with any argument whose conclusion is that a certain kind of knowledge, or a certain range of knowledge, etc., is logically impossible for a single being, there would seem to be a plausible reply which can be made in defense of omniscience. This sort of response is in fact commonly made by philosophical theologians in response to difficulties with the doctrine of divine omnipotence (see Article 28, OMNIPOTENCE). The latter doctrine initially seems to claim that God can do absolutely everything, since He is all-powerful. Can God therefore draw a square circle, make a mountain whose slopes run only uphill, etc.? At least since the time of Thomas Aquinas, most theologians have held that omnipotence need not be construed as a claim about the power to do logically impossible things. It is enough that omnipotence extend over the realm of the logically possible. That is what would be a perfection of power.

In a similar way, a perfect-being theologian could argue that perfect knowledge would range over all those things which it is logically possible to know, but there is no need for it to encompass the things which it is not possible to know. And so if either (or both) of the technical lines of argument summarized above should turn out to be correct, then the doctrine of divine omniscience would be re-stated. The unrestricted reference to "all truths" would be replaced by "all the truths which it is logically possible for any one being to know," or something of the sort. And it would be argued that such a power of knowing would be sufficient to satisfy the requirements for cognitive power, for being a perfect knower, in a high concept of God.

The third sort of difficulty which some philosophers find in the idea of divine omniscience goes back at least to medieval times. It does not allege that omniscience is logically impossible, but rather that it is logically incompatible with human free will (see Article 37, FOREKNOWLEDGE AND HUMAN FREEDOM). Jonathan Edwards (1957 [1754]) formulated a powerful version of this argument, and summarized it as follows:

[I]f there be a full, certain and infallible Foreknowledge of the future existence of the volitions of moral agents, then there is a certain infallible and indissoluble connection between those events and that Foreknowledge; and . . . therefore . . . those events are necessary events; being infallibly and indissolubly connected with that, whose existence already is, and so is now necessary, and cannot but have been.

Consider, for example, something which is being done right now, apparently by free will, by a free choice. I am right now writing this paper (w), though (I suppose) I might have chosen to take a nap instead. But God, if He is omniscient, knew yesterday that I would now be writing (*k*). The Edwards line of argument can then be represented as follows:

(1)   Necessarily, if *k* then *w*.
(2)   Necessarily, *k*.
(3)   Therefore, necessarily *w*.

But if I am doing something *necessarily* then I have no choice about doing it. Since the action is necessary, I cannot avoid it. It cannot be a free action. It was already determined at least as far back as yesterday (and indeed, from everlasting to everlasting). So I have no real alternative to it now, and no real choice about it now.

If we wish, we can modify the argument above simply by replacing the word "necessarily" with the clause "I cannot now do anything about the fact that. . . ." The logic of that analogous argument is the same as that of the original, and perhaps it brings out more clearly the intended connection with the possibility of a genuine human free will, of genuine choices.

The argument, as formalized above, is logically valid. That is, it is logically impossible that the conclusion be false if the premises are true. What do the two premises come to?

Premise (1) represents Edwards's "infallible and indissoluble connection" between the divine foreknowledge and the events which are foreknown. It asserts a necessary connection between the divine foreknowledge of an event and that event's actually happening. Edwards derives this premise from God's necessary infallibility, and it does seem to follow from that. It also follows, perhaps more prosaically, from a rather common conception of knowledge (whether divine or human).

What about (2)? Taken without any modalizing expression, such as "necessarily" (or the analogue which I suggested above), premise (2) is simply *k*. And that is just the claim that there is a divine foreknowledge of the act in question. It is just a special case of the doctrine of divine omniscience, here applied to a divine knowledge of some human act before that act is done. *k* is the substantive content of (2).

The modalization of (2) however – the introduction into it of necessity or some similar notion – is required for the validity of the argument. For the unmodalized version of (2) will not yield the modalized version of the conclusion. Instead, the conclusion which could validly be drawn would simply be *w* – which is just the observation that I am now writing this paper. In that case the necessity would have disappeared from the conclusion, and with it would have disappeared the suggestion that this conclusion is incompatible with genuine choices, free will, etc. The modalized version of (2), however, will support the modalized version of the conclusion.

Edwards defends the necessity in (2) on the grounds that the knowledge of God *is already in the past* – it is something "whose existence already is." He says that "in things which are past, their past existence is now necessary: having already made sure of existence, it is too late for any possibility of alteration in that respect." This principle, which seems crucial to the argument, is now often referred to as the "principle of the fixity of the past" (PFP). Premise (2), therefore, can be thought of as being a combination of two factors – the substantive element is the doctrine of omniscience applied to future events, and the modal element is provided by the PFP.

A variety of responses have been made to arguments of this sort. One may accept the core of the argument as it stands, holding that it is logically valid and that its premises are true, and that therefore its conclusion, (3), is also true. Some will go on to the further conclusion that there is therefore no human free will. This is a strong form of theological determinism. But it differs from other strong theological determinisms, in that the deterministic conclusion is not drawn from any theory or claim about the divine causation of events. This version of determinism does not appeal to God's power to cause or prevent future events, nor does it claim that future events are determined by *causes* which lie in the past. It is drawn, rather, merely from the divine *foreknowledge* of human choices, acts, etc. And it does not claim that the divine foreknowledge causes the future event.

Others who accept the core argument may go on to argue that there is a suitable sense of freedom which is compatible with determinism. If that is so, then human actions, such as my now writing this paper, can be free actions even if they are also determined and necessary. Compatibilist claims are common in connection with other forms of determinism, and they are also vigorously disputed by the partisans of "libertarian" conceptions of freedom. The contest between libertarian and compatibilist views is probably much the same in this context as in the others.

Philosophers who reject the core argument generally do so by rejecting premise (2) in one way or another. Since (2) includes two factors, and each of them may be rejected in more than one way, there is considerable variety in these contrary views.

Some philosophers reject (2) because they reject the substantive element in it. They claim, that is, that there are some things about the future which God does not know. At the very least, He does not know what the free actions of human beings will be. And so God did not know yesterday whether I would write this paper today or take a nap instead.

In turn, there are at least three ways in which this denial may be further explained or defended. Some philosophers appeal to an idea which seems to go back at least to Aristotle, the idea that future-tense sentences, at least if they refer to events whose determining causes are not already in the past, are neither true nor false – they have no truth value at all. They will come to have a truth value only when the event actually happens or the time for it passes, or when something else happens which will definitely cause or prevent the event. But if there was nothing yesterday which causally determined or prevented my choice and action today, then yesterday it was neither true nor false that I would write today. The divine omniscience, however, is said to be a knowledge of truths. If there was no truth yesterday about my actions today, then there was nothing relevant for God to know yesterday, and His failure to know what I would do today is not a failure of omniscience.

240

Some other philosophers hold that these future-tense propositions do have a truth value, and that God *could* know the true ones. But He voluntarily refrains from knowing them (perhaps in order to leave room for free will). On this view, omniscience is construed as a *power* of knowing, rather than as an actual knowing. God has this power, even with respect to future human choices, but He may not exercise this power in one or another particular case. This would be analogous to claiming that God, because He is omnipotent, is able to perform miracles (see Article 46, MIRACLES). But in fact He does not perform every miracle which is within the range of His omnipotence. So also, on this view, He (voluntarily) does not know everything which lies within the cognitive power of His omniscience.

There seems also to be a (miscellaneous) third group of philosophers who deny that God knows all future human choices and actions, but who do not cite either of these reasons or explanations. For further discussion of these various ways of denying the "full" omniscience involved in premise (2), see Swinburne (1977).

The other element in (2) is the modality of necessity, and some philosophers deny this premise because they deny the modality (though they may accept the substantive element). This position also has several variants.

One variant holds that the substantive element in (2) is not a proposition about the past (or that it is not *wholly* about the past, etc.), and therefore the PFP does not apply to it. This variant itself has at least two subvariants.

One of these holds that God is an eternal being (rather than, say, an everlasting temporal being). As an eternal being, no temporal descriptions apply to Him (see Article 32, ETERNITY). He has knowledge of all events, including those in the future (our future, that is, but not God's future), but none of this knowledge is *fore*knowledge. He does not know anything *before* it happens (or after it either). On this view an eternal being is, in some obscure and difficult sense, contemporaneous with every temporal event. So (2) is not a proposition about the past, and therefore it does not inherit any necessity on account of pastness. But there is no other reason for thinking that (2) is necessary. So we can reject the modality in (2). For further discussion of this idea of eternity see Stump and Kretzmann (1981).

The other subvariant makes no appeal to the alleged eternity of God, but distinguishes two (or more) sorts of propositions about the past. It is claimed that some propositions are *entirely* about the past, in the sense that they have no entailments about future events, etc. Other propositions may be *partially* about the past, but – if they have entailments about the future – they are partially about the future too. And it is then said that the PFP applies only to propositions which are *entirely* about the past. These are now often called "hard facts about the past." If (2) reports merely a soft fact about the past, and not a hard fact, then the PFP does not apply to it, and there is no reason to think that it is necessary.

There has been a large amount of recent controversy about the right way to make the hard/soft distinction, what its significance is, etc. For further discussion and references see Zagzebski (1991).

Still another way of denying the modality in (2) (and the last to be mentioned here) is simply to deny the PFP. People who hold this view maintain (contrary to, say, Edwards) that the mere pastness of an event or state of affairs does not confer any necessity on it. If it does not inherit necessity from some other source then it simply is not necessary at all. It is a contingent element in the past history of the world, an event which might have been different from what it actually was.

Someone who holds this view would say that God indeed knew yesterday that I would write today. But why did He know *this*, rather than knowing, say, that I would be taking a nap right now? God did indeed have the knowledge that He had yesterday. But there was no inherent necessity that He should have *that* particular piece of knowledge, rather than have some alternative to it. What determined that God have that particular item of knowledge is my decision today to write rather than to nap. The particular features of the divine knowledge yesterday are determined by my choices and actions today.

If this is the way things are, then the divine foreknowledge about future human acts and decisions *depends* on those acts and decisions, and it imposes no constraint or necessity on them. If there are any such constraints, they must derive from some source other than the divine knowledge. For further discussion and references see Zagzebski (1991).

Bibliography

Edwards, J.: *A Careful and Strict Inquiry into the Modern Prevailing Notions of that Freedom of Will which Is Supposed to Be Essential to Moral Agency, Virtue and Vice, Reward and Punishment, Praise and Blame* (1754); ed. P. Ramsey, *Freedom of the Will* (New Haven and London: Yale University Press, 1957).

Grim, P. and Plantinga, A.: "Truth, omniscience, and Cantorian arguments: An exchange," *Philosophical Studies*, 71 (1993), pp. 267–306.

Stump, E., and Kretzmann, N.: "Eternity," *Journal of Philosophy*, 78 (1981), pp. 429–58.

Swinburne, R.: *The Coherence of Theism* (Oxford: Clarendon Press, 1977).

Wierenga, E. R.: *The Nature of God* (Ithaca: Cornell University Press, 1989).

Zagzebski, L. T.: *The Dilemma of Freedom and Foreknowledge* (New York: Oxford University Press, 1991).

30

Goodness

PAUL HELM

In Judeo-Christianity and philosophical reflection upon it "perfect goodness" may be thought of as a separately identifiable attribute of God, or as characterizing other divine attributes, or as that standard of value which only God can exemplify. God is said to be good in a wider or narrower sense; wider, when this indicates the fullness and completeness of his being, his self-sufficiency and freedom from want or deficiency of any kind. In this sense of "perfect goodness" it has the same reference as "perfect being," though a different sense. Divine perfection provides the conceptual link between being and goodness in God's case; God alone is, and can be, good. In the narrower sense God's goodness is an aspect of his moral character, and he communicates this goodness to his creatures in acts of creation and redemption. The source of these views lies in the scriptural ideas of the goodness of God (e.g. Psalm 119:68, Matthew 19:17) and of the creation (Genesis 1: 1 Timothy 4:4), but the expression of them in philosophical terms, as well as some of the characteristic philosophical problems that the idea of divine goodness gives rise to, owes much to Neoplatonic influences flowing through such theological fountainheads as Boethius and Augustine.

Of these two senses, the metaphysical sense of "goodness" is the less familiar. According to it, goodness is not a separate quality or property but, like existence, it transcends all the categories of being. Goodness is a property which belongs to every contingent being in virtue of being created, but especially to humankind, created morally upright. Since according to Judeo-Christian theism everything that exists contingently owes its existence to the Creator, anything, to the degree that it exists, participates in the goodness of its creator.

So divine goodness is at the center of a complex web of ideas, linking together real existence, createdness, and moral character. On this view it is better, though not necessarily morally better, to be than not to be; existence is an intrinsic good, even though the individual in question may be morally wicked. (The idea of evil as a deficiency may be regarded as a platonizing of the scriptural idea of iniquity, a falling short of the mark.) At the point at which an individual became wicked to a completely unrelieved or unqualified degree he or she would no longer exist. There are degrees of being, and so degrees of goodness. For example the goodness of a material body, liable to decay, corruption, and death, is less good than the goodness of a spirit which, though existing contingently, has no such natural liability.

In the moral sense of "goodness" God is said to be good in that he has no moral deficiency; his benevolence or justice or wisdom (or any other moral character or trait) are good in that they, in turn, are perfect exemplifications of these qualities, part of the fullness of being which he, as the supreme being, enjoys. In the Anselmian tradition of perfect-being theology, God is said to be perfectly good in that goodness to a perfect degree is a necessary part of God's overall perfection.

You are only one supreme good, altogether sufficient unto Yourself, needing nothing else but needed by all else in order to exist and to fare well.   (*Proslogion, ch. 22*)

Now, one thing is necessary, viz., that one necessary Being in which there is every good – or better, who is every good, one good, complete good, and the only good.   (*Proslogion, ch. 23*)

In this tradition, the metaphysical and the moral senses of goodness, though conceptually distinct, can be seen to come together in the following way. God is perfectly good not only in the senses described but also in that in him existence and essence are one. In him there is nothing that is unactualized. This reveals another feature of this idea of goodness, that it is telic in character. To be good is to achieve one's end. In God's case, his end is himself. In the case of creatures who necessarily participate in divine goodness, their good is to be on the way to achieving their end. This general thesis about goodness and purpose, when it is applied to human beings, yields a meta-ethic: to be morally good is to fulfill one's potential.

There is a strong conceptual connection between the goodness of God and the fullness of his being, his self-sufficiency. This connection is made via the idea of God as the creator. For if there are created things that are good, and (following 1 Timothy 4:4) good because they exist, even though transient and perishing, then *a fortiori* their imperishable and eternal creator must be the supremely good, not supremely good because he is the best of a genus, but, being outside all genera, God is goodness itself. Thus Augustine:

This thing is good and that good, but take away this and that, and regard good itself if thou canst; so wilt thou see God, not good by a good that is other than Himself, but the good of all good. For in all these good things, whether those which I have mentioned, or any else that are to be discerned or thought, we could not say that one was better than another, when we judge truly, unless a conception of the good itself had been impressed upon us, such that according to it we might both approve some things as good, and prefer one good to another.   (*De Trinitate* 8.3)

And Aquinas says that since God is "the primary operative cause of everything, goodness and desirability fittingly belong to him" (*Summa Theologiae* 1a.6.1). What makes something good is that it is desirable; the supremely existing and supremely good being is supremely desirable; lesser beings less so. So for Aquinas the good and the desirable have the same reference, but a different sense (*Summa* 1a.5). Goodness has the sense of completeness; God, being supremely perfect, is supremely good.

Some philosophers have resisted the consequences that would seem to follow from this, that God is necessarily good, on the grounds that if a property x is possessed necessarily by *a*, then *a* cannot be praised for having *x*. And since God is praised for his goodness, he cannot have that goodness necessarily. So they have argued that the being who is God is contingently good. But this reasoning is not altogether convincing. For one thing, the sense in question is not causal necessity, but ontological necessity. Further, God is not praised for achieving moral goodness, or for retaining it, but for being it, as a beautiful landscape may evoke expressions of admiration and praise.

Tensions may be observed between other elements in this web of ideas. For example, if the goodness of created things and the divine goodness are linked, is a created thing good merely in virtue of having been created by God, regardless of what it is like? Put slightly differently, is a creature good simply in virtue of being created by God or because it participates in the divine goodness? At least in the case of humankind, which according to the Judeo-Christian tradition is created in the image of God, it is hard not to conclude that human goodness is such in virtue of certain intrinsic features possessed by humankind.

Another tension concerns the relation between the divine goodness and the divine freedom. If God is all good, the fullness of being, what reason might he have for creating anything distinct from himself? A standard answer to the first question is that goodness has a tendency to diffuse itself and the creation is a diffusion of the divine goodness.

Thus Jonathan Edwards:

God's disposition to cause his own infinite fullness to flow forth, is not the less properly called his goodness, because the good he communicates is what he delights in, as he delights in his own glory. . . . Nor is this disposition, in God, to diffuse his own good, the less excellent, because it is implied in his love to himself.

Creatures, even the most excellent, are not independent and self-moved in their goodness; but in all its exercises, they are excited by some object they find: something appearing good, or in some respect worthy of regard, presents itself, and moves their kindness. But God, being all, and alone, is absolutely self-moved. The exercises of his communicative disposition are absolutely from within himself; all that is good and worthy in the object, and its very *being*, proceeding from the overflowing of his fullness.   (*God's Chief End in Creation*, ch. 1, sect. iv (in *Works*, ed.; Hickman (London, 1834), vol. 1, p. 105)

But if this is so, how can the theologically unwelcome conclusion be avoided that the divine act of creation is not a free act, but that the creation is a necessary emanation from the fullness of the divine being?

The idea that goodness, and especially divine goodness, is essentially diffusive has played an important role in speculations about the internal coherence of the Christian doctrine of God as a trinity of persons. God is not a solitary, undifferentiated God; the goodness of God is thus exemplified in the life of reciprocal love of the divine tri-personal life. And this diffusive goodness is further seen in the creation of a universe in which exist individuals made in the image of God, and so capable of receiving and reciprocating that love.

Divine goodness may be said to represent an *a priori* standard of perfection to which actual goods may or may not attain. But what sort of standard is it? There are three main problems that arise in answering this question. The first is semantic. How does the goodness of God relate to the goodness of which men and women have a more ready experience, cases of human goodness? Is God, being good, good in precisely the same sense in which a particular human being, or human action, may be said to be good? Or is his goodness *sui generis*, unrelated, or perhaps only partly related, to human goodness? The second question is: if there is some positive relation, even if only an analogical relation, between divine and human goodness, is the goodness in question moral goodness, or goodness in some other sense? And third, if the divine goodness is moral goodness, what is the relevant standard of goodness? Does God set the standard of moral goodness in question, or does his goodness merely follow or exemplify that standard? This question, Does God command something because it is good, or is it good because he commands it?, is a special case of the more general issue: Does God decree the existence of *a* because it is good, or does the goodness of *a* consist simply in its being created by God? Let us look at each of these three questions in turn.

First, the semantic question. If God's goodness is totally unrelated to human goodness, then it is a misleading linguistic accident that the same word may be used of diverse things. If divine and human goodness have nothing in common, why call both *goodness*? It is sometimes argued that since God is not part of the human moral community no moral attributes of the sort that arise in that community can be ascribed to him. But if divine goodness means something completely different from human goodness, then what sense does it make to praise God for his goodness? Why should his being good not be a reason not for praising but for withholding praise?

Aquinas, among others, has stressed the need to distinguish between the order of being and the order of knowing. Creatures are good in so far as they participate in the divine goodness, but the divine goodness is known only by extrapolation from human experience of creaturely goodness (*Summa* 1a.13.2). So there must be at least an analogical relation between divine goodness and human goodness; perhaps goodness in each case is being used univocally, each being conditioned by the respective metaphysical circumstances in which the goodness is exemplified. What it is for x to be good will not be the same as what it is for y to be good if x and y are instances of different kinds of thing. The goodness of God and of humankind are qualitatively the same, but human goodness, unlike divine goodness, is exemplified in a finite, contingent, and (in this life at least) a defective manner.

In the philosophy of Kant and philosophies influenced by him the goodness of God has a dramatically different character, and plays a radically different role. Goodness is not an essential part of divine perfection, the fullness of his being of which we may dimly become aware through the use of models or analogies. Rather, that God is good is not known, or knowable, but rather postulated by pure practical reason. It is a requirement for the rationality of human ethics that God be postulated as the *summum bonum*, as the rewarder of virtue and the punisher of vice. "But where do we get the concept of God as the highest good? Solely from the *Idea* of moral perfection" (Kant 1948 [1785], p. 73). The idea of a purely moral God exercises only a regulative role; Kant can find no comparable role for any other, metaphysical, attributes of God, and so the God postulated has been fairly characterized as "purely moral."

Once the goodness of God is disconnected from its scriptural and ontological roots, as it is in the philosophy of Kant and in the theologies of those who have been strongly influenced by him, there is scope to impute to God any of the varieties of goodness found in human life. Thus the goodness of God may be thought to lie in fulfilling an instrumental or organic function, or working to the advantage or pleasure of people, like a good knife or a good wine. Or perhaps God is good because he is good at his job, like a good salesman!

One answer to our second question has already been suggested. If the goodness of God is said to bear an analogical relation to what people regard as good, then which of the many sorts of goodness is this to be?

In contemporary philosophy of religion, most attention has been paid to the third question. For it appears to raise crucial issues of metaphysical and moral superiority and inferiority, a special case of the Euthyphro dilemma (see Article 57, DIVINE COMMAND ETHICS). Is some human action morally good because it exemplifies the moral goodness of God, or is God morally good because his character and actions exemplify human goodness? If God's goodness merely follows some independent standard of goodness, then it appears that his sovereignty and independence are compromised; if God himself sets the standard, by his command, then it appears that whatever God commands would *ipso facto* be good.

Various responses to this dilemma have been proposed. All solutions appear to allow for the distinction between positive and natural law, and to have no problem with the idea that God may command what is otherwise morally indifferent, for example, command a certain kind of priestly dress. The most prominent responses to the dilemma are the following.

Since moral values are metaphysically necessary, not even God can will or command what is evil. Since cruelty is necessarily evil, not even God can, by his command, make an act of cruelty permissible or obligatory. What God can do, by his command, is to emphasize the obligatoriness of certain particular actions in a given set of contingent circumstances. Thus by bringing about the contingent circumstances in which I have borrowed ten dollars, he may be said to make the repayment of the money obligatory.

Another approach emphasizes the unity and simplicity of the divine character and argues that the distinction between the power and the goodness of God is artificial and inadmissible. As a simple being, God could not command, or propose to command, a course of action that was inconsistent with his moral nature. So no counterfactual of the form "what if God were to command an act of theft?" could be true. Others have argued that a divine command would only be a "live option" if it is believed to be the command of a loving God. Should this belief be unwarranted then the concept of what was ethically wrong would break down.

Whatever solution to the Euthyphro dilemma is favored, care must be taken to avoid the view that reflection on the character or commands of God cannot be the source of fresh moral insight. For it does not follow from the view that God can only will what is morally good, that each human being knows, in advance of

247

God's command, what goodness requires in any given situation which he or she is likely to be confronted with. Necessary truths may be learned *a posteriori* , and so may the implications of the necessary truth (if it is one) that God commands only what is morally good.

The tension between divine goodness and divine freedom noted earlier surfaces again in connection with THE PROBLEM OF EVIL (see Article 50). For if God is perfectly good, how, if he creates anything at all, could he fail to create the best of all possible worlds? Perhaps there is no best of all possible worlds, because, for any possible world, a better can always be imagined. Or perhaps possible worlds that God might create necessarily contain features which are incommensurable. But then why create *this* world?

There is only a problem of evil, a problem of why an all-good God permits or ordains evil, either natural evil or moral evil or both, if the goodness of God bears some similarity of character to human goodness. It is frequently assumed in modern discussions of the problem of evil that the divine goodness consists in benevolence which God intends to distribute equally to all his human creatures. But perhaps, in this world and any world closely similar to it, an equal distribution of benevolence is impossible.

So the problem of evil, considered as an issue of logical consistency, is more or less acute depending upon what the moral values which comprise the divine goodness are thought to be. If divine goodness is divine equi-benevolence, then the problem of evil is at its most acute, particularly if it is also held that whoever is benevolent must act for the immediate moral good of others. If, however, the divine goodness comprises other values besides or other than egalitarian benevolence, justice say, then the problem of evil is less acute; and even less acute if part of God's goodness is that he has obligations to others besides his human creatures, obligations to himself, say, which take precedence over other obligations. Perhaps a good God has purposes wider than or different from those which are concerned with human happiness (the fulfillment of which is often thought to be the sole criterion of the operation of divine goodness), to which human happiness is subordinate.

What these reflections reveal is that the idea of goodness as a perfection of God, while being indisputable, is far too indefinite and vague an idea to be of real value in articulating divine goodness. Not only is it impossible to derive one unitary concept of divine goodness from the idea of divine perfection, there are, as we have seen, various concepts of divine goodness, each depending on the different values which such goodness is held to entail.

Bibliography

Anselm: *Proslogion*, tr. J. Hopkins and H. Richardson (London: SCM Press, 1974).

Aquinas, Thomas: *Summa Theologiae*, vol. 2, *The Existence and Nature of God*, tr. T. McDermott (London: Eyre & Spottiswoode, 1964).

Augustine: *On the Trinity*, tr. A. W. Haddan: (Edinburgh: T. & T. Clark, 1872).

Helm, P. (ed.): *Divine Commands and Morality* (Oxford: Oxford University Press, 1981).

Kant, I.: *The Moral Law: Kant's Groundwork of the Metaphysic of Morals*, tr. H. J. Paton (1785) (London: Hutchinson, 1948).

Kretzmann, N.: "Goodness, knowledge and indeterminacy in the philosophy of Thomas Aquinas," *Journal of Philosophy*, 80 (1983) pp. 631–49.

MacDonald, S. (ed.): *Being and Goodness* (Ithaca: Cornell University Press, 1991).

Morris, T. V.: "Duty and divine goodness." In *The Concept of God*, ed. T. V. Morris (Oxford: Oxford University Press, 1987).

Murdoch, I.: *The Sovereignty of Good* (London: Routledge & Kegan Paul, 1970).

Quinn, P.: *Divine Commands and Moral Requirements* (Oxford: Clarendon Press, 1978).

31

Simplicity

ELEONORE STUMP

The concept and difficulties associated with it

Among the traditionally recognized divine attributes regularly discussed by medieval theologians and accepted by them as part of orthodox religious belief, the strangest and hardest to understand is simplicity. None the less, for all the difficulty of the doctrine of simplicity, philosophers and theologians in all three major monotheisms – Judaism, Christianity, and Islam – have seen it as foundational for understanding the divine nature. In their view, God is an absolutely perfect being, and absolute perfection requires simplicity.

The doctrine of simplicity is the doctrine that God is one in a radical sort of way; a simple God lacks composition of any sort. The doctrine can be thought of as comprising four claims.

1   God cannot have any spatial or temporal parts.
2   God cannot have any intrinsic accidental properties.
3   There cannot be any real distinction between one essential property and another in God's nature.
4   There cannot be a real distinction between essence and existence in God.

These claims rule out composition in increasingly strict ways.

Claim (1), which is the easiest to understand, rules out the possibility that God is a physical entity or even is spatially locatable, as immaterial ghosts are sometimes supposed to be (see Article 34, INCORPOREALITY). Claim (1) has also regularly been taken to imply that God is eternal rather than temporal: on the doctrine of simplicity, the life of a simple God is not spread out over time, any more than God is spread out over space (see Article 32, ETERNITY). Although the idea that God is not corporeal is familiar, not everyone finds the doctrine of God's eternality comprehensible or consistent. Some philosophers have supposed that an eternal God couldn't act in time, and some philosophers have argued that the notion of an atemporal life is incoherent.

Claim (2) presupposes the familiar distinction between intrinsic and extrinsic properties, or between real properties and Cambridge properties (as they are sometimes called). Although this distinction is widely used and often easy to apply, it is difficult to give a precise and satisfactory account of it. The basic notion behind it is, roughly, that a change in s's extrinsic properties can occur without a change in s, while a change in s's intrinsic properties is a change in s. The intrinsic properties of an abstract geometrical figure are all essential to it. On the doctrine of simplicity, God is like this, too, in the sense that none of his intrinsic properties is accidental. Like every other entity, however, God has extrinsic accidental properties, such as his being mentioned on this page.

The implications of claim (2) are, on the face of it, counterintuitive. They are also difficult to square with the traditional account of God, according to which God freely chooses to do some things, including responding to human free choices. So, for example, God has the property of being such that he freely answers the prayer Hannah freely chooses to pray by bringing about the birth of her son Samuel. But, according to claim (2), any such property is essential to God. Presumably, then, it is not possible for God to exist and not have such a property, and therefore God has no choice about whether he has it or not. It is hard to see, then, in what sense God's response to Hannah can be free or dependent on Hannah's freely choosing to pray her prayer.

Such difficulties are only exacerbated by claim (3), which denies the possibility of distinguishing one essential attribute of God's from another. From this claim it seems to follow that God's being such that he answers Hannah's prayer must be identical with any other attribute of God's, including, for example, being such that he talks with Rebecca about her pregnancy. Furthermore, any such attribute of God's will be identical with any of the more widely recognized divine attributes, like OMNISCIENCE (see Article 29); and omniscience will be identical with OMNIPOTENCE (see Article 28), which will also be identical with perfect GOODNESS (see Article 30) and every other property of God's.

Finally, claim (4) makes it clear that all talk of attributes is misleading, on the doctrine of simplicity. If we could distinguish attributes within God, then we could also make a distinction within God between the existent God and the essence that God has. But according to claim (4), God is so radically one that there is no composition in him even of essence and existence. Consequently, God does not have an essence; instead, he is identical with his essence, and even his existence cannot be distinguished from that essence.

Many but not all of these apparently counterintuitive consequences can be warded off by clarifying the view of God's nature that the doctrine of simplicity is meant to express. On the doctrine of simplicity, it is misleading to think of God's answering Hannah's prayer as, literally, one of the things God does. Rather, strictly speaking, the one thing that atemporal God has is a variety of effects in time: a promise to Hagar at t_1, a conversation with Rebecca at t_2, and a response to Hannah at t_3. The absence of real distinction among divine attributes such as omniscience and omnipotence can be explained analogously. What human beings distinguish conceptually as divine omnipotence and omniscience is the single thing that is God but recognized by us under differing descriptions or different manifestations. On the doctrine of simplicity, although all the designations for divine attributes are identical in reference, they are none the less not synonymous but are rather different in sense, just as "the morning star" and "the evening star" are non-synonymous expressions designating the same thing under different descriptions or in different manifestations. Furthermore, that omnipotence and omniscience are different manifestations of the same thing doesn't entail that power and knowledge are the same.

The most recalcitrant difficulties generated by the doctrine of simplicity are those that result from combining the doctrine with the traditional ascription to God of free will. How can it be both that God freely willed to create (see Article 39, CREATION AND CONSERVATION), for example, and also that God has no intrinsic accidental attributes? If God freely willed to create, isn't it the case that he might have willed not to create, so that there are possible worlds in which God doesn't create? But if that is so, then God isn't the same in all possible worlds; in some worlds, he has an attribute, namely, the attribute of being such that he creates, which he doesn't have in other worlds. But then it does seem that God has intrinsic accidental attributes.

Part of the trouble here comes from combining the medieval terminology of the doctrine of simplicity with contemporary understandings of the same terms. Although Thomas Aquinas, for example, denies that God has any intrinsic accidental attributes, he does not mean that God is the same in every possible world in which he exists. For much of the medieval period, modalities were not thought of in terms of sameness or difference across possible worlds but rather in terms of branching timelines of the actual world. So, for example, although Aquinas sees God's not creating as logically possible, God's creating is none the less not an accident of God's but is rather necessary to him – in the sense that there is no branch of this world's timeline on which not willing to create is correctly ascribable to God. For Aquinas, then, to deny that God has intrinsic accidents is to hold that God's nature is immutably and determinately the same for all time in this world, not that it is the same across all possible worlds.

Someone might none the less object that the difference between those of God's attributes which are the same in all possible worlds and those which aren't marks a real distinction in God's nature, between the metaphysical "softness" of willing to create, for example, and the metaphysical "hardness" of God's omnipotence. It isn't clear, however, that this conceptual distinction constitutes a metaphysical distinction in God. Although some of the objects of God's will might have been different, it isn't the case that there are parts of the divine will which are more mutable or less ineluctable than others (see Article 40, IMMUTABILITY AND IMPASSIBILITY). What the conceptual distinction picks out is a difference in the ways in which God is related to himself and to other things, but being related differently to different things doesn't entail that there are distinct intrinsic properties in God.

Many philosophers none the less suppose that these difficulties and others as well are fatal to the doctrine of divine simplicity. Some argue that the doctrine is incoherent, and others maintain that it is inconsistent with certain other traditionally held claims about God. To some philosophers, for example, a simple God seems to have more the nature of an abstract object than the character of a person. Still others suppose that there is no way of reconciling the doctrine of simplicity with the doctrine of the Trinity (see Article 66, TRINITY).

The history of the concept

The concept of simplicity can be found in Plotinus (see, for example, *Enneads* V.1–3), who attributes it to Parmenides and Plato, although it is perhaps more accurately attributable to earlier commentators on Plato. For Plotinus, the doctrine of divine simplicity is a powerful impetus to negative theology, showing that God is to be understood only in terms of what he is not, rather than in terms of any positive attributes which can be correctly applied to him. (The same impetus to negative theology can also be seen clearly in the use Maimonides (see Article 11, THE JEWISH CONTRIBUTION TO MEDIEVAL PHILOSOPHICAL THEOLOGY) makes of the doctrine.) The Church Fathers also have a notion of simplicity and apply it to God. It or something ancestral to it can be found in Origen (see, for example, *Peri Archon* I.1.6). Athanasius supposes that accepting composition of essence and qualities in God will be generally shocking to the orthodox (*Epistola ad Afros Episcopos* 8).

The concept receives a good deal of attention in the work of Augustine, who combines the logic of Aristotle's *Categories* with Neoplatonic attitudes towards metaphysics and theology. So, for example, Augustine argues that in God there is none of the difference between accident and substance of the sort that characterizes creatures; rather, as Augustine puts it, God is what he has (*De Civitate Dei* XI.10). Augustine recognizes a worry about the compatibility of simplicity and Trinity, but he sees the difficulties more in the doctrine of the Trinity itself than in the combination of the two doctrines. According to the doctrine of the Trinity, God is three persons but only one substance; the persons of the Trinity are distinguished from one another only by relational attributes and not by any intrinsic essential or accidental properties, all of which are identical among the three persons. Augustine recognizes the perplexing nature of these claims, but he sees no special difficulty in holding that the one thing that all the persons of the Trinity are is itself simple (see, for example, *De Trinitate* VI.6–8).

Anselm takes any composition to be incompatible with aseity. If God is just because he has justice, then he has justice from something external to himself, on which he is dependent, Anselm thinks, and so he is not self-sufficient, contrary to what we suppose about the deity. Since similar considerations apply to any property attributed to God, Anselm holds that anything that can be truly said of God is the same as God's essence and that God is without any composition at all (*Monologion* 16–18). In the *Proslogion*, he deduces God's simplicity from the characterization of God as "that than which nothing greater can be conceived of" (*Proslogion* 12).

The culmination of medieval Latin discussions of simplicity comes in the work of Aquinas. In *Summa Theologiae* I.3, Aquinas presents the notion of divine simplicity by denying composition of God in increasingly strenuous ways. There is in God, he says, no composition of matter and form, so that God is not material. Furthermore, God is identical with his nature, and his nature is identical with his existence. Consequently, he has no accidents, and his essence cannot be divided into various attributes. In *Quaestiones Disputatae de Potentia* he argues that although the words characterizing divine attributes refer to one and the same

253

thing, they are not synonymous (I.7.6). Furthermore, although these terms cannot be predicated of God and creatures univocally, it must not be thought that they are therefore predicated equivocally. Instead, they are predicated analogously, so that, for example, while divine and human justice cannot be defined in exactly the same way, divine justice is analogous to human justice.

Aquinas's account of simplicity is informed not only by the work of his Christian predecessors but also by a long tradition of philosophical and theological discussion among Jewish and Islamic philosophers. In the opening chapter of his work on the *Mishnah Torah*, Maimonides considers the command to the Jews to worship only one God. He sees the commandment not only as forbidding polytheism, but also as warding off wrong views of the nature of God. According to Maimonides, the commandment mandates ruling out any sort of composition in God. In *The Guide of the Perplexed* Maimonides spells out his interpretation of the doctrine of simplicity, including a denial of any distinction between essence and existence in God (chs. 14–18). Furthermore, he thinks that because God is simple, terms applied to God and creatures are used equivocally, and the only attributes which can be predicated of God strictly speaking are negative attributes. We are none the less not left without knowledge of God, because the negative attributes, in showing us what God is not, give us some significant information about him. Positive attributes customarily applied to God are to be understood in a negative way; so, for instance, when we say that God is living, what we should understand by this expression is that it is not the case that God is dead (ch. 18). Although Aquinas accepted a great deal of Maimonides's interpretation of simplicity, he rejected this way of understanding predicates applied to God and creatures.

Maimonides was himself reacting to an important controversy within Arabic philosophical theology (see Article 10, THE ISLAMIC CONTRIBUTION TO MEDIEVAL PHILOSOPHICAL THEOLOGY). Islamic philosophers (*falasifa*), such as al-Farabi, Avicenna, and Averroës, accepted the notion of divine simplicity, whereas the Muslim theologians (*mutakallamin*) tended to reject it. Avicenna went so far as to deny that God has an essence at all. Averroës rejected this view as well as related views of Avicenna, but he, too, emphasized the importance of divine simplicity. Averroës saw simplicity and Trinity as opposed to each other; allowing composition in God would, in his view, open the way for supposing that God is triune as Christians think, contrary to the Qur'an's insistence on the unity of God. Arguing against "the philosophers," al-Ghazali, on the other hand, thought he could demonstrate that there must be composition in God, at least the composition between essence and existence.

Even in the medieval Christian tradition there wasn't universal acceptance of the doctrine of simplicity. Although he was officially condemned for this view, Gilbert of Poitiers in the twelfth century held that there is a real distinction in God between his essence and his attributes. A century later, John Duns Scotus spoke of a "formal" distinction among God's attributes, which he thought allowed him both to admit the doctrine of simplicity and also to distinguish among divine attributes. Partly in consequence of this subtle weakening of the doctrine of simplicity, Scotus thought that some terms can be applied to God and creatures univocally. William of Ockham rejected Scotus's notion of a formal distinction, but he agreed with him that some terms can be applied to God and creatures univocally, and he maintained that we can properly cognize God's essence in a concept which is both proper to it and composite.

Applications of the concept to issues in the philosophy of religion

The doctrine of divine simplicity makes a difference to several issues in the philosophy of religion, including the problem of the apparent incompatibility of omnipotence and impeccability, the seeming paradox of essential goodness, the question of God's relationship to morality, and issues related to the cosmological argument. Here I will focus just on the last two.

First, the question of God's relation to morality has typically been thought to have two possible answers. God's will is sometimes taken to create morality, in the sense that whatever God wills is good just because he wills it. This is the fundamental approach of divine command theories of morality (see Article 57, DIVINE COMMAND ETHICS). Alternatively, morality is taken to be grounded in principles transmitted by God but independent of him, so that a perfectly good God frames his will in accordance with those independently existing standards of goodness. Either of these answers seems to have a high cost attached to it. The first seems to make morality arbitrary, so that apparently anything at all could turn out to be moral (although there are sophisticated theories of divine command morality that attempt to avoid this implication). The second seems to deprive God of his sovereignty, since even God looks to standards external to him for morality. Furthermore, although this answer yields an objective morality, it does so at the cost of destroying any essential connection between morality and God.

If the doctrine of simplicity is coherent and consistent with other theistic doctrines, it can provide a third alternative. Because God is simple, he is identical with perfect goodness. Thus there is an essential relationship between God and the standard for moral goodness, and that standard is not external to God. On the other hand, because it is God's nature and not his will that is the standard, not just anything could turn out to be moral. For a simple God, then, the relation of God to perfect goodness is such that both God's sovereignty and the objectivity of morality are preserved.

Second, in the modern period, philosophers such as Gottfried Leibniz and Samuel Clarke rested their versions of the cosmological argument on the principle of sufficient reason (see Article 42, COSMOLOGICAL ARGUMENTS). On their view, God is a necessary being, and unless we admit the existence of a necessary being, we will be unable to give a reason for the existence of something rather than nothing; in that case, contrary to the principle of sufficient reason, we will be saddled with a brute fact. One problem with this strategy for the cosmological argument is that it seems unable to account for the necessity of God's existence, which looks like a brute fact of a theological sort. If it is, then theists are in no better a position than atheists: each group has a brute fact it can't explain.

255

The doctrine of simplicity supplies what is lacking in versions of the cosmological argument such as Clarke's, namely, an explanation of the necessity of God's existence. Like properties, natures or essences exist in all possible worlds, if they are consistent. A simple God is identical with his nature, and so God's existence is necessary also. Someone might suppose that this line of argument just trades the brute fact of divine necessary existence for the brute fact of divine simplicity. But in fact the medievals thought that being simple was entailed by being absolutely perfect. According to them, absolute perfection requires absolute invulnerability and absolute independence, each of which is incompatible with composition. Since they also held that "God is an absolutely perfect being" is as close as we can come to a definition of "God," divine simplicity on their view is entailed by our very notion of God. Given the doctrine of simplicity, then, God is an entity whose necessary existence is self-explanatory in the sense that the explanation of it is provided entirely by the nature of the entity. Consequently, the doctrine of simplicity supplies what is missing in some modern versions of the cosmological argument. If God does not exist, then the search for an explanation of all contingent facts leaves at least one inexplicable contingent fact, namely, that there is something rather than nothing. But if there is an absolutely simple God, the chain of contingent facts has its ultimate explanation in a cause that is necessary and self-explanatory.

Bibliography

Hughes, C.: *On a Complex Theory of a Simple God* (Ithaca: Cornell University Press, 1989).

Leftow, B.: *Divine Simplicity* (forthcoming).

Mann, W.: "Divine simplicity," *Religious Studies*, 18 (1982), pp. 451–71.

——: "Simplicity and immutability in God," *International Philosophical Quarterly*, 23 (1983), pp. 267–76.

Morris, T.: "On God and Mann: A view of divine simplicity," *Religious Studies*, 21 (1985), pp. 299–318.

——: *Anselmian Explorations* (Notre Dame: University of Notre Dame Press, 1987).

Plantinga, A.: *Does God have a Nature?* (Milwaukee: Marquette University Press, 1980).

Stump, E., and Kretzmann, N.: "Absolute simplicity," *Faith and Philosophy*, 2 (1985), pp. 353–81.

32

Eternity

BRIAN LEFTOW

Western theists agree that God is eternal. They disagree over what "God is eternal" asserts. The Old Testament seems to take "God is eternal" to say that

(BE) God exists without beginning or end,

through everlasting time. Influenced by Platonic philosophy, Christian thinkers came to treat "God is eternal" as saying that God is timeless, i.e. that

(GT) God's existence does not endure through, and has no location in, time.

(GT) profoundly alters one's concept of God.

A timeless God does not remember, forget, regret, feel relief, or cease to do anything. For a timeless God has no past, and one can remember, forget, etc., only what is past. A timeless God does not wait, anticipate, hope, foreknow, predict, or deliberate. For a timeless God has no future, and one can anticipate, etc., only what is in one's future. A timeless God does not begin to do anything, if one can begin to do only what one then continues to do. If timeless, God does not change: what changes first has, then lacks, some property, and so must exist at at least two times. Thus a timeless God never learns or changes His attitudes or plans. All His knowledge and intentions are occurrent, not dispositional. Further, if God is timeless, there is no temporal gap between His forming a plan and executing it, or executing it and seeing all its consequences.

If timeless, God's life lasts forever in the sense that at every time, it is true to say that, timelessly, God exists. Yet in itself, God's life is neither long nor short. We may say that a timeless God is forever unchanging. But from His own perspective, He knows and does what He does in the flash of a single now. A timeless God lives His whole life in a single present of unimaginable intensity.

(GT) and its concept of God reigned unchallenged from Augustine to Aquinas. Duns Scotus was the first to break ranks on (GT). His example was contagious, and (GT)'s foes now far outnumber its friends. Some who deny (GT) argue that while God is in time, His time is unlike ours. Some say that it is "metrically amorphous," i.e., that while events in God's life take time, there is no determinate amount of time they take. Some claim that God's time was amorphous until He created, at which point God entered ordinary time. Either proposal tries to save one benefit of (GT), that one need not say for how much of His life God waited before creating the universe.

Some argue that while God has a past, His "specious present" is unlike ours. To experience an extended event in one "specious present" is to presently experience a stretch of it, as when we seem to see motion. This seems to involve seeing a moving thing in a series of positions *in one present experience*, and so having a present perception which includes some of the moving thing's immediate past states. This "specious present" encompasses for us perhaps 0.05 seconds of the object's motion. God's (some say) encompasses His entire life. This proposal seeks to save an implication of (GT), that in some sense God never ceases to live any part of His life.

Debate over God's eternality has centered on whether to accept (GT). So I explore God's eternality by first examining two reasons to affirm (GT), then considering reasons to deny it.

Limits and life

We begin and cease to live. Thus there are points in time beyond which we do not live: our life has limits. The writers of Scripture see God as unlimited, free from creaturely constraints. Thus (BE) was their way to say that God's life is boundless or limitless. Scriptural authors found it natural to gloss "without beginning or end" in terms of everlasting life in time.

Yet a life can have two kinds of limit. A life can have *outer* limits, a beginning or end. A life can also have *inner* limits, boundaries between parts, e.g. that between one's first and second year. If a life lasts forever in time, always one part of it is past and another is future. So any life in time contains at least one limit, an inner boundary dividing its past from its future. This inner limit is as real a constraint as outer limits are. For it walls us off from parts of our lives. We no longer live what is past, but can only recall it. We have not even memory's flawed access to our futures.

We are sometimes glad of this. Our pasts contain episodes it is good to be done with, and our futures contain events we might dread if we knew of them. But there are also past events we wish we could relive, and future days we are eager to see. Now God is perfect, and so lives a perfect being's life. What is a perfect being's life like? Plausibly, no part of such a life is on balance miserable: each part's balance of good and evil, or the qualities of its specific goods, are such that on balance, the perfect being is better off living that part of its life than not living it. If this is true, having a past and a future would be at best an only partly compensated loss for God. In not living part of His life, God would lose some good involved in living it. If God is on balance better off living than not living each part of His life, the loss of any evils that part of His life brings Him would not wholly compensate for the loss of that good. Thus having a past and a future would limit the perfection of God's life.

Some suggest that this does not follow if God's "specious present" holds His whole past and God has perfect predictive knowledge or literal prevision of His future. But as time passes, we regret losing not just vivid experience of events but the events themselves – losing parts of our own lives. A continuing hallucination of the past would content nobody who knew that what seemed to be happening really was not. This holds *a fortiori* for a future one has yet to live at all. And what would it say about God if it made no difference to Him whether we lived with Him or ceased to exist, as long as His memory/prevision of us was intact?

Such thoughts have led many to hold that if God is a wholly perfect being, He has no past or future. If He does not, God is not in time. Note that if He is not in time, (BE) remains true. For only temporal lives begin or end. A life's beginning is earlier than its end, and any life with parts earlier than other parts is temporal.

The creation of time

Theists think that God is the source of whatever is not God. Time is not God. So theists want to see God as the creator not just of temporal things, but of time itself. This does not require theists to say that time is an independent thing, a container of events which exists whether or not filled. For God might create time *by* creating temporal things. If (say) for time to exist is for there to be events related as earlier and later, God may create time by causing such events to occur, or causing the existence of beings which do so. Whatever time's precise status, though, theists want to trace to God not just concrete things, but the most general conditions under which concrete things exist, time and space themselves.

Most theists think that God's creative activity is wholly free. As part of this, most think God is able to refrain from all creating. If He is, and time is a creature, it is possible that God exists even if no time exists: God is at least possibly timeless, and had He created nothing, He would have been timeless.

If this is so, the real question about God and time is whether God becomes temporal by creating time. This can seem true. If God exists and a minute goes by, it is natural to infer that God existed through that minute. All the same, we might want to resist this inference.

"God becomes temporal" suggests that God's life has first a timeless and then a temporal part. But God cannot first be timeless, then later be temporal. For then God's timeless phase is earlier than His temporal phase, and whatever is earlier than something else is in time. Nor can God be timeless during the time He is temporal. If *t* is a time at which God is timeless (as distinct from a time at which it is true to *say* that God is timeless), then God's timeless state, supposedly not earlier than anything, is earlier than every time after *t*. So the most "God becomes temporal" can mean is that God's life always consists of two temporally disconnected parts, one of which would not have existed had He not created time. But this is not what "God becomes temporal" tries to say. It tries to say that "before" there was time, God was timeless and not temporal, and once there was time, God was temporal and not timeless. What we have found is that there is no coherent thought here to express.

A second try at saying that making time makes God temporal goes this way: God is never anything but temporal, but He is only contingently so, and is so because He is always making time. This view also faces problems. If time is God's free creation and God is contingently temporal by making time, presumably God decided to be temporal. He could not have done so timelessly, for then He would

259

have had to become temporal. But then when did He decide? If He did so at any time, it was then too late. As He was already *at* that time, He was already temporal.

But the temporalist has a reply here. It is that God's decision to become temporal would not have been temporal save for God's deciding to become temporal. Because God decided to make time, there came to be events or times later than this decision. So the decision came to *have been* temporal. Had God not decided to make time, nothing would have been later than this decision. This decision would then have been atemporal. So it is God's decision which accounts for His being in time.

This move works only at the price of denying (BE). Consider the instant of God's life which supposedly is temporal but could have been timeless. This instant either is or is not the first of God's temporal life. If it is not, then God was temporal before this instant. If so, a decision located at this instant can account for God's being temporal only by being effective *before* it occurs, i.e., by a backward causal relation which brings it about that God was temporal before He decided to be. This is unacceptable. If the instant in question is the first instant of God's temporal life, God's life has a beginning, and so (BE) is false. Without (BE), God's life is not temporally unlimited. So this temporalist reply saves God's creation of time only by giving up temporalism's version of the claim that God is eternal.

It seems, then, that if God is eternally temporal, God cannot have decided to create time. But if not, and time is something God creates, then God cannot have decided to create *simpliciter*, i.e., to create anything rather than nothing. For at any time, He has already created something – time – without having decided to do so. But then God's creating *simpliciter* seems neither intentional nor free. Again, most Western theists think that God could have refrained from creating *simpliciter*. If God is eternally temporal and time is something God creates, it has always been too late for God to refrain from creating *simpliciter*. He may always have had the power to exist without a creation, but He has never had the opportunity to use it. However, when theists say that God was able to refrain from creating, they seem to mean that He had both power and opportunity.

Conjoined, then, (BE), the claim that God creates time, and the claim that God could have refrained from creating *simpliciter* seem to yield (GT). For it is not clear that God could become temporal by creating time.

Problems for timelessness

Critics of (GT) argue that features of the Western theist concept of God require that God exist in time. Such arguments as these are current:

a God is alive. But living involves changing. So God must change. Only beings in time can change. So God is in time.
b God is alive. Lives are events. Events must occur in time. So God is in time.
c God coexists with temporal things. So God's properties change: first He coexists with Abraham and not Moses, later with Moses and not Abraham. So God is in time.

d   God is omniscient (see Article 29, OMNISCIENCE). Thus God knows what time it is
    now. But only someone who exists now can know what time it is now. For
    whoever knows that it is now noon can say with truth, "it is now noon." But
    only at noon can someone say this with truth. So God is in time.

e   If God is omniscient, He knows human actions which to us are future. If He is
    essentially omniscient, He cannot hold a false belief. If God is timeless, His
    knowledge cannot change, or depend on temporal events: what is eternal is as
    fixed as what is past. Were we to do other than God believes we will, either God
    would come to hold a false belief, or we would change God's timeless knowl-
    edge, or God's timeless knowledge would have been different because our tem-
    poral action was to be different, and so would have depended on our temporal
    action. Hence we cannot do other than God believes we will. So if God is time-
    less and essentially omniscient, we are not free. But we are free and God is
    essentially omniscient. So God is in time.

f   If God is timeless, all He knows, He knows at once. So either His knowledge is
    all prior (in some non-temporal sense) to all temporal events or it is all (non-
    temporally) posterior to all temporal events. If the first, matters are as in (e). If
    the second, God knows what He does because temporal events turn out as they
    do. If so, His knowledge comes "too late" for Him to interfere providentially in
    time (see Article 72, PROVIDENCE AND PREDESTINATION). God knows that Hitler kills
    Jews by seeing it happen. What one sees happen, one is too late to prevent. By
    contrast, if God is temporal, we are free, yet He can predict what we are likely
    to do and (if He chooses) act in time to save us or our victims.

g   God acts. Actions are events. Again, events must occur in time.

h   God is a cause. Either causal relations link only events, or they also link agents
    to events ("agent causality"). If the first, then as events occur only in time,
    God is in time. If the second, the agent's action is dated at the time of the effect.
    So if God has any temporal effects as an agent cause, He is again in time.

i   God interacts with temporal things: we pray, He hears and responds. If God
    first hears, then responds, He hears before He responds. So He hears and
    responds in time.

j   God became incarnate. So events in God's life have temporal dates. Whatever
    lives through temporally dated events exists in time.

k   If God loves His creatures, He reacts appropriately to their present suffering: it
    pains Him. In the final state of things, "the Kingdom of Heaven," creatures no
    longer suffer, and so if God is perfectly rational, He feels less pain then than is
    appropriate while they suffer. So if God always loves His creatures and is per-
    fectly rational, God changes between now and then. If God timelessly beheld
    both present suffering and future happiness, His single, changeless overall
    state of feeling would be inappropriate to at least one of them.

Limits of space preclude my tackling all of these arguments. I choose to address
the metaphysical worry behind (b), (g), and (h), that only occurrences in time can
be events. I do so by exploring some arguments for this conclusion.

One might argue that:

(1) Necessarily, any event which is a change in the things to which it happens occurs in time;

(2) Necessarily, all events are such changes;

(3) So necessarily, all events occur in time.

But theists deny (2). Theists hold that God has created some things *ex nihilo* (from nothing). This cannot be a change in the things created, for they do not exist before being created.

Again one might reach (3) from

(4) Necessarily, any event which occurs before or after another event occurs in time, and

(5) Necessarily, any event occurs before or after another event.

But (5) is false. The mereological sum of all events is an event. So is the existing of all of spacetime. No event occurs before or after either.

One might reach (3) from

(6) Necessarily, any event with parts which follow one another occurs in time, and

(7) Necessarily, all events have such parts.

But (7) is false. Consider a car continuously decelerating from 10 mph to zero. The car cannot do this without at some time having a speed of 5 mph. If the deceleration was continuous, though, the car was at 5 mph for only an instant. So the car's traveling at 5 mph was an instantaneous event, one without parts.

One might reach (3) from

(8) Necessarily, any event which either follows or precedes another event or has parts which do so occurs in time, and

(9) Necessarily, any event follows or precedes another or has parts which do so.

But (9) appears false. Many think it a live possibility that there be a topologically closed space-time, one structured like a circle, not a line. No event would occur before or after the existing of all of such a space-time, or the sum-event of its events. But neither event would have parts before other parts. The "before" relation is asymmetric (if A is before B, B is not before A) and irreflexive (A is never before A). Suppose, then, that space-time has a circular structure. If A and B are points in a circular space-time, then by proceeding around the circle in the direction time goes, we get from A to B *and* from B to A – time does both if it completes a circle from A back to A. Thus if in such a case A is before B, B is also before A and A is before itself. So in a circlelike space-time, nothing is before anything else.

Finally, one might reach (3) from

(10) Necessarily, every event has a date and

(11) Necessarily, every date is the date of a temporal event.

Chisholm explicates the concept of an event without supposing that events have dates (Chisholm 1990). If his account is coherent, it is not clear why (10) should be true. Further, arguably (11) is false: eternity is itself a date.

A date is an answer to the question "when?" Asked when God knew that He would speak to Moses, a Hebrew Bible author might well have replied "eternally" or "from eternity." These answers give dates. Effectively, they say "at every earlier time." Later thinkers took (GT) as their account of God's eternality, but continued to see "eternally" as answering "when." Boethius' *De Trinitate* details the way statements about God fall into Aristotle's categories. When he turns to the category of "when," Boethius takes "God exists always" as his sample statement and explicates it in terms of God's timelessness (Boethius 1926, p. 20). The shift to a different doctrine of divine eternality did not change the question the doctrine answered. Thus if events require dates, "eternally" will serve.

If the arguments surveyed fail, it is not clear why one should deny that something atemporal could count as an event. Nor need the concept of a timeless happening cause pain. An event is something that happens at some present. An eternal event is just one which happens at a peculiar present, the eternal present. In a less liberal sense, an event is something *new* that happens. However, nothing is earlier than God's life if God is timeless. So for any f, if God is timelessly f, God is f, and nothing was f before God was. So arguably, God's eternally being f has the newness we associate with a happening. We do not think of it thus because we tend to think of whatever is eternal as infinitely old. What is old has a long past. But what is timeless cannot be old. There is no past in eternity.

Bibliography

Boethius: *The Theological Tractates*, tr. H. F. Stewart and E. K. Rand (New York: G. P. Putnam's Sons, 1926).

Chisholm, R.: "Events without times," *Nous*, 24 (1990), pp. 413–28.

Helm, P.: *Eternal God* (New York: Oxford University Press, 1988).

Leftow, B.: *Time and Eternity* (Ithaca: Cornell University Press, 1991).

Padgett, A.: *God, Eternity and the Nature of Time* (New York: St Martin's Press, 1992).

Pike, N.: *God and Timelessness* (New York: Schocken Books, 1970).

Stump, E., and Kretzmann, N.: "Eternity," *Journal of Philosophy*, 78 (1981), pp. 429–58.

Swinburne, R.: "God and time." In *Reasoned Faith*, ed. E. Stump (Ithaca: Cornell University Press, 1993), pp. 204–22.

Yates, J.: *The Timelessness of God* (Lanham, MD: University Press of America, 1990).

33

Necessity

WILLIAM E. MANN

Philosophical reflection on theism has produced two controversial theses connecting the concepts of God and necessity. Many theists, emphasizing the difference between God and creatures, have insisted that although the existence of creatures is a contingent matter, God's existence is necessary. Some theists, in an effort to stress God's sovereignty over everything, have claimed that God's creative activity is responsible not only for all contingent matters, but also for all necessary matters. Taken separately, each thesis has drawn philosophical criticism. Taken together, they appear to be incompatible. If God's existence is necessary, then there would seem to be at least one necessary truth for which God is not responsible – the truth that God exists necessarily. Someone inclined to defend both theses must be prepared to argue that God's necessary existence is compatible with God's complete sovereignty. Philosophical assessment of the theses requires analysis of the notion of necessary truth.

Prospects are bleak for producing a definition of necessary truth that does not presuppose the concept under definition (Adams 1983). For example, the characterization of a necessary truth as a proposition, p, whose negation entails a contradiction is doubly indebted to the concept. For what distinguishes a contradiction from other types of proposition that might be entailed by the negation of p is the fact that a contradiction is *necessarily false*, a notion scarcely intelligible apart from the notion of necessary truth. Moreover, the relation of entailment employed in the characterization is such that for two propositions, q and r, q entails r if and only if it is *impossible* for q to be true and r false, that is, if and only if the conjunction of q with the negation of r is necessarily false. This kind of definitional circularity does not seem to be vicious. It may merely be symptomatic of how fundamental the notion of necessity is to our thought. Even without a definition, most people believe that some propositions are true necessarily. Tautologies – sentences like "Either the earth has an atmosphere or the earth does not have an atmosphere" and "If the atomic number of gold is 79, then it is not the case that the atomic number of gold is not 79" – appear to constitute the clearest examples. Other putative but more controversial cases of necessary truths include "$1 + 2 = 3$," "Everything that is red is extended in space," and "All cows are ruminants."

Despite the presumptive case in favor of necessary truths, some philosophers have found reason for questioning whether any proposition is necessarily true, especially if there is an omnipotent God. It will be convenient to examine the issues in the context of Gottfried Leibniz's imagery of possible worlds (see Mates 1986, chs. 4 and 6). Many contemporary philosophers have characterized contingent truths as propositions that are true in some possible worlds and false in others, while necessary truths, if there are any, are propositions true in every possible world. This characterization still involves circularity if the explication of the notion of a possible world involves, for instance, the concept of a maximally consistent set of propositions, because propositions p and q are consistent if and only if the conjunction of p and q is not necessarily false. Even so, the notion of possible worlds has heuristic value, emphasizing that necessity involves invariability throughout all possible situations.

Several remarks made in the writings of René Descartes (for texts, see Frankfurt 1977, and Curley 1984) have led interpreters to ascribe to him the doctrine that whether there are or can be any necessary truths depends somehow on God's omnipotence. Let us call the general principle that God's omnipotence makes a difference to the status of necessary truths "the Cartesian principle." Its most radical version is the thesis that there are no necessarily true propositions if an omnipotent God exists. That $1 + 2 = 3$ is true is as contingent upon God's omnipotent creative activity as is the proposition that grass is green. If we inject Leibniz's idiom of possible worlds into this version of the Cartesian principle, we can say that according to it, no proposition is true in every possible world. There are worlds God could have created in which $1 + 2 \neq 3$. Because this version of the Cartesian principle entails that every proposition is such that there is some possible world in which it is true and some possible world in which it is false, Alvin Plantinga has called this version *universal possibilism* (Plantinga 1980). A slightly more modest version of the Cartesian principle maintains that some propositions are necessarily true and exempt from God's unlimited power, although perhaps not the proposition that $1 + 2 = 3$. Obvious candidates are propositions that express necessary truths about God's existence and nature. This version of the Cartesian principle might maintain, for example, that God cannot fail to exist, to be omniscient, and to be omnipotent; that in every possible world it is true that God exists, is omniscient, and is omnipotent. Yet another version of the Cartesian principle maintains that although some propositions are necessary, they are necessary because God conferred their necessity on them: no proposition is *necessarily* necessary. If no proposition is necessarily necessary, every proposition is possibly possibly true (and possibly possibly false). Plantinga has called this position *limited possibilism*. It can be understood in the following way. Suppose that not every world is possible relative to every other possible world. It might then be the case, for example, that although a proposition is true in every world possible relative to the actual world, there are still other worlds, not possible relative to the actual world but possible relative to some of the worlds that *are* possible relative to the actual world, in which the proposition is false. There are consistent systems of modal logic that allow for this sort of case. Perhaps the best way of interpreting limited possibilism is to connect its notion of possibility to conceivability. In making the proposition that $1 + 2 = 3$ necessary, God has made it, and us, such that we cannot conceive how it could be false. That is, in every world conceivable by us, "$1 + 2 = 3$" is true. In some of the worlds conceivable by us in which "$1 + 2 = 3$" is true, however, there are beings with conceptual capacities different from ours who can genuinely conceive "$1 + 2 = 3$" to be false. It is important to stress that these beings' capacities are *genuine* capacities: it is not merely that they *think* that they can conceive 1 plus 2 not equaling 3; they can successfully comprehend what it would be like for 1 plus 2 not to equal 3. These beings thus have conceptual access to worlds in which "$1 + 2 = 3$" is false. In this situation, then, although "$1 + 2 = 3$" is necessarily true (true in every world conceptually accessible to us), it is not necessary that "$1 + 2 = 3$" be necessarily true, that is, "$1 + 2 = 3$" is not true in every world conceptually accessible to beings, conceivable by us, who have conceptual capacities that we cannot fully comprehend.

One may suspect that the Cartesian principle, which promotes divine omnipotence over necessary truth, is misguided. If the goal of the Cartesian principle is to present a conception of a God who can do or have done literally anything, then not only has that goal not been attained, but each of the three versions of the principle presents reasons for thinking that the goal is unattainable. If universal possibilism is correct, then there is one large class of things that God cannot do or have done, namely, make any truth to be a necessary truth. In particular, God cannot make it necessarily true that $1 + 2 = 3$, or that he exists or is omnipotent. If limited possibilism is true, then although God can establish some truths as necessary, he cannot make any truth to be necessarily necessary. On the analysis of limited possibilism that identifies possibility with relative conceivability, even if God cannot conceive himself as not existing, God can conceive of beings with conceptual capacities different from his who can genuinely conceive of him as not existing. These beings thus can do something that God cannot do.

Nor will it help to seek refuge in the position that exempts only some truths, including truths about God's existence and nature, from the class of truths that are contingent upon God. For this position sustains for a vast number of propositions the same criticism that applies to universal possibilism: try as he might, God cannot make or have made "$1 + 2 = 3$" into a necessarily true proposition. Moreover, the position must provide an account of what it is that makes the exempt truths exempt. Simply to stake out truths about God's essence and existence is too *ad hoc* a procedure. But to the extent to which the position might allow for necessary truths about other kinds of entities – for example, sets or numbers – the position will approximate to commonsense intuitions about necessity but raise anew questions about the scope of God's omnipotence.

An alternative to the Cartesian principle is to attempt to explicate divine sovereignty over necessary truth by appealing not to God's omnipotence but rather to God's mental activity. Elements of this view can be found in the thought of St Augustine and perhaps also in Leibniz. Although Leibniz's imagery includes the vision of God choosing from among the infinitely many different possible worlds which world would be actual, that is, which world God would create, the imagery does not require that possible worlds exist independently of God. One could maintain, as Leibniz comes close to maintaining, that possible worlds are merely conceptual entities residing in the divine mind. Centuries earlier, Augustine had identified the Platonic Forms – the abstract, perfect exemplars of concrete things and properties which concrete things and properties deficiently resemble – with *ideas* in the divine intellect. Augustine's doctrine and Leibniz's tendency can be viewed as examples of a theistic strategy that would make the existence of abstract objects depend on the divine mind. Let us call the strategy "the Augustinian strategy," recognizing that instances of it, such as Leibniz's tendency, might never have been thought of by Augustine. If propositions are the bearers of truth and falsity, and if propositions are themselves abstract objects, then on the Augustinian strategy, for a proposition to exist is just for it to be thought by God. (The strategy can be tailored to accommodate St Thomas Aquinas's view that although normal human knowledge is propositional in content, God's knowledge is not. Aquinas believes that because propositions are complex objects and God's mode of knowing is simple both in its operation and in its representational content, God does not know by means of propositions. One can on Aquinas's behalf express more perspicuously the thesis that propositions exist only in the mind of God by maintaining that whatever it is that provides the grounds for the existence of propositions in human knowledge exists in the mind of God.)

Although the Augustinian strategy accounts for the existence of propositions by lodging them or the entities on which they depend in God's mind, it does not account for the distinction between contingent and necessary propositions. Can one consistently maintain that although all propositions depend on God's activity for their existence, some propositions nevertheless cannot fail to be true (and some propositions cannot fail to be false), no matter what? It would appear that a positive answer to this question requires that the proposition that God exists itself be necessarily true. For if God could fail to exist, then, on the hypothesis that all propositions depend on God for their existence God's non-existence would be a circumstance under which propositions would also fail to exist. If one assumes that no proposition can be either true or false if it does not exist, then it follows that if God can fail to exist, no proposition can be necessarily true (or necessarily false), that is, no proposition can be true in every possible world (or false in every possible world). The Augustinian strategy applied to propositions thus seems to entail that if it is possible for God to fail to exist, then universal possibilism is true. (The converse also seems to hold: if universal possibilism is genuinely universal, then it applies to the proposition that God exists, entailing that there are possible worlds in which God does not exist.)

The Augustinian strategy must explain how it can be that there are truths that are genuinely necessary which depend, none the less, on God's mental activity for their necessity. Let us begin by asking how the strategy might depict the relationship between God and contingent propositions. As a result of creating the actual world, God acted in such a way that a number of propositions became true – for example, the proposition that the earth is the third planet from the sun – and a number of propositions became false – for example, the proposition that the moon has an atmosphere. We need not suppose that these propositions somehow existed before God's creative act made them true (or false). Nor need we suppose that the act of creation is simply or even primarily a matter of making propositions true. In particular, followers of Aquinas might want to say that the portrayal of creation as making certain propositions true is an artifice of human intellects, whose understanding is propositional in nature. Bearing these caveats in mind, we can continue by supposing that the strategy depicts God's creative activity with respect to the contingent features of the world as God's *choosing* which propositions would become true and which would become false. Choice, we may suppose, is an operation whose input is beliefs and desires and whose output is action. A proponent of the strategy will most likely want to make two observations, at a minimum, about divine beliefs and desires. First, God's beliefs cannot be false or incomplete, and thus God's choices cannot suffer from the cognitive deficiencies of being erroneous or based on ignorance. Second, although it would be presumptuous to claim to know the exact content of God's desires in choosing to create, a defender of the Judeo-Christian tradition will insist that God's desires are directed toward the good. Leibniz is notorious for carrying the second observation to its logical extreme, arguing that since God is perfect, God would choose only the best; it follows that the actual world must be the best possible world. Other accounts of God's goodness have denied the assumption behind Leibniz's claim, namely, that perfect goodness entails maximization. But theistic dissent from Leibniz's view has not consisted in denial of the fundamental point that God's desires are desires for the good (see Kretzmann 1991, Mann 1991).

The Augustinian strategy can thus account for the truth and falsity of contingent propositions by making actual truth and actual falsity depend on God's creative choosing, a choosing that is cognitively perfect and directed toward the good. The strategy would thus maintain that a proposition, p, is contingent if and only if whether p is true or false depends on God's choice. But this thesis does not in itself show how the *contingency* of contingent propositions depends on God. Nor does the thesis in itself guarantee that the Augustinian strategy is independent of the Cartesian principle. Let us take the latter point first. It would help to show the independence of the Augustinian strategy from the Cartesian principle if one could show how God's freedom of choice grounds contingency without lapsing into universal possibilism or limited possibilism. One might begin by noting that the account of divine choice sketched above precludes some propositions from being possibly true, *if* propositions about God's existence and nature are necessarily true. Not only will the proposition that God does not exist be necessarily false, but so also will the proposition that God creates an irredeemably corrupt world. Many theists will not find these consequences unwelcome. One might continue by pointing out that God's being responsible for the contingency of contingent propositions need not be understood to entail that there is some proposition, p, that is in fact contingent but might have been necessary. Two of the consequences of standard interpretations of modal logic are that (1) any proposition that is possibly necessary is necessary, and (2) any necessary proposition is necessarily necessary. The first consequence rules out universal possibilism. (Recall that universal possibilism asserts that no proposition, p, is necessarily true. If p is not necessarily true, then the contrapositive of (1) entails that it is not possible that p be necessarily true. But if that is so, then it follows by the interdefinability of possibility and necessity that it is necessary that *p* not be necessarily true, a result that establishes a necessary truth, contrary to universal possibilism.) The second consequence obviously rules out limited possibilism. The Augustinian strategy can pay respect to standard modal logic by allowing that not even God could have promoted a contingent proposition into a necessary proposition. A defender of the Augustinian strategy can claim instead that the dependency of contingent propositions on God's activity can be illustrated by appeal to the asymmetry of explanation. An analogy may be helpful. Given Newtonian mechanics, one can deduce the period of a pendulum from the pendulum's length. Because the relevant mathematical operations are symmetrical, one can also deduce the pendulum's length from its period. It is obvious, however, that the pendulum's length explains its period, not vice versa. In similar fashion, a defender of the Augustinian strategy can claim that for any true contingent proposition, *p*, although "*p* is contingently true" and "God chooses that *p* be true and could have chosen that *p* be false" entail each other, it is the latter claim that explains the former, not vice versa.

Further articulation of the Augustinian strategy would require showing how this particular explanatory asymmetry is embedded in a general theistic theory of God and the world. But we have enough before us now to see how the Augustinian strategy might explicate the relation between God and necessary truth. We may suppose that every necessary truth is necessarily necessary, and that just as God cannot have altered the status of a contingent proposition, so God cannot have altered the status of a necessary proposition. Because the necessary truths cannot vary across possible worlds, the Augustinian strategy cannot explicate their relation to God in terms of choice, if choice presupposes the ability to have chosen otherwise. Most theists would agree that if God is omniscient, then for any necessarily true proposition, *p*, "*p* is necessarily true" and "God knows that *p* is necessarily true" entail each other. The distinctive contribution of the Augustinian strategy is to insist that it is God's knowing that *p* is necessarily true that explains *p*'s being necessarily true rather than the other way around. It is not that God's intellectual activity *discovers* that $1 + 2 = 3$. But neither is it correct to say that God's activity *invents* the truth that $1 + 2 = 3$, if invention entails either that the truth came into existence at some time or that it might have been false. God thoroughly understands that $1 + 2 = 3$ with a sweep of intellectual comprehension that sees all the implications of that truth for all the rest of the truths. In understanding "$1 + 2 = 3$" in this way, God understands something about himself as the supremely rational being. The necessary truths occupy an important place in the structure of rational thought. According to the Augustinian strategy, the structure of rational thought is either the structure of the divine mind or the divine mind itself, actively and essentially engaged in thinking.

One important class of necessary truths, according to the tradition informing the Augustinian strategy, are truths about God's nature. For example, God is necessarily or essentially omniscient, omnipotent, and perfectly good. Any being who lacked one of these attributes, or who possessed one of them only accidentally, would not be God. (Defenders of the tradition typically insist that these sorts of attributes cannot be possessed accidentally.) If, in addition, God's existence is necessary, it follows that God cannot nullify his own existence or abrogate his essential attributes: God exists and is omniscient, omnipotent, and perfectly good in every possible world. On a theology based on the Cartesian principle, these consequences can appear to place limitations on the divine power and make God depend on his attributes for his being what he is. The Augustinian strategy can embrace the consequences while dispelling the appearance of limitation by deploying the following two tactics. One is to argue that, surface grammar to the contrary notwithstanding, propositions like "God cannot cause his own non-existence" do not specify any real restriction on God's power. The other is to argue that, unlike created beings, the metaphysical distinction between a substance and its attributes does not apply to God. God is perfectly simple, in such a way that the expressions, "God," "Perfect goodness," and "God's perfect goodness" do not refer to three things but rather to one thing specified in three ways. In this case, then, God does not *depend* on perfect goodness; God *is* perfect goodness itself (see Article 31, SIMPLICITY).

Bibliography

Adams, R. M.: "Divine necessity," *Journal of Philosophy*, 80 (1983), pp. 741–52.

Curley, E. M.: "Descartes on the creation of the eternal truths," *Philosophical Review*, 93 (1984), pp. 569–97.

Frankfurt, H.: "Descartes on the creation of the eternal truths," *Philosophical Review*, 86 (1977), pp. 36–57.

Kretzmann, N.: "A particular problem of creation: Why would God create this world?" In *Being and Goodness: The Concept of the Good in Metaphysics and Philosophical Theology*, ed. S. MacDonald (Ithaca: Cornell University Press, 1991), pp. 229–49.

Mann, W. E.: "Modality, morality, and God," *Nous*, 23 (1989), pp 83–99.

——: "The best of all possible worlds." In *Being and Goodness: The concept of the Good in Metaphysics and Philosophical Theology*, ed. S. MacDonald (Ithaca: Cornell University Press, 1991), pp. 250–77.

Mates, B.: *The Philosophy of Leibniz: Metaphysics and Language* (New York: Oxford University Press, 1986).

Plantinga, A.: *Does God Have a Nature?* (Milwaukee: Marquette University Press, 1980).

34

Incorporeality

CHARLES TALIAFERRO

Traditional forms of Judaism, Christianity, and Islam each conceive of God as an immaterial, nonphysical reality. If "the incorporeality of God" means the denial that God is physical, then all three monotheistic religions accept the incorporeality of God. However, if we follow the etymology of the term and define "incorporeality" as "without body" (from the Latin *incorporale*), Christianity takes exception to a strict adherence to belief in God's incorporeality when it comes to the Incarnation. According to traditional Christianity, in the Incarnation, the second member of the TRINITY (see Article 66) became infleshed (the Latin meaning of *incarnātus*) and thus, in a sense, came to be "with body". While this pivotal claim about the union of God and man at the heart of Christianity marks a dramatic departure from a radical transcendent theology of God according to which any such union is metaphysically impossible, it does not commit Christians to denying God's immateriality. In traditional Christianity, God the Father, God the Holy Spirit, and God the Son (apart from the Incarnation) are clearly understood as lacking material structure and composition. Because of their shared conviction that God is immaterial, Christians along with Jews and Muslims have historically opposed material conceptions of God or gods such as one finds in Stoicism, according to which God is a vast material being, a world soul or animal, and in polytheism, according to which there are hosts of material deities. God's immaterial reality has also been used to articulate an important difference between monotheism and versions of pantheism according to which the material world either is God or a part of God. (For advocates of divine incorporeality outside of religious monotheism, see Article 8, ANCIENT PHILOSOPHICAL THEOLOGY.)

In this article I understand the claim that God is incorporeal to mean that God is not material. A "corporealist" maintains God is a material reality, while an "incorporealist" maintains God is immaterial. I follow the common, current practice of treating "material" and "physical" as synonyms, though it should be noted that it was once customary to use "material" to refer to matter alone and "physical" to cover both matter and energy. There will be three sections in what follows. The first considers reasons that have been advanced on behalf of divine incorporeality. The second considers objections to these arguments and the project of articulating a corporeal view of God. In a final section, I consider a version of divine incorporeality that may accommodate an important motivation behind corporealism.

271

Arguments for divine incorporeality

While "incorporeal" is a negative term, marking God's *not* being material (or *not* having a body), it has been advanced by philosophers and theologians on the basis of arguments from a wide range of positive attributions to God, namely God's NECESSITY (see Article 33), ETERNITY (see Article 32), IMMUTABILITY (see Article 40, IMMUTABILITY AND IMPASSIBILITY), OMNIPOTENCE (see Article 28), SIMPLICITY (see Article 31), GOODNESS (see Article 30), and OMNIPRESENCE (see Article 36), and on the basis of the belief that God is not a being, but BEING (see Article 27) itself. Divine incorporeality has also been defended on the basis of the testimony of REVELATION AND SCRIPTURE (see Article 74) and RELIGIOUS EXPERIENCE (see Article 47). These arguments are advanced in light of certain theories about the material world and human nature. Many of the traditional theistic arguments in natural theology, the ONTOLOGICAL (see Article 41), COSMOLOGICAL (see Article 42), TELEOLOGICAL AND DESIGN ARGUMENTS (see Article 43), have all been formulated as arguments for believing there is an immaterial God. The concept of the incorporeality of God is therefore at the intersection of many divine attributes and it plays a central role for theistic conceptions of God's relation to the cosmos. Its place is so embedded in theistic philosophical literature that incorporeality is sometimes cast as a defining characteristic of God, such that the proposition "God is incorporeal" is treated as analytically true rather than as a proposition entailed by other, more central theistic claims. As we shall see in the next section, it has also been a pivotal target for anti-theistic philosophers who argue that the very idea of an incorporeal God is conceptually absurd.

Consider the eight pairs of attributions below. If it is plausible to believe any one set of these joint attributions according to which something is true of God that is not true of the material world as a whole nor any of its parts, then it is plausible to believe that God is not the material world as a whole nor any of its parts. Arguments may be strengthened to deliver a more robust conclusion, should one have reason to believe that these pairs describe essential properties. That is, if you believe God is essentially eternal and the material world is essentially not eternal (or essentially temporal), then you may conclude that it is impossible for God and the material world to be the very same thing. In either case, the reasoning rests on the principle of the indiscernibility of identicals (if A is B, then everything true of A is true of B).

God necessarily exists	Neither the material cosmos as a whole nor any of its parts necessarily exists
God is eternal	Neither the material world as a whole nor any of its parts is eternal
God has no beginning	Neither the material world as a whole nor any of its parts is without a beginning
God is immutable	Neither the material world as a whole nor any of its parts is immutable

God is omnipotent	Neither the cosmos as a whole nor any of its parts is omnipotent
God is simple (i.e. God contains no parts)	Neither the material world as a whole nor any of its parts is without parts
God is perfectly good	Neither the material world nor any of its parts is perfectly good
God is Being	Neither the material world as a whole nor any of its parts is Being

Arguments based on these incompatible attributions may be spelled out in different ways. Thus, the argument from simplicity above is based on the notion that God is not a compound. The simplicity of God can be given other interpretations, however, one of which is that there is no distinction between subject and attribute in God. Granted that there is always such a distinction in material things, the appeal to this understanding of divine simplicity provides an additional reason for concluding that God is not material. Arguments from God's perfect goodness also allow for different versions. "Perfect goodness" may be analyzed as supreme value or maximal excellence. Divine incorporeality may then be advanced on the basis of the belief that God has such supreme value or maximal excellence and the material world either does not or cannot. Alternatively, the argument can be shifted to fit an analysis of "perfect goodness" in terms of not being subject to corruption. If material things are subject to corruption and God is incorruptible, then God is not a material thing. Such a construal of the argument would make it similar to (though not the same as) the argument from necessary existence noted first on the list.

Historically, many of the arguments for divine incorporeality have been built on the supposition that a material God would either limit God or entirely eclipse the creation. As for the first, it has been argued that the materiality of God is incompatible with God's omnipotence (including God's power to know of the world and, thus, God's omniscience). As for eclipsing the creation, it has been argued that if God is material, there can be nothing created that is not God. Assume that it is an essential feature of a material being to be dense and impenetrable. If God is a material being and omnipresent, then it seems to follow that there is no material being other than God. Such a conclusion runs up against a fundamental monotheistic claim that not everything that exists is God. For many traditional theists, belief in divine omnipresence and a distinction between the Creator and creation has seemed to fare better on the supposition that God is incorporeal.

Some influential arguments for divine incorporeality have been built on dualist theories of human nature combined with an appeal to revelation. The belief that we are singled out of the created order as made in the image of God (Genesis 1) prompted Jews and Christians to use what they believed distinguished us from

273

other created beings in developing their understanding of God. On the grounds that this distinction lay in our possessing intellect and reason (in having a human soul or mind) which are immaterial, philosophers and theologians argued that this immaterial nature was a reflection of God's immateriality. Augustine counseled believers as follows: "Descend into thyself; go to thy secret place, thy mind . . . to give thee some similitude to thy God . . . because surely not in the body, but in that same mind, was man made after the image of God" (*Lectures or Tractates on the Gospel of John* XXIII.10). This reverses the position of the Stoic Chrysippus who partly based his belief in the materiality of God on the materiality of human persons.

Other arguments for divine incorporeality include the appeal to religious experience, according to which God is said to be beyond all created, material form. Idealist arguments are also worthy of note. If God exists and a form of idealism is true according to which there are no corporeal objects, then God is incorporeal.

Arguments against divine incorporeality

A major objection to theism from the mid-twentieth century onward among English-speaking philosophers of religion has been that it makes no sense to posit an incorporeal God. This position is advanced by those who contend that the concept of a person is the concept of a physical being. To attribute intelligence and personal agency to a thing which has no physical body is a category mistake. Analytical forms of behaviorism support such a stance. The positivist movement also underwrites a critique of theism on conceptual grounds at precisely this point with the charge that claims about the activities of immaterial spirits are immune to empirical confirmation or disconfirmation and hence empty of content.

These objections have been addressed in different ways. Verificationism has met with many objections, as outlined in Article 25, THE VERIFICATIONIST CHALLENGE, and its advocates today, such as Michael Martin, rarely advance it as possessing more than *prima facie* force. The reply to materialist theories that entail the impossibility of there being an incorporeal God have been addressed by some theists who argue that materialism is, at best, only contingently true. If it is true that human persons and all their activities are physical this is a contingent state of affairs and not one that has a bearing on the coherence of the claim that there is a non-physical person or person-like reality. William Alston takes this stance, while others (Richard Swinburne, Alvin Plantinga, and John Foster; see references in Taliaferro 1994) adopt a more aggressive tactic of arguing that materialism is not true even of human beings. Some of the issues at stake are addressed in Article 55, THEISM AND THE SCIENTIFIC UNDERSTANDING OF THE MIND, and Article 38, DIVINE ACTION.

Is a corporealist view of God an entirely rogue thesis, unheard of within the great monotheistic religious traditions? The sacred scriptures of these traditions, the Hebrew and Christian Bibles and the Qur'an, each contain vivid corporeal imagery for God. There are many highly anthropomorphic references to God; God is said to have a head, eyes, fingers, arms, and so on. To be sure, theologians and philosophers in these traditions have gone to great lengths in arguing that such language is to be read as highly metaphorical references to an incorporeal reality. But this appears to constitute some evidence that arguments of this type were needed and therefore that the belief in God's corporeality has not been altogether absent. Famously, Thomas Hobbes contended that the God of Christianity should be understood as a corporeal being, albeit one that is pure, simple, and invisible. More recently, Grace Jantzen has developed a theology in which the material world is God's body. This is a thesis advanced by some contemporary defenders of PROCESS THEOLOGY (see Article 16).

Those defending corporealism have sought to reply to the arguments cited in the first section by overturning at least one of the pair of attributes on the list. In this endeavor they are assisted by some incorporealists. Each of the following has been held by theists today who believe God is incorporeal: God does not necessarily exist, God is not eternal, God changes, God is not simple, God is a being, not Being. In these respects, then, incorporealists have removed some of the barriers to conceiving of God as a material reality. Views of the physical world have likewise been advanced of late that may assist corporealism. Thus, some hold that the material world is limitless, that it has always existed, and even that it necessarily exists.

As for the intelligibility of the God–world relation, some corporealists claim that God either is or contains the cosmos and that this does not compromise the distinctive identity of the different things making up the cosmos. Defenders of this position such as Jantzen seek to preserve the distinction between God and creation at the level of free agency (God does not directly control God's creatures; there are free, independent sources of action). They also seek to secure a more general independence of the world from God. Not all that occurs is the outcome of God's omnidetermining causation. By allowing for this relative independence, corporealists hope to avoid the thesis that the omnipresence of God precludes the existence of other, non-divine creatures. For Jantzen, God's omnipresence in the cosmos may be interpreted as a function of God's knowledge (God knows all that occurs at every point in creation), God's power (God can act upon any part of the cosmos), and God's constitution (God is the whole cosmos; no part of the cosmos would exist if God did not). God's identity as the world does not amount to either the world or God being a dense, impenetrable object filling all things. Rather, God's omnipresence amounts to God's being metaphysically constituted by the cosmos and the cosmos being open to God's omniscient, omnipotent, conscious care. For Jantzen, God is in some sense more than the material world taken as a collection of objects and yet not an independently existing, immaterial subject or being.

Do corporealists make God dependent on the physical cosmos in a fashion that undermines the divine attributes of omnipotence and omniscience? The fact (if it is one) that God's corporeal nature would generate some restrictions for God may be no worse than if God is assumed to be incorporeal. Thus, if God is a corporeal being, God cannot survive the destruction of all corporeal beings. But if God is an incorporeal being, God cannot survive the destruction of all incorporeal beings. It may also be argued that in attributing omniscience to a corporeal God, one does not necessarily attribute to God certain limitations such as the supposition that God must use eyes to see the cosmos, nerve endings to feel it, a brain to think about it, and so on. So long as incorporealists are prepared to acknowledge important disanalogies between divine and human embodiment, some of the embarrassments of anthropomorphism seem avoidable.

There remain some difficulties with the corporealist position. First and foremost, there is the problem of being able to surmount the cogency of all the arguments from divine attributes listed in the first section. While some incorporealists have joined corporealists in calling these into question, it has yet to be established that they have overturned these and thus defeated the cumulative case for divine incorporeality (see Wainwright 1974). It is also not clear whether corporealism has significant advantages over traditional incorporealism. Jantzen, for example, contends that her theory of God has the advantage of eliminating the radical disparity between God and the cosmos that is at the heart of traditional incorporealism. It is not obvious, however, whether she has entirely eliminated a radical disparity between God and the cosmos in so far as she grants that God has states and activities that are not exclusively material. In so far as corporealists such as Jantzen and others preserve theistic notions of omnipotence and omniscience and do not wish to identify these as states of the world (i.e. God's intentions and knowledge are not the very same things as, say, certain explosions among the stars, earth tremors and the like; one cannot scientifically observe God's intentions, knowledge, and so on), corporealists seem to be left with the idea that there is something radically different about God transcending the physical cosmos when it is conceived of as only a huge, perhaps limitless material expanse. Their distinction between the material world taken as merely material on the one hand, and taken as God's constitution and the bearer of the divine attributes (omniscience, love, and so on) on the other, marks a profound difference that does not give it a clearcut advantage over traditional incorporealism. Corporealists thereby still retain a fundamental, deep division between the material and the immaterial.

Corporealists have, however, brought to light some of the difficulties of maintaining traditional incorporealism and the Christian understanding of the Incarnation. Thus, if one adopts incorporealism on the basis of the incompatible attributions cited in the previous section, it becomes difficult to see one's way to arguing that God can have become embodied as a human being. Can God be eternal as well as incarnate as a temporal being? Can God be changeless and yet incarnate as a being who was subjected to enormous change? Similar, tough questions await the traditionalist in working out conceptions of God's necessity, perfect goodness, simplicity, Being, and omnipotence. Some of the ways to address these problems are covered in Article 67, INCARNATION. I note here that philosophical efforts to articulate an understanding of the Incarnation along traditional lines have led some theists either to modify their view of divine attributes (understanding God as being subject to time and change, for example) or to modify their view of the material world. Reflection on the latter, though, has tended to bolster a non-physicalist (typically dualist) theory of human persons rather than advance the cause of materialism. Many of the philosophical theists who articulate accounts of the Incarnation that secure God's pre-existence as the Son of God as well as God's solidarity with all humans in the Incarnation hold that both human persons and the divine person in the Trinity are non-physical (see Swinburne 1994).

The immanence of God

There may be a way for incorporealists to accommodate some of the motivation behind corporealism. Notwithstanding the resultant radical difference that corporealists retain between the material world and God's states, they set out to develop a profoundly immanent picture of the God–world relation. On their view, one may readily do justice to recognizing that in God we live and move and have our being (Acts 17:28). Can traditional incorporealists provide as rich an immanent picture of God's relation to creation?

Should one embrace a traditional incorporealist understanding of God along with a passibilist treatment of God's perfect goodness, there may be a way to understand the creation, not as literally God's body or material composition, but as the affective equivalent of this. According to passibilism, God is affected by the world's states such that God takes pleasure in the goods of the world and sorrows over its ills. This responsiveness or, as Richard Creel puts it, this being "touched" by the world's states, may be understood as a manifestation of God's perfection (see Article 40, IMMUTABILITY AND IMPASSIBILITY). Being affected by the states of one's own body appears to be one of the defining conditions for one's having a body (or being embodied) and this relation may provide one way of articulating in analogical terms God's proximate, caring presence to the world.

Augustine complained that the identification of God and the world was monstrous. "When anyone tramples on anything, he tramples on God; when he kills any living thing, he kills God! I refuse to set forth all the conclusions which thinking men can draw, but which they cannot express without shame" (City of God, IV:2). Some theists today do not seem to think it a shame to contend that God sorrows when creatures are unjustly killed and trampled and that this constitutes a profound affective bond between God and the world that approaches (but is not the same as) thinking of the world as God's body. From the standpoint of traditional theism, the analogy between God and the world and a person and her body needs to be very carefully formulated so as not to supplant the freedom and autonomy of created individuals. The resultant passibilist identification of God with the world sketched here is not metaphysical, but ethical and psychological, and it may thereby prove to be less of a threat to individual freedom than extant versions of corporealism. See Article 64, THEISM AND ENVIRONMENTAL ETHICS for further work on this view of the God–world relation.

Bibliography

Alston, W. P.: "Functionalism and theological language," American Philosophical Quarterly, 22 (1995) pp. 221–30.
Augustine of Hippo: City of God, tr. C. G. Walsh et al. (Garden City: Doubleday, 1958).

——: *Lectures or Tractates on the Gospel of John*, tr. P. S. Schaff (New York: Christian Literature Co., 1988).

Jantzen, G.: *God's World, God's Body* (Philadelphia: Westminster Press, 1984).

Paulsen, D.: "Must God be Incorporeal?," *Faith and Philosophy*, 6 (1989), pp. 76–87.

Swinburne, R.: *The Christian God* (Oxford: Oxford University Press, 1994).

Taliaferro, C.: *Consciousness and the Mind of God* (Cambridge: Cambridge University Press, 1994).

Wainwright, W. J.: "God's Body," *Journal of the American Academy of Religion*, 42 (1974), pp. 470–81.

35

Beauty

PATRICK SHERRY

Beauty is probably today the most neglected of the divine attributes. Yet many of the early Christian Fathers and the medievals regarded it as central in their discussions of the divine nature, and they have been followed by a few significant later writers, including Jonathan Edwards and Simone Weil. In this article I shall discuss briefly the historical background and the reasons given traditionally for ascribing beauty to God, raise some issues and difficulties, and end by outlining a few positive suggestions.

Sources and arguments

The ascription of beauty to God in Western religious traditions can be traced back historically to two main sources, Plato and the Bible. The most important Platonic text is the so-called "ladder of beauty" in the *Symposium*, where Socrates reports the advice of the priestess Diotima that lovers of beauty should ascend from beautiful bodies to beautiful souls, laws, institutions, and fields of knowledge, until they come to Beauty itself (*Symposium* 210–11; it should be noted that the Greek *kalos*, like *beau* in French, has wider connotations than the English "beautiful"). It became common practice among early Christian writers, e.g. St Augustine, to identify Beauty itself with God, just as they identified Plato's Form of the Good with Him, often using his analogy (in *Republic* VI.509) between this Form and the sun.

The most influential of these early treatments occurs in *The Divine Names*, a treatise written round about CE 500 by a Syrian monk known nowadays as Pseudo-Dionysius. In it, he says that the Good (which is one of his names for God) is called beauty because it imparts beauty to all things according to their natures. Furthermore, it is "the all-beautiful and the beautiful beyond all. It is forever so, unvaryingly, unchangeably so . . ." It is not beautiful in only one part or aspect, for "in itself it is the uniquely and eternally beautiful . . . the superabundant source in itself of the beauty of every beautiful thing" (Pseudo-Dionysius 1987, IV.7).

St Thomas Aquinas's fullest treatment of divine beauty comes in his commentary on *The Divine Names*, especially chapter IV, *lectio* 5. Like Pseudo-Dionysius he describes God as not only beautiful, but as beauty itself, the source of beauty in all things. He does not, however, make there or in any of his other works the claim which was made by some other medieval thinkers, that beauty is one of the transcendentals, i.e. those concepts which apply to all being as such. Some of his later followers argued both that it is so and that this claim is implicit in what Aquinas says.

Most of the texts in the Hebrew Bible which ascribe beauty to God are to be found in the Psalms, e.g. Psalm 27:4, 71:8, 90:17, 145:5 – though again we must be careful about using the term "beauty" here, for the relevant terms can also be translated as "sweetness," "splendor," and "majesty." Sometimes beauty is ascribed to places associated with God: thus in Psalm 50:2 we read, "Out of Zion, the perfection of beauty, God shines out"; the term *yŏphee* used here is in later Hebrew probably the nearest term to "beauty" in the aesthetic sense. But the most important Biblical concept in this connection is probably that of "glory" (Hebrew *kabod*). The earliest texts using it with reference to God associate it with visible phenomena like a cloud, fire, and the manifestations on Mount Sinai (Numbers 14:2); later it is used more generally of God's power and splendor, especially in the Psalms (e.g. 96:3).

This usage forms the background to the ascription of divine glory to Christ in the New Testament, especially in the Epistles, e.g. in 2 Corinthians 4:6, where St Paul describes the glory of God as shining forth on the face of Christ. This, in turn, led to a long tradition of Christian theology which associates beauty particularly with the second Person of the Trinity. St Augustine, for example, ascribes beauty to the Son, as being the exact image of the Father and also the "perfect Word and, so to speak, art of the almighty and wise God" (*On the Trinity*, VI.10.11). Similarly, when Aquinas gives his best-known analysis of beauty, in terms of integrity or completeness, right proportion or harmony, and radiance, he immediately goes on to say that these three characteristics make it particularly appropriate to associate beauty with the Son (*Summa Theologiae*, 1a.39.8).

It should be said that such theologians did not wish to ascribe beauty *only* to the Son, for there is also a long tradition which associates beauty with the Holy Spirit. As time went on, specifically Trinitarian theologies of beauty were worked out, e.g. in terms of the glory of the Father being manifested in that of the Son, which in turn is illuminated and shed forth in the world by the Holy Spirit. Perhaps the fullest such theology is to be found in Hans Urs von Balthasar's *The Glory of the Lord.*

It should also be pointed out that theologies of beauty are by no means restricted to Christianity. Later Jewish mystical traditions developed the Hebrew Bible's teaching on the radiant glory of God and its manifestation in creation. Hinduism celebrates the interplay between the beauty of the world and the presence of the beauty of the Lord Krishna.

In traditional theistic accounts three kinds of reason are offered for ascribing beauty to God: the arguments of natural theology, appeals to experience, and the claims of revelation.

On natural theology, towards the beginning of his *Summa Theologiae* Aquinas outlines a two-pronged argument for ascribing perfections to God: He must have all perfections because of His very nature as self-subsistent being; and He must have them because He is the cause of perfections in creatures, and any cause must always have the perfections of its effects (1a.4.2). He applies this argument specifically to beauty in his commentary on *The Divine Names*. There he says that God is most beautiful and super-beautiful, both because of His exceeding greatness (like the sun in relation to hot things) and because of His causality, as source of all beauty. Because God has beauty as His own, He wishes to multiply it by communicating His likeness; hence He is the exemplary cause of all beauty in things (IV.5). Similarly, in the *Summa* Aquinas argues that God contains all perfections in His essence, and in his *Commentary* he says that beautiful and beauty are not to be separated in God, because the First Cause, on account of His simplicity and perfection, comprehends all in one.

Appeals to experience: such arguments from natural theology as those just summarized, even if valid, leave the nature of divine beauty unclear. At best, they tell us *that* God is beautiful or beauty. But many traditional treatments of the question also appeal to experience, both of God and of great worldly beauty, which is taken to be a manifestation of divine glory. An example of the first kind of experience is given in St Gregory of Nyssa's treatise *On Virginity*, in which he describes King David as having been lifted out of himself by the power of the Holy Spirit, so that he saw in a blessed state of ecstasy the boundless and incomprehensible Beauty, a Beauty which is invisible and formless (chapter 10). A few pages later Gregory, following Plato, exhorts his readers to mount a ladder from earthly beauty to the vision of Beauty itself, with the aid of the Holy Spirit (chapter 11).

Other similar accounts of such visions of beauty, often regarded as anticipations of the Beatific Vision, are to be found in mystical literature. But more commonly the divine beauty is said to be discerned in some powerful experience of natural or artistic beauty, which is regarded as reflecting the nature of its Creator. Thus the Psalmist exclaimed, "The heavens declare the glory of the Lord" (Psalm 19:1). Similarly, later poets like Gerard Manley Hopkins expressed their wonder and joy at God's glory manifested in nature.

Claimed revelations: experiences like those described above may be regarded as revelations of God. But the term "revelation" usually has a more restricted sense in Christian theology: many theologians would prefer to confine revelations of divine beauty to the epiphanies of the divine glory in the Old Testament, culminating in the manifestation of this glory in the Incarnation, or at least to regard these as the normative examples. For Balthasar, for instance, Christ is the paradigm of all beauty, and thereby the justification for ascribing beauty to God.

Problems and issues

The three kinds of approach which I have just summarized are analogous to ones found in other areas of theology and philosophy of religion, and they encounter some familiar objections. Aquinas's two-pronged argument raises the questions of what a self-subsistent being is, and whether causes must always have the qualities of their effects and, if so, why. The appeals to experience raise questions about the veracity of mystical experiences, and about whether the Psalmist, Hopkins, and others were not just interpreting familiar experiences of natural beauty in terms of their prior religious beliefs (see Article 47, RELIGIOUS EXPERIENCE.) And the more directly theological approach raises a vast range of questions about the nature of revelation (see Article 74, REVELATION AND SCRIPTURE) and how it is recognized, and about the theology of the INCARNATION (see Article 67).

But besides these general difficulties and objections, the appeal to divine beauty raises problems of its own. It is often said today that beauty is simply a matter of what pleases people, that what pleases them differs from person to person and from culture to culture, and that in any case the concept is an outmoded one. Certainly the concept seems to create many problems: what is beauty, why do we find it so difficult to define and judge, why do people disagree so much about it, and is it in things themselves or rather, as people say, "in the eye of the beholder"? Modern philosophical aesthetics regards the nature and grounds of aesthetic judgment as only one topic among many, and even here it allots to the consideration of beauty only a minor role, perhaps following the example of much art and literature, which rejects or disregards the traditional view that its role is to celebrate the beauty of creation.

Moreover, the idea of divine beauty seems to raise further difficulties. We commonly think of beauty in terms of colors, shapes, sounds, and so forth – things experienced through the senses. So how can God, who has no body or matter, be described as beautiful? Of course, similar problems arise with other divine attributes, like wisdom, power, and love. But theistic believers get some handle on these other attributes by trying to discern the relevant divine actions, e.g. God's wise governance of the world, His power manifested in natural phenomena or in holiness, and His love shown in Providence and especially, Christians say, in the life and work of Christ. In the case of beauty, however, it is difficult to find any corresponding actions other than God's creation of beauty in the world. Those who try to fill in the picture here tend to say that God's beauty is inexpressible, or else to produce something rather formal, for instance by applying Aquinas's threefold analysis of beauty to the divine Being.

At the root of many of these problems, I think, is the fact that we lack a proper vocabulary to support our ascriptions of beauty to God. We usually employ the term "beautiful" in two ways: as an overall verdict on a work of art or a natural phenomenon, or to qualify another term, as in "beautifully structured." Either way, the term is supported by a vast range of concepts: by other aesthetic ones like "elegant" and "graceful," or by particular words describing the qualities of colors, sounds, and so on. Much of this vocabulary, however, is inappropriate for describing God – what would a pretty, handsome, or elegant God be like? In the case of divine beauty the neighboring or supporting concepts are drawn from elsewhere: from the language of power (the Biblical term "glory" suggests power as well as beauty, and goes along with terms like "majesty," "splendor," and "strength" – see Article 28, OMNIPOTENCE), from that of ethics (those who speak of Christ's beauty commonly stress his moral and spiritual qualities), or from the more general divine attributes of holiness, perfection, goodness, and excellence (see Article 30, GOODNESS). God's beauty is also often related to light, in the sense of intellectual or spiritual illumination, and hence to wisdom, knowledge, and truth (see Article 29,

OMNISCIENCE). It seems, therefore, that the concept of divine beauty is obscure both in itself and in its relation to more familiar kinds of beauty.

Some suggestions

The difficulties which I have summarized are formidable, but they may not be insuperable. Although twentieth century aesthetics allots a lesser role to beauty than that of earlier centuries, the concept is still the subject of much philosophical reflection and writing. After all, the term is in common use, both among ordinary people and among artists and writers. Moreover, it is not true that beauty is ascribed *only* to colors, lines, sounds, and so forth: people commonly speak of the beauty of scientific theories and of the elegance of mathematical proofs. Also, although the beauty of good deeds and of virtues is more rarely hymned today than in the ancient world or even as late as the eighteenth century, we still speak of beautiful personalities, sweetness of character, and moral deformity. If, therefore, we still recognize moral and intellectual beauty, there may be no good reason for excluding beauty *a priori* from God.

Still, it is difficult to see how one might go on from this point, given the paucity of recent reflection on divine beauty in both philosophical and popular literature. One might use recent work defending the claims of religious experience against skeptical objections, e.g. by arguing that its being different from ordinary sense experience is not sufficient warrant for rejecting it and that it should be regarded as "innocent until proved guilty," and thereby defend the propriety of appealing to visions of divine beauty. But this strategy, even if successful, still leaves the nature of divine beauty unclear to those who have not had such visions.

There are, in principle, two other possible starting points for a philosopher here: the divine nature itself and the beauty of creation. As regards the first, it may be that God's beauty could be construed in terms of the relationship between His attributes: Edgar de Bruyne, in discussing some remarks of Duns Scotus, mentioned the idea that God's beauty is the harmony in the "ocean" of divine perfections, which are formally distinct but are united in the simplicity of the divine essence (Bruyne 1946, pp. 356, 359). He did not, however, develop this idea – to do so would require a full discussion of the various divine attributes and their relation to the simplicity of the divine nature.

A discussion of the topic which started from our apprehension of beauty in nature and in art would naturally relate this to a doctrine of Creation (see Article 39, CREATION AND CONSERVATION). Again, one should first scrutinize some of the common objections put forward. It is not true, for example, that all modern thinkers have found the ascription of beauty to God more problematical than, say, power or wisdom. Simone Weil, as we shall see, found the luminosity of beauty and its ability to excite wonder and spiritual longing a particularly apt starting point for considering God's presence in the world. And is it true that the Psalmist, Hopkins, and others were offering a religious "interpretation" of the world when they saw its beauty as a manifestation of divine glory? If they were, it was not quite in the way that people do so when they see some fortunate occurrence as the working of

Providence (see Article 72, PROVIDENCE AND PREDESTINATION), for there is an ambiguity in the latter case which is not present in the case of beauty. When Hopkins exclaimed, in his poem "God's Grandeur,"

> The world is charged with the grandeur of God.
> It will flame out, like shining from shook foil . . .

he was not, I think, offering us an *interpretation*; for God's glory seemed to him to shine out through nature, just as it did for the Psalmist in the heavens.

We find a philosophical presentation of this line of thought, and a very bold and simple one, in the work of Simone Weil. She describes the beauty of the world which attracts us as the appearance of divine beauty, a "snare" through which God captures the soul in spite of itself. Indeed, she continues, it is a kind of incarnation:

In everything which gives us the pure authentic feeling of beauty there really is the presence of God. There is as it were an incarnation of God in the world and it is indicated by beauty.

The beautiful is the experimental proof that the incarnation is possible.   (Weil 1952, p. 137)

She goes a stage further when she describes beauty as an attribute of God Himself, and as the attribute in which we see Him: writing of the "ladder of beauty" in the *Symposium*, she says that we are not dealing here with a general idea of beauty, but with "the beauty of God; it is the attribute of God under which we *see* him" (Weil 1968, p. 129). She agrees with Plato that beauty is the only one of the "lovable realities" (*Phaedrus* 250d) that is seen, unlike attributes such as wisdom: for her, the beauty of the world *is* God's own beauty, made manifest to the senses.

It is this very bold account of beauty that enables Weil, in an argument reminiscent of recent theological theses about "implicit" or "anonymous" Christianity, to claim that the love of beauty may be what she calls a "form of the implicit love of God." In her essay on this topic she says, "The Beauty of the world is Christ's tender smile for us coming through matter. He is really present in the universal beauty" (Weil 1959, p. 120). This seemingly irenic argument, however, has some harsh implications: for Weil, those who ignore or deface beauty are committing a religious fault.

Although Weil's treatment is much influenced by Plato, especially the *Symposium*, she does not share his anxiety to mount from earthly beauty to Beauty itself as quickly as possible. Rather, she seems more interested in the traffic *down* the ladder, i.e. in the ways in which beauty is, as she says, "incarnated" in this world. This is partly, I think, because of her admiration for ancient Stoicism with its love for the world, our universal homeland (see Weil 1959, pp. 131–2); but more so because of her strong doctrine of Creation. She takes the myth of creation in the *Timaeus*, according to which the Demiurge made the world through what Plato calls the Soul of the World and the Model of Creation, and she identifies this trio with the Christian Trinity (Weil 1968, pp. 132–3). For her, again, God's beauty is, through Christ and the Holy Spirit, immanent in the world, because of the Creation.

Weil's approach is strikingly bold. If she is right, she has in the simplest possible way solved our problem of explaining what the divine beauty is, and how it is related to worldly beauty. She has also explained why aesthetic experience is for many people also a religious experience; and by treating the beauty we perceive as a mode of God's presence she has avoided the seeming emptiness of both inferences to divine beauty and second-hand reports of mystical experiences.

Her position is, however, elusive at times, largely because of the aphoristic style in which she writes. She treats beauty in an abstract way, giving few examples either from nature or from art, and is not concerned with the relationship between it and other aesthetic concepts. In so far as she relates beauty to other concepts, it is to ones like truth, eternity, and goodness. But her approach is, I think, right in that she sees that any account of divine beauty must relate it to the beauty we perceive, and that a doctrine of Creation plays a central role here. Any further philosophical treatment of the question will need to deal with the relationship between God's beauty and the other divine attributes, as well as to elucidate further the relationship between God and the world.

Bibliography

Aquinas, St Thomas: *In Librum Beati Dionysii De Divinis Nominibus Expositio* (Turin: Marietti, 1950).

Balthasar, H. U. von: *The Glory of the Lord: a Theological Aesthetics*, tr. J. Riches et al., 7 vols. (Edinburgh: T. & T. Clark, 1982–91).

Bruyne, Edgar de: *Études d'esthétique médiévale*, vol. III (Bruges: de Tempel, 1946).

Pseudo-Dionysius: *The Divine Names*, in *The Complete Works*, tr. Colm Luibheid (London: SPCK, 1987), pp. 47–131.

Sherry, P.: *Spirit and Beauty: An Introduction to Theological Aesthetics* (Oxford: Clarendon Press, 1992).

Weil, S.: *Gravity and Grace*, tr. E. Craufurd (London: Routledge & Kegan Paul, 1952).

——: *Waiting on God*, tr. E. Craufurd (London: Collins Fontana, 1959).

——: *On Science, Necessity and the Love of God*, tr. R. Rees (London: Oxford University Press, 1968).

36

Omnipresence

EDWARD R. WIERENGA

Omnipresence is naturally understood as being everywhere present. Thus, to say that God is omnipresent is to say that he is present everywhere. But what does it mean to say that God is present at *any* place, much less at *every* place?

St Anselm, writing in the eleventh century, struggled with this issue. In chapter 20 of his *Monologion* he offered an argument for the conclusion that "[t]he Supreme Being exists in every place and at all times." In the following chapter, however, he argued that God "exists in no place and at no time." Anselm then attempted to reconcile these "two conclusions – so contradictory according to their utterance, so necessary according to their proof" – by providing interpretations of them according to which they are both true, and, thus, not incompatible after all. This Anselm did by distinguishing two senses of "being wholly in a place," namely, being contained in a place and being present at a place. In the first sense, those objects are wholly in a place "whose magnitude place contains by circumscribing it, and circumscribes by containing it." Ordinary physical objects are thus contained in regions of space. In this sense, however, God is not in any place, for it is "a mark of shameless impudence to say that place circumscribes the magnitude of Supreme Truth." On the other hand, God *is* in every place in the sense that he is *present* at every place. In this sense, Anselm held, "the Supreme Being must be present as a whole in every different place at once . . ." But this second sense of "being present," the sense in which God *is* present in every place, is just the concept that was in question, and Anselm said very little explicitly to make it clearer.

St Thomas Aquinas added some details here. He agreed that God is present in space in a different sense from that in which ordinary objects are. But Aquinas further specified this sense, claiming that God's presence is to be understood in terms of God's power, knowledge, and essence (see Article 28, OMNIPOTENCE; Article 29, OMNISCIENCE; and Article 39, CREATION AND CONSERVATION). More precisely, Aquinas held that "God is in all things by His power, inasmuch as all things are subject to his power; He is in all things by His presence in all things, inasmuch as all things are bare and open to His eyes; He is in all things by His essence, inasmuch as He is present to all as the cause of their being" (*Summa Theologiae* I.8.3). Aquinas's illustration of this point is suggestive, if not entirely satisfactory. He held that "how [God] is in other things created by Him may be considered from human affairs. A king, for example, is said to be in the whole kingdom by his power, although he is not everywhere present. Again, a thing is said to be by its presence in other things which are subject to its inspection; as things in a house are said to be present to anyone, who nevertheless may not be in substance in every part of the house. Lastly, a thing is said to be substantially or essentially in that place where its substance is."

Perhaps a king may be said to be present wherever his power extends. At any rate, it is clear that Aquinas took this to be a kind of presence. In his *Summa contra Gentiles*, for example, Aquinas contrasted the "contact of dimensive quantity" that a physical object has to the place it is in with the "contact of power" that an incorporeal object has in a place, and he added that "an incorporeal thing is related to its presence in something by its power, in the same way that a corporeal thing is related to its presence in something by dimensive quantity" (see Article 34, INCORPOREALITY). And he concluded that "if there were any body possessed of infinite dimensive quantity, it would have to be everywhere. So, if there be an incorporeal being possessed of infinite power, it must be everywhere" (*Summa contra Gentiles*, III.68.3).

The third condition Aquinas gave, that of presence by essence or substance, can perhaps be assimilated to the condition of power. If God is present in things by his essence "inasmuch as He is present to all as the cause of their being," then it is in virtue of an exercise of his power, namely, creating and sustaining things, that he is present.

However, Aquinas's explanation of his second condition, namely presence through knowledge, is puzzling. The things in a house that are present in virtue of being "subject to inspection" seem a poor analogy for God, who, if anything, is more like the inspector than that which may be inspected. So perhaps Aquinas should be taken as holding that God is present everywhere in the sense that everything is open to his inspection ("bare and open to his eyes"), rather than that he is open in this way to others. Another way of putting this idea, then, is to say that God is present everywhere in virtue of his knowledge of everything in any place.

This way of conceiving of God's presence by reference to his knowledge and power assumes that the predicate "is present" as applied to God is *analogical* with its application to ordinary physical objects. The term is neither univocal (used with the same meaning as it is in ordinary contexts), nor equivocal (used with a completely unrelated meaning). Rather, the meaning of "is present" or, better, "is present at place *p*" when applied to God, can be explained by reference to its ordinary sense, as follows: God is present at a place (in a special sense) just in case there is a physical object that is present at that place (in the ordinary sense) and God is able to control that object, God knows what is going on in that object, and God is the cause of the existence of that object. Conceiving of God's presence in this way, however, would seem to limit him to those places that are actually occupied by some object or other. Perhaps this is in fact what such philosophers as Anselm and Aquinas intended; Anselm, after all, said that "the supreme Nature is more appropriately said to be everywhere, in this sense, that it is in all existing things, than in this sense, namely that it is merely in all places" (*Monologion* 23). On the other hand, if God is present at places not otherwise occupied, the classical account can accommodate this simply by not insisting that "is present" as applied to God is strictly analogical with its application to ordinary objects; it is instead to be defined in terms of God's knowledge and power.

Twentieth century commentators on divine omnipresence have also held that God's presence is analogical. As Charles Hartshorne (1941) put it, "The relation of God to the world must necessarily be conceived, if at all, by analogy with relations given in human experience." But rather than taking divine presence to be analogical to the location in space of ordinary objects, philosophers like Hartshorne have assumed that God's relation to the world is analogous instead to a human mind's relation to its body.

Hartshorne held that among the things that human beings know, some are known immediately – by "vivid and direct intuition" – while other things are known only by inference. The former knowledge is infallible: it includes knowledge of one's own thoughts and feelings, as well as knowledge of changes going on in one's body. Since such immediate knowledge is the highest form of knowledge, it is the kind of knowledge God has. In God's case, moreover, he has immediate knowledge of the entire cosmos.

Hartshorne made similar claims about power. Some of what people have power over, they control directly. Other things can be controlled only indirectly or through intermediaries. Human beings have direct or immediate power only over their own volitions and movements of their own bodies. Again, however, since immediate power is the highest form of power, it is the kind of power appropriate to God. Accordingly, God has immediate power over every part of the universe. Hartshorne may thus be seen as elaborating the medieval view of divine omnipresence: God is present everywhere in virtue of having *immediate* knowledge and power throughout the entire universe. However, Hartshorne endorsed a surprising addition. He held that, by definition, whatever part of the world a mind knows and controls immediately is its body. He thus drew the conclusion that the world is God's body.

Richard Swinburne (1977) also approached the question of what it is to be an omnipresent spirit by asking what it is for a person to have a body. Swinburne's view differs from Hartshorne's in certain respects, but Swinburne, too, was willing to accept what he called a "limited embodiment" of God. Swinburne appealed first to the notion of a basic action – an action one does but not by doing something else. For example, raising one's arm is typically a basic action, whereas making the same arm rise by lifting it with one's other arm is not a basic action. According to Swinburne, God can move any part of the universe directly, as a basic action. Moreover, God "knows without inference about any state of the world." Thus, Swinburne concluded that the doctrine of divine omnipresence is the claim "that God controls *all* things directly and knows about *all* things without the information coming to him through some causal chain." This summary of Swinburne's position may be slightly inaccurate, because presumably Swinburne did not really mean to say that God controls directly the free acts of other agents. Perhaps, then, his thesis is that God *can* control directly what happens at any place (see Article 38, DIVINE ACTION).

It is rather implausible to claim, on the basis of the knowledge and power

Hartshorne and Swinburne each attribute to God, that the world is his body, even in only a limited respect. One way to see this is to notice that on their views, God bears the same relation to unoccupied regions of space that he does to occupied regions. That is, for any place, God knows immediately what is happening at that place and he is able to control directly what happens there. It is surely unmotivated, then, to say of such a region that if there is some physical thing there then it is a part of God's body, when God would have the same epistemic access to that region and control over it if the physical object were not there. The presence of the object makes no contribution to God's abilities.

Hartshorne's view has a further implausibility, not shared with Swinburne's. Hartshorne attempted to attribute to God maximal immediacy with respect to knowledge and power. However, what he took to be immediate, at least in the case of knowledge, included both a more immediate and a less immediate component. Attributing only the more immediate component would better accord with Hartshorne's aim of ascribing maximal immediacy to God's knowledge. Doing so, however, undercuts Hartshorne's definition of one's body as whatever part of the world one's mind knows and controls immediately. This point needs explanation. Hartshorne had described immediate knowledge as infallible, indicating that it includes knowledge of one's own thoughts and feelings, as well as knowledge of changes in one's body. On the sort of mind–body dualism Hartshorne seems to presuppose, however, only the knowledge of one's own mental states would count as infallible. Knowledge of changes in one's body, dependent as they are on various causal processes, are neither infallible nor as immediate as knowledge of one's mental state. What one has the most immediate knowledge of, then, is not one's body.

A similar, although perhaps less convincing, point can be made with respect to power. According to Hartshorne, one's most immediate power is with respect to one's volitions and with respect to movements of one's body. In this case, too, control over volitions would seem to be more immediate than control over one's body, especially if voluntary bodily movements are causal effects of volitions. So what one has most direct control over need not be one's body.

Swinburne's view avoids this objection by defining immediate knowledge as information which does not come to the subject through a causal chain. Accordingly, it should follow that anything of which one has immediate knowledge is *not* one's body, since knowledge of our own bodies always arises through a causal chain.

If Swinburne's view of divine omnipresence is thus stripped of its admission of God's "limited embodiment," it seems to be the medieval view strengthened with the requirement that the knowledge and power that constitute God's presence be immediate or direct. In fact, however, the medievals also held that God's knowledge and power were immediate or direct, even if they did not emphasize this in their discussions of omnipresence. Thus, despite the fact that Aquinas spoke of things "being open to God's eyes," suggesting that God saw or perceived what was happening in order to have knowledge of it, in fact Aquinas did not believe that God acquired his knowledge in this way. God does not acquire knowledge by being

289

acted upon causally by the world. Rather, "he sees other things, not in themselves, but in himself, inasmuch as his essence contains the likeness of things other than himself" (*Summa Theologiae* I.14.5). Moreover, God's omnipotence is an "active power of the highest degree" (*Summa* I.25.2), and this is naturally understood as direct or immediate power. Thus, Swinburne's explication of omnipresence as *immediate knowledge and power extending everywhere* may be seen as making explicit the standard medieval understanding of that divine attribute. (For another development of omnipresence in terms of God's knowledge, power, and conservation of the cosmos and its constituents, together with the assumption that God is thereby related to the cosmos in a way analogous to the way human persons are related to their bodies, see Taliaferro (1994) esp. ch. 5.)

Bibliography

Anselm: *Saint Anselm: Basic Writings*, tr. S. N. Deane (La Salle: Open Court, 1962).
Aquinas, Thomas: *Basic Writings of St Thomas Aquinas*, 2 vols., ed. A. C. Pegis (New York: Random House, 1944).
Hartshorne, C.: *Man's Vision of God and the Logic of Theism* (New York: Harper & Brothers, 1941).
Swinburne, R.: *The Coherence of Theism* (Oxford: Oxford University Press, 1977).
Taliaferro, C.: *Consciousness and the Mind of God* (Cambridge: Cambridge University Press, 1994).
Wierenga, E.: "Anselm on omnipresence," *New Scholasticism*, 52 (1988), pp. 30–41.

37

Foreknowledge and human freedom

LINDA ZAGZEBSKI

The apparent incompatibility of divine foreknowledge and human free will has produced a long and impressive history of reflection on the modalities of time, the nature of OMNISCIENCE (see Article 29), and the sense in which human persons are free. Roughly, the problem is that if there is an omniscient God, his knowledge would presumably encompass all of the future, including the future acts of human beings. And we would expect an omniscient deity's powers of knowing to be so strong that not only does he have no false beliefs, it is *impossible* for him to have false beliefs. But if it is impossible for God's belief about a future human act to be false, it seems to be impossible for that person to do otherwise. How, then, can her act be free?

The mere assumption that God has foreknowledge in the sense of having justified true beliefs about the future does not create any difficulties for human freedom since a belief can be justified and true even though, at the time of the belief, it *can* turn out to be false. What generates the dilemma in its strongest form is the assumption that God's past beliefs about the future are *infallible* and the principle of the necessity of the past, along with some general logical principles and principles that purportedly follow from the definitions of infallibility and the notion of free will. To say that a believer *s* is infallible is to say that *s* cannot make a mistake in his beliefs; necessarily, if *s* believes *b*, *b* is true. So the proposition *s believes b* strictly implies *b*. The principle of the necessity of the past is the principle that past states of affairs have a form of necessity simply in virtue of being past; that is to say, what is past is fixed and beyond the power of any being. William of Ockham called the necessity of the past necessity *per accidens*, and the contemporary literature has adopted his usage in calling it accidental necessity.

The argument that these assumptions lead to the denial of human freedom proceeds as follows:

Let three moments of time be ordered such that $t_1 < t_2 < t_3$.

(1) Suppose that God infallibly believes at time t_1 that I will do c at t_3. (*premise*)
(2) The proposition *God believes at* t_1 *that I will do* c *at* t_3 is accidentally necessary at t_2. (*from the principle of the necessity of the past*).
(3) If a proposition *p* is accidentally necessary at *t* and *p* strictly implies *q*, then *q* is accidentally necessary at *t*. (*transfer of necessity principle*)
(4) *God believes at* t_1 *that I will do* c *at* t_3 entails *I will do* c *at* t_3. (*from the definition of infallibility*)

(5)   So the proposition *I will do* c *at* t_3 is accidentally necessary at t_2.   (2–4)

(6)   If the proposition *I will do* c *at* t_3 is accidentally necessary at t_2, it is true at t_2 that I cannot do otherwise than to do c at t_3.   (*premise*)

(7)   If when I do an act I cannot do otherwise, I do not do it freely.   (*principle of alternate possibilities*)

(8)   Therefore, I do not do c at t_3 freely.   (5–7)

Since an omniscient God is assumed to have previous infallible beliefs about every act of every human person, it follows by parity of reasoning that no act of any human person is free. It appears, then, that either humans do not act freely or else God does not have infallible knowledge of future human acts. Let us call the above argument *D*, the dilemma argument.

Some "solutions" to the dilemma of divine foreknowledge and human free will reject or weaken the assumption of divine foreknowledge or of human freedom. For example, on the standard interpretation of Aristotle's sea battle argument in *De Interpretatione* 9, Aristotle denies a truth value to future contingent propositions. This has the immediate consequence that no future contingent proposition is knowable, not even by an omniscient knower. Alternatively, future contingents may be declared logically unknowable, even if they have a truth value (e.g. Swinburne 1977, Hasker 1989). A third move is to give an account of human freedom that is weaker than the one embraced by causal indeterminists (e.g. Kenny 1969). Just as so-called soft determinists argue that causal determinism is compatible with free will, what we might call soft theological determinists can argue that theological determinism is compatible with free will in a strong enough sense of freedom, but one that is weaker than desired by those who find determinism threatening. Each of these moves concedes that infallible divine foreknowledge is incompatible with a strong sense of human freedom, and simply attempts to make that palatable.

There are three major traditional solutions to the foreknowledge/freedom dilemma which purport to retain both a strong sense of God's omniscience and a strong sense of human freedom. Each of them rejects the soundness of argument *D* by introducing special positions on the relationship between God and time, the principles of modality, or both. The first solution comes from Boethius (6th century) and Thomas Aquinas (13th century). According to this solution, God is timeless (see Article 32, ETERNITY). God and all of his states, including his states of knowing or believing, exist outside of time altogether. God does not actually have beliefs *at* a time t_1. This means that premise (1) in argument *D* is false, not because God is ignorant of my act c at t_3, but because God does not know my act or any act *as future*.

The second solution comes from William of Ockham (14th century), who made use of the concept of accidental necessity, the necessity of the past. According to this solution, not all of the apparent past is really, or strictly, past. God's past beliefs about the contingent future are not past in the sense relevant to accidental necessity, and so propositions that say they occurred are not accidentally necessary. Premise (2), then, is false.

The third solution comes from the Jesuit philosopher Luis de Molina (16th century), who denied (3), the transfer of necessity principle (see Freddoso, in Molina 1988, pp. 57–8). Molina developed the idea of divine *scientia media*, or middle knowledge, to explain how God can secure infallible knowledge of contingent future human acts. The idea is that God knows what any possible free creature would freely choose in any possible circumstance. By combining his knowledge of the circumstances he has willed to create with his middle knowledge, God can know the entire future, including that part of it consisting of free human acts.

I will not examine these traditional solutions here. Instead, I propose that we look at another place in which argument *D* goes awry.

Let us begin by looking at determinism, its forms, and its difficulties. I will propose two innocuous principles, each of which is connected with a form of determinism. First, there is the *principle of the necessity of the past*: the only possible futures are ones that are compatible with the actual past. The form of determinism connected with this principle is what we might call *accidental determinism*. This is the position that there is only one possible future compatible with the actual past. Argument *D* allegedly shows that divine foreknowledge leads to accidental determinism on theological grounds. Second, there is the *principle of causation*: The only possible futures are ones that are compatible with the causal history of the actual world. The future must include the effects of all past causes. The form of determinism connected with this principle is *causal determinism*. This is the view that there is only one possible future compatible with the causal history of the world at any given time. That is, every future event is causally determined by events in the past. While these two principles and the two forms of determinism connected with them are conceptually distinct, causal determinism is committed to accidental determinism. If it is true that there is only one possible future compatible with the causal history of the world, there is only one possible future compatible with the entire past history of the world, which includes the causal history as a part.

It is often thought that causal determinism precludes human freedom. If so, the reason it does so ought to be examined since it may show us what is threatening about accidental determinism. Argument *D* employs a well-known principle that is frequently used to show the incompatibility between causal determinism and free will – the principle of alternate possibilities in (7). Harry Frankfurt (1969) has a famous series of examples intended to falsify a related principle, the principle that I am not *responsible* for an act if I am not able to do otherwise. The principle used in (7) concerns human freedom rather than responsibility, but Frankfurt-style examples can also be used to falsify (7).

Here is a Frankfurt-style counterexample to (7). Suppose that Black is an insane neurosurgeon who wishes to see White dead, but is unwilling to do the deed himself. Knowing that Jones also despises White and will have a single good opportunity to kill him, Black inserts a mechanism into Jones's brain that enables him to monitor and to control Jones's neurological activities. If Jones's neurological activity suggests that he is on the verge of deciding not to murder White when the opportunity arises, Black's mechanism intervenes and causes Jones to decide to commit the murder. On the other hand, if Jones decides to murder White on his

293

own, the mechanism does not intervene at all. It merely monitors, but does not affect Jones's neurological activity. Now suppose that when the occasion arises, Jones decides to murder White without any help from Black's mechanism. Intuitively, it seems that Jones acts freely. He brings about his act in exactly the same way as he would have if he had been able to do otherwise. None the less, he is unable to do otherwise since if he had attempted to do so, he would have been thwarted by Black's device. If this interpretation of the situation is justified, (7) is false, and argument D is fallacious.

The Frankfurt cases are counterexamples to (7) and to the principle which was Frankfurt's intended target:

(7') If when I do an act I cannot do otherwise, I am not morally responsible for it.

They are also counterexamples to a number of variations on (7) that might be proposed by a believer in the incompatibility of infallible foreknowledge and human freedom such as:

(7") If I cannot freely refrain from doing an act, I do not do it freely.

Frankfurt-style cases, then, seem to block a number of reasonable moves from (6) to (8) in argument D.

A possible problem with the Frankfurt-style case as a counterexample to (7) is that it seems to presuppose causal determinism. Frankfurt argues that his cases can be made to fit a non-deterministic world, but in the case just described, it is hard to see how Black can be a perfect predictor if Jones's choice is not causally determined. If Jones shows signs of making the "wrong" choice, Black can intervene with the device to cause him to make the other choice, but when Jones shows every sign of being about to make the "right" choice, the device does nothing. However, if it is never more than probable that Jones will make the "right" choice or any particular choice in a non-deterministic world, Jones retains the ability to change his mind right up to the moment he makes the actual choice. It appears, then, that when Jones shows signs of being about to choose to murder White, he is able to do otherwise after all.

My response to this potential problem is that it does not really matter whether or not Frankfurt cases in a non-deterministic world are literally such that the agent cannot do otherwise. As Wesley Morriston of the University of Colorado, Boulder, has pointed out to me, the importance of Frankfurt's examples is that they show us that the ability to do otherwise is beside the point. They get us to see that what makes Jones's act free is not the presence or absence of alternate possibilities, but something else – the fact that he does it "on his own" without the operation of any conditions which make it the case that he cannot do otherwise. Jones does not act *because of* these conditions. As Frankfurt puts it (1969, p. 837):

Now if someone had no alternative to performing a certain action but did not perform it because he was unable to do otherwise, then he would have performed exactly the same action even if he *could* have done otherwise. The circumstances that made it impossible for him to do otherwise could have been subtracted from the situation without affecting what happened or why it happened in any way.

Here Frankfurt says that the point is that Jones would have done the same thing even if he had been able to do otherwise. What he should have said if he is not presupposing determinism is that Jones *might* have done the same thing if he had been able to do otherwise. Under the assumption of a non-deterministic universe, Jones might or might not have done the same thing in counterfactual circumstances. But Frankfurt's basic point is sound: whatever Jones does is unaffected by any conditions which make it the case that he cannot do otherwise.

The moral of the story from Frankfurt's point of view is that since the principle of alternate possibilities is false, causal determinism is not so bad. Frankfurt assumes, then, that indeterminists are squeamish about determinism only because of its denial of alternate possibilities. From the point of view of the foreknowledge/free will incompatibilist, the moral is different. Frankfurt has shown that (7) is false, but that means that if causal determinism is bad, it must be bad for some other reason than the fact that it entails the inability to do otherwise. It is, then, all the more important that we identify what is wrong with causal determinism because accidental determinism may have a parallel problem.

The problem has already been identified in part. If the world is causally determined, my act does not really originate in *me*. For my act really to be my own, it must have a certain kind of independence of any conditions which make it the case that I cannot do otherwise. My act must be unaffected by the presence or absence of these conditions; the explanation for its occurrence must not include these conditions to any significant degree. If my act is causally determined, however, it would not have occurred without its causes (suitably described), and the explanation for its occurrence gives a central place to its causes.

To insure my freedom, then, we must make sure that my act, or, more precisely, the choice to perform the act, originates in me, that it is not causally determined, and if there are non-causally necessitating features of the situation, i.e. conditions that make it the case that I cannot choose otherwise, it must be true that my act is as independent of those conditions as Jones's choice to murder White is independent of Black's mechanism. This suggests that free choice requires the following:

S chooses c freely only if (i) s brings about the choice of c, (ii) s is not causally determined to choose c, and (iii) s might have chosen c even if able to do otherwise, i.e. s might have chosen c even if any non-causally necessitating conditions had not obtained.

Since the only non-causally necessitating condition we are considering is divine foreknowledge, it follows that my choice is free only if (i) I bring it about, (ii) my choice is not causally determined by God or anything else, and (iii) I might have made the same choice even if God had not foreknown what I would choose. That is to say, it would have made no difference to my choice if God had refrained from believing what I would choose.

Now a believer in God's essential omniscience can certainly question whether God *could* withhold belief about my choice c. Arguably, to do so is to give up his omniscience. If so, to ask what would or might have happened if God had refrained from having a belief about c is to ask what would or might have

295

happened if the impossible had obtained, and that is a nettlesome topic, which I have examined elsewhere (Zagzebski 1990). But notice that if this is a problem, it is Frankfurt's problem also. To what possible world is Frankfurt referring in the passage quoted above? Given that Frankfurt is a causal determinist, a world that is qualitatively almost identical to the actual world but in which Jones can do otherwise must be a causally determined world in which, miraculously, Jones is able to escape the confines of causality in this one instance. It is not at all clear that that is a possible world at all on Frankfurt's view, yet his point is not difficult to understand. There must be some way of expressing the fact that certain states of affairs, even if necessary, make no difference to the occurrence of a human act. It is this independence of my act from God's omniscience that is maintained in the partial definition of free choice just given.

This leads us to see that on the assumption of divine foreknowledge, both causal determinists and causal indeterminists have a false picture of the range of possible worlds close to the actual world. According to the causal determinist, there are no close possible worlds in which I make a different choice than I make in the actual world since the making of a different choice would involve a difference in the causal sequence; and since every link of that sequence is necessitated by previous events, the world could only have been different at any point if something had been different at the beginning of the world, or if there had been different causal laws. In contrast, the causal indeterminist says that there is a world exactly like the actual world up to the moment at which I choose c, but in which I choose not-c instead. The foreknowledge advocate must say that they are both wrong, but the indeterminist is much closer to being right since there is another possible world that has the following feature: the only difference between it and the actual world up to the moment I choose c is that God believes that I choose not-c instead of c, and in this world I choose not-c. This means that there is a significant difference between the Frankfurt cases and the foreknowledge case. In the Frankfurt cases someone is prepared to thwart my will, and succeeds in doing so in close possible worlds. But in the foreknowledge case no such thing occurs since it is true in every possible world that God believes that I will do what I decide to do. This feature, of course, strengthens the claim that infallible foreknowledge does not take away freedom, but since it is difficult to see how a Frankfurt-style example can be coherently emended to include this feature, it appears that we have reached the limit at which analogies with other cases of being unable to do otherwise are useful.

In conclusion, even if (5) is true and all of my acts, both past and future, are accidentally necessary, this fact does not take away my free will in a sense of freedom strong enough to be incompatible with the existence of any necessitating conditions, causal or otherwise, which are such that the subtraction of those conditions from the situation would effect my choice. So accidental determinism itself is no threat to human freedom. What is unacceptable is not the idea that there is only one future compatible with the past; what is unacceptable is that there is a certain kind of dependency between human acts and prior conditions. The lack of alternate possibilities itself is not the problem.

The considerations of this article cast suspicion on the common idea that there is a modal asymmetry between past and future according to which the past has a kind of necessity that the future lacks. Rejecting the modal asymmetry of time would permit us to resolve another foreknowledge dilemma (discussed in Zagzebski 1991, Appendix). This dilemma is not directly related to freedom, and is more vexing because it has fewer premises and fewer ways out. This dilemma is as follows:

New foreknowledge dilemma

(1)   There is (and was in the past) an essentially omniscient foreknower.
(2)   It is now possible that Jones will murder White next Friday, and it is now possible that Jones will not murder White next Friday.

On the assumption that the essentially omniscient foreknower exists in every world in which Jones exists and is in a position to decide whether or not to murder White next Friday (a reasonable assumption if the foreknower is identified with God), the proposition, *Jones will murder White next Friday*, is strictly equivalent to the proposition, *the essentially omniscient foreknower believes Jones will murder White next Friday*. This makes (1) and (2) strictly imply

(3)   It is now possible that the essentially omniscient foreknower believed before now that Jones will murder White next Friday, and it is now possible that the essentially omniscient foreknower believed before now that Jones will not murder White next Friday.

From (1) and the law of excluded middle we know that

(4)   Either the essentially omniscient foreknower did believe Jones will murder White next Friday before now or he did not.

But the principle of the necessity of the past entails

(5)   If he did, it is not now possible that he did not, and if he did not, it is not now possible that he did.

(4) and (5) entail

(6)   Either it is not now possible that he did not, or it is not now possible that he did.

But (6) contradicts (3). Assuming that the law of excluded middle is unassailable, it follows that (1), (2), and (5) are inconsistent.

The rejection of the modal asymmetry of time would have the consequence that there is no sense of "possible" that makes both (2) and (5) true. (2) says that the future has alternate possibilities, while (5) says that the past does not. There are, of course, many different ways of understanding what it means to have alternate possibilities but the application of the Frankfurt examples to the foreknowledge dilemma gives us reason to think that whatever sense there is to the non-existence of alternate possibilities in the past also applies in the future. And, presumably, if there is a sense in which alternate possibilities apply to the future, it would also apply to the past, although I have not investigated such a sense here.

Bibliography

Aquinas, St Thomas: *Summa Theologiae*, 1, q. 10, 14, and 25.

——: *Summa contra Gentiles*, chapter 65.

Boethius: *The Consolation of Philosophy*, Book 5.

Fischer, J. M.: "Responsibility and control," *Journal of Philosophy*, 79 (January 1982), pp. 24–40.

Frankfurt, H. G.: "Alternate possibilities and moral responsibility," *Journal of Philosophy*, 66 (December 1969), pp. 829–39.

Hasker, W. J.: *God, Time and Knowledge* (Ithaca: Cornell University Press, 1989).

Kenny, A.: "Divine foreknowledge and human freedom." In *Aquinas: A Collection of Critical Essays*, ed. A. Kenny (Notre Dame: University of Notre Dame Press, 1969).

Molina, Luis de: *On Divine Foreknowledge*, (Part IV of the Concordia), tr. and introd. A. J. Freddoso (Ithaca: Cornell University Press, 1988).

Ockham, William of: *Predestination, God's Foreknowledge and Future Contingents*, tr. M. McC. Adams and N. Kretzmann (Indianapolis: Hackett, 1969).

Swinburne, R.: *The Coherence of Theism* (Oxford: Oxford University Press, 1977).

Zagzebski, L.: "What if the impossible had been actual?" In *Christian Theism and the Problems of Philosophy*, ed. M. Beaty (Notre Dame: University of Notre Dame Press, 1990).

——: *The Dilemma of Freedom and Foreknowledge* (New York: Oxford University Press, 1991).

38

Divine action

THOMAS F. TRACY

It has often been noted that the God of the theistic traditions in the West is pre-eminently a God who acts. The sacred texts and liturgical practices of these religions vividly depict God as an agent whose purposes are enacted in a drama of universal scope, stretching from the creation to the consummation of all things. There are, to be sure, other ways of representing God in these texts and traditions: for example, as impersonal or supra-personal ground of being. The theme of divine action, however, is woven so deeply into the fabric of these faiths that any adequate account of theistic beliefs must take it into account.

Varieties of divine action

Divine action in these traditions takes a number of different forms. First and foremost, there is God's action of creating and sustaining the world, i.e. the totality of non-divine things (see Article 39, CREATION AND CONSERVATION). This creative action has been understood in more than one way, but we can identify three elements in the classical theistic view. First, most theists have held that there would be no world, not even an unformed and chaotic one, apart from God's creative action; God creates *ex nihilo* (out of nothing). Second, this act of creation is not a single event completed at some point in the past. God does not impart to creatures a power of existence which they then possess on their own. Rather, creatures depend absolutely upon God for their existence at every moment, so that if God should cease to sustain (or "conserve") them, they would cease to be. Understood in this way, creation is the ongoing, continuous action by which God brings about the very existence of the world. Third, theists have usually said that this divine creative activity is not a necessity of the divine nature, but rather expresses God's free decision. God could exist without a world of finite beings but chooses, for the creatures' sake, to bring the world into being. This stands in contrast, for example, to a Neoplatonic conception of creation as a necessary emanation of the self-sufficient but inherently diffusive divine perfection. The finite world, on a Neoplatonic account, is generated by an outflowing of the divine being that does not involve will or purpose. Over against this, most theists have held that God, in an act of free generosity, intentionally and voluntarily causes the world to be.

    Contemporary process, or neoclassical, theologians have offered a significantly different account of God's creative action (see Article 16, PROCESS THEOLOGY). The Whiteheadian metaphysical scheme requires that every existing individual, including God, must be a creative integration of relations to other individuals. On this view, God and the world are mutually dependent and co-eternal, and God's distinctiveness as a creative agent lies in the universal scope of God's relatedness to others and the unique role God plays in contributing an "initial aim" to the development of each individual. The existence of the world cannot be attributed to God's action, on this account, but God acts pervasively in the world's creative becoming.

The theistic traditions characteristically have affirmed that in addition to creating and sustaining all finite things, God governs the processes of nature and the dramas of human history, acting to assure that the divine purposes for creation will be fulfilled. Having called the world into being, God does not then become a detached observer, but remains intimately involved in history. Indeed, it is a corollary of the doctrine of creation *ex nihilo* that nothing in the course of events occurs without God's will or permission.

A distinction is sometimes made between general and particular providence. In general providence God establishes the fundamental principles and basic dynamics by which the history of the created world will unfold: e.g. the causal structures and boundary conditions of the natural order, the possibilities and limitations of human nature, and the powers of action bestowed on creatures of all kinds. God has so arranged the world that various natural goods can be realized (for example, that human beings thrive on the earth), and these goods may be understood to be brought about by God's provident design.

Beyond establishing and superintending the overall course of history, God acts at particular times and places to achieve specific ends; this is particular providence. The narratives of the Hebrew Bible, for example, portray God as engaging human beings through a series of revelatory and redemptive actions in history. God calls Abraham and his descendants into a covenant relation; God rescues the Hebrew people from slavery in Egypt and gives the law at Sinai; God raises up kings and prophets; God acts in myriad ways to judge, sustain, and redeem this people through all the vicissitudes of their history. Christianity and Islam incorporate much of this history of divine action, and because each tradition develops these stories in a different way, they generate distinctive understandings of God's purposes and identity. The canonical narratives of each theistic tradition shape general views of what God is doing in history, and these views generate a wide range of specific claims about divine action. Theists typically affirm that the God depicted in their sacred texts acts in the familiar world around them, in their communities of worship, and in their own lives. The life of faith can be understood as an ongoing relationship of interaction with God in which, for example, God calls, inspires, strengthens, chastens, forgives, saves, sanctifies, and may respond to human intercessions and petitions.

The distinction between general and particular divine providence has often been collapsed in modern theology (e.g. by Schleiermacher 1963 [1830]), so that particular providence is understood exclusively as the outworking of general providence in specific cases. For example, an event in the natural world (say, a strong east wind as the fleeing Jews approach the sea of reeds) may be the result of the ordinary operations of natural law and yet also be understood to express God's particular purposes for the community whose destiny is especially affected by that event. Indeed, the entire history of the world, to the extent that it flows from causal laws and initial conditions established by God, can be regarded as an extended act of God mediated through natural processes. On this account, events can be identified as "special divine acts" in so far as they play a distinctive role in revealing and/or advancing divine purposes that were initially written into the program of history. Such a view denies, however, that God acts within historical processes to turn events in a new direction, bringing about developments that would not have occurred but for this particular divine initiative. The elimination of special divine action, in this strong sense, has theologically significant consequences (for example, in Christology and soteriology), and so is a matter of debate in contemporary theology.

These rich patterns of talk about divine action raise a number of compelling philosophical and theological questions. There are, in the first place, puzzles about the coherence of the concept of God as an agent of intentional actions. Are some of the properties that theists have traditionally ascribed to God incompatible with the claim that God acts? Second, questions arise about the relation of God's actions to the operations of created causes in the natural order. This question has especially dominated modern considerations of particular divine action, given the rise of the natural sciences and the "disenchantment" of nature as a scene of supernatural activity.

God as agent of intentional actions

A number of the properties that many (but not all) theists have ascribed to God may be thought to be inconsistent with the claim that God is an agent of intentional actions. Consider, for example, the claims that (a) God is incorporeal and is not located in space, and (b) God is not in time but exists in timeless eternity. Can a being that is in neither space nor time coherently be said to act?

Turning first to the claim of divine incorporeality, it is of course true that the agents with whom we are most familiar are bodily agents whose powers of action are rooted in the capacities of the organism that bears their life and who affect the world around them through physical interactions. This alone, however, does not warrant the conclusion that embodiment is a necessary condition of agency generally, rather than a contingent matter of fact about agents of our type. Clearly, the concepts "agent" and "action" are logically linked; an intentional agent must be able to bring about at least some states of affairs "on purpose" (that is, roughly, because the agent believes that doing so will satisfy the action description which expresses the agent's aim). But is talk of intentional action inseparably linked to talk of bodily behavior? Even in our own case we are able to act without undertaking any intentional bodily motion, e.g. in various mental acts. I intend a movement of my body in intentionally raising my arm, but I do not intend any bodily event in working out a bit of mental arithmetic, even though this no doubt involves electrochemical processes in the brain. Our mental activities may be

301

dependent upon brain events, but the description of such an activity (say, counting backward from 100) does not, by itself, entail any statements about brain events. Although there are many action descriptions (such as "waving to a friend") that do refer to some form of bodily behavior, this is not a feature of every action type. Even actions that intend changes in the physical world need not specify that these changes are brought about by the motions of an agent's body. We may not be able to explain *how* an incorporeal agent brings about physical effects, but talk of such agency poses no readily discernible problem of internal consistency (see Article 34, INCORPOREALITY; and Article 36, OMNIPRESENCE).

What of the claim that God exists in timeless eternity? Can a timeless being be said to act and, in particular, to act in history? Actions would appear to take time and to take place in time; that is, they are temporally extended and temporally located. If God brings about an event that occurs within a temporal series and occupies a portion of that series (one of God's "mighty acts in history," for example), then must the divine agent also be located in time? Note, in particular, that if some of God's actions are responses to human actions, then it would seem that (1) they must be undertaken by God after the human actions to which they respond, and (2) God undergoes a temporal transition from not-acting to acting.

Considerations like these have led some theists to grant that God exists in time. To say that God is eternal is then to say that God exists at all times without beginning or end. Against this, defenders of divine atemporality have insisted that God's creative act must include the creation of time itself, whether time is understood as a function of the relations between finite things or as an entity (space-time) in which other finite things are located. God can create time, however, only if God exists outside time. There are, of course, profound limits on our ability to imagine and express the notion of timeless existence, and most theorists who defend the coherence of this concept appeal to analogies drawn from spatial relations in which an observer takes in an extended series at a single moment (for example, observation from high ground of a line of travelers on a road; simultaneous viewing of a length of unwound motion picture film). Analogies of this sort suggest that we think of the whole temporal order as immediately present to God, so that God is simultaneous with every event in time even though these events are not all simultaneous with each other. God will have access, then, to the entire course of history all at once, and can act at every point in the time series simultaneously from the eternal now. Considered from the divine agent's side, none of God's acts is before or after any of the others; all are initiated at once outside time. Each of their effects, however, occurs at its appropriate moment in history.

In this account of timeless divine action, a distinction is at work between God's agency (God's decree) and the effect brought about by that agency (the event decreed). The events that God decrees unfold in time as a history of divine action. But all of God's acts, from creation to redemption and consummation, are decreed in the timeless unity of the eternal now. These divine acts stand in relations of logical and explanatory priority both with one another and with events in history. If, for example, God acts in response to a free human action, the human action is prior (in the order of explanation) to the divine response. But there will be no temporal succession in God's life; the whole of history and all of God's actions are contained within the unitary present of eternity. It hardly needs to be said that this concept of atemporal divine agency is a rich source of philosophical puzzles, and it is the subject of ongoing and vigorous debate (see Article 32, ETERNITY; and Article 37, FOREKNOWLEDGE AND HUMAN FREEDOM).

Divine action and created causes

A second set of questions about divine action has to do with the relation of God's activity to the operations of created causes and to the order of nature. It is often said that God acts in and through the processes of nature and history. How might this be understood? What is the relation between traditional theistic affirmations of particular divine action in the world, on the one hand, and scientific descriptions of the world as an intelligible law-governed structure, on the other?

In approaching these questions, it is useful to make a distinction between actions that are direct, or basic, and those that are indirect, or mediated. Agents often perform one action (opening a window) by doing another (moving the body in the required ways). An indirect action is brought about by means of action under another description, and any action of this sort must, on pain of infinite regress, originate in an action that the agent undertakes without having to perform any prior intentional action as the means to it. This will be the agent's basic action.

Theists typically have held that God acts both directly and indirectly, choosing in creation to establish and then to act through an order of created causes. God's creative act of calling the world into being is a direct, or basic, action; the divine agent decrees that the world shall be, and it is. So, too, the action of sustaining the world in existence will be direct; if God were no longer to conserve the existence of finite things, they would instantaneously cease to be. Not all of God's actions need be direct, however. God may choose to bestow various causal powers upon created things, and to bring about effects by means of these "secondary" causes. Rather than producing each finite event directly (e.g. causing water in a kettle to boil spontaneously), God endows created things with causal efficacy of their own, instituting a natural order in which the water is heated by means of a flame. God alone directly and at every moment causes finite things *to be* (that is, to be *ex nihilo*, rather than merely to undergo change). But God empowers creatures to cause *changes* in other existing things, including the changes that we ordinarily call "coming into (or passing out of) existence," as in birth and death. These effects are brought about both by God and by the finite cause, though on different levels (for example, see Aquinas, *Summa Theologiae*, Ia.105.5). God is the primary cause, whose creative action establishes and sustains the network of secondary causes through which the history of the world unfolds. Creatures, in exercising the causal powers God has given them, are the instruments of God's indirect action.

It might be held that this account does not fully convey the depth of creatures' dependence upon God in their operation as secondary causes. According to medieval scholastic theologians, it is not enough that God creates and sustains finite entities and structures their causal powers. Beyond this, God must also act directly with creatures if they are to exercise those powers. This divine concurrence, or cooperation, is a necessary but not sufficient condition for the finite cause to produce its effect. God acts as a general cause, empowering all creatures in their causal operations. Since the divine concurrence is universal and uniform, the difference in the effect from case to case reflects the specific nature of the creaturely cause. Without this direct divine cooperation, it was claimed, creatures will simply fail to produce effects at all. The idea of divine concurrence has received relatively little attention in modern discussions of divine action, in part because it is unclear what concurrence amounts to and why it is needed over and above the affirmation that God creates and sustains a world in which creatures possess and exercise causal powers.

These basic affirmations about God's direct and indirect agency make possible an account of particular, or special, divine action in the world. Note, in the first place, that if the causal history of the world is strictly deterministic, then every event within it can be regarded as an indirect act of God mediated through the operation of secondary causes. God can realize particular divine purposes simply by designing the causal laws and initial conditions of the natural order so as to guarantee that the intended result will be achieved. If one holds that all of God's actions in the world take this form, then the result (as we noted above) is to absorb particular providence entirely into God's general providence in creation and conservation.

Traditionally, however, theists have affirmed that God also acts directly within the world to serve particular purposes not built into history at the beginning. In a deterministic universe, such actions must constitute miraculous departures from the ordinary course of nature (see Article 46, MIRACLES); this will be the case whether these divine interventions are overtly spectacular "mighty acts" or exquisitely subtle contributions to the mental or spiritual lives of human agents. For this reason, a succession of modern theologians have held that we can no longer affirm direct and particular divine action in history. They have been led to this view, at least in part, by their belief that universal causal determinism either has been established by the natural sciences or is presupposed by scientific methods of inquiry. There are good reasons, however, to deny both these claims about the sciences; indeed, there currently are compelling scientific grounds (for example, in the dominant interpretation of quantum mechanics) for thinking that universal determinism is false.

In a non-deterministic universe, the simple picture of God's indirect action through the causal structures of nature is complicated by the fact that at least some of these causal chains will be incomplete. Events will lack causally sufficient antecedent conditions in the natural order when there is an element of indeterministic chance in their history and/or when they result from human actions that are free in the strong (i.e. "libertarian") sense. God could choose to determine events of either sort; they would then be chance or (more controversially) free only in their relation to other finite events. When God does not do this, however, these undetermined events may initiate causal chains in the world which cannot simply be attributed to God as (indirect) divine acts, though God directly gives them their being and permits them to play this role in history.

Note that the integration of chance into the order of nature provides a structure within which God's particular providential actions need not involve any miraculous suspension of natural law. In selectively determining events that occur by chance on the finite level, God does not displace natural causes that would otherwise have determined that event, and God's activity could be entirely compatible with whatever the sciences may tell us about the distribution of such events in regular probabilistic patterns. In this way, the world God has made could display both a reliable causal structure and an inherent openness to novelty, allowing for a seamless integration of natural law and ongoing direct involvement by God in shaping the course of events.

Theists, then, may affirm both that God acts universally in the creation and conservation of all things and that God acts in particular events in history. The latter may be understood in several ways: (1) as indirect action through secondary causal chains that extend from God's direct actions; (2) as direct action that brings about events outside the regularities of nature; and (3) as direct action that determines natural indeterminacies within the regular structures of nature. In any or all of these ways, God can affect the course of history and interact with human beings to achieve particular divine purposes.

See also Article 72, PROVIDENCE AND PREDESTINATION.

Bibliography

Aquinas, Thomas: *Summa Theologiae*, Ia, QQ. 103–19, ed. T. McDermott (London: Blackfriars, 1964).

——: *Summa contra Gentiles*, III, 64–77, tr. V. J. Bourke (Notre Dame: University of Notre Dame Press, 1975).

Calvin, J.: *Institutes of the Christian Religion* (1559), book 1, 16–17; ed. J. T. McNeill (Philadelphia: Westminster Press, 1960).

Morris, T. V. (ed.): *Divine and Human Action* (Ithaca: Cornell University Press, 1988).

Russell, J. R., Murphy, N., and Peacocke, A. R. (eds): *Chaos and Complexity: Scientific Perspectives on Divine Action* (Rome: Vatican Observatory, 1995).

Schleiermacher, F.: *The Christian Faith* (1830); ed. H. R. Macintosh and J. S. Stewart (New York: Harper & Row, 1963).

Thomas, O. C. (ed.): *God's Activity in the World* (Chico, CA: Scholars Press, 1983).

Tracy, T. F. (ed.): *The God Who Acts* (University Park: Pennsylvania State University Press, 1994).

39

Creation and conservation

HUGH J. McCANN

Popular beliefs about creation typically accord God a more active role in the foundation of the universe than in its preservation. It is generally allowed that God may annihilate the world, but its continued existence is not viewed as owing directly to His creative activity. The assumption is rather that once in place, the universe can continue to exist on its own, and that divine involvement is required only for special acts of providence and mercy. This is not, however, the view of traditional Western theology. There, the typical account has it that God is as much responsible for the continued existence of the world as for its inception, and that His activity in both creating and sustaining the universe is essentially the same. Associated with this position is the idea that God's sovereignty over the world is complete: that He is the "first cause" of all that is and occurs, and that His providence guides directly every detail of the entire history of the universe. This sort of view has a number of controversial implications, not all of which can be discussed here. It is possible, however, to set forth the main considerations that motivate it, and address some of the more obvious difficulties.

Initial reservations

It is as well to begin by looking at the difficulties. Some objections to divine conservation are theologically motivated. The narrative of creation in the Hebrew Bible seems clearly to portray God as bringing forth new things; it does not postulate any activity of sustenance, but rather states that after the initial production of things "He rested" (Genesis 2:2). Likewise, God is not, at least usually, portrayed as actively involved in the daily maintenance of creation. That He observes all, that He knows the fall of every sparrow, is certain; but His active engagement is reserved for special occasions. The titanic events of the exodus and of the conquest of Canaan, the miraculous cures that occur throughout Scripture, and the redemptive acts of the New Testament are all portrayed as divine *interventions* in the normal course of events. To think of God as equally involved in all that occurs in the world would seem, therefore, to blur the distinction between miracles and ordinary events. Furthermore, it places God uncomfortably close to the untoward occurrences of the world, particularly moral wrongdoing. If His creative activity is directly responsible for all that takes place, human freedom appears to be threatened, and with it the free will defense against THE PROBLEM OF EVIL (see Article 50).

Equally problematic considerations arise on the cosmological front. If the conservation of the world is of a piece with its creation, we may be headed for a "continuous creation" theory of the sort held by Jonathan Edwards, wherein the world is held to pass away and be recreated at each moment of its existence. There are considerable conceptual difficulties here, and in any case such a view seems empirically false. What is more, the conservation doctrine appears to conflict with conservation principles in science. If mass/energy is preserved in all physical processes and interactions, what need is there for God to preserve it? Finally, making God the first cause of all that occurs threatens the efficacy of secondary causes in nature. If He is the producer of everything, what is left for them to produce?

Coming to be and being

One can begin to address these concerns by considering what the result of God's creative activity must be. It is natural to think of coming to be as a process, in which the material of which a thing is made undergoes transformation until it becomes the thing produced. That is the way it is when things are produced in nature, and when we do things like build houses or sculpt statues. But creation cannot be understood in this way. It occurs *ex nihilo* (from nothing): it involves no pre-existing "matter," no transformation of any underlying stuff of which the universe is made. Therefore, even if the world had a temporal beginning, what is brought about in creation is not any process wherein it came to be, and its appearance was not a change in which any thing changed. Quite the opposite: there is nothing short of the *being* of things that can constitute the product of creation. Even in the beginning, if there was one, there was nothing else for God to bring about.

Once this is realized, the problem with Edwards's sort of theory emerges. The world is not in any process of continually passing away and being re-created: there can be no process of the world's passing away, just as there can be none of its coming to be. Rather, any time at which the world does not fully exist must be a time at which it does not exist at all. So we can think of the world as being continually brought into existence, in the strict sense, only by postulating its repeated complete demise – a view which, amid other difficulties, seems quite false. "Continuous creation" should not, then, be interpreted to mean that the world is continually passing away and coming to be. Rather, it is simply a way of making the point that as creator, God is directly responsible for the entire existence of the universe. And on this score, the continuous creation view turns out to be very much on the right track.

Here, too, the fact that the coming to be of the universe is not a process is important. If it were a process, we would have reason for thinking that as creator, God is more directly involved in the first appearance of things than in their continuance. For the coming to be of the universe would then be a phenomenon different in kind from its being, and so might call for more direct or active engagement on God's part. But that is precisely what is false. Even at a supposed first moment of the world's existence, God is simply responsible for its being. There is no procedure to be gone through, no transitional phases that need to elapse, only the existence of things which stands as the result of creation. But if this is so, then to make God responsible for the sustenance as well as the emergence of the world is not to impute to Him a different activity from that in which He is supposed to have engaged "in the beginning." On the contrary: His creating and conserving the world are, from the point of view of the act itself, indistinguishable, a seamless endeavor consistent with the divine SIMPLICITY (see Article 31), and responsible for every instant of the world's existence. Indeed, it is hard to see how we could require less. If, from the perspective of creation, a first moment of the world's history is the same as any other, how can God's activity as creator not be as vital to getting the world beyond the present instant as to its being here at all?

Self-sustenance

Perhaps, however, there is some capacity of things to sustain themselves in existence, or an inertia-like tendency to remain in being once they appear. The endurance of the world is, after all, a common enough fact of experience, whereas we detect no independent activity of God to keep it there. Furthermore, there are scientific laws that call for the conservation of mass and energy, and surely in this regard science does not take itself to be dealing with supernatural phenomena. So we seem to have good reason for expecting the persistence of the world to have a natural explanation, not a divine one.

However, once we consider what the explanation might be, we are in trouble. Scientific laws do not explain things by being "out there" dictating that certain events must happen. They explain by describing processes and dispositions which belong to the nature of things, and which are ontologically prior to the laws that describe them. But when it comes to the sheer persistence of the world, this is an empty idea. There could not, first of all, be any active process by which things are somehow able to sustain their own existence, propelling themselves from the present into the future. Such a claim would be utterly without empirical backing. We know of no such process, nor is it possible even to imagine what it would be like. We can successfully envision processes that account for the descriptive features of the world – processes that underlie chemical reactions, for example, or which account for the occurrence of economic recessions. But what natural process could account simply for the continued existence of things? None, it would seem, for the sheer existence of things cannot be a manifestation of their behavior. Their behavior, and their interaction with other entities, can account for the ways in which the items that make up the world manifest themselves, but it cannot account for the sheer fact that they are there, or continue to be there.

There are, in addition, metaphysical difficulties attending the idea that there is a process of self-sustenance to be found in the world. Presumably, any entity manifesting such a process would do so in virtue of its internal organization. That is, there would have to be some structure of the entity – some machinery, as it were – through which the operation of self-sustenance is carried out. Otherwise, it would be hard to see how it could count as a process at all. But even if, *per impossibile*, we were able to imagine such structures, we would then have to ask how they are sustained in existence. If they are sustained by God, we will have gotten nowhere; if, on the other hand, a further substructure is needed for their sustenance, we are headed for an infinite regress. Furthermore, it is difficult to see how any such process could succeed. In order to do so, the operation of the process at a time t would have to have as its effect the existence of the entity at some later time t^*. Otherwise, the endurance of whatever entity is at issue will go unaccounted for. But since time is a continuum, there is no temporal instant immediately adjacent to t. There must, therefore, be an interval between t and t^*. This in turn requires that our supposed process act at a temporal distance: that is, any instance of its operation must have direct effects at times distant from the operation. And this surely is impossible.

It does not appear, then, that the created world could have an active capacity to sustain itself. Would another conception have more success? Perhaps we should view the supposed ability of things to sustain themselves as a mere disposition rather than an active power – a simple capacity to continue in existence, rather like the tendency in classical physics for an object to continue at rest or in motion unless acted upon. But while this conception may look more promising, in the end it fares no better. In themselves, dispositions cannot explain anything. The solubility of salt no more explains its dissolving in water than the dormitive virtue of morphine explains its putting people to sleep. Rather, when dispositions are associated with good explanations it is because they are grounded in structural elements of the situations in which they are found, elements which *act* in appropriate circumstances to produce a characteristic result. Thus salt is water-soluble because it and water are so structured atomically that when they are combined there occurs a *process* in which the salt is dissolved. We cannot, however, understand the alleged disposition for self-sustenance in this way, for this would not be a purely dispositional account. Rather, it would reduce self-sustenance to the sort of active power considered above, and we have already seen that this approach must fail.

What would a purely dispositional account look like? We would have to postulate a strictly metaphysical disposition, one that has no supervenience base and is manifested in no process or activity, but which we nevertheless claim explains the endurance of the created world. In fact, however, there is no difference, scientific or philosophical, between this kind of disposition and no disposition at all. Remember that the endeavor here is to explain the continued existence of things. For that, the alleged disposition has to come to more than the fact that things do continue – a fact that would hold whether the explanation were divine or natural. And a purely metaphysical disposition comes to no more. Without a supervenience base, it can have no ontological foundation in things, and with no characteristic activity its sole manifestation must lie precisely in the world's continued existence. Clearly, there is no reason to suppose that such a disposition amounts to anything whatever that is real. Even if it did, we would have to ask what in turn, other than God's creative activity, enables it to persist. Still less is there reason to suppose that such a disposition could explain anything. In this respect the comparison with inertial movement turns out to be quite apt, since the latter was notoriously left unexplained in classical physics. And just as it is no explanation of inertial movement to say things tend to move that way, so it is no explanation of the continuance of the world to say it tends to continue. What is needed is an account of this phenomenon based on the intrinsic nature of things. A purely metaphysical disposition amounts to a refusal to provide that, and so leaves the "self-" in self-sustenance with no meaning. We can only conclude, therefore, that the continued existence of the world can have no explanation based on features intrinsic to it. That the world persists must be explained in the same way as the fact that it exists at all: through the creative activity of God.

Conservation principles and secondary causes

What are we to say, then, about conservation principles in science? These appear to call for the preservation of mass/energy – to make it, in fact, a matter of natural law. Are they simply mistaken? Or are we brought to the unlikely conclusion that they turn out to concern a supernatural process of divine conservation? The answer is neither. Such principles would indeed be mistaken if taken to postulate a natural power of self-conservation in things, but that is a mistaken interpretation. The law of conservation for mass/energy does not, as usually formulated, call for the preservation of anything *tout court*. There are two qualifications. First, mass/energy is held to be preserved in closed systems, which are *defined* as systems in which mass/energy is neither gained nor lost. This alone shows that the principle at issue is not aimed at accounting for the persistence of things. If it were, this proviso would reduce it to the vacuous claim that the amount of mass/energy in the world remains the same unless it doesn't.

What then is the aim of the principle? The answer is to be seen in the second qualification usually found in formulations of the conservation principle, which is that the amount of mass/energy is preserved *in all physical interactions*. What this implies is that the conservation law is concerned not with the persistence of the world, but rather with the transformations it undergoes. And what it holds, in effect, is that there is no physical process for either the creation or the destruction of mass/energy. But that is precisely what was argued above. The very idea of such a process is impossible, for there is nothing it could consist in. Far from being in disagreement, therefore, the claim that divine conservation is responsible for the persistence of the world dovetails completely with the law of conservation for mass/energy.

There is equal reason for optimism on the subject of secondary causation. Strong doctrines of divine conservation are sometimes associated with a simplistic occasionalism, in which it is concluded that since God is the cause of all, the things He creates must have no real nature or powers. However, this too is mistaken. It is true that God is responsible for the existence of everything, and that this has to include the characteristics of things as well as the things themselves. Otherwise we are left with an untenable doctrine of bare particulars, in which God is responsible only for the existence of substances, any one of which might have any nature you please, or for that matter none at all. But to make God responsible for the existence of everything is hardly to say that there is no such thing as chemical bonding, or electromagnetic waves, or the forceful interactions of physics. Laws that describe the nature and behaviour of created things have all the significance they ever did, even in a world whose entire being is owing to God.

What makes it seem otherwise is a misunderstanding, wherein scientific laws are associated with views on which the past is "causally" responsible for the existence of the future. As David Hume clearly saw, however, there is no such relationship. Nothing in our experience answers to it. And although space does not permit a full treatment of the issue, neither do scientific laws call for some sort of causal glue that binds the universe together over time. Scientific laws are synchronic, not diachronic: they call for actions and reactions that are simultaneous rather than sequential, and measure relationships between variables that coexist rather than succeed one another. It is true that if we *assume* the world will persist, such laws enable us to predict and control the future. But there is nothing in that which gainsays the idea of divine conservation. Indeed, the idea that God, not nature, is responsible for the existence of things may actually help to avoid some embarrassments over event causality.

Divine intervention

What, finally, are we to say about scriptural accounts which portray God as more active at some points in history than at others – as intervening to perform miraculous and/or redemptive acts in human history? There are at least two ways of understanding divine intervention that the above account of creation leaves untouched. First, certain manifestations of divine providence may be of special significance, both in making God's loving concern especially apparent to us, and in that had they not occurred, human history would have been vastly different (see Article 72, PROVIDENCE AND PREDESTINATION). The rise of Israel in the Hebrew Bible, and the introduction of Christian salvation in the New Testament, can certainly be viewed in this light. It is impossible to imagine what the world would be like today without them, and that remains true even if in fact God's creative activity is equally responsible for everything that has occurred. Second, even though making God the first cause of all does not undermine a correct understanding of secondary causation, there is no reason why every event He produces must be so related to others that no departures from the natural order are possible. There can still occur events that involve such departures, if that is what the concept of a miracle requires (see Article 46, MIRACLES). So the parting of the Red Sea, or the transforming of water into wine at Cana, can still count as divine interventions in the strong sense that the regular course of events is interrupted.

But what is not possible is to think of divine intervention as a phenomenon in which God bestirs Himself from a period of non-engagement with the course of events in our world. If the above argument is correct, the universe could not survive for an instant were God to cease His activity as creator. And there is a lot more that is wrong with viewing God as mostly withdrawn from the world's affairs. Merely occasional engagement is not possible for a God who is eternal and

unchanging, as the tradition took Him to be (see Article 32, ETERNITY; and Article 40, IMMUTABILITY AND IMPASSIBILITY). Nor is the disinterest this view imputes to God compatible with a providence grounded in complete love, which should rather require His complete and intimate involvement with all that takes place. Finally, a great deal of Scripture speaks of God as fully involved in the course of history. Far from being remote and disinterested, He is held to be the foundation for the being of all things (Romans 11:36), to uphold all things through His power (Hebrews 1:3), and even to have wrought all our works in us (Isaiah 26:12). It is not possible to deal here with the problems concerning freedom and evil implicit in these claims. Whatever their solution may be, it is clear that much of Scripture finds no distance at all between the ongoing career of the world or of anything in it and the creative will of God. The metaphysics of the world's persistence supports such a view.

Bibliography

Aquinas, Thomas: *Summa contra Gentiles*, book III, chs 64–70; *Basic Writings of Saint Thomas Aquinas*, vol. 2, ed. A. C. Pegis (New York: Random House, 1945).

Edwards J.: *The Great Christian Doctrine of Original Sin Defended* (1758); *Works*, vol. 3, ed. C. A. Holbrook (New Haven: Yale University Press, 1970).

Farley, B. W.: *The Providence of God* (Grand Rapids: Baker Book House, 1988).

Freddoso, A. J.: "God's general concurrence with secondary causes: Why conservation is not enough," *Philosophical Perspectives*, 5, ed. J. E. Tomberlin (Atascadero, CA: Ridgeview Publishing, 1991), pp. 553–85.

Kvanvig, J. L., and McCann, H. J.: "Divine conservation and the persistence of the world." In *Divine and Human Action*, ed. T. V. Morris (Ithaca: Cornell University Press, 1988), pp. 13–49.

Malebranche, N.: *Entretiens sur la métaphysique* (1688); tr. W. Doney, *Dialogues on Metaphysics* (New York: Abaris Books, 1980).

Quinn, P. L.: "Divine conservation, continuous creation, and human action." In *The Existence and Nature of God*, ed. A. J. Freddoso (Notre Dame: University of Notre Dame Press, 1983), pp. 55–80.

40

Immutability and impassibility

RICHARD E. CREEL

Immutability and impassibility have been attributed to God by thinkers including Aristotle, Philo, Boethius, Augustine, Maimonides, Anselm, Aquinas, and, in the twentieth century, Eleonore Stump and Norman Kretzmann. There was not much discussion of these attributes between the medieval period and the nineteenth century because by the end of the Middle Ages they were standard conclusions of Judeo-Christian philosophical theology. None the less, these attributions have always had their critics, and there has been growing criticism from twentieth century thinkers such as A. N. Whitehead, Charles Hartshorne, and Richard Swinburne.

This article explores the concepts of immutability and impassibility, sets forth arguments for and against attributing these properties to God, and discusses how these properties relate to one another and to some of the other attributes widely thought to apply to God. "God" shall be used herein to mean an absolutely perfect being.

Immutability

That which is immutable is that which cannot change. To say that God is immutable is to say that God cannot change. It would not be enough to say that God *does* not change. That would leave unanswered, "But *could* God change?" The point of the doctrine of divine immutability is that it is logically impossible for God to change.

Three of the more frequently deployed arguments for attributing immutability to God are as follows. First, there is the argument from God's *absolute perfection* (see Article 30, GOODNESS). Anything that is absolutely perfect cannot change by way of getting better, since that which is perfect cannot be improved upon; nor can it change by way of getting worse, since that which is absolutely perfect cannot deteriorate. But if that which is absolutely perfect cannot get better or worse, then it must stay the same and cannot change. Therefore, since God is absolutely perfect, God cannot change.

Second, there is the argument from God's *absolute simplicity* (see Article 31, SIMPLICITY). Change can occur only in a thing that has parts. But that which is absolutely simple has no parts; therefore it cannot change. Further, that which is composite, i.e. made up of parts, depends on its parts for its nature and existence, and it depends on something to hold its parts together. But that which is

313

absolutely perfect cannot depend on anything for its nature, existence, or unity. God is absolutely perfect. Therefore God must be absolutely simple. Therefore God cannot change.

Third, there is the argument from God's *eternality* (see Article 32, ETERNITY). In order for change to take place, something which does not possess a certain property must subsequently come to possess it. Hence, change can take place only in things that exist in time. But according to the classical tradition of Boethius, God is eternal in the sense that he must possess all of his life all at once, i.e. without succession. This absolutely inclusive simultaneity of the divine life is incompatible with existing in time. Therefore God must be immutable.

Two arguments for divine mutability are as follows. First, consider this argument from *the nature of agency* (see Article 38, DIVINE ACTION). Surely an absolutely perfect being (hereafter APB) will have the power of agency, i.e. be able intentionally to cause things to happen. But for an agent intentionally to cause something to happen which was not happening requires that he was not willing it and then began to will it – but to change from not willing something to willing it is to change. Therefore, in order to have this power of agency, an individual must be able to change. God, as the APB, must have this power of agency. Therefore God must be able to change. Therefore God must be mutable.

Second, consider *perfection in knowledge* (see Article 29, OMNISCIENCE). In order to be perfect in knowledge, God must know things as they are. Some things are changing; therefore God must be aware of things as changing. But awareness of change in an object requires change in the subject that is aware; the subject must change from being aware that x is not happening to being aware that x is happening, or vice versa. This argument applies to God even if God knows eternally all that will ever happen, for he must also know what is happening now, and if what is happening now is changing, then the content of God's awareness must change as what is actual changes. In brief: the real world is changing; perfect knowledge of a changing world requires change in the knower; God must know the world perfectly; therefore God must be mutable.

Impassibility

Philosophers have divided sharply over whether God is immutable, but they generally agree on what they mean by immutability. Regarding impassibility, however, they are divided over what to mean by it, as well as whether to attribute it to God. The definition which I think is most basic and useful says that impassibility is the property of being insusceptible to causation. To say that God is impassible is to say that God cannot be affected by anything, i.e. cannot be passive in relation to anything. Hence, it is not sufficient to say merely that God has not been or never will be affected by anything. Impassibility means it is logically impossible for God to be affected by anything.

Three arguments for divine impassibility go as follows. First, consider *divine infinitude*. To be passible requires a limitation by virtue of which a thing can be affected by something else, as when pressure from a finger changes the shape of a balloon or when a breeze changes the location of a balloon. But God is absolutely perfect. Therefore God is infinite and has no limitation by virtue of which he can be affected by a finger, a breeze, or anything else. Hence God is impassible.

Second, God is *pure act*. God exists causally prior to everything else; everything else depends on God's initiative for its existence, so God must be the pure act of being, and that which is pure act cannot be passive in any way. Hence, as the only being that exists by virtue of its own essence and as the creator of all else that exists, it is impossible that God could have been or could be moved by anything to exist, act, be, or change in any way. Necessarily, God's act precedes all other acts. Hence God is impassible.

Third, an APB must by its very nature be *perfectly blissful*. Being unhappy, sad, miserable, melancholy, regretful, etc., in any way or to any extent would be incompatible with absolute perfection. Hence, the inner quality of God's life should be thought of as impassible, i.e. beyond the influence of this world.

Three arguments for divine passibility are the following. First, an APB must be *perfect in love*. Necessarily, a perfect lover is sympathetic to the beloved. Any being which is insensitive or indifferent to the joys and sufferings of others is unloving and therefore unworthy of the title "God." Consequently, God must be affected by the joys and sorrows of his creatures, which is to say that God must be emotionally passible in relation to his creatures.

Second, an APB must be able to enter into the give and take of *personal relations*. In order to communicate with persons, God must be sensitive to input from them and take such input into account in decisions about and responses to them. Hence God must be passible in order to be able to interact with persons.

Third, in order to be *omniscient*, God must be passible, i.e. God's knowledge of the world must be caused by the world. If it were not, God would be ignorant of the world, since if God did not know the world directly, no one and nothing could mediate knowledge of the world to him.

It might be argued that God knows the world by way of knowing his will, which creates the world, and not by way of direct awareness of the world, but that is unsatisfactory for at least three reasons. First, such knowledge of the world would be indirect (God would know the world by knowing his will). Such indirect knowledge would be inferior to direct knowledge and would therefore be unworthy of God. Second, indirect knowledge of the world would smack of Manicheanism, suggesting that God would not soil himself by direct noetic contact with the world. Third, God so conceived would be religiously inadequate. God would not know *me*; he would know only his will that I exist. Therefore I could not presume to relate to God personally.

Toward a unified position

Whether God is immutable or mutable, impassible or passible must be deduced from his nature as an APB. Prior to deduction we must stay open to all the possibilities, namely that God is both immutable and impassible, or neither, or one but not the other. Further, we must stay open to the possibility that we can distinguish various aspects in God, and that God is both immutable and impassible in one of those aspects, neither in another aspect, and one in a third aspect but not the other in that same aspect. Finally, it may be the case not only that immutability and impassibility apply differently to different aspects of God, but also that there are different facets of these different aspects and that immutability and impassibility apply differently to different facets of the same aspect. Let's look at some specifics.

In Creel (1986) I argued that to discuss the issues of divine immutability and impassibility satisfactorily, we need to distinguish the following aspects of God: his nature, knowledge, will, and feeling. It seems universally agreed that the *nature* of an APB must be impassible and immutable, i.e. the nature of God cannot change and is not determined in any respect by anything external to God. But is God immutable and impassible in *knowledge?*

If God is eternal in Boethius' sense, then God must be immutable in knowledge. We have, however, seen reasons to think that perfection in knowledge is incompatible with immutability. Hence, we should hold that God is mutable in that facet of his knowledge that pertains to actualities. But in addition to actualities, there are necessary truths and basic possibilities, both of which are immutable. Hence, these facets of God's knowledge must be immutable, since God must always know all basic possibilities and atemporal truths, and therefore cannot change by virtue of forgetting one or learning a new one.

However, just as God's knowledge of actualities must change as actualities do, so God's knowledge of temporal possibilities must change as they come into existence. For example, it is eternally possible that there be grandchildren, but it is not eternally possible that *I* have grandchildren. Once upon a time I was a mere possibility, and it is impossible for a mere possibility to have grandchildren, or even the possibility of having grandchildren. But now I am actual and have adult children, so now it is possible that I have a grandchild. To be sure, God knew eternally of the possibility of there being humans who had grandchildren, but he did not know eternally of the temporal possibility of *me* having grandchildren. Hence, God's knowledge of temporal possibilities must be mutable and passible since it must change as old possibilities pass out of existence and new possibilities come into existence, and those changes in God's knowledge must be caused by the changing world of which God is aware.

Further, must not God be mutable in order to be a person and have the power of agency, i.e. to be able to make decisions and implement them, and to engage in personal relations with others? Here I think the argument for immutability is stronger. Given God's eternal knowledge of possibilities, God does not have to wait on history in order to decide his will. God can index his will to all possibilities that can be actualized in the world that he intends to create, and he can do this independently of the existence of the world.

But even if God's will is immutable, must not God change in order to *implement* his will once the possibilities of the world become actual? Imagine I sin and God begins punishing me, and then I repent and God ceases punishing me. Even if God has eternally decided to punish me if I commit such a sin in such circumstances and to forgive me if I repent, must not God change from *not* punishing me to punishing me and then from punishing me to not punishing me? I think not. It seems more compatible with the notion of God as infinite pure act to think of ourselves as continually wrapped in the unchanging will of God, so that neither God's decision nor God's will ever changes. What changes is the way we experience the will of God. How we experience it is contingent on how *we* change in relation to God's unchanging will.

Some critics object that this is an impersonal conception of God. But what could be more intimate than to think of oneself or to feel oneself as wrapped in the eternal, exhaustive, providential will of a loving God who wants the best for us, who is and always has been willing the best for us, and who continually accompanies, surrounds, and feels us in our actuality, somewhat like an omniscient loving mother would feel the developing fetus in her womb?

One who concedes that God's will could be indexed to all possibilities and therefore need not change in that respect might none the less argue that God *could* change his will, and so is not immutable. I do not agree. God's will could have been *different*, i.e. God could have decided to actualize a different possible world. But if God's will is eternally decided, then to say that God could *change* his will would show conceptual confusion on the part of the claimant. If God is eternally decided about absolutely everything, then there is no remaining possibility with regard to which he could change his will.

Parenthetically, to believe that God could have decided differently presumes that there are different possible worlds that God could have actualized. However, if Gottfried Leibniz was correct that there is only one best possible world and that God could will nothing else, then if it is true that it is better that there be a world than not, it also seems clear that God's will is immutable, since there is nothing else God could do but will that uniquely best possible world.

Finally, the question as to whether God should be thought of as impassible in *feeling* is closely tied to the question of the religious adequacy of a conception of God. Properly formulated, the concept of an APB should describe a being worthy of unqualified awe, admiration, and devotion. Therefore, according to the classical tradition, God should be conceived as eternally, perfectly, impassibly blissful. A deficiency in God's happiness would have to result from his very nature or be caused by something external, but God's nature cannot be deficient, so any deficiency would have to be caused by creatures, which are the only things external to God. It seems improper, however, to think that the happiness of an APB could be hostage to the actions or experiences of its creatures. Hence, the most worthy way to conceive of an APB is as perfectly blissful. Further, it is this conception which best assures that, by the grace of God, creatures may taste of God's perfect bliss now and someday share in it fully.

None the less, many contemporary thinkers object that God cannot be both perfectly blissful and perfectly loving. A perfectly loving, omniscient being, as God must be, would be perfectly sensitive to the joys and sufferings of his creatures. Because God is loving, he could not but be emotionally affected by, e.g. the cruelties, horrors, and cravenness of the Nazi Holocaust. Similarly, God cannot but rejoice when a sinner repents or justice wins out over injustice. If we believed that God were not moved emotionally by such things, he would not be someone by whom we could feel loved or from whom we could seek companionship and solace or for whom we could feel unqualified admiration and devotion. Feeling is the subjective facet of evaluation, and surely an APB would not evaluate things in a purely intellectual or behavioral way.

Critics, however, object that it is inappropriate to think of God as emotionally buffeted by what goes on in the world. Further, because God knows he is in ultimate control of history and will make sure that good triumphs over evil, he can take abiding joy in that knowledge, and therefore not be affected emotionally by what goes on in the world from day to day – even as an experienced swimming teacher of able young children is not callous or remiss in not being emotionally troubled by the children's fear and choking as they learn to swim. She knows she will not let the children suffer irredeemable harm and that eventually they will learn to swim and be delighted to have done so.

To some people, then, the impassibly blissful God seems emotionally indifferent to the world, and that makes God seem impersonal, alien, and therefore religiously unapproachable and inadequate. To other people the passibilist conception of God makes God seem pathetic in the sense of pitiful, as God grieves over lost sinners and acts of evil and, according to some passibilists, does so forever. But surely the felt quality of an APB's emotional life would not be pitiable or depend upon its creature's choices.

Perhaps we can save what is most important on each side of this conflict by distinguishing between God being emotionally "touched" and emotionally "crushed" by the experiences and actions of his creatures. What I think we should save out of the impassibilist position is that God in himself is not emotionally "crushed" by what goes on in the world. God in himself is perfectly, imperturbably happy through enjoyment of his own perfection, through knowledge of the goodness of his creation, through enjoyment of his creation, and through knowledge of his ultimate control over history.

What I think we should save out of the passibilist position is that God is emotionally "touched" by the joys and sufferings, the good and the evil actions of his creatures. This was not my position in Creel (1986), but now, thanks to my critics, I think an adequate conception of God must include the notion that God is touched by our sufferings and joys, victories and defeats – though not necessarily in the same ways as we are. In his relation to us, God, as supreme knower, feels all our joys and sorrows just as we feel them, but in himself he may feel sad about some of our joys and may rejoice over some of our sufferings. In brief, that God is touched by our joys and sorrows is what must be saved out of the passibilist position in order that we may believe that God cares about us in the deepest sense and therefore is approachable for companionship in the richest sense.

Bibliography

Creel, R. E.: *Divine Impassibility* (Cambridge: Cambridge University Press, 1986).

Dodds, M. J.: *The Unchanging God of Love: A Study of the Teaching of St. Thomas Aquinas on Divine Immutability in View of Certain Contemporary Criticism of this Doctrine* (Fribourg, Switzerland: Editions Universitaires Fribourg Suisse, 1986).

Fiddes, P. S.: *The Creative Suffering of God* (Oxford: Clarendon Press, 1988).

Fretheim, T. E.: *The Suffering of God: An Old Testament Perspective* (Philadelphia: Fortress Press, 1984). [The Western controversy over divine immutability and impassibility has been motivated in part by Biblical statements that seem to go in opposite directions. Scholars generally agree that the controversy cannot be resolved by simply citing scripture. Fretheim, like Abraham Heschel in *The Prophets*, argues for a passibilist conception of God.]

Hallman, J. M.: *The Descent of God: Divine Suffering in History and Theology* (Minneapolis: Fortress Press, 1991).

McWilliams, W.: *The Passion of God: Divine Suffering in Contemporary Protestant Theology* (Macon, GA: Mercer University Press, 1985).

O'Hanlon, G. F., SJ: *The Immutability of God in the Theology of Hans Urs von Balthasar* (Cambridge: Cambridge University Press, 1990).

Sarot, M: *God, Passibility, and Corporeality* (Kampen, Netherlands: Kok Pharos, 1992). [Concludes with a valuable discussion of whether a passible God must be corporeal.]

Stump, E., and Kretzmann, N.: "Eternity, awareness, and action," *Faith and Philosophy*, 9/4 (1992), pp. 463–82.

Taliaferro, C.: *Consciousness and the Mind of God* (Cambridge: Cambridge University Press, 1994), ch. 6.

Weinandy, T.: *Does God Change?* (Still River, MA: St Bedes Publications, 1984). [Much of the Western discussion of immutability and impassibility has been motivated by the Christian doctrine of divine incarnation. Weinandy's book is a valuable introduction to this discussion.]

319

PART VI

THE JUSTIFICATION OF THEISTIC BELIEF

41

Ontological arguments

CLEMENT DORE

Arguments from the concept of a supremely perfect being to the existence of such a being (called the "ontological argument" by Kant) were first expounded by St Anselm in his *Proslogion* and *Response to Guanilo*. John Duns Scotus, St Thomas Aquinas, René Descartes, Baruch Spinoza, Gottfried Leibniz, and Immanuel Kant have all made major contributions to the historical literature on ontological arguments. Moreover, in the twentieth century we have important contributions from Charles Hartshorne, Norman Malcolm, James Ross, and Alvin Plantinga (see the bibliography).

It would be impossible even to begin to do justice to these thinkers within the scope of this article. Rather, I shall discuss a version of the ontological argument which was advanced by Descartes in the seventeenth century (see Article 12, EARLY MODERN PHILOSOPHICAL THEOLOGY). Though it is very succinct, it captures, I think, the essence of all ontological arguments.

In *Meditation V*, Descartes argues that "there is not any less repugnance to our conceiving a God (that is to say a Being supremely perfect) to whom existence is lacking (that is to say to whom a certain perfection is lacking), than to conceive of a mountain without a valley." And he draws the conclusion that "existence is inseparable from Him and, hence, that He really exists." (Descartes responded to a critic that by "a mountain without a valley," he meant an uphill slope without a downhill slope.)

The following is an elaboration on this argument.

(1) The concept of a supremely perfect being is, in part, the concept of a person who has all those properties which are such that it is better than not that a person jointly possesses them. Wisdom and power are examples. (I say "jointly" because, for example, power without wisdom is not a perfection.)

(2) The concept of existence is the concept of such a property.

So

(3) it is a conceptual truth that a supremely perfect being possesses the property of existence.

Hence

(4) a supremely perfect being exists.

Since Kant, many philosophers have rejected arguments of this sort, on the

323

ground that existence is not a property of persons. But it is also widely agreed that Gottlob Frege was right in supposing that existence is a property of concepts, namely, the property of being instantiated (see Article 27, BEING). And my interpretation of Descartes's argument (call it "OA₁") can be reformulated with that in view:

(1) The concept of a supremely perfect being is the concept of a being who has all supreme perfection-making properties.

(2) The concept of the concept of such a being being instantiated is the concept of a supreme perfection-making property (one that is necessary, though not sufficient, for supreme perfection).

So

(3) it is a conceptual truth that the concept of a supremely perfect being is instantiated.

Hence

(4) the concept of a supremely perfect being is instantiated, i.e. a supremely perfect being exists.

However, for verbal economy, I shall continue to say simply that the concept of existence *simpliciter* is the concept of a property which is such that it is better than not that a supremely perfect being possesses it.

Another objection to OA₁ is this: "It is analogous to the following argument:

(a) The concept of a centaur is the concept of a being with the torso of a human being and the normal hindparts of a horse.

(b) The concept of the normal hindparts of a horse is, in part, the concept of something which has a tail.

So

(c) it is a conceptual truth that centaurs have tails.

Hence

(d) centaurs have tails

"It is as clear as can be that all that step (c) warrants is the conditional proposition that *if* there are any centaurs, *then* they have tails. For surely steps (a) through (c) (all of which are true) do not entitle us to conclude that there are in fact centaurs.

"But now, by parity of reasoning, all that steps (1) through (3) of OA₁ warrant us in concluding is that *if* a supremely perfect being exists, *then* a supremely perfect being exists. And this is a far cry from being able to conclude that there actually *is* a supremely perfect being."

The following is a reply to this objection: Sentences of the form "*s* is *p*" express a conceptual truth if and only if the explanation of the fact that they express a truth lies entirely in the *concept* of *s* and the *concept* of *p*. Thus, the explanation of the fact that "Centaurs have tails" expresses a conceptual truth lies entirely in the concept of a centaur and the concept of having a tail. But it is false that the explanation of the truth of "If a supremely perfect being exists, then he exists" lies entirely in the concept of a supremely perfect being and the concept of existence. The concept of a supremely perfect being has no bearing whatever on the truth which is expressed by that sentence, since it would continue to express a true proposition, no matter what syntactically correct substitutions for "supremely perfect being" we might make in it. The same does not hold true for the sentence, "If centaurs exist, then they have tails."

But now (1) and (2) appear to have the same kind of epistemic bearing on (3) as do (a) and (b) on (c), i.e. it looks as if (1) and (2) entail that it is in fact a conceptual truth that a supremely perfect being exists. However, as we have just seen, "A supremely perfect being exists" does not express a conceptual truth if it means "If a supremely perfect being exists, then he exists." It looks, then, as if OA$_1$ really does establish the existence of God.

But here my critic may wish to continue as follows: "All conceptual truths are analytic. Thus, it is a conceptual truth that centaurs have tails because 'centaur' means 'creature with the normal hindparts of a horse and the torso of a human being,' and the latter means in part 'creature with a tail.' And all analytic statements are reducible to ontologically insignificant conditions. For let 'x-centaur' mean 'an existent centaur.' Then 'An x-centaur exists' is analytic. But unless it is equivalent to an ontologically insignificant conditional, namely, 'If an x-centaur exists, then it exists,' then a mere stipulative definition has existential significance.

"But now it must be the case that the reason that it is conceptual truth that a supremely perfect being exists is that 'supremely perfect being' means in part 'a being which exists,' so that 'A supremely perfect being exists' is reducible to 'A being which is supremely powerful, *and which exists*, exists.' And this latter plainly has no more existential clout than does 'An x-centaur (i.e. an existent centaur) exists.' "

However, this argument (call it "the analyticity argument") can be seen to be a failure. For let "x has actual existence" mean "The sentence, 'x exists' (1) expresses a truth and (2) is not equivalent in meaning to an ontologically insignificant conditional sentence." Then we can advance the following argument (call it "OA$_2$"):

(1) The concept of a supremely perfect being is the concept of a being who has all supreme perfection-making properties.
(2) The concept of having actual existence is the concept of a supreme perfection-making property.

So

(3) it is a conceptual truth that a supremely perfect being has actual existence.

Hence

(4) a supremely perfect being has actual existence, i.e. the sentence, "A supremely perfect being exists," expresses an ontologically significant proposition.

325

Now suppose that my critic maintains, as against OA$_2$, that since it is, indeed, a conceptual truth that a supremely perfect being has actual existence, it must be true that "supremely perfect being" means, in part, "being which has actual existence," so that "A supremely perfect being has actual existence" means "A being who is supremely powerful, etc., and *who has actual existence*, has actual existence." It is clear that the latter sentence is strongly analogous to "*x*-centaurs (existent centaurs) exist," so that if all that OA$_2$ warrants is the envisaged conclusion, then it is ontologically defunct.

But now consider the following definition. Let "*x* has real, actual existence" mean " '*x* has actual existence' (1) expresses a truth and (2) is not equivalent in meaning to any ontologically insignificant conditional sentence." Then we can set out the following argument (call it "OA$_3$"):

(1)   The concept of a supremely perfect being is the concept of a being who has every supreme perfection-making property.

(2)   The concept of having real, actual existence is the concept of a supreme perfection-making property.

So

(3)   it is a conceptual truth that a supremely perfect being has real, actual existence.

So

(4)   a supremely perfect being has real, actual existence, i.e. "a supremely perfect being has actual existence" expresses an ontologically significant proposition, i.e. the conclusion of OA$_1$ is ontologically significant.

Now if my critic maintained at this point that "supremely perfect being" means "being who is supremely powerful, etc., *and who has real, actual existence*," so that all that OA$_3$ entitles us to conclude is the ontologically insignificant proposition that a being who has real, actual existence has real, actual existence (i.e. that if such a being exists, then he has real, actual existence), then I would reply by introducing the concept of actual, real, actual existence; and, as we progressed, it would become more and more incredible that "supremely perfect being" has such a grotesquely bloated meaning. (This is not a double-edged sword. Indeed, my meta-proofs are intended to show that the conclusions of the immediately preceding proofs are not analytic, but, rather, synthetic, conceptual truths.)

But is it the case that, say, "A supremely perfect being has real, actual existence" differs in meaning from, say, "A supremely perfect being has actual existence"? If not, then my rebuttal is a failure. But the answer is that they do differ in meaning, inasmuch as they refer to different sentence types and tokens. "A supremely perfect being has actual existence" ascribes the property of ontological significance to the sentence (type and token), "A supremely perfect being exists," whereas "A supremely perfect being has real, actual existence" ascribes ontological significance to a *different* sentence (type and token), namely, "A supremely perfect being has actual existence." And so on for "A supremely perfect being has actual, real, actual existence," etc.

It should be stressed that we are not confronted by an unacceptable regress here, since once my critic grows weary, there are no further sentence tokens to enter into the regress; and surely sentence types do not exist in the absence of corresponding sentence tokens.

But is it not the case that there are no *other* instances of conceptual truths which are not clearly essentially conditional truths? And does that not render my arguments suspect? The answer to the former question is "no." For it is far from clear that, say, "It is a conceptual truth that the whole number between the number eight and the number ten is odd" means the same as "It is a conceptual truth that if there is a whole number between the number eight and the number ten, then it is odd" or "If the number eight and the number ten exist and there is a whole number between them, then it is odd." And such examples can, of course, be multiplied indefinitely.

Another reply to my critic is now available. Not only must he reject OA_1, but an indefinitely large number of meta-proofs, until he grows weary. He, on the other hand, has only one argument on behalf of his position, namely, the argument that there are no other instances of non-conditional conceptual truths. And, as we have just seen, that is far from clearly cogent.

Here my critic may wish to argue that, none the less, it has some cogency, and, since it refutes OA_1, it *ipso facto* refutes all of the envisaged meta-proofs; so that my multiplying the latter results in no epistemic gain. But, as every philosopher knows, one person's *modus ponens* is another person's *modus tollens*. And I submit that it is incredible that the envisaged argument refutes *all* of the meta-proofs, and, hence, that it is incredible that it refutes OA_1.

But don't the envisaged arguments establish, not just the existence of one supremely perfect being, but the existence of an indefinitely large number of supremely perfect beings? And isn't that a good reason to suppose that something is wrong with them? The answer is that since the concept of a supremely perfect being is, among other things, the concept of a being who is the uncreated creator of everything else, it is a conceptual (necessary) truth that any supremely perfect being there may be is the uncreated creator of everything else, and, hence, positing two or more supremely perfect beings commits one to the logically absurd conclusion that there are beings who are both created and uncreated (see Article 39, CREATION AND CONSERVATION).

Let me elaborate. Let us individuate the envisaged supremely perfect beings by naming them. Call one of them "God_1," another "God_2," and yet another "God_3," and so on. And suppose that God_1 is necessarily an uncreated creator of everything else. Then God_2 and God_3, etc., are both created (by God_1) and yet, *qua* supremely perfect beings, uncreated by anyone else. Hence, they are logically impossible. And what is logically impossible is surely not something with respect to which existence is a perfection, i.e. the concept of a logically impossible state of affairs is not such that the concept of its obtaining is the concept of a perfection relative to that state of affairs. Logically impossible states of affairs are such that it is better than not that they do not obtain. The reason is this: a necessarily false proposition entails every proposition. So if a logically impossible state of affairs obtained, then the world would be intolerably chaotic.

327

It is, of course, true that since "a logically impossible state of affairs obtains" is itself a necessary falsehood, it entails as well that the world would *not* be intolerably chaotic. But, since it *would* be intolerably chaotic none the less, it is clearly better than not that no logically impossible state of affairs obtains, i.e. other things being equal, a world which is not intolerably chaotic *simpliciter* is better than a world which is both *not* intolerably chaotic *and* intolerably chaotic, or, at any rate, other things being equal, a world, *in which only one supremely perfect being exists*, and is not intolerably chaotic *simpliciter* is better than a world, in which there is *more* than one supremely perfect being, and which is both not intolerably chaotic and intolerably chaotic.

But now what about *nearly* supremely perfect beings – beings who have all of the perfections of a supremely perfect being *except* being the uncreated creator of everything else? The answer is that the concept of a supremely perfect being is also the concept of a being who cannot possibly be surpassed *or even rivaled* with respect to the number and degree of his perfections, and, hence, that nearly supremely perfect beings are also logically impossible, so that it is not better than not that they exist.

But suppose that someone introduces the concept of *minor deities*, i.e. beings who possess *some* properties which are perfections relative to a supremely perfect being, including existence, but far fewer and to a far less degree. How are we to deal with this concept? The answer is that, on this definition, "Minor deities exist" means, in part, "Existent beings, who possess some of a supremely perfect being's perfections, exist"; and that sentence would continue to express a truth under any syntactically correct substitutions for "beings who possess some of a supremely perfect being's perfections." But vacuous truths of this sort are subject to translation into vacuous, ontologically sterile conditionals. Otherwise, sentences such as "Existent centaurs (dragons, etc.) exist" would commit us to a distressingly bloated ontology. It follows that "Minor deities exist" is equivalent in meaning to the ontologically sterile conditional sentence, "If minor deities exist, then they exist." "Minor deities [thus defined] exist" is demonstrably and, indeed, intuitively, ontologically sterile.

It would also be unacceptable to define "minor deities" as "beings who possess all properties (whatever they may be) which are perfections relative to a supremely perfect being, except . . ." where "existence" is not a fill-in. For the concept of supreme perfection is such that the number of perfections which we would be able to fill in is a mere drop in the ocean with respect to the totality of the perfections of a supremely perfect being: it is physically impossible for us to fill in enough exceptions to render minor deities, defined in the envisaged manner, logically possible. This is because the number of perfections, which we could fill in, constitutes just a small percentage of the perfections of a supremely perfect being, and hence, any possible world, in which a supremely perfect being and a minor deity existed, would be a world in which the latter possessed a high percentage of the perfection of a supremely perfect being and there is no such possible world. But since, as we have seen, it is a conceptual truth that a supremely perfect being exists, and, hence, a supremely perfect being exists in every possible world, there is no possible world in which a minor deity exists. Minor deities, like nearly supremely perfect beings, are logically impossible, and so it is not better than not that they exist.

If my arguments are sound, then "God exists" is intuitively an ontologically significant conceptual truth: it is intuitive that God exists necessarily. But if a proposition, p, is, if true, necessarily true, then p is, if false, necessarily false. For suppose that there is a possible world in which p is true. Then in that world it is necessarily true. And what is necessarily true in one possible world (e.g. "$7 + 5 = 12$") is necessarily true in the actual one. (There is no possible world in which what is a contingent proposition in the actual world, e.g. "Grass is green," is necessarily true.) It follows that if p is false, then it is not (even) possibly true.

So we can construct an additional argument for God's existence:

(1)   If God is not logically impossible, then God exists necessarily.
(2)   God is not logically impossible.

Hence

(3)   God exists necessarily.

Of course, this argument does not constitute an epistemic gain unless (2) is subject to defense. But in fact a defense is available:

(a)   The concept of a supremely perfect being is the concept of a being which has all supreme perfection-making properties.
(b)   The concept of the concept of such a being *being logically coherent* is the concept of a supreme perfect-making property.

So

(c)   it is a conceptual truth that the concept of a supremely perfect being is logically coherent.

Hence

(d)   the concept of a supremely perfect being is in fact logically coherent.

Once again, someone may claim at this point that all that (c) actually warrants is the ontologically insignificant conclusion that *if* the concept of a supremely perfect being is instantiated, *then* that concept is logically coherent. But meta-proofs, which are analogous to the meta-proofs envisaged earlier, are available at this point. Thus let "The concept of x is *actually* logically coherent" mean "The sentence, 'The concept of x is logically coherent,' (1) expresses a truth and (2) is not reducible to an ontologically insignificant conclusion." Then we can get a meta-proof of the envisaged sort simply by noting that the concept of its concept being *actually* logically coherent is the concept of a supreme perfection-making property. And until my critic grows weary, I can fall back on *real*, actual logical coherence; and so on indefinitely.

Bibliography

Anselm, St: *Proslogion II and Response to Guanilo.* In *Basic Writings*, tr. S. W. Deane, introduction by C. Hartshorne (La Salle: Open Court, 1962).

Descartes, R.: *The Philosophical Works of Descartes*, vol. 1, ed. Haldane and Ross (New York:
   Dover, 1955).

Hartshorne, C.: *Anselm's Discovery* (La Salle: Open Court, 1965).

Kant, I.: *Critique of Pure Reason*, book II, ch. 3, tr. N. Kemp Smith (New York: St Martin's
   Press, 1963).

Leibniz, G. W.: *New Essays Concerning Human Understanding*, book 4, ch. 10 and appendix
   X, tr. A. G. Langley (La Salle: Open Court, 1949).

Plantinga, A.: *The Nature of Necessity* (Oxford: Clarendon Press, 1974).

Plantinga, A. (ed.): *The Ontological Argument from St. Anselm to Contemporary Philosophers*
   (New York: Doubleday, 1965). [Much of the writing which I have cited in the text can be
   found in this anthology.]

Ross, J.: *Philosophical Theology* (Indianapolis: Bobbs-Merrill, 1969).

Spinoza, B.: *Ethics*, Part I, Everyman Edition, tr. A. Boyle, rev. C. H. R. Parkinson (London:
   Dent, 1989).

42

Cosmological arguments

WILLIAM L. ROWE

Within philosophy of religion, a cosmological argument is understood to be an argument from the existence of the world to the existence of God. Typically, such arguments proceed in two steps. The first step argues from the existence of the world to the existence of a first cause or necessary being that accounts for the existence of the world. The second step argues that such a first cause or necessary being has, or would very likely have, the properties associated with the idea of God. Cosmological arguments appeared in Plato and Aristotle, played a prominent role in Jewish, Christian, and Islamic thought during the medieval period, and were forcefully presented in the eighteenth century by Gottfried Leibniz and Samuel Clarke. In the modern period these arguments, particularly as presented by Thomas Aquinas, Leibniz, and Clarke, have been severely criticized by David Hume, Immanuel Kant, and others. In the last few decades of the twentieth century, however, there has been a revival of interest in cosmological arguments, and several challenges to the major criticisms of these arguments have appeared.

Cosmological arguments may be divided into two broad types: those that depend on a premise denying an infinite regress of causes and those that do not depend on such a premise. Among the former are contained the first "three ways" presented by Aquinas, as well as an interesting argument, developed by Islamic thinkers, that the world cannot be infinitely old and, therefore, must have come into existence by the creative will of God (see Article 9, THE CHRISTIAN CONTRIBUTION TO MEDIEVAL PHILOSOPHICAL THEOLOGY; and Article 10, THE ISLAMIC CONTRIBUTION TO MEDIEVAL PHILOSOPHICAL THEOLOGY). An important difference between the arguments represented by Aquinas's first "three ways" and the Islamic argument is that while both reject an infinite regress of causes, only the latter bases the objection on the alleged impossibility of an infinite *temporal* regress. Unlike Bonaventure who adopted the Islamic argument, Aquinas did not think that philosophy could show that the world had a temporal beginning. He rejected an infinite regress of essentially ordered causes (a *non-temporal* causal series), identifying God as the first cause in such a non-temporal series. Leibniz and Clarke, however, allowed an infinite regress of causes, arguing only that there must be a sufficient reason for the existence of such a series of causes. Thus the eighteenth century arguments of Clarke and Leibniz do not depend on rejecting an infinite regress of causes. Appealing to the principle of sufficient reason, Clarke and Leibniz insist only that such a series could not be self-explanatory and, therefore, would require an explanation in the causal activity of some being outside the series (see Article 12, EARLY MODERN PHILOSOPHICAL THEOLOGY).

Cosmological arguments relying on philosophical objections to an infinite temporal series of causes typically proceed as follows:

(1)   Whatever begins to exist has a cause.
(2)   The world began to exist.
(3)   Therefore, the world has a cause of its existence.

The philosophical argument for premise (2) is based on the alleged impossibility of an infinite series of past events. Why is such a series thought to be impossible? If we begin with some present event and consider further events proceeding endlessly into the future, such a series is *potentially infinite*. For at any future event in the series there will have actually occurred only a finite number of events between that event and the present event. But if we think of events receding endlessly into the past from the present, we would be thinking of an infinite series that has actually occurred, a series that is *actually infinite*. The claim is that while a series of events can be potentially infinite, it cannot be actually infinite. So, the world could not have always existed.

It must be admitted that it is difficult to imagine an absolutely infinite number of temporally discrete events having already occurred. But what is the philosophical objection to it? It is sometimes suggested that if the series of events prior to the present is actually infinite, then there must be events in the past that are separated from the present by an infinite number of events. However, this suggestion is mistaken. No past event is separated from the present by an infinite number of events. It is also sometimes suggested that if the past is actually infinite then new events cannot be *added* to the series, for the series thus added to would be the same size as the series before the addition was made. The response to this objection is that one can add to an infinite collection even though the number of entities in the collection before the addition will be the same as the number of entities in the collection after the addition. The fact that this is so does not prevent the old collection from being a proper subset of the collection composed of the old collection and the new member. For reasons such as these, most philosophers who have studied these matters remain unconvinced that an actual series of past events is impossible.

In addition to the philosophical argument against the possibility that the world has always existed, some proponents endeavor to support premise (2) by appealing to scientific theories that imply that the world had a beginning. For example, they appeal to the big bang theory according to which the universe probably began to exist some 15 billion years ago. There is a growing body of literature that endeavors to assess the implications of such theories for this particular cosmological argument.

A good example of a cosmological argument based on a rejection of a *nontemporal* infinite regress of causes is Aquinas's second way. This argument may be summarized as follows:

(1)   Some things exist and their existence is caused.

(2) Whatever is caused to exist is caused to exist by something else.

(3) An infinite regress of (non-temporal) causes resulting in the existence of anything is impossible.

(4) Therefore, there is a first cause of existence.

There are two major difficulties in assessing the third premise of this argument. First, there is the difficulty of understanding exactly what a non-temporal causal series is. Second, there is the difficulty of determining exactly why such a series cannot proceed to infinity. To resolve the first difficulty we must distinguish the *earlier* cause that brought some presently existing object into existence from whatever *presently existing* things that are causally responsible for its existence at this very moment. The basic idea is that if A (a human being, say) now exists, A is right now being caused to exist by something else B, which may itself be simultaneously caused by C to be causing A to exist. Although A would not exist now had it not been brought into existence by something else that existed temporally prior to A (a temporal causal series), it is also true, so Aquinas thought, that A would not now exist were it not now being caused to exist by something else B (a non-temporal causal series). In such a non-temporal series of causes of A's present existence, Aquinas held that the cause of any member in the series either is the first cause in the series or is itself being caused to cause that member by some non-temporally prior cause in the series.

Although Aquinas allowed that it is theoretically possible for a temporal series of causes to proceed backwards to infinity, he thought it obvious that a non-temporal causal series must terminate in a first member, itself uncaused. Why is this supposed to be obvious? Presumably, the idea is that it is obvious that if B is right now causing A to exist, and C is right now causing B to be causing A to exist, then if C and every prior member in the series were to have the same status as B, no causing would be occurring at all. Or, to put it differently, if there were no first cause in this series it would be simply inexplicable that such a series of causings is actually occurring. But once the argument is put in this fashion it invites the skeptical challenge that the fact that such causing goes on may simply be inexplicable. Thus, understanding the third premise of this argument and determining exactly why it must be true has proved to be difficult. And, of course, it would be question-begging to simply *define* a non-temporal causal series as one that terminates in a first cause. As a result, many philosophers find the argument unconvincing.

As noted above, the cosmological arguments developed by Leibniz and Clarke do not depend on a premise that rejects an infinite regress of causes. What they do depend on is a rather strong explanatory principle according to which there must be a determining reason for the existence of any being whatever. If we think of a *dependent being* as a being whose determining reason lies in the causal activity of other beings, and think of a *self-existent being* as a being whose determining reason lies within its own nature, the first step of Clarke's cosmological argument can be put as follows.

(1) Every being (that exists or ever did exist) is either a dependent being or a self-existent being.

(2)   Not every being can be a dependent being.
(3)   Therefore, there exists a self-existent being.

While the principle that there must be a determining reason for the existence of any being whatever immediately yields premise (1), it is difficult to see how it establishes premise (2). For if we allow for an infinite regress of dependent beings, each having the reason for its existence in some preceding member of the series, it is difficult to see how any being exists that lacks a reason for or explanation of its existence. Of course, if we view the infinite series of dependent beings as itself a dependent being, we might argue that unless there is a self-existent being there would be no determining reason for the existence of the series itself. But it does not seem right to view the succession or series of dependent beings as still another dependent being. So, as strong as the principle we are considering appears to be, it does not appear to be strong enough to do away with the supposition that every being that exists or ever did exist is a dependent being. To carry out this task the cosmological arguments of Clarke and Leibniz required a stronger principle, the principle of sufficient reason (PSR).

The explanatory principle we have been considering is restricted to requiring an explanation for the existence of individual beings. PSR is a principle concerning facts, including facts consisting in the existence of individual beings. But PSR also requires an explanation for facts about individual beings, for example, the fact that John is happy. In addition, PSR requires an explanation for general facts such as the fact that someone is happy or the fact that there are dependent beings. Leibniz expresses PSR as the principle ". . . that no fact can be real or existent, no statement true, unless there be a sufficient reason why it is so and not otherwise . . ." (Leibniz 1951 [1714], para. 32). And Clarke asserts: "Undoubtedly nothing is, without a sufficient reason why it is, rather than not; and why it is thus, rather than otherwise" (Clarke and Leibniz 1956 [1717], third reply).

If we understand a contingent fact to be a fact that possibly might not have been a fact at all, it is clear that Leibniz held that every contingent fact has a sufficient reason or explanation. And so long as we restrict ourselves to contingent facts concerning the existence of things, it is clear that Clarke held that all such facts must have a sufficient reason. If either view should be correct, it does seem that Clarke's premise (2) must be true. For if every being were dependent it does seem that there would be a contingent fact without any explanation – the fact that there are dependent beings. If PSR is true, the fact that there are dependent beings must have an explanation or sufficient reason. So, given Clarke's convictions about PSR, it is understandable why he should hold that not every being can be a dependent being. For if every being that exists or ever did exist is a dependent being, what could possibly be the sufficient reason for the fact that there are dependent beings? It won't do to point to some particular dependent being and observe that it produced other dependent beings. The question why there are any dependent beings cannot be answered by appealing to the causal activity of some particular dependent being any more than the question why there are any human beings can be answered by appealing to Adam and Eve and their causal activity in producing other human beings. Nor will it do to observe that there always have been dependent beings engaged in causing other dependent beings. The question why there are any dependent beings cannot be answered by noting that there always have been dependent beings any more than the question why there are any elephants can be answered simply by observing that there always have been elephants. To note that there always have been elephants may explain how long elephants have been in existence, but it won't explain why there are elephants at all.

Should we conclude that Clarke's cosmological argument is sound? Not quite. For all we have seen is that his argument is sound *if* PSR is true. But what of PSR itself? Is it true? In its unrestricted form PSR holds that every fact has an explanation; in its restricted form it holds that every contingent fact has an explanation. Even if we take PSR in its restricted form, there are serious objections to it.

An explanation of one fact in terms of another fact that is a *sufficient reason* for it would be one in which the explaining fact *entails* the fact it explains. One objection to PSR is that it cannot avoid the dark night of Spinozism, a night in which all facts appear to be necessary. This difficulty was particularly acute for Leibniz. He explained God's creation of this world by this world's being the best and God's choosing to create the best. But what accounts for God's choosing to create the best, rather than some inferior world or none at all? God chooses the best because of His absolute perfection – being absolutely perfect He naturally chooses to create the best. The difficulty is that God's being perfect is, for Leibniz, a necessary fact. It seems, then, that God's choice to create the best must also be necessary and, consequently, the existence of this world is necessary. If we avoid this conclusion by saying that God's being perfect is not the sufficient reason of His choice to create the best we run into an infinite regress of explanations of His choice to create the best. For suppose we say that it is God's perfection in conjunction with His choice to exercise His goodness that constitutes the sufficient reason for His choice to create the best. What then of His choice to exercise His goodness? A similar problem would arise in providing a sufficient reason for it. And we seem to be off to the races, each reason determining a choice only by virtue of a prior choice to act in accordance with that reason.

A second and more serious objection to the restricted form of PSR is that it appears to be impossible for every contingent fact to have an explanation. Consider the huge conjunctive fact whose conjuncts are all the other contingent facts that there are. This huge conjunctive fact must itself be a contingent fact, otherwise its conjuncts would not be contingent. Now what can be the sufficient reason for this huge conjunctive fact? It cannot be some necessary fact. For the sufficient reason for a fact is another fact that entails it; and whatever is entailed by a necessary fact is itself necessary. The huge conjunctive fact cannot be its own sufficient reason since only a necessary fact could be self-explanatory. So, the sufficient reason for the huge conjunctive fact would have to be one of the contingent facts that is a conjunct of it. But then that conjunct would have to be a sufficient reason for itself, since whatever is a sufficient reason for a conjunctive fact must be

335

a sufficient reason for each of its conjuncts. It follows, then, that the huge conjunctive fact cannot have an explanation. It thus appears that PSR is false.

In the above argument it is important not to confuse the huge conjunctive fact constituted by every other contingent fact with the general fact that there are contingent facts. The latter fact – that there are contingent facts – is not itself a contingent fact. It is a necessary fact. For every possible world contains some contingent fact or other. Consider the contingent fact that there are elephants. That there are elephants is a fact in the actual world. But if some possible world in which there are no elephants were to be actual, it would be a fact that there are no elephants. So, no matter what possible world is actual, either that there are elephants will be a fact or that there are no elephants will be a fact. Thus, that there are contingent facts is itself a necessary fact. But the huge conjunctive fact described above is itself a contingent fact. Had some other possible world been actual, the huge conjunctive fact described above would not have been a fact.

Our conclusion concerning the eighteenth century argument developed by Clarke is that its second premise – not every being can be a dependent being – has not been proved to be true. As opposed to Hume and many modern critics, we have defended Clarke's view that if every being were dependent there would be a fact – that there are dependent beings – that would lack a sufficient reason. But since PSR is the only reason given to reject the idea that every being could be dependent, and since PSR, even in its restricted form, is open to serious objections, we must conclude that the second premise of Clarke's argument has not been established. This does not mean that his argument is unsound. It only means that it has not been shown to be sound and, therefore, fails as a proof of the existence of a self-existing being.

As we noted at the outset, cosmological arguments involve two steps: proving that there exists a first cause or self-existent (necessary) being, and proving that such a being would possess the properties commonly associated with God – infinite power, wisdom, and goodness (see Article 28, OMNIPOTENCE; Article 29, OMNISCIENCE; and Article 30, GOODNESS). Since philosophers have been mainly concerned with assessing the first step, we have focused our attention on it. It is important to recognize, however, that even if some argument for the first step should be entirely successful, there remains the difficult task of establishing that the first cause or self-existent being is God.

Bibliography

Aquinas, T.: *Summa Theologiae* (London: Eyre & Spottiswoode; New York: McGraw-Hill for Blackfriars, 1964).

Clarke, S.: *A Discourse Concerning the Being and Attributes of God*, 9th edn (London, 1738).

——, and Leibniz, G.: *The Leibniz–Clarke Correspondence* (1717), ed. H. G. Alexander (Manchester: Manchester University Press, 1956).

Craig, W.: *The Cosmological Argument from Plato to Leibniz* (London: Macmillan Press, 1980).

Hume, D.: *Dialogues Concerning Natural Religion* (1779), ed. N. Kemp Smith (Oxford: Clarendon Press, 1935).

Leibniz, G.: *Monadology* (1714), in *Leibniz Selections*, ed. P. P. Wiener (New York: Charles Scribner's Sons, 1951).

Rowe, W.: *The Cosmological Argument* (Princeton: Princeton University Press, 1975).

Smith, Q., and Craig, W.: *Theism, Atheism and Big Bang Cosmology* (Oxford: Clarendon Press, 1993).

43

Teleological and design arguments

LAURA L. GARCIA

Teleological arguments make a case for the existence of God based on examples of apparent design or purposiveness in the natural world. These arguments are normally inductive in nature, taking as their starting point features of the world difficult to explain within a purely naturalistic model. Design arguments have appealed to such general features of the universe as its beauty, its orderly or law-like operations, the interconnectedness of its parts, and its intelligibility; or to more specific features such as its suitability for life, its providing the right conditions for moral growth, or its including conscious beings. Many find this evidential approach to the existence of God more persuasive than the ONTOLOGICAL (see Article 41) or COSMOLOGICAL ARGUMENTS (see Article 42); it appeals to concrete instances of order common to our experience, so that few are inclined to dispute the premises. Instead, discussion revolves around whether or not the examples of apparent design in nature are caused by an intelligent being or are simply a matter of chance.

Traditional analogical arguments

Early versions of the argument from design took the form of an *analogy* between human productions and the universe as a whole. Writing at the end of the eighteenth century, the English philosopher and theologian William Paley famously compared the universe to a watch, noting that "the contrivances of nature . . . are not less evidently mechanical, not less evidently contrivances, not less evidently accommodated to their end or suited to their office than are the most perfect productions of human ingenuity" (Paley 1972 [1802], p. 14). Since Paley's examples of apparent purpose in nature, or means adapted to ends, were largely drawn from the biological realm (he was especially impressed with the human eye), they became less convincing after the advent of evolutionary theory. Darwin's theory provided an explanation of the adaptation of organisms to their environments and of organic parts to their functions that required no appeal to a designing intelligence or orderer. Purely random mutations and the process of natural selection might produce these same results, so a theistic explanation of the data, while possible, is not required. Darwin's theory also undermines Paley's analogy between human artifacts, such as a watch, and natural, living organisms. Watches contain no internal principles of adaptation or variation, while organisms do.

Some defenders of the design argument respond to this criticism by viewing the entire evolutionary process as another instance of nature operating to achieve an end, since it results in organisms of increasing complexity and capacity. Richard Swinburne suggests that the theory of evolution shows the natural universe to be "a machine-making machine" (Swinburne 1979, p. 135). Alternatively, one might shift from the organic realm to focus on the motions of the planets in the solar system or the process of crystal formation or the way in which the universe as a whole has evolved to make life possible. Formulated as an analogical argument, it would start with similarities or *initial likenesses* between the two items (e.g. the planetary system and a clock) and conclude that they will probably be similar in a further respect as well, the *terminal likeness*. Analogical arguments are strongest when (1) there are few or no instances where the initial likenesses are found *without* the terminal likeness (so that the initial likenesses seem clearly relevant to the terminal likeness, and (2) the items being compared have few major *dissimilarities*.

The most famous critic of the design argument, David Hume (see Article 12, EARLY MODERN PHILOSOPHICAL THEOLOGY), focused especially on (2), finding many differences between products of human design and the universe as a whole – for example, the uniqueness of the universe, the epistemic inaccessibility of its origins, its apparent flaws or defects, and so on (see Hume 1980 [1779]). Those defending the analogical approach seek to minimize these differences or to show their irrelevance to the conclusion. Recently some have proposed that a better analogy might be between the universe and a work of art, rather than between the universe and a machine, since this would allow a greater appeal to the beauty of the universe and would avoid some of Hume's criticisms about the unsuitability of the universe for certain human purposes. It would also serve to blunt the objection that an intelligent and all-powerful being (see Article 29, OMNISCIENCE; and Article 28, OMNIPOTENCE) would not use a mechanism as inefficient as the evolutionary process to produce the universe. Works of art, especially those of narrative form, are evaluated by very different criteria than mechanical efficiency. Swinburne's reflections on what God's purposes might be in creating free, personal, embodied agents also undercut some of Hume's complaints about the unsuitability of the universe as a place for human flourishing. Similar points about the kind of universe most conducive to personal and moral growth appear in the work of F. R. Tennant (1930) and John Hick (1981).

Arguments to the best explanation

Current versions of the design argument proceed not in terms of analogies between the universe and human artifacts, but as arguments to the best explanation of the data of our experience. They claim that the theistic hypothesis of an intelligent creator is a better explanation of these data than is the naturalistic hypothesis that the features of the universe are due to the chance operation of blind natural forces. One advantage of the explanatory model of argumentation is that it allows for a cumulative case to be made in favor of the theistic hypothesis; distinct and apparently unrelated aspects of the universe can be presented as evidence of intelligent purpose. An important example of the cumulative case approach can be found in the work of F. R. Tennant early in this century. Tennant appealed especially to the fitness of the earth as a home for living and conscious beings, including the adjustment of the many physical variables required to make life possible. But he also emphasized the rational structure and intelligibility of the universe, its suitability as an arena for moral development, and its being "saturated with beauty" at every level, from the microscopic to the macroscopic (see Tennant 1930, vol. 2, ch. 4).

This approach finds greater precision in the recent work of Richard Swinburne, who appeals especially to the "temporal order" of the universe, by which he means "its conformity to formula, to simple, formulable, scientific laws" (Swinburne 1979, p. 136). He points out that this order does not admit of a scientific explanation, since science cannot explain why the most general laws of nature operate as they do. Since the only alternative to scientific explanations are personal explanations, Swinburne argues that the theistic hypothesis is more probable given the evidence. "Either the orderliness of nature is where all explanation stops, or we must postulate an agent of great power and knowledge who brings about through his continuous action that bodies have the same very general powers and liabilities (that the most general natural laws operate)" (Swinburne 1979, pp. 140–1).

The orderliness of the universe can be seen as an end in itself, from the point of view of an intelligent world-maker, or it can be seen as a means to further ends. The fact that the universe is intelligible makes possible the existence of finite rational creatures who can grow in knowledge and power, and who can make a difference to their surroundings. If one takes the existence of creatures like ourselves to be a good thing and a possible reason for creating, then the fact that the world is governed by predictable laws becomes evidence for intelligence in a further sense. This feature of the universe, then, supports the theistic hypothesis in a double way – it seems to require a personal agent as its cause, and a personal agent would have reason to design a law-governed universe.

Part of the perennial appeal of the design argument is the sense we sometimes have (Hume notwithstanding) that the universe must have been made with human beings in mind. It is not that a designer would have *no* reason to make an intelligible universe of great beauty and variety unless it includes conscious beings like ourselves, but there is power in the realization that only rational beings can understand and appreciate the universe. As the poet Gerard Manley Hopkins put it, "These things were here, and but the beholder wanting" (Hopkins, "Hurrahing in Harvest," 1877). Only rational creatures can stand in an internal relationship to the world, and can learn and grow and imitate their maker in creating new things as a result of this knowledge.

Arguments from the sciences

Just as the earliest versions of the design argument drew much of their material and impetus from discoveries in the sciences, especially the study of anatomy and botany, so the argument has received new life from the vast expansion of scientific knowledge in the last twenty or thirty years concerning the origins of the universe and of life on earth. Many of these discoveries are summarized by M. A. Corey and brought together into a teleological argument for the existence of God. Drawing on the work of scientists such as Paul Davies, Sir John Eccles, Fred Hoyle, and Robert Jastrow, Corey argues that the factors necessary to make life possible are enormously varied and are causally independent of one another. Even minute deviations in any one of them would have rendered life impossible. Thus, either we are faced with a truly astonishing amount of lucky coincidence in our universe, or the universe was caused by a being who intended it to produce life. Corey proposes the following argument (1993, p. 203):

(1)   Life-facilitating coincidences between distant and causally unrelated branches of physics could not come about by chance, but only by Intelligent Design.
(2)   Our universe has a large number of these coincidences.
(3)   Therefore, our universe was Intelligently Designed.

Corey includes in his data pool evidence for big bang cosmology, the origin of living from non-living matter, and various leaps in the evolutionary process, including the shift to human life, which he claims have no satisfactory explanation within the traditional evolutionary model of gradual change (see Article 53, THEISM AND PHYSICAL COSMOLOGY; and Article 54, THEISM AND EVOLUTIONARY BIOLOGY).

Scientists and philosophers on the other side of the debate respond by offering naturalistic models for some of the developments in question, or by attributing the surprising outcomes to chance or coincidence, that is, leaving them unexplained for the time being. Some clearly hope for a naturalistic model to arise that will do what Darwin did for Paley's arguments – render them less compelling by providing a plausible non-theistic explanation of the same facts. Even in the absence of such an explanation, naturalists can resist the claim that the data require further explanation, especially since science can proceed without answering the deeper metaphysical questions raised by Corey and others.

The introduction of considerations about the origin of the universe into the design argument returns the discussion to the "best hypothesis" strategy for proving the existence of God. Positing a personal cause to account for the intelligibility and orderliness of the universe would also explain the sheer existence of a contingent universe, and the reverse is also true. That is, the cosmological argument for God and the teleological argument are mutually supportive under this model of explanation. Similarly, any evidence from the sciences for purpose within the natural processes at work in our universe can be seen as offering confirmation for the theistic hypothesis, if it appears that they are more likely under that hypothesis than under a purely materialistic model. This cumulative case approach also allows the inclusion of evidence from moral experience or from religious experience, even from purported miracles, since each of these points to something in our experience which, it claims, is better explained by theism than by naturalism (see Article 46, MIRACLES; and Article 47, RELIGIOUS EXPERIENCE). This mode of reasoning, familiar from court cases and from detective work, has the advantage of not resting the entire case for God on any one piece of evidence, and of better capturing the way in which most people decide significant questions.

Probability and world hypotheses

Swinburne credits his argument from the orderliness of the universe with the status of *confirming* the existence of God, even if it does not by itself make the existence of God more probable than not. Swinburne reasons that the orderliness of the universe is not at all likely on the naturalistic view and it is at least somewhat likely on the theistic view, so it increases the probability of the theistic view. A similar strategy could be offered in defense of the scientific arguments advanced above. One must show that the level of cooperation among causally independent physical factors necessary to produce organized, living, conscious beings is (1) not particularly likely from a naturalistic perspective, and (2) quite likely on the assumption of God's existence. Swinburne's efforts to show that a designer would have good reason to make rational creatures is relevant to (2).

John Hick objects to any attempt to compare the probability of theism versus naturalism, viewed as hypotheses which can explain all our knowledge and experience: "There can be no prior corpus of propositions in relation to which a total interpretation could be judged to be probable or improbable, since all our particular items of information are included within the totality which is being interpreted. There can, in other words, be no evidence in favour of one total interpretation over against another" (Hick 1970, p. 29). But later on Hick offers the existence of suffering in the world as evidence counting against the theistic hypothesis, while certain features of our moral experience count in its favor. Clearly, then, there are propositions common to both interpretations which can be used to evaluate the evidence under consideration. One such proposition would be that an all-powerful, all-knowing, perfectly good being would not allow the existence of gratuitous suffering (see Article 30, GOODNESS; and Article 50, THE PROBLEM OF EVIL). But another would be the claim found in Aquinas's Fifth Way: "Whatever lacks knowledge cannot move towards an end, unless it be directed by some being endowed with knowledge and intelligence" (*Summa Theologiae*, I.Q.2.a.3).

One might also appeal to canons of scientific rationality, as does Swinburne in contending that the theistic hypothesis is superior on grounds of simplicity. Theism postulates one personal agent to explain the complex, ordered universe, whereas naturalism must postulate a variety of different basic entities with various powers and liabilities, with no apparent reason why there are just these and no others. Further, the agent posited by theists is the simplest sort of personal agent possible, says Swinburne – namely, one who has infinite knowledge and power, and who possesses these properties essentially (see Article 31, SIMPLICITY). Otherwise more complicated explanations would be needed of why there are exactly *n* deities, why and how they cooperate in their efforts, why they have *n* level of power or knowledge and no more, and so on (Swinburne 1979, p. 141).

Unless its perfections are essential to it, we would also need an explanation of why the being has the perfections it does.

Critics of Swinburne contend that the kinds of simplicity he appeals to are more at home in the physical sciences and may not be relevant to metaphysical problems. In a more direct attack, J. L. Mackie argues that personal agency is not well understood by us, and that positing a disembodied spiritual being who acts on the material world by unmediated intentional states loses in plausibility whatever it gains in simplicity (Mackie 1982, ch. 8). If the postulated being is outside of time and yet acts in such a way as to affect the temporal order, the conceptual difficulties are even greater (see Article 32, ETERNITY). Mackie also invokes the Humean claim that the organizing capacities of an infinite mind would be just as much in need of explanation as the organized material world that results from its activity. Swinburne could reply that while we experience the organizing capacities of minds in the case of our own activity, we do not experience a similar purposive operation in unconscious natural systems.

Mackie's final complaint is that since Swinburne posits only a *contingently existing* being behind the natural universe, he has simply pushed the need for explanation back a step. The existence of this being will remain unexplained, so it will be a matter of preference whether to choose one unexplained element (God) in one's metaphysical picture of things or several (the most basic material particles). Further, for any theist committed to divine freedom, God's choice to create the universe itself requires an explanation (see Article 39, CREATION AND CONSERVATION). This means that theists must defend a notion of personal explanation that accepts intentions as explanations of actions even when there is no lawlike or logically necessary connection between those intentions and the resulting actions.

In assessing the dispute between the world-hypotheses of theism and naturalism, John Hick argues that the choice is not between having an explanation (God) and having no explanation, but rather between rival explanations. "Since theism and naturalism can each alike lay claim to prima facie evidences and must each admit the existence of prima facie difficulties, any fruitful comparison must treat the two alternative interpretations as comprehensive wholes, with their distinctive strengths and weaknesses" (Hick 1970, p. 31). But it seems more accurate to see the choice in this debate as similar to that involved in the cosmological argument. To say that apparent design is a result of chance or coincidence is in fact to leave it unexplained. The question, then, is whether the human mind can rest in this sort of final inexplicability, or whether reason requires us to postulate a cause of the highest-order contingent facts of our experience.

Is the designer God?

Since Hume it has been popular to dismiss the teleological argument on the grounds that even if it succeeds in its goal of showing that there is some sort of intelligence behind the orderliness of the universe, it can show little or nothing about the nature or even the present existence of the designer, including the number of beings involved in the creative effort. The most detailed reply to Hume comes from Swinburne's argument that considerations of simplicity would lead to the hypothesis of one intelligent being whose faculties are infinite and are held essentially.

As to the moral attributes of God, Swinburne argues that omnipotence and omniscience entail perfect goodness, so that if the natural properties of the deity are probable to a given extent, the moral properties will have that same level of probability. One might instead argue for the benevolence of God by noting various features of the world itself, including its fitness for the development of moral agents. Finally, some would look for elaboration of the nature of God to the cosmological or ontological arguments, since these conclude to a necessary being on the one hand and to a being with every perfection on the other. Since the ontological argument in Plantinga's formulation rests on the acceptance of its first premise (that maximal greatness is possibly exemplified), one might argue that inductive evidence for an omniscient, omnipotent creator adds to the plausibility of that premise and thus lends *inductive* support to its conclusion.

Another advantage of the cumulative case approach, then, is that the emerging concept of God need not rest on one piece of evidence or one isolated proof. Instead, it emerges from a consideration of many different kinds of evidence, all of which point to a similar conclusion. These considerations may undermine some of Hume's complaints, but they do not fully overturn them. The presence of evil in the world does seem to count against the perfect goodness of the designer. However, Swinburne contends that the existence of evil in the world does nothing to disconfirm theism, but leaves its epistemic probability untouched (Swinburne 1979, ch. 11).

Since much of the current excitement surrounding design arguments has been generated by scientists, it is likely that the debate will center for the near future around the controversies in physics and biology over the evidence for purpose in nature. More philosophical precision should be brought to bear on the kind of probability involved in the testing of metaphysical hypotheses, on the epistemic value of what Swinburne calls "confirming" arguments, and on the interrelations between deductive and inductive arguments for God's existence.

Bibliography

Corey, M. A.: *God and the New Cosmology* (Lanham: Roman & Littlefield, 1993).

Hick, J.: *Arguments for the Existence of God* (London: Macmillan, 1970).

——: "An Irenaean theodicy," In *Encountering Evil*, ed. S. T. Davis (Westminster: John Knox Press, 1981).

Hume, D.: *Dialogues Concerning Natural Religion* (1779) (Indianapolis: Hackett, 1980).

Mackie, J. L.: *The Miracle of Theism* (Oxford: Clarendon Press, 1982).

Paley, W.: *Natural Theology* (1802) (Houston: St Thomas Press, 1972).

Swinburne, R.: *The Existence of God* (Oxford: Clarendon Press, 1979).

Tennant, F. R.: *Philosophical Theology* (Cambridge: Cambridge University Press, 1930).

44

Moral arguments

C. STEPHEN EVANS

Moral arguments for God's existence are for lay people among the most popular reasons for belief in God, though they have often been neglected by philosophers. The germ of this kind of argument is simple enough to be grasped by a child; it lies in the conviction that God is in some way the basis of morality, or, as Ivan put it in *The Brothers Karamazov*, "without God everything is permitted." However, this core intuition can be developed in multiple ways, with greater or lesser degrees of sophistication. Thus, there are probably even more different kinds of moral arguments for theism than there are different forms of the cosmological and teleological arguments (see Article 42, COSMOLOGICAL ARGUMENTS; and Article 43, TELEOLOGICAL AND DESIGN ARGUMENTS).

Theistic arguments in general

Before looking at moral arguments one must first think about the functions of arguments for God's existence in general. Few philosophers today would view a single argument for God's reality as a *proof*. This is partly because of a recognition that even good philosophical arguments rarely amount to a proof, and partly because of a recognition of the complexity of belief in God. "Theism" does not refer to a single proposition but a complex web of assertions about God's reality, character, and relations with the universe. It is unreasonable to think that a single argument could establish such a complicated theoretical network. Rather, particular theistic arguments should be seen as providing a lesser or greater degree of support to segments of the network and therefore support for the web as a whole only indirectly.

Many common criticisms of theistic arguments seem not to appreciate this point. For example, the teleological argument is often criticized on the ground that even if sound it would only establish a divine designer and not a creator. However, no single argument can be expected to establish all the attributes of God. Similarly, it would be a mistake to reject moral arguments on the ground that such arguments do not prove the existence of a God with all of the attributes of classical theism. Rather, such arguments will be useful in a "cumulative case" for theism if they increase the plausibility of belief in God by providing support for at least some elements of the theistic web.

Difficulties with moral arguments

As I have noted, moral arguments have not been discussed by philosophers as much as their popularity would suggest. This is likely due to a widespread sense that such arguments are vulnerable to devastating objections, even though a careful look reveals that these objections are not necessarily decisive. One problem is that many philosophers think such arguments are tied to "divine command" theories of morality, and that these theories are both philosophically and religiously flawed (see Article 57, DIVINE COMMAND ETHICS). A line of thought that stems from Plato's *Euthyphro* holds that an action is not morally wrong merely because God forbids it, or permissible merely because he does not forbid it. Would gratuitous torture be morally right if God commanded such actions to be done? Religious believers often hold that God commands certain actions because of their right character; that is partly why they see God as good and worthy of worship (see Article 30, GOODNESS). However, if this is so, then it is not the fact that those actions are commanded that makes them right.

These kinds of considerations certainly create difficulties for certain forms of divine command theories of morality. However, Philip Quinn (1978) has argued very powerfully that such objections, as well as several others commonly made against divine command theories, are by no means decisive. Even aside from whether the difficulties can be surmounted, there are, as we shall see below, types of divine command theories to which such objections do not apply. Furthermore, even though it is clear that a divine command theory of morality certainly can provide the basis for a moral argument, it is by no means the case that all moral arguments depend on a divine command theory of morality.

A second type of objection, also discussed by Quinn, stems from Immanuel Kant's doctrine of moral autonomy. Kant held that a person should be devoted to morality for duty's sake alone, but some philosophers believe that if morality is thought to depend upon God, then one's commitment to morality would not be unconditional. However, as the example of Kant himself shows, it is far from clear that a belief that morality is somehow linked to God necessarily violates autonomy. Even if connecting morality to belief in God creates a problem for autonomy in some senses, it is not obvious that autonomy in these senses is truly essential for the moral life.

Richard Swinburne (1979, pp. 175–9) rejects moral arguments for a very different reason. In his overall case for theism, he claims that basic moral principles are analytic in character and necessarily true. We have no need of any explanation of such truths, any more than we need to explain why a brother is a male sibling, and therefore no need of any theistic explanation. Swinburne argues that a world in which the basic moral principles did not hold can not be coherently conceived.

However, this does not appear to be correct. There are many people, moral nihilists and relativists for example, who appear coherently to conceive of the world as one in which no objective moral principles at all hold. Even people who do agree with Swinburne about the basic principles of morality sometimes worry, after reading such thinkers as Sigmund Freud and Friedrich Nietzsche, that such beliefs might be an illusion. Furthermore, even if Swinburne were correct that many moral principles are necessary truths, it would not necessarily follow that such principles are purely analytic. Many philosophers would argue that "water is H_2O" is a necessary truth, but it is hardly analytic. Furthermore, the fact that water is necessarily H_2O by no means rules out the need for an explanation for the existence or the structure of water. Moral arguments may fail, but there is no obvious reason to think they must.

Types of moral arguments

The most famous and influential moral arguments were those offered by Kant (1956 [1788]). However, the fourth of Thomas Aquinas's "Five Ways" is best understood as a type of moral argument, and this argument itself seems to rest on ideas traceable to Plato and Aristotle. Other philosophers and theologians who have developed or defended moral arguments include Cardinal Newman, Hastings Rashdall, W. R. Sorley, A. E. Taylor, Austin Farrer, and H. P. Owen. The moral argument presented by C. S. Lewis (1952), in his amazingly popular *Mere Christianity*, though of course not directed to a philosophical audience, is very likely the most widely-convincing apologetic argument of the twentieth century.

The most fundamental distinction to be drawn between types of moral arguments is that between theoretical and practical. Theoretical arguments are aimed at showing that some propositions about God are true, or at increasing the likelihood or probability of their truth. Such arguments typically take some feature of morality or moral experience as data to be explained and try to show that God provides the best explanation of those data. For example, if one believes that people are sometimes obligated to act in certain ways, and one also holds a divine command theory of obligation, one might hold that the fact that people are under obligation is best explained by the fact that God issues certain commands.

Within the general category of theoretical arguments there is tremendous variety. Such arguments may vary by taking different features of the moral life as the data to be explained, by having different accounts of that feature of the moral life, or by offering different accounts as to how that feature is related to and thus explained by God. For example, a philosopher might begin with the sheer fact that some states of affairs have moral value, or the existence of obligations, or such concrete phenomena as conscience or guilt. Very different accounts of the nature of each could be offered, as well as different theories as to how God is supposed to ground or provide an explanation of the feature in question. The overall project will likely include a defense of the reality or objectivity of the feature in question against the moral skeptic, as well as a critique of rival, secular explanations. Some contemporary versions of this type of moral argument will be examined below.

Practical moral arguments aim not at establishing the truth or probability of some propositions about God but rather at making evident the reasonableness of belief on practical grounds (see Article 45, PRAGMATIC ARGUMENTS). Some feature of my situation as a moral agent makes belief reasonable or perhaps even necessary for me. The conclusion of such an argument is not "(Probably) God exists," but something like "(Probably) I ought to believe in God."

Kant's practical moral argument

Though the most famous proponent of a practical moral argument was Kant (1956 [1788]), at times he presents arguments of a more theoretical character as well. He rejected all theoretical attempts to show that God's existence could be known, but held nevertheless that a rational moral agent should believe in God. Kant believed strongly in autonomy and thus held that I as a moral being should seek to do my moral duty because of duty and not because of any particular end that I desire. An action is obligatory because of the formal maxim it expresses rather than the end the maxim enjoins. Nevertheless, whenever I act, and therefore whenever I act from duty, I necessarily seek an end.

Since Kant held that happiness is a good that all human beings seek, he believed that the supreme end of the moral life, the complete or highest good, is a world where people are both morally virtuous and happy, and where their happiness is proportional to their virtue. He claimed that one could not reasonably believe that such an end is attainable unless God exists. Empirically there is little reason to think that the world proportions happiness to virtue. However, if the world itself is the creation of a morally good being then there is a basis for hope that my efforts to bring about the highest good will not be wasted or completely ineffectual in the long run.

The heart of Kant's argument is the principle that "ought implies can." If I am obligated to seek to bring about the highest good, then the highest good must be attainable. If it is attainable only if God exists, then it is reasonable for me to believe that God exists.

Kant's argument is vulnerable at a number of points and has often been criticized. Opponents have argued that the highest good in his sense is not really a required moral goal, and that even if it is, the possibility of its attainment requires only the possibility of God's existence rather than God's actual existence. Nevertheless, even if this particular argument is not successful, the core intuition that seems to underlie it retains force, and thus there are other practical versions of the argument that can be formulated. (Kant himself develops the argument in a number of interesting ways.)

That intuition could be stated like this: If I am truly to live as a moral being, I must be able to believe that the world of which I am a part and in which I must act must in some sense be a moral world, even if all appearances are to the contrary. It is difficult for a moral agent to strive for moral ends in the world and at the same time believe that the world is fundamentally alien to those ends. To live the moral life I must believe that the causal structure of nature is such that progress toward certain ends can be achieved through moral struggle, but that in turn requires that I conceive nature itself as in some way containing a moral order. There may be various ways of conceiving such a moral order, but the theistic understanding of nature as the creation of a morally good being is surely one way of doing so.

It may be objected that such an argument is not purely practical in nature but also theoretical. This seems correct, since the argument really points out an oddity in the situation of a moral agent that can be resolved by thinking of nature in a particular manner. Nevertheless, conceiving of the argument as purely theoretical fails to capture some of its appeal; what is at stake is not merely the resolution of an intellectual puzzle but the possibility of moral action itself.

Other philosophers object to practical arguments on the grounds that such arguments are immoral or irresponsible in that they justify belief without justifying the truth of what is believed. Certainly such arguments should not be employed to evade evidence. Nevertheless, William James (1897) argued that where certain conditions are met, such a prudential or pragmatic argument is a reasonable basis for belief. For James, these conditions included the following: (1) the believer must find the hypothesis being considered believable yet find that the question cannot be decided on purely theoretical grounds; (2) the believer must be in a situation where some decision is practically required; and (3) the option must involve some momentous good. Because of the last two conditions, agnosticism is not a practical option.

Some contemporary moral arguments

Though moral arguments for theism have not been a major focus of philosophical discussion in the latter half of the twentieth century, there have been some interesting treatments. Robert Adams (1987, pp. 144–63) has developed both a theoretical and a practical form of the moral argument. His theoretical argument is closely linked to his defense of a "modified" divine command theory of ethical wrongness. According to this theory, in its final form (pp. 139–43), ethical wrongness is identical with the property of being contrary to the commands of a loving God. If there is no God, or if a God exists but is not loving, then nothing would be morally right or wrong. Adams's version of the divine command theory is not vulnerable to the objection that divine commands are arbitrary since they are rooted in God's loving character. Such a theory does not attempt to explain the whole of morality, but only the specific qualities of moral rightness and wrongness. It presupposes that some things, such as love, have value independently of God's commands.

The strengths of this theory, according to Adams, lie in its ability to make sense of both the objective cognitive status of judgments about ethical wrongness, and in the fact that such judgments appear to state "non-natural" facts, a non-natural fact being one that cannot be completely stated in the languages of the natural sciences, including psychology. Some other meta-ethical theories, such as prescriptivism, capture the non-natural aspect of morality at the expense of cognitivity; others, such as hedonistic naturalism, make such judgments cognitive at the expense of reducing them to judgments about natural facts.

If Adams's divine command theory is true, then a sound moral argument can easily be constructed. If some actions are morally wrong, and moral wrongness consists in being contrary to the commands of a loving God, then there must be a

349

loving God. If such a theory is not only true but plausible, then the corresponding argument must have some force as well. Actually, in order to mount a moral argument for God's existence on the basis of a divine command theory, it is not even necessary for such a theory to cover all moral rightness and wrongness. It will be sufficient if there are some moral obligations known to hold which depend on God's commands.

George Mavrodes (1986) has developed a theoretical version of the moral argument that does not rest on a divine command theory. Mavrodes's argument takes the form of an attempt to show that certain moral facts, specifically the existence of some moral obligations, would be strange and inexplicable in a naturalistic universe. He begins by describing what he calls a "Russellian universe," the kind of universe that a philosopher such as Bertrand Russell believed was the actual universe. In such a universe, everything that exists and occurs is ultimately the result of "accidental collocations of atoms," and there is no hope for life after death or any ultimate future for the universe.

Mavrodes argues that common naturalistic explanations of moral obligations fail, by trying to show that morality in a Russellian universe would be strange or absurd. For example, he argues that moral obligations cannot consist solely of feelings of obligation, because real obligations can be present where such feelings are absent, and feelings of obligation can exist even where no actual obligations hold. Naturalistic attempts to explain morality as a kind of enlightened self-interest fail as well. It may be true that it is in the best interests of everyone *collectively* for every individual to act morally, but it does not follow from this that it is always in every individual's interest to act morally. Even if it were true that it would be in the individual's interest to act morally if everyone else would do so, it is difficult to see how such a conditional claim could produce real obligations in the actual world, where it is certain that not everyone else will act morally.

Nor is it the case that morality can be explained in terms of evolutionary theory (see Article 54, THEISM AND EVOLUTIONARY BIOLOGY). Evolution could perhaps explain why certain creatures with moral beliefs and feelings have evolved if we assume that having such beliefs and feelings would have some survival advantage. However, such an explanation does not enable us to understand actual moral obligations. It would appear to explain, not moral obligations, but only the illusion that there are such things.

As Mavrodes sees it, the problem with all such naturalistic views is that they make morality ultimately a superficial, rather than fundamental, aspect of the universe, since what is ultimate on such a view is "accidental collocations of atoms." Morality makes much more sense in a universe in which things like persons, minds, and purposes are "deeper." A theistic universe is clearly one of the ways in which that might be the case. In so far as moral obligations revolve around respecting the value and worth of persons and the creations of persons, it makes sense to say such obligations must be taken seriously. After all, such a universe is one where a personal God is the ultimate reality (see Article 15, PERSONALISM). Theistic religious traditions have usually viewed the natural world as having value because it is God's creation, and human persons and human creations as having special value and dignity because they are created in God's image.

Bibliography

Adams, R. M.: *The Virtue of Faith and Other Essays in Philosophical Theology* (Oxford: Oxford University Press, 1987).

Evans, C. S.: *Subjectivity and Religious Belief: An Historical, Critical Study* (Grand Rapids: Eerdmans, 1978).

James, W.: *The Will to Believe and Other Essays in Popular Philosophy* (New York: Longmans, Green, 1897).

Kant, I.: *Critique of Practical Reason* (1778), tr. L. W. Beck (Indianapolis: Bobbs-Merrill, 1956).

Lewis, C. S.: *Mere Christianity* (London: Collins, 1952).

Mavrodes, G. I.: "Religion and the queerness of morality." In *Rationality, Religious Belief and Moral Commitment*, ed. R. Audi and W. J. Wainwright (Ithaca: Cornell University Press, 1986).

Quinn, P. L.: *Divine Commands and Moral Requirements* (Oxford: Oxford University Press, 1978).

Swinburne, R.: *The Existence of God* (Oxford: Clarendon Press, 1979).

45

Pragmatic arguments

JEFFREY JORDAN

Pragmatic arguments, unlike ontological, cosmological, or teleological arguments, are not, at least not primarily, truth-directed. A pragmatic argument is primarily benefit-directed. A truth-directed argument is definable as a set of propositions, consisting of premises and conclusion, such that the premises are supposed to confer justification for thinking that the conclusion is true. The goal of a truth-directed argument is the acquisition of a true belief. A benefit-directed argument, on the other hand, seeks to motivate the acquisition of a belief because of the benefits possibly generated by holding that belief. A pragmatic argument, then, is one which seeks to support the formation and maintenance of a certain belief, primarily because of the beneficial consequences generated by acquiring that belief.

There are two broad kinds of pragmatic arguments. The first is one which recommends believing some proposition p because, if p should turn out to be true, the benefits gained from believing that p will be impressive. We can call this kind a "truth-dependent" pragmatic argument since the benefits are obtained only if a favorable state of affairs occurs. The predominant example of a truth-dependent pragmatic argument is one which uses a calculation of expected utility to recommend belief. The expected utility of a proposition involves the probability of a proposition being true and the benefits, or utility, gained if that proposition is true. The expected utility of a proposition is calculated simply by discounting the utility of that proposition, if true, by its probability (and subtracting any costs attached to believing it). To illustrate: suppose one will wager on either of two horses, A or B. The probability of A winning is p and the probability of B is q. The payoff if A should win is a; while the payoff of B is b. Moreover, the cost of wagering on A is c_1; while the cost of B is c_2. According to the principle of maximizing expected utility, one should bet on A as long as $(pa - c_1) > (qb - c_2)$. A calculation of expected utility recommends that one should act upon, or believe, as the case may be, whichever of the doxastic alternatives carries the greater expected utility. Perhaps the best-known example of an expected utility argument is found in Pascal's *Pensées*, the famous wager argument for Christian belief (see Pascal 1966 [1670]).

The second kind of pragmatic argument, which we will call a "truth-independent" pragmatic argument, is one which recommends believing some proposition p because of the benefits gained simply by believing that p, whether or not p should turn out true. This is an argument which recommends the adoption of a belief because of the psychological, or moral, or religious, or maybe even social benefits gained immediately by adopting that belief. In David Hume's *Dialogues Concerning Natural Religion*, for example, the character Cleanthes asserts that "religion, however corrupted, is still better than no religion at all. The doctrine of a future state is so strong and necessary a security to morals that we never ought to abandon or neglect it" (Hume 1947 [1779], p. 219).

Truth-dependent pragmatic arguments differ from truth-independent ones. Being pragmatic, they are not truth-dependent in an evidential sense; yet they do carry a connection to truth: the benefits mentioned within a particular truth-dependent argument are gained only if the recommended belief turns out true. In truth-independent pragmatic arguments, conversely, the benefits are gained whether or not the recommended belief is true.

Because pragmatic arguments are benefit-directed, it is natural to ask, what constitutes a benefit in this context? A benefit can be seen as a satisfied preference. Benefits, since they are measured by the preferential ranking of the person involved, are largely person-relative, though a case can be made that some preferences are attributable to any person, at least in so far as that person is rational. Further, the benefits invoked by a particular pragmatic argument need not be self-centered prudential benefits only. They may involve the good of other persons, and even the common good of a large number of people. Thus, pragmatic arguments cannot be easily dismissed as morally suspect, selfish appeals to base considerations.

Pascal's Wager

The most celebrated example of a truth-dependent argument is from the French philosopher Blaise Pascal (1623–62).

Let us examine this point and declare: "Either God is or He is not." But to which view shall we incline? Reason cannot decide this question. Infinite chaos separates us. At the extremity of this infinite distance a game is in progress, where either heads or tails may turn up. How will you wager? . . . Let us weigh the gain and the loss involved by wagering that God exists. Let us assess the two cases: if you win, you win all; if you lose, you lose nothing. Do not hesitate then, wager that He does exist.   (Pascal 1966 [1670], pp. 150–1)

There are at least three different versions of the wager found in the complete *Pensées* passage (see Hacking 1972, McClennen 1994). One version, which might be called a *weak dominance* argument, can be paraphrased thus:

Wagering on the existence of God, rather than against it, is a sure thing. In the event that God exists, one who believes does very well; in the event that God does not exist, one who believes does no worse than one who does not believe.

The idea behind this argument is that the one wagering in favor of God existing will, by believing, in no case be in a position worse off than one who does not. The one who wagers against, however, will in some cases be worse off. A weak dominance argument is, then, a "sure-thing" appeal: one cannot lose by wagering in favor of God existing (see Pascal 1966 [1670], pp. 150–1).

353

A second version adds probability values to the wagering context, which allows a calculation of expected utilities:

If the probability of God existing is equal to that of God not existing, and given that the utility of theistic belief, if God exists, is infinite, then the expected utility of believing swamps that of disbelief.

The key idea of this version is that, since the expected utility of disbelief is, presumably, finite, theistic belief will always be recommended since its expected utility is infinite (see Pascal 1966 [1670], p. 151).

A third version of the wager, and perhaps the best-known version, does not presuppose an equiprobability between God existing and not existing:

As long as there is some positive probability that God exists, it follows, since infinity multiplied by any finite amount generates an infinity, that the expected utility of believing that God exists swamps that of disbelief.

The idea here is that no matter how small one takes the odds to be that God exists, believing that God exists none the less carries an infinite expected utility (see Pascal 1966 [1670], p. 151).

Pascal's wager is not an argument that God exists. It is an argument that it is rational to believe that God exists and that it is positively irrational to be irreligious. Rationality is understood in this context as a kind of prudential rationality as opposed to what could be called epistemic rationality. Prudential rationality concerns what is in one's interest, while epistemic rationality is strictly connected to evidence. The distinction between prudential and epistemic rationality is a more general form of the distinction made above between pragmatic and truth-directed arguments.

It may, in fact, be more accurate to say that the wager is an argument in support of trying to believe. The wager provides prudential reason why one should try to bring it about that one believes that God exists. Pascal recognized that belief was not a voluntary matter, at least not directly and immediately so. He suggested that one could inculcate proper belief via roundabout and indirect methods of belief-formation.

One objection to the wager is a partitioning complaint: the wager, as it is framed, neglects all sorts of relevant alternatives. Possible religious hypotheses include not just the existence of the Christian God, but also that of the Islamic God, and the god of the Druids, and even the deity, if such should exist, who would grant eternal life to atheists and condemn to perdition all who believe in any other deity. Indeed, given the cooked-up hypothesis just mentioned, we could come up with any number of incompatible god-possibilities, each one condemning the devotees of every other deity to perdition. This objection to the wager is called the "many-gods objection" and the point of it is that the wager proves too much: given a possible infinite utility and a positive probability, no matter how small, an infinite expected utility is generated. Hence, the wager, instead of uniquely picking out one religious hypothesis to believe, is left with any number of incompatible religious hypotheses, each with an infinite expected utility, and no obvious way to choose among them.

354

The friend of the wager has at least two ways of dealing with this embarrassment of Pascalian riches. The first is to deny that mere logical possibility entails a positive probability. Or, to put the point another way, when calculating probabilities it is common and proper to ignore remotely small probabilities. Consider flipping a coin thought to be fair. When doing so, we say it's fifty–fifty heads or tails, even though there are innumerable other possible occurrences: the coin might land on its edge, it might vanish, it might transform itself into an elephant, and so on. This point holds even if we accept the notion of an infinite utility since when deliberating whether to take an umbrella or not, we ignore the vanishingly small possibility that doing so, or not doing so, could generate an infinite disutility.

A second way of saving Pascal's partitioning of the alternatives is to limit the relevant choices to "live hypotheses" only. A live hypothesis is any proposition not thought to be false and is such that one could believe it without extensive and far-reaching revisions in one's web of beliefs. A live hypothesis can be accommodated more easily than one which is not. The restriction to live hypotheses only entails a person-relativity – a hypothesis live for one person may not be so for another. Understood this way, the wager would be a last step in an apologetic case rather than the first: since the relevant alternatives have been narrowed down to theism and naturalism, the wager is a tie-breaker that recommends theistic belief.

A second objection to the wager involves its use of infinite utilities. The problem here is twofold: what sense, if any, can be made of the idea of an infinite utility, and can standard, axiomatic decision theory accommodate infinite utilities?

The key to understanding Pascal's contention that theistic belief carries, if true, an infinite utility is to remember that, according to Christian theology, afterlife is an endless, sublime existence of which each succeeding moment is as saturated in happiness as each preceding one. Since the idea of afterlife is unending, summing to infinity as it were, it is not too much of a stretch to term this mode of existence an infinite gain. It is a payoff which surpasses any finite good. Is the idea that there are infinite utilities compatible with standard axiomatic systems of standard decision-theory? It is not. The introduction of infinite utilities will generate problems with several of the axioms found in the standard constructions. Is this an intractable problem for the Pascalian? Probably not. For one thing, there is no construction of decision-theory which is without controversy. Further, it is not surprising that theories constructed for finite utilities cannot accommodate infinite ones (see McClennen 1994). Moreover, remembering that the wager is protean, the Pascalian can point out that rational decisions can be framed independent of the standard axiomatic theories, especially since the Pascalian can present the wager-argument in any of its several guises, being neither limited to any one version of the argument nor, apart from the concept of an infinite utility, dependent upon any controversial decision-theoretic principles.

Other prominent pragmatic arguments

Another example of a pragmatic argument is the "will-to-believe" argument of the American pragmatist William James (1842–1910). According to James, there

355

are occasions on which it is rationally and morally permissible to believe a proposition, even in the absence of adequate evidence supporting that proposition (see James 1959 [1897], p. 11).

It is important to notice that James does not endorse the idea that one can properly believe a proposition despite the evidence against it. In the essay "The will to believe," James specifies two conditions that must apply before one can properly believe a hypothesis, James's term for a proposition that lacks adequate evidence (see James 1959 [1897], pp. 2–4). The first condition concerns the evidence for or against a proposition. According to James, whenever a proposition cannot by its nature be declared true or false on intellectual grounds, it is intellectually indeterminate. A proposition is intellectually indeterminate in either of two ways. The first includes situations in which the evidence, pro and con, is balanced. This would be a case of epistemic parity: a tie situation between the evidence pro and con. The second way occurs when there is no evidence known, whether evidence against or in support of the proposition. The two ways can both be understood as involving intellectual indeterminacy in either an in-principle sense, or an in-practice sense, and James's argument can use either sense of indeterminacy. The first condition is, then, that a proposition is intellectually indeterminate.

The second condition concerns what James would call a "genuine option." An option is a choice concerning which of two propositions to believe and it is genuine in the case that it involves a choice which is living, momentous, and forced. An option is living whenever the choice involves propositions that are real possibilities of belief. For example, whether or not to be a theist is probably a real possibility for most Westerners; but the option of being a Druid or not is so remote a possibility that it is dead. Momentous options are those choices upon which something of great importance depends, which are irreversible once made, and which are unlikely to be repeated. A forced option obtains whenever one cannot avoid making a decision by suspending judgment. With regard to any proposition, the choice of whether to believe it true or false is avoidable: one can suspend belief regarding its truth-value. However, if some significant consequence can be had only if one believes a certain proposition, then the choice of whether to believe that proposition or not is forced. If one can receive x only by believing that p, then whether or not to believe that p is forced: if one suspends judgment toward p, one will not receive x.

The principle endorsed by James can be stated thus: *for any person* s *and proposition* p, s *can permissibly believe* p *if* p *is (1) intellectually indeterminate, and (2) is part of a genuine option* (James 1959 [1897], p. 11). Notice that this principle is compatible with the rule that one should believe a proposition if that proposition has the support of evidence in its favor. The normative concept involved in James's principle is best understood as including both rational and moral permissibility.

The application of James's principle to philosophy of religion is as follows. The religious option, according to James, consists of two claims. The first is that what is best or supreme is eternal, and the second is that we are better off even now if we believe the first claim (James 1959 [1897], pp. 25–6). Though vague, the idea, when expressed differently, is that God exists and, if we believe, we are the immediate recipients of assurance and hope and other beneficial states of mind. Also, according to James, the option of whether to believe the religious option or not is living, momentous, and forced – in a word, a genuine option. Moreover, the evidence, pro and con, is undecidable and thus intellectually indeterminate. From this it follows that the religious believer is well within her intellectual rights by believing that God exists.

James's argument provides us with an example of a truth-independent pragmatic argument. James, unlike Pascal, is not gambling on the truth of the claim that God exists. He is banking that theistic belief provides immediate benefit. There is also a hint in James, which he does not formulate fully, that it is only by believing that one will have any real chance of discovering decisive intellectual evidence concerning the existence of God. Believing in the absence of adequate evidence may be, the argument goes, necessary in order to get oneself in a perspective from which adequate evidence is finally obtainable (see James 1959 [1897], pp. 24–5, 27–8). If something like this is correct, then the chasm between prudential rationality and epistemic rationality is, at certain points, bridgable.

In his posthumously published essay *Theism*, J. S. Mill (1806–73) proffers two truth-independent pragmatic arguments in support of the legitimacy of hoping that an attenuated form of theism might be true. The first of Mill's two arguments is similar to James's argument, though unlike James, Mill neither carefully crafts the circumstances in which it is rationally permissible to adopt a positive stance toward theism, nor does he believe that one can permissibly believe religiously. Mill advocates the adoption of hope toward the doctrines and ideals of theism. Like James, Mill is clear that it is permissible to invoke pragmatic considerations only in the absence of strong evidence contra theism (see Mill 1957 [1874], p. 81).

Mill's second pragmatic argument is that theistic belief serves the important function of undergirding morality:

There is another and a most important exercise of imagination which, in the past and present, has been kept up principally by means of religious belief and which is infinitely precious to mankind, so much so that human excellence greatly depends upon . . . it. This consists of the familiarity of the imagination with the conception of a morally perfect Being, and the habit of taking the approbation of such a Being as the *norma* or standard to which to refer and by which to regulate our own characters and lives.   (Mill 1957 [1874], p. 82)

Mill does not argue that religious belief is logically necessary for moral reasoning, but he does argue that it has historically facilitated moral motivation. That is, though one could reason morally independent of religious belief, religion plays a beneficial, causally productive role. Religious belief provides a moral heuristic and an ideal, both of which render moral reasoning more concrete and more accessible. Religious belief provides some content to moral reasoning. So, according to Mill, although there is not enough evidence to render religious belief rationally permissible, one can hope that theism is true and this hope will provide the same benefits that religious belief historically provided (see Mill 1957 [1874], pp. 82–7).

Pragmatic arguments and the ethics of belief

There is a widespread and influential tradition found in Western philosophy, a tradition that we can call "evidentialism," which holds that:

for all persons s and propositions p, it is permissible for s to believe that p only if p is supported by adequate evidence.

Endorsing this evidentialist imperative, many philosophers have held that pragmatic reasons for belief-formation are illegitimate since such reasons do not themselves provide adequate evidence for the truth of the belief. Perhaps the most-quoted statement of the evidentialist imperative is that of W. K. Clifford (1845–79): "it is wrong always, everywhere, and for any one, to believe anything upon insufficient evidence" (Clifford 1879, p. 186). Clearly enough, Clifford formulated the evidentialist imperative in a moral sense: it is morally impermissible to believe something which lacks sufficient evidence. Contrary to Clifford, the normative sense of the imperative can be understood as a cognitive standard: it is irrational to believe something which lacks sufficient evidence. Understood in either sense, is the evidentialist imperative an obstacle to a principled use of pragmatic arguments?

Though one might suppose that employing pragmatic arguments is a clear violation of the evidentialist imperative, it is far from clear that it is. For one thing, the evidentialist imperative is, if it is an obligation, at most a *prima facie* obligation. And if the evidentialist imperative is a *prima facie* obligation, then it is possible, if the pragmatic considerations were to override the epistemic ones, that a use of pragmatic arguments would be compatible with the evidentialist imperative.

Moreover, depending on the precise sense of *adequate* used in the imperative and remembering both Pascal's second version of the wager and the "will-to-believe" argument of James, pragmatic arguments can be used even if the evidentialist imperative is true and is one's actual duty. As long as pragmatic arguments are employed only when a situation of evidential parity exists, there will be no violation of the evidentialist imperative since the pragmatic arguments are employed merely as tie-breakers.

Finally, some philosophers have argued that the evidentialist imperative, though venerable, is in sore need of revision. In particular, some have argued that pragmatic reasons can supplement epistemic reasons in determining whether it is rational to believe a proposition. This idea is based upon the distinction between (1) a proposition p being rational to believe, and (2) believing p being the rational thing to do. Although a particular proposition may not be rationally believable, it could be, none the less, that believing that proposition may be the rational thing, all things considered, to do. In this way the acquisition of a particular belief can be rationally mandated by either (1) or (2), depending upon the circumstances and the person involved (see Nozick 1993, pp. 64–93). If this proposal is correct, then the distinction between epistemic rationality and prudential rationality is narrowed once again.

Bibliography

Clifford, W. K.: *Lectures and Essays*, vol. 2 (London: Macmillan, 1879).

Hacking, Ian: "The logic of Pascal's wager," *American Philosophical Quarterly*, 9 (1972), pp. 186–92.

Hume, D.: *Dialogues Concerning Natural Religion* (1779), ed. N. Kemp Smith (Indianapolis: Bobbs-Merrill, 1947).

James, W.: "The will to believe." In *The Will To Believe and Other Essays in Popular Philosophy* (1897) (New York: Dover, 1959), pp. 1–31.

McClennen, E.: "Pascal's wager and finite decision theory." In *Gambling on God: Essays on Pascal's Wager*, ed. J. Jordan (Lanham: Roman & Littlefield, 1994), pp. 115–37.

Mill, J. S.: *Theism* (1874), ed. R. Taylor (Indianapolis: Bobbs-Merrill, 1957).

Nozick, R.: *The Nature of Rationality* (Princeton: Princeton University Press, 1993).

Pascal, B.: *Pensées* (1670), tr. A. J. Krailsheimer (London: Penguin, 1966).

46

Miracles

GEORGE N. SCHLESINGER

What is a miracle?

The word "miracle" originated from the Latin word for a wonderful thing or a surprise. However, to have religious significance, it is not sufficient that an event be merely wonderful. If the desk in front of me suddenly turned into a water buffalo, I would certainly be stupefied. But since such a fantastic metamorphosis would appear not to serve any divine purpose, the theist would not view it as a miracle.

In the Hebrew Bible a miracle is designated by the word *nes* or *oth* both meaning a sign. The major function of a miracle is to serve as a spectacular manifestation of God's direct intervention in promoting a divine plan, and thus inspire religious sentiments.

There were some who thought that there is an inherent contradiction in the very notion of a "miracle," since a miracle is commonly thought of as a violation of some of nature's laws. However, a regularity which may be broken fails by definition to be a law. Among the various replies to this objection, the one suggested by Richard Purtill is likely to be found fairly congenial. The United States, Purtill points out, has a large set of laws regulating human behavior, but occasionally exceptional procedures are introduced, like presidential pardons. A miracle may be compared to a presidential pardon, in that the origin of the pardon is outside the ordinary legal procedures. It is unpredictable, and plays no role in the maneuvering of a lawyer in the court, since it cannot be brought about by the means available to him during a court procedure. Similarly, the creation of miracles is not within the scope of a scientist's activities. Yet, a presidential pardon does not constitute a violation of the legal system: it is not illegal, it is *outside* the legal system. In a comparable manner a miracle does not violate, but is outside, the system of nature's laws (Purtill 1978, p. 70).

It is important to emphasize that in spite of the widespread belief to the contrary, an event may be the source of marvel and elicit genuine religious response, not only without violating any natural law, but even if all its details may be explained by known laws. As long as an event is genuinely startling and its timing constitutes a mind-boggling coincidence, in that it occurs precisely when there is a distinct call for it to promote some obvious divine objective, then that event amounts to a miracle. The promotion of a divine objective may take many forms: it could be a spectacular act of deliverance of the faithful from the evil forces ranged against them, it might come as a highly unusual meteorological event through which the priests of Baal are discredited, or as a swift, clear, and loud answer to the prayers of the truly pious. However, whatever form the wondrous event takes, it should have a religious impact on its witnesses.

Hume's challenge

Arguably, the most widely discussed challenge to the belief in miracles has been the ingenious, highly compact, epistemological objection by David Hume. A wise man proportions his beliefs to the evidence, says Hume. Wisdom therefore should teach us that,

... no testimony is sufficient to establish a miracle, unless the testimony['s] ... falsehood would be more miraculous, than the fact, which it endeavors to establish.   (Hume 1748)

It will be admitted by those of us lucky enough to have some exceptionally trustworthy friends, that none were so very reliable that any lie or erroneous statement escaping their lips would be no less of a marvel than, say, the sun standing still for Joshua. Thus a rational individual will refuse to give credence to a miracle story which is less probable than a human agent testifying incorrectly.

For over two centuries many attempts have been made to blunt the sharp blow dealt by Hume to the credibility of miracle stories. Some have tried to counter Hume by saying that while he is right in claiming that "... someone who has a strictly scientific view of the world ... can never be convinced of the truth of religion by testimony in favor of miracles" (Dawid and Gillies 1989, p. 64), an individual living in a religious cultural climate, in which the probability of occasional direct divine intervention in the physical world is not believed to be too small, is not prevented from entertaining the possibility of a miracle.

It turns out then that Hume's argument might be circumvented by someone who allowed the possibility of religious knowledge as distinct from empirically based scientific knowledge.   (1989, p. 64)

This suggestion does not seem to help much. Recall that Hume said,

... upon the whole we may conclude that the Christian religion not only was at first attended with miracles, but even at this day cannot be believed by any reasonable person without one.   (Hume 1748)

Clearly miracles occur not for the benefit of the converted but for those who are meant to be attracted to religious belief for the first time. Thus if an agnostic brought up in a secular cultural climate could indeed never be induced through a miracle to change his or her position, then the authors' argument has not succeeded in strengthening, but rather in destroying, the foundations of theism.

Price's argument

A contemporary of Hume, R. Price, devised an argument showing that a fairly reliable individual's testimony is often accepted as adequate evidence even for the most improbable event. He argued that in the case of a lottery where, say, as many as 10^8 tickets have been sold, if an ordinary newspaper reports that ticket number n won the main prize, we believe it without a moment's hesitation. It seems to be of no concern to us that the prior probability for ticket number n to land the biggest amount, was negligibly small, that is 10^{-8} (Price 1767, pp. 410–11).

Price's putative counterexample to Hume's argument does not work. Obviously, the newspaper's report has to be accepted: if it were legitimate to doubt it, we would be committed to the absurdity that we are capable of prophesying at any time before the draw takes place that all the papers will print false information concerning the winner! This follows from the obvious fact that someone is bound to win, yet no matter who is claimed to have done so we are obliged to disbelieve it.

The case of the church choir

Let me cite an actual example which is likely to throw light on some important aspects of a miracle. *Life* magazine (March 27, 1950, p. 19), reported that all fifteen members of a church choir in Beatrice, Nebraska, came at least ten minutes too late for their weekly choir practice that was supposed to start at 7:20 p.m. on March 1, 1950. They were astonishingly fortunate, because at 7:25 the building was destroyed by an explosion. The reasons for the delay of each member were fairly commonplace: none of them was marked by the slightest sign of any supernatural cause. However, nothing remotely resembling the situation that *all* members were prevented from being on time on the same occasion, had ever happened before. Furthermore, this singular event took place precisely when it was needed, on the very night on which they would otherwise have perished. Consequently, some people were inclined to see the incident as a clear instance of divine intervention and a compelling manifestation of God's care and power for everyone to see. How else should one explain such a spectacular coincidence which turned out to be the deliverance of people who were regarded as the most pious, and most intensely devoted to any church-associated work, and thus the most truly worthy to be saved, in a manner which (though it did not violate any law of nature) was too startling to be a mere happenstance?

First of all, let us note that even if the probability of any one member having a compelling reason to arrive late at the devotional activity of choir practice is as much as one in four, the probability that just ten of them should have independent reasons for delay is $(1/4)^{10}$ which is less than one in a million, while for twelve people to have independent reasons for lateness is less than one in 16 million. Thus two important questions arise. First, why is it that practically nobody used Hume's famous argument to cast doubt on *Life*'s story? Second, why was the religious impact of this extraordinary event confined to only a very few people?

Through the answer to the first question, a fairly sound answer to Hume's famous objection will emerge. Some skeptics were reluctant to see a heavenly manifestation in what took place, since they were troubled by the fact that equally "deserving" individuals are only too often abandoned to their bitter fate. Why, then, should certain devout people in Beatrice, Nebraska, be singled out for such special treatment? Others, who assumed that it is inherent in the very nature of miracles not to observe any regularities, were not so much concerned by this, but instead by the problem that the deliverance of the 15 could in fact have occurred in many other ways. For instance, it could have been that all 15 people arrived at the usual time, 7:20, and the explosion took place earlier, at 7:15. However, the church clock which was taken by everyone to be showing the right time was in fact running 10 minutes late. If any such account is correct, there is not that much room to marvel about the way the congregants escaped harm.

At the same time, the grounds for rebutting Hume should now become evident. If the choir members were inclined to give a fantastic account of their delivery, there is no limit to the number of stories they could have invented. They might have claimed that everyone arrived on time, but a few seconds before the explosion, a monstrous apparition frightened them so greatly that they all dashed outside just in time to be away from the explosion. Or they could have claimed that the support beams happened to fall precisely so as to form a fully effective shield against the falling debris, and so on, and so on. Clearly, no more than one account of their deliverance could be true, while there is an infinite scope for fictitious accounts. If the widely advertised story was not true then there is an exceedingly small probability that among the infinitely many possible stories, that particular fabrication (the purely chance synchronization of 15 people's tardiness) is going to be fed to the readers of *Life*. But if the printed story is true there was no choice about what to put in the magazine: there was no more than one true story. Thus here, as in the context of many other miracle stories, it is not the case that, as Hume claimed, we are confronted by a contest between two factors (one being more probable than the other), but between one adverse factor and two supportive factors. The credibility of the miracle story is supported first of all by the assumption that the witnesses are fairly reliable, but also by another very significant factor based on the principle that what has a larger probability is more likely to have happened than what has a smaller probability. Obviously, if the printed story was true and they wanted to make sure to give a truthful report. then the probability that it would be the printed report, was one. However, if the reported story was false, because the people chose to give a false report, then the probability that this particular story was going to be printed (rather than one of its million equally false and dramatic rival fabrications) was exceedingly small.

Acknowledging miracles

There are many more powerful examples to show that no matter how great a miracle may seem to some, others who are bent upon denying it can always explain it away. For instance we read in 1 Kings 13:6 that the wicked king Jeroboam was about to strike the Prophet, and was instantaneously punished by having his outstretched arm paralyzed. This experience shook the king up so much that he suffered a sudden onslaught of piety manifested by his humbly beseeching the prophet: "Entreat now the Lord . . . that my hand may be restored to me." The king's request was granted, and yet in verse 33 we are told ". . . Jeroboam did not turn from his evil way . . ." But what about the sudden paralysis, occurring precisely at the moment when the king was about to strike the holy man, and the equally swift restoration of the king's arm due to the latter's temporary repentance? Was this not a conspicuous enough manifestation of divine intervention? We are not given any account of the King's thought processes, but we know the human mind has sufficient resources to explain away any evidence that runs counter to what it is anxious to believe.

Thus the reasonable theist will acknowledge the existence of three types of individuals: the pious, whose belief is firm enough without being given any extraordinary signs; the pliable agnostic on whom the impact of a prima facie miracle may have a transforming effect; and those who will insist on explaining away any miraculous phenomenon.

Arguments for and against

A source of serious puzzlement has been that if spectacular miracles like the splitting of the Sea of Reeds which was witnessed by over a million people and lasted for several hours are to be believed, why is it that for centuries nothing comparable has been recorded as having happened? It may be noted that this problem constitutes part of the pressure on theists to renounce their belief that such fantastic events are genuinely historical. And indeed in the last hundred years or so the denial of miracles has not been universally regarded as incompatible with theistic belief. No less a person than the Anglican bishop of Birmingham said that "miracles as they are narrated [in the Scriptures] cannot in the light of our modern knowledge of the uniformity of nature, be accepted as historical." Obviously, therefore, this problem, like any other problem concerning miracles is of interest only to believers, who are not prepared to demythologize sacred literature.

Those theists (sometimes labeled "fundamentalists") who read the stories of the Scriptures as literal reports of what actually took place may be able to meet the challenge just described. They could suggest that signs of a divinely ruled universe are evenly distributed throughout history. However those signs assume different forms, forms that are best suited to the prevailing cultural climate. This point merits elaboration.

In several papers, one of the greatest physicists of this century, E. P. Wigner, mentioned a number of phenomena which he called "miracles we neither understand nor deserve." It is only because the features of the universe he was referring to are so familiar that we fail to be astonished by them, but since they are unique in their usefulness, while their possible, unuseful alternatives are vastly more numerous, their actual presence is from an objective point of view very surprising. One of these remarkable features is that at distant places and remote epochs of time the same kind of experiments yielded the same results. Were it otherwise, the scientist's task would most likely lie beyond the powers of human intellect (Wigner 1967).

He also pronounced it simply "unreasonable," in that same famous lecture, that the imaginative creations of mathematicians, prompted by no practical need or purpose, virtually always turn out sooner or later to be of vital use to the empirical scientist. He produced some truly staggering examples, but I shall cite only the simplest one. It was known already in antiquity, that the square root of $+1$ is both $+1$ and -1. Since there is no number which when multiplied by itself results in -1, mathematicians calmly accepted the fact that -1 does not have a square root. Consequently, the Indian mathematician's assertion that an equation like $x^2 = -1$, is impossible to solve, was universally agreed to. But then, in the sixteenth century, an Italian, Rafael Bombelli, said that though in reality there is no number to represent the square root of -1, let us *imagine* what would happen if there *was* a number i such that $i^2 = -1$. Thus began a new branch of mathematics dealing with imaginary numbers and their combinations with real ones, to be called "complex numbers."

Within 300 years this fantasy-born branch of mathematics turned out to be a very important tool in different areas of physics. Is it not simply miraculous, Wigner asked, that ideas not rooted in any facts at all, should turn out to be so much in harmony with the empirical features of the universe?

It seems natural that not everyone was thrilled with Wigner's arguments; his ideas would appear especially repugnant if "miracles" were interpreted in a religious sense, namely as divine manifestations. Michael Gullien, for instance, insisted that we should not read anything supernatural into the mathematician's imagination-spawned abstract results eventually turning out to be indispensable practical tools. He says,

The coincidence between the natural world and the mathematical world is not any more mysterious than the coincidence between the natural world and the auditory, tactile and olfactory worlds. (Gullien 1983, p. 71)

This argument rests on mistakenly regarding all our precious faculties as indispensable weapons in the struggle for survival. It is easy to see how vulnerable the human race would be to adverse forces without the capacity to hear. On the other hand, without the fascinating results of Euler, Gauss, Cantor, and other great mathematicians, though we would be much poorer intellectually and many of the fruits of advanced technology would not be available to us, yet these were not essential for the survival of the human race which flourished for thousands of years with a minimal knowledge of mathematics.

Conclusion

An inquiry into the nature of miracles is bound to illuminate some of the broader aspects of the nature of religious faith. Believers have found a great variety of supportive evidence for their position. Among them are ancient arguments like the argument from design and more recent ones like Pascal's wager. Miraculous events are merely one kind of factor a believer may cite as testifying to the credibility of his or her position. Each one of these factors may have an impact on those susceptible to it. However, none are compelling: anyone resolutely set against the

365

idea of theism is able to resist the power of the best argument or the most wondrous features of the universe. Hence, it is not implausible for the theist to claim that in fact there is no radical difference between different epochs in history with respect to the availability of support for the existence of a perfect being, but the form it may take is bound to vary with the particular stage of development of the human race at any given time. Pascal's wager would have been of little use, say, a thousand years ago when people's notions of the concept of probability and of expected utilities was still confused. The implications of the many exciting features of the physical universe would have been lost on an audience even as late as the sixteenth century, when modern science was at a very early stage. Thus the sources of religious inspiration are bound to vary with the varying stages of knowledge and cultural climate.

Bibliography

Books

Gullien, M.: *Bridges to Infinity* (Los Angeles: Tatcher, 1983).
Hume, D.: *An Inquiry Concerning Human Understanding* (1748), sect. X.
Price, R.: *Four Dissertations* (London: Millar & Cadell, 1767).
Purtill, R. L.: *Thinking about Religion* (Englewood Cliffs: Prentice-Hall, 1978).

Articles

Dawid, P., and Gillies, D.: "A Bayesian analysis of Hume's argument concerning miracles," *Philosophical Quarterly*, 39 (1989), pp. 57–65.
Wigner, E.: "The unreasonable effectiveness of mathematics in the physical sciences," lecture reprinted in *Symmetries and Reflections* (Bloomington: Indiana University Press, 1967).

47

Religious experience

KEITH E. YANDELL

Having an experience

In the sense relevant to religion, to "have an experience" is to be in a conscious state which one is at least somewhat capable of describing. "Having a religious experience" is being in a conscious state that is *soteriologically essential* within a *religion* or *religious conceptual system*.

Religion

A religion or religious conceptual system has two essential components, a *diagnosis* and a *cure*. The diagnosis asserts that every human person has a basic non-physical illness so deep that, unless one is cured, one's potential is unfulfilled and one's nature cripplingly flawed. Then a cure is proffered. Having an experience is, from the perspective of a particular religious tradition, soteriologically essential if and only if one's having it is (according to that religion's proposed cure) a necessary component in being cured of one's illness (as that tradition diagnoses it).

Describability

Religion often is thought of as mainly about the mysterious and incomprehensible. However correct that is so far as it goes, obviously it cannot be the whole story. The claim: "There is something mysterious and incomprehensible," even if sincerely believed, does not have enough content to distinguish a religious devotee from a seeker of the Loch Ness monster or a reader of Sherlock Holmes mysteries who supposes *The Hound of the Baskervilles* to be sober history. Religions offer cures to diagnosed spiritual illnesses, and hence assume sufficient accessible knowledge to make understanding the diagnosis and the cure a possibility. This is why religious traditions tend to describe the achievement of soteriologically essential experiences in cognitive terms, as involving the achievement of knowledge, enlightenment, or understanding. Religious traditions typically talk, not (or not merely) of middle-sized physical objects, but about God, Brahman, Nirvana, and the like. In so far as God, Brahman, Nirvana, or the like are to play any role whatever in either diagnosis or cure, God, Brahman, Nirvana, or the like must be accurately describable relative to the diagnosis or cure. At least some religious traditions are ambivalent about such matters, in effect insisting on indescribability (ineffability) when under the pressure of a "how different from ourselves is ultimate reality" line but presupposing describability (effability) when pursuing a "how relevant to our deepest needs is ultimate reality" theme.

Phenomenology

A phenomenological description of an experience is one given by its subject that says how things experientially seem to the subject. If Mary knowingly sees a mirage, she will not believe that she sees an oasis, but it will experientially seem to her that she does, just as it will experientially seem to her that she sees an oasis when she does. A phenomenological description will be cast in language neutral as to whether things are as they seem to the subject. The claim that Mary has an experience in which she seems to see an oasis leaves it open whether or not there is an oasis that she sees. Phenomenological descriptions of religious experiences allow for descriptive accuracy in the absence of commitment, for or against, regarding the reliability of the experiences described.

It is important to have cross-cultural information about religious experiences. This helps one avoid conclusions that depend on the peculiarities of one particular cultural setting. The primary source for cross-cultural information regarding religious experiences is descriptions of such experiences in sacred texts, religious writings, and the like. Some scholars are deeply suspicious of such reports, believing that the experiences in question are so "contaminated" by their being reported in the sort of language native to the subject's own religious tradition as to be worthless as reliable clues to what the experiences were really like. Other scholars take the view that the concepts and expectations learned from a subject's religious tradition are so constitutive of her experiences that they are its creatures, produced by the tradition in question in conjunction with the subject's needs, and thus possessed of a sort of internal uniqueness peculiar to whatever tradition or even subtradition she belongs to. The former sort of scholar wants to prise off the alleged conceptual overlay to see the experience in its naked form; the latter sort of scholar holds that nothing would survive the prising off process.

Each perspective has its point, and its limitation. Consider one's consciously seeing, in imagination with one's eyes closed, a red dot against a white background. In order to perform this modest feat, one must have the concepts *red*, *white*, *dot*, and *background*. The features of the experience that render these concepts applicable are essential to the experience; remove them and there is no experience to be had. Accessibility to these concepts is constitutive of the experience. But this need introduce no epistemological contamination; the subject who reports "I am imagining a red dot against a white background" reports accurately, even if she belongs to a strange cult in which such imaginings are alleged to yield instant immortality. If she belongs to such a cult, and reports the experience by saying "I have achieved immortality," she overreports, going considerably beyond her own phenomenology. Here, one can see the point of insisting that the phenomenology of the experience is accurately captured by the first report, and left well behind by the second. Even if she, upon her imagining, feels as if she has achieved immortality, a sheer report will come in some such terms as "I feel as if I have just become immortal."

I draw two morals. No experience lacks features that make concepts applicable to it; such accessibility is an inherent feature of experiences. Being accessible to concepts is no barrier to an experience being reliable, and no reason by itself to think an experience a mere artifact of the subject and his background. These morals apply to religious experiences as much as to any others.

Criteria for kinds: content

The experiences that persons have, religious or not, fall into different kinds by virtue of two different features: structure and content. Auditory experience differs from visual, tactual experience from olfactory, by virtue of content. Similarly, joy differs from guilt, awe from disgust, pleasure from pain, by virtue of content. In more general terms, aesthetic appreciation differs from moral obligation, perceiving physical objects differs from reflecting on modal logic, sadly reflecting on the current condition of the Boston Celtics differs from remembering their glory days, by virtue of content. The prima facie evidence is that religious experiences differ in kind by virtue of content.

Criteria for kinds: structure

Experiences also differ by virtue of structure. Feeling nauseous, dizzy, or lonely has a different structure than seeing a tree, hearing a bell, or smelling the perking coffee. The former experiences are *subject/content*; the experience's "owner" feels a certain way. The latter experiences are *subject/consciousness/object*; the experience's "owner" senses (or seems to sense) a particular object – a tree, a bell, or coffee. To have generalized anxiety or euphoria, panic attacks, or a headache, is to have subject/content experience. To be anxious about the large dog pulling at his chain, euphoric at the thought of buttermilk doughnuts, or pained by a friend's harsh words, is to have a subject/consciousness/object experience. The prima facie evidence is that religious experiences differ in kind by virtue of structure.

Object claims

All religious traditions make what we might call object claims. An item O is an object relative to Mary if and only if "Mary does not exist," by itself or with any set of truths, *does not* entail "O does not exist." God, Brahman, Nirvana, and so on through the beings and states that various religious traditions talk about in ways centrally relevant to the diagnoses and cures they offer are, in this sense, *objects* relative to human beings. An *object claim* asserts that some object exists or has some quality; an *experiential object claim* is an object claim made by someone on the basis of some experience that he has had. A mind-body materialist will want to

369

add to our definition of object claim some such phrase as "*O* is not one's body" or "*O* is not one's brain," though I will not.

It is a consequence of this definition that, if a robust theism is true, Mary is not an object relative to God. A robust theism is true if and only if either (i) *God exists* is a necessary truth or (ii) *God exists* is a logically contingent truth, and (iii) *Anything that logically possibly depends on God for its existence does depend on God for its existence* is a necessary truth. But if either (i) and (iii), or (ii) and (iii) are true, God's non-existence will entail Mary's non-existence. This definition would be problematic, at least for a theist, if it entailed that Mary could not be a *creature* relative to God or Mary must be a *mode* or *state* of God rather than a *substance*. But none of these things do follow. Mary need not, in my technically defined sense, be an *object relative to God* in order for Mary to be, say, *a libertarianly free self-conscious substance* (i.e. a person). It does follow that God will not be in a position to use the principle of experiential evidence in which our notion of an *object* plays a role as part of God's basis for knowing that Mary exists. But it would be an odd notion of divine knowledge on which that was necessary.

Aspect claims

An item *a* is an aspect relative to Mary if and only if "Mary does not exist," by itself or with some set of truths, *does* entail "*a* does not exist." God, Brahman, Nirvana, and so on through the beings and states that various religious traditions talk about in ways centrally relevant to the diagnoses and cures they offer are not, in this sense, *aspects* relative to human beings. An *aspect claim* asserts that some aspect exists or has some quality; an *experiential aspect claim* is an aspect claim made by someone on the basis of some experience that he has had.

Relevance conditions

Seeing my computer screen does not provide me with evidence that the next president of the United States will be a Martian; not every experience is evidence for every claim. How does one tell what the evidential potential of an experience is? The answer is fairly simple: Mary's experience *e* provides evidence that some object or aspect exists or has some quality only if Mary's having *e* is a matter of its experientially seeming to Mary that the object or aspect in question exists or has the quality in question. Such experiences meet the appropriate relevance conditions for such claims.

Content, structure, and evidence

The structure of an experience is relevant to what it can be evidence for. Subject/aspect experiences can be non-inferential evidence for experiential aspect claims. Subject/consciousness/object experiences can be non-inferential evidence for experiential object claims.

Having an experience can provide one with evidence in favor of some claim in either of two ways. The evidence can be *direct* or *indirect*. Feeling dizzy provides direct evidence for "I am dizzy." Were there a well-established theory, known to me as such, to the effect that *Feelings of dizziness arise because of chocolate deprivation*, my feeling dizzy would provide indirect evidence for "I am chocolate deprived." Subject/content experiences, if they provide direct evidence for anything, can provide direct evidence for claims about their owners. Subject/consciousness/object experiences, if they provide direct evidence for anything, can provide direct evidence for claims about things other than their owners. Our focus here is only on religious experiences as possible direct evidence. Obviously, what indirect evidence they provide depends on what theories are known to be well-established, and that is a large topic on its own, beyond our concerns here.

A modest typology

Exactly how many basic kinds of religious experience there are, or how many sub-types fall under a given kind, is a more complex, but also less central, issue than whether there is more than a single basic kind. Given their structure and content, it is tolerably clear that there is more than one basic sort of religious experience.

There is *enlightenment experience* – Nirvana is central in the Buddhist traditions, *kevala* in the Jain tradition, *moksha* in Advaita Vedanta Hinduism (see Article 1, HINDUISM; and Article 2, BUDDHISM). Briefly described in terms of their religious significance according to their own traditions, these can be characterized as follows. Nirvana experience is constituted by an awareness of the fleeting states of consciousness, or else of their cessation and the inner stillness that this involves. Kevala experience is an awareness of the abiding self that underlies our fleeting conscious states and is presupposed by, though ignored in, Nirvana experiences. Moksha experience involves an awareness of the identity of oneself with quality-less Brahman. As even these brief characterizations suggest, these experiences differ significantly in content from one another, let alone from the other proposed types. Each of them seems to be subject/content rather than subject/consciousness/object in structure.

There is *numinous experience* which, according to monotheistic traditions, is awareness of God (see Article 5, JUDAISM; Article 6, CHRISTIANITY; and Article 7, ISLAM). Reliable or not, it is subject/consciousness/object in structure. The subject experiences an awesome, overpowering, majestic, holy, living, personal Being who elicits awe, a sense of one's creaturehood and dependence, an awareness of one's sinfulness, repentance, and worship. God may be experienced as stern judge or as loving savior. But the subject of numinous experience does not suppose herself to be experiencing an aspect of her own being or something with which she is identical.

There is *nature mysticism* which involves a sense of empathy with nature directed at whatever part of nature is perceptually available to the subject of the experience while she has the experience. Perhaps the greatest barrier to viewing this as a religious experience is its relative lack of a tight connection to religion conceived as a set of institutions and practices. Given attention to experiential structure and phenomenology, religious experiences seem to belong to at least three different types.

Explanations

If Mary is having an experience (of whatever sort), there will be various sorts of explanation relevant to her doing so. Presumably her body is in some states such that, were it not in those states or in some similar ones, she would not be having that experience – at least not in the particular way in which she is in fact having it. Suppose that Mary is having the experience *seeing her first gray hair*. She would not be having this experience if, for example, she had been decapitated, were brain dead, or suffered blindness; there will be physiological conditions requisite to, and to that degree physiological explanations of, her having her gray-hair experience. There will be features of her physical environment that are also requisite conditions of her having her experience; were it dark, were there no adequately reflecting surface, or were she wearing a paper bag over her head, she would not be seeing her first gray hair. In so far as features of her physical environment are requisite conditions of her having her experience, reference to such features has explanatory relevance to her having her experience. Perhaps Mary's experience is more fully described as *seeing with horror her first gray hair* or as *seeing with delight her first gray hair*. If her experience is of the former sort, perhaps Mary has been raised in a culture that makes a fetish of youth and thinks of the un-young as ugly and worthless; if of the latter, perhaps Mary dwells in a culture in which age is associated with wisdom and authority, whereas the young are viewed as frivolous creatures not to be taken seriously. In either case, there will be sociological features that are requisite conditions of Mary having the particular experience that she has, and which thus have explanatory relevance to its occurrence. Perhaps Mary's experience is more fully described as *seeing, with resolute rebellion, her first gray hair* or as *seeing, with philosophical resignation, her first gray hair*. If her experience is of the former sort, perhaps Mary is the sort of person whose self-image is of one with vibrant youth and before long she will be having another experience describable along the lines of *noting with satisfaction that the dye has erased all traces of gray*; if it is of the latter sort, perhaps Mary views herself as one who takes what comes, accepting what is natural, and it simply would not occur to her to dye her hair. In either case, there will be requisite psychological conditions of Mary having the particular experience that she has, and which thus have explanatory relevance to its occurrence. Yet none of these explanations in any way calls into question whether Mary actually did see a gray hair on her head.

Similarly, any religious experience that a human person has will be accessible to multiple sorts of explanation. For example, a numinous experience may be so expressed that God is described as a king, a father, a mother, or a rock. God's power may be characterized by saying that God can make a camel go through the eye of a needle or as God's having a thousand arms, and divine knowledge as God's knowing the end from the beginning or as having a thousand eyes. A religious experience may relieve a deep anxiety, remove fear of death, provide

372

release from a sense of guilt, give new meaning to one's life, create a sense of vocation, or function in various psychologically significant ways. The social and political structures of one's culture, metaphors drawn from one's experience of nature and society, one's psychological needs, the ways in which persons are conceived in one's culture, and the like, inevitably play a role in the descriptions a subject offers of his religious experiences. There is nothing in this that inherently robs religious experience of whatever evidential force it might have.

The doctrines of the traditions

The doctrines of the traditions generally thought of as religious – including those constitutively involved in their proffered diagnoses and cures – understandably concern matters other than the immediate conscious awareness of human persons. No religion of interest could be woven from threads so thin as those provided by "I do not feel tired at the moment," "I feel slightly nauseous," or "I feel calm." The same holds for experiences reported by "It is as if I were distinctionlessly united with nature" or "I seemed to be in the presence of God" unless it is somehow to be a live option that one was distinctionlessly united with nature or in God's presence. Losing all sense of time has no religious significance unless it is a matter of *seeming to be timeless* in such a manner that what seemed so might be so. Whatever their actual status, religions do not typically purport to be systematizations of peculiar feelings or sensations – a sort of lake of data to be drained by abnormal psychology. The diagnoses and cures are supposed to be appropriate, given persons and their cosmic environment – matters plainly not limited to the feeling contents of the subjects of religious experience or to such introspectively evident features of their psyches as that they do not feel weary, do feel nauseous, or are enjoying calm. This is highly relevant when one asks what sorts of claims, if any, enjoy evidential support based on religious experience.

The appropriateness of asking about evidence

Three perspectives find questions of evidence irrelevant if not destructive. A purely secularist, opposed-to-all-religion position takes it to have been established that all religious doctrines yet offered have been shown to be false, and is quite willing to infer that any doctrinal replacements will suffer a similar fate. Since the great work in which it was shown that all religious doctrines are false is uncommonly hard to locate – it is hard to think of any barely plausible candidates – pure secularism possesses an unfounded optimism about its status and prospects.

Fideism, secular or religious, proclaims matters of religion inherently inaccessible to issues of evidence. Fideism rests on a skepticism itself hard to support, and dubiously compatible with any one having any reason to be a fideist. Nor, of course, is it inappropriate to ask for reasons for fideism, which is not itself a religion but a theory about religions.

Purely pragmatic practitioners purport to care only for the psychological and physical benefits alleged to be provided by religious experiences, and evaluate

373

such experiences only in terms of the emotional support and curative power they believe such experiences to have. While one of course can pursue a purely pragmatic approach if one wishes, it is hard to see why that possibility should get in the way of the possibility of considering questions concerning the evidential force, if any, of religious experience. Further, the very assumptions about what is beneficial, what needs to be cured or healed, and what counts as curing or healing, are all likely to be in the same epistemological boat as the religious diagnoses and cures themselves. Are we then to adopt a second-order pragmatism about these assumptions, and perhaps a third-order pragmatism about that perspective? It seems perfectly in order to query whether a proposed cure is, even if achieved, worth the having, and whether, if so, it is accessible by the proposed means – and one may as well raise these questions at the ground floor level. In so far as practitioners claim any success, they make claims that immediately go beyond sheer pragmatism.

A principle of experiential evidence

A principle of experiential evidence, if it gets things right, tells us when an experience is evidence for a claim based on it. It should recognize two fundamental points: that things experientially seem to be a certain way is evidence that things are as they seem, at least provided we do not have reason to think the experience in question unreliable; none the less, an experience may be unreliable. Here is one such principle:

(P)   Mary's experience *e* provides evidence for claim *c* if and only if (1) *c* is an experiential object or aspect claim made by Mary, (2) *e* meets the relevance conditions regarding *c*, and (3) Mary has no reason to doubt *e*'s reliability.

Subject/consciousness/object experiences with monotheistic content, for example, could provide evidence that God exists; subject/content experiences could provide evidence that the subject of an experience possessed certain aspects. By contrast, qualities such as *being immortal* or *being omniscient*, which are aspects of anything that has them, have this feature: one's seeming to oneself to be immortal or omniscient is no evidence whatever that one is immortal or omniscient, nor – in contrast to such features as *feeling calm* or *being in pain* – is there phenomenological content directly connected with such features. No religious experience could provide direct evidence that its subject had such aspects as *being immortal* or *being omniscient*.

Here is one way of thinking about experiential evidence: an experience *is evidence* for a claim if it is reliable and meets the requisite relevance conditions; it is *properly accepted as evidence* by one who knows the experience has occurred, that it meets the requisite relevance conditions, and non-culpably has no reason for thinking it unreliable; an experience is *good evidence* if it *is* evidence and is properly accepted by the person who appeals to it.

Subject/consciousness/object religious experiences, then, have positive direct evidential potential regarding religious beliefs actually held within religious traditions. Subject/aspect experiences do not possess direct positive evidential potential.

Bibliography

Beardsworth, T.: *A Sense of Presence* (Oxford: Religious Experience Research Unit, 1977).

Bowker, J.: *The Sense of God* (Oxford: Clarendon Press, 1973).

Griffiths, P. J.: *On Being Mindless* (LaSalle: Open Court, 1986).

Hardy, A.: *The Spiritual Nature of Man* (Oxford: Clarendon Press, 1979).

Pike, N.: *Mystic Union: An Essay in the Phenomenology of Mysticism* (Ithaca: Cornell University Press, 1992).

Wainwright, W. J.: *Mysticism* (Madison: University of Wisconsin Press, 1981).

Wood, T.: *Mind-Only* (Honolulu: University of Hawaii Press, 1991).

Yandell, K. E.: *The Epistemology of Religious Experience* (Cambridge: Cambridge University Press, 1993).

48

Fideism

TERENCE PENELHUM

Philosophical defenders of faith have commonly tried to show that it is not at odds with reason: that it is internally consistent, that it accords with scientific knowledge, or even, more positively, that some of its tenets can be established independently by philosophical reasoning. Fideists reject this mode of apologetic argument, and maintain, in contrast, that faith does not need the support of reason, and should not seek it.

Moderate and radical fideism

There are many possible forms of fideism, because the concept of reason is so multifaceted. We may also class a fideistic position as moderate or radical. Probably the least radical is one which merely denies the possibility or the need of justifying theistic belief through argument (that is, of natural theology). Such a denial may have theological reasons (such as the claim that human reason is too corrupted by sin to attain to knowledge of God on its own) or be based on epistemological considerations. One can reject natural theology for reasons such as these without supposing that faith collides with reason in any other way – by being an inevitable source of paradox, for example, or by being at odds with the canons of prudence.

If we call an apologetic fideistic merely because it rejects the demand for natural theology, two well-known contemporary positions must be classed as forms of fideism. One is Reformed epistemology, which does not hold natural theology to be impossible, but rejects the foundationalist (or evidentialist) thesis that faith can only be judged rational if independent non-theistic grounds can be offered for it (see Article 49, REFORMED EPISTEMOLOGY). It is not committed to other, more radical fideistic doctrines (Plantinga 1983). Another is what has been called Wittgensteinian fideism: the position that religious discourse has its own logic that can only be appreciated by a participant, and must not be judged by criteria derived from other kinds of discourse or confronted by questions about the existence of God. The rejection of traditional existence-questions has led proponents of this position to adopt an antirealist understanding of religious language that contrasts sharply with that of Reformed epistemology (Nielsen 1967). Both these positions, while questioning traditional supports of faith, emphasize that faith has, or is, its own form of rationality. So it is necessary to be cautious about where fideism, in its moderate form, begins.

There is, however, no doubt what some of its radical versions tell us. We find (in

Tertullian and Søren Kierkegaard) the view that any proper understanding of faith shows that it inevitably generates paradoxes. We find (in Kierkegaard) the view that faith is prudentially and morally foolish. Although claims like these oppose faith and reason, it is important to recognize that they can still be argued on philosophical grounds. To claim that faith cannot make rational sense is analogous to the claim that morality cannot be justified by the criteria of rational self-interest, even though many philosophers have tried to give it credentials by arguing that it can. It is a consequence of such a view that the transition to faith from a life lived hitherto without it cannot be a reasoned transition but only a "leap" from one mode of personal being to another – a sort of rebirth.

A fideist, then, will hold that faith does not need, or does not manifest, some form of rationality, and will proclaim this in its defense. Most commonly the fideist will hold that faith does not meet standards of evidence or proof, but may go further and maintain its proclamations are paradoxical. In both its moderate and its radical form, fideism will involve the denigration of reason as a source of spiritual truth, and will find grounds in the nature of faith for holding that its support is a liability rather than an asset.

Fideism and skepticism

If this understanding of the fideistic tradition is sound, it is not hard to see why it has shown an otherwise strange affinity for skepticism. The skeptic claims to expose fundamental weaknesses in the power of reason to lead us to knowledge of reality, and these claims are readily seen by the fideist as opening the way for faith by undermining philosophical attempts to establish it in the wrong way. Hence the phenomenon, striking in the early modern era, of *skeptical fideism*.

Skeptical fideism took two forms. Some fideists sought to present faith as a non-dogmatic acceptance of traditional conventions and practices, much as the Pyrrhonists of antiquity abandoned the philosophical search for truth and acquiesced in the local pieties of their culture. I have elsewhere called this *conformist fideism*; it is to be found (at least intermittently) in Michel Montaigne and Pierre Bayle. Other fideists, recognizing that the enervating conventionality of the conformist stance is deeply at odds with the commitment of real faith, see the skeptic as an unwitting ally who exposes the pretensions of reason so that faith can then step in and fill the spiritual gap the skeptic has helped to create. We find this position, which I have called *evangelical fideism*, in Blaise Pascal and Kierkegaard. The arguments I shall examine here are all to be found in their writings. Only some of them depend on the concessions they make to skepticism.

Some key fideist arguments

The core of fideism is the insistence that faith is not a mere matter of assent to doctrines, but a state of trust and commitment of which the object is God himself, not a series of propositions about him. The obstacle to faith in each of us is a sinful self-centeredness that makes us reject the signs of God's presence that he has revealed

377

to us. While faith is the only cure for human ills, humans have elected to use their intellectual powers to seek a cure on their own. Reason requires an objectivity and detachment that is appropriate in science but is an evasion of the passionate involvement required to attain salvation. Faith requires rebirth and submission. Without these, God's presence will remain hidden from us.

These arguments do not show the undesirability of attempts to support faith by argument. The implied censure of the motives of philosophers who have attempted this may fit the attitudes of René Descartes and G. W. F. Hegel, who were the models of rationalism for Pascal and Kierkegaard, but they fail to fit those of Anselm and Thomas Aquinas. The intellectual objectivity necessary for the consideration of philosophical arguments no more shows the pridefulness of those who engage in them than the detachment of medical researchers shows them not to care for healing. It is indeed true that faith and intellectual assent cannot be equated; but this does not show that the trust and submission of faith cannot follow from a recognition of God's reality and love, and that these cannot be shown to us through the intellect. And if it is true that the barrier to faith is pride and sinfulness, these would not show that God's reality and love could not be proved to us by argument: only that if they were, we would exercise our freedom in the wrong way and refuse to concede that they had been. In fact, the existence of proofs of God would help to show that unbelief was indeed due to sin, since only some form of willful self-deception could explain why those to whom his reality was demonstrated refused to concede it. Failing this, unbelief would always have another excuse. This last also shows that the skeptic is not the real ally of faith, since if skepticism is true then unbelief could be explained by our intellectual incapacity as well as by our wickedness.

In short, if it is indeed human corruption that keeps us from God, it is more likely to be manifested in our refusing to concede the cogency of arguments in faith's support than in our laboring to create them.

In addition to arguments based on the supposed motives of a philosophical search for God, Pascal and Kierkegaard maintain that failure in such a search is inevitable because of God's hiddenness. This theme is perhaps the most enduring legacy of fideism. Pascal holds that God discloses himself when he chooses, and that the signs of his presence are clear to those who earnestly seek him, but not to those hindered by their unwillingness to acknowledge him. Kierkegaard, in his parable of the prince who woos the humble maiden (see Kierkegaard 1985), tells us that God enters history in a way that seeks a loving response from his creatures. Since revealing himself in his full power and glory would overwhelm us and elicit a response based on fear or self-interest, he must necessarily appear in disguise, as a humble servant. While their views differ importantly, they concur in saying that there can be no clear sign for those who do not turn to him for rescue from their corrupt condition. There can be no signs that reveal God unambiguously. In Kierkegaard's language, faith does not only require passionate commitment, but a commitment in the face of objective uncertainty.

But if God hides himself from any of his creatures because of their corruption, he may hide himself from them even if there are phenomena that prove his reality conclusively: for their corruption would prevent their heeding the clear implications of these phenomena. If the signs are indeed inconclusive, then this very fact would give those who are confronted with them a reason for conscientious hesitation. (This is a necessary truth.) While it is true that an overwhelming manifestation of God's presence would take away his creatures' freedom and lead to responses based on fear, there is no reason to suppose that every phenomenon that placed his presence beyond reasonable doubt would have to be overwhelming. Not all miraculous occurrences need be overwhelming; and certainly philosophical demonstrations would not be. The claim that God must be hidden because if he were apparent, even to the intellect, our freedom to respond to him in loving submission would be taken away, confuses the epistemic requirements of proof with other circumstances that have attended some major revelatory events. And the fact that it would, in some circumstance, be perverse or unreasonable to say no to a sign or an argument, does not show that human beings do not have the freedom to say no in spite of this. Our very ability to be unreasonable in this way is surely one of the manifestations of the corruption in our natures.

The classic fideistic arguments against the use of philosophical reasoning in apologetics are therefore weak ones, even though the fideist is right to emphasize that faith in God is far from identical with assent to the conclusion of an argument. While the demands of faith make it understandable that arguments for God should encounter widespread rejection, they do not make it necessary that they should be probative failures. If they are probative failures, this rather constitutes a *problem* for the apologist, for whom it should be puzzling that doubters have good reason for their hesitations.

Radical fideism

There are two views of the "leap" of faith. While the moderate fideist, like Pascal, will emphasize that faith and philosophical reasoning are incompatible in their motive and the truths of faith are beyond the power of reason to attain, the radical fideist tells us that faith is flatly contrary to reason, involving those who have it in the passionate espousal of paradox and the active flouting of reason's canons. Tertullian, Bayle, and Kierkegaard insist that Christian proclamations, most notably those of the Incarnation and the Trinity, do not merely look paradoxical but must genuinely be so, and that the believer must knowingly brush aside the claims that reason makes when faith confronts it. Tertullian, notoriously, said that he believed not although, but because, it was absurd. Bayle says there is a religion of the heart as well as of the head, and that one must believe even though the light of reason teaches that what one believes is false. Kierkegaard argues that Christian faith is doubly paradoxical: the divine act of Incarnation that the believer acknowledges is paradoxical; and the acknowledgment of it, which involves a leap of acceptance in the face not merely of inadequate evidence but of sheer contradiction, is a logical scandal that resists all attempts of rationalizing apologists to domesticate it.

It is hard for the philosopher to respond to radical fideism, since the radical fideist seems to reject all the rules to which a philosopher can appeal. The fideist seems on the surface to have chosen to accept the claims of one authority and to have brushed aside the protests of another: to have decided to treat the urgings of his or her own intellect as though they are like the urging of those residual sinful desires that faith helps believers to overcome. But this appearance is deceptive.

There is no logical difficulty in the suggestion that one might hold, even with passion, some doctrine that is self-contradictory, yet not realize it. Consciously living inconsistency is another matter. If I myself think that something I believe is truly paradoxical, then, although I may indeed come to believe it from a variety of causes (including the encounter with someone I think has divine authority), I will also have come to believe in its falsity. I will then have a conflict of beliefs. To say that I have come to embrace it wholeheartedly in all its paradoxicality is to say that I do not, after all, have the belief in its falsity with which the belief in its truth is contending in my psyche. The radical fideist evinces an inner conflict but maintains verbally that it is resolved. One cannot resolve such a clash by denying its presence. One can, of course, over time, weaken, and even extinguish, one of the competitors (through inattention, compartmentalization, or sheer recitation of its contrary), but in this case that would necessarily mean that one no longer judges the faith-commitment to be paradoxical. To say before that happens that one has chosen faith over reason is to indulge in a self-deceiving denial of an inner conflict that is bound to continue as long as the consciousness of reason's negative judgment does. That the conflict is less than agonizing in some people (that the passion is a happy one) merely shows that self-deception is often successful. For all its insistence on the spiritual purity of faith, radical fideism is a form of false consciousness.

Parity

There is an important argument that both Pascal and Kierkegaard use, which I have elsewhere called the *parity argument*. As found in their work, it includes the skeptical premise that many commonsense beliefs share with faith the feature that they are beyond rational justification. If this is so, the situation of faith is no worse than that of many secular forms of belief, and they should be recognized to involve faith also. (Kierkegaard speaks of secular faith as well as religious.) This argument, in spite of appearing in many facile forms in popular preaching, is fundamentally a sound one: there is an obvious inconsistency in dismissing faith as irrational merely because of the fact (if it is one) that it involves a leap beyond evidence in the way that perceptual or inductive beliefs are thought to do. But in spite of the soundness of the argument as an apologetic maneuver, it can be, and has been, detached from its fideistic connections. The analogy between religious beliefs and those dependent on perception or memory or induction is a staple of Reformed epistemology, where the skeptical overtones are eliminated: it is now maintained that just as these secular beliefs do not need the independent support of philosophical argument to be properly classified as rational, or even as forms of knowledge, the same is true of those beliefs that form the cognitive core of faith. The analogy is used as an argument for holding that the evidentialist criteria of rationality are too narrow. It could well be maintained that the appeal of fideism derives from assuming the correctness of these criteria and then reacting in the wrong way to their implications. (It can also be noticed that once these criteria of rationality are abandoned, there is no reason to reject any independent philosophical support for faith that natural theology might offer, since it need not be offered as a guarantee of faith's reasonableness, but only as an additional sign of its truth.)

Faith and practical reason

Discussions of faith and reason usually center on how far faith does or should conform to standards of cognitive rationality. But the fideist tradition also has things to say about how far the life of faith conforms to standards of practical rationality.

Pascal tells us that faith is God known by the heart, not the reason, and (more famously) that the heart has its reasons that reason does not know. But the passage in the *Pensées* that has always engaged the philosophers' attention is the wager argument, in which Pascal urges a serious but unbelieving reader to recognize the advantages of faith over unbelief as a way of minimizing the risks one runs in the face of eternity (see Article 45, PRAGMATIC ARGUMENTS). This is a clear appeal to prudence (and is based on the stated assumption that there are no better theoretical grounds for belief than for unbelief). Pascal urges his unbeliever to adopt various devices to induce belief in himself in spite of the absence of convincing grounds for it. Pascal's critics think this appeal compromises the spiritual purity of any belief that could result from it. However, Pascal's understanding of faith is not thus compromised. For the unbeliever is urged to take steps that might lead to faith; it is no part of Pascal's case that someone following this prudential course already has it. We may assume that if genuine faith were to result from the course of action Pascal recommends, the prudential motive will have been replaced. On the other hand, it is true that by using this argument Pascal has emphasized one form of rationality that can assist faith's emergence; and we can suppose that even if similarly impure motives (such as curiosity) might inspire thinkers to study the cognitive credentials of faith, they too could be succeeded by a faith that was sustained by quite different motives.

Are fideists right to suppose that faith itself does not satisfy the standards of practical rationality? Notoriously Kierkegaard thinks this. He believes faith to be a passion; and his panegyrics on Abraham, the paradigm of faith, emphasize that his unanxious response to the command to sacrifice Isaac is unintelligible to prudential and to moral reason. But it is not obvious that someone who has come to think that the claims of the faith are true, or even, less definitely, that there is some degree of likelihood that they are true, should not respond passionately to this, and should not have his or her life transformed by this. For we judge passions, and the lives based on them, as being foolish or wise, in the light of how the person who feels them and lives them is responding to the truth as he or she perceives it. And given what believers come to believe, or even think may be likely, faith and personal transformation may well be fully reasonable responses. The

381

caricature of faith as a passionate and wholehearted certainty about matters that are uncertain is a deeply mistaken one. Fideism, unfortunately, has helped create and perpetuate it.

Bibliography

Kierkegaard, S.: *Concluding Unscientific Postscript*, tr. D. F. Swenson and W. Lowrie (Princeton: Princeton University Press, 1941).

——: *Fear and Trembling*, tr. H. V. Hong and E. H. Hong (Princeton: Princeton University Press, 1983).

——: *Philosophical Fragments*, tr. H. V. Hong and E. H. Hong (Princeton: Princeton University Press, 1985).

Nielsen, K.: "Wittgensteinian fideism," *Philosophy*, 42 (1967), pp. 191–209.

Pascal, B.: *Pensées*, tr. A. Krailsheimer (Harmondsworth: Penguin, 1966).

Penelhum, T.: *God and Skepticism* (Dordrecht: Reidel, 1983).

——: *Reason and Religious Faith* (Boulder: Westview, 1995).

Plantinga, A.: "Reason and belief in God." In *Faith and Rationality*, ed. A. Plantinga and N. Wolterstorff (Notre Dame: University of Notre Dame Press, 1983), pp. 16–93.

49

Reformed epistemology

ALVIN PLANTINGA

One of the main disputed questions since the Enlightenment has been the question whether religious belief – Christian belief, let's say – is *rational* or *reasonable* or *acceptable* or *justified*. Reformed epistemology (so called because some of its adherents taught at Calvin College and to some extent looked for inspiration to John Calvin and others in the tradition of Reformed theology) is a position in the epistemology of religious belief. Despite its evocation of the Protestant Reformation, the name is *not* meant to suggest that Roman Catholic theology or epistemology stands in need of reformation. Among the architects of Reformed epistemology are Nicholas Wolterstorff and Alvin Plantinga, both long-term professors at Calvin College, and William P. Alston, who, while showing little interest in the label (holding out for "Episcopalian epistemology"), has written (*Perceiving God*) one of the most powerful developments of some of the main themes of Reformed epistemology.

Reformed epistemology has focused on belief in God as conceived in traditional Christianity, Judaism, and Islam: an almighty, all-knowing, wholly benevolent and loving immaterial person (see Article 28, OMNIPOTENCE; Article 29, OMNISCIENCE; and Article 30, GOODNESS) who has created the world, created human beings in his own image, and continues to act in the world by way of providential care for his creatures (see Article 39, CREATION AND CONSERVATION; Article 38, DIVINE ACTION; and Article 72, PROVIDENCE AND PREDESTINATION). And its principal claim is that belief in God (so thought of) can be "properly basic." What does that mean, and why is it important?

To give an answer requires us to make a brief historical excursion. Note first that for most of the twentieth century, discussion of the rational acceptability of belief in God centered on the question whether there was adequate *evidence* for the existence of God; if there *is* adequate evidence, then belief in God is rationally acceptable; if there isn't, then it *isn't*, the viable alternatives being atheism and agnosticism. And the proper way to address *this* question, so it was thought, is to consider the arguments for and against the existence of God. On the pro side, the most popular theistic proofs or arguments have been the traditional big three: the ontological, cosmological, and teleological arguments, to use Immanuel Kant's terms for them, together with the moral argument (see Article 41, ONTOLOGICAL ARGUMENTS; Article 42, COSMOLOGICAL ARGUMENTS; Article 43, TELEOLOGICAL AND DESIGN ARGUMENTS; and Article 44, MORAL ARGUMENTS). The first of these is an argument for a first cause or first mover; the second is a fascinating but puzzling argument for the existence of a being than which none greater can be conceived; the third is an argument from the apparent design the world displays; and the moral argument contends that there couldn't really be any such thing as genuine moral obligation if there were no such being as God. Of these, the teleological argument, the argument from design, is perhaps both the most popular and the most convincing; one of the most recent and perhaps the best statement of this argument is to be found in the work of Richard Swinburne (*The Existence of God*).

On the other side, the anti-theistic side, the principal argument has traditionally been the *deductive argument from evil* (see Article 50, THE PROBLEM OF EVIL): the argument that the existence of an omnipotent, omniscient wholly good God is logically inconsistent with the very existence of evil, or at any rate with the vast extent of pain, suffering, and human wickedness actually to be found in the world. The deductive argument from evil has fallen out of favor over the last quarter-century as philosophers have come to think there is no inconsistency here; it has been replaced by the much messier and (from the atheologian's point of view), less satisfactory *probabilistic* argument from evil, according to which it is *unlikely* that there is such a person as God, given all the evil the world in fact displays. The argument from evil is flanked by subsidiary arguments, such as the claim that the very concept of God is incoherent, or the claim that modern science, or perhaps the habits of thought engendered by modern science, or perhaps some particular conclusion of modern science (evolution, say) or at any rate *something* in the neighborhood, makes the existence of God unlikely.

And the question is: which of these groups of arguments is the stronger? If the arguments *for* the existence of God are stronger, then (depending upon how *much* stronger) belief in God is rationally justified; if the arguments against are stronger, the rational conclusion is that probably there is no such person as God; if they are more or less equal in strength, then the right position is agnosticism, believing neither that there is such a person as God, nor that there isn't. Call this claim – that belief in God is rationally acceptable if and only if there is adequate evidence in the form of good arguments for it – *evidentialism*. Now why, according to the evidentialist, must there be a good argument for the existence of God if belief in God is to be rationally acceptable? After all, hardly anyone thinks you need a good argument for the existence of the past if you are to be rational in thinking you had breakfast this morning.

The answer lies in a more general line of thought (a picture, a way of conceiving our whole intellectual life) often called "classical foundationalism." Classical foundationalism goes back to the Enlightenment and to those twin towers of western epistemology, René Descartes and John Locke. This picture starts from a distinction between beliefs that are accepted in the basic way and those that are not accepted in that way. To accept a belief in the basic way is to believe, but not believe on the evidential basis of other things you believe; a basic belief is a sort of starting point for thought. Thus I believe the proposition $(6 + 1 = 7)$ in the basic way; I don't reason or argue to it from other propositions I believe; my belief is immediate, unmediated by other beliefs serving as premises in an argument of which the belief in question is the conclusion. On the other hand, I believe the proposition $341 \times 269 = 91,729$ (I've just calculated it) on the basis of other propositions: such propositions as that $1 \times 269 = 269$, $4 \times 9 = 36$, and the like. Alternatively, I might use my calculator, in which case I would believe the proposition on the basis of such other beliefs as that my calculator is reliable, at least for calculations of this sort, that I properly entered the numbers, and that it yielded the result in question. This is an arithmetical example, but of course there are many more examples from every area of thought.

The second and more characteristic claim of the classical foundationalist is that only *some* propositions can be *rightly*, or *properly*, or *justifiably* accepted in that basic way. The fundamental idea is that the only propositions I can justifiably accept in the basic way are propositions that are *certain* for me. What kinds of propositions *are* certain for me? Two kinds. First, there are some propositions about my own mental life that are certain: for example, the proposition *it seems to me that I see a horse*. (Not *I see a horse*; unlike *it seems to me that I see a horse*, this proposition is not certain for me; I could be hallucinating or dreaming and think I see a horse when there isn't one there to be seen.) Second, "self-evident" propositions are certain for us: ones like $2 + 1 = 3$ or *if all men are mortal and Socrates is a man, then Socrates is mortal*. These are propositions so utterly obvious that one can't even understand them without seeing that they are true. And according to the classical foundationalist's picture, it is only beliefs of these two sorts that are properly basic, that is, properly accepted in the basic way. Beliefs of other kinds, in a well-run cognitive structure, will be accepted on the evidential basis of other beliefs – ultimately on the basis of beliefs of the two sorts mentioned above.

Now my belief that there is such a person as God is neither self-evident (it is possible to understand it but not accept it) nor about my own mental life. Therefore belief in God, on this picture, is properly accepted only if it is accepted on the evidential basis of other beliefs. This picture has been dominant from the Enlightenment on, and has been dominant throughout most of the twentieth century. Of course it has had variations and spinoffs, analogically related positions that differ in various ways; there is no space here to go into the squalid details. For most of the twentieth century this way of thinking was orthodoxy.

It is precisely this orthodoxy that the Reformed epistemologist disputes. As she sees it, belief in God is perfectly proper and rational, perfectly justified and in order, even if it is not accepted on the basis of such arguments, even if the believer doesn't know of any such arguments, and even if in fact there *aren't* any such arguments. This is not because, like certain theologians, she *redefines* "belief in God" so that it really amounts to something quite different, perhaps something like sitting loose with respect to the future and being authentic in the face of illness, death, suffering and the other ills our flesh is heir to, or perhaps believing in the historical evolutionary process that has brought us all into being. No: the Reformed epistemologist is talking about God as conceived in traditional Christianity, Judaism, and Islam: an almighty, all-knowing wholly good and loving person who has created the world and presently upholds it in being. And it is her claim that belief in such a being is properly basic.

What does it mean? And how can it be true? What, in particular, does "properly" mean here? Well, what, according to the classical picture, would be wrong with you if you believed a proposition in the basic way when it wasn't properly basic? Descartes and Locke and most of their successors thought of propriety in terms of *duty* or *obligation*: they thought that there are duties and obligations (right ways and wrong ways) with respect to *belief* as well as with respect to *action*. These duties specify how we ought to govern or regulate belief; and the particular duty in question is just to make sure that you don't believe in the basic way a proposition that isn't certain; the only right way to believe propositions that aren't certain is on the evidential basis of propositions that are. So what is wrong with you, if you accept as basic a proposition that is not properly basic, is that you are going contrary to your epistemic duties: you have violated a requirement or obligation; you are living in epistemic sin.

It is just this claim that the Reformed epistemologist disputes. She insists on two things: first, the classical foundationalist is mistaken in thinking that there is a duty to try to accept only those two kinds of propositions in the basic way: there simply is no such duty. She holds that there is nothing whatever immoral in believing, say, that you had an orange for lunch yesterday, even if you don't believe in it on the basis of an argument from premises that are certain for you. The fact is there isn't a good (non-circular) argument from such propositions to any past phenomena; but that doesn't mean that you are flouting duty or obligation in forming such beliefs. She holds that there is nothing whatever immoral in believing in material objects in the basic way – in particular, given, as the history of modern philosophy from Descartes to David Hume and Thomas Reid indicates, that there is no good (non-circular) argument for the existence of material objects from propositions that are properly basic by classical foundationalist standards. And she also believes that there is nothing immoral, contrary to duty, in believing in God in the basic way. For first, it may not be within my power *not* to believe in this way. But second, suppose that after careful reflection and consideration it just seems obvious to me that there *is* such a person as God (perhaps I have the sort of rich interior spiritual life depicted in Jonathan Edwards's *Religious Affections*): how could I possibly be going contrary to duty in holding the belief? Accordingly, the Reformed epistemologist thinks it clear that belief in God is properly basic in the sense that one can be perfectly justified in holding this belief in the basic way. Indeed, not only is this clear, it is *obvious*, and it is hard to see how the evidentialist could have thought otherwise.

Reformed epistemology began life as a response to evidentialism, with its concern for justification; the question was: "Can I be justified in believing in God in the basic way, or do I have to have arguments if I am to be justified?" But Reformed epistemology has gone beyond questions of justification to other questions about positive epistemic status, or questions about other sorts of positive epistemic status. Among other sorts of positive epistemic status, two of the most important would be *internal rationality* and *warrant*. The first has to do with the sort of doxastic response you make to the evidence that is available to you – the sorts of beliefs you do or do not form in response to that evidence. And here *evidence* includes not just other propositions that you believe (although it does include that) but also your current experience: the ways in which you are being appeared to, for example, when you look out at your backyard and your visual field is filled with that highly detailed and intricate pattern of light, color, and shape. (That is just one kind of experience; there is also, for example, *moral experience*: certain actions just seem right and others seem wrong.) And you are internally rational when your doxastic response to your evidence is appropriate or right. Well, when is such a response appropriate or right? The first thing to see is that what is involved here is not a matter of duty or obligation. It is instead, broadly speaking, a matter of health, sanity, proper function. A doxastic response is appropriate or right when it is among the responses that could be made to that situation by someone who was completely rational – suffering from no cognitive dysfunction.

But now we can turn to our question: suppose I believe in the basic way that God loves me, or that God was in Christ, reconciling the world to himself: could I be internally rational in thus believing? Again, the answer seems easy: *of course* I could. For suppose again I have that rich interior spiritual life mentioned above: it seems to me that I am in communion with God, and that I see something of his marvelous glory and beauty, that I feel his love and his presence with me. Then (unless I've got some powerful defeater, and we need not hypothesize that I do) a response that involves believing that there *is* such a person is clearly perfectly sensible: there is nothing whatever pathological about it. Perhaps there is something pathological about having that sort of experience in the first place: that is as may be. But *given* the experience, there is nothing pathological in that doxastic response.

Finally, what about *warrant*, the last member of our trio? Warrant, we may say, is what separates knowledge from mere true belief. Warrant is the answer to Plato's question in the *Theaetetus*: what is it that must be added to true belief to get knowledge? Warrant is a name for that quantity or quality, whatever exactly it is. Well, what *is* warrant? Here I shall have to be brief and dogmatic, assuming a certain view as to what warrant is. (The same conclusion would result if we thought of warrant in the other presently plausible ways.) As I see it, then, the warrant enjoyed by a belief has to do with the status of the faculties or belief-producing processes or mechanisms that are responsible for the production of that belief. More exactly, a belief has warrant only when it is produced by cognitive faculties that are functioning properly (note the connection with internal rationality), in the sort of cognitive environment for which they have been designed (by God or evolution).

These are the first two conditions of warrant; there are two more. Some faculties or belief-producing processes, as far as we can see, have the production of true beliefs as their function: they are aimed at the production of true belief. Here we think of perception, memory, and the processes, whatever exactly they are, by virtue of which we know simple arithmetical and logical truths. But other belief-producing processes seem to be aimed at something other than true belief. For example, there is wishful thinking; the function of this mode of belief-production isn't the production of true belief, but of belief with some other virtue – perhaps belief that will enable you to carry on in the sad and difficult world of ours. There is also the alleged mechanism whereby women don't remember childbirth to be as painful as it actually is; perhaps this is aimed at willingness to have more children. Other belief-producing mechanisms might be aimed at the production of beliefs that permit and enhance friendship; a real friend will give you the benefit of the doubt and continue to believe in your honesty after a careful and objective look at the evidence would have dictated a reluctant change of mind. The third condition of warrant, then, is that it be produced by cognitive faculties or belief-producing processes that are aimed at the production of true belief (and not survival or psychological comfort). And the fourth and final condition is just that the process or faculty in question be *successfully* aimed at the production of true belief: there must be a high probability that a belief produced by the process in question (when it is functioning properly in the right kind of environment) will be true.

Well, then, *do* Christian and theistic belief meet these conditions? According to Sigmund Freud and Karl Marx, they do not. The heart of Freud's criticism of religious belief (especially belief in God) is that religious belief is produced by the process of *wish-fulfillment* or wishful thinking, a process that is aimed at psychological comfort in the face of a natural world that seems indifferent or hostile. According to Freud, therefore, belief in God doesn't meet the third condition of warrant. And according to Marx, belief in God (and other religious belief) is produced by way of psychological malfunction on the part of people who live under conditions of societal malfunction; so it doesn't meet the first condition of warrant. If either Freud or Marx were correct, therefore, theistic belief would not have warrant; it wouldn't be produced by the right kind of faculty or belief-producing process (see Article 51, NATURALISTIC EXPLANATIONS OF THEISTIC BELIEF).

Of course neither Freud nor Marx gave any reason to *believe* these suggestions of theirs; they simply *announced* them. And in announcing them, they were really assuming that theistic belief is in fact false. For suppose theistic belief is true: then we human beings have been created by a loving God who would be interested in our knowing about him, and would almost certainly have provided a way by which we could come to know him and know about him. He would therefore have created us in such a way that under the right conditions we would come to know him and know about him. Since many of us (again, assuming that theism is true) *do* in fact know him and know about him, the natural thing to think, surely, is that the processes or faculties by which these beliefs are formed are functioning properly in the sort of environment for which they were designed; further, they are successfully aimed at the production of true belief, i.e. those beliefs involved in knowing God and knowing something about him. If theistic belief is true, therefore, then in all probability it meets the conditions of warrant; on the other hand, if it is false, then in all probability it does not meet those conditions. So in simply announcing that theistic belief lacks warrant, Freud and Marx and their followers are simply assuming that theistic belief (and other religious belief) is in fact false.

Of course one who thinks theistic belief *true* (as do the Reformed epistemologists) will not follow Marx and Freud here; such a person will not have Marx and Freud's reason for thinking theistic belief without warrant. Instead, the Reformed epistemologist will point out that (in all probability) theistic belief has warrant if and only if it is true; since she thinks it *is* true, she will also think it has warrant, and has it in the basic way. Here she can't claim (as with justification) that it is just *obvious* that theistic belief has warrant; for it isn't just obvious that theism is true. Instead, she points out that theistic belief has warrant if and only if it is true; hence whether one thinks it has warrant will depend upon whether one thinks it true.

Bibliography

Alston, W. P.: *Perceiving God* (Ithaca: Cornell University Press, 1991).

Edwards J.: *Religious Affections* (New Haven: Yale University Press, 1959).

Freud, S.: *Civilization and its Discontents*, tr. Joan Riviere (London: Hogarth Press, 1949).

Hoitenga, D.: *From Plato to Plantinga: An Introduction to Reformed Epistemology* (Albany: State University of New York Press, 1991).

Kenny, A.: *The God of the Philosophers* (Oxford: Clarendon Press, 1979).

McLeod, M.: *Rationality and Theistic Belief: An Essay on Reformed Epistemology* (Ithaca: Cornell University Press, 1993).

Marx, K.: "Contribution to the critique of Hegel's philosophy of right." In *On Religion* by Karl Marx and Friedrich Engels, ed. R. Niebuhr (Chicago: Scholar's Press, 1964).

Plantinga, A.: *Warranted Christian Belief*, forthcoming.

——, and Wolterstorff, N. (eds): *Faith and Rationality* (Notre Dame: University of Notre Dame Press, 1983).

Swinburne, R.: *The Existence of God* (Oxford: Clarendon Press, 1991).

Wolterstorff, N.: *Divine Discourse* (Cambridge: Cambridge University Press, 1995).

PART VII

CHALLENGES TO THE RATIONALITY
OF THEISTIC BELIEF

50

The problem of evil

MICHAEL L. PETERSON

For almost two thousand years in the West, the problem of evil has persisted as a serious challenge to traditional belief in God. The God of classical theism is believed to be omnipotent, omniscient, and wholly good (see Article 28, OMNIPO-TENCE; Article 29, OMNISCIENCE; and Article 30, GOODNESS). Many thoughtful people maintain that such beliefs are in tension with certain beliefs about evil. When this tension is given more exact shape and structure, we have a specific formulation of the problem of evil and have the stage set for certain kinds of responses to it.

The logical problems of evil and the free will defense

During the 1960s and 1970s, philosophers concentrated a great deal of attention on the logical problem of evil (also called the a priori problem and the deductive problem). The logical problem revolved around the charge that propositions

(1)   God is omnipotent, omniscient, and wholly good

and

(2)   Evil exists

are logically inconsistent. Sometimes the claim that there are large amounts and extreme kinds of evil is substituted for (2). Clearly, the issue is one of deciding whether or not the relevant claims about God and evil can be clarified and reconciled.

Critics such as J. L. Mackie argued that the theist *qua* theist must believe both that God exists and that evil exists, but cannot do so consistently. The alleged inconsistency, however, is not obvious; it is neither explicit nor formal in nature. In order to make the implicit inconsistency explicit, some additional propositions must be specified, for instance, "a good thing always eliminates evil as far as it can" and "there are no limits to what an omnipotent thing can do." Mackie argues that (1), properly supplemented, entails:

(−2) Evil does not exist.

Since the theist is also committed to (2), we have what Mackie heralds as the *reductio.*

While George Mavrodes, Keith Yandell, and other theistic thinkers offered important responses, Alvin Plantinga emerged as the foremost theist to address the logical problem. Plantinga (1967) laid down conditions which any auxiliary propositions specified by the critic must meet: they must be "necessarily true, essential to theism, or a logical consequence of such propositions." Theists generally argue that such propositions offered by critics either beg the question by specifying propositions that are not essential to theism or lift out of context propositions that are essential to theism but impute new meanings to them which the theist need not accept.

Plantinga maintained that, if the critic is to win the debate over the logical problem, he will have to show that a proposition very much like

(3)   If evil exists, then it is unjustified

is a necessary truth. Plantinga claims that it is extremely difficult to know how the critic could show that this proposition is necessary and thus that theism is inconsistent. On the other hand, Plantinga envisioned a method – now known as the free will defense – for showing that (3) is not a necessary truth and thus that (1) and (2) are indeed consistent.

Plantinga's famous free will defense was produced in both 1967 and 1974 renditions, with the latter exploiting the power of ideas about possible worlds and modal logic. The free will defender aims to show that (1) and (2) are consistent by showing that there is a possible world in which both propositions are true. The underlying strategy is this: in order to show that two propositions p and q are consistent, one must find a third proposition r which is consistent with p and, conjoined with p, entails q. This would show that p and q are possibly true together. Hence, in order to rebut the alleged inconsistency, Plantinga's approach is to find a proposition whose conjunction with (1) is consistent and entails (2). He carefully argues that it is possible that God has a morally sufficient reason for creating a world containing moral evil. He provides a scenario in which God brings about a world containing significantly free moral beings because no other moral good can exist without freedom. He further argues that, while it is possible that there be a world containing significantly free creatures who only do what is right, it is not within God's power to bring this about. What significantly free beings do is up to them.

Plantinga maintains that a proposition much like the following is entirely possible:

(4)   Every person goes wrong in every possible world.

Thus, he claims that the heart of his free will defense is that the following proposition is possible:

(5)   It was not within God's power to create a world containing moral good but no moral evil.

The free will defender need not claim that this proposition is in fact true or even probably true; he need only claim that it is possibly true in order to rebut the logical argument from evil.

Antony Flew and J. L. Mackie continued to oppose the free will defense on the grounds that it rests on an incompatibilist view of human freedom whereas compatibilism (which claims that free will is compatible with determinism, even divine determinism) is a more plausible position (see Article 72, PROVIDENCE AND PREDESTINATION). If compatibilism is true, then an omnipotent God can create a world in which free persons always do what is right. Another debate arose regarding God's omniscience, which would allow him to foreknow what evils his creatures will bring about. Thus, God could choose to actualize a better world, i.e., one with less evil. Many theists now avoid this criticism by saying that it is not logically possible for God to foreknow future contingent free actions (see Article 37, FOREKNOWLEDGE AND HUMAN FREEDOM). The outcomes of these and other debates have been so favorable to theists that it is reasonable to say that the logical problem has been laid to rest.

Probabilistic arguments from evil and the use of reformed epistemology

Through the decade of the 1980s, the evidential problem of evil – often called the inductive problem and the a posteriori problem – rose to prominence. Neither theists nor their critics felt that the conundrum of evil is exhausted by debating the internal consistency of theism. The evidential problem articulates inductive grounds for rejecting theistic belief. In this context, some proposition about evil, say,

(2)   Evil exists,

counts as evidence against the proposition

(1)   God is omnipotent, omniscient, and wholly good.

As interest in the logical problem was declining, one of the first renditions of the evidential problem was cast in terms of a probabilistic argument from evil. Early on, Plantinga rightly observed that what it means to say that (2) counts probabilistically against (1) depends on the particular theory of probability one adopts: personalistic, logical, or frequency. Probabilistic arguments from evil can be read as assuming one of these three interpretations of the probability calculus.

The critic's ability to assign a relatively low probability value to proposition (1) soon becomes problematic. All the personalistic theory really allows the critic to say is that (1) is improbable with respect to all of the propositions which he already accepts. This is interesting autobiography, but is hardly a problem for the theist. The logical theory of probability, which asserts that one proposition just has a certain objective probability with respect to another proposition, enables the critic to claim that (1) just has a low probability given (2). However, there is no clear method for assigning probabilities to one proposition on the basis of another, and there is no convincing reason to think that propositions have a priori probabilities at all. The frequentist critic must argue that the relative frequency with which universes with as much evil as this world contains are created by a theistic deity is low. But this approach fares no better, as it encounters the problem of the single case. Ours is the only actual universe in the reference class, unless one risks dangerous subjectivity by including hypothetical universes.

Continuing refections on the probabilistic argument from evil brought to light the fact that, in the final analysis, any proposition must be probabilistically assessed on the basis of all the propositions one knows or justifiably believes – the "total evidence." Discussions came to be couched in terms of what probability proposition (1) has on the basis of one's "epistemic framework" or "noetic structure." Some theists pointed out that what propositions one takes to be basic in one's noetic structure differ from person to person, such that proposition (1) will have a different degree of probability (if it makes at least rough sense to talk this way) for each person. The theist and atheist have such differing noetic frameworks that they are inevitably going to assign drastically different probabilities to (1).

So far, of course, the activity of trying to assess the probability of (1) in reference to propositions already taken as basic in one's noetic structure is not in question. However, critics such as Antony Flew argued that there are certain propositions that ought to be in the foundation of every well-formed noetic structure (i.e., every rational person's storehouse of beliefs that he takes as basic) and that the denial of (1) is among them. Flew's point is that if atheism is normal, natural, and rational to presume, then the burden of proof is on the theist to produce a very convincing argument for (1) in order to be rationally entitled to believe it (see Article 52, THE PRESUMPTION OF ATHEISM).

Alvin Plantinga, Nicholas Wolterstorff, George Mavrodes, William Alston, and some other theists began to pay attention to the whole idea of what it means for a person to be rationally entitled to hold a belief. Sophisticated epistemological studies were produced accenting difficulties in classical foundationalism and evidentialism (which are assumed by the project of classical natural theology) and recommending the advantages of an alternative view labeled REFORMED EPISTEMOLOGY (see Article 49); it recognizes that our native noetic powers provide us with basic beliefs not countenanced by classical foundationalism. This analysis of what it means for a belief to be "properly basic" permits proposition (1) to be properly basic if it is produced in us by the normal functioning of our noetic powers, in normal circumstances, etc. Classical foundationalism, by contrast, restricts properly basic beliefs to those which are self-evident or incorrigible or evident to the senses, and thus prevents (1) from being considered basic.

Clearly, if belief in God can indeed be properly basic then Flew and others cannot insist on a presumption of atheism. Reformed epistemologists argue that we are within our epistemic rights to hold (1) "basically," that is, without arguments. One would be obligated to engage in discursive reasoning to justify it only if one felt the probative force of some objection or potential "defeater." If one can overcome or defeat the objection, then one is entitled to continue holding the belief. For present purposes, the problem of evil is a potential defeater of belief in (1). The theistic believer, then, has the rational obligation to defeat the defeater in order to be justified in continuing to believe (1). So, the Reformed epistemologist engages in defensive tactics only when a belief like (1) is under attack. The free will defense against the logical problem of evil can be seen in this light. Likewise, when an argument is constructed to establish that theistic belief is made improbable by evil, Reformed epistemologists counter by showing that theistic belief is not improbable, by defeating another potential defeater. Reformed epistemology obviously has more general application to a wide range of topics in philosophy of religion than lie beyond the scope of this essay.

The evidential problem of gratuitous evil

A number of atheistic thinkers (e.g., Edward Madden and Peter Hare, Michael Martin, William Rowe) have tried to establish the evidential relevance of evil to theistic belief without appealing to probabilistic logic. Reformed epistemology notwithstanding, they hold the conviction that it is proper to ask theists to make some sense of their beliefs in light of the broad facts of experience, particularly the facts of evil. Fundamentally, proposition (1) – or some expanded set of theistic propositions – is treated as a kind of global hypothesis which can be evaluated in broadly inductive terms. Theism, either restricted to (1) or expanded by other propositions, would seem to imply that the world should be different from what it really is, particularly in regard to the evil it contains. Hence, evil tends to count as evidence against it.

Many critics have also concluded that there is little or no positive evidence for divine existence. Obviously, this matter must be settled through philosophical appraisal of the key theistic arguments (see Part VI: The Justification of Theistic Belief), but it none the less provides a premise in an inductive argument from evil. Then, by arguing that all theistic reasons for evil are insufficient, critics take themselves to have mounted strong inductive support for atheism. Again, this matter must be settled through philosophical interchange with those proposing theodicies. So, the whole process becomes nothing other than the employment of classical philosophical dialectic, the process of offering argument and counterargument in relation to a stated thesis.

Furthermore, theists and critics alike are admitting that the toughest construal of the evidence is what appears to be pointless or gratuitous evil, evil for which there seems to be no good explanation or justification. Even if God could have good reasons for allowing some evil, why is there so much apparently pointless evil? The adequacy of all explanations for evil must be determined through philosophical give-and-take. Eventually, if theistic explanations cannot withstand scrutiny, then it seems that critics are justified in holding that the evils under consideration are gratuitous and thus detrimental to religious belief.

One important discussion pertains to the precise definition of gratuitous or pointless evil. Glossing definitions from David Basinger, Randall Basinger, Keith Chrzan, and others, we may here define gratuitous evils to be states of affairs for which there is no good explanation, no adequate justification. Generally, an adequate explanation is considered to be one which cites some greater good that could not have been achieved or some greater evil that could not have been avoided without the existence of the evil (or class of evils) in question. Through the centuries, it has been the burden of theodicy to give some account of evil along these lines, thus specifying the point or purpose of evil.

Another intense debate regards the factual premise: that there is, or appears to be, gratuitous evil. This claim is incorporated into formulations of the evidential argument which reflect the intuition that gratuitous evil tends to disconfirm theism. William Rowe cites the example of a helpless fawn suffering for days in a forest fire and then dying. Rowe indicates that we are unable to perceive any outweighing goods connected to the suffering that would justify an omnipotent, omniscient, wholly good being in permitting it; such an evil appears to be pointless. Focusing discussion on the epistemic status of the "appearance-claim," Stephen Wykstra pointed out that if there were justifying goods we would not be able to know them because God's ways are inscrutable. Hence, our inability to see such justifying goods is not a real problem for theistic belief because this epistemic situation is exactly what theism would lead us to expect.

Rowe replies that we must distinguish between "restricted standard theism" (which is the view that an omnipotent, omniscient, wholly good God exists) and "expanded standard theism" (which is restricted standard theism conjoined with other theological propositions about sin, God's general purposes, after-life, etc.). Rowe admits that restricted standard theism implies that God's mind grasps goods that lie beyond our ken, but denies that it implies that the goods in relation to which God permits many sufferings are such. Furthermore, there are other versions of expanded standard theism which, contrary to Wykstra's own version, imply that we might be able to detect some of the goods connected to the world's evils (e.g., because it is God's good pleasure to let us dimly sense his purposes, because we are created in his image, etc.). Rowe acknowledges that evil for which we cannot see the existence of a greater good or prevention of a greater evil counts only against restricted standard theism and not against some versions of expanded standard theism.

Still another discussion relates to whether a theistic conception of deity really requires that God allow no gratuitous evil. The enterprise of theodicy has typically aimed at providing explanations for evils or whole classes of evils, driven by an underlying intuition that an omnipotent, omniscient, wholly good God would have some reason for the evils in the world, a reason typically conceived as specifying some good to which they are connected. Theodicists have drawn from the logic of the divine attributes as well as Scripture and tradition in order to explain God's ways. Yet there is evil in the world that seems to defy all reasonable explanation and it is this evil that seems particularly damaging to theistic belief. In reacting to this problem, I have previously argued that God, by creating a moral context for free, mature persons which is defined by natural and moral laws, has thereby accepted the possibility of gratuitous evil. William Hasker has likewise contended that these structural features of the world make the possibility of gratuitous evil necessary. Peter van Inwagen has proposed that, because sin has ruptured creaturely relations to God, he allows us to live in a world in which some evil things happen to us by chance, that is, for no reason at all (see Article 68, SIN AND ORIGINAL SIN). Obviously, if a theistic conception of deity allows the possibility of gratuitous evil, then gratuitous evil does not count as heavily against theistic belief as initially thought (see bibliography in Peterson 1992).

The task of theodicy

Apart from recent discussions regarding whether a theistic universe includes gratuitous evil, theists through the centuries have assumed that there is no ultimately gratuitous evil. Keith Yandell has pointed out that all theistic defenses against the problem of evil – and, by implication, all theodicies – assume that there is a "greater good" that justifies the evils of our world. Hence, it would seem that, for the classic tradition in theodicy, there is no ultimately gratuitous evil – even if an evil that seems gratuitous at one level must be justified by a good at another level (e.g., as undeserved hardship stimulates the virtue of perseverance). The traditional task of the theodicist is to tell a story (whose elements are drawn from Scripture, church doctrine, our common moral experience, etc.,) which makes sense of why God allows evil in the world. It gives evil some point or some purpose. One thinks readily of the two most famous traditional theodicies, Augustine's which explains evil as a fall from a previously perfect state and Leibniz's which explains the amount of variety of evil in the world as the least possible that is still commensurate with a world that is best on the whole. In the late twentieth century, perhaps the three best known theodicies have been John Hick's soul-making theodicy, Richard Swinburne's theodicy for natural evils, and Whiteheadian process theodicy.

In *Evil and the God of Love*, Hick argued that God's main purpose in creation is to bring human beings from animal self-centeredness into moral and spiritual maturity. Since this quality of personal life cannot be created by fiat, God has designed an environment in which human beings can gradually develop the desired attributes. Unlike Augustinian theodicy, Hick's Irenaean-type theodicy regards evil in the world as an inevitable stage in the gradual improvement of the race. Important elements of Hick's theodicy include "epistemic distance" which involves the existence of God not being strongly impressed upon creaturely consciousness, significant free will which involves great risks as well as opportunities, and an eschatological fulfillment which envisions God bringing about the redemption of the race.

Swinburne's theodicy for natural evils is based on the presumption that some kind of free will theodicy is viable. Swinburne argues that, in order to be significantly free, human beings must know how to bring about good and evil. For God to reveal this knowledge directly would be to overwhelm us and impair our freedom; so we must gain it inductively from past experience, and this experience includes learning what causes pain and suffering. In other words, natural evil is necessary in a world characterized by significant freedom. Thus, if free will theodicy works for moral evil, it works also for natural evil.

Although many theodicies are rooted in what William Rowe calls expanded standard theism, that is, the core belief that God is omnipotent, omniscient, wholly good, conjoined with one or more other theological beliefs, the tradition of process

399

theodicy modifies the core theistic belief. Following Alfred North Whitehead's process metaphysics and Charles Hartshorne's modifications of it, process theists reject the classical concept of omnipotence as unlimited coercive power as both metaphysically impossible and morally unacceptable, and replace it with the concept of unlimited persuasive power (see Article 16, PROCESS THEOLOGY). They also modify classical theistic concepts such as knowledge and goodness. Thus, the overall process vision of the world, out of which their theodicy comes, is one in which God cannot unilaterally bring about his will because creatures possess the inherent power of self-determination. Therefore, in order to accomplish his goals for the world, which are conceived in terms of the realization and maximization of values, God lovingly seeks to persuade creatures to achieve their most valuable opportunities. Process theists (such as John Cobb, David Ray Griffin, and Lewis Ford) believe that they solve the problem of evil largely by denying that God is omnipotent. Evil in the world, then, is explained in terms of negative creaturely actions which are not in God's power to control. One important criticism which has been offered is that the process deity is not worthy of worship, a criticism that can be launched from many angles. First, is a deity who is not all-powerful a fitting object of worship? Second, if process thought construes God's values for the world in largely aesthetic terms (e.g., increased order and significance), how can it handle the problem of evil as a moral objection? Third, if process theists do not conceive of God as personal but rather as a principle how can they make sense of anything close to theistic worship?

The existential problem of evil

Since the 1970s, the taxonomy of the problem of evil has become increasingly well defined. We now have firm distinctions between the logical and evidential problems of evil as well as between defense and theodicy. We also have classified many of the standard theodicies. However, there is still relatively uncharted territory which we might denominate the existential dimension of the problem of evil. This territory consists of assorted discussions: Kenneth Surin's "practical problem of evil" (which pertains to what we can do to combat oppressive and destructive evils in the world), Alvin Plantinga's "religious problem" (which relates to the need for pastoral counseling in order to maintain a right attitude toward God), and Marilyn Adams's "pastoral problem" (which involves providing some conceptual explanations about God's goodness in an evil world in order to encourage trust in him).

One person-relative expression of the problem of evil is found in articles by Robert Adams and William Hasker. Hasker actually calls this the "existential form of the problem of evil." Adams and Hasker observe that happy people who do not regret their own individual existence cannot meaningfully raise a problem of evil, since their existence and identity are causally dependent upon certain past evil events in world history. Thus, in so far as the problem of evil is raised as a personal and moral complaint against God and the world he has created, answers to it will satisfy those who are happy that they exist and fail to satisfy those who are willing to say that they regret their existence.

Other issues related to God and evil deserve careful consideration, such as whether God must or can create the best of all possible worlds. And new issues are already on the horizon, such as comparative studies of the problem of evil in non-Christian religions and the relation of the doctrine of hell to the problem of evil (see Article 71, HEAVEN AND HELL).

Bibliography

Griffin, D. R.: *Evil Revisited* (Albany: State University of New York Press, 1991).

Hick, J.: *Evil and the God of Love*, 2nd edn, 1978 (San Francisco: Harper & Row, 1966).

Madden, E., and Hare P.: *Evil and the Concept of God* (Springfield: Charles C. Thomas, 1968).

Peterson, M. L.: *The Problem of Evil: Selected Readings* (Notre Dame: University of Notre Dame Press, 1992). [Extensive bibliography.]

Plantinga, A.: *God and Other Minds: A Study of the Rational Justification of Belief in God* (Ithaca: Cornell University Press, 1967).

——: *The Nature of Necessity* (Oxford: Clarendon Press, 1974).

Rowe, W.: "The problem of evil and some varieties of atheism," *American Philosophical Quarterly*, vol. 16, 4 (October 1979), pp. 335–41.

51

Naturalistic explanations of theistic belief

KAI NIELSEN

Naturalism denies that there are any spiritual or supernatural realities. There are, that is, no purely mental substances and there are no supernatural realities transcendent to the world; or at least we have no sound grounds for believing that there are such realities or perhaps even for believing that there could be such realities. It is the view that anything that exists is ultimately made up of physical components.

Naturalism sometimes has been reductionistic (claiming that all talk of the mental can be translated into purely physicalist terms) or scientistic (claiming that what science cannot tell us humankind cannot know). The more plausible forms of naturalism are neither across-the-board reductionistic nor scientistic (Nielsen 1996, ch. 1). Most claims that people make are not scientific; yet they can, for all that, be true or false. Many of them are quite plainly and uncontroversially in place. That it snows in Ontario in winter, that people very frequently fear death, that keeping promises is generally speaking a desirable thing are some unproblematic examples. And very frequently mentalistic talk in terms of intentions, thoughts, beliefs, feelings, and the like is not only useful, but indispensable if we are to make sense of human life and of the interactions between people. Such remarks are typically true or false and again sometimes unproblematically so. But such talk is, for the most part, hardly scientific, though from this, of course, it does not follow that it is anti-scientific talk – it is just non-scientific. There we are, however, still talking, under different descriptions, about the same physical realities as we are when we give macroscopic descriptions of bodily movements, though in using the mental terms we are usually talking for a different purpose and from a different perspective. These descriptions are different, and usefully so, but, all the same, only one kind of reality is being described, namely physical reality. There are no *purely* mental realities in a naturalistic account of the world.

Religions, whether theisms or not, are belief-systems (though that is not all that they are) which involve belief in spiritual realities. Even Theravada Buddhism, which has neither God nor worship, has a belief in spiritual realities; and this is incompatible with naturalism, as also is theism which is a form of supernaturalism (see Article 2, BUDDHISM). Naturalism, where consistent, is an atheism. It need not be a militant atheism and it should not be dogmatic: it should not claim that it is certain that theism is either false or incoherent. Yet, unlike an agnostic, a naturalist, if she is consistent, will be an atheist arguing, or at least presupposing, that theism is either false or incoherent or in some other way thoroughly unbelievable. But naturalists will argue for atheism in a fallibilistic, and *sometimes* even in a moderately skeptical, manner: one that is characteristic of modernity or of the peculiar form of modernity that some call postmodernity.

Atheism has a *critical* side and an *explanatory* side. (With many naturalistic theorists, atheists engage in both of these tasks. And sometimes it is not as clear as it should be which they are doing.) The critical side is classically exemplified in the works of Baron d'Holbach, Thomas Hobbes, Pierre Bayle, and most profoundly in David Hume, and in our period by (among others) Axel Hägerström, Bertrand Russell, J. L. Mackie, Wallace Matson, Paul Kurtz, Richard Robinson, Antony Flew, Ingemar Hedenius, Kai Nielsen, and Michael Martin (see Article 25, THE VERIFICATIONIST CHALLENGE; and Article 52, THE PRESUMPTION OF ATHEISM). Such an atheism gives, in one way or another, grounds for the rejection of all belief in supernatural or spiritual beings and with that, of course, a rejection of Judaism, Christianity, and Islam with their common belief in a God who created the universe out of nothing and has absolute sovereignty over his creation (see Article 39, CREATION AND CONSERVATION).

It will also be the case that naturalistic explanations will become of paramount interest only when the critique of theism has been thought to have done its work. Karl Marx's and Sigmund Freud's accounts of religion, as they were themselves well aware, gain the considerable significance they have only after we have come to believe that the Enlightenment critiques of religion by Bayle and Hume, perhaps with a little contemporary rational reconstruction, have successfully done their work. But it is not implausible to think that in our situation, coming down to us from the Enlightenment, there is what in effect is a cumulative argument (more literally a cluster of arguments with many strands and a complex development) against theism that has with time increased in force (Nielsen 1996). Starting with the early Enlightenment figures, finding acute and more fully developed critiques in Hume and Kant (see Article 12, EARLY MODERN PHILOSOPHICAL THEOLOGY), and carried through by their contemporary rational reconstructers (e.g., Mackie and Martin), the various arguments for the existence of God (including appeals to RELIGIOUS EXPERIENCE, see Article 47) have been so thoroughly refuted that few would try to defend them today and even those few that do, do so in increasingly attenuated forms. The move has increasingly been in religious apologetic (see Article 48, FIDEISM; and Article 18, WITTGENSTEINIANISM) to an appeal to faith or to arguments that claim that without belief in God life would be meaningless and morality groundless: that is, that naturalism leads to nihilism or despair.

Naturalists in turn point to the fact that such theistic responses do not face the fact that a perfectly reasonable and morally compelling secular sense can be made of morality, that alleged revelations and faiths are many and not infrequently conflicting, and moreover, and distinctively, that the very concept of God is problematical. To turn to the part about problematicity, where the theisms are plainly anthropomorphic, where we have something like a belief in a Zeus-like God, then religious claims are plainly false. Where theisms, by contrast, are more theologically elaborated and the religion, at least in that sense, is more developed, theistic religions move away from anthropomorphism to a more spiritualistic conception of God, for example, "God is Pure Spirit," "God is not a being but Being as such," "God is the mysterious ground of the universe." But with this turn (an understandable turn for theism to take given the pressure of philosophical thought, science, and secular outlooks) religious claims, though becoming thereby not so clearly, or perhaps not even at all, falsifiable, are threatened with incoherence.

As we move away from anthropomorphism to claims that God is Unlimited, Ultimate Being transcendent to the universe, we no longer understand to *whom* or to *what* the term "God" refers. If we try to think literally here we have no hold on the idea of "a being or Being that is transcendent to the universe." And to try to treat it metaphorically is (1) to provoke the question *what* is it a metaphor of, and (2) to lose the putatively substantive nature of the claim. God, in evolved forms of theism, is said to be an infinite individual who created the universe out of nothing and who is distinct from the universe. But such a notion is so problematical as to be at least arguably incoherent (Nielsen 1996, ch. 14). So construed, there could be no standing in the presence of God, no divine encounters and no experiencing God in our lives. With anthropomorphism we get falsification; without it we get at least apparent incoherence and religious irrelevance.

At the core of theistic belief there is a metaphysical belief in a reality that is alleged to transcend the empirical world. It is the metaphysical belief that there is an eternal (see Article 32, ETERNITY), ever-present, creative source and sustainer of the universe. The problem is how it is possible to know or even reasonably to believe that such a reality exists, or even to understand what such talk is about. Naturalists believe that if we continue to try to see through *Judeo-Christian spectacles*, there is nothing to understand here. We are faced with the hopeless task of trying to make sense out of an incoherent something, we know not what. Yet religious belief, much of which in one way or another is theistic belief, is culturally speaking pervasive even with the continuing disenchantment of the world.

Many contemporary naturalists believe that with the critical work – the critique of the truth-claims of theism – essentially done by Hume, we should turn, setting both metaphysical speculation and fideistic *angst* aside, to naturalistic explanations of religious beliefs. The main players here from the nineteenth century are Ludwig Feuerbach, Friedrich Engels, Karl Marx, Max Stirner, and Friedrich Nietzsche; and from the twentieth century Emile Durkheim, Max Weber, Axel Hägerström, Sigmund Freud, Bronislaw Malinowski, and Antonio Gramsci. Their accounts, although varied, are all thoroughly naturalistic.

These naturalists assume that by now it has been well established that there are no sound reasons for religious beliefs: there is no reasonable possibility of establishing religious beliefs to be true; there is no such thing as religious knowledge or sound religious belief. But when there are no good reasons, and when that fact is, as well, tolerably plain to informed and impartial persons, not crippled by ideology or neurosis, and yet religious belief (a belief that is both widespread and tenacious) persists in our cultural life, then it is time to look for the *causes* – causes which are not also reasons – of religious belief, including the causes of its widespread psychological appeal for many people. And indeed, given the importance of religious beliefs in the lives of most human beings, it is of crucial importance to look for such causes. Here questions about the origin and functions of religion become central, along with questions about the logical or conceptual status of religious beliefs.

Let us see how some of this goes by starting with Feuerbach and then, going to our century, moving on to Freud. (We will later turn to other such naturalists.) For Feuerbach religion is the projected image of humanity's essential nature. To understand what religion properly is, its explanation and elucidation must be taken out of the hands of theology and turned over to anthropology. Feuerbach sees himself, *vis-à-vis* religion, as changing profoundly the very way things are viewed and reacted to, changing religion's very object, as it is in the believer's imagination, into a conception of the object as it is in reality, namely that God is really the species-being (the idealized essence) of human beings rather than some utterly mysterious supernatural power. To talk about God, for him, is to talk about human beings *so idealized.*

Freud also discusses religion in psychological and anthropological terms. Religion in reality is a kind of mass obsessional delusion; though for understandable, and often very emotionally compelling reasons, it is, of course, not recognized as such by believers or at least not clearly and stably so. What religious beliefs and practices in reality do, according to Freud, is to depress the value of life and distort "the picture of the real world in a delusional manner" – which, Freud has it, comes to "an intimidation of the intelligence." By so functioning, religion has succeeded in "sparing many people an individual neurosis. But hardly anything more" (Freud 1930, pp. 31–2). Religion, on Freud's account, is the universal obsessional neurosis of humanity. It emerges out of the Oedipus complex – out of the helpless child's relation to what understandably seems to the child an all-powerful father. "God," Freud tells us, "is the exalted father and the longing for the father is the root of the need for religion" (Freud 1957, p. 36). Religious beliefs and doctrines "are not the residue of experience or the final result of reflection; they are illusions, fulfillment of the oldest, strongest and most insistent wishes of mankind; the secret of their strength is the strength of these wishes" (Freud 1957, p. 51).

In many circumstances of life we are battered and to some considerable extent helpless. Faced with this helplessness, we unconsciously revert to how we felt and reacted as infants and very young children when, quite unavoidably, given the kind of creatures we are, we were subject to a long period of infantile dependence – a period when we were utterly helpless – and, given the sense of security that we need because of this helplessness, we develop a father-longing. We need someone who will protect us. Freud believes that human beings come to believe that this is what the father does. Coming to recognize in later life that our fathers are by no means perfect protectors, nor could they be even with the best of motivations, still, in a world replete with threatening circumstances that we cannot control, we, unconsciously reverting to our infantile attitudes, create the gods (Freud 1957, p. 27). Thus religion functions to exorcize the terrors of nature, to reconcile us to the "cruelty of fate, particularly as shown in death" and to "make amends for the sufferings and privations that the communal life of culture has imposed on man" (1957, p. 27). To speak of God is in reality not to speak, as believers believe, of a supernatural creator and sustainer of the world – there are no such spiritual realities – but of an imagined idealized father, all-knowing, all-powerful and all-good, who deeply cares for us and who can and will protect us (see Article 29, OMNISCIENCE; Article 28, OMNIPOTENCE; and Article 30, GOODNESS).

For Feuerbach and Freud religious ideas were about psychological–anthropological realities. There is a stylized, and I believe a misleading, difference (alleged difference) characteristically thought to obtain between them and Engels, Marx, and Durkheim. For the latter, by contrast with Feuerbach and Freud, religion is taken instead to be about *society* – about social realities. For Marx all precommunist societies are class societies, driven by class struggles, where the class structures are epoch-specific and are rooted in the material conditions of production. Religions, in his conception, and also Engels's conception of things, function principally to aid the dominant class or classes in mystifying and, through such mystification, controlling the dominated classes in the interests of the dominant class or classes. Members of the dominating classes may or may not be aware that religion functions that way. But, whether they are aware of it or not, it so functions. Religion, as ideology, serves to reconcile the dominated to their condition and to give them an illusory hope of a better purely spiritual world to come, after they depart this veil of tears. This works, in the interests of the dominant class or classes, as a device to pacify what otherwise might be a rebellious dominated class, while at the same time "legitimating" the wealth and other privileges of the dominating class or classes. In this peculiar way – definitely an ideological way – religion works to "unify" class society, while at the same time giving expression to distinctive class interests. It serves, that is, both to "unify" class society and to sanction class domination, while giving the dominated class an illusory hope, though, of course, not one seen by them to be illusory, of a better life to come after the grave (Marx and Engels 1958, Nielsen 1996, chapter 15).

Durkheim, though in a rather different way, saw religion as unifying society. In his view, however, it *genuinely* unified society. As Steven Lukes put it, Durkheim "saw religion as social in at least three broad ways: as socially determined, as embodying representations of social realities, and as having functional social consequences" (Lukes 1985, p. 462). In all these ways, talk of God is in reality talk about society, but they are none the less different ways and only the part about embodying representations of social realities is *necessarily* naturalistic. However, if a naturalistic turn is taken, questions about the social determination and the social function of religion, rather than questions about the truth of religious beliefs, come to the forefront, gaining a pertinence that they did not have before. Still, (1) questions about what are the causes of religious beliefs and practices and what sustains them, (2) questions about the role they play in the life of human beings, and (3) questions about their truth, should be kept apart, though admittedly (1) and (2) are intertwined. But at least initially, they should be held apart in our thinking about them and examined separately.

Durkheim sought to give an utterly naturalistic account of what we are talking about when we speak of God. God and the religious beings of other religious systems "are nothing other than collective states objectified; they are society itself seen under one of its aspects" (Durkheim 1912, p. 590: tr. p. 412). Religion, for him, was a mode of comprehending social realities. To put matters again in a stylized way, while for Freud religious realities were psychological realities and for Feuerbach they were anthropological, they were for Durkheim sociological realities. Two points are relevant here: (1) *all* of these accounts are *reductionistic*, and (2), for Durkheim, in reality, his sociological notions about religion were suffused with psychological notions. There is no keeping these matters apart in the way Durkheim wished to and his *conception* of sociology required. (Here his practice was better than his belief about religious practices.) However, it goes the other way as well. Freud's "psychology of religion," and Feuerbach's anthropological account, were also sociological accounts. So with all the figures discussed above we have a social-psychological, sometimes socio-economic, account of the origin of religion. the status of religious ideas and the function of religion. They. of course, differently emphasize this and that, but they have an underlying common conception of religion. What Lukes says of Durkheim was common to all the above naturalistic theoreticians of religion, namely that, refusing to take religious symbols at what orthodox believers would take to be their face value – to see the world through Judeo-Christian spectacles – they sought "to go 'underneath' the symbol to the reality which it represents and which gives it its 'true meaning' and (they sought to show as well) that all religions 'answer, though in different ways, to the given conditions of human existence' " (Lukes 1985, p. 482).

If such a naturalistic account of religious representations is sound, or at least on its way to being sound via some more sophisticated restatement, we can then appropriately turn our attention to the social and psychological functions of religion: the roles it plays in the lives of human beings. These are things that naturalists have characteristically taken to be at the very heart of the matter in thinking about religion. Our attention turns now, that is, not to questions concerning the truth or coherency of religious beliefs, but to an attempt to understand their role in life, *whether the beliefs themselves are coherent or not.*

We have set out a range of naturalistic explanations of religion. It is frequently argued, or sometimes just rather uncritically believed, that naturalistic explanations of religion in effect, and unavoidably, destroy the very subject matter they are designed to explain. Religion, it is frequently claimed, must be believed to be properly understood. Durkheim's own insight that "whoever does not bring to the study of religion a sort of religious sentiment has no right to speak about it" shows, some believe, that neither his own naturalistic analysis nor any other naturalistic account could be adequate (cited by Lukes 1985, p. 515). No matter how we cut it, religious beliefs, on such an account, are in error and religious beliefs could have no sound claim to be true. His very explanation (as all naturalistic explanations) is incompatible, where accepted, with the person who accepts it continuing to be a religious believer, if he would be at all consistent. Thus, naturalistic explanations, if correct, or even widely just thought to be correct (on the not implausible assumption that people have some minimal concern with consistency) would undermine religion itself – the very phenomena it purports to explain. Who, a philosopher (Gustave Belot) asked Durkheim, putting forth in discussion with Durkheim what Belot took to be a *reductio*, "would continue to pray if he knew he was praying to no one, but merely addressing a collectivity that was not listening?" Where is the person, Belot went on, who would continue to take part in "communion if he believed that it was no more than a mere symbol and that there was nothing real underlying it?" (cited by Lukes 1985, p. 515). Explanation, given Durkheim's way of going about things, becomes identical with naturalistic critique here, and that very fact, the claim goes, reveals its *explanatory* inadequacy.

The naturalist should respond that it is false to say that there is nothing real underlying religious symbols. There is something there very real indeed – facts about human beings and society – only the reality is not what the believer takes it to be. Rather than its being the case that understanding religion requires belief, understanding religion, in a genuine way, is incompatible with believing it. Moreover, this secular understanding can be a sensitive empathetic understanding attuned (as Durkheim thought it must be) to the realities of religious experience and sentiment. This is shown most forcefully in the accounts of religious experience and sentiment given by Feuerbach, Hägerström, and Ronald Hepburn. Having a feel for religion does not require having the related belief, but it does require the having of a sense of what it is that makes religion so compelling, and so psychologically necessary, for so many people, indeed historically speaking for most people.

Naturalistic explanations are, of course, incompatible with religious belief. But they are not *thereby* inadequate explanations. They do not explain religion *away* in explaining or presupposing that religious claims could not be true, for the account explains religion's origins, explains its *claim* to truth, explains how that very claim is in error, the depth of that error, its persistence, in spite of that, in various institutional contexts and in the personal lives of human beings, its various cultural and historical forms, how and why it changes and develops as it does, and its continuing persistence and appeal in one or another form. An account which does these things well is a good candidate for a viable conception of religion, yielding an adequate range of explanations of the phenomena of religion. It seems to me that the naturalistic explanations we have discussed, particularly when taken together, do just that.

Bibliography

Durkheim, E.: *Les Formes élémentaires de la vie religieuse* (Paris: Alcan, 1912), tr. J. A. Swain, *The Elementary Forms of the Religious Life* (London: Allen & Unwin, 1915).

Feuerbach, L.: *The Essence of Christianity*, tr. G. Elliot (New York: Harper & Brothers, 1957).

Freud, S.: *Civilization and its Discontents* (1919), tr. W. D. Robson-Scott (London: Hogarth Press, 1930).

———: *The Future of an Illusion* (1927), tr. W. D. Robson-Scott (Garden City: Doubleday, 1957).

Hägerström, A.: *Philosophy and Religion* (1964), tr. P. T. Sandin (London: Allen & Unwin, 1964).

Lukes, S.: *Emile Durkheim* (1973) (Stanford: Stanford University Press, 1985).

Marx, K., and Engels, F.: *On Religion* (London: Lawrence & Wishart, 1958).

Nielsen, K.: *Naturalism without Foundations* (Buffalo: Prometheus Press, 1996).

52

The presumption of atheism

ANTONY FLEW

This presumption is not that presumptuous insolence of which, at the beginning of the final Book of *The Laws* (885A), Plato accuses those who dare to disbelieve in "the existence of the gods" and in their salutary and inflexible interventions in human affairs. Here the presumption of atheism, like the presumption of innocence under the English Common Law, is a principle prescribing who should bear the burden of proof. Whereas the presumption of innocence stipulates that accused persons shall be presumed to be innocent until and unless their prosecutors have succeeded in proving them guilty, the presumption of atheism stipulates that it is up to believers in the existence and activities of the gods or of God to provide good reason for believing rather than to unbelievers to provide positive reasons for not believing.

To perfect the parallelism the word "atheist" has in the present context to be construed in an unusual way. Nowadays it is normally taken to mean someone who explicitly denies the existence and activities of God as conceived within the three great Mosaic traditions – Judaism, Christianity, and Islam. But here it has to be understood not positively but negatively, with the originally Greek prefix "a-" being read in the same way in "atheist" as it customarily is in such other Greco-English words as "amoral," "atypical," and "asymmetrical." In this interpretation an atheist becomes not someone who positively asserts the non-existence of God, but someone who is simply not a theist. The former may be distinguished as the positive sense of the term and the latter as the negative.

It is important to notice that this class of negative atheists embraces some members who cannot properly be described as, in the modern understanding, agnostics. In this understanding agnostics have already conceded that there is, and that they have, a legitimate concept of God such that, whether or not this concept does in fact have actual application, it theoretically could. But negative atheists, unlike positive, have not as such necessarily conceded even this. Indeed the class of negative atheists includes as perhaps its most intellectually stimulating sub-class that of all those who have never encountered the concept in question, and who therefore require some account of how it can be introduced and can be shown to be coherently applicable.

We may distinguish three elements of analogy between the presumption of atheism and the presumption of innocence. The first is that in both of these contentions about the burden of proof the word "proof" is being used in the ordinary, wide sense in which proofs embrace any and every variety of sufficient reason. It is not limited to the sort of deductive, demonstrative proof in which the conclusion proved cannot be denied without thereby contradicting at least one of the premises.

In the Article of the *Summa Theologiae* immediately preceding that in which St Thomas Aquinas claimed that "There are five ways in which one can prove that there is a God" (I.ii.3), he certainly did maintain that this is something which "can be demonstrated" (I.ii.2). But, equally certainly, he did not mean this in the narrowest sense of "demonstrated." It was no doubt in order to avoid possible confusion there that when the First Vatican Council of 1870–1 proclaimed as an essential dogma of the Roman Catholic faith that "the one and true God our creator and lord can be known for certain by the natural light of human reason" (Denzinger 1953, Section 1806), the words "can be known for certain" replaced the reading "can be demonstrated" of an earlier draft.

A second element of positive analogy between these two presumptions is that both are defeasible; and that they are, consequently, not to be identified with assumptions. The presumption of innocence indicates where the court should start and how it must proceed. Yet the prosecution is still able, more often than not, to bring forward what is in the end accepted as sufficient reason to warrant the verdict "guilty;" which appropriate sufficient reason is properly characterized as a proof of guilt. Were the indefeasible innocence of all accused persons an assumption of any legal system, then there could not be within that system any provision for any verdict other than "not guilty." To the extent that it is, for instance, an assumption of the English Common Law that all citizens are cognizant of all which the law requires of them, that law cannot admit the fact that this assumption is, as in fact it is, false. The presumption of atheism is of course similarly defeasible, and requires no assumption of atheism whether positive or negative.

The third element in the positive analogy is a perhaps paradoxical consequence of the second. Because these are not assumptions but contentions about the burden of proof, that people succeed in proving what they are thus challenged to prove does not even begin to show that the burden was wrongly placed upon their shoulders. Yet although such contentions make no disputatious assumptions but are concerned only with proper procedures, their acceptance or rejection can nevertheless produce very substantial differences in the eventual outcomes.

To adopt a presumption about the burden of proof is to adopt a policy. And policies have to be assessed by reference to the objectives and the priorities of those for whom they are proposed. Thus the policy of presuming innocence is rational for all those for whom it is more important that no innocent person should ever be convicted than that no guilty person should ever go free, but irrational for those harboring the opposite priorities. If such people proposed or adopted a presumption of guilt, then upon whatever other grounds they might be faulted it could not be for their irrationality in so doing.

The objective by reference to which the policy of accepting the presumption of atheism has to be justified is the attainment of validation of knowledge about the existence and activities of God, if such knowledge is indeed attainable. The

411

inquiries pursued under this procedure are directed towards either acquiring such knowledge or showing who if anyone is already possessed of it.

Knowledge is of course crucially different from mere true belief. All knowledge that, as opposed to knowledge how, involves true belief. But not all true belief constitutes any kind of knowledge. To have a true belief is simply and solely to believe that something is so, and to be in fact right. But someone may believe that this or that is so, and the belief may in fact be true, without its thereby and necessarily constituting knowledge. If true beliefs are to achieve this more elevated status, then their believers have to be properly warranted so to believe. True believers must, that is to say, either have sufficient evidencing reasons or else in some other way be in a position to know.

Evidencing reasons, which constitute evidence for some supposed matter of fact, must be distinguished from motivating reasons, which in the present context constitute motives for self-persuasion regardless of the adequacy or inadequacy of the available evidence. For Blaise Pascal's wager argument began by stating that "Reason [by which he meant evidencing reason] can decide nothing here," and proceeded to the conclusion that the only safe, indeed the only sane bet is placed by persuading ourselves of the truth of Roman Catholicism (see Article 45, PRAGMATIC ARGUMENTS).

The question whether anyone does actually possess positive knowledge of the existence and activities of God can be illuminatingly approached by applying two passages from the *Discourse on Method* to the present case, and bringing out their true implications. The first comes from Part I, where René Descartes wrote:

For it seemed to me that I might find much more truth in the reasonings which someone makes in matters that affect him closely, the results of which must be detrimental to him if his judgment is faulty, than from the speculations of a man of letters in his study; which produce no concrete effect. . . .

In the second passage, which comes from Part II, he starts from the assertions of philosophers. But his conclusions apply with even greater force to religious beliefs:

. . .While traveling, having recognized that all those who hold opinions quite opposed to ours are not on that account barbarians or savages, but that many exercise as much reason as we do, or more; and, having considered how a given man, with his given mind, being brought up from childhood among the French or Germans becomes different from what he would be if he had always lived among the Chinese or among cannibals. . . . I was convinced that our beliefs are based much more on custom and example than on any certain knowledge.

When in Part IV Descartes undertakes to doubt everything which he can doubt, his supposedly almost all-embracing skepticism is directed primarily at beliefs of a kind which, in the first passage quoted, he had given good reason to adjudge the least dubious. For in Part I he had – ineptly but in his day prudently – granted immunity to locally established religious beliefs. So, "on the grounds that our senses sometimes deceive us," he proceeds to conclude that perhaps there is not "anything corresponding to what they make us imagine." He then attempts to prove, indeed by means of an ontological argument to demonstrate, the existence of a good God who as such cannot permit him to be comprehensively deceived by always delusive sense-data (see Article 41, ONTOLOGICAL ARGUMENTS).

This entire exercise manifests the need to accept the presumption of atheism. And that requires us to begin by examining any proposed or presupposed conception of God as if we were meeting it for the first time; considering, that is to say, whether it is coherently applicable and, if so, inquiring what evidencing reasons would be necessary and sufficient to establish that it does in fact have application. By contrast Descartes continues to take absolutely for granted the conception of God with which he was equipped by his Jesuit tutors. Later, in the third of his *Meditations on First Philosophy*, he argues that that conception is an innate idea imprinted upon every individual human soul as – as it were, and this is Descartes's own image – its Maker's trademark. Descartes thus both attempts to demonstrate that the doubtfully coherent conception of a logically necessary Being must have actual application and then goes on to assert, recklessly and falsely, that it is one with which we are all furnished at or before our births.

Suppose instead that we work with the definition of the word "God" offered at the beginning of the latest and most powerful philosophical defense of theism. It reads:

A person without a body (i.e., a spirit), present everywhere, the creator and sustainer of the universe, able to do everything (i.e., omnipotent), knowing all things, perfectly good, a source of moral obligation, immutable, eternal, a necessary being, holy, and worthy of worship.   (Swinburne 1977, p. 2)

The first difficulty is the identification of the intended subject of these various attributes. For both all the persons who we severally are, and all those others with whom we are variously acquainted, are creatures of flesh and blood. It is indeed only from our experience of such creatures of "too, too solid flesh" that we are able to acquire our ideas of persons. So how would it be possible to identify such immaterial spirits or – still more difficult – reidentify them after a lapse of time as being the same individual spirits?

In the present special case this difficulty can be conveniently resolved by making the intended subject the hypothesized ultimate cause of everything else, and therefore identifiable by reference to the Universe as a whole. It was a maneuver of this sort which allowed David Hume, in Part II of his posthumous masterpiece, the *Dialogues Concerning Natural Religion*, to make Philo insist "that the question is not concerning the *being* but the *nature* of God" (emphasis original). Until some characteristics are attributed to this hypothesized cause the hypothesis of its existence must remain as uncontentious as it is uninteresting. Philo – and, consequently, Hume – thus becomes able to deny the dangerous charge of atheism while proceeding to argue that it is impossible validly to infer from the observable Universe any conclusions about "the *nature* of God."

When we go on to ask what characteristics we might be rationally justified in attributing to this hypothesized subject it ought to become immediately obvious that it might conceivably possess one or more of the attributes listed in Swinburne's definition without necessarily possessing all or even any of the others. So what might constitute a sufficient evidencing reason for believing in the existence of a Being possessed of one of those defining characteristics will not necessarily be any sort of good reason for believing in the existence of God as thus defined.

The grossest and most flagrant example of failure to appreciate this is provided by those who assume that they are both entitled and required to move directly, and without evidencing support from some supposed prior Revelation, from the Big Bang of contemporary cosmology to Swinburne's God as its probable cause. For the whole history of natural science should suggest that, if it ever does become possible to discover the cause or causes of that explosive beginning, then it or they will most likely be impersonally and finitely physical (see Article 74, REVELATION AND SCRIPTURE).

In the *Summa Theologiae* Aquinas attempts to defeat the presumption of what Hume, following Pierre Bayle and in deference to Strato of Lampsacus, calls Stratonician atheism:

Now it seems that everything we observe in this world can be fully accounted for by other causes, without assuming a God. Thus natural effects are explained by natural causes, and contrived effects by human reasoning and will. There is therefore no need to suppose that a God exists.   (I.ii.3)

Aquinas in his response to this challenge takes his conception of God as an unquestionable given, and proceeds immediately to deploy his five promised proofs. These are in fact presented as proofs of the existence of five entities which are described very differently. These different descriptions are then simply assumed to apply to one and the same Supreme Being. Indeed four of the five conclude with "and this is what everybody understands by God" or some equivalent expression.

It is remarkable, yet rarely remarked, that in that same article Aquinas undertakes to meet a second challenge – that of reconciling the abundant evils of the Universe with its alleged total dependence upon a Creator both omnipotent and perfect (see Article 50, THE PROBLEM OF EVIL). Suppose that the existence of a "creator and sustainer of the universe, able to do everything (i.e., omnipotent)" and "knowing all this" can be "known for certain through the creation by the natural light of human reason" (see Article 28, OMNIPOTENCE; and Article 29, OMNISCIENCE). Then unless natural reason was being somehow supplemented and reinforced – whether by a supposed supernatural Revelation or in some other way – it would scarcely be possible to come even to suspect that that "creator and sustainer" might also be "perfectly good" (see Article 39, CREATION AND CONSERVATION; and Article 30, GOODNESS).

Consider, for example, how Joseph Butler in *The Analogy of Religion: Natural and Revealed*, believing that he has succeeded in showing that what he sees as "ten thousand instances of design cannot but prove a Designer," immediately mistakes it that he has at the same time proved: not only "that there is a God who made and governs the world;" but also that that God "will judge it in righteousness" (I, p. 371).

(Butler had, however, earlier asserted that this "moral government must be a scheme quite beyond our comprehension," and drawn the conclusion that "this affords a general answer to all objections against the justice and goodness of it" (I, p. 162). What he apparently did not appreciate was that, by thus making the claim that "God who made and governs the world will judge it in righteousness" humanly unfalsifiable, he necessarily deprived it of any humanly intelligible substance.)

Only claims to enjoy knowledge of God from the evidences of natural reason have so far been considered. But the presumption of atheism is equally relevant to claims to possess such knowledge either upon the basis of some supposed Revelation or through allegedly enjoying a kind of knowledge by acquaintance. For those sincerely desiring to know the truth of these most important matters must draw and act upon the moral implicit in Descartes's observations of "how a given man, with his given mind, being brought up from childhood among the French or Germans becomes different from what he would be if he had always lived among the Chinese or among cannibals. . . ."

For how, in the light of this observation, can any of us continue to assume that we happen to be members of a uniquely privileged set to whom an authentic Revelation has been vouchsafed? If commitment to a system of religion supposedly constituting or containing a Revelation is not to be arbitrary, irrational and indeed fundamentally frivolous, then the presumption of atheism has to be defeated by showing that there is good reason to believe that this particular pretended Revelation is actually authentic.

It is difficult if not impossible to suggest any sufficiently good reason other than that the teachings in question were and/or are Supernaturally endorsed by the production of miracles. Consider, for instance, one of the dogmatic definitions of the First Vatican Council: "If anyone shall say that miracles cannot happen . . . or that miracles can never be known for certain nor the divine origin of the Christian religion be proved thereby: let them be anathema" (Denzinger 1953, Section 1816).

To establish the authenticity of some particular pretended Revelation it would be necessary first to solve the problems of establishing the occurrence of any miracles at all by the methods of critical history – problems first indicated by Hume. Next it would be necessary to show that miracles had actually occurred as apparent supernatural endorsement of the particular teachings in question. But even that would still not be sufficient. For it would also be necessary to establish that no miracles had ever occurred to provide seeming supernatural endorsement for any other, inconsistent teachings.

Finally, consider the case of those who think to defeat the presumption of atheism by referring to what they apparently see as their enjoyment of a kind of knowledge by acquaintance with God. They believe and maintain that they have had, and continue to have, direct experience of God; and they sometimes go on to assert "that you too can have Jesus for a friend."

415

The crucial distinction here is between two senses of the word "experience," and of its semantic associates. In the ordinary, everyday, objective sense to claim to have had experience of cows or of computers is to claim that you have had dealings with real flesh and blood cows or with real chips and wires computers. In the other sense, which we might dub the subject sense, people can truly claim to have had experience of cows or of computers providing that they have dreamed, or had hallucinations of cows or of computers; and even though they have never actually seen and touched and manipulated a single, real, flesh and blood cow or a single, real, chips and wires computer.

Someone's honest claim to have had experience of some sort of objects, in the first sense of the word "experience," may be shown – perhaps by someone else – to have been mistaken. But someone's honest claim to have had experience of that same sort of objects, in the second sense of the word "experience," constitutes the irrefutable last word. For those who fail to make and maintain this crucial distinction it becomes all too easy to assume that claims to have had experience of something, in the first sense of "experience" possess the same irrefutability as they would have were the same word being construed in the second sense. If people make that mistaken assumption, then they may be misled to believe that those challenging their claims are implying that they are lying.

To all atheist observers those who claim to be having experience of God, and perhaps receiving communications from the same source, appear to be enjoying or suffering experience only in the second, subjective sense; and experience of that second kind constitutes no reason at all for believing in the objective existence of its reported objects. As Thomas Hobbes put it in chapter 32 of his *Leviathan*:

For if a man pretend to me, that God hath spoken to him supernaturally and immediately, and I make doubt of it, I cannot easily perceive what argument he can produce, to oblige me to believe it. . . . To say that he hath spoken to him in a dream is no more than to say that he dreamed that God spoke to him.

Bibliography

Aquinas, St Thomas: *Summa Theologiae* (Garden City: Doubleday, 1969).

Butler, J.: *The Works of Joseph Butler*, ed. W. E. Gladstone (Oxford: Clarendon Press, 1896).

Denzinger, H.: *Encheiridion Symbolorum Definitionum et Declarationum de Rebus Fidei et Morum* [*Handbook of the Texts of Definitions and Declarations concerning Matters of Faith and Morals*] (Barcelona, 1854), ed. C. Rahner (Freiberg-in Breisgau: Herder, 1953).

Descartes, R.: *The Philosophical Works of Descartes*, tr. E. S. Haldane and G. R. T. Ross (Cambridge: Cambridge University Press, rev. edn 1931).

Hobbes, T.: *The Leviathan* (1650) (London and New York: Dent and Dutton, 1914).

Hume, D.: *Dialogues Concerning Natural Religion* (London, 1779), ed. N. Kemp Smith (London: Nelson and Sons, 2nd edn 1946).

Plato: *The Laws*, tr. R. G. Bury (London, and Cambridge, MA: Heinemann and Harvard University Press, 1952).

Swinburne, R.: *The Coherence of Theism* (Oxford: Clarendon Press, 1977).

PART VIII

THEISM AND MODERN SCIENCE

53

Theism and physical cosmology

WILLIAM CRAIG

Physical cosmology is that branch of science which studies the origin, structure, and evolution of the universe as a whole. It is a field which has intimate connections with both philosophy and theology. Historically, cosmology finds its origin in religious doctrines concerning the foundation of the world, such as ancient Near Eastern creation stories. The cosmological speculations of the pre-Socratics were, in turn, the womb in which Western philosophy was conceived (see Article 8, ANCIENT PHILOSOPHICAL THEOLOGY). Together philosophy and theology dominated cosmological thinking until the technological advances begun in the Renaissance enabled cosmology to become in time a full-fledged empirical science. Nevertheless, it remains a field rich in issues of philosophical importance, both in its presuppositions and implications, and is also the scientific field which perhaps most overlaps the concerns of theology, given Christian theism's doctrines of creation and last things, which correspond to cosmology's subdivisions of cosmogony and eschatology.

The big bang origin of the universe

Although deeply influenced by Greek philosophical thought, the early Church Fathers stoutly opposed the Aristotelian doctrine of the eternality of the universe. From the first century on, with few exceptions, the Fathers held to the biblical doctrine of temporal *creatio ex nihilo* (creation from nothing; Genesis 1:1; Proverbs 8:22–31; Isaiah 44:24; John 1:1–3; Hebrews 11:3). Given this unanimity, no council pronounced on the doctrine until the Fourth Lateran Council (1215), which declared God to be "Creator of all things, visible and invisible, . . . who, by His almighty power, from the beginning of time has created both orders in the same way out of nothing." By this time there also existed a strong tradition, fueled by Islamic scholasticism, that the finitude of the past could be philosophically demonstrated. Such a beginning of the universe seemed to point ineluctably to its Creator (see Article 39, CREATION AND CONSERVATION). Even Thomas Aquinas, who was skeptical of arguments for the finitude of the past and so accepted the beginning of the universe on the basis of Scripture and church teaching, admitted, "If the world and motion have a first beginning, some cause must clearly be posited to account for this origin of the world and motion" (*Summa contra Gentiles*, 1.13.30).

Seven hundred years later the expansion of the universe predicted by the Russian mathematician Alexander Friedman in 1922 on the basis of a cosmological application of Einstein's general theory of relativity and first verified by Edwin Hubble's observation of the galactic red shift in 1929, coupled with the Hawking-Penrose singularity theorems of 1968, pointed via a time-reversed extrapolation of the expansion to the conclusion that the universe did in fact begin to exist at a point in the finite past before which it literally did not exist. That cosmic explosion of the universe into existence has come to be known as the "big bang." The initial cosmological singularity in which the universe originated marked the beginning, not only of all matter and energy in the universe, but of physical space and time themselves. The big bang model thus provided dramatic empirical verification of the biblical doctrine of *creatio ex nihilo* and the missing evidence for a sound cosmological argument.

Of course alternative models aimed at eliminating the absolute origin of the universe have been proposed. Two alternative models – the steady state model and the oscillating model – are now generally recognized to have failed as plausible attempts to avoid the beginning of the universe. The marriage of the general theory of relativity to quantum theory has resulted in the conception of a third alternative to the standard big bang model: quantum models of the universe. Prior to 10^{-43} seconds after the big bang quantum physics must be employed to describe the universe, and the goal of the union of relativity theory and quantum theory is to describe this brief moment. Unfortunately, this period is so poorly understood that it has been aptly compared with the regions on the maps of ancient cartographers marked "Here there be dragons!" – it can be filled with all sorts of fantasies.

One class of quantum models may be called vacuum fluctuation models. These theories hold that our observable universe is a tiny part of a wider universe-as-a-whole, which is itself a vacuum in a steady state. Throughout this vacuum subatomic energy fluctuations are conceived to be occurring, by means of which material particles are created out of the energy contained in the vacuum. These then grow into separate mini-universes within the whole, our observations pertaining to the expansion of our mini-universe alone.

One obvious question arises in connection with such models: since all the evidence we have indicates that the universe is expanding, why should we suppose that it is merely our part of the universe that is expanding rather than the *whole* universe? This hypothesis seems to violate the Copernican principle, which dictates that unless there is some compelling evidence to the contrary, we should assume that our observations of the universe are typical and that the observable universe is therefore not fundamentally different from the whole. But there is no evidence that the universe beyond the limits of our observations does not share in the expansion we observe or that this wider universe has the special properties necessary to spawn local universes via vacuum fluctuations. Indeed, it is difficult to see how we ever could have such evidence.

In any case vacuum fluctuation models have been shown to be incompatible with observational cosmology. On such scenarios it is impossible to specify exactly when and where a fluctuation in the primordial vacuum will occur which will grow into a universe. Within any finite interval of time there is a positive probability of such a fluctuation occurring at any point in space. It follows that given infinite past time, universes will spring into being at every point in the vacuum and, as they expand, will begin to collide with one another. But we do not observe anything of this sort happening in nature. About the only way to avoid the difficulty is to postulate that the background vacuum space is itself expanding – but then we are constrained to posit some origin of the wider universe itself, and we are right back where we started.

Most cosmologists believe that a final theory of the origin of the universe must await the as yet undiscovered quantum theory of gravity. The quantum gravity model which has drawn the most attention in recent years is that proposed in various versions by Stephen Hawking. By means of introducing imaginary numbers (multiples of $\sqrt{-1}$) for the time variable in his equation describing the wave function of the universe, Hawking drafts a model in which time becomes "imaginary" prior to 10^{-43} seconds, so that the singularity is rounded off. Space-time in this early region is geometrically the four-dimensional analogue of the two-dimensional surface of a sphere. Any point on a sphere which one chooses to be a "beginning" point, such as the North Pole, is really just like every other point on the sphere's surface. In particular, it does not constitute an edge or boundary to that surface. Thus, on Hawking's model, the past is finite, but boundless. Moreover, since imaginary time is not distinguishable from space, it would be improper to regard any point on this sphere-like surface as actually *earlier* than any other point on that surface. Hawking claims that if the universe is as he describes it, then it has no need of a creator.

Wholly apart from the scientific problems attending his model, however, it is evident that Hawking faces acute philosophical difficulties in commending his theory as a realistic account of the origin of the universe. For example, his uncritical use of so-called "imaginary time" is clearly problematic. First, Hawking has the burden of explaining what physical reality corresponds to the mathematical notion of "imaginary time." It is not any more evident what an imaginary interval of time is than, say, the imaginary volume of a glass or the imaginary area of a field. Second, the use of imaginary numbers for the time variable makes time a spatial dimension, which is metaphysically suspect. Time is ordered by a unique relation of *earlier/later than* and also, plausibly, by the relations *past/future* with respect to the present. Thus, space and time are essentially distinct. To make time a dimension of space or to claim that space can be converted into time, as Hawking's model does, is therefore just bad metaphysics.

Significantly, this philosophical critique applies to all quantum gravitational models, since they all share the common feature of having real space-time originate in a quantum mechanical region which is a four-dimensional space involving imaginary time. Of course, if some such model is interpreted non-realistically, then no metaphysical objection arises; but then neither does such a model abrogate the need for a creator.

The claim that God created the universe raises a host of important philosophical questions. We may consider briefly two.

First, since a cause must precede its effect in time and there is no time prior to the initial cosmological singularity, how can God be causally related to the big bang? The theist could answer this question by holding that God existed prior to the big bang in metaphysical time, which is distinct from the physical times posited in cosmological theory. But why think that causes must precede their effects temporally? The cause of the big bang could be simultaneous with it. On a relational view of time, God may be conceived to exist changlessly and, hence, timelessly *sans* creation, and to enter into time at the moment of creation (see Article 32, ETERNITY).

Second, why think that the universe's having a beginning implies that it literally *came into being* at the big bang and so requires a cause? This question suggests a view of time according to which the distinction between past, present, and future is merely a subjective feature of consciousness and temporal becoming is an illusion. On this view of time, the universe never really came into being, but just subsists tenselessly as a four-dimensional whole. Such a metaphysic of time requires that we regard all our experiences of tense and temporal becoming, both in our apprehension of the external world and in the inner life of the mind, as illusory, a conclusion comparable to Zeno's denial of the reality of motion. Moreover, it seems incoherent, in that even our illusion of temporal becoming involves an objective becoming in the contents of consciousness, so that temporal becoming is not eliminated. Much more needs to be said on this head, but the question at least serves to illustrate the intimate connection between cosmology and profound metaphysical issues in the philosophy of space and time.

The fine-tuning of the universe for intelligent life

In recent years the scientific community has been stunned by its discovery of how complex and sensitive a nexus of initial conditions must be given in the big bang in order for the universe to permit the origin and evolution of intelligent life. In the several fields of physics and astrophysics, classical cosmology, quantum mechanics, and biochemistry, various discoveries have repeatedly disclosed that the existence of intelligent carbon-based life on earth at this time depends upon a delicate balance of physical quantities, which is such that were any one of these quantities to be slightly altered, the balance would be destroyed and life would not exist. A life-prohibiting universe is inconceivably more probable than a life-permitting universe like ours.

Many scientists have felt compelled to conclude that such a delicate balance cannot be simply dismissed as coincidence, but requires some sort of account. Traditionally, such considerations would have been taken as evidence of divine design. Loath to admit the God-hypothesis, however, some thinkers have sought a way out by appealing to the so-called anthropic principle. First proposed by Brandon Carter in 1974, the anthropic principle has assumed a number of different forms, generating a great deal of confusion concerning what it is precisely that the principle means to assert. Fundamentally, it states that any observed properties of the universe which may initially appear astonishingly improbable can only be seen in their true perspective after we have accounted for the fact that certain properties could not be observed by us, were the universe to possess them, because we can only observe properties which are compatible with our own existence.

422

Anthropic theorists contend that the principle implies that no explanation of the basic features of our universe need be sought. We ought not to be surprised at observing the universe to be as it is, for if it were not as it is, we could not observe it. While this fact does not explain the origin of those features, it shows that no explanation is necessary. Hence, to posit a divine Designer is gratuitous (see Article 43, TELEOLOGICAL AND DESIGN ARGUMENTS).

This reasoning, however, is invalid. Certainly we should not be surprised that we do not observe features of the universe which are incompatible with our own existence. But it does not follow that we should not be surprised that we *do* observe features of the universe which *are* compatible with our existence, in view of the enormous improbability that the universe should possess such features.

Proponents of the anthropic principle will respond that such surprise is justified only if the basic features of our observable universe are coextensive with the basic features of the universe-as-a-whole. The anthropic principle is, however, typically conjoined to the hypothesis that our observable universe is but one member of a collection of diverse universes (a world ensemble) that go to make up a wider universe-as-a-whole. Given the existence of this wider universe, it is argued that all possible universes exist within it and that the anthropic principle reveals why surprise at our being in a universe with basic features essential to life is inappropriate.

Various theories, some of them quite fantastic, have been offered for generating a world ensemble. It needs to be emphasized that there is no evidence for any of these theories apart from the fact of intelligent life itself. But any such evidence for a world ensemble is equally evidence for a divine Designer. Moreover, each of the proposed scenarios faces formidable scientific and philosophical objections. The many worlds interpretation of quantum physics, for example, is so fantastic that philosopher of science John Earman characterizes its postulated splitting of space-time as a "miracle." "Not only is there no hint as to what causal mechanism would produce such a splitting," he complains, "there is not even a characterization of where and when it takes place" (Earman 1987, p. 312).

Even if we conceded that a multiple universe scenario is unobjectionable, it is not at all obvious that such a move would succeed in rescuing us from a cosmic Designer. The fundamental assumption behind the anthropic philosopher's reasoning seems to be that if the universe contains an exhaustively random and infinite number of universes, then anything that can occur with non-vanishing probability will occur somewhere. Why, though, should we think that the number of universes is actually infinite? And why should we think that the multiple universes are exhaustively random? These are not necessary conditions of many-worlds hypotheses. In order to avoid the hypothesis of intelligent design, one must assume much more than the mere existence of multiple universes.

The point is that the anthropic principle is impotent unless it is conjoined with a profoundly metaphysical vision of reality. Indeed, compared to the bloated ontology required by a world ensemble, the metaphysical postulate of theism might seem considerably more economical and therefore preferable.

423

WILLIAM CRAIG

Quantum physics and quantum cosmology

In writing the laws of quantum mechanics, Erwin Schrödinger treated quantum entities as waves, such that associated with every quantum system is a particular wave, called its wave function, the square of which at any location gives the probability of the associated entity's being located there if a measurement were carried out. Prior to the measurement, the entity literally has no precise position, but a range of positions varying in probability. Once a measurement has been carried out and the entity's position detected, however, then the probability of the entity's being at that location is 1; the wave function is said to have collapsed. What brought about this collapse is the measurement carried out on the quantum system. This led Niels Bohr to conclude that dynamic properties are not intrinsic properties of the quantum system itself, but relational properties with respect to the entire measurement situation.

Since the classical measuring device is also describable by the equations of quantum mechanics, it, too, has a wave function associated with it. But then the following question arises: if the measuring device itself is not a classical system, then what collapses its wave function? Bohr never answered this question. He just took for granted the existence of the classical measuring apparatus. Bohr's Copenhagen interpretation of quantum physics dealt only with the interrelation between the quantum and classical realms without shedding light on either realm in itself.

Johann von Neumann proposed to break the measurement chain at the point where human consciousness makes an observation of the quantum system. Reality thus depends at least with respect to its dynamic properties on human observers. However, this solution seems both unbelievable and unavailing. It implies that Schrödinger's cat, enclosed in a box with a potentially deadly quantum device, is neither dead nor alive until I open the box and look in, which just seems incredible. Moreover, since my consciousness is at least linked to a human brain, which, as a physical entity, can be described by the Schrödinger equation, what collapses the wave function of the system of me observing the cat? Positing a community of other human observers only perpetuates the regress.

It is at this point that the theist may offer a way of escape. For why must the conscious observer be a human observer? Why may not God act as a sort of Cosmic Observer who collapses the wave function in any measurement situation or even who would collapse any wave-functions in the universe with respect to any possible measurement? Since God is unembodied Mind, He cannot be described by the equations of quantum mechanics and so is utterly unaffected by quantum physical indeterminacy. Hence, the regress is broken (see Article 34, INCORPOREALITY).

One need not hold that God determines which of the possible states of a quantum system will be actual, but merely that He actualizes whichever one chances to result from a measurement situation by His observation of that measurement. An observer serves merely to objectify or actualize the outcome, to make reality determinate in the relevant respect. In order for God to do that, all that seems to be

424

required is that He be aware of the outcome of any measurement situation, that He have a true belief with respect to the result of that measurement. As a cosmic observer, God is non-mediately aware of the outcome of every measurement situation, so that His observation of a quantum measurement involves no intermediate links in the measurement chain.

On the orthodox Copenhagen interpretation, apart from a measurement situation there literally is no reality corresponding to the dynamic properties of quantum entities. At best these properties are relational properties involving the entire measurement situation. Hence, God need not be conceived to collapse the wave functions of unmeasured quantum systems. Rather what He knows is either the outcome of every quantum measurement actually made in the history of the universe or else the outcome which would result from any quantum measurement that could be made on any quantum system in the universe. Such knowledge is entailed by any adequate doctrine of divine OMNISCIENCE (see Article 29).

Such a conclusion has striking cosmological implications. The crucial assumption of quantum cosmology is that the universe at its inception possesses a wave function, and the collapse of this wave function is a necessary condition of the existence of our universe. But then on the traditional Copenhagen interpretation, the inevitable question cannot be suppressed: who or what collapses the wave function of the universe? Since all spatiotemporal observers are contained in the universe itself, the answer can only be: an observer who transcends space and time and who brings the universe into being by His reduction of its wave function. Apart from anti-supernaturalistic bias, there is no reason at all to prefer the exorbitant ontology of the many worlds interpretation over theism, which supplies a mathematically consistent picture of creation, is simpler, and enjoys independent support from other sources. By contrast, the many worlds interpretation, in apparently requiring a time beyond time, may not even be coherent.

Bibliography

Barrow, J., and Tipler, F.: *The Anthropic Cosmological Principle* (Oxford: Clarendon Press, 1986).

Craig, W. L., and Grünbaum, A.: "Creation and big bang cosmology," "Comments," "Response," *Philosophia naturalis*, 31 (1994), pp. 217–49.

Craig, W. L., and Smith, Q.: *Theism, Atheism, and Big Bang Cosmology* (Oxford: Clarendon Press, 1993).

Earman, J.: "The SAP also rises: A critical examination of the anthropic principle," *American Philosophical Quarterly*, 24 (1987).

Hetherington, N. S. (ed.): *Encyclopedia of Cosmology* (New York: Garland, 1992).

Kanitscheider, B.: *Kosmologie* (*Cosmology*) (Stuttgart: Philipp Reclam, 1984).

Leslie, J.: *Universes* (London: Routledge, 1989).

Russell, R. J., et al. (eds): *Quantum Cosmology and the Laws of Nature* (Vatican City: Vatican Observatory, 1993).

54

Theism and evolutionary biology

WILLIAM HASKER

This article will discuss the relationship between biological evolution and the traditional theistic conception of God; in particular, the doctrine of God as the creator of the natural world. We will not consider the numerous ideologies which have been erected on the basis of evolution, such as social Darwinism a century ago or the contemporary claim of sociobiology to explain nearly all human behavior in terms of patterns inherited from prehuman ancestors. Such ideologies are nearly always inimical to theistic religion, and they are at best weakly supported by the scientific theory of evolution. So we turn our attention to the relation between the scientific theory and theistic belief.

Theism and common ancestry

Evidently there is no inherent difficulty in the idea that God might create the universe and its contents through a gradual evolutionary process. Indeed, if theism is true, well-confirmed theories of geology, astronomy, and cosmology seem to show that God has done just that. The most vocal opposition to biological evolution comes from fundamentalist "creation science," and is based on a literal interpretation of the scriptural creation story. Its proponents reject not only evolution but mainstream geology and astronomy as well in order to secure the "young earth" (roughly 6,000 to 10,000 years of age) their theory demands. But there also exists a group of more sophisticated creationists who accept the geological timescale and the gradual appearance of more complex forms of life. They argue that: (1) The fossil record does not show the innumerable gradual transitions Darwin's theory requires, but rather, in many cases, the sudden appearance of major new forms without identifiable ancestors. (2) The high degree of certainty often claimed for belief in evolution rests in large part on the prior assumption that there does not exist a God who is capable of creating advanced forms *ex nihilo* (from nothing). (3) Once we acknowledge the possibility of divine creation, the fossil record is better explained by assuming that God did in fact specially create major new kinds of creatures from time to time, than by postulating unbroken genealogical continuity and a common ancestry for all living creatures.

The first two of these three contentions arguably contain a good deal of truth, but it is extremely questionable whether the best response is to deny the common evolutionary ancestry of life on earth. The strong scientific consensus in favor of common ancestry, and the lack of any well-developed creationist alternative, strongly suggest that it is a more prudent strategy for the theist to accept common ancestry, at least as a working hypothesis, and to explore the relationships between theistic religion and various aspects of evolutionary thought.

Evolution and divine purpose

What is essential for an acceptable religious interpretation of evolution is that the evolutionary process must be seen as the means selected by God for fulfilling God's creative purposes. This does not necessarily mean that God must be seen as having actively intervened in the process (though that is certainly not excluded a priori). God is no less the creator of stars and mountains because we have adequate naturalistic explanations of the origins of stars and mountains. However, for evolution to be "the means by which God created," it must be the case both that the results of evolution do in fact coincide with (what may be reasonably taken to be) God's purposes, and that it would have been possible for God to know in advance that this would be the case. The serious challenges to a theistic interpretation of evolution are those which dispute one or the other of these claims. We will consider several such challenges.

Evolution and the "objectivity of nature"

An initial objection to the project of a religious interpretation of evolution lies in the claim that science as such is committed to a view of nature as "objective" or non-teleological. According to Jacques Monod, "The cornerstone of the scientific method is the postulate that nature is objective. In other words, the *systematic* denial that 'true' knowledge can be got at by interpreting phenomena in terms of final causes – that is to say, of 'purpose.' " He goes on to say that this postulate is "consubstantial with science"; to abandon it means "departing from the domain of science itself" (Monod 1971, p. 21). Monod traces this idea (with dubious historical warrant) to the formulation of the principle of inertia by Galileo and René Descartes.

Monod takes his principle to imply not only that final causes are banished from physics – which was indeed the contribution of Galileo and Descartes – but that nothing whatever in nature is properly interpreted in terms of purposes of any kind. But this "postulate" has never been accepted generally by scientists, and is routinely violated today, especially in Monod's own field of biology. (A major purpose of his book is to resolve this "epistemological contradiction.") If Monod's principle is accepted in its full generality, the project of theistic interpretation of evolution is doomed from the start, but is there good reason to accept it? We will consider several reasons that have been given.

Evolution as cruel and wasteful

One objection to a theistic and teleological interpretation of evolution that surfaced early on is that evolution is too cruel and wasteful to be seen as the fulfillment of a divine purpose. Darwin wrote to Asa Gray, "I cannot persuade myself that a beneficent and omnipotent God would have designedly created the Ichneumonidae with the express intention of their feeding within the living bodies of Caterpillars, or that a cat should play with mice" (quoted in McMullin 1985, p. 139). Still earlier we have David Hume's famous complaint about a "blind nature . . . pouring forth from the lap, without discernment or parental care, her maimed and abortive children." As the latter quotation shows, this objection does not depend essentially on evolution, but is rather an aspect of the general problem of natural evil (see Article 50, THE PROBLEM OF EVIL). The objection seems to have been especially salient in the nineteenth and early twentieth centuries, perhaps as a reaction to the excesses of a natural theology in which, as Holmes Rolston has pointed out, "the idea of a perfect machine was transferred to that of a perfectly designed organism . . . [and] the then-current paradigm for design persuaded thinkers to overlook not only anomalies and misfits, mutations and monstrosities, but, more importantly, struggle, gamble, and loss" (Rolston 1987, p. 90).

It should be noted that this objection, if pursued relentlessly, harbors within itself value judgments that are highly suspect; it implies not only the rejection of divine creation but a deep antipathy to nature itself. One may be led to hold that it would be better that there be neither hawks nor hares, than that hawks should live by preying upon hares; and the destruction of the rain forests may come to seem, on the whole, a beneficent act, in that it greatly reduces the number of creatures that will suffer, die, and be preyed upon (see Article 64, THEISM AND ENVIRONMENTAL ETHICS).

Once irrelevant models are discarded (the prairie is not a garden, the jungle is not a zoological park), this objection seems not to be insurmountable. It may not be necessary to ask why God specifically chose to create Ichneumonidae or the HIV virus; presumably parasites and disease organisms, like other organisms, evolve so as to exploit an available ecological niche. More generally, John Hick has well argued that a world of objective difficulties and dangers, with its attendant suffering, is a central means for bringing human beings to moral and spiritual maturity. Similarly, in the broad evolutionary context, "Life is advanced not only by thought and action, but by suffering, not only by logic but by pathos" (Rolston 1987, p. 144). This theme resonates deeply with the Christian conception of God, who "is not in a simple way the Benevolent Architect, but is rather the Suffering Redeemer." And "Life is a paradox of suffering and glory, and this 'secret of life' remains hidden in God, unresolved by biochemistry or evolutionary theory. The way of nature is the way of the cross; *via naturae est via crucis*" (Rolston 1987, pp. 144, 146).

Evolution as random and contingent

In contemporary discourse the "cruelty" of evolution tends to recede into the background; what is most often said to defeat a religious interpretation of evolution is its random, unplanned character. Darwinian orthodoxy stresses that the results of evolution, which convey the impression of intelligent design, are in fact the outcome of a random natural process which had no end in view. Evolution is, in Richard Dawkins's phrase, the "blind watchmaker." This line of argument has been underscored by an emphasis on the contingency of the evolutionary process and its results. Stephen Jay Gould, in particular, insists that the directions of evolutionary change are in no way inevitable. The survival of various lineages at times of catastrophic mass extinction (such as marked the ends of the Permian and Cretaceous periods) depends as much on luck as on adaptation understood in conventional terms. If we were able to rewind the tape of life and play it again from the beginning, there is no guarantee whatever that human beings, or any other form of intelligent life, would emerge.

Gould seems to think this change in evolutionary theory is fatal to any attempt to understand evolution in terms of divine purpose. If we were able to see evolution as the majestic unfolding of a preordained pattern (as many 19th century evolutionists understood it), then a theological interpretation might make sense. But if in fact it has a radically contingent character, it is no longer a matter of divinely ordained inevitability but rather of simple good luck that we are here with our opposable thumbs and enlarged brains to talk about it.

This way of thinking is highly contestable. Biblical religion places tremendous emphasis on God's working through a historical process that is contingent, unpredictable, and at times extremely surprising. Why then should God not also work through a contingent, inherently unpredictable process of evolution? In either case, to be sure, it will be necessary to affirm God's active intervention to shape events into the desired pattern – though one need not claim to know much about the details of such intervention. Yet to affirm any kind of divine "steering" of the process brings one sharply into conflict with the regnant evolutionary orthodoxy. Some, perhaps, will not find this price too high to pay.

It is worth pointing out that the highly contingent character of evolution, if accepted, puts some pressure on Darwinism itself. Darwinian selection, enhanced by modern genetics, is quite convincing in its account of gradual modification through the accumulation of minor variations. But it continues to have difficulty in accounting for major evolutionary "breakthroughs" – large changes which cannot readily be seen as the accumulation of minor variations, and for which evidence of gradual transition is lacking. Add to this the stress on the contingency of evolution, which means that theory is powerless to predict the major directions of evolutionary change, and we arrive at a situation in which evolutionary theory really has *very little explanatory power* with regard to the overall process. Now, it could be that this is the best that can be done. If we know a priori that neo-Darwinian explanations are the only ones possible, then we might have to accept the fact that the features of the process we are most interested in are simply the result of a series of highly improbable coincidences – in other words, of luck. But of course, we do *not* know this, either a priori or in any other way. And it is difficult to distinguish, empirically, between a situation in which the best possible explanation still leaves a great deal unexplained, and one in which a better explanation exists but we have so far been unable to find it.

429

Evolution and human nature

It is often thought that evolution poses a problem for a religious understanding of the nature of human beings. The acceptance of evolution seems to push one in the direction of a naturalistic, reductivist view of human nature which contrasts sharply with the religious view of humankind as bearers of the divine image.

Almost certainly, this is a mistake. The difficulty here does not lie in evolutionary science as such, but rather in the naturalistic philosophies which underlie some interpretations of evolution (including interpretations given by prominent scientists). Evolution does force one to recognize affinities between humans and other animals, but the fact that humans are animals comes as no surprise; it was well known, for instance, to Aristotle. Also, the major differences between humans and other animals – developed rationality, the use of language, the development of culture, moral and spiritual awareness – are empirically evident. The interpretation of these differences – for instance, whether ordinary morality, with its belief in an objective difference between right and wrong, is a massive illusion, as J. L. Mackie among others has urged – is a matter for philosophical and religious debate (see Article 55, THEISM AND THE SCIENTIFIC UNDERSTANDING OF THE MIND). But to assume that common biological descent forces one to accept a naturalistic account of human beings is a classic instance of the genetic fallacy.

Evolution, physicalism, and purpose

Thus far, we have found no clear confirmation for Monod's assertion that true knowledge of nature cannot be found by interpreting it in terms of purposes, including and especially God's purposes. The suffering found in nature may give one pause, but does not in the end defeat a theistic interpretation. The randomness and unpredictability of evolution are perfectly compatible with viewing it as an arena of divine activity. And the widespread impression that evolution supports a naturalistic, reductionist account of human nature is seen to be due more to the naturalistic philosophies embraced by some evolutionists than to the scientific theory of evolution.

We have yet to consider what may be the strongest motivation for evolutionists to reject explanation in terms of purpose. This is the commitment to physicalistic explanation, a commitment which is considered to be normative for science generally and has been strengthened for biology in particular by recent progress in molecular genetics and biochemistry. Maintaining this commitment allows biology to be integrated into the powerful explanatory paradigms of the physical sciences in a way that would otherwise be impossible.

In light of this commitment, the overall structure of evolutionary theory looks something like this: Certain complex assemblages of organic chemicals develop a kind of dynamic stability in their interactions with the environment, together with a capacity for self-replication, which leads us to say they are alive. A variety of random physical forces leads to variations in the self-replicating assemblages, and some of the assemblages are more successful than others in maintaining and replicating themselves. Over time, some of these assemblages become more complex than the earliest forms by many orders of magnitude, and their behaviors and interactions with the surrounding environment also become more complex. Nevertheless, the entire process is governed by, and explicable in terms of, the ordinary laws of physics and chemistry. Put differently, it is never necessary to go outside of the physical configurations and the physical laws in order to predict the future behavior of these assemblages; this is the "closure of the physical."

No one would claim that this goal of comprehensive, unified scientific explanation is close to being realized in practice, but enough has been accomplished to make it more than a pipedream. And if the objective of a "theory of everything" is to be realized, this sort of unification must be held possible. However, there is an epistemological price to pay for these benefits. In the physicalist picture, intentional states are physical states of the organism, primarily of the brain and central nervous system. Some of these physical states are believings, doubtings, fearings, desirings, and the like – that is, they are propositional-attitude states. Now, epistemology in an evolutionary context invariably invokes natural selection as a guarantor of the general reliability of our epistemic faculties. Organisms which, in the presence of a saber-toothed tiger, form the belief that a woolly lamb stands before them and experience a desire to cuddle it, are unlikely to pass on these unfortunate epistemic propensities to offspring. So our belief-dispositions, like our behavioral dispositions, are subject to selection pressures, and their general reliability is thereby guaranteed, at least for beliefs which have some fairly direct connection with survival and reproductive success.

When this evolutionary epistemology is combined with the commitment to physicalistic explanation, a startling fact emerges: belief-states and desire-states as such have no effect on behavior and are not subject to selection pressures! The rejoinder to this is that belief-states are in fact identical with brain-states and as such they do indeed influence behavior and are subject to selection pressures. This is true, however, only in a Pickwickian sense. The belief-state *considered as a physical brain-state* does indeed interact causally with other physical states of the organism and the environment. But *the intentional content of the belief-state is irrelevant to its causal interactions*; in a conceivable world in which the identical physical state was attended by no conscious awareness, the organism would still flee from danger, seek food and sex, and complain about the weather (or, emit sounds interpretable as complaints about the weather) just as it does in the actual world. The selection pressures ensure that the physical state of the organism will be such as to give rise to appropriate behavior, but they have no tendency whatever to ensure that the intentional content of belief-states corresponds with objective reality. And since, in the physicalistic evolutionary scenario, selection pressures are the *only* factor tending to guarantee the reliability of our epistemic faculties, it follows from that scenario that we have no reason whatever to trust their reliability. Of course, it might be the case, as a result either of a continual miracle or of some kind of pre-established harmony, that what our brains cause us to believe does after all generally coincide with what is really the case. But we can have no reason to think that this really is so – and if it were so, such otherwise inexplicable epistemic success would in itself be a powerful argument for theism.

Assuming these consequences are unacceptable, the alternative is to admit that the intentional content of mental states really does influence behavior – which is to say, that desires and beliefs as such really are relevant to what people do and say. (This of course is what all of us believe all of the time anyway, except for short stretches when we are in the grip of physicalist dogma.) However, this also comes at a price. It means that the physicalistic dream of a theory of everything based on the principles of physics must be given up; those principles need to be supplemented in some way (just how will be a matter for further discussion) to allow for the role of the mind in guiding behavior. Some human and animal behavior really is teleological (not just "teleonomic"). It means also that we may need to consider seriously the possibility of irreducibly teleological explanation even where consciousness is not directly involved; the unconscious and pre-conscious striving of unminded creatures is similar enough to conscious striving to make this a live option. And, finally, once the door has been opened to seeing individual organisms as genuinely purposive, it becomes once again an open question whether we can see purpose on a broader scale, namely in the purposes of the creator.

We have seen that the most common objections to a religious reading of evolution are of little force, and it has been argued that a strictly physicalistic version of evolution leads to unacceptable paradox and must be modified in such a way as to allow for irreducible teleology in the world of nature. If this is so, then the way is open for the development of a constructive religious interpretation of evolution, one that will not merely remove evolution as a threat to faith, but will exploit its possibilities for the enhancement of a theistic worldview.

Bibliography

Barlow, C. (ed.): *Evolution Extended: Biological Debates on the Meaning of Life* (Cambridge, MA, and London: MIT Press, 1994). [Excellent collection of statements on the meaning of evolution.]

Gould, S. J.: *Wonderful Life: The Burgess Shale and the Nature of History* (New York and London: W. W. Norton, 1989). [Classic statement on the contingency of evolution.]

Johnson, P. E.: *Darwin on Trial*, 2nd edn (Downers Grove, IL.: InterVarsity Press, 1993). [Advocates "old-earth" creationism.]

McMullin, E. (ed.): *Evolution and Creation* (Notre Dame: University of Notre Dame Press, 1985).

Monod, J.: *Chance and Necessity: An Essay on the Natural Philosophy of Modern Biology*, tr. A. Wainhouse (1970) (New York: Knopf, 1971).

Rolston, H., III: *Science and Religion: A Critical Survey* (New York: Random House, 1987).

Ruse, M.: *The Darwinian Paradigm: Essays on its History, Philosophy, and Religious Implications* (London and New York: Routledge, 1989).

Teilhard de Chardin, P.: *The Phenomenon of Man*, tr. B. Wall, (1955), rev. tr. (New York: Harper Row, 1965). [Classic, though somewhat dated, attempt to incorporate evolution into a constructive religious worldview.]

432

55

Theism and the scientific understanding of the mind

ROBERT AUDI

The relation between religion and science has long been a major concern of the philosophy of religion, particularly since Charles Darwin. There are many elements in the relation, but the most important ones may be those connected with the concept of mind. In an unqualified form, the central question here is whether the truth of theism can be squared with a scientific conception of mind, or, to change at least the emphasis of the question, whether there is a scientifically acceptable conception of mind that squares with a plausible theistic concept of a person – human or divine. One difficulty in answering the question is that we cannot presuppose any widely accepted definitions of "theism," "science," "mind," or other pivotal terms. Even the most plausible definitions of these terms remain highly controversial. The best course here is to establish, for each pivotal term, a working characterization that enables us to address the most important philosophical issues associated with the problem. This is our first task.

The terms of the problem

To make the issue manageable, and to maintain contact with the mainstream of discussion on our problem, we shall consider only monotheism and indeed what might perhaps be called "standard" Western theism, the kind illustrated by Christianity, Judaism, and Islam and centering on God as the omniscient, omnipotent, omnibenevolent creator of the universe (see Article 29, OMNISCIENCE; Article 28, OMNIPOTENCE; and Article 30, GOODNESS). If these four terms are taken to imply, as they commonly are in the philosophy of religion, more than what intelligent lay people would ordinarily mean by "all-knowing," "all-powerful," "wholly good," and "creator" – if, e.g., omnipotence entails being able to do anything "logically possible" and "creator" implies producing the universe "from nothing" (see Article 39, CREATION AND CONSERVATION) – then it is arguable that the God of standard Western theism is a philosophical construction and hence the concept of God is not (or not entirely) a religious notion rooted in scripture or everyday religious practice. Even if this "deflationary" view is correct, however, the traditional notion of God as creator of the universe and as having these four attributes is both central in the literature on our problem, and one that ordinary theists readily arrive at upon reflecting on what is implicit in their initially simpler conception of

God. One need not start with a philosophical conception of the divine attributes to find the path thereto almost irresistible once reflection begins. By contrast, a brief discussion of theism and the scientific understanding of the mind need not presuppose that God has certain other, more "technical" attributes often considered essential, for instance impassibility, necessary existence, simplicity, and timelessness (see Article 40, IMMUTABILITY AND IMPASSIBILITY; Article 33, NECESSITY; Article 31, SIMPLICITY; and Article 32, ETERNITY).

It may seem that science is less difficult to characterize than theism, but that is by no means clear. Again, it is best to center on some of the natural and social sciences as paradigms – particularly biology, chemistry, physics, and psychology – and frame the discussion with reference to them. We may also presuppose some widely accepted basic properties of scientific theorizing: (1) it aims at providing an account of the phenomena of experience, psychological as well as physical, and (2) it seeks an account that has explanatory and predictive power and is in some way testable through the use of observation or experiment. There is less agreement on what constitutes a scientific understanding – the kind that is an upshot of successful scientific theorizing. Some would say that we understand phenomena, such as those of human behavior, only if we can predict them from underlying states or processes. There would, however, be disagreement about whether the relevant underlying states or processes are causal. There is even disagreement over whether the basic, unobservable items that, at any given time, are explanatorily fundamental are real or, instead, to be understood instrumentally, say as posits that facilitate the activities of explanation and prediction crucial for negotiating the world. There is also disagreement over the status of scientific generalizations: do they express necessary connections or simply *de facto* regularities? *Must* metals expand when heated or is this simply a regular pattern that we have confirmed sufficiently to warrant our accepting it?

It is impossible to resolve these disagreements here, but we may be guided by the idea that the degree of harmony between science and theism is most readily probed if we consider rich conceptions of each. Standard Western theism is a rich version of theism, giving God not only far-reaching attributes but, by implication, the associated mental properties of (minimally) knowledge and good will. If there is not an equally standard conception of science, we may certainly say that for many who understand science its theories do provide an account of phenomena which has explanatory and predictive power, represents events as playing causal roles, and, commonly, describes them as falling into patterns that admit of explanation in terms of underlying states or processes, such as those involving configurations, movements, and forces among elementary particles. Taking this fairly rich conception of science together with the comparably rich conception of theism enables us to address a number of the persistent problems centering on the relation between scientific and religious conceptions of mind.

The scientific understanding of the mind

Even with a conception of science before us, there remains much to be said about what would constitute a scientific understanding of mind. The first point to be made here is that neither psychologists nor biological scientists interested in mind need countenance any *substance* that can be called "the mind." Rather, talk of the mind – e.g. of someone's having a good mind – is considered a kind of discourse about people and their mental properties, such as thinking. To be sure, many educated people tend to think of the mind as the brain. This is not, however, a considered view: it comes of oversimplifying the multitude of connections between our brains and our mental properties, and (outside philosophy) it is not often put to the basic test it must pass as a serious identity claim – every property of the brain must be a property of the mind and vice versa. Do we want to assign the mind a weight in grams? Can it be dyed bright red, as the brain can? Can we, as in the case of the brain, remove parts of the mind, hold them in our hands, and discard them, without affecting its mental function? And when the mind is wholly occupied with the relation between religion and science, must the brain be also? Given what we know about what the brain must do to keep us alive, the answers are surely negative.

There may be a few who will dig in their heels and defend the view that the mind is the brain. Rather than continue to discuss this, we would do better to note that what, in a scientifically minded person, motivates the brain-mind identity view is the desire to construe a person as a physical system. *That* desire can be accommodated by simply taking every mental property to be some kind of brain property – a view commonly called the *identity theory*. The identity theory goes well with a materialistic conception of the universe, and that, in turn, seems to go well with a scientific worldview. Physics, for instance, is commonly taken to understand phenomena in terms of matter and motion, especially contacts between concrete material entities. This conception is, however, naive: even Newtonian physics countenanced action at a distance, and the relevant gravitational forces do not require a stream of material particles traversing the entire distance.

As scientists report progressively smaller and less "corpuscular" elementary particles, we may wonder how material the basic entities postulated by current physics *are*. We might also ask what scientists must say about the status of numbers, which are indispensable for their work. The number 3 is not a numeral or even a set of numerals (destroying all of these symbols for the number would not destroy it, or undermine the truths in which it figures). Granted, a scientific materialist may care only about concrete entities; but even if all of these can be conceived as material, numbers and properties (such as the property of being square) are at best not easily interpreted as such. The point is that while materialist *metaphysicians* want to conceive everything real as material, this aim is not essential to science, which, arguably, presupposes rather than seeking to explain the nature and truth of pure mathematics, and appears quite uncommitted to restricting its posited entities to those properly conceived as material.

A natural step to take here is to distinguish the material from the physical and to maintain simply that mental properties are physical. Now, however, the contrast between the mental and the canonical basic elements of science is weakened. Suppose, e.g., that physical properties are understood as those having causal and explanatory power with respect to observable events. "Mentalists" – those who believe mental properties like thinking and sensing are real – will respond that, clearly, mental properties have this kind of power. But, one might ask, how can a mental phenomenon like a decision, cause a physical phenomenon like my telephoning a friend? With action at a distance, there are two physical phenomena in a causal relation; here, the relation is cross-categorial. There may be no obviously cogent answer to this question, but it should help to recall that physics itself seems to be appealing to less and less familiar kinds of entities in explaining observable events. It should also be said that if there is something mysterious here, a mystery is not an impossibility. Indeed, there is, as David Hume saw, something mysterious about causation of any kind once we look for more than a mere regularity linking causes to their effects.

Suppose, however, that it should be true that a scientifically minded thinker must opt for the identity theory. Is there good reason to think the theory true? It has been ably and plausibly attacked in the literature and is presently not held by most scientifically minded philosophers who count themselves physicalists. There are many other conceptions of the mental available to such philosophers. Two should be noted here: *philosophical behaviorism*, roughly the view that mental properties are behavioral (and hence physical) properties; and *eliminative materialism*, roughly the view that there are no mental properties, and hence mental terms represent false postulations (usually accompanied by the hypothesis that neuropsychology will ultimately enable us to do without those terms in explaining behavior). Philosophical behaviorism is widely agreed to have been refuted; and eliminative materialism, though currently defended by a small number of theorists, does not provide a positive conception of the mental that can be readily used in pursuing the problem central here. Even if it should be successful in showing that certain apparently mental concepts are empty, its proponents have not provided a plausible general account of the concept of the mental and shown that this broad concept is empty.

A view that may promise to avoid the pitfalls of both behaviorism on one side and the identity theory on the other is *functionalism*, roughly the thesis that mental properties are to be understood in terms of certain input–output relations; e.g. to be in pain is to be in a state of the kind caused by a burn and causing outcries. Mental properties are, as it were, *role-defined* rather than defined in terms of any quality they have or type of material constituting them. On this view, a person has only physical and functional properties, and the latter are defined in terms of relations among the former. Functionalism is defensible, but is widely (though not universally) agreed to leave us at least unsatisfied with respect to understanding qualities of experience, such as the painfulness of pain and the redness of an afterimage. Whereas the identity theory could claim that the experience of (say) being in pain is identical with a brain state, functionalism must maintain that there is nothing it "is like" to be in pain, no intrinsic character of the experience: talk of the experience is talk of mediation between inputs and outputs, and that mediation has no intrinsic character. Thus, if my sensory impressions of red and green were inverted with respect to those of normal people, functionalism would apparently have to say that I am still having the same experience (am in the same perceptual mental state) when I approach a red light because, being taught in the same way as everyone else, I respond to red stimuli as they do regardless of my internally "seeing green."

These and other difficulties with the identity theory and functionalism have led a number of scientifically minded philosophers to maintain a *non-reductive materialism*: mental properties are grounded in (supervene on, in a currently much-discussed terminology) physical ones, but are not identical with them, hence not reducible to them. This view allows us to anchor the mental in the physical and biological world without either the difficulties of identifying mental with physical properties or those of trying to account for qualities of experience. However, granting that this view does not have to countenance mental *substances*, such as Cartesian minds, it remains a *property dualism*. It will thus be unsatisfactory to those who take physical properties to be the only kind, as well as those who do not see how mental phenomena as such can have any explanatory power if they are not really physical. If, e.g., my decision to telephone someone merely depends on my brain properties and is identical with none of them, how does my decision produce my physical behavior, as opposed to being, say, a mere shadow of the real productive work done by something in my brain which really has the power to move my fingers over the buttons?

This kind of problem is receiving much discussion, and non-reductive materialism is still in development. What has not been generally noticed that is highly relevant to our problem is that if there should be mental substances, their mental properties might still depend on physical ones in much the way posited by non-reductive materialists. Nothing prevents my mind from being integrated with my body so as to respond to neural stimuli, say from my color perception, just as reliably as, for an identity theorist, the brain responds to them by going into "color states." If the non-physical property of having a red sensation or being in pain can depend on a brain property, then in principle it can do this even if it is a property of a Cartesian mind. René Descartes famously said (in *Meditation VI*) that we are not lodged in our bodies merely as the captain of a ship is lodged therein; and if one thinks there are mental–physical causal interactions, one might well suppose that the mental depends on the physical even if it also has causal powers over (other) physical phenomena. Reflection on this sort of possibility may lead to the hypothesis that in the end one must either live with a deep mystery in non-reductive materialism or choose between a version of the identity theory and a version of substance dualism.

Is a substance dualism compatible with a scientific worldview? If such a worldview includes the metaphysical drive for monism, and especially for materialism (or at least physicalism) that is so prominent among philosophers of science, it is not. But if one conceives science as seeking a testable, explanatory account of the phenomena we experience and appealing to causal connections with underlying states or processes as basic, then there is no strict incompatibility. Indeed, one can do psychology, and scientifically connect the brain with our mental life, in all the ways psychologists do, without presupposing either that substance dualism is right or that it is wrong. In framing an overall conception of the human person, much depends on the status of the principle of intellectual economy, which tells us not to multiply kinds of entity beyond necessity. This is a widely accepted principle, especially among the scientifically minded. But when is it *necessary* to posit a kind of entity? That is simply not obvious. The jury seems to be still out on the question of what philosophy of mind, taken together with all the scientific data, best harmonizes with this principle.

Theism and the philosophy of mind

We may assume (for our purposes here) that standard Western theism centers on a personal God, a God conceived as having a sufficiently rich set of mental properties to count as a person of a special kind. Usually, God is conceived as a spiritual being; commonly, God is also considered a non-physical substance (see Article 34, INCORPOREALITY). If, however, one wants to say that in the "typical" view God is a kind of Cartesian mind, this would go too far. Those who speak, religiously and not philosophically, of the divine mind do not conceive it as identical with God but as essential to God. It is not common, however, for believers – apart from special cases like the Incarnation of Jesus – to speak of God as embodied, and we may leave the Incarnation aside in order to avoid presupposing any specific theology. Still, any theist convinced that a person must have a body can make a case for God's having a body – for instance, the world as a whole. At least three points are important if this view is to be taken seriously: God can move any part of the world at will, as we can move our limbs at will; God has non-inferential knowledge of the position of every part of the world, as we (often) have such knowledge of the position of certain of our limbs; and in so far as God has experiences (which might be taken to be a matter entirely up to God), the entire world might be experienced in the divine mind in something like a perceptual way, producing the appropriate sensations with phenomenal qualities as rich as God wishes them to have. To be sure, it is not clear how the states of the divine mind *depend* on anything physical; on one view, they would immediately depend on the physical, as where a divine perception is produced by my moving my head, but *ultimately* depend on God, as (at least the sustaining) creator of everything physical. The view in question also implies that we human beings are part of God. This consequence brings its problems, but most of them, such as the harmony between divine sovereignty and human freedom, are already with us (see Article 37, FOREKNOWLEDGE AND HUMAN FREEDOM).

Still another possibility is that the notion of a body need not be tied to that of physical matter. As some philosophers imagine resurrection, it takes place not by disembodiment of the mind or soul and the person's survival therein, but through God's providing a resurrection body in place of the physical one (note that in 1 Corinthians 15:43–4, Paul speaks of a "spiritual body" as what is "raised"). Theism as such, however, does not immediately entail the possibility of personal resurrection; it entails this only on the assumption that such resurrection is logically possible. If one's philosophy of mind forced one to conclude that it is not, unless some suitable physical embodiment occurred, then one could harbor a hope of resurrection only in so far as one took God to supply an appropriate body (see Article 70, SURVIVAL OF DEATH). That, however, is apparently logically possible, as are various kinds of embodiment on the part even of God.

So far, our discussion has presupposed a kind of realism: that there are things, such as physical objects, whose existence is mind-independent and material. For idealists, such as George Berkeley, this view is a mistake; and currently some anti-realists also reject such views. One intelligible form of antirealism would be, like Berkeley's, theistic: the primary reality would then be not only mental but the divine mind. Such a view, with or without the idea that the world is God's "body," can make sense of both the relation of God to human persons and the common-sense world known through perception and scientific investigation. The central problem here is to make good sense of the regularity and familiar features of experience. If the picture is as coherent as it seems, the task is arguably quite within the scope of omnipotence.

Compatibility, harmony, and mutual support

Several points seem clear from our discussion above: that standard Western theism, taken apart from specific theological commitments which cannot be addressed here, provides considerable latitude in the conception of God, that there is no universally acceptable notion of science which rules out the existence of God, and that most of the leading views in the philosophy of mind are either not materialist at all or non-reductively so. Even reductive materialism is not strictly incompatible with theism: God could have created us as material systems, and God could also have a body some of whose properties would be the physical identicals of divine mental properties. We are speaking, of course, about sheer logical compatibility between theism and various conceptions of mind. As important as compatibility is by itself, one naturally wants to ask whether there can be something more: a harmony between theism and the scientific conception of mind.

Here we might begin with a question so far left in the background: does a scientific conception of *anything*, mental or physical, require the assumption that all explanations of its existence and career must be natural? It is by no means clear that this is so, in part because it is not clear what counts as a natural explanation. It is certainly not clear that if a mental property, such as my making a decision, is not identical with a physical one, then that property's explaining something, such as my telephoning a friend, is not natural. Suppose, then, that a divine decision explains a physical event. It might be said that this *must* be a non-natural explanation because it is supernatural. That may seem true if God has no body, but even on that assumption there is a danger of going too fast. If it is even possible that we human beings are essentially mental substances, then the way events in our minds cause physical events could be a model for one way in which divine decisions do: cross-categorially. This could be harmonized with the view that we are created in God's image. There remains the disanalogy concerning the different kind of dependence of our mental states on the physical and God's mental states on the physical (or anything else outside God). But it is not clear that a scientific approach to the world – as opposed to certain metaphysical interpretations of such an approach – cannot accommodate that disanalogy. Causations across different metaphysical categories may be mysterious, but causation may be somewhat mysterious in any case. If a scientific worldview is possible without it, that would at least not be a typical case of such a view. To many scientifically minded people, moreover, it would seem explanatorily impoverished.

At least three further responses to our problem should be mentioned if we are to indicate the range of main options. First, a person attracted both to theism and to a scientific worldview and unable to harmonize them could agnosticize: simply hold theism as a hypothesis deserving regular reflection and meriting certain responses in one's daily life. Second, one could treat one's favorite position in the philosophy of mind similarly, being agnostic about that while taking one's theism to be true. Third, one could opt for *non-cognitivism*, roughly the view that religious language is expressive rather than assertive: providing a picture of the world and prescriptions for human life, but not describing how reality in fact is (see Article 26, THEOLOGICAL REALISM AND ANTIREALISM). Here the task is to harmonize religious *attitudes* with scientific *beliefs*, rather than to harmonize two sets of beliefs having apparently disparate kinds of content. The former task is less demanding, intellectually at least, than the one we have been exploring.

There is a bolder approach for those who want to be both theists and scientifically minded: to employ the points made here (and others) in working toward not only a harmony between the two sets of commitments but also mutual support between them. From this perspective, scientific discovery is viewed as a prima facie indication of God's structuring of the world; divine sovereignty is seen as an assurance that the search for truth will tend to lead to valuable results; the intimate connection between one's physical and one's mental life, and especially our autonomy in directing our conduct, are conceived as possibly reflecting agency in a sense that is applicable to divine sovereignty over the world. For people proceeding in this way, scientific results may lead to revisions in theology, as theology may lead to scientific hypotheses or changes in scientific direction. Different people with different theologies and philosophies of science will proceed in diverse ways; but so far as we can see, the compatibility between the two worldviews is clear, and possibilities for harmonious interactions between them are wide.

Bibliography

Alston, W. P.: *Perceiving God* (Ithaca and London: Cornell University Press, 1991).

Gustafson, J. M.: *Ethics from a Theocentric Perspective*, vol. 1 (Chicago: University of Chicago Press, 1981).

Hempel, C. G.: *Aspects of Scientific Explanation* (New York: Macmillan, 1965).

Hick, J.: *Philosophy of Religion*, 2nd edn (Englewood Cliffs: Prentice-Hall, 1973).

Lycan, W. G.: *Mind and Cognition* (Oxford: Basil Blackwell, 1990)

Plantinga, A.: "How to be an anti-realist," *Proceedings and Addresses of the American Philosophical Association*, 56 (1982), pp. 47–70.

Swinburne, R. G.: *The Coherence of Theism* (Oxford and New York: Oxford University Press, 1977).

Taliaferro, C.: *Consciousness and the Mind of God* (Cambridge and New York: Cambridge University Press, 1994).

Van Inwagen, P.: *Material Beings* (Ithaca and London: Cornell University Press, 1990).

Wainwright, W.: "God's body," *Journal of the American Academy of Religion*, 62 (1974), pp. 470–81.

56

Theism and technology

FREDERICK FERRÉ

Theism normally entails that the religious believer's highest value-commitments be centered in God, who is considered (at a minimum) to be an effective, creative agent intimately concerned about and aware of creaturely actions and attitudes. The compatibility of such strongly focused commitments with other, subordinate values has long been in question. Should God be trusted *alone* or *along with* other objects of trust? This issue can be seen first in connection with ancient arts and crafts as a premodern spiritual concern, second in relation to science-based "high" technology as a modern debate, and third with reference to possible future technologies as a postmodern hope.

Technology and premodern concern

The ancient concern is dug deep into the biblical tradition. We find it vividly in the story of the Tower of Babel. There human technological prowess is depicted as a challenge to God. The tower, which was to have its "top in the heavens" (Genesis 11:4), was just a sample of what human beings could do if they should remain united on a technical project. Such prowess was clearly not permissible – so clearly that no reason is thought necessary to be given for its impermissibility.

More generally, the technologies of civilization itself – the word *civil* coming from the Latin for "city" – are deeply suspect in the early stories of scripture. Who, after all, is responsible for the first city? It was the major artifact of the murderous Cain. Thus civilization itself bears the mark of Cain. The theme of the wicked city – Sodom, Nineveh, Babylon – runs as a deep pedal point through the biblical saga. We are situated by these stories just outside the urban technological enterprise, positioned with the viewpoint of a suspicious desert nomad looking askance at the corruption brought about by too much ease and too much fancy know-how.

One might extend this viewpoint still further, arguing that the "knowledge of good and evil" against which Adam and Eve were warned in the Garden of Eden could not have been knowledge of *moral* good and evil, since being able to know that it was "wrong" to eat the fruit of the forbidden tree required prior *moral* comprehension of exactly the same sort. Instead, the forbidden fruit had to be a kind of knowledge that both characterizes God and might be considered wrong to fall into human possession. This double criterion rules out the notion that *sexual* knowledge was at issue, since such knowledge could hardly lead to becoming "like God" (Genesis 3:5). If not sexual and not moral, then perhaps the essence of the forbidden fruit was *technical* knowledge – *how* to do "good and evil" things, as God alone properly should know how to do. Original sin on this hypothesis would be technical hubris.

This is, of course, highly speculative (Ferré 1988, pp. 107–8). It is an interesting speculation, however, despite its variance from the received tradition in which moral, not technological, innocence was lost in Eden. It does cohere well with many other biblical themes, and with myths of other cultures, like the Prometheus story in which fire, the symbol of technological capacity, was stolen from heaven at great cost for human benefit. If it is at all correct, it would place biblical theism on an unalterable collision course not only with technological faith but also with technology itself.

Technology and modern debate

Technology has changed its character since the rise of modern science. Far more powerful than the ancient arts and crafts, modern technology has been deliberately designed under the leading conceptualities and values of the modern era: analytical, non-traditional, "value-free," quantitative, and oriented toward the maximization of power not only for warfare but also for control of nature for "helps to man" (Bacon 1960 [1620], p. 23). Some theist voices have welcomed modernization as compatible with theism; some have denounced it.

One of the welcoming voices was that of Harvey Cox. Though Cox himself has become more cautious, his initial position stands as a reminder that theists may not always feel obliged to remain aloof from the technological world – what Cox calls the "technopolis" – to which they have contributed so much (Cox 1965). In fact, if Cox's reading of scripture is correct, biblical spirituality was the key factor in freeing the human spirit from domination by local "divinities" and allowing the full technological expression of human intelligence to get under way. In the Hebrew–Christian scriptures it is made perfectly clear that God, the only proper object of worship, is not nature but is the transcendent creator of nature. This liberating realization of the transcendence of the sacred had the effect of "desacralizing" the natural resources needed by technological society. God's clarion call to humanity, that we "subdue the earth," made biblical theism, in contrast to nature-worship or polytheism, the primary spiritual vehicle for the coming of the present technological age.

To Cox's Protestant position can be added the Roman Catholic views of Norris Clarke. Clarke chooses a different theological starting place. He does not begin with the "disenchantment" of nature but with the story of the creation of Adam and Eve in the "image" of God. If humanity is to live up to its status, reflecting in a lesser way the character of God, then the human mission must include God's aspect both as contemplator and as creative worker. As Clarke writes:

... God is at once contemplative and active. He has not only thought up the material universe, with all its intricate network of laws, but he has actively brought it into existence

443

and supports and guides its vast pulsating network of forces. God is both a thinker and a worker, so to speak. So, too, man should imitate God his Father by both thinking and working in the world.   (Clarke 1972, p. 252)

The subordinate human role is indicated by the fact that we do not, like God, create *ex nihilo* (from nothing). Our materials must be found and simply refashioned. But the analogy between our technological work and God's making and doing remains. Furthermore, Clarke points out, the biblical story of creation includes the human vocation to co-create with God. The first humans – significantly, before the Fall – were given a garden to "till and keep" (Genesis 2:15). The incarnate God-man, too, was depicted as a tool-user.

Thus the labor of the young Jesus as a carpenter in Nazareth already lends, in principle, a divine sanction to the whole technological activity of man through history.   (Clarke 1972, p. 252)

Clarke is conscious of the tendency of humans to abuse technological powers and to exploit them for selfish advantage, Theists cannot be naive. Every aspect of human life and practice is subject to distortion and abuse. But, Clarke argues, such a warning is properly against the *mis*use of technology, not against the technological enterprise as a whole or in principle.

The other, highly critical, side of the debate is voiced by Jacques Ellul, who founds his wholly different evaluation of technology on a different rendering of some of the same scriptural passages noted by Cox and Clarke. Ellul, a Calvinist, makes much of the radical break that entered history with the Fall. In Paradise, before the estrangement that forced us to survive by the sweat of our brows, there was no laboring, no use of tools. It is impossible for us now, with sin-laden minds, to think back across the bottomless chasm of Original Sin to imagine how Adam and Eve "tilled and kept" the Garden of Eden (see Article 68, SIN AND ORIGINAL SIN). But Ellul uses a *reductio ad absurdum* argument to show how wrong it would be to imagine Adam and Eve working with tools in the Garden, as Clarke seems to suppose. "Keeping" or "guarding" Eden (different versions translate this word differently) could not – certainly not in *Paradise* – have involved the use of swords or spears or other weapons. That much is ruled out by the total inappropriateness of armaments in God's pre-Fallen, perfect environment. But if "guarding" allows of no weapons, then "tilling" allows of no farm machinery. If one is absurd, so is the other. If Paradise is to be even gropingly thought about as a true Paradise, Ellul concludes, we must resolutely omit technology from the picture.

No cultivation was necessary, no care to add, no grafting, no labor, no anxiety. Creation spontaneously gave man what he needed, according to the order of God who had said, " I give.. . ."   (Ellul 1984, p. 129)

Technology, then, is *tout court* in the domain of sin. It had no place in Paradise and arose only because of the Fall. To think of human efforts as "co-creating" with God, Ellul holds, is blasphemy. God's creative activity before the Fall was not in need of completing or perfecting. We must not, in our pride over our human technological abilities, forget that "creation as God made it, as it left his hands, was *perfect and finished*" (Ellul 1984, p. 125). We put on airs when we tell our-selves that we are "working along with" God. If it had not been for human sin, there would have been no need for technology, because "God's work was accomplished, . . . it was complete, . . . there was nothing to add" (Ellul 1984, p. 125). Ellul's theological condemnation of the technological imperative is complete. In his well-known sociological analyses he makes further important distinctions between the tools of the craft traditions and the all-devouring efficiencies of modern "technique" (Ellul 1964). The former are less objectionable, though by no means theologically mandated; the latter are demonic and out of human control. Both as sociologist and as theologian, Ellul provides no comfort and gives no quarter to the defenders of technology.

Technology and conceptual issues

This survey of the debate between theists on the proper stance toward technology and the technological society makes clear how urgently thinking in this area requires continuing clarification. Some of the debate may rest on differing conceptions of what "technology" is. Perhaps a reconciling suggestion may be offered as follows. When we speak of "technologies" in general we must include all the ways in which intelligence implements practical purposes (Ferré 1988, ch. 2). To include less would be to create an insupportable bifurcation between premodern and modern ways of implementing our purposes. Modern automobiles are different, but not absolutely different, from horse-drawn carriages or chariots. On the other hand, it is neither ethnocentric nor myopic to insist on recognizing the vast changes introduced into our practical means by the rise of modern science. A radio bears some, but not much, similarity, for example, to a jungle drum. Therefore the *genus*, "technology," should stand for all practical implementations of intelligence; the *differentia* should be the kind of intelligence involved, whether habitual-traditional, on the one hand ("craft" technologies), or analytical-scientific ("high" technologies) on the other.

Having a definition that firmly roots the technological phenomenon in human purpose and intelligence helps make it clear that technology is nothing alien to the categories of religion and ethics. Indeed, looked at in this way, coming to terms with technology is part of the age-old task of theistic religion's coming to terms with culture itself. Theisms of various sorts have yet to complete the long process of self-definition vis-à-vis the works of human hands. Theisms of the prophetic tradition, standing outside culture and thundering against its perceived defects, contrast with theisms of the priestly tradition, serving inside culture and seeking to relate the ideals of religion to the realities of social life. Both are part of the fabric of standard forms of theism.

Questioning in a new way, however, and with a new sense of urgency, may elicit fresh insights. First, theists cannot, without grave danger to their own faith, embrace the pagan quasi-religion of "technologism." Its anthropology is uncritical; its soteriology is unidimensional; its cosmology is reductionist. Placing unqualified confidence in the works of human hands is technolatry (Ferré 1993,

445

ch. 11), and is unworthy of theism. Second, theists cannot participate in whole-sale gnostic rejection of intelligent methods for dealing with the material order. Such rejection of materiality is tantamount to the rejection of the reality or impor-tance of creation. Gnostic absolute dualisms of good and evil are tantamount to despair over the redeemability of all creation. Somehow the balance between appropriate humility and responsible engagement with creation must be main-tained.

In the search for such balance, the argument over technology's ethical norms must take place on two distinct levels: the first is on the question of identifying the good, *what* ought to be sought; the second is on the question of defining the right, *how* the good should be distributed, and among whom. For most of the history of the modern period, since the rise of modern science and its accompanying posi-tivism and utilitarianism, it has been widely accepted that the good can be defined in terms of human happiness, and that the right can be fulfilled by building up the greatest quantity of such happiness for the greatest number. This fits well with the modern intellectual norms of simplification, quantification, and maximization we noted earlier. This is no accident. It is a case in which a *style of knowing* has influ-enced (through its implicit norms) a society's *style of valuing*.

Unfortunately, both for the adequacy of the ethical norms themselves and for the sustainability of the modern technologies embodying them, the taken-for-granted modern stress on *human* happiness left the rest of nature's good out of account. And the modern stress on maximizing the *quantity* of happiness left out also the qualitative issue of fairness in the distribution of this good, in relation not only to the rest of the non-human world but also to future human generations. The modern attraction to simplicity and analysis in thinking led to our engineer-ing technologies becoming highly efficient in attaining want-values, simply defined, but overlooking larger ramifications and causal connections that have a way of ambushing the unwary.

Unfortunately, our norms of thinking have tended to make us systematically unwary, the more we have been led into modern knowledge-ideals of constantly narrower specialization; our norms of proper investigation have diminished the status of "tenderness"; our moral norms have emphasized anthropocentric inter-ests at the expense of the rest of the world. There is little wonder, then, in the fact that the triumphs of modern human technological values seem so often to turn to terror. We are in need of a fuller, richer set of ideals which can sustain and restrain the planetary adventure through the next century. What might such postmodern norms be like?

Technology and postmodern ideals

Fresh postmodern "ideals of doing," i.e. more adequate ethical norms needed for a healthier future, frankly rest on new "ideals of being," new ecological and theo-logical insights into how things fundamentally are. Ethics and worldview inter-twine; the times seem ripe for changes in both. In particular, this seems to be a moment of special opportunity for the organismic theism offered by such thinkers as Alfred North Whitehead (Whitehead 1978) and his contemporary interpreters (Cobb 1992). (See Article 16, PROCESS THEOLOGY.)

Theism of this sort might make the ancient Hebrew word *shalom* again central. *Shalom* means "health" or "wholeness." The New Shalom is a vision of health among humans living with tenderness and compassion under the gentle guidance of a nurturing God on a whole earth. It is faith in creativity expressed through living organisms, and faith also in the proven capacity of healthy life to sustain and limit itself, through internal homeostatic controls, even as it extends itself over evolutionary time: quantitatively, from niche to niche, and qualitatively, in its capacity (through some species, more than others) to achieve ever finer intrinsic qualities of experience.

From this new theistic "ideal of being," important consequences flow for postmodern ideals of doing. First, in the future we should regard and respect intrinsic value wherever it is found. Such value will not be limited to human persons. God cares for all centers of value; correspondingly, we are under obligation to give ethical consideration to good of every sort, not just to human good.

Second, however, we should be careful to give qualitative, not only quantitative, good its due. This means that we must not lapse into undiscriminating egalitarianism in our treatment of competing goods. Organismic good is real and important, even when it appears outside human persons; but God's aim is for ever-increasing intrinsic fineness of experience. Persons, beyond all other organisms, are capable of immense qualitative achievements in mental creativity and richness of intrinsic consciousness. This makes it possible to make not merely self-serving but principled theocentric ethical choices between human persons and other centers of value.

Third, in the future, once we recognize the inherently long-term, continuous temporal character of the divine lure toward increasing finite value, we are obliged to give adequate recognition to ecological requirements and to intergenerational justice. The present generation is actual, of course, and has actual need- and want-values. These values have their own urgency and must not be ignored or roughly sacrificed (as in the brutal Stalinist destruction of real persons in favor of a vaguely defined posterity); but the temporal breadth of the relevant community under the theistic vision of personalistic organism must be drawn more inclusively, to ensure that the need-values of future persons and other future life-forms are included in our technological calculations.

Technologies for the future

New ideals and worldviews are important, but they are not enough; they need to be implemented in practices and artifacts if the society we hope for in our future is to be realized.

First, what are the implications of the holistic norms of organismic theism for teaching and learning? One thing should be clear by now: modern norms of knowing, for all the brilliance of scientific achievements, have infected typical modern technologies with profound flaws. In place of excessive admiration of "misplaced concreteness" in simple abstractions, we need appreciation of real complexity; in place of near-exclusive emphasis on quantity, we need rich stress on quality; in place of knowledge by rational analysis and specialization, we need new wisdom, including methods of insight, synthesis, and integration.

There is everything to gain, on this theistic vision, by abandoning the rigid distinctions between "disciplines" and "fields" and the many self-imposed barriers to integrated learning across traditional boundaries. These boundaries exist only within technologies of learning that are modeled on the preference for specializations and rigid separations that arose with modern science in the seventeenth century. But these rigid boundaries are radically challenged by a worldview entailing the intimate interconnectedness of all things. Ecology, the postmodern science of integrated understanding, should be the model for our new curriculum, not reductionist physics. Even physics, today, is far more like ecology than its various specializations make apparent. Academic departments, creatures of outdated (and now dangerous) epistemological norms, could well disappear. In their place, constantly self-transforming networks of integrative understanding are required for both research and teaching. In that integration, quantitative and qualitative understanding – what we today call the sciences and the humanities – will be fully incorporated. Team projects, especially team teaching, would then become the rule, not the exception. Understanding complexity and connectedness, not analyzing simplicity and "purity," could become central ideals of knowledge.

The technologies of modern specialization – the ones we live with today – have tended to launch into the environment with cold, Cartesian linear logic; postmodern technologies, embodying organismic theism's ideals of complex, integrative understanding, instead will relate more fittingly and wisely to the vastly complex web of relationships that all human interventions into the environment involve. Human beings cannot live without disturbing the environment. No species does. But we can, by adopting richer ideals of knowing, appropriate to organismic theism, understand far better what our (necessary) disturbances will mean for other co-dwelling centers of value and for future generations. The technologies that will embody such fuller understanding cannot help being enormously different from the great planet-altering machinery that our simplifying, tenderness-free values have produced to rip and tear the earth in service of our modern want-values. It would be reasonable to hope that they may be redemptive technologies that will shape a new world under an ecologically responsible form of organismic theism.

Bibliography

Bacon, Sir Francis: *The Great Instauration* (London, 1620), ed. F. H. Anderson (Indianapolis: Bobbs-Merrill, 1960).

Clarke, W. N.: "Technology and man: A Christian vision." In *Philosophy and Technology: Readings in the Philosophic Problems of Technology*, ed. C. Mitcham and R. Mackey (New York: Free Press, 1972).

Cobb, J. B., Jr: *Sustainability: Economics, Ecology, and Justice* (Maryknoll, NY: Orbis, 1992).

Cox, H.: *The Secular City: Secularization and Urbanization in Theologi450 cal Perspective*, rev. ed. (1966) (New York: Macmillan, 1965).

Ellul, J.: *The Technological Society*, tr. J. Wilkinson (New York: Vintage, 1964).

——: "Technique and the opening chapters of Genesis." In *Theology and Technology: Essays in Christian Analysis and Exegesis*, ed. C. Mitcham and J. Grote (Lanham: University Press of America, 1984), pp. 123–37.

Ferré, F.: *Philosophy of Technology* (Englewood Cliffs: Prentice-Hall, 1988).

——: *Hellfire and Lightning Rods: Liberating Science, Technology, and Religion* (Maryknoll, NY: Orbis, 1993).

Whitehead, A. N.: *Process and Reality: An Essay in Cosmology*, ed. D. R. Griffin and D. W. Sherburne (New York: Free Press; London: Collier Macmillan, 1978).

PART IX

THEISM AND VALUES

57

Divine command ethics

JANINE MARIE IDZIAK

Different ethical theories postulate different groundings for rightness and wrongness. A divine command moralist holds that the standard of right and wrong is constituted by the commands and prohibitions of God. According to the divine command theory, "an action or kind of action is right or wrong if and only if and *because* it is commanded or forbidden by God" (Frankena 1973, p. 28). In other words, the theory stipulates that "what ultimately *makes* an action right or wrong is its being commanded or forbidden by God and nothing else" (1973, p. 28). According to the divine command theory, it is *not* the case that God commands a particular action because it is right, or prohibits it because it is wrong; rather, an action is right (or wrong) because God commands (or prohibits) it. An ethics of divine commands is often expressed in terms of right and wrong being determined by the *will of God*.

Within the last quarter of the twentieth century there has been a revival of interest in divine command ethics (hereafter DCE) among analytic philosophers. Of particular note is the work of Robert Merrihew Adams, Philip Quinn, and Richard Mouw (see Quinn 1990). In fact, DCE has a long history.

The idea of DCE is traced back to Plato's *Euthyphro*, which raises the question of whether something is holy because the gods approve it or whether they approve it because it is holy. Among early church and medieval writers isolated texts indicative of DCE are found in the writings of Augustine, Ambrose, Gregory the Great, the Pseudo-Cyprian, Isidore of Seville, Hugh of St Victor, and Anselm. DCE became more prominent and more extensively discussed in the late Middle Ages. John Duns Scotus showed proclivities towards it, and William of Ockham clearly espoused it. The theory received its fullest articulation in the work of Andrew of Neufchateau and Peter of Ailly, and after them it was adopted by Jean Gerson and Gabriel Biel (see Idziak 1980, 1989).

DCE also played a part in Reformation theology. Remarks characteristic of this position are found in the writings of Martin Luther and John Calvin. The theologian Jerome Zanchius explicitly followed Luther in endorsing this position while, among English Puritans, it was espoused by William Perkins and John Preston. In twentieth century Protestant theology DCE has continued in the work of Karl Barth, Emil Brunner, and Carl F. H. Henry (see Idziak 1980, 1989).

DCE was the subject of vigorous debate among British moralists of the modern period. Ralph Cudworth, Thomas Chubb, George Rust, Anthony Earl of Shaftesbury, Francis Hutcheson, Richard Price, and Jeremy Bentham all argued against it. On the other hand, René Descartes was perceived as a divine command moralist, John Locke showed inclinations towards this ethical theory, and William Paley clearly advocated it. In discussing the prominent moral standards of his day, John Gay delineated a hierarchical scheme in which these standards are all ultimately founded on the criterion of the will of God (see Idziak 1980, 1989).

The idea of basing morality on divine commands has been formalized, elaborated, and refined in various ways. In the contemporary literature DCE was first introduced as a *metaethical* theory about the meaning of fundamental moral terms (Adams 1973, pp. 318–47), an orientation undoubtedly reflecting the philosophical framework of linguistic analysis. Analytic philosophers have subsequently worked with normative theories of various types. Quinn, for example, has formulated theories based on *logical relations* such as strict equivalence between requirement, permission, and prohibition and divine commands (Quinn 1978, p. 30). He has also construed the relation between divine commands and moral duty in *causal* terms in order to capture an intuitive picture of God as an agent *bringing about* or *creating* moral obligations and prohibitions by means of his legislative activity (see Idziak 1980, pp. 305–25).

Historically, Andrew of Neufchateau formulated a purely *voluntaristic* version of DCE in which the divine will, without the divine intellect, issues the commands constituting the moral law (*Primum Scriptum Sententiarum*, d.48, q.1, a.2, concl.3). A recurrent objection to DCE is that it makes morality *arbitrary* (Idziak 1980, pp. 14–15). As stated by one critic, "it would appear that God is a being that on the basis of whim or fancy approves of some things, disapproves of others . . ." (Haines 1990, p. 23). While this criticism may hold true of Andrew's voluntarism, it does not apply to all versions of DCE. Peter of Ailly incorporated the *divine simplicity* into DCE. Since the divine will which does the commanding is identical with the divine intellect, God's commands are not arbitrary products of will alone (see Idziak 1980, pp. 15–16, 60–1). Others have contended that divine commands are not arbitrary because God wills in accord with other divine attributes, such as knowledge, justice, and love (Idziak 1980, pp. 250–1). This approach has been turned by Adams into a *modified* DCE in which ethical wrongness is explicitly explicated in terms of what is contrary to the commands of a *loving* God (Adams 1973, pp. 320–4).

The defense of any ethical theory operates on two levels: the refutation of objections brought against the theory, and the presentation of reasons in support of the position and for preferring it to other ethical systems. We will begin by considering putatively *good positive* reasons for adopting DCE.

This project also has implications for a criticism leveled against DCE. It is sometimes objected "that one must have some reason for obeying God's commands or for adopting a divine command ethics, and that therefore a nontheological concept of moral obligation or of ethical rightness and wrongness must be presupposed, in order that one may judge that one ought to obey God's commands" (Adams 1973, p. 332). In other words, it is claimed that we decide to adhere to divine commands because we see that what God wills is good, but making this judgment assumes a moral standard independent of divine commands according

454

to which God is judged. Finding cogent reasons of a *non-moral* variety for adopting DCE would serve to undercut this criticism.

Taking divine commands as normative for human conduct has been related to *our dependency on God as creator* (see Article 39, CREATION AND CONSERVATION). According to Locke, "it is proper that we should live according to the precept of His [God's] will" because "we owe our body, soul, and life – whatever we are, whatever we have, and even whatever we can be – to Him and to Him alone." Since "God has created us out of nothing and, if He pleases, will reduce us again to nothing," we are, Locke contends, "subject to Him in perfect justice and by utmost necessity" (quoted in Idziak 1980, p. 182). However, it has been objected that the mere fact that *A* made *B* is not a good reason for *B* to obey *A* as illustrated by the hypothetical case of a couple who conceive children specifically to use them as child prostitutes and live off their earnings (Haines 1990, p. 25). An advocate of DCE might in turn reply that it is not only God's status as creator but the *gracious way in which God has dealt with us* which is important. According to Barth, for example, the basis of God's ethical claim on us lies in the fact that God "has given Himself to us," that "although He could be without us He did not and does not will to be without us," that "He has taken our place and taken up our cause" (quoted in Idziak 1980, p. 130).

DCE has been regarded as a correlate of the divine power (see Article 28, OMNIPOTENCE). Thus some might maintain that God's commands are authoritative "only because God has power to enforce them," including the bestowal of eternal rewards and punishments (Barcalow 1994, pp. 24–5). Such a view, however, has occasioned harsh criticism of DCE as a "might makes right" doctrine (Idziak 1989, pp. 60–1). In another way, the *rejection* of DCE has been seen as *compromising and limiting God's power*. As Andrew of Neufchateau argues, if rightness is based on the nature of things and hence on something external to God, then God is subject to laws which are not enacted by his will and are not in his power (*Primum Scriptum Sententiarum*, d.48, q.1, a.2, concl.3). Or again, God would be "limited in that if he is to urge men to do what is obligatory he has to urge them to do what is obligatory independently of any action of his" (Richard Swinburne in Idziak 1980, p. 287). Not all theists, however, have found such restrictions on divine power unacceptable. As Rust comments, "it is no imperfection for God to be determined to Good; it is no bondage, slavery, or contraction, to be bound up to the eternal Laws of Right and Justice . . ." (quoted in Idziak 1980, p. 196). Indeed, some advocates of DCE, such as Barth, explicitly reject appeal to divine power as a basis for adherence to this theory (Idziak 1980, pp. 126–7).

In the historical literature are found arguments for DCE which draw from the realm of metaphysics. An analogy between the metaphysical notion of God as *first being* and the ethical notion of God as *first good* forms the basis of an argument presented by Andrew of Neufchateau to support the conclusion that God is the contingent and free cause of all other goods and the Being on account of which each good is such a good (Idziak 1989, p. 56). Peter of Ailly constructs an ethical analogue of a cosmological argument for God's existence in support of the conclusion that just as the divine will is the first efficient cause, so it is the first law or rule (Idziak 1989, pp. 57–8).

The dependency of morals on divine commands has been discussed in connection with God's status as *first and uncaused cause* by both medieval and Protestant writers (Idziak 1989, pp. 48–51). The Puritan John Preston, for example, reasons in the following way. God being the *first cause* implies that God is *uncaused*, that is, that God cannot be causally affected by anything. If God were to choose something because he perceived it to possess goodness or justice, then God would be causally affected by something external to himself, which is impossible (see Article 40, IMMUTABILITY AND IMPASSIBILITY). Therefore, it is not the case that God wills something because it is good or just; rather, something is good or just because God wills it (Idziak 1989, pp. 50–1).

DCE has also been connected with the metaphysical issue of the *status of the essences*, morality being treated as one instance of this more general problem. Cudworth interprets Descartes as having espoused DCE because the natures and essences of all things depend on the will of God. The reason is that, if such dependency were not the case, it would follow that, "something that was not God was independent upon God" (Idziak 1989, p. 54). Price likewise considers whether "we must give up the unalterable natures of right and wrong and make them dependent on the Divine will" in order to avoid "setting up something distinct from God, which is independent of him, and equally eternal and necessary" (Idziak 1989, p. 54). The suggestion that DCE must be adopted in the realm of ethics because *there cannot be anything which is independent of God* may be interpreted as an attempt to capture the religious insight of the *absolute primacy and centrality of God*.

The defense of DCE is not limited to arguments of a philosophical sort. The theory is grounded as well in the *experience of the faith community*.

It has been claimed that DCE is *biblically based*. On one level, there are particular incidents recorded in the Hebrew Bible in which an apparently immoral act was made the right thing to do by a divine command, thereby indicating that God is the source of moral obligation (Quinn 1990, p. 355). Cases cited include Abraham's planned sacrifice of Isaac, an instance of murder; the Israelites plundering the Egyptians on their way out of Egypt, a case of theft; the prophet Hosea taking a wife of fornication; Jacob lying to deceive his father; the patriarchs engaging in polygamy; the Israelites divorcing foreign wives; and Samson committing suicide (see *Primum Scriptum Sententiarum* d.48, q.2, a.2, concl.2; Quinn 1990, pp. 354–9). On a global level, the Hebrew Bible portrays God as a commander legislating about all sorts of things, including clearly moral matters (Quinn 1990, p. 355). Concomitantly, the whole of human duty is summarized in the injunction to "fear God and keep his commandments" (Ecclesiastes 12:13) (see Mouw 1990, p. 6). Accounts of the giving of the Decalogue picture God as revealing his will and not merely transmitting information so that "it is natural enough to suppose that the authority of the Decalogue depends upon the fact that it is an expression of the divine will" (Quinn 1990, p. 355). Behavioral prescriptions continue to be connected with the divine will in the New Testament, such as the exhortation for

456

gratitude in 1 Thessalonians 5:18: ". . . give thanks in all circumstances, for this is God's will for you in Christ Jesus."

Moreover, DCE is grounded in *Christian spirituality*. Spiritual leaders, writers, and directors have maintained that "human beings are at their best when they are surrendering to the will of God in all things" (Mouw 1990. p. 6). Illustrative of this sense of complete abandonment to God's will is the late medieval classic *The Imitation of Christ* in which Thomas à Kempis depicts Christ counseling a disciple "to learn perfect self-surrender, and to accept My will without argument or complaint" (1978 [1441], p. 174). In a meditation on the phrase of the Lord's Prayer, "Your will be done on earth as it is in heaven," Teresa of Avila muses (1964 [1583], p. 215):

"Fiat voluntas tua": that is, may the Lord fulfill His will in me, in every way and manner which Thou, my Lord, desirest. If Thou wilt do this by means of trials. give me strength and let them come. If by means of persecutions and sickness and dishonor and need, here I am, my Father, I will not turn my face away from Thee nor have I the right to turn my back upon them. . . . Do Thou grant me the grace of bestowing on me Thy kingdom so that I may do Thy will, since He has asked this of me. Dispose of me as of that which is Thine own, in accordance with Thy Will.

Or again, the colonial American saint Elizabeth Seton enjoins that "the first purpose of our daily work is to do the will of God; secondly, to do it in the manner he wills; and thirdly, to do it because it is his will" (Pennington 1988, p. 7).

And it is not the case that a sense of conformity to God's will characterizes only extraordinary Christians. The same theme is found in liturgy. It is found in traditional hymns:

> Father, who didst fashion man
> Godlike in thy loving plan,
> Fill us with that love divine,
> And conform our wills to thine.
> > (*Father, we thank thee who has planted . . .*)
>
> Watch o'er thy Church, O Lord, in mercy,
> Save it from evil, guard it still;
> Perfect it in thy love, unite it,
> Cleansed and conformed unto thy will.
> > (*On this day, the first of days . . .*)

Perusal of a worship book such as the Presbyterian *Daily Prayer* provides examples of how the notion of conformity to God's will figures in Christian prayer: "Eternal God, send your Holy Spirit into our hearts, to direct and rule us according to your will . . ." (Office of Worship 1987, p. 192); "God of love, as you have given your life to us, so may we live according to your holy will revealed in Jesus Christ . . ." (p. 134); "Purify our desires that we may seek your will . . ." (p. 222); ". . . give us patience to be diligent and to labor according to your will . . ." (p. 224). Thus DCE can be defended *as a formalization of an important theme of Christian spiritual life, namely, conformity to the divine will* (Idziak 1991, pp. 547–8).

457

On the other hand, a problem raised for DCE is that theists may disagree about the content of divine law. One can think of honest disagreements among theists on such issues as capital punishment, artificial birth control, abortion, and homosexuality. Exactly how do we determine what God permits and forbids? (Barcalow 1994, p. 26). If we cannot reliably determine what the divine commands are, then DCE is effectually useless as an action guide and will only lead to skepticism about morals.

Some advocates of DCE from the Protestant tradition place heavy emphasis on the Bible as the source of our knowledge of divine commands (Mouw 1990, pp. 8–10). Other divine command moralists look to official Church teachings or to the possibility of personal revelation (e.g. through prayer) (Idziak 1980, p. 251). It must be acknowledged, however, that some people express skepticism about the reliability of these religious sources of knowledge (Barcalow 1994, pp. 26–8). Individuals of this persuasion can take note of Patterson Brown's suggestion that "one can *infer* by means of reason alone . . . what God would command." For "we can presumably ratiocinate . . . what a supremely intelligent, loving, and just being would will; and that is by definition what God would will . . ." (quoted in Idziak 1980, p. 251).

Another problem posed for DCE is that it does not permit a coherent account of the moral attributes of God to be formulated. Specifically, if *x* being morally good is explicated in terms of *x* doing what God wills, then the claim that God is morally good reduces to the trivial claim that God does what God wills (Adams 1973, p. 337). Adams responds to this criticism by suggesting that, when a divine command moralist calls God good, she or he is expressing a favorable emotional attitude towards God and ascribing to God certain qualities of character regarded as virtuous, such as kindness, benevolence, faithfulness, a forgiving disposition, or love. Adams also contends that these attitudinal and descriptive features of his analysis are part of the ascriptions of goodness to human beings (1973, pp. 338–41).

Quinn broadens this line of criticism by raising a question about the possibility of DCE allowing *any* moral virtue to be attributed to God. For DCE makes obedience to God the fundamental human virtue, other virtues being explicated with reference to such obedience (e.g. courage is obedience to divine commands requiring us to act bravely in hazardous situations). However, it makes no sense to suppose that God (or anyone else) commands himself to do certain things and then obeys the commands he has addressed to himself. Hence, DCE seems to deprive God of the very moral virtues which make God worthy of worship (Quinn 1978, pp. 130–5). However, Quinn attempts to defeat this objection by describing divine *analogues* for human moral virtues. For example, divine love might consist in unselfish concern for the welfare of the recipient, in which respect it resembles the virtue of human love although lacking two properties of human love, namely, "being commanded by God" and "being a moral virtue" (Quinn 1978, pp. 135–64).

An objection against DCE which recurs in the historical and contemporary literature is that the theory has *counterintuitive consequences*. Since divine commands create morality, this means that if God prohibited honesty and promise-keeping, then honesty and promise-keeping would be wrong. Concomitantly, if God were to command such actions as theft, adultery, rape, cruelty for its own sake, torturing young children, or even the hatred of God himself, then these intuitively abhorrent and immoral acts would become the right actions to perform (Adams 1973, pp. 320–1; Quinn 1978, pp. 28–9, 53–6, 58–61; Idziak 1980, p. 16; Barcalow 1994, p. 28). The most plausible response to this criticism is that the commands God issues are consonant with God's nature and character as, for example, loving and benevolent, so that the aforementioned types of commands will not in fact occur (Idziak 1980, pp. 15–16). Thus Adams's modification of DCE which makes explicit that our commitment is to commands emanating from a *loving* God is crucial to the plausibility of this ethical theory (Adams 1973, pp. 320–4).

Bibliography

Adams, R. M.: "A modified divine command theory of ethical wrongness." In *Religion and Morality*, ed. G. Outka and J. P. Reeder, Jr. (Garden City: Anchor, 1973), pp. 318–47.

Andrew of Neufchateau: *Primum Scriptum Sententiarum* (Paris: Granjon, 1514).

Barcalow, E.: *Moral Philosophy: Theory and Issues* (Belmont: Wadsworth, 1994).

Frankena, W. K.: *Ethics*, 2nd edn (Englewood Cliffs: Prentice-Hall, 1973).

Haines, B. L.: *Ethics: Elementary Readings* (Dubuque: Kendall/Hunt, 1990).

Idziak, J. M.: *Divine Command Morality: Historical and Contemporary Readings* (New York and Toronto: Edwin Mellen, 1980).

——: "In search of 'good positive reasons' for an ethics of divine commands: A catalogue of arguments," *Faith and Philosophy*, 6 (1989), pp. 47–64.

——: review of *The God Who Commands* by Richard Mouw, *Faith and Philosophy*, 8 (1991), pp. 545–8.

Mouw, R.: *The God Who Commands* (Notre Dame: University of Notre Dame Press, 1990).

Office of Worship for the Presbyterian Church (USA) and the Cumberland Presbyterian Church: *Daily Prayer* (Philadelphia: Westminster Press, 1987).

Pennington, M. B., OCSO: *Through the Year with the Saints* (New York: Doubleday, 1988).

Quinn, P. L.: *Divine Commands and Moral Requirements* (Oxford: Clarendon Press, 1978).

——: "The recent revival of divine command ethics," *Philosophy and Phenomenological Research*, 50 (suppl.) (1990), pp. 345–65.

Teresa of Avila: *The Way of Perfection* (1583), tr. E. A. Peers (Garden City: Doubleday, 1964).

Thomas à Kempis: *The Imitation of Christ* (1441), tr. L. Sherley-Price (New York: Penguin, 1978).

58

Natural law ethics

Natural law is the body of moral norms and other practical principles which provide reasons (including moral reasons) for action and restraint.

The most basic precepts of natural law direct people to choose and act for *intelligible* ends and purposes. These precepts, which Thomas Aquinas called "the first principles of practical reason," refer to the range of "basic" (i.e. non-instrumental or not-merely-instrumental) human goods for the sake of which people can intelligently act. In so far as a possible action promises to instantiate at least one such good, performing it has an intelligible point.

However, the diversity of goods which provide non-instrumental practical reasons, together with the range of subrational factors which can motivate people to act in ways contrary to the prescriptions of practical reason, make it unavoidable that people will face morally significant free choices. Moral norms, including such very general moral principles as the Golden Rule of fairness and the Pauline Principle that evil may not be done even to achieve good consequences, guide choice in such circumstances (though they do not always narrow the range of fully reasonable, morally good options to one) by providing conclusive reasons to choose certain options and to refrain from choosing others. Moral norms are needed in addition to the most basic practical principles because the latter exclude only those possibilities for choice which lack an intelligible point (and, as such, are the objects of merely emotional as opposed to rational motivation).

Paradigmatically, moral norms guide choices between possibilities both (or all) of which provide *reasons* for action, one (or some) of which, however, are *defeated* (giving the chooser a conclusive reason to choose the, or an, alternative). Immoral choosing is possible (though, by definition, never justified) because people often have powerful emotional motives to act for goods they cherish or desire despite the fact that any reasons for acting here and now provided by those goods are defeated by moral norms which exclude the contemplated action.

Of course, emotion figures in all human action, and, far from being the enemy of reason, gives support (albeit not undivided) to reason's prescriptions. In immoral choosing, however, the proper relation of reason and emotion is reversed: reason allows itself to be harnessed by emotion in the cause of producing rationalizations for choices which are, in truth, practically unreasonable (i.e. immoral).

A theory of natural law is a critical, reflective account of the principles which guide sound practical reasoning and moral judgment. A complete natural law theory will identify, in addition to (1) the basic human goods which provide non-instrumental reasons for acting, (2) the moral norms which follow from the integral directiveness of the principles which prescribe choosing for these goods. Such a theory will also identify (3) the virtues which sustain morally good individuals and groups in upright choosing (see Article 59, VIRTUE ETHICS); explain and defend (4) the possibility of free choice; and (5) meet the criticisms of skeptics who deny the possibility of free choice or doubt that free choice can be guided by moral norms and other practical principles which are objective (as opposed to subjective), natural (as opposed to merely conventional), universal (as opposed to individually or culturally relative), or, in short, *true*. Thus, complete natural law theories include both *practical* (i.e. normative, prescriptive) propositions identifying certain choices, actions, and dispositions as reasonable or unreasonable, good or bad, right or wrong, permitted, forbidden, or required; and *theoretical* (i.e. descriptive) propositions about the truth, objectivity, and epistemological warrant for the practical propositions, and the real possibility of freely choosing in conformity with their prescriptions.

Natural law theories characteristically identify principles relevant not only to personal morality, but also to politics and law. Historically, the term "law" in the phrase "natural law" has been the source of some confusion. For example, natural law is sometimes conceived as analogous to legislation, creating the misimpression that moral norms and other practical principles have their prescriptive force as dictates of the will of a superior authority. The truth is that even natural law theorists who affirm (as most, but not all, do) that these norms and principles have their ultimate source (as do all realities) in a transcendent divine Creator, typically do not endorse "voluntarist" accounts of obligation which depict norms and principles as binding *because* they are commanded by that Creator (see Article 57, DIVINE COMMAND ETHICS). The better account of obligation presents the prescriptivity of moral and other practical principles as a matter of *rational* bindingness or necessity: to fly in the face of moral prescriptions is to be (practically) *unreasonable*. The term "law" in the phrase "natural law" recalls that moral norms are prescriptions common, in principle, to all members of the human community, namely, the community of the human species.

Another confusion arises from the claim (found in Plato and Cicero as well as Augustine and Aquinas) that an unjust law is not (or seems not to be) a law. A simplistic understanding of this claim has led certain "legal positivist" critics to suppose that natural law theory either (1) treats every law, in so far as it is a law, as necessarily just (thus undermining the serious moral criticism of law), or (2) refuses to treat as "law" social rules which are, their more or less manifest injustice notwithstanding, treated precisely as law by actual citizens as well as by judges and other officials who apply law and act under its authority.

A careful reading of leading theorists of natural law through the ages makes plain, however, their recognition that the injustice of a law, while vitiating its proper moral authority, does not necessarily render it invalid by the legal system's own criteria of validity. Hence, an actor in the system (or a sociologist or legal scholar whose objective is to give a rich and accurate account of how the system

461

functions) may reasonably treat even an unjust law as "law" in a perfectly mean-ingful sense. Indeed, even an unjust law may, depending on the gravity of its injustice and certain other factors, retain some measure of moral bindingness. The prima facie moral obligation to obey the law remains intact, for example, where it would be unfair to others for a citizen or official to disobey or disregard the law, its relatively minor injustices notwithstanding. The classical saying *lex iniusta non est lex* (an unjust law is not a law), then, presents no denial of the significance of law's positivity or the legitimacy and value of the study of positive law as such. (In fact, Aquinas's attention to the positivity of law and its significance constituted a major advance in legal theory for which modern legal positivists are in his debt.) It is, rather, a reminder of the *conditional* nature of the moral obligatoriness which attaches to positive law.

The term "natural" in "natural law" has been a source not only of confusion but also of division. According to the scholastic tradition of thought about natural law founded by Francisco Suarez (1548–1617), knowledge of the reasonable, the good, and the right is derived from prior knowledge of human nature or what is "natural" for human beings. This tradition reverses the understanding of Aquinas, according to whom something in the moral domain is "natural" for human beings and in accord with human nature precisely in so far as it can be judged to be *reasonable*; and something in this realm of discourse is "unnatural" and morally wrong just in so far as it is *unreasonable*. Contemporary thinkers in the tradition of Aquinas argue that practical knowledge (i.e. knowledge of human goods and moral norms and the reasons they provide) is a *source* of our knowledge of human nature, i.e. the nature of beings whose capacities are fulfilled by actions directed toward the ends of friendship, knowledge, aesthetic achievement and appreciation, personal authenticity and integrity, and the like goods.

Not every non-skeptical theory of personal or political morality or law is rightly denominated a "natural law theory." Theories of natural law must be distin-guished, for example, from Kantian theories which neglect, or even deny, the basic human goods to which the first principles of practical reason and basic pre-cepts of natural law direct choice and action, and which, taken together, generate an ideal of *integral* human fulfillment – the fulfillment of all human persons and their communities. According to what is perhaps the most prominent contempo-rary natural law theory (that defended by Germain Grisez, Joseph Boyle, and John Finnis among other philosophers, theologians, and legal scholars), the most fun-damental and abstract *moral* principle prescribes choosing (and otherwise willing) precisely in harmony with this ideal. All more proximate and specific moral norms, even if identified prior to this principle, constitute specifications of (and are, in that sense, derived from) it.

Natural law theories must also be distinguished from theories of the "intuition-ist" sort (with which they are frequently confused). The basic human goods to which action is directed by the first principles of practical reason and basic pre-cepts of natural law, and the moral norms which follow from the integral direc-tiveness of these goods, are *reasons*, not intuitions. They are grasped in intellectual acts by practical understanding in reflection on *data* provided by natural and sensory appetites and emotional responses, and by theoretical knowledge of possibilities provided by learning and experience.

This is not to say, as certain neo-scholastic thinkers say (or suppose Aquinas to have said), that basic *practical* knowledge is deduced, inferred, or in any logically significant sense derived from methodologically antecedent *theoretical* (or "factual") knowledge of human nature. As Aquinas taught (following an axiom of Aristotle's method), while the nature of a thing or being is ontologically fundamental, human knowledge of natures (including human nature) is derived. An entity's nature is understood by understanding its potentialities or capacities; these are in turn understood by understanding its activities or performances; and these finally are understood by understanding the *objects* of its acts or performances. Human nature, then, is known by understanding the objects of human acts; and these are the basic human goods which, by providing non-instrumental reasons, give human acts their intelligible point.

Finally, natural law theories must be distinguished from utilitarian, consequentialist, proportionalist, and other theories which propose aggregative accounts of justice and moral goodness. Although different schools of thought about natural law differ on the question of how, if at all, it can make sense to speak of a hierarchy of *basic* human goods, virtually all reject emphatically the idea that alternative options for morally significant choice can be commensurated in such a way as to make workable (even in "hard" cases) a principle which directs people to choose that option which promises to conduce to the best net proportion of benefit to harm overall and in the long run. Natural law theorists emphasize the "intransitive" (self-shaping, character-forming) significance of morally significant choices for (or against) human goods which, *qua intrinsic* (and, precisely in that sense, *basic*), are never rightly treated as mere means to other basic goods or to some putative "overall," "comprehensive," or "greater" good.

Grisez and Finnis have criticized proportionalist theories and the like, which currently enjoy a significant measure of support not only from secular thinkers in the tradition of Jeremy Bentham and J. S. Mill but also among moral theologians, for confusing human and divine responsibility in regard to bringing about "optimal" states of affairs. The *ideal* of integral fulfillment, though people are capable of respecting the rational principle enjoining them to choose consistently with a will toward it, cannot be an operational objective or goal of human choosing. If this ideal is to be *realized*, it is up to God to bring about its realization. For humans to choose to destroy, damage, or impede one or some of the goods which constitute the basic aspects of human well-being and fulfillment for the sake of an allegedly "greater good" is (in addition to many other failings) to usurp vainly the divine office. Among the specifications of the principle that one ought always to choose (and otherwise will) consistently with a will toward integral human fulfillment, are the norms against direct killing and other choices to damage persons in any basic aspect of their well-being either as one's end or as a chosen means to other ends.

Notwithstanding their rejection of voluntarist accounts of obligation, most natural law theorists hold, with Aquinas, that human beings have the duties they have because they have been created with a particular nature (which, again, in no way suggests that practical knowledge, including knowledge of *natural law*, is derived from prior theoretical knowledge of human nature). As a theological matter, they typically hold that God directs people to their proper ends, not by instinct (as in the case of brute animals), but rather by (practical) *reason*. In this way, human beings are made "in the image of God" (Genesis 1:27) and act, as God acts, *freely*, and as co-creators with Him. Christian natural law theorists interpret St Paul's reference to a "law inscribed on the hearts even of the Gentiles" (who do not have the law revealed through Moses) (Romans 2:14–15), as a reference to the natural law which can, in principle, be known by unaided reason. The moral law is "natural," then, in so far as it does not depend on supernatural revelation. Knowledge of the natural moral law is sufficient, according to St Paul, for divine judgment. Thus, Pope John Paul II teaches in the encyclical letter *Veritatis Splendor* (1993) that the way of salvation open even to those who do not have biblical faith is to act in conformity with the moral requirements of the natural law.

What, then, for religious believers is the relationship between natural and divine law? According to Aquinas, human persons, by understanding and doing what is reasonable and right, participate in God's providential direction of the whole of creation according to a plan conceived in wisdom and love. This participation of rational creatures in God's eternal plan, and, thus, in divine providence, is identified by Aquinas as the natural law. Of course, Aquinas, like all Christians, holds that reason has been weakened and distracted by sin; and he in no way denigrates revealed moral teaching which, in his view and the view of the larger tradition of natural law thinking, reinforces and illuminates what can be known of moral truth by reason alone. Neither Aquinas nor the tradition holds that natural law renders divine moral commands superfluous.

Although the Roman Catholic Church has been the principal institutional bearer of the tradition of natural law theory in the modern world, understandings of natural law were developed before Christ by Greek and Roman thinkers, whose influences persist to this day, and even today there are Protestant, Jewish, and unbelieving natural law theorists. The prominence of Catholic teaching about natural law, combined, no doubt, with the claim of the *magisterium* of the Catholic Church to teach its precepts authoritatively, has, however, led to its association in the public's mind with Catholicism. An influential strain of Reformation theology rejects natural law teaching on the ground that it overestimates the reliability of reason in the fallen condition of humanity (and on other grounds). But the teaching is scarcely a "sectarian" or narrowly Catholic one.

Bibliography

Boyle, J. M., Jr., Grisez, G., and Tollefsen, O.: *Free Choice: A Self-Referential Argument* (Notre Dame: University of Notre Dame Press, 1976).

Donagan, A.: *The Theory of Morality* (Chicago and London: University of Chicago Press, 1977).

Finnis, J.: *Natural Law and Natural Rights* (Oxford: Clarendon Press, 1980).

——: *Fundamentals of Ethics* (Washington, DC, and Oxford: Georgetown University Press and Oxford University Press, 1983).

Fuchs, J., SJ: *Natural Law: A Theological Investigation* (New York: Sheed & Ward, 1965).

George, R. (ed.): *Natural Law Theory: Contemporary Essays* (Oxford: Clarendon Press, 1992).

Grisez, G.: *The Way of the Lord Jesus*, vol. I: *Christian Moral Principles*, and vol. II: *Living a Christian Life* (Chicago: Franciscan Herald Press, 1983 and 1993).

Simon, Y. R.: *The Tradition of Natural Law* (1965); new edn with intro. by R. Hittinger (New York: Fordham University Press, 1992).

59

Virtue ethics

JEAN PORTER

Generally speaking, a virtue is an admirable or desirable trait of character. Virtue ethics may therefore be understood as a form of moral reflection which gives a central place to such traits of character. As such, it is often contrasted with approaches to ethics which emphasize rules, duties, or a general obligation of beneficence, although the proper relationship among these various notions is itself a matter of dispute.

Moral philosophy, considered as a systematic discipline, began with reflections on the nature of the virtues and their place in an overall conception of human excellence. Under the influence of Stoicism and then Christianity, moral reflection increasingly addressed the nature of duty and the moral law as well (see Article 58, NATURAL LAW ETHICS), but the idea of virtue and related notions continued to dominate reflection on the moral life through the end of the Middle Ages. With the rise of modernity, however, the concept of virtue gradually lost its central place in moral reflection, to be supplanted by notions of law, duty, and obligation. In this century, the topic of virtue was almost ignored by moral philosophers until the 1950s. Although reflection on the virtues cannot be said to have regained its original centrality, it is certainly one of the dominant topics of interest among contemporary moral philosophers, especially younger scholars.

History of the topic

The concept of virtue (*aretē*) plays a central role in Homer's writings, where it connotes excellence or manliness, rather than what we would ordinarily think of as properly moral virtue. In the heroic period, "virtue" could refer to any quality which enabled an individual to perform his or her role in society in a praiseworthy fashion. Thus, courage and strength are the characteristic virtues of aristocratic warriors, and faithfulness and modesty are the characteristic virtues of women.

In Athenian society in the fifth century BCE, the virtues appropriate to a more warlike society were gradually supplanted or transformed in the context of urban life. These social changes, in turn, led to attempts to provide a systematic account of the nature of virtue. Socrates is thought of as the prototypical moral philosopher of this period, but as scholars have recently reminded us, other philosophers and also the Athenian tragedians laid the foundations for systematic reflection on the virtues (MacIntyre 1984, pp. 131–45; Nussbaum 1986, pp. 23–84).

Socrates' most famous pupil, Plato, offers the first extended philosophical exploration of the virtues to have survived intact. Throughout his writings, we see the efforts of a brilliant and subtle mind to come to terms with the inconsistencies and gaps in his own received tradition of the virtues. Briefly, he argued that virtue, correctly understood, is essentially knowledge or insight into what is truly good. The individual who possesses this knowledge is enabled to bring the different components of his soul into right relation with one another, and to act in accordance with his vision of the good. Because the virtues are forms of knowledge, they are all essentially one; thus, Plato asserts the much-disputed doctrine of the unity of the virtues. Furthermore, he held that virtue can be taught, that all wrongdoing results from some sort of ignorance, and that only the virtuous person is truly happy (Nussbaum 1986, pp. 85–234).

In turn, Plato's disciple Aristotle offered an alternative account of the virtues, which also attempted to come to terms with the inconsistencies of the heroic tradition. Aristotle grounded his account of the virtues in a metaphysically informed account of the human good, in terms of which he systematized current ideals of virtuous behavior and offered criteria for distinguishing true virtues from their similitudes (MacIntyre 1984, pp. 146–64; Nussbaum 1986, pp. 235–372). His normative account of the virtues includes the much-misunderstood claim that virtuous behavior represents a mean, which refers to an appropriate balance among competing claims as determined by practical wisdom (Stocker 1990, pp. 129–64). He also argued, contrary to Plato, that it is possible to know the good and yet to act contrary to it, thus initiating an extended discussion on the problem of weakness of the will.

Subsequently, all the major philosophical schools, and many of the religious traditions, of the Hellenistic and Roman worlds contributed to the ongoing tradition of reflection on the virtues. The most influential authors in this period, at least within the medieval West, would include the Stoic Seneca, the eclectic Cicero (whose moral writings were much influenced by the Stoics), and the Christian theologians Gregory the Great and Augustine. Medieval reflection on the virtues continued along the same lines, incorporating the distinctively Christian ideals of the theological virtues (faith, hope, and charity) into a tradition which had come to focus on the cardinal virtues of prudence, justice, temperance, and fortitude. The best-known medieval discussion of virtue is that of Thomas Aquinas, who synthesized Aristotelian and Neoplatonic elements, the latter being mediated to him through Augustine, Pseudo-Dionysius, and a number of other early Christian authors. However, it would be a mistake to assume that reflection on the virtues was limited to Christian theology in this period. To mention one notable example to the contrary, the Jewish philosopher and rabbi, Moses Maimonides, also developed a theory of virtue which combined philosophical and traditional Jewish elements in a distinctive and original way.

During the modern period, through the early nineteenth century, moral philosophers continued to devote much attention to the virtues. After this point, however, Kantianism and utilitarianism came to dominate moral philosophy, and interest in the virtues as an independent topic for reflection faded, whether because Enlightenment concepts of the individual rendered the idea of virtue incomprehensible (MacIntyre 1984, pp. 36–61), or because traditions of the virtues could not accommodate the complexity of modern moral discourse (Schneewind 1990).

The neglect of virtue among moral philosophers began to change after the appearance of Elizabeth Anscombe's well known essay, "Modern Moral Philosophy" (1981 [1958]). In that essay, Anscombe argues that the central concepts of the moral philosophy of her time, duty and moral law, are no longer credible; the idea of a moral law makes no sense unless we believe in a divine lawgiver, which many of us do not, and the Kantian idea of a self-legislating reason is simply incoherent. Given this situation, she argued, we should turn to an Aristotelian account of the virtues to provide a starting point for an alternative moral philosophy, grounded in a renewed philosophical psychology. Subsequently, Alasdair MacIntyre, in *After Virtue*, argued that contemporary morality consists of nothing more than fragmentary survivals from earlier traditions, and for that reason, it cannot sustain rational discourse, either at the public or the philosophical level (MacIntyre 1984, pp. 51–78). In his view, coherence in moral discourse can only be attained within the context of particular traditions, which are given concrete moral content by the virtues which they commend and the vices which they reject (pp. 204–43).

The subsequent influence of these authors indicates that they expressed a widely shared dissatisfaction with the direction that moral philosophy had taken since the beginning of the nineteenth century. In addition, they drew upon, and helped to foster, a renewed interest in the classical authors as resources for contemporary moral thought. Aristotle in particular began to be reappropriated as a source for moral reflection. This reappropriation both presupposed a willingness to examine his theory of the virtues on its own terms, and served to promote further philosophical work on the virtues.

Contemporary developments

Since the work of Anscombe and MacIntyre, there has been a considerable amount done on the virtues and related topics, including the moral significance of character, the nature of judgment, the moral significance of the emotions, and the importance of particular commitments, relationships, and roles for the moral life (see Article 60, NARRATIVE ETHICS). Most of the authors contributing to these conversations see themselves as reacting, at least in part, to mistakes or distortions introduced by the dominant schools of moral philosophy. For this reason, the contemporary discussion can be organized in terms of what its various interlocutors are reacting against. This may seem excessively negative, but it does at least have the advantage of identifying what various authors see as the significance and point of virtue ethics. At the same time, any such classification can only offer a rough guide to what is a very complex set of discussions, and most of the major philosophers who have contributed to this discussion could be classified in more than one way.

One perspective in this discussion is shaped by the view that there is something fundamentally wrong with the conception of morality that dominates industrial societies today. Both Anscombe and MacIntyre hold this view; more specifically, they agree that we have lost the traditional framework of practices and beliefs within which alone cogent moral discourse would be possible. For these authors and those who follow them, therefore, the point of virtue ethics may be said to be the revival or construction of a framework for normative analysis, within which rational, cogent moral discourse would once again be possible.

Another group of philosophers, although similar to the first in many respects, differ in what they see as the central problem to be addressed. For these authors, the difficulty is not so much that the general concept of morality is incoherent, as that the academic discipline of moral philosophy is misguided. The most influential advocates of this point of view would include Bernard Williams (1985) and Martha Nussbaum (1986), but a number of other important moral philosophers could also be included here. These authors all agree that the modern project of arriving at a theory of morality is wrong-headed, and should be abandoned in favor of an appeal to notions of virtue and related concepts; thus, they have come to be known, perhaps unfortunately, as moral anti-theorists.

It is important to note that Williams, Nussbaum, and most of the others who share their views do not reject the possibility of fruitful philosophical work on morality. Williams, at least, does not even deny the possibility of developing a constructive account of moral judgment (Williams 1985, p. 17). "Theory" has come to have a more specific meaning in this context. That is, these authors understand a moral theory to be a systematic account of moral judgment which locates all such judgments in some one fundamental moral principle (for example, obligation, or the maximization of well-being), and offers a procedure for resolving all moral problems on that basis. Typically, anti-theorists deny that there is one fundamental moral principle, or they deny that there can be a decision procedure for moral judgments, or (usually) both.

The point of virtue ethics as these authors develop it can accordingly be understood in terms of what they affirm, in contrast to what they take to be the mistaken approach of moral theorists. Although most of the authors associated with moral anti-theory would agree that moral theory is mistaken in both of its basic assumptions, it is possible to identify certain differences of emphasis among them, both in terms of what they are concerned to deny, and in terms of what they affirm. Thus, for some, virtue ethics is attractive because it reflects the fact that our normative judgments are irreducibly pluralistic. Others are more concerned to draw on virtue ethics to provide an alternative to the decision procedures of modern moral theory. Usually, this alternative is developed in terms of an account of judgment which draws on Aristotle, although important accounts of judgment have also been offered which draw on Ludwig Wittgenstein or David Hume.

A third group of philosophers who have contributed to virtue ethics are not so thoroughgoing in their rejection either of our general concept of morality, or of moral theory as it is usually practiced. However, they claim that recent philosophy has neglected important aspects of the moral life, and virtue ethics offers a way to address these issues. In addition, a growing number of philosophers have turned to virtue ethics as a framework for exploring specific moral ideals and issues. Finally, a number of studies attempt to draw on virtue ethics as a basis for social critique. MacIntyre connects his defense of the virtues to a critique of liberalism (MacIntyre 1984, pp. 244–55), thus fostering the widespread view that virtue ethics has a natural affinity for a conservative or communitarian political vision. However, some political philosophers have challenged this assumption by developing accounts of the virtues which are characteristic of liberalism as a way of life. It should also be noted that a number of feminist thinkers have drawn on virtue and related categories to develop critiques of dominant ideals and practices.

Current issues

The issues which informed classical reflection on the virtues are still discussed among philosophers today. Thus, it is still possible to find extended discussions on the relationship between the virtues and reason or knowledge, on the one hand, and the passions and emotions, on the other. There are also discussions on Aristotle's claim that virtue attains a mean between different sorts of moral failures; and on the thesis that the virtues are united or connected, in such a way that whoever truly has one virtue, necessarily possesses them all. However, many of the central issues for contemporary virtue ethics did not arise, or arose in a significantly different form, among classical authors.

Among the issues which are central for the contemporary discussion, one set might be described as conceptual. What do we mean by a virtue, and how is the concept of a virtue related to such notions as habit and disposition? It is generally agreed that virtues cannot be reduced to tendencies to perform certain kinds of actions, but what then are the criteria by which we determine whether a person has a given virtue, or is virtuous *tout court*? As Anscombe observed, many of these issues are questions for the philosophy of mind, as well as (or instead of?) questions for moral philosophy (1981 [1958], pp. 41–2).

A related set of questions arises when we ask how we are to conceptualize specific virtues. What does it mean to be courageous, or temperate, or kind? A number of authors have understood virtues as being necessarily conflictual, that is, as being characterized by the recurrent temptation or the negative emotion that they correct. On this view, for example, temperance would be understood in terms of a contrast with greed, courage would be understood in contrast to fear, and so forth. The difficulty with this approach, aside from the fact that important figures in this tradition rejected it (both Aristotle and Aquinas, to name two), is that it does not work at all for justice, and on close examination, it does not work very well even for courage or temperance. Yet it does not seem that specific virtues are tied conceptually to particular kinds of actions, at least, not in such a way that there are determinate kinds of acts which are always associated with, or always contrary to, specific virtues.

One very important conceptual issue concerns the relationship between having or practicing the virtues and following moral rules. No one who defends virtue ethics would be willing to accept the reduction of virtue to a disposition to follow moral rules, but there is considerable debate over how the relationship is to be understood. For some, moral rules are at best rough guidelines or "rules of thumb" which can and should be supplanted by the prudential judgment of the individual of mature practical wisdom. Others are willing to allow for an independent place for rule-governed behavior in the moral life, although rule-following is still thought to be linked to such virtues as justice or conscientiousness. For still others, the moral rules are seen as practices which sustain and foster the virtues.

A second set of issues might be described as normative, although they are obviously linked to the conceptual issues discussed above. One obvious question that arises in this connection concerns the relationship between received traditions of the virtues, and their contemporary defenders. Can the traditional identification of prudence, justice, temperance, and fortitude still be defended, or if not, which virtues are central for us? Indeed, does it even make sense to attempt to identify certain virtues as primary or most important?

Furthermore, how far should we take the virtues to be morally desirable qualities? To some extent, this question is pursued in terms of defending or rejecting the traditional doctrine of the unity or connection of the virtues. Most virtue ethicists would now reject the classical view that the possession of one virtue necessarily implies the possession of all of them (for a rare defense of the classical view, see Stocker 1990, pp. 129–64). Some virtue ethicists, most notably Michael Slote (1992) would go beyond the rejection of the classical view, insisting that virtues need not be morally praiseworthy qualities at all. On this view, the category of the virtuous should include, or should be developed solely in terms of, notions of what is admirable or praiseworthy, rather than in terms of what is morally good.

A third set of issues might be described as social. The identification of virtue ethics with conservative and communitarian policies (although challenged by some liberal virtue ethicists, as noted above) has led some critics to question whether the traditions of the virtues offer a sufficient basis for a thoroughgoing social critique. Similarly, it has been argued that traditions of the virtues do not offer sufficient resources for mediating social conflict in complex industrial societies. Finally, virtue ethics has been criticized as promoting a sectarian morality, or else it has been argued that the close identification of the virtues with particular traditions is just mistaken.

Virtue ethics and the philosophy of religion

It might seem strange that so little has been said about the relationship between virtue ethics and religious thought. In fact, however, in this century theologians and philosophers of religion have been even slower than moral philosophers to appreciate the potential importance of virtue ethics. Some work has been done on the relevance of the virtues to the philosophy of religion or to Christian theology. However, philosophers of religion who are interested in moral issues tend to give most of their attention to other issues such as divine command theories of morality (see Article 57, DIVINE COMMAND ETHICS). A growing number of Christian theologians are exploring the relevance of classical and contemporary virtue ethics for their own distinctive concerns. The revival of a distinctively theological exploration of the virtues only began in earnest in the 1970s, and it remains to be seen how extensive its influence will be, or what will be its most important distinctive contributions.

It would seem that Aquinas might exercise an influence in favor of virtue ethics among theologians and philosophers of religion, analogous to the influence which Aristotle has had on moral philosophers. To some extent, this has in fact been the case. During the first decades of the twentieth century, a number of distinguished Catholic scholars offered important new readings of Aquinas's theology, including his moral theology and his treatment of the theological virtues. This work was one of the important sources for the renewal of Catholic moral theology later in the twentieth century. More recently, a number of younger scholars have turned their attention to a retrieval of Aquinas's virtue ethics. However, interest in Aquinas as an independent source for virtue ethics has been somewhat limited, even among theologians, and certainly among philosophers, due perhaps to the fact that he is widely, although mistakenly, thought to follow Aristotle in every aspect of his moral thought which is not explicitly theological (see Article 19, THOMISM).

Perhaps the most important original contribution that virtue ethics has made to the philosophy of religion has come through Lee Yearley's work, particularly his *Mencius and Aquinas* (1990). On one level, this book is a comparative study of the accounts of virtue developed by the Chinese philosopher Mencius (371–289 BCE) and by Aquinas (see Article 78, COMPARATIVE PHILOSOPHY OF RELIGION). In addition, however, Yearley develops a methodology for the comparative study of different religious accounts of virtue and morality out of Aquinas's analysis of the virtues, placed in the context of contemporary anthropological theories (1990, pp. 169–203). In this way, he claims to offer an approach which avoids seeing surface similarities as definitive, but which uncovers surprising points of contact in the midst of seemingly radical differences. Only time will tell how far the promise of Yearley's original and important work is vindicated.

Bibliography

Anscombe, E.: "Modern moral philosophy," in *Collected Philosophical Papers*, vol. III: *Ethics, Religion and Politics* (1958), ed. G. E. M. [Elizabeth] Anscombe (Minneapolis: University of Minnesota Press, 1981), pp. 26–42.

MacIntyre, A.: *After Virtue*, 2nd edn (Notre Dame: University of Notre Dame Press, 1984).

Nussbaum, M. C.: *The Fragility of Goodness: Luck and Ethics in Greek Tragedy and Philosophy* (Cambridge: Cambridge University Press, 1986).

Schneewind, J. B.: "The misfortunes of virtue," *Ethics*, 101 (October 1990), pp. 42–63.

Slote, M.: *From Morality to Virtue* (Oxford University Press, 1992).

Stocker, M.: *Plural and Conflicting Values* (Oxford: Clarendon Press, 1990).

Williams, B.: *Ethics and the Limits of Philosophy* (Cambridge, MA: Harvard University Press, 1985).

Yearley, L. H.: *Mencius and Aquinas: Theories of Virtue and Conceptions of Courage* (Albany: State University of New York Press, 1990).

60

Narrative ethics

ROBERT C. ROBERTS

Introduction

In both theological and non-theological ethics the concept of narrative has recently gained in prominence. This gain is due in part to a change of focus. In the first two-thirds of the twentieth century ethicists took little interest in issues of character and the concepts of virtue and vice, being interested instead in the rightness or wrongness, the goodness or badness of actions and policies, and correspondingly in the rules and principles governing actions. Since Elizabeth Anscombe's "Modern Moral Philosophy" (1958) and its call for attention to moral psychology, ethicists have increasingly focused on the concept of character and on the particular virtues, such as courage, truthfulness, generosity, humility, and practical wisdom, and their vice counterparts. Traits of character are not, like actions, datable occurrences in a person's history, but dispositions: temporally extended qualities that are *exhibited* occurrently in action, intention, thought, and emotion. One of the most basic and natural media for presenting such qualities is narrative, in which connected sequences of actions, intentions, thoughts, and emotions are depicted in life-contexts that are the natural settings of such occurrences. The psychologizing of ethics has meant that novels and biographies in which characters are narratively depicted, sometimes with great moral psychological insight, have become important resources for thinkers about ethics.

Related to this first reason is a second. The revival of the ancient ideal of the good person as the healthy, fully functioning, self-realized person has caused the concerns of ethics to intersect with those of psychotherapy, some branches of which have long employed narratives. Psychotherapeutic narrative characteristically tells the story of the person whose improvement is chiefly in view, and so is reminiscent of the spiritual diary and autobiography found in some parts and times of the Christian Church, famously with St Augustine and among the Puritans. In these cases vices and other defective dispositions and their historical antecedents and consequences are especially of interest, as areas of prospective moral improvement and clues to strategies for effecting it.

With the undermining of the Enlightenment ideal of universal Reason and culture-independent access to ethical norms, narratives reflecting various ethical and religious traditions have drawn greater interest. Some philosophers (e.g. D. Z. Phillips and Martha Nussbaum in their very different ways) have used fictional narratives to complicate and enrich the overly tidy, simple, rationalistic, and

473

psychologically and culturally thin accounts of morality that have been offered by modern philosophers.

When Christian and Jewish ethicists place the narratives constitutive of their moral traditions at the center of their accounts of the moral life, they can declare a certain independence from reigning philosophical thought about ethics and exploit the rich particularities and distinctives of their traditions.

What is a narrative?

A narrative is a verbal account (oral or written) of a temporally connected series of events, including mental events (e.g. plans, assessments, emotions) and actions, including speech acts. It shows connections (continuities and changes, antecedents and consequences) between the past, the present, and the future within and beyond the bounds of the narrative. It depicts characters, in their con- tinuities and changes, through depiction of their actions, interactions, and reac- tions (e.g. emotions), their thoughts, desires and intentions at different points in time.

Narratives can be historically true, or fictional. If fictional, they can still be more or less "true to life," that is, represent real (human) possibilities or at any rate by their exaggerations and unreality, illuminate real human possibilities and actual human beings. They can have the character of myth or allegory, in which case the characters are not in the last analysis individuals, but purportedly univer- sal types of persons or of aspects of persons (e.g. virtues and vices, as in Bunyan's *The Pilgrim's Progress*). Or the narrative may be realistic (even if fictional), in that its characters are individuals. Oral and written history (of which biography is of special interest here) and most novels are largely composed of realistic narratives. In the following discussion of the relations of ethics to narrative I shall have realis- tic narratives, fictional and otherwise, chiefly in view.

Narratives and the concept of a self

In the opinion of many recent ethicists, the idea of a self as something to which its history is merely accidental does not do justice to the concept of a self with which we daily do business. (Examples would be a Cartesian "thinking substance" which would be the same regardless of what actions, undergoings, thoughts, and pas- sions its past is composed of, or an existentialist/emotivist "agent [which], thin as a needle, appears in the quick flash of the choosing will" [Murdoch 1971, p. 53].) A person's identity is constituted, in significant part, of his or her history. Thus if someone says, "Tell me about yourself; who are you, anyway?" we may begin by giving our name and physical appearance, but we will go on to tell about our con- nections with other people, our relations with institutions, things we have done (some quite long ago), things that have happened to us, and so on. Much of this account will necessarily take narrative form. If the incidents so narrated are not just epiphenomenal of the real self, but are constitutive of who we are, then we can speak of the narrative nature of the self. We are not just beings who *have* a past; our past makes up, in part, what we *are*. I am the one who was born to such-and-such parents, who married so-and-so twenty years ago. My identity has a "narrative structure," not in the sense that it is a *narrative*, but in the sense that it is in part a *history* which can only be properly displayed in a narrative.

One of the kinds of things that would have to be given account of in answer to the question, "Tell me about yourself; who are you?" is your character. Character is of special interest to the ethicist. One's character is an aspect of one's identity. We might *explain* a person's present character by reference to his or her past. For example, we might think that if he had not chosen a certain courageous course of action at an earlier juncture, he would not now be the courageous, self-confident person he has become; his character is (partially) *caused* by his past. But we would not say that his courage is *constituted* of his past. It is constituted, instead, of his present dispositions to do, think, desire, and feel in characteristic ways, given a context appropriate to the display of courage. (Certain kinds of situation elicit displays of courage from the courageous person; other kinds elicit displays of compassion; yet others, of truthfulness, and so forth for all the virtues.) But a person's character, just because it is a set of dispositions, is most naturally displayed in a narrative. Novelists like Charles Dickens, Leo Tolstoy, and George Eliot are astute presenters of character, and they ply their craft largely by narrating, *in situ*, the characters' actions, thoughts, emotions, and desires.

Jane Austen comments, "Vanity was the beginning and the end of Sir Walter Elliot's character; vanity of person and of situation" (*Persuasion*, ch. 1). This sentence, like any mere ascription of a trait to a person, is not itself a narrative presentation of Sir Walter's character, though it is embedded in the narrative which is the novel, and it invites such a narrative as a clarification. Austen gives us narrative proper when she recounts particular actions, emotions, and thoughts of this man as in the opening lines of the novel. He was, she tells us,

a man who, for his own amusement, never took up any book but the Baronetage; there he found occupation for an idle hour, and consolation in a distressed one; there his faculties were roused into admiration and respect, by contemplating the limited remnant of the earliest patents; there any unwelcome sensations, arising from domestic affairs, changed naturally into pity and contempt, as he turned over the almost endless creations of the last century. . . .

Here Austen is telling us, even if in generalities, what Sir Walter did and thought and felt. Such things are the indicators of his character, the events in which his traits are exemplified. His conceit about his good looks and rank come out further in his reaction to the proposal that he should economize to relieve his financial distresses (ch. 1), his expressions of contempt for the navy as "the means of bringing persons of obscure birth into undue distinction" and as causing men to lose their good looks early (ch. 3), and his thinking it will look better to let his house to somebody with "Admiral" before his name than to a mere "Mr" (ch. 3).

Narratives and the ethics of character

The concepts of person, character, self, and other related ones provide the most fundamental connection between narratives and contemporary ethics. The influence is reciprocal: because contemporary ethics is more psychological than that of the recent past, it is more interested in narratives; and this interest tends to make it more richly and concretely psychological. We can imagine a kind of philosophical ethics that uses narrative examples to pose or illustrate problems of action and rules for action (What should one do in such-and-such a situation, and how would one know what to do? Did so-and-so act rightly when she did thus and such? Why or why not? Consider the narratives with which Lawrence Kohlberg (1984) presents moral dilemmas to train in moral reasoning and test for it.) But this is not, for the most part, the way present-day ethicists use narratives.

While present-day ethicists interested in character pursue many different goals in their work, some of which are narrowly "professional" or continuations of the "ethical theory" enterprise of discovering the universal conceptual foundations of ethical discourse and thought, it seems to me that an intrinsically central purpose of any ethics of character must be to understand better the moral life – in particular, to understand the human virtues such as courage, compassion, humility, generosity, justice, truthfulness, practical wisdom, the sense of duty, and so forth, and their counterpart vices. A deep grasp of the nature of these traits is a significant part of what has been called "wisdom" in many traditions, and so character ethics is naturally a return to the notion that the philosopher is in the business of discovering and purveying ethical wisdom – a knowledge of the good life for human beings.

I have said that narratives are a natural and powerful way to display virtues and vices. Great narrativists like Austen, Henry James, Dostoevsky, Tolstoy, and Eliot are also, in their own way, great moral psychologists. In their fashion they are what Aristotle calls *phronimoi* (people of practical wisdom) because they are able to present, with great delicacy and subtlety of nuance, the variants of human moral success and failure. But just as philosophers are not very often good narrativists, so the best narrativists are not very often excellent philosophers (the philosophical sections of Tolstoy's *War and Peace* only mar the book by injecting third-rate work into a great novel). It seems that a *coordination* between philosophical and narrative presentations of the virtues and vices is needed. (Martha Nussbaum, 1990, has argued for such a coordination.) What is a philosophical presentation of a virtue or vice, and why is it needed, in addition to excellent narrative presentations?

The trait terms are regulated by what Wittgenstein (1953) would call a "grammar." (On the notion of the grammar of a trait, see Roberts 1991, 1994, 1995.) A term's grammar consists in the rules for its application. The grammar of a trait term, which will vary from one moral tradition to another (Aristotelian generosity differs in grammar from Christian generosity, and both differ from Nietzschean generosity), determines such things as the kind of actions and emotions (*in situ*), of motives and reasons, that characteristically exemplify the trait. For example, acts exemplifying generosity belong in the category of "givings" and thus are performed in situations where a good (time, money, praise, attention) can benefit another or at least be perceived by the agent as capable of doing so, and the motive for giving must include the well-being of the recipient. Certain versions of emotions such as regret that one has given the benefit or resentment about giving it are excluded by generosity, and certain versions of gladness at giving or regret at not being able to give or give more exemplify the virtue. (The above sketch does not apply to Nietzschean generosity.)

The grammar of a virtue is related in the following ways to the narrative display of the same virtue. The narrated incidents that display the virtue (say, the acts, thoughts, and emotions exemplifying the generosity of John Jarndyce in Dickens's *Bleak House*) mark grammatical features of it; if they did not, they would not exemplify the virtue. Philosophical analysis of the virtue consists in identifying its grammatical features, and may be aided by, and based on, narrated incidents that exemplify the virtue. Provided that the narrator has narrative practical wisdom, the narrative provides a basis for philosophical analysis superior in some ways to everyday life. The philosopher profits from the close and sensitive observation of the other *phronimos*, from the fact that the incidents are set in a rich yet compactly presented lifelike setting, and even from the idealization that often characterizes fictional characters. On this last point, one might think that the unrealism of the idealized character would be likely to mislead the philosopher, but this is not so, since the kind of "psychology" the philosopher engages in is itself ideal. He or she is engaged in the analysis of the *concept* of generosity, humility, or courage, concepts which are not often exemplified in any very pure way in actual life. (As a colleague once remarked to me, Dorothea Brooke of George Eliot's *Middlemarch* is "too good to be true." True, but she is not too good to be true to the *concept* of moral goodness.) The narrativist might conceivably mislead the philosopher by getting the grammar of the moral life wrong in some way or other, but in that case the narrativist would be a defective one and ought not to be employed as philosopher's sidekick. Good narrativists are not likely to get the grammar of the moral concepts wrong if they stick to writing narrative and leave the philosophizing to us.

The narrative display of a virtue is warmer, more immediately appealing, and more vivid than the philosophical display of it. For these reasons it enlivens the philosopher's imagination, and speaks to his heart, and keeps him close to the earth, thus correcting his occupational tendency to lose himself in the dusty clouds of abstract inference. For the same reason it can enliven his writing or oral teaching, if used by way of illustration. Alcibiades reports that Socrates did ethics by talking "about pack asses and blacksmiths and shoemakers and tanners" (*Symposium* 221e), and it was perhaps in part this concreteness that gave his philosophizing the *ethical* immediacy that Alcibiades complains of and profits from. One would think that wisdom (even if philosophical!) ought to make an impact on people.

So far I have talked about the importance of narratives to philosophical ethicists. But why philosophize about the virtues at all? If we have narrative displays of the virtues, what good are philosophical ones to us? Why not just read Sophocles and leave Aristotle on the shelf? Why read *Either/Or* when we have *Middlemarch*? The answer, I think, is that we human beings come to understand in a variety of ways, which are mutually supplementary. We would never get any very adequate understanding of Paris by sitting in our hotel room exploring the *Plan Taride*. But without such a map (or at least one that we construct for ourselves from a great deal of ground-level exploring) we would not know as well where we are in our ramblings about Paris. The map is a more abstract, schematic representation of the very same Paris that we see and hear and smell as we walk along the Seine or wander the markets and neighborhood streets of some out-of-the-way *arrondissement*. Philosophers from Plato to Wittgenstein have felt that to understand is somehow to display the essence of whatever it is they were trying to understand. The representation of a virtue in terms of its grammar presents its outline, its schema, its structural features. As Wittgenstein says, "*Essence* is expressed by grammar" (1953, Part I, §371, his italics). We all have a more or less inarticulate conception of the grammar of the virtues, acquired by living and speaking the language of morals, just as a resident of Paris, even without a paper map, has some sense for where things are relative to one another. But just as the map makes that implicit understanding much more definite and clear, so the philosophical display of a virtue concept orients one to the virtue in a way that common experience, including the reading of excellent narratives in which the virtues are displayed, cannot by itself do.

Constitutive narratives

So far I have focused on realistic narratives in which persons – and thus their virtues and vices – are exhibited. Such narratives not only display virtues and vices concretely, but do so in the matrix of some cultural understanding – either that of the various characters in the novel or history, or that of the narrator, which may or may not be the outlook of the characters. Thus in the narrative we have concreteness in at least two dimensions that are important for moral philosophy: an account of particular moral *persons*, given in the matrix of one or another particular moral *outlook*. In so far as the narratives are composed by astute observers of persons and deep understanders of their moral tradition, narratives are a great source of wisdom and an indispensable resource for moral philosophy. But in some moral traditions some narratives play a role that goes beyond that of *displaying* virtues. They make up a part of what is culturally distinctive about a set of virtues, by entering into the very grammar of those virtues.

The narrative of the Hebrew people's exodus from Egypt displays virtues and vices of the people and their leaders, but that is far from its most basic moral function. The story recounts the actions of God in owning the people of Israel as God's own. God is shown identifying in a special way with the people of Israel and blessing and disciplining them by his actions. The story is thus about Israel's formation as a people; about their identity as God's. It is led up to by the stories of the patriarchs and succeeded by narratives of judges, kings, and prophets, all of which are about God's faithfulness to and judgment of his chosen people. If an ordinary narrative displays the self-understanding of its characters, this one structures a self-understanding in its believing reader or hearer. This narrative does not just *exemplify* a moral tradition, in the way that, say, the characters of Alyosha and Father Zossima in Dostoevsky's *The Brothers Karamazov* exemplify Russian Orthodox Christianity and the virtues of its most exemplary adherents; it *founds* one or at least represents a crucial stage in its founding. But the founding has a special status here, which affects the function of the narrative in the community. Stories of foundings are not all constitutive of the founded outlooks in the way this one is. The story of the career, trial, and death of Socrates is a story of a founding, yet is not constitutive of the Socratic morality in the way the Exodus narrative is of the Hebrew. For it is an essential part of Jewish faithfulness to God to remember this event, while it is not essential to Socratic morality, but only helpfully edifying, to remember the story of Socrates. The identity of the God in whom the Jew hopes, and whose worship is the highest virtue, is provided (revealed) in the events here narrated. Jewish gratitude is in significant part gratitude for the very acts of God recounted in this narrative. The Hebrew sense of self that is involved in one way or another in all the Jewish virtues – hospitality to the foreigner, generosity, trust and humility, the praise of God, just treatment of fellows, contrition, truthfulness, marital fidelity, honor of parents, etc., etc. – is in essential part the sense of belonging to the people whom God made his own in this special way.

The story that is recorded in the four Gospels is similarly constitutive for the Christian outlook and virtues. It too tells of an act of God, not now for a selected population but for the entire world. It too tells of the founding of a community and a new way of life, yet is more than just the story of a founding. The narrative of the incarnation, death, and resurrection of the Son of God does not just dramatically display a set of virtues with a special grammar, but is itself taken up in the grammar of the virtues of those who accept the story and become members of the community. Compassion is seeing in the faces of the sufferers one ministers to the face of the incarnate Son who died for them; contrition is both sadness for sins committed against the God whose Son is the main character in the story and comfort that this man's death is one's own righteousness; gratitude is first of all for the act of God recounted in the story; hope is first of all for the resurrection of which the risen Jesus is the first fruits. Jesus does exemplify some of the Christian virtues – say, forgivingness, humility, compassion, courage, and longsuffering – but the main function of the narrative in the Christian community (a function strongly suggested by the content of the narrative) is not to display the Christian virtues, but to take its place in the grammar of those virtues.

The distinctiveness of the Christian virtues, as compared with their counterparts in other moral outlooks, is largely provided by the gospel narrative. Jonathan Edwards's *Charity and its Fruits* is a good example of a grammatical display of several virtues (e.g. longsuffering, humility, generosity) in their distinctively Christian lineaments. The humility whose grammar he exhibits is a special one that is implied by and derives from a love of God. This love is a response to the gospel narrative, and Edwards describes it in several connections using the locution "love . . . as. . . ." The Christian's humility is implied by his loving "God as an infinitely condescending God" (p. 149), loving "Christ as an humble person" (p. 150), "Christ as a crucified Saviour" (p. 151), "Christ as one that was crucified for our sakes" (p. 152). The "as" in each case is followed by a reference to some feature of the gospel narrative. It is "in terms of" these features that the Christianly humble person counts himself as no greater than any of his human fellows (even if he is wealthier and smarter than any of them) and infinitely inferior to God. To be humble in *this* way is to see oneself and one's world in the light of *that particular story.*

Bibliography

Anscombe, E.: "Modern moral philosophy," *Philosophy*, 33 (1958), pp. 1–19.

Edwards, J.: *Charity and its Fruits* (Edinburgh: Banner of Truth Trust, 1969).

Frei, H.: *The Identity of Jesus Christ* (Philadelphia: Fortress Press, 1975).

Kohlberg, L.: *The Psychology of Moral Development: The Nature and Validity of Moral Stages* (San Francisco: Harper & Row, 1984).

MacIntyre, A.: *After Virtue*, 2nd edn (Notre Dame: University of Notre Dame Press, 1984).

Murdoch, I.: *The Sovereignty of Good* (New York: Schocken Books, 1971).

Nussbaum, M. C.: *Love's Knowledge* (Cambridge: Cambridge University Press, 1990).

Phillips, D. Z.: *Interventions in Ethics* (Albany: State University of New York Press, 1992).

Plato: *Symposium*, tr. M. Joyce; in *The Collected Dialogues of Plato*, ed. E. Hamilton and H. Cairns (New York: Random House, 1961).

Roberts, R. C.: "Virtues and Rules," *Philosophy and Phenomenological Research*, 51 (1991), pp. 325–43.

——: "The philosopher as sage," *Journal of Religious Ethics*, 22 (1994), pp. 409–31.

——: "Kierkegaard, Wittgenstein, and a method of 'virtue ethics,'" in *Kierkegaard Post/Modernity*, ed. M. Matustic and M. Westphal (Bloomington: Indiana University Press, 1995).

Rorty, A.: "Characters, persons, selves, individuals," in *Mind in Action: Essays in the Philosophy of Mind* (Boston: Beacon Press, 1989).

Wittgenstein, L.: *Philosophical Investigations*, tr. G. E. M. Anscombe (New York: Macmillan, 1953).

61

Agapeistic Ethics

GENE OUTKA

This subject takes depictions of love in the Bible as its point of departure. Matthew records Jesus' insistence that on two great commandments – to love God with all your heart, soul, and mind, and to love your neighbor as yourself – "depend all the law and the prophets" (Matthew 22:37–40; see Deuteronomy 6:5 and Leviticus 19:18). Paul holds that "love is the fulfillment of the law" (Romans 13:10), and praises love more highly than even faith and hope (I Corinthians 13). John takes love to be constitutive of God's own action toward the world (3:16). Such passages fittingly pervade the consciousness of those in the Christian tradition.

Attempts to heed the particularity of Biblical depictions are crucial, since the word "love" appears indispensable to human beings, but is notoriously imprecise. One such attempt draws on ancient linguistic practices. Commentators routinely point out that among three Greek words for love, *eros*, *philia*, and *agape*, it is *agape* that predominates in the books of the New Testament. *Philia* appears too, though far less frequently, while *eros* never appears. How far the New Testament authors are deliberately selective is hard to determine. They do link what they say about love to the life, death, and teaching of Jesus. And they take care generally to appropriate from surrounding social worlds only what coheres with their basic convictions.

However we understand its genealogy, this usage figures prominently in later developments. *Agape* becomes a key term to refer to the love shaped by Christian convictions. Moreover, the several Greek words for love furnish a convenient philological base for conceptual distinctions between types of love. It is frequently held for example that *eros* connotes desire and longing and *philia* connotes fondness and liking. To invoke such distinctions clarifies further what *agape* is and is not, by comparing how it is like and unlike other kinds of love. Yet in execution this procedure permits appreciable room for maneuver. The distinctions themselves afford interpretive leeway. And they often reflect differences among discrete theological and philosophical traditions.

In the narrative we have now positioned ourselves to tell, we will focus on *agape* within Christian ethics or moral theology. We examine under "agapeistic ethics" therefore "the law of love" as a *practical* doctrine to which Christians are necessarily committed. And we focus on twentieth century discussions. A larger narrative lies in the background, one that draws on the writings of major historical figures, e.g. Augustine, Thomas Aquinas, Martin Luther, John Calvin, Jonathan Edwards,

481

Søren Kierkegaard. Still, "agapeistic ethics" has reached a distinct level of explicitness since 1930. That this is so is due to Anders Nygren, above all, whose *Agape and Eros* appeared in that year. He radically contrasts two loves in ways that receive continuous criticism. But no one disputes his seminal importance, and we go first to him.

The content of God's agape

Nygren tends to equate God's grace and God's *agape*. Since he likewise views God's *agape* as pattern and prototype for the love that Christians show, much depends on the content he attributes to it. He lists four features. First, God's *agape* is "spontaneous and unmotivated." God loves because of who God is, but God does not love particular human beings by virtue of character traits that distinguish them from other human beings. Such traits may affect how God loves but not whether God loves. God's independence and sovereignty are disclosed in love directed to the unworthy. Jesus is the paradigm in that he consorts with publicans and sinners and seeks out the lost. Second, God's love is "indifferent to value." This affirms again that God refuses to limit love to the virtuous. Third, God's love is "creative," that is, it is "value-creating." Such love does not depend on recognizing value in the object. Rather, it imparts value. Human beings acquire value precisely because God loves them. Fourth, God's love is the "initiator of fellowship" with God. By their own resources, human beings cannot know or enjoy fellowship with God. The reality of communion with God is due to God's own action.

Eros-love assumes entirely contrary features. It represents for him a fundamental religious and moral orientation. Such love is not spontaneous but is evoked and conditioned by the values it discovers. It judges degrees of worth and orders its attachments accordingly. It moves upward not downward, and by dint of its own efforts. In its sublime no less than its vulgar forms, it is acquisitive rather than other-regarding. It authorizes ethical egoism in human interaction and spiritualized egoism in relation to God. Efforts by Christians to accommodate it have failed and must fail.

Those who have come after Nygren rarely contrast the loves so totally. Some selectively appropriate and extend his account of *agape* as it pertains to neighbor-love. In addition to efforts to interpret neighbor-love, many have constructive things to say about three matters that Nygren neglects or inadequately treats: the first great love commandment, self-love, and *philia*. They contend that agapeistic ethics should incorporate or remain congruent with all three.

The neighbor as irreducibly valuable

We turn then to an attempt to extend the continuities between God's love and neighbor-love on which Nygren insists, to an understanding of neighbor-love itself. The attempt bears a selective and critical relation to parts of Nygren's program. It assumes that we may extend his account of God's *agape* and reject his account of self-love, for example, or that these need not stand or fall together. It assumes as well, however, that his account of God's *agape* is not some quixotic teaching of his own, but that he points to central Christian convictions.

To say that *agape* is "unmotivated" means at a minimum that the recipient of love is regarded for his or her own sake. We should concern ourselves with what the other may want or need, and not solely for the sake of gain to the lover. The neighbor constitutes a terminal point for another's attitudes and actions. Yet arguably other-regard may be genuine and still restricted to one's own people or friends or comrades. And it would be idle to deny that many act on the belief that we may do anything to those outside in order to strengthen bonds among those inside. So we go on to consider Biblical passages that generate normative pressures toward greater inclusiveness. One passage enjoins a love that extends beyond relations of undemanding, safe, assured reciprocity: "For if you love those who love you, what reward have you? Do not even tax collectors do the same?" (Matthew 5:46; see also Luke 6:32–4). Neighbor-love should then include unilateral efforts on the agent's part to establish and enhance personal relations marked by closeness and social relations marked by concord. In brief, *agape* does not await, anticipate, or demand a response in kind, though it may compatibly desire and hope for such a response, and take actual attainment as the fruition it seeks. Another passage directs attention to those who emphatically do not reciprocate. It is the injunction to "love your enemies and pray for those who persecute you" (Matthew 5:43–4). That is, care about those who do not wish you well, who themselves actively dislike or oppress you. Still another passage enjoins active promotion of the well-being of others who are simply in need. It is the parable of the Good Samaritan (Luke 10:29–37) which concludes: "Go and do likewise." That is, actively help even those who are not members of your community and have no natural claim on your assistance, for they too are fit recipients of neighbor-love.

Such normative pressures toward inclusiveness prompt certain interpreters of *agape* to extrapolate as follows (Outka 1972, pp. 9–24, 260–74). To correspond to grace means that we do not debate whether to love the neighbor but only how to love him or her. What a person does in particular should not determine by itself whether he or she is cared about *at all*. *Agape* includes both agent-commitment and recipient-evaluation. The goodwill enjoined involves permanent stability on the agent's part. Permanence means persistence in the face of obstacles. Even when the agent does not approve of the neighbor's behavior, it still makes sense to talk of regarding the neighbor as worthwhile and of caring what happens to him or her. The agent ought to be "for" the neighbor, whatever the particular changes in him or her, for better or for worse. Thus the neighbor should be regarded as irreducibly valuable prior to doing anything in particular that marks him or her off from others. To affirm this means that we cannot restrict our love to those we find lovable in so far, and only in so far, as they are good, enjoyable, or useful, or members of groups with which we identify. For now, explicitly, the neighbor as an object of *agape* is any human being.

Again this depiction of neighbor-love aims to correspond and attest, on our own level and with our own limited capacities, to God's *agape* (Barth 1958 [1955]). The shorthand referent for it is "equal regard." Points to be developed and difficulties that arise are legion. Here is a partial list. (1) Do the two accounts, of God's *agape* and corresponding human *agape*, dwell excessively on a unilateral feature? Is the importance of attained fellowship, with God and among human beings, given proper weight? (2) Is the egalitarian element in this depiction (where one neighbor's well-being is judged to be as valuable as another's) continuous after all with God's *agape*? What if we read the Bible to affirm that God's love is partial, e.g. toward Israel and toward Jesus? Should we distinguish between the neighbor as irreducibly valuable and as equally valuable, and press only the former? (3) Who qualifies as a neighbor? Are there physical limits below which a living being no longer possesses or does not yet possess the necessary characteristics to warrant assigning irreducible value to his or her well-being? For example, does a fetus qualify? (4) How actively should we try to take every neighbor into account? Should we attend to *all* neighbors whose well-being we can affect, or to *any* neighbor we happen to meet? (5) How close is *agape* as neighbor-love to other central normative conceptions, e.g. to justice, to Kantian "respect for persons," to utilitarian beneficence? (6) What of multilateral cases where the well-being of two or more neighbors conflicts and choice is unavoidable? How far may we compromise and dirty our hands? (7) Is the universal scope of *agape* misleadingly indiscriminate with respect to ties of consanguinity and marriage and other special relations? Can *agape* incorporate a recognition that the closer the relation the greater the degree of personal responsibility and the richer the significance of exchanges?

In our narrative here we can only pose such questions, to suggest a range of issues internal to agapeistic ethics. Let us go now to the three matters that are not necessarily at odds with a claim that the neighbor is irreducibly valuable but that further complicate the considerations that those concerned with agapeistic ethics should weigh.

God as the subject of unique veneration

The first great love commandment means that love for God remains the most basic and comprehensive human love of all. God demands absolute attachment and devotion, adoration of a kind that we transfer to our neighbors or ourselves on pain of idolatry. How we conceive such adoration depends, however, on how active or receptive in relation to God we judge human creatures to be. An active element appears in Thomas Aquinas's account of charity. We are to love God above all things, and subject ourselves to God totally, by referring all that is ours to God. The first love commandment retains a necessary discreteness in our actual manner of life. It generates attitudes and actions for which it alone supplies the final rationale. And it subtends our other loves. A receptive element appears in Nygren's preference for "faith" as the more fitting term to refer to love for God. Faith includes adoration, but underscores the purely receptive character of our relation to God. It also encourages us to note the greater material continuity between God's love and neighbor-love than between love for God and neighbor-love.

To many, active love for God is more integral to agapeistic ethics than Nygren allows (Outka 1972, pp. 44–54, 214–20). This complicates the continuities and discontinuities between God's love and ours in ways we do best to face. To pay homage to God as the subject of unique veneration is what the first great commandment requires. Such homage need not jeopardize the claim that all human life in relation to God is responsive. Yet response is more than the receptivity of faith, though it surely is that. Love for God attests to the active element in this response, where one meaningfully gives rather than withholds one's final loyalty and deepest devotion to God and only to God.

Self-love

Nygren finds acquisitive self-love in *eros*, and finds no positive place for self-love in *agape*. His pessimistic estimate explains why he refuses to accord the "as yourself" clause the status of another command alongside or equal in nominative weight to love of neighbor.

Many reject such unrelieved pessimism that fails even to consider respects in which neighbor-love is both like and unlike self-love (Santurri and Werpehowski 1992, pp. 1–103). Nygren bypasses two other highly plausible value judgments of self-love, each of which can find a place in agapeistic ethics. First, self-love is taken as normal, reasonable, prudent. The second commandment is interpreted here as "you shall love your neighbor as you *now* love yourself." We do not require in general to be urged to attend to our own well-being, for we are attached immediately and unreflectively to it. But our self-love can serve as a model for what neighbor-love involves. We then transfer prudential reasoning into moral reasoning by invoking some variant of the Golden Rule.

Second, self-love is positively valued as revering one's individual identity and particular life, a life non-interchangeable with others. To be concerned about one's own flourishing is a substantive religious and moral claim along with concern about neighbors. The enemy of self-love in this sense is sloth more than pride. And the temptations of sloth are ones to which feminist writers give special attention. Sloth refers to a peculiar state of the self, one governed by passivity and torpor. Though it encompasses inaction and laziness, its operations range further. It includes activities, but activities without direction or focus. Its most typical operation is the dispersal of whatever energies the self has at its disposal. Sloth involves a mysterious but culpable absence of intra-psychic vitality. It violates the agency which those who commend such self-love believe each person has religious and moral reasons to honor.

Philia

Apart from affirming that God's love is the initiator of fellowship with God, Nygren accords little space to mutualist accounts of love. To many, this neglect is a profound mistake. The accent in *philia* falls distinctively on the relation it creates, the bond *between* parties. We are *with* others and not simply *for* them or receiving *from* them (Vacek 1994, p. 280). Here let us distinguish vertical and horizontal levels.

There is the level of communion between God and human beings. Aquinas affirms that charity signifies friendship with God, mutual communion, and a mutual return of love. M. C. D'Arcy (1959) and John Burnaby (1947) reaffirm such communion, and criticize Nygren for failing to give it its due. On this level, we can say that God desires fellowship for its own sake and that this desire involves God no less than ourselves. Indeed, the concern to keep human love responsive traditionally means that even when no positive human response takes place, God's love perdures. From God's side, the will to communion is irrevocable, and the grace it reveals is prevenient. The friendship between God and ourselves is mutual, where mutuality precludes undifferentiated unity and includes genuine interaction. Still the friendship is not reciprocal, where reciprocity means that mutual needs are met, assistance rendered, or enrichment provided. However, some draw back from certain aspects of traditional teaching, e.g. the doctrine of divine immutability in classical theism, and opt instead for a metaphysics that is a form of process theology. Edward Vacek says for instance, that "when we colove with God's love, we effectively cooperate with God in redeeming the world" (Vacek 1994, p. 57). While he upholds differences between Creator and creature, he rejects one-sided obedience and enlarges our powers to cooperate with and affect God. Charity is for him a matter of mutual affirmation and mutual perfecting. Others think that traditional teaching retains an integral place for personal communion between God and human beings, but that it is vital to reiterate that God establishes covenant, God brings redemption.

There is the level of communion with one another. Here reciprocity reigns, precisely in the sense that mutual needs are met, assistance rendered, and enrichment provided. We may distinguish three claims. First, to stress the importance of mutual giving and receiving pays tribute to elementary features of human existence. Our sociality goes all the way down. Our special bonds and affections shape by necessity rather than by accident our religious and moral and psychic identities. To suppose that we can only be givers in our relations with others denies the constituted nature of creaturely life. It tempts us to be condescending. And as feminist ethicists like Beverly Harrison (1989) maintain, it threatens to block the deepest experiences of mutuality that are available as we acknowledge our own vulnerability and need. Second, those with whom we share particular bonds, e.g. our co-religionists, family members, fellow-citizens, and friends, matter especially to us in ways that a simplified egalitarianism misses. We can love more complexly in these special relations. The possibility of injustice increases with the closeness of the relation. Such closeness makes us not only more vulnerable, it heightens and orders our expectations. Our capacity for reciprocal help and harm is deeper and more varied with those closely related to us. Third, friendship as a bond of personal communion is particularly prized. That *philia* has long been associated with friendship is therefore apt. By our own cultural reckonings, friendship differs from special relations given by ties of blood or political association. Not only does it require free assent on both sides, but in the case of the highest kind, it requires virtue on both sides. To remove preference and discrimination from friendship would be self-defeating.

The status of agapeistic ethics

The claims we have canvassed indicate that no formal answer will do to the question of how central *agape* is to Christian ethics as a whole. For the question remains abstract until we specify the content we ascribe to *agape*, and we can never separate this content from other convictions we hold. Yet our findings cut against a widespread impression that agapeistic ethics is tantamount to "love-monism," i.e. to a drive toward unification that makes *agape* the one "basic reason" around which the entire Christian life is organized. Two more modest possibilities suggest themselves.

First, to say that *agape* has an authoritative status in that it should govern on every occasion and toward all persons is not to say that it alone has status. Paul announces that faith, hope, and love possess such centrality. Even as he ranks love as the greatest of all three, he attests to their relative discreteness and anticipates their status as theological virtues. Again, Eric Osborn (1976) locates four main patterns in early Christian thought, "righteousness (or justice)," "discipleship," "faith," as well as "love." We should reject love-monism that endeavors to reduce these patterns to one alone, and instead trace connections, including reciprocal influences.

Second, to affirm that the neighbor is irreducibly valuable and that this forms part of the content of *agape* is not to say that it is the sole originating source of all other religious and moral claims. Put differently, *agape* as the kind of love we can and should have with any human being is not the only kind of love to which we ascribe religious and moral significance. Indeed, we have seen that the first great commandment takes precedence over all our other loves; we should always love God above all else. And *agape*, self-love, and *philia* stay distinct, although we should bring them into mutually constructive interplay. What is then left unclear is whether we should order these human loves. Two paths lie open.

Down one path we keep the loves distinct and decline to order them. We love the other for the sake of the other (*agape*), for our own sake (*eros*), and for the sake of a relationship we have with the other (*philia*) (Vacek 1994, pp. 157–8). We establish no priority-rule among the three loves when we make particular decisions. Each love may be a form of cooperating with God.

Down another path we keep the loves distinct but establish a priority-rule for *agape* in all our human interactions. We include the self within *agape*, yet acknowledge differences as well as similarities between neighbor-love and self-love. The relation of *agape* to *philia* is intricate. As we noticed earlier, reciprocity is the internal ideal fruition of *agape*. Unrequited love is hardly superior to communion. It is better to have friends than enemies and to seek to turn the enemy into the friend. The one who loves agapeically is interested in a response, and is not unaffected by whether a response ensues. Yet the tests of *agape* remain: it is unqualified and all-embracing, in correspondence to God's love. These tests retain a certain priority with reference to the special relations included under *philia*. The priority obtains because *agape* sets the boundaries within which special relations come into their own and can go beyond the limits these relations may impose (Outka 1972, pp. 268–74). To set boundaries includes the minimal moral prohibitions against our doing anything whatever to those outside the personal relations and social groups with which we identify, for the sake of those inside. In the case of friendship, *agape* allows us to prefer some to others, but enjoins us "to remain open to those others and refuse to harm them for the sake of those we prefer" (Meilaender 1981, p. 31). Still, *agape* is the guardian in, rather than the direct inspiration of, every special relation. Special relations furnish their own substantive considerations on the basis of which we often justifiably act. Which of these two paths we take, or some other, is centrally important within a subject that continues to evoke wide discussion.

Bibliography

Allen, J. L.: *Love and Conflict: A Covenantal Model of Christian Ethics* (Nashville: Abingdon Press, 1984).

Barth, K.: *Church Dogmatics IV/2* (1955), tr. G. W. Bromiley (Edinburgh: T. & T. Clark, 1958).

Burnaby, J.: *Amor Dei* (London: Hodder & Stoughton, 1947).

D'Arcy, M. C.: *The Mind and Heart of Love* (New York: Meridian, 1959).

Harrison, B. W.: "The power of anger in the work of love, Christian ethics for women and other strangers." In *Weaving the Visions: New Patterns in Feminist Spirituality*, ed. J. Plaskow and C. P. Christ (San Francisco: Harper, 1989), pp. 214–25.

Meilaender, G.: *Friendship: A Study in Theological Ethics* (Notre Dame: University of Notre Dame Press, 1981).

Nygren, A.: *Agape and Eros* (1930), tr. P. S. Watson (London: SPCK, 1957).

Osborn, E.: *Ethical Patterns in Early Christian Thought* (Cambridge: Cambridge University Press, 1976).

Outka, G.: *Agape: An Ethical Analysis* (New Haven: Yale University Press, 1972).

Ramsey, P.: *Basic Christian Ethics* (New York: Scribner's, 1950).

Santurri, E., and Werpehowski, W. (eds): *The Love Commandments: Essays in Christian Ethics and Moral Philosophy* (Washington, DC: Georgetown University Press, 1992).

Vacek, E. C., SJ: *Love, Human and Divine: The Heart of Christian Ethics* (Washington, DC: Georgetown University Press, 1994).

62

Theism, law, and politics

PAUL J. WEITHMAN

Religion is among the most potent political forces in the contemporary world and the claims religious believers make on their institutions raise some of today's most pressing political questions. These include whether government can serve explicitly religious purposes, what sort of autonomy religious organizations should enjoy, when claims by religious minorities are unreasonable, and how institutions should accommodate religious diversity. Addressing such questions is the business of practical politics; it is also the task of political philosophy, the normative study of politics.

Contemporary political philosophy in the English-speaking world is dominated by liberalism, a family of political theories which claim that government should insure a significant degree of individual autonomy. This requires, liberals argue, that government guarantee citizens various rights, including freedom of speech, press, assembly, and conscience, and the right to vote. A number of philosophers have contested particular points of liberal theory. Some have developed rival accounts of the nature and purposes of government. But none has dislodged liberalism from its dominant position. When asking about theism's implications for contemporary political philosophy, it is therefore appropriate to begin by querying its implications for liberalism.

Political philosophy's development has been largely independent of Judaism, Byzantine Christianity, Islam, and the great religions of Asia. I shall therefore construe theism as equivalent to the organized religions descended from Latin Christianity. Focusing on theism so construed illuminates the characteristic motives, strengths, and weaknesses of a number of philosophical views. It casts light on liberalism's motives because liberalism began as an attempt to accommodate the religious diversity consequent on the Protestant Reformation. It also sheds light on the motivations of the other views I will discuss. These developed in reaction to liberalism and, in some instances, in reaction to liberalism's treatment of religion. It spotlights the strengths and weaknesses of various political theories because political philosophy has traditionally assumed both explanatory and normative tasks. Since Plato, political theorists have exploited philosophically compelling accounts of human nature to explain political phenomena. They have relied upon those accounts to defend moral claims about the goods to be realized in political life and the means by which political authorities ought to pursue them. One measure of a political theory's adequacy is its ability to offer compelling explanations of tenable prescriptions for the place of religion in political life.

Liberalism

Before the sixteenth century, it was possible to conceive of Europe as a single spiritual community united by religion. No one denied the reality of Europe's political and ethnic divisions. It was none the less possible to maintain that human beings had common spiritual ends which were to be promoted by diverse political authorities. The advent of Protestantism introduced religious pluralism to Europe on a large scale. Catholicism and the various forms of Protestantism held out different conceptions of human nature and sin, of liturgy and redemption. Their adherents made claims to worship as their religion dictated and urged that those with whom they differed have their rites suppressed. The ensuing conflicts marked the end of a spiritually unified Christendom and posed new philosophical problems. European political theorists had to ask themselves how governmental institutions could remain stable and function effectively in the face of such pluralism.

Some philosophers in the early modern period defended policies of religious suppression. The dominant liberalism of contemporary political philosophy, however, has its origins in the doctrine of religious toleration (see Article 65, THEISM AND TOLERATION). John Locke and other champions of toleration argued that religious practice is a legitimate matter of governmental concern only when it is disruptive of public order. Otherwise, Locke argued, religious practice should no more concern the government than should any other private pursuit. Liberal theories descended from the defense of toleration aspire to an even-handed treatment of religious diversity. Government should, their proponents say, neither discourage nor promote various religious and moral views. In the name of individual autonomy, it should guarantee the right to pursue any of them.

Let us say that the scope of a moral doctrine is given by the areas of human life to which its values apply. A moral doctrine is comprehensive in scope if all of human life is covered by its values. Liberalism is itself a moral view. The notion of scope therefore enables us to distinguish, following the American philosopher John Rawls (b. 1921), between *comprehensive* and *political* liberalisms. Comprehensive liberalisms are liberalisms whose normative claims extend to all of human life. According to some comprehensive liberalisms, for example, autonomy is not simply a political value. Its realization is a necessary condition of a well-lived human life; political arrangements which promote it are therefore necessary for human beings to lead the best life of which they are capable. Political liberalisms, by contrast, are moral doctrines of narrow scope: their values and prescriptions apply only to political life and political institutions. They make no claims about the true human good, and present a political morality which purports to be compatible with a variety of philosophical and religious claims about private life.

Many religious believers find comprehensive liberalisms less even-handed than their proponents claim. Critics charge that liberals committed to realizing autonomy in all areas of life are equally committed to government attempts to promote it in ways detrimental to religion. Thus many liberals' commitment to autonomy implies limits on parental control of education. Democratic education, they claim, should be geared to producing citizens capable of critical reflection on all the ways of life available to them. The problem is that some religious believers do not attach high value to critical reflection. Many religious believers conclude that a political theory which purports to treat all religions equally is in fact detrimental to them. Comprehensive liberalisms, framed to accommodate religious and moral diversity, are themselves insufficiently sensitive to it.

Because political liberalism is of more restricted scope, religious citizens in democratic societies might find it more promising. The most sophisticated of the political liberalisms is that recently propounded by Rawls, and critical reaction to it is in a very early stage. It is possible, however, to distinguish two lines of religiously-based criticism.

The first concerns the role political liberalism accords private associations, including religious associations. The thought of these associations belongs to what Rawls calls "the background culture," which he contrasts with "the public culture," the culture of the political. Some critics have argued that there is no clear distinction between the two. The background culture, including its religious elements, plays an important role in citizens' formation. It is as participants in the background culture, critics argue, that citizens acquire the qualities of character constitutive of good citizenship. A liberalism which ignores the political role of these associations therefore ignores an important source of its own stability. The problem with this criticism is that Rawls does not ignore the importance of private associations in moral education. He does argue that democratic citizens should learn to reason about political matters without relying on their religious views. This does not imply that religious associations cannot play a crucial role in teaching them to do this.

Rawls's treatment of public political discussion opens the second line of criticism. He argues that such discussion should proceed on the basis of a common political morality; religious views may be introduced into public discussion only to defend conclusions that can be supported on the basis of that common morality. Some have argued convincingly that these restrictions impose too great a limitation on religious language. Citizens with religious convictions, they say, should be able to introduce them in public argument. Moreover, Kent Greenawalt has argued that any political morality uncontentious enough to be common lacks sufficient content to settle important political issues. Citizens, legislators, and judges have no alternative but to rely upon other views, including religious views.

Theism, nationalism, and citizenship

The English political theorist John Gray has argued that what he calls "the new liberalism," while ostensibly addressed to all mature democracies, is in fact thoroughly American in its presuppositions and arguments. The charge that contemporary political philosophy is parochially American is an important one for present purposes. Political liberalism's treatment of religion might seem geared to religion's role in American public life and is insensitive to its functions in politics outside the United States. Much contemporary political philosophy might seem insensitive to the ways in which religiously motivated political argument and

491

action result from the combination of religion with the particularities of local, regional, and ethnic culture.

This insensitivity shows itself in the limited explanatory ambitions of contemporary political philosophy. One of the most salient features of politics is the vigor of various forms of religious conservatism. Fundamentalism, the most powerful of these, is too often dismissed as a form of irrationality or wished away by those who hope that the spread of democracy will ameliorate it. Yet the worldwide resurgence of religious fundamentalism and its ability to exacerbate class, ethnic, and national tensions, reveal a deep-seated alienation from modernity and liberalism. One of the traditional tasks of political philosophy is to explore moral psychology, drawing out its implications for the stability of regimes; this is as true of the early John Rawls as it was of Plato. Why fundamentalism should be so appealing to so many is in part a question of moral psychology; its popularity has implications for the viability of democratic liberalism. It is therefore problematic that contemporary political philosophers should pay it so little sustained attention.

How might liberals remedy this problem? Focusing on his native Canada, Charles Taylor (b. 1931) has argued that American-style liberalism is unable to conceptualize and accommodate the needs of ethnic and tribal communities. He attributes this inability to the conception of citizenship on which such liberalism is premised. Crudely put, citizens are conceived of as having moral capacities necessary for social cooperation and for embracing some comprehensive moral view. They are also conceived of as having the rights necessary to protect the exercise of those capacities. Those capacities are, however, characterized without reference to the particular ends and attachments citizens actually have. According to Taylor, political philosophy appropriate to a pluralistic society would begin with a very different conception of citizenship, one which defines citizenship with reference to the sub-communities to which citizens belong, the ties they have, and the goods they pursue in common. Taylor argues that liberals could adopt this conception of citizenship without surrendering their traditional commitment to the most cherished individual rights and liberties.

Philosophers concerned with nationalism and ethnicity are debating the nature of citizenship, and many have put forward variants of Taylor's suggestion. Their proposals are interesting and important, and promise to shed some light on the role of ethnic sub-communities within liberal democracies. They are, however, at a preliminary stage of development. If their details can be worked out, it is possible that philosophers interested in religion's political role could make use of them. It is possible that a theory which defines citizenship with reference to ethnic and national attachments could define it with reference to religious ones as well. This, in turn, raises the possibility that liberalism could more adequately treat religion's role in world politics than it currently does.

Theism and public philosophy

As mentioned above, contemporary liberals pay little heed to religious fundamentalism and assume that liberalism is compatible with many forms of theism. In recent years, there has been renewed interest among American religious ethicists in John Courtney Murray's attempt to show the compatibility of Catholicism and American democracy. Murray (1904–67), a Jesuit priest, argued that American democracy depends upon what he called a "public consensus." Among the objects of this consensus are principles of justice, the ideal of civility, and values associated with education and public morality. These norms provide the basis for "the public philosophy," a working philosophy for American public life.

The scope of the public philosophy, while not comprehensive, is considerably broader than that of political liberalism. Civility, for example, is a value that should be realized, not only in public political argument, but in much other interaction among citizens as well. This breadth of scope, Murray thought, is crucial to the transmission of the public philosophy and the maintenance of the American moral consensus. Citizens learn to participate in the moral consensus only if its constitutive values are systematically fostered by and realized in a wide range of institutions. Murray argued that the core values of the American public philosophy can be found in the NATURAL LAW ETHICS (see Article 58) explicitly embraced by Roman Catholicism and congenial to many other religions as well. It follows that these religions are not merely compatible with liberal democracy, but also supportive of it. Murray concluded that churches and religious schools are among the institutions which form and transmit the American public philosophy.

A generation later, a number of American religious thinkers have returned to Murray's work for inspiration. Religious thought and language, they argue, can inspire innovative policy and help to build political coalitions in support of social justice. Religious ties, they maintain, can rebuild a sense of community eroded by social mobility and an emphasis on autonomy. Religious education can foster the virtues of self-sacrifice and commitment to the common good on which liberal democracy depends. The attempt to update Murray's thought and elucidate its implications for contemporary American politics is among the most exciting projects in religious social ethics. It is not, however, without its critics.

Some criticize Murray for focusing on religious liberty and neglecting economic justice. Others read his defense of rights as an endorsement of modernity's most corrosive ingredient, the element of modern politics that destroys bonds of community. David Hollenbach, one of the most notable thinkers associated with the Murray revival, has replied that human rights should be understood as "the minimum conditions for life in community." Among these conditions, Hollenbach argues, are a guaranteed standard of living and the opportunity to use one's gifts in community life. Hollenbach's theory of rights is therefore sensitive to the distribution of wealth and opportunity. Because human rights have an irreducibly communitarian element, Hollenbach argues, their defense is not a commitment to the individualism that weakens communal bonds.

The Murray revival faces other serious difficulties. First, recall that consensus on a public philosophy is consensus on a moral view with broad though not comprehensive scope. Such consensus requires agreement on the values to be fostered in public education and media of communication; important among these values, Murray thought, were values connected with human sexuality. The diversity of mores in the contemporary United States poses serious obstacles to such a consensus. Second, organized religions in the United States exercise looser control over their members in the 1990s than they did in Murray's time. This diversity of opinion within churches extends to the very issues on which Murray thought there should be a public consensus among religions. The Catholic Church, for example, has been unable to build consensus on sexual morality among its American members despite vigorous efforts. This suggests that even if there were moral consensus among the official representatives of various organized American religions, religious organizations would be incapable of building a consensus that includes most of their members.

Anti-liberalism

I have so far focused on political philosophers sympathetic to liberalism in some form. There are, however, many thinkers who are unsympathetic to it because of the moral culture fostered by liberal democratic politics. In the name of toleration, these thinkers claim, citizens of liberal democracies come to believe that virtually any way of life is as morally worthy as any other, and that matters of public morality should be left to individuals. As a consequence, they say, liberal democratic societies are insufficiently respectful of inviolable moral norms like those forbidding euthanasia, abortion, and assisted suicide, and insufficiently committed to traditional values.

Many of these critics are religious, spanning the doctrinal spectrum. Pope John Paul II (b. 1920) of the Roman Catholic Church has written a series of public letters called "encyclicals" that have been sharply critical of the capitalist and democratic West. The culture of the West, John Paul argues, inclines increasingly to materialism, moral relativism, and the worship of technology (see Article 56, THEISM AND TECHNOLOGY). It thereby neglects the essential spirituality of humankind and leaves human beings spiritually hungry. Culture can be renewed, John Paul says, only by turning to God and returning to the moral absolutes articulated in scripture, the Christian tradition, and the natural law. The evangelical Protestant Stanley Hauerwas argues that the cultures of liberal democracies like the United States systematically misunderstand and trivialize religion. In response, Hauerwas calls on religious citizens to maintain a separatist and critical attitude toward secular liberal society. He urges them to dedicate themselves to communities animated by religious faith where traditional values are nourished.

The most philosophically powerful of liberalism's critics is Alasdair MacIntyre (b. 1929). MacIntyre recognizes the pluralism of large industrial democracies, but argues that liberals have drawn the wrong conclusion from it. While liberals hope to build on a common political morality, MacIntyre argues that any such morality relies upon what he calls "essentially contested concepts." Even concepts like "justice" and "equality" on which liberals like Rawls hope to secure agreement are, MacIntyre contends, used differently by those who endorse different moral views. Some might hope to settle this disagreement by looking at paradigmatic cases in which the demands of justice are satisfied. MacIntyre argues in reply that agreement on the requisite paradigms is impossible to secure. Liberalism presents itself as a moral view neutral among various contending theories. MacIntyre concludes that, as a view committed to its own ways of life and paradigms of justice, it is but one more contender in a series of deep moral disagreements.

MacIntyre argues that the human good consists in a life characterized by the cultivation and harmonious exercise of the moral virtues (see Article 59, VIRTUE ETHICS). From this claim, plus MacIntyre's analysis of moral disagreement, three consequences follow. First, in large and pluralistic societies, there can at present be no meaningful and terminable debate about how those societies might promote the true human good. Second, different and incompatible values regulate the public life of liberal societies on the one hand, and smaller communities, including religious communities, within such societies on the other. Consider, for example, MacIntyre's penetrating studies of truth-telling, written in the early 1990s. Truth-telling, he argued, imposes different requirements and admits of different exceptions in different spheres of life. It is therefore extremely difficult for citizens to develop consistent attitudes toward truth-telling, to exercise the virtue of veracity consistently or to combine that virtue with others. Similar claims are, he says, true of the other virtues. Third, because of the impossibility of realizing and combining the virtues under modern conditions, it follows that the true human good is unavailable, or available with great difficulty, in the most developed societies. MacIntyre echoes Aristotle in claiming that a life of virtue is most easily led in relatively small communities with a high degree of moral consensus. Since the modern state is far from being such a community, MacIntyre like Hauerwas counsels withdrawal to what cultural, religious, and intellectual enclaves persist in liberal societies.

MacIntyre is more interested in the question of what communities are necessary for realizing the true human good than he is in the reform of practical politics. This distance from politics is both a strength and a weakness of anti-liberalism generally. The anti-liberals are at their best as religiously-motivated social critics. They very effectively point out that, from the vantage point of various religious traditions, there appear to be deep human needs unfilled by liberal politics and deep moral problems with the culture it fosters. Political philosophy should, however, play a constructive as well as a critical role. The prevalence of theism and its profound impact on contemporary politics pose powerful challenges to political philosophers. Religion challenges them to explain the persistence of fundamentalism and the alienation from liberal politics experienced by many religious believers. It challenges philosophers to develop new ways of thinking about human rights and the distribution of wealth, about the political promise and spiritual limitations of liberal democracy. In sum, the challenges of theism for politics, and the problems with contemporary political philosophy, show how much remains to be done.

Bibliography

Douglass, R. B., and Hollenbach, D., SJ: *Catholicism and Liberalism* (Cambridge: Cambridge University Press, 1993).

Greenawalt, K.: *Religious Conviction and Political Choice* (New York: Oxford University Press, 1988).

Hauerwas, S.: *A Community of Character* (Notre Dame: University of Notre Dame Press, 1981).

John Paul II: *Evangelium Vitae* [*The Gospel of Life*] (New York: Random House, 1995).

MacIntyre, A.: *After Virtue* (Notre Dame: University of Notre Dame Press, 1981).

Murray, J. C., SJ: *We Hold These Truths* (New York: Sheed & Ward, 1960).

Rawls, J.: *Political Liberalism* (New York: Columbia University Press, 1993).

Taylor, C.: *Reconciling the Solitudes* (Montreal and Kingston: McGill-Queen's University Press, 1993).

63

Theism and medical ethics

JAMES F. CHILDRESS

Medical ethics often refers to ethics for physicians, parallel to ethics for other health care professionals, such as nurses. A broader conception, often called "bioethics" or "biomedical ethics," emerged in the late 1960s and early 1970s to deal with the moral perplexities occasioned by new medical technologies that could prolong life far beyond previous expectations, transplant organs from one person to another, detect certain fetal defects in utero, offer new reproductive possibilities, and the like. Bioethics or biomedical ethics involves an interdisciplinary and interprofessional approach to ethical issues in the life sciences, medicine, and health care (see Reich 1995).

Medicine deals with birth, illness, suffering, and death, all matters that regularly fall under primary systems of belief and ritual and moral practice within theistic traditions. This essay will consider what selected theistic beliefs imply about morally right actions, practices, and policies in medicine and health care (as well as, more briefly, the biological sciences). Theism includes not only monotheism, but also pantheism and polytheism (represented, for instance, in the ancient Hippocratic oath, which refers to several Greek deities), among others. Since theism is multifarious, it is necessary to concentrate on *selected* theistic beliefs in *selected* theistic traditions. This essay will focus on Judaism, Roman Catholicism, and Protestantism. Despite their important differences, these three traditions tend to share certain major perspectives, themes, and general norms that bear on biomedical ethics.

One broad theme is that of *covenant* as represented, for instance, in God's covenant with humanity following the Flood, with Israel as the chosen people, and, for Christians, in Christ. Sometimes covenant is used as a general category for various relationships with God as creator, provider or orderer, and redeemer, and with other creatures who also image God (Bouma et al. 1989). One of the most influential Protestant works in modern medical ethics. Paul Ramsey's *The Patient as Person* (1970), presents covenant faithfulness as the primary category for understanding medicine's responsibilities in light of the Christian faith. Human covenants, such as medicine, can mirror and reflect God's covenants, and such covenants share several features: rootedness in events or actions; creation of moral community; endurance over time; and, in contrast to contracts, incomplete specifiability (Bouma et al. 1989).

God's covenantal action, Christianity and Judaism agree, begins with his creation of human beings in his own *image* (see Article 39, CREATION AND CONSERVATION).

According to the papal encyclical, *Evangelium Vitae* (John Paul II 1995), "in the biblical narrative, the difference between man and other creatures is shown above all by the fact that only the creation of man is presented as the result of a special decision on the part of God . . . to establish a *particular and specific bond* with the Creator. . . . The life which God offers to man is a gift by which God shares something of himself with his creature" (emphasis added). As the biblical account puts it, "Then God said, 'Let us make man in our image, after our likeness; and let them have dominion. . . .' So God created man in his own image, in the image of God he created him; male and female he created them. And God blessed them, and God said to them, 'Be fruitful and multiply, and fill the earth and subdue it; and have dominion over . . . every living thing that moves upon the earth' " (Genesis 1:26ff; cf. 5:1 and 9:6; see also 1 Corinthians 11:7 and James 3:9).

Although the image of God has been variously interpreted as reason, free will, and spiritual capacities, including the capacity for self-transcendence, among other possibilities, the major strands of both Judaism and Christianity do not neglect the human body in favor of such intellectual and spiritual characteristics. Instead, they view the human person as a psychophysical unity, as an animated body or embodied soul (Ramsey 1970).

The image of God structures theistic biomedical ethics from two perspectives: the direction of the agent and his/her actions, and the evaluation of the patient, toward whom the agent acts. While these perspectives are closely connected, their emphases are different. For instance, in the debate about abortion, some theologians argue that the basic question is "not just whether fetuses or infants image God, but whether we image God in responding to their presence and their needs" (Bouma et al. 1989, pp. 47–8), but others insist that whether an agent's actions image God will depend in part on whether the other is an imager of God (Reichenbach and Anderson 1995). Hence, both standpoints are important.

Scriptural directions for agents to image God target dominion along with being fruitful and multiplying and filling the earth. The authorization of human dominion, which presupposes that human beings are in, but also distinguished from, the rest of nature, is critically important, for instance, in debates about developing and using biomedical technologies to extend human life, to enhance its quality, and to meet various human needs and desires. Dominion is most often interpreted as trusteeship or stewardship. For example, one theistic approach consists of an ethic of stewardship based on the three commands found in or derived from the Genesis account: to fill the land, where filling has qualitative as well as quantitative dimensions and thus indicates an obligation to improve the human condition; to rule over the land as God's representative, which includes both scientific knowledge and some forms of control; and to care for what falls under human stewardship (Reichenbach and Anderson 1995).

It is common to hear charges that scientists or physicians are "playing God," by usurping God's power over life and death, by using new reproductive technologies, by genetic interventions, or by ending life. In general the charge of "playing God" identifies two features of divine activity that should not be imitated: God's unlimited power to decide and unlimited power to act (see Article 38, DIVINE ACTION).

Thus, critics of "playing God" usually demand scientific and medical accountability along with respect for substantive limits, such as not creating new forms of life. Objections to this metaphor often challenge the rationale for holding that a particular course of action is wrong. In addition, on the positive side, the image of God provides a warrant for "playing God." Hence, rather than rejecting "playing God," Paul Ramsey (1970) calls on those who allocate health care to play God in a fitting way: we should emulate God's indiscriminate care by distributing scarce lifesaving medical technologies randomly or by a lottery rather than on the basis of social worth.

Because the biblical story connects dominion with the responsibility of procreation, of multiplying and filling the earth, it is not surprising that modern reproductive technologies – artificial insemination, in vitro fertilization, surrogacy, with all their spin offs – provoke vigorous debates about when human beings are most distinctively human and most distinctively image God. At opposite ends of the spectrum are the pro-technologists, such as Joseph Fletcher, who view artificial reproduction as more human than natural reproduction, precisely because of the use of human reason to control nature through technology, and the anti-technologists, such as Leon Kass, who view reproductive technology as intrinsically inhuman. In between are those who view some reproductive technologies as potentially but not necessarily dehumanizing and their use as sometimes morally justified; hence they recommend caution and regulation rather than prohibition.

Theistic perspectives that operate with some versions of natural law (see Article 58, NATURAL LAW ETHICS), as in Roman Catholicism, tend to stress natural limits, often set by the God-created ends of sexual organs, sexual activities, marriage, etc. Thus, according to the Vatican's *Instruction on Respect for Human Life in Its Origin and on the Dignity of Human Procreation* (Congregation for the Doctrine of the Faith 1988), just as contraception wrongly pursues the unitive while thwarting the procreative purpose of marital sexual intercourse, so artificial reproduction wrongly pursues the procreative apart from the unitive purpose. The only acceptable forms of artificial reproduction *assist* but do not *dominate* nature. Otherwise the suffering occasioned by infertility should be borne in the light of Christ's suffering.

In contrast to official Roman Catholicism, neither Protestantism nor Judaism accords so much value or weight to nature in setting limits on the use of reproductive technologies. Working mainly within command/obedience models (see Article 57, DIVINE COMMAND ETHICS), rather than models of natural law, both allow more extensive interventions into nature. Despite such variations there is widespread opposition to surrogacy, particularly commercial surrogacy, as well as considerable concern about respect for spare extracorporeal embryos after in vitro fertilization. Disputes about reproductive technologies often hinge on whether the offspring can still be viewed as "gifts" rather than as "products."

In Genesis (9:6) creation in God's image is connected with the prohibition of taking human life. Various theists stress that the sanctity of human life derives from the fact that it is God's creative gift. Hence, the obligation to protect human life, including one's own, grows out of God's gracious gift of life. According to the papal encyclical, *Evangelium Vitae* (John Paul II 1995, p. 703), "Man's life comes from God; it is his gift, his image and imprint, a sharing in his breath of life. God therefore is the sole Lord of this life: Man cannot do with it as he wills . . . the sacredness of life has its foundation in God and in his creative activity. . . ."

Metaphors of property (life is a "loan," "trust," "temple," "handiwork," etc.) and relationship (human beings are God's "children," "sentinels," "servants," "trustees," etc.) are central in theistic debates about suicide. Construing life as a "gift" invokes both sorts of metaphor. Debates about suicide, life-sustaining treatment, and the like often probe these metaphors. For instance, are there limits on what a recipient may do with a gift? If the gift is faulty (e.g. there are serious genetic defects) may it be returned or destroyed? Or is the gift then viewed as a way for God to test or educate the recipient?

Despite the widespread affirmation of the sanctity of life, usually held to be knowable outside theistic contexts, it is not viewed as an absolute – for example, martyrdom is permitted and even encouraged in some contexts, killing in war and in self-defense is usually accepted, and capital punishment is often admitted. According to *Evangelium Vitae* (1995, p. 708), "Christian reflection has sought a fuller and deeper understanding of what God's commandment [not to kill] prohibits and prescribes." Its meaning is specified through various distinctions, which are particularly important in Roman Catholicism, but which also have parallels in other religious and secular traditions. (Protestant ethics, with some exceptions, such as the work of Paul Ramsey (1970), tends not to stress precise distinctions as much as either Jewish law, the *halakhah*, or Roman Catholic moral theology.)

In the latter, the prohibition against taking human life is further specified as the prohibition against directly taking innocent human life. Then the debates focus on distinctions between direct killing and indirect killing and between innocence and guilt. First, it is wrong directly to kill a suffering patient even at his or her request, but it may be permissible to relieve a patient's suffering through medications that will probably, but indirectly, hasten his or her death. In addition to consent from the appropriate parties, the rule of double effect requires that the action causing death be good, or at least indifferent, in itself; that the agent intend only the good effect, not the bad effect; that the bad effect not be a means to the good effect; and that the good effect outweigh the bad effect.

Second, Catholic moral theology also distinguishes ordinary from extraordinary or, in more recent language, proportionate from disproportionate means of treatment. If patients forgo ordinary or proportionate treatments, their actions constitute suicide, or if families and clinicians withhold or withdraw such treatments, their actions constitute homicide. However, if patients forgo, or families and clinicians withhold or withdraw, extraordinary or disproportionate treatments, which are sometimes called "heroic" or "aggressive," their actions do not constitute suicide or homicide. And they may be morally justifiable. Controversies continue about the criteria for drawing these distinctions, but, in general, treatments with no reasonable chance of benefit or with burdens to the patient and others that outweigh their benefits may be considered extraordinary or disproportionate and thus morally optional. Nevertheless, it may be difficult to classify some medical technologies such as artificial means of nutrition and hydration.

500

According to some ethicists, the criteria for distinguishing ordinary and extra-ordinary treatments involve judgments about quality of life; according to other ethicists who worry that quality of life judgments would subvert the absolute value of (innocent) life, these distinctions concern treatments, not persons. Another effort to reduce the risks of quality-of-life judgments restricts decisions to withhold or withdraw treatments to patients who are irreversibly and imminently dying. Using modern technologies to extend the dying process would, for some theists, deny our mortality and our finitude, would make an idol of life itself, and would amount to (inappropriately) "playing God" – just as much as directly taking human life. Not all letting die is acceptable, because euthanasia can occur by omission – euthanasia is defined by the *Evangelium Vitae* as "an action or an omission which of itself and by intention causes death, with the purpose of eliminating all suffering." Letting nature take its course, letting God's will be done, is usually viewed as appropriate for the irreversibly and imminently dying patient.

In contrast to the breadth of the Roman Catholic criteria for extraordinary treatments, the Jewish tradition puts maximal weight on the category of the imminently dying patient, a *goses*, in part because it views each moment of life as equally valuable (Rosner 1991; Rosner and Tendler 1980). Only a patient whose death is imminent and irreversible may be allowed to die under some circumstances. Thus, in general, Judaism recognizes a more extensive obligation to use technologies to prolong life than does either Roman Catholicism or Protestantism. But even the Orthodox branch of Judaism allows withholding "any additional non-routine medical services, so as to permit the natural ebbing of the life forces" for a *goses* (Rosner and Tendler 1980, p. 56). However, particularly among Orthodox Jews, there is opposition to withdrawing or stopping such treatments once they have been started. Many other religious and philosophical bioethicists deny the moral relevance of the distinction between withholding or not starting treatments, on the one hand, and withdrawing or stopping treatments, on the other hand, contending that the same criteria should apply to both actions.

Obviously, the obligation to sustain an individual's life ceases at his or her death. However, the line between life and death is by no means uncontroversial, and debates hinge in part on conceptions of the image of God, or essential human characteristics, because human death involves the irreversible loss of qualities associated with human life. Traditionally, the irreversible cessation of spontaneous respiration and heartbeat marked death, but these cardiopulmonary standards became somewhat problematic with the use of new technologies to maintain respiration. Then the conception of whole-brain death emerged; it involves the irreversible cessation of the activity of the whole brain, including the brain stem, as measured by neurological tests, even if technologies can temporarily maintain respiration and heartbeat. This conception has been widely accepted by religious communities, even though controversy continues, for instance, in Orthodox Judaism, which still favors cardiopulmonary standards.

Parallel in part to debates about the image of God, questions arise about whether a higher-brain death standard – the irreversible cessation of the capacity for consciousness and social interaction – would be defensible, particularly in view

501

of the instability of the whole-brain death standard, which was established in part in order to provide organs for transplantation. By and large, however, the higher-brain death standard has not been accepted, in part because it would count as dead anencephalic newborns and patients in a persistent vegetative state. Such a standard would, in principle, permit the burial or the removal of organs from an individual who is still breathing on his or her own, without mechanical assistance, but who has lost higher-brain functions.

The conviction that human beings are created in the image of God also has implications for the appropriate treatment of the corpse. Respect for the corpse is required because the dead human body is still symbolic or emblematic of the living human person, an imager of God. In Judaism, three prohibitions against the desecration of the corpse derive from the image of God: it is impermissible to mutilate, to use or derive any benefit from, or to delay the burial of the corpse or any of its parts (Rosner and Tendler 1980). Hence, for Judaism autopsies pose problems that do not arise for Christianity. However, all prohibitions in Jewish law, except for murder, idolatry, and certain sexual offenses, such as incest, may be overridden to save human life – "Thou shalt not stand idly by the blood of thy neighbor" (Leviticus 19:16). Hence, many rabbinic authorities permit the transplantation of organs from cadavers, with appropriate consent, because of the responsibility to save human life. Some rabbinic authorities have permitted the use of corneas from cadavers on the grounds that corneal transplants are potentially life-saving because totally blind people are at risk of death through accidents (Rosner 1991).

Part of what it means to image God is to care for the neighbor. In both the Hebrew Bible/Old Testament and the New Testament, this theme is prominent. According to Leviticus 19:18, "you shall love your neighbor as your self," and this norm is reiterated in the New Testament, for instance, in connection with the parable of the Good Samaritan, who has compassion and renders care to a victim of robbers' violence (Luke 10:25–37). Even though such norms and stories motivate and direct care, including health care, they are silent on several conflicts that have troubled contemporary biomedical ethics. Hence, further reflection is required. For instance, the parable of the Good Samaritan does not address the conflict between the victim's needs and desires, between caring for the neighbor and respecting the neighbor's decisions, that would have arisen if the victim had refused further treatment. Now health care professionals are often perplexed about when if ever they may override a patient's wishes, choices, and actions in order to benefit that patient – when, in short, they may be paternalistic.

The image of God frequently appears as the theological basis for the ethical norm of respect for persons. However, it is usually interpreted to entail respect for embodied persons, not merely for their wills. And autonomy, as self-rule, is limited by God's will as expressed in creation and other ways. Hence, theists often oppose strong liberal views of autonomy, in part because of their convictions about human dependence on God (as well as on others) and in part because of their convictions about human sinfulness. Hence, paternalistic interventions may be easier to justify in some theistic contexts because of the significance of the obligation to care for the neighbor and the limitations on human autonomy.

A second potential conflict left unresolved by the parable of the Good Samaritan and by other scriptural passages on neighbor-love concerns just access to and just allocation of health care. After all, the Good Samaritan did not encounter several victims in need of extremely costly medical technologies. While convictions about the universality of the image of God, and about the universal scope of the norm of neighbor-love, may support universal access to health care, they do not necessarily determine appropriate allocations of resources for and within health care. Paul Ramsey (1970), as noted above, claimed that random selection is an appropriate way to image God's indiscriminate care in micro-allocation decisions regarding scarce lifesaving medical resources, but he also explicitly argued that basic theistic convictions do not dictate specific macro-allocation policies, for instance, regarding how much of society's resources should go into health care versus other social goods. For such issues neighbor-love must be supplemented by a norm of distributive justice.

Abortion, perhaps the most controversial and divisive issue in contemporary biomedical ethics, involves convictions about the way both agents and fetuses image God. Various methodological and substantive differences appear within and among the traditions in debates about abortion even though there is a strong consensus that, at a minimum, abortion is morally undesirable. While a few theists hold that the fetus is mere tissue, with no moral significance, most theists divide into two other camps: (1) those who hold that abortion is prima facie wrong because the fetus is a potential human being, but accept some abortions as morally justifiable even though tragic; and (2) those who hold that abortion is absolutely wrong because the fetus is a full human being from the moment of conception.

While many, perhaps most, Protestants view the fetus as potential rather than full human life, the official Roman Catholic position is that the fetus is a full human being from the moment of conception. Hence, for Roman Catholics, abortion is morally wrong as a sin of homicide and murder because it involves directly taking the life of an innocent human being. The hierarchy has rejected developmental views of humanhood, which some theologians now support, in part because identical twinning may occur up to about fourteen days. (St Thomas Aquinas and others had held a view of mediate animation, according to which the fetus became ensouled later in pregnancy.) The Church has also rejected interpretations of the fetus as an aggressor, who may be justly opposed with force because of its attack on the pregnant woman.

Instead, the only morally justified actions that result in fetal deaths fall under the rule of double effect (see p. 500). This rule appears to permit abortions in situations of ectopic pregnancy and cancer of the uterus, because the legitimate medical actions are good or indifferent, the agents do not intend the fetal deaths, which are effects rather than means, and there is proportionate reason to accept those deaths. Critics challenge the narrowness of these exceptions, particularly when there are threats to maternal life and health. And some go farther and justify abortion in cases of serious genetic problems for the fetus and rape and incest. Such exceptions create internal problems for any position that views the fetus as a

503

full human being, but not for a position that views the fetus as a potential human being.

By and large Jewish authorities do not view the fetus as a full human being until the head or the greater part has emerged (Rosner 1991). However, they generally oppose abortion because the fetus is a potential human being, even though it is "mere fluid" until forty days after conception. Abortion is permissible and sometimes even obligatory where there is a threat to maternal life and health – health is defined more broadly in Conservative and Reform branches than in the Orthodox branch of Judaism. In contrast to Roman Catholicism, neither the Jewish nor the Protestant tradition places much weight on the rule of double effect in connection with abortion.

Recent studies suggest that liberals and conservatives in different theistic traditions may share more with their counterparts in other traditions than with their own religious colleagues. Nevertheless, the debates within and across these traditions often turn on interpretations of common perspectives, themes, and norms from scripture and tradition, such as God's creation of human beings in his own image and likeness and neighbor-love, frequently supported or supplemented by reason and experience.

Bibliography

Bouma, H., III, Diekma, D., Langerak, E., Rottman, T., and Verhey, A.: *Christian Faith, Health and Medical Practice* (Grand Rapids: William B. Eerdmans, 1989).

Congregation for the Doctrine of the Faith: *Instruction on Respect for Human Life in Its Origin and on the Dignity of Human Procreation* (Vatican, 1988).

John Paul II: *Evangelium Vitae* [The Gospel of Life], *Origins*, 24 (April 6, 1995).

Ramsey, P.: *The Patient as Person* (New Haven: Yale University Press, 1970).

Reich, W. T., (ed.): *Encyclopedia of Bioethics*, rev. edn, 5 vols. (New York: Simon & Schuster/Macmillan, 1995). [This important reference work contains fine entries on major religious traditions and their responses to major issues and problems in bioethics.]

Reichenbach, B. R., and Anderson, V. E.: *On Behalf of God: A Christian Ethic for Biology* (Grand Rapids: William B. Eerdmans, 1995).

Rosner, F.: *Modern Medicine and Jewish Ethics*, 2nd rev. edn (Hoboken: KTAV Publishing; New York: Yeshiva University Press, 1991).

Rosner, F., and Tendler, M. D.: *Practical Medical Halacha*, 2nd edn (Jerusalem and New York: Feldheim Publishers, 1980).

64

Theism and environmental ethics

GARY L. COMSTOCK

It is not easy to define theism, but the term generally refers to a range of different metaphysical theories which share either the idea that the structure of reality includes a single perfect divinity (God or Goddess) or the idea that it includes one or more imperfect divinities (gods, goddesses, angels, local spirits, trickster figures). Theists generally hold that there is a divine being or beings, beings more powerful than humans and capable of contravening at least occasionally some of the laws of nature.

It is also not easy to define environmental ethics, but the term generally refers to a range of different moral theories which share either the idea that humans have direct duties to nature or the idea that humans have significant indirect duties regarding nature. Environmental philosophers generally hold that moral agents ought to be constrained in their behavior to some degree by the welfare of wild animals, plants, and natural processes, or what the American conservationist Aldo Leopold called "the land."

Let us call *ecocentric* any ethical theory that places highest value on policies to prohibit the development of wilderness areas and to preserve endangered species, and *anthropocentric* any ethical theory that reverses these priorities, placing highest value on policies that encourage economic development and employment. Both kinds of environmental ethicists may appeal to similar grounds to justify their positions, or they may appeal to different grounds. Both may appeal, for example, to theistic principles. When ecocentrists or anthropocentrists appeal, for example, to the will of God (see Article 57, DIVINE COMMAND ETHICS), to justify their practical moral judgments, then the relation of theistic metaphysics to environmental ethics comes into play.

In the contemporary secular academy, however, environmental ethics typically proceeds on assumptions that are *not* theistic. This fact might tempt us to think that theism and religion have little to do with environmental ethics, but this is not true. First, many religious people are atheists. On traditional interpretations of Madhyamaka BUDDHISM (see Article 2) for example, Buddhists believe there is a "sacred" or "divine" dimension to reality but no transcendent beings and in other non-theistic religious traditions, such as Confucianism (see Article 3, CHINESE CONFUCIANISM AND DAOISM), the Advaita Vedanta HINDUISM of Sankara (see Article 1), and some liberal forms of CHRISTIANITY (see Article 6) and JUDAISM (see Article 5), the central tenet of theism, belief in divinities, is also denied. These religious traditions each have distinctive attitudes toward nature, suggesting that atheism provides a

505

useful starting point for our discussion. Second, the potential contributions of theism to the secular discussion of environmental ethics will best stand out in relief if the backdrop of atheism is in place.

No God, only nature

Atheistic ecocentrists will not appeal to divine sanctions or desires to justify their ecological principles. If there is no God but only material processes, the integrity of which should figure in our moral deliberations, then environmental values will have to be justified in other ways, such as by appealing to the intrinsic value of nature, the demands of enlightened self-interest, the rights of individual humans and future human generations, the moral standing of non-human animals, or considered intuitions brought into reflective equilibrium with scientific knowledge and moral principles. Atheists who value nature highly may on occasion speak of the "sacrality" or "divinity" of nature, but these evaluations should probably be understood as rhetorical appeals meant to underscore the intensity of the speaker's regard for the inherent worth of nature.

Atheists need not be ecocentrists at all, of course, and may be strict anthropocentrists, holding that the circle of morally considerable beings extends no further than the limits of the species *Homo sapiens*. Nothing about atheistic metaphysics seems to require the adoption of any particular position in environmental ethics.

Adherents of religions that do not believe in divinities may, like their secular counterparts, appeal to the "transcendent" beauty and value of nature without thereby positing the existence of beings more powerful than humans. Consider Madhyamaka Buddhism again, in which the self, or *atman*, is understood to be identical with the impersonal absolute, or *Brahman*. This claim is sometimes interpreted to mean that *Nirvana*, the ultimate good, is attained only if individuals allow their particular identities to become absorbed into a supreme spirit. Such metaphysical commitments might be thought to lead to a devaluing of nature in so far as the Buddhist's ultimate aim seems to be to overcome all attachment to the material world. If Nirvana means to extinguish one's self in world-denying meditation then there seems to be little point in positive political action to protect moral goods such as the integrity of a virgin prairie.

The interpretation of Buddhism just offered, however, is deficient. As mentioned previously, Madhyamaka Buddhism does not endorse the idea of a transcendent being, nor the ideas that individuals should aim at annihilating themselves and disavowing politics. The Buddhist goal of Nirvana is a state of freedom from the cyclical path of birth, decay, and death, but the desirability of this end-state does not imply something disvaluable or suspect about nature. Indeed, Nirvana once obtained entails a life of respect for all creatures and the cultivation of civic virtue so that, properly understood, atheistic Buddhist metaphysics may incline strongly to an ecocentric view. There seems to be no necessary entailment, either in academic environmental ethics or in non-theistic religious traditions, between the rejection of theism and either a pro- or anti-environmentalist ethic.

When we turn to the relation of theism to environmental ethics we immediately encounter the problem of speaking of God. By its very nature, a being that transcends the categories of language cannot be described in literal terms and direct propositions. To describe God's attributes, most theists acknowledge the need to use indirect speech: metaphors, analogies, and narratives (see Article 24, RELIGIOUS LANGUAGE). Six metaphors recur as theists attempt to conceptualize God's relation to nature: God as the enemy, owner, redeemer, husband, embodiment, and identity, of nature. The various metaphors seem associated, if only loosely, with different attitudes to the environment, suggesting that some versions of theism correspond with particular versions of environmental ethics.

God the enemy of nature

Cosmological dualists see the material world as God's adversary, a necessary evil God must wrestle into submission. Manicheans, for example, convinced that matter is bad, practiced a form of world-denying asceticism and celibacy in which sex was considered unholy and unnecessary. To consider pleasure morally wrong and flesh itself inherently corrupt is not to have a view of nature that will readily lend itself to endorse the celebration of natural processes or the preservation of endangered species. When nature is regarded as God's adversary, divine permission to exploit nature for human purposes is not far behind.

Christian apocalypticists who anticipate Jesus' imminent return and the end of history, for example, envision nature as the scene of an evil god's activities, a drama in which Satan is responsible for the illness, decay, and suffering that leads to death. On the adversarial view, nature can be escaped either at the end of time as in Christian eschatology or immediately, through enlightenment. Ascetics in many traditions, including Hinduism and other forms of Buddhism, believe that attachment to nature, the body, and its desires is thoroughly evil, to be renounced and overcome in enlightenment. By contrast, consider the eschatologies of some American Indian traditions in which time is not expected to end soon and flesh and death are not regarded as matters to be transcended. For those Indians, the future value of creation is so high that no actions with deleterious effects for future generations are allowed, even if the effects do not surface for seven generations. If, as on the Christian apocalyptical view, the seventh generation hence is likely never to exist and the present world is the territory of a devil soon to be defeated, there is little reason to be concerned with nature or future generations. Seeing God as the enemy of nature seems to leave little room for ecocentrism.

God the owner of nature

Traditional Christian theology acknowledges the existence of Satan but emphasizes God's role as creator of a perfect cosmos, a cosmos fallen from its idyllic state when humans exercised their freedom and fell from grace. On this view, God takes an interest in human welfare because humans are created in God's image and charged to act as stewards to manage the animal and plant kingdoms. As an owner takes an interest in maintaining and improving private property for its extrinsic and instrumental value, so humans may take an interest in nature because of the good purposes to which it can be put.

The historian Lynn White, Jr, focused attention on this view of God and its causal relation to environmental degradation in a famous 1967 essay, "The historical roots of our ecologic crisis." White alleged that the biblical view of God as owner of nature and humans as its divinely appointed managers, led Jews and Christians to adopt an environmental attitude similar to that found in the God as nature's enemy camp. White pointed to the first chapters of Genesis as the biblical basis of this problem (White 1967, p. 1204). There we read that God, exercising the right of ultimate authority, gives humans dominion over nature, permitting them to eat plants and name animals. After expulsion from the Garden and survival of the Flood, humans are also given animals to eat.

If God gives humans dominion over the material order there can be little argument against humans exploiting nature to satisfy desires so long as they do not transgress the bounds of the contractual agreement. The ownership model, wrote White, divorces humans from nature, separating them from creation in a hierarchical dualism of spirit and matter, souls and bodies, in which it is believed that spirit ought to rule matter and humans ought to rule nature. Whereas pre-Christian pagans lived in harmony with the land because they believed there were spirits inhabiting the wolves and trees and brooks, White alleged, Christian dualists came to regard wild animals as machines and the entire organic and plant world as inert, dead.

White's thesis provoked enlightening debate about our topic. Not all participants agreed with his analysis; he was criticized for postulating a reductive causal relation between two very complex things: first, an amalgam of diverse religious beliefs, traditions, practices, and institutions (i.e. Judaism and Christianity), and, second, an equally complex set of ecological states and consequences (i.e. the so-called environmental crisis). The causes of environmental degradation are more complex than White allowed, and factors other than Judeo-Christian metaphysics almost certainly played a role in the evolution of the present state of the environment, including colonialism, urbanization, the growth of the market economy, increasing democratization, and consumeristic attitudes (Moncrief 1970, p. 510). It seems the divine ownership model need not bear full responsibility for causing this or that ecologic state.

The weakness of White's argument aside, those who see God as owner of nature are unlikely to share radically pro-environmentalist intuitions. If human responsibility for the earth derives from a contractual agreement with its owner rather than from features intrinsic to the earth itself, then humans seem to be permitted any action not explicitly ruled out by the agreement.

God the redeemer of nature

There are several powerful metaphors for God in the Bible. White's argument may have been stronger had he focused on the theistic metaphysics of the New

Testament author Paul instead of the writers of the first chapters of Genesis. Paul reinterpreted the Genesis creation myth in the light of the life, death, and resurrection of Jesus Christ, arguing that Christ was the New Adam who will eventually restore nature to its original pre-Fall condition. For Paul, the original condition of nature excludes death and all processes involving decay, pain, suffering, predation, and mortality. The original and final environmental state, according to Pauline Christianity, will not include mortality. Therefore, on Paul's view, the present state of nature cannot present us with moral standards because it is a pitiful shadow of its former self, a decrepit structure in need of razing and reconstruction. Moral guidance must come from special Revelation from God (see Article 74, REVELATION AND SCRIPTURE).

The Pauline Christian view that death is unnatural, a distortion of God's perfect world, is found in the prophet Isaiah as well. Isaiah seemed to see the elimination of predation and carnivorism in his vision of the peaceable kingdom. Apparently, herbivores are present when nature is redeemed, but raptors, predators, and other carnivores will be changed from their present state. If God is construed as redeemer of nature, nature as we know it ends with the redemption, but nature itself is not replaced. On the redeemer model, nature, although fallen, is fundamentally good. "The creation waits with eager longing for the revealing of the children of God," writes Paul, "in hope that the creation itself will be set free from its bondage to decay and will obtain the freedom of the glory of the children of God" (Romans 8:19, 21).

The redemption view may be like the enemy and ownership views in being susceptible to blanket condemnations of all theism as preventing strong positive attachments to land. If nature is fallen, then our allegiance must be to nature in its future perfect state, not its present condition. None the less, the blanket condemnation is probably less applicable here than with the first two perspectives. It may not apply at all to the next three perspectives.

God the husband of nature

Owners may be distant managers and redeemers may tarry, but good husbands are constant and intimate lovers. As a good husband takes an intimate and immediate interest in his wife's welfare, so the divine husband loves his wife, the material earth. When the biblical author who calls God by God's personal name "Yahweh," and is therefore referred to as "Y," recounts the creation story in the second chapter of Genesis, Y depicts God as a farmer who creates his wife using the materials and skills of husbandry: topsoil, clay, water, and creative selection (2:7, 19). The divine wife of a single perfect God must be similarly perfect, so that nature with its rhythmic cycles, pain and death for animals and humans, must be considered on this view the best possible world. Here matter is not evil and flawed as it is in the redeemer model; it is God's perfect partner unaffected by the fall of humanity (Rolston 1994, pp. 216–17).

If God is construed as marriage partner intimately and physically involved with the reproduction and evolution of plants, animals, and humans, then suffering, decay, and death cannot be perceived as features that compromise the goodness of nature. Sex, seeds, and husbandry practices are the tools by which God's creative activity must proceed. Because God is divine husband and humans are the highest achievement of the union of God and earth, humans are by extension God's stewards of all life, expected to reproduce their own kind, filling the earth, through monogamous sexuality, with future generations of their own species and, through husbandry, with future generations of other species.

When the ongoing cycle of life is thought to be a partner equal in marriage to the holy one, the idea that nature must be redeemed or transcended is inappropriate. For the Yahwist, death seems not to be the result of a catastrophic Fall brought into the world by human disobedience but a necessary and good part of God's design for nature. In this vision, humans are not distanced from the rest of the animal kingdom, as may be the case in the first chapter of Genesis where humans assume a priestly role as a distinct class created in the image of God. Whereas human managers of God's property are expected to exploit the earth and turn it to *their* ends, human subjects in God's procreative husbandry are expected to act in concert with nature, making it more productive by helping it to achieve its *own* ends. On the husbandry model, God has made nature the best of all possible worlds, a view that may strongly incline to an ecocentric ethic.

The models of God as owner, redeemer, and husband assume the truth of the theory of divine passibility, the theory that God can change and experience emotions (see Article 40, IMMUTABILITY AND IMPASSIBILITY). If God is a being who cares about nature, then the importance of caring for the earth is magnified by the fact that God takes pleasure when the earth fares well and suffers when the earth fares poorly. Passibilistic forms of theistic environmental ethics may intensify the importance of caring for the earth in a way that atheistic forms do not (Taliaferro 1992, p. 77).

God embodied in nature

Animists hold that local spirits are active in specific aspects of the environment. In some American Indian cosmogonies, nature is depicted as created by an animal-like creature that dives to the bottom of a primeval ocean and drags up mud which then becomes the cosmos. In other myths, twin gods, a sky-father and an earth-mother, join in a sexual act that results in the birth of the world. And in some contemporary Christian theologies, God is construed as nature or, more precisely, nature is thought to be the body of God (McFague 1993). In each of these traditions, God is less the husband of nature than its internal spirit. Nature is the outward form and embodiment of God; no part of God exists anywhere except in nature, but the material world is not thought to exhaust God's identity because God also has an intellectual or spiritual dimension (see Article 34, INCORPOREALITY). A view of human identity in which humans are thought to consist both of bodies and minds may be an appropriate analogy for this conception of God.

The ethical implications of the embodiment view seem to be clearly pro-environmental. Just as others should respect our bodies because our bodies are the material form of ourselves, so humans should respect the earth because it is the material form of God. But a different view of the god embodied might entail different consequences, depending on the character of the god and the god's relationship to the land. If God is the traditional Judeo-Christian God, possessing OMNIPOTENCE (see Article 28) and GOODNESS (see Article 30), humans would be expected to reverence the earth because it is a perfect God's body. If the gods are less than perfect, then attitudes may change. In some polytheistic traditions, for example, local deities may inhabit nature and be eager to work to enhance the happiness of people. Here again nature will deserve respect. But local deities may alternatively be malevolent, needing to be pacified with sacrifices so that they do not destroy crops or animals. In this case, nature might be regarded with some suspicion, less as a perfect God's body than as a highly charged but ambiguous source of good or evil. Here nature may not be thought intrinsically valuable, even if it is the body of the gods.

The embodiment view does not identify God with nature, thereby allowing embodiment theorists to distinguish between God and nature, a possibility not open to the final position.

God nothing but nature

Pantheists hold that God *is* nature, that there is no transcendent God "above" nature. Rather, life and feeling pervade everything in the cosmos, even apparently lifeless entities such as rocks and empty space. Some formulations of ecofeminist pagan spirituality teach, for example, that God and nature are strictly identical. The earth is our Divine Mother but not in the sense that she is married to a Divine Father; Nature is herself the only Goddess, a divinity who regulates her own processes and responds to any threat in ways that maximize the possibility that life will survive on the planet (Starhawk 1990). The idea that nature is self-regulating and self-preserving calls to mind the Gaia hypothesis in which nature protects herself from all human and non-human onslaughts.

Identity theorists generally believe that because we are all interconnected parts of a divine whole we should care for nature in all of its complexity, not only because it is beautiful and useful to us but because it *is* us. John Seed puts this sentiment powerfully when he writes: "[the statement] 'I am protecting the rainforest,' develops into 'I am part of the rainforest protecting myself. I am that part of the rainforest recently emerged into thinking' " (Seed 1985, p. 253). If I am the rainforest and the rainforest, as part of nature, is the Goddess, then I must protect the rainforest not only because I must protect myself but also because I must protect the Goddess. Indeed, we are the Goddess's best instruments of self-defense.

The identity view is likely to lead to a robust ecocentrism. Indeed, if "nature is God" then nature is a process that ought always to be allowed to take its own course. According to this line of radical ecoholism, humans should not seek to fight famines or kill cancers in their own bodies because starvation and disease are the Goddess's way of maintaining harmony in the balance of populations. Far from being evils, cancer and death are flowerings of the divine will of Nature.

The "God is nothing but nature" view is similar to the embodiment view except in one important respect. According to the law of the indiscernibility of identicals, if x and y are identical, then x has every property that y has, and y has every property that x has. If God and nature are identical, God does not have any properties the material world lacks, and there can be no "spiritual" dimension to coexist with God's material dimension. While embodiment theorists think of nature as God's body but not God's entire personality, identity theorists are committed to the view that nature is the whole of God. If there is no aspect of God outside nature, and if belief in God's transcendence leads inevitably, as ecofeminists assert, not only to human exploitation of the earth but to men's exploitation of women, then there are powerful practical reasons to deny the existence not only of the traditional God of Judaism, Christianity, and Islam but of all possible gods that would transcend nature (see Article 76, FEMINISM).

How then does identity theory differ from the position with which we began? The only apparent difference is that whereas atheists explicitly deny the existence of a Supreme Being, identity proponents want to insist that nature properly construed *is* the Supreme Being, Mother Earth with her own internal consciousness. However, unless in asserting "God is nature" the identity theorist is simply giving a metaphoric twist to a view of God *as* nature – in which case the identity proponent would in fact better be described as an embodiment proponent – one may be left wondering just how the identity view differs from a particularly poetic expression of atheism.

Conclusion

Theistic metaphysical beliefs that construe God as enemy, owner, and redeemer of nature seem to incline more to an anthropocentric environmental ethic while those that see God as nature's husband, embodiment, or identity seem to lean more to ecocentrism. However, there seems to be little in the way of necessary or logical entailment between one's view of God and one's environmental ethics. Note, finally, that the psychological dependence may run in exactly the opposite direction; our intuitions about the environment may do more to shape our views of God than our intuitions about God do to shape our attitudes to nature.

Bibliography

Berry, W.: "The gift of good land." In *The Gift of Good Land: Further Essays, Cultural and Agricultural* (San Francisco: North Point Press, 1981).

Leopold, A.: *A Sand County Almanac* (New York: Oxford University Press, 1949).

McFague, S.: *The Body of God: An Ecological Theology* (Minneapolis: Fortress Press, 1993).

Moncrief, L. W.: "The cultural basis of our environmental crisis," *Science*, 170 (1970), pp. 508–12.

Rolston, H.: "Does nature need to be redeemed?" *Zygon*, 29 (1994), pp. 205–29.

Seed, J.: "Anthropocentrism," appendix E in B. Devall and G. Sessions, *Deep Ecology: Living as if Nature Mattered* (Salt Lake City: Peregrine Smith Books, 1985).

Starhawk: "Power, authority, and mystery: Ecofeminism and Earth-based spirituality." In *Reweaving the World: The Emergency of Ecofeminism*, eds I. Diamond and G. Feman Orenstein, (San Francisco: Sierra Club Books, 1990), p. 73.

Taliaferro, C.: "Divine agriculture," *Agriculture and Human Values*, 9 (1992), pp. 71–80.

White, L. Jr.: The historical roots of our ecologic crisis," *Science*, 155 (1967), pp. 1203–7.

65

Theism and toleration

EDWARD LANGERAK

Toleration is the enduring of something disagreeable. Thus it is not indifference toward things that do not matter and it is not broad-minded celebration of differences. It involves a decision to forgo using powers of coercion, so it is not merely resignation at the inevitability of the disagreeable, although begrudging toleration can be granted when one believes that coercion, while possible, would come at too high a price. Tolerating another's actions is quite compatible with trying to change another's mind, as long as one relies on rational persuasion – or, perhaps, emotional appeals – rather than blunt threats or subtle brainwashing.

Religious toleration generally applies to *expressing* or *acting upon* theologically-related beliefs, although the mere *holding* of beliefs or the *persons* holding them have also been the objects of intolerance and toleration. In any case, religious toleration is not to be confused with secularization or erosion of religious devotion, although the resulting indifference toward another's religious expression may have behavioral manifestations that overlap those of toleration. And, in spite of some behavioral similarities, toleration is distinct from the sort of pluralistic ecumenicism that seeks consensus on central religious matters or views other religious beliefs as simply different routes to similar goals. We can take religion extremely seriously, believe that we are clearly right and others are egregiously wrong on a matter of huge and holy significance, and still decide to tolerate their propagation of the error.

Story of theistic intolerance

But why would we do that? Here is a widely accepted story about theistic intolerance (see, for example, Rawls 1993, pp. xxi–xxiv, and Fotion and Elfstrom 1992, pp. 75–8). When humans thought the gods were local and their concerns provincial, we could pledge allegiance to them without insisting that everyone else do so. Hence polytheism was quite compatible with religious toleration or, just as likely, indifference toward the other's belief. (Of course, the human tendency throughout most of our history to be suspicious and disdainful of differences made it also compatible with religious intolerance, especially since religious differences tend to rationalize and to pump up the intensity of dislikes that might begin with ethnic, economic, or other differences.) Even when some of us thought our god was the most powerful among many gods – and a jealous god at that – we did not require outsiders to agree. In fact, even when we worshiped the one true, Creator God, we did not insist or even desire that everyone else do so, especially since God's call seemed directed primarily to our own group. Hence, even a monotheism with universal implications can avoid clashing with unbelievers.

However, when God revealed to us a universal doctrine and called on us to teach it to all peoples as the exclusive way to eternal salvation, mandating us to make disciples of all nations, then we could not have a *laissez faire* attitude toward unbelief or apostasy. Why should we allow pernicious error a chance to mislead the gullible into perdition or to sow confusion and disorder? A righteous society, after all, is devoted to what God declares is right rather than to what humans declare as rights. And in so far as compassion compels us, we must consider primarily the eternal destiny of those in error or, if they are beyond redemption, the souls of those they might corrupt.

Thus the motivation for intolerance intensified when monotheism became not just universalistic but also exclusivistic and expansionistic, as it did with Christianity and, later, Islam. When the fighting and forced conversions occurred primarily at the borders, society could still flourish away from the infidels. However, when such religions turned religious wars in upon themselves – for example, as Islam did briefly after Muhammad's death in 632, and Christianity did at great length after the Reformation – life became uncertain at best and, at worst, nasty, brutish, and short. Indeed, even those theists who were disposed to be somewhat lenient toward unbelievers (especially if the latter professed a different sort of theism) on the grounds that unbelievers are generally inculpable for their erring ways, often became brutally intolerant toward apostasy; once one knows the truth, only culpable corruption could motivate rebellion against it.

Locke, liberalism, and the rise of toleration

One can debate many aspects of the above story, but it is close enough to the truth for one to appreciate John Locke's task as he wrote his *Letter Concerning Toleration* (1689). England was going through the throes of the Restoration and the Glorious Revolution, including the conflicts between the state church (Anglican) and the dissenters, and worrying about a possible Catholic heir to the throne. Thirty years earlier, in *An Essay in Defence of the Good Old Cause*, Locke had argued that religious toleration was impractical because it would lead to civil unrest. But in the *Letter* he argues that what we know about history and human nature shows that toleration is necessary for civil peace:

It is not the diversity of Opinions, (which cannot be avoided) but the refusal of Toleration to those that are of different Opinions, (which might have been granted) that has produced all the Bustles and Wars, that have been in the Christian World, upon account of Religion. The Heads and Leaders of the Church, moved by Avarice and insatiable desire of Dominion, making use of the immoderate Ambition of Magistrates, and the credulous Superstition of the giddy Multitude, have incensed and animated them against those that dissent from themselves; by preaching unto them, contrary to the Laws of the Gospel and to the Precepts of Charity, That Schismaticks and Hereticks are to be outed of their Possessions, and destroyed.   (Locke 1983 [1989], p. 55)

This pragmatic appeal to prudence probably was the most persuasive point to those exhausted by the carnage and terror of religious wars that, at best, produced uneasy and distressingly temporary truces. But Locke spent much of his *Letter* on the more principled point that true religion inherently requires "the inward persuasion of the Mind . . . [making] Penalties in this case absolutely impertinent; because they are not proper to convince the mind" (p. 27). So coerced conversions are irrational not only because they are imprudent, they are also downright self-contradictory:

I may grow rich by an Art that I take not delight in; I may be cured of some Disease by Remedies that I have not Faith in; but I cannot be saved by a Religion that I distrust, and by a Worship that I abhor. It is in vain for an Unbeliever to take up the outward shew of another mans Profession. Faith only, and inward Sincerity, are the things that procure acceptance with God. (p. 38)

Locke's "inward persuasion" argument is forceful, but it does require a few more premises to yield anything like a liberal argument for full religious toleration. What if theological truth were obvious to the unbiased mind? Then one could accept the need for inward persuasion and still force the unbeliever to give the truth a fair hearing. Thus Locke requires an epistemology that rubs against the view (arguably his own) that reason alone is sufficient for Christian belief. Interestingly, earlier theologians such as Thomas Aquinas and John Calvin used the inwardness argument (Little et al. 1988, pp. 15–20). Indeed, Aquinas accepted the added epistemological point that an unbeliever's conscience could be inculpable when it rejects Christ, as well as the theological and moral claim that such a conscience should remain free. This latter claim involves a normative principle for toleration that goes beyond Locke's point about the logical irrationality of coercion. However, Aquinas's and Calvin's epistemology did not allow that a believer could become an apostate or heretic with an inculpable conscience, so they had trouble extending toleration to important intramural Christian differences. Thus, for the toleration of different sects, Locke must argue that intelligent people of good will can be equally well informed and still differ on important points of doctrine and liturgy, points that each side regards as crucial to salvation.

Even then, Locke's pragmatic and logical arguments would hardly yield toleration in the sense of equal religious liberty. Locke notoriously argued for intolerance of Catholics and atheists, his reasons combining a purely practical concern about public order and safety with the quaint view that the promises of Catholics and atheists could not be trusted, the former because they pledged allegiance to a foreign prince (the Pope) and the latter because only those who believe in divine reward and punishment have sufficient motive for fidelity. These latter views are peripheral to Locke's main position on toleration – he probably would allow empirical evidence to change his mind as he did on the causes of civil unrest – but even then he would need further considerations for full religious tolerance. So far his view is quite compatible with various forms of discrimination against religious minorities. Islam, for example, has traditionally allowed other theists to practice their faith, but has usually discriminated against them with special taxes and with restrictions on propagating their views. Indeed, the Qur'an states that there can be no compulsion in religion (2:256). It thereby agrees with Locke and Aquinas and Calvin about the need for inward freedom, although, for reasons similar to those of Aquinas and Calvin, not allowing it for apostates. But the "no compulsion" view is quite compatible with many forms of discrimination that do not coerce belief. Islam means "surrender" and, although belief (*imam*) cannot be coerced, Muslims can use coercion, even holy war (*jihad*), to subdue unbelievers to a particular polity (Little et al. 1988, pp. 66–7). To reject such discrimination, one needs something like liberalism's separation of church and state.

Here arises an important historical difference between Christianity and Islam. It can be argued that, until recently, Islam has never had to confront the issue of separating church and state because, until recently, there were not two institutions about which the question of separation could be raised. As Islam delivered the message, it also set up political structures (using tribes and caliphs) that embodied its moral and social implications, appealing to a religious law (*Shari'a*) that tends not to distinguish religious, moral, and political duties. Thus Islam did not develop an institutional church distinct from its development as a political reality (Little et al. 1988, p. 85). Christianity, on the other hand, was an often-persecuted minority for several hundred years after its founding, and it quickly developed an ecclesiastical hierarchy that argued for the wisdom of mutual respect between the two different institutions of church and state. The early Christians appealed to the teachings of both Jesus and Paul to argue for a distinction between the realms of Caesar and of the church, although there was room for debate about how to handle overlapping responsibilities. Thus any later tendencies toward theocracy had to develop in spite of rather than because of Christianity's scriptures and early history. And when the consequences of religious wars showed them to be folly, Christianity had the theological resources to take seriously not just Locke's arguments about the irrationality of religious persecution but also his advocating the separation of church and state, a doctrine that developed into liberalism's demand for a religiously neutral state.

The classic statement of this demand is J. S. Mill's *On Liberty* where, right after he notes that intolerance is so natural to humans that religious freedom owes more to religious indifference than to principle (Mill 1978 [1859], p. 8), he asserts his "one very simple principle" that "the sole end for which mankind are warranted, individually or collectively, in interfering with the liberty of action of any of their number is self-protection" (p. 9). This principle by itself will not yield religious freedom because even the Inquisition could be defended in terms of society's self-protection from the harmful effects of heresy. So Mill also needs his controversial distinction between conduct that concerns others and that which concerns only oneself (p. 73), and his even more improbable relegation of most religious matters – including monogamy – to the latter, private sphere (p. 89). Combine this understanding of the relationship between society and the individual with a moral principle of respect for the individual and her conscience and autonomy and we get classical liberalism's case for full toleration of religious practices – the contentious but peaceful coexistence of different religions in a neutral state.

Although the early history and teachings of Christianity enabled it to become quite receptive to this separation of church and state, we should note that it need not accept classical liberalism's reasons for the division of labor. For example, communitarians, who have a more organic view of society and thereby reject Mill's individualism, can ground their toleration of religious expression in religious awe toward persons they perceive as imagers of God. Indeed, Tinder has persuasively argued that reverence toward the sanctity of God's children is a much firmer foundation for toleration than is Mill's dubious appeal to utility or secular appeals to a universal dignity that empirically seems quite unequal (Tinder 1976, p. 114). Of course, not all Christians noticed this aspect of their doctrine during the sad story of religious intolerance, and prudence probably did more than principle to stop the carnage of religious wars. But if Mendus is right in thinking that stable toleration must be based on respect rather than expediency (Mendus 1989, p. 111), then it is important to notice that the religious and moral implications of being created in God's image provide many theists with a robust reason for principled toleration. Imagers of God are hearers and givers of reasons and, especially regarding decisions that are central to their identity, one may not overly manipulate them, even out of love. A related, distinctly theological rationale for toleration is that this limitation on coercion out of reverence toward God's imagers also implies respect for God's own spiritual power and is more consistent with the prophetic faith that God's word "shall not return to me empty, but it shall accomplish that which I purpose" (Isaiah 55:11).

Toleration, tolerance, and affirmation

The arguments for religious toleration mentioned so far can be placed on a spectrum from the purely pragmatic, on one side, to the purely principled on the other. Although there are no sharp divisions in this spectrum, toleration based on protecting one's own self-interest (should the wrong sect get into power) is grounded quite differently from toleration based on an analysis of the character of true religious belief or on an appeal to moral or religious obligation. But all of these arguments must be distinguished from another consideration that Mill introduced, namely the positive appreciation of diversity. Notice that Locke was not one to celebrate plurality; he merely argued the irrationality of not enduring it. One could go further than Locke and argue for actually cooperating with disagreeable practices. Thus an employer might cooperatively set up work schedules that accommodate an employee's disagreeable Sabbath day practices and a society may empower minorities to broadcast disagreeable viewpoints. Mill and others have argued that it is prudent for individuals and societies to cooperate with the airing of what they see as errors, because that is how we correct our mistakes and arrive at better reasons and more truth. Theists also can argue for this motivation for cooperation if they have a view of revelation and hermeneutics which implies that human comprehension of God's will is inherently limited and fallible. This view would yield a theologically based, epistemological humility that not only tolerates but also enables the expression of what seems to be heresy, since the latter might give new insights into truth or, at least, the reasons for accepting it. But even such cooperation is consistent with viewing the other as being wrong in a disagreeable way.

Beginning with Mill, however, we see arguments not simply for enduring diversity as conducive to peace or progress, but also for celebrating, approving, and affirming it. Thus he claimed that public opinion, and not just legal coercion, was an undesirable constraint on human flourishing (Mill 1978 [1859], p. 9). Indeed, he argued that society's being judgmental about diversity maimed individuals in a way similar to the Chinese practice of foot-binding (p. 66). Such broad-minded affirmation of differences should not be confused with toleration. Some have suggested we use "tolerance" to refer to the welcoming of differences and reserve "toleration" for merely enduring them, arguing along Mill's line that liberal democracies should nurture such tolerance in ways that would make toleration unnecessary and even offensive (Fotion and Elfstrom 1992, p. 124). Others have suggested that "tolerance" should simply refer to the character disposition that inclines one toward acts or practices of toleration (Newman 1982, p. 5). It does seem that tolerance sometimes connotes broad-minded approval of important differences and not merely the tendency to put up with them. However the verb "tolerate," the adjective "tolerant," and the noun "intolerance" seem to associate with both toleration and tolerance, so linguistic legislation aimed at separating them is unlikely to succeed. Moreover, Mill and some liberals may underestimate how personal integrity and group identity require the judgment that many important differences are disagreeably wrong, even if tolerable. One may be able to welcome any number of ethnic, cultural, and lifestyle diversities as adding spice to a pleasing pluralism and yet regard many moral and religious differences as sad and disagreeable wrongs that one should argue against even while tolerating them (Mouw and Griffioen 1993, p. 18). Rawls, for example, while not giving up his hope that political liberalism can rely on an overlapping agreement about central issues of justice, now believes that the differences we find in our pluralistic society are so deep and so wide and concern matters that are so central to what makes life meaningful, that we cannot hope for an emerging consensus about ethics and the good life (Rawls 1993, p. xvi). And this conflict is between what he calls *reasonable* doctrines, not just between reasonable views and those of Nazis or the Ku Klux Klan. Thus one can respect a position as reasonable but also regard it as wrong and disagreeable. One can tolerate people's acting on such positions while not approving of them and, indeed, while trying to change their minds through rational persuasion or even public opinion.

Instead of hoping that toleration will gradually be replaced by approval, affirmation, and admiration of differences, it may be more realistic as well as more consistent with personal integrity and cultural identity to cultivate the attitude of tolerance as the limited but valuable disposition toward appropriate toleration. It is important to underscore *appropriate*, since there are many behaviors – not all of them criminal – toward which tolerance would not be a virtue. It is also important to notice that one can respect another's holding a view that one regards as wrong. Often the mistake one thinks the other is making is clearly not the result of culpable ignorance, stubborn prejudice, or corrupt consciousness. Rather, one can see that the other's believing the error is quite reasonable from the other's point of view, and also that the other's point of view is itself what a reasonable person might accept. An orthodox Jewish physician, for example, might respect the decision-making of a Jehovah's Witness who refuses a lifesaving blood transfusion for an infant and still regard the decision as disagreeably – even tragically – wrong. Indeed, the physician may be intolerant of the other's action, seeking a coercive court order to override it, and still respect the other's view as reasonable. What Rawls calls "comprehensive doctrines" (1993, p. 58) are often simultaneously reasonable and conflicting. In a pluralistic society this sort of conflict will usually call for mutual and respectful toleration. But sometimes it may call for respectful intolerance, especially when innocent third parties may be harmed by a reasonable but wrong decision. Such respect is not the same as the refusal to blame or the willingness to forgive, which can apply to people holding unreasonable views. And respect need not be predicated on skepticism, relativism, or nihilism, since it can regard the other as definitely wrong, albeit in a reasonable way.

Thus one can retain in tolerance the notion of enduring disagreeable error and still be open-minded about whether the error is reasonable. And one can do this without a generalized broad-minded delight in all tolerable diversity. Moreover, the criteria one uses for deciding what is reasonable and the different (though perhaps overlapping) criteria one uses for deciding what one can tolerate – or even cooperate with – imply that in a pluralistic society various combinations of these attitudes (or their opposites) are quite possible.

Religion and the public square

For theists, theologically based values are quite likely to influence what one regards as reasonable. This influence is not a deep issue in a pluralistic society because it is distinct from the more political decision about what is tolerable. So the remaining question concerns the extent to which theological beliefs should influence decisions about coercive legislation. This debate has lately been labeled "Religion and the public square" (Mouw and Griffioen 1993, ch. 3).

Islamic fundamentalism, uninfluenced by the Western debate about the separation of church and state, a question it may find unintelligible (see above), contends that the religious law (*Shari'a*) of the Qur'an does not distinguish theological from moral or political grounds for law and thus is normative for a country's legislation. However, many Muslims now live in countries with fairly secular governments, so they eventually may have to resort to the sort of prudential and principled separation of powers that is a continuing process and debate for theists in Europe and America.

In the United States the debate is often framed by the First Amendment protection of "the free exercise" of religion and the prohibition of laws "respecting an establishment of religion." Does this mean a complete separation of church and state, and a religiously neutral state? Does it mean that citizens must ignore their deeply religious beliefs, which shape their identity and inform their idea of the good, when voting for legislation and legislators? Or does it mean that they can use such beliefs when making up their own minds but that the "public square" debates may appeal only to "public reasons," even when the debaters themselves are less motivated by them than by their own religious beliefs? Or, even more restrictively, should citizens limit the public square debates – on abortion, for example – to reasons that not only are completely independent of any theologically based beliefs but which also provide sufficient political motivation for themselves?

Rawls is perhaps the most influential philosopher in this debate, arguing (1993, Part II) for a political conception of liberalism that may overlap, but which can also stand free of, all of the reasonable and conflicting comprehensive doctrines about the good life that one finds in a democratic, pluralistic society. Others argue that a thicker conception of the good is necessary for politics, a conception that may include irreducibly religious – even theistic – elements (Mouw and Griffioen 1993). The question is whether and how one can allow religious beliefs into public discussions or decisions about what is tolerable without thereby impinging on appropriate "free exercise" of minority religious outlooks. The history of the debate over monogamy in the United States illustrates the difficulty of drawing an uncontroversial line. This difficulty is multiplied when citizens of a democratic and pluralistic society must decide how to respond to what they regard as oppression in other societies. For Western theists, at least, such issues are the main focus of the current debate about theism and toleration.

Bibliography

Fotion, N., and Elfstrom, G.: *Toleration* (Tuscaloosa and London: University of Alabama Press, 1992).

Little, D., Kelsay, J., and Sachedina, A. A.: *Human Rights and the Conflicts of Culture: Western and Islamic Perspectives on Religious Liberty* (Columbia: University of South Carolina Press, 1988).

Locke, J.: *A Letter Concerning Toleration* (London, 1689), ed. J. H. Tully (Indianapolis: Hackett, 1983).

Mendus, S.: *Toleration and the Limits of Liberalism* (Atlantic Highlands: Humanities Press, 1989).

Mill, J. S.: *On Liberty* (London, 1859), ed. E. Rapaport (Indianapolis: Hackett, 1978).

Mouw, R. J., and Griffioen, S.: *Pluralisms and Horizons* (Grand Rapids: William B. Eerdmans, 1993).

Newman, J.: *Foundations of Religious Tolerance* (Toronto: University of Toronto Press, 1982).

Rawls, J.: *Political Liberalism* (New York: Columbia University Press, 1993).

Tinder, G.: *Tolerance: Toward a New Civility* (Amherst: University of Massachusetts Press, 1976).

PART X

PHILOSOPHICAL REFLECTION ON CHRISTIAN FAITH

66

Trinity

DAVID BROWN

Historical background

Though the doctrine of the Trinity may be loosely defined as "three persons in one God" (Father, Son, and Holy Spirit), some knowledge of the historical background is required, if misrepresentation or caricature is to be avoided. While the New Testament contains ascriptions of divinity to Christ and to the Holy Spirit, as well as occasional uses of formulae which mention all three persons (e.g. Matthew 28:19), the classic formulation of the doctrine only emerged as a response to the Arian controversy in the fourth century. The result was the first two ecumenical councils of the Church at Nicaea (325) and Constantinople (381) and what we now know as the Nicene Creed, though it only reached its present form (with one exception noted later) at the second council. Any philosophical assessment of trinitarian claims needs to take seriously this context and the fluidity of the conceptual language employed.

Arians used texts such as John 14:28 ("My father is greater than I") to argue that the Son was a creature, not co-eternal with the Father. Nicaea used the non-biblical phrase *homoousios* (literally "of the same being") to refute the claim, but it was only by the time of the Council of Constantinople, largely thanks to the work of the three Cappadocian Fathers (Basil, his younger brother Gregory of Nyssa, and their friend Gregory Nazianzen), that a precise terminology was worked out: Father, Son, and Holy Spirit are three *hypostases* in one *ousia*. In Latin this came to be expressed as three *personae* in one *substantia*: hence the normal English pattern of "three persons in one substance."

The meaning of these terms is a potential minefield of misunderstandings, as they were only given a more precise signification as discussion continued. Thus at Nicaea *hypostasis* ("entity") and *ousia* ("existent") were still being used as equivalent terms, while the Latin Fathers were eventually to use *substantia* as the equivalent of *ousia* despite the fact that its more literal meaning accords exactly with *hypostasis* (both literally mean "that which stands under," i.e. something which supports attributes or predicates). The net result is that it is not always very easy to determine the precise and intended meaning of our patristic sources before these questions of terminology had been clarified.

In the past, the tendency was to assume an inevitable progression from Nicaea through Augustine to the Fourth Lateran Council (1215). Nicaea, it was said, already endorsed numerical identity between the three persons. Augustine explained how this was possible (the persons were differentiated only in their

525

relations). This then received the official endorsement of the Church at the medieval council. But it is now clear that the fluidity of the terminology helped conceal considerable divergence of views. Indeed, the current assumption is that the majority at Nicaea would probably have accepted a generic view of what was meant by *homoousios*: each of the persons are the same kind of thing (divine), not the same thing (God: numerical identity). This is, for instance, the conclusion reached by the patristic scholar Christopher Stead in his *Divine Substance* (1977). Expressing it in the philosophical terminology of the time, what we have is a case of Aristotelian second substance, and not first (*Categories* 5): that is, a genus like animal, and not a particular, like this horse. The point is made not to exclude the later numerical identity of the Lateran Council as a legitimate option, but as a way of insisting that generic identity and the more social conception of the godhead that goes with it are just as firmly embedded within the Christian tradition.

A further word of caution on terminology is necessary, which tells against a purely generic account. This concerns the meaning of *persona* and its Greek equivalent *prosopon*. For it cannot be too strongly emphasized that there is no simple equivalence with our modern understanding of "person." The latter is strongly individualistic, and the primary reference is to a self-reflective and self-determining center of consciousness. Some would trace the origins of such a conception back to René Descartes; others to the twelfth century renaissance; others still earlier, to Augustine. But what at any rate is clear is that the Cappadocians reflect the then prevalent use, to mean a being in social relation to others. Why it should bear that meaning is readily explicable in terms of the history of the use of *prosopon*. Originally it meant "face"; then the "mask" held in front of the face in Greek drama. From that usage came the notion of "character," the public projection of the form of one's relationship to others; then, finally, the ontological bearer of that character. The Latin *persona* had a similar history, though it never seems to have meant "face." However, that the social or relational element was also to the fore is well illustrated by the fact that in Roman law slaves could not be described as *personae*, because their social relations with others were entirely determined by their masters.

In the fourth century, discussion focused on securing the full and equal divinity of the Son and Holy Spirit. With Augustine in the fifth century, the question of the unity of the three persons takes first place. For him this meant challenging the appropriateness of the term "person." It should not be read generically but without any precise meaning and merely as a way of indicating that distinctions do exist within the godhead: "When it is asked, 'what three?', human speech suffers from a considerable disability. 'The persons' are mentioned, less in order that something be said, than that silence be avoided" (*De Trinitate* 5, 10, my translation). So rather than *persons* in relation, Augustine insists, the stress should be upon differentiated relations. Whether that is the price that must be paid in order to preserve divine unity is the question that exercised the medieval Church, and so led to the rather different formulation of the Fourth Lateran Council and its claim to numerical identity: "we believe and confess that there is one supreme reality, at once three persons taken together and each of them singly, because each of the three persons is that reality, that is the divine substance, essence, or nature."

Conceptual arguments for trinitarianism

Overwhelmingly it has been the case that such a conception of God has been seen as dependent upon revelation, but there are two important exceptions: Richard of St Victor (d. 1173) and G. W. F. Hegel (1770–1831).

Richard's argument (*De Trinitate* 3) has been revived recently by Richard Swinburne (1988 and 1994). In outline, the argument is that if God is loving, then he must share (hence the Son); and cooperate in sharing (hence the Holy Spirit). One advantage the argument brings is the support it gives to the Western addition to the Nicene Creed, the *Filioque*, which talks of the Holy Spirit proceeding from the Father *and the Son*. However, there are also difficulties. It robs divinity of its most obvious characteristic, aseity (being dependent upon nothing other than itself). It assumes that for love to be present it must be other-regarding. But is not self-love only wrong if others' interests are neglected? It assumes that cooperation in love must generate a third person. However, even if we confine ourselves to the marriage analogy, is this necessarily so?

A very different form of argument is offered by Hegel. As in his famous master–slave analogy (*Phenomenology of Spirit*, pp. 178–96), his argument is that it is only possible to come to self-consciousness through projection of oneself on to something other than oneself. Putting this in trinitarian terms (*Lectures on the Philosophy of Religion*, Part 3), it was necessary for the Father to have the Son as other than himself before a coming to full self-consciousness could occur in the life of the Holy Spirit (Hegel's *Geist*). The argument plays a major role in Hegel's philosophy since it is used to justify belief not only in the Trinity but also in the necessity of the world. The crucifixion is the culmination of a general pattern of divinity essaying into something other than itself. As a claim about human self-consciousness, Hegel's contention is on strong ground; our self-understanding is only forged through interaction with others. But that is surely a function of the way we as humans think, not an essential feature of all thought. It is only if all divine thinking is seen as instantaneous that OMNISCIENCE (see Article 29) and aseity would be preserved. One's assessment of the plausibility of the argument is also likely to be affected by one's acceptance or otherwise of Hegel's general revision of patterns of argument through dialectic (thesis, antithesis, synthesis). However it is viewed, it is important to note the argument, as it has had major influence on much contemporary, especially German, theology. It is implicit in much of Jürgen Moltmann's writings, and explicit in Eberhard Jüngel's *God as the Mystery of the World* (1983; German 1977).

Criteria of differentiation

The New Testament sometimes suggests very little difference between the persons. It is not always easy to tell when God as Spirit is the intended reference and when the Holy Spirit; the Gospel of John often moves indifferently between Father and Son. At other times quite a sharp distinction is implied: the Son praying to the Father; the Resurrection as a unique experience of the Son, as Pentecost is of the

527

Spirit; references to the Spirit making possible an experience of the relation between Son and Father (Romans 8:14–15; Galatians 4:6–7). However, to safeguard the unity it was eventually accepted that all the persons were involved in any external act of the godhead, and so as the basis of differentiation an appeal instead was made to the relationships of sonship and procession, the latter being derived from John 14:26. This had the advantage of identifying a non-contingent difference, one which applied to the immanent and not just the economic Trinity (God "in himself" as distinct from how he "manages" or relates to the world).

Sonship and procession are both metaphors. But if the persons do not literally "generate" or "send," what have we left as the distinction between them? All we seem to have is them relating to one another. It was in response to an Arian challenge along these lines that Augustine made use of the *Filioque* as a means of uniquely identifying each member of the Trinity (*De Trinitate* 5, 12). His point may be put more formally as follows. The Father relates and yet is not related (he actively does something – "generates" a Son – but is not passively at the end of any process). The Son both relates and is related (along with the Father he "sends" the Holy Spirit, but he is also passively at the end of a process in being "generated"). The Holy Spirit does not relate and yet is related. The importance of the *Filioque* thus lies in the fact that without it one would have no way of distinguishing Son and Spirit; both would be at the end of a process and neither would actively relate. The issue is one which the Cappadocians did not directly face. Had they done so, so firm was their conviction that the Father was the sole *archē* or source of the godhead that their answer would have been rather different: the Holy Spirit is the unique passive recipient of a relation which goes from the Father through the Son. The Holy Spirit would then be unique in being the passive recipient of a mediated relation, but unlike the Western tradition, the Eastern creed was never altered.

Some philosophers have been so convinced of the appropriateness of applying the more specific relational terms to the immanent Trinity that they have even concluded that it gives irrefutable grounds for insisting that only one of the persons could have become incarnate. So, for instance, Anselm in *Cur Deus Homo* (2,9) observes against the Father becoming incarnate that there would then be two grandsons in the Trinity: the "Father" as grandson of the parents of the Virgin, and the "Son" as grandson of the Virgin, since he would then be Son of her son! Were one to follow Augustine and interpret the relations less literally, on the positive side could be set the fact that such an approach does assume the simplicity of one divine person coming first (at any rate, logically and non-temporally), and historically simplicity has played a major role in theological explanation. But, on the other side, it should be noted that thereby an ineliminable element of hierarchy is introduced between the persons, and hierarchy would seem incompatible with any notion of full divinity. Not only that, should not God have within himself maximal richness without any need to "create" or "generate" it? For reasons such as these, other trinitarians would prefer to leave the distinction between the persons in the immanent Trinity unanalyzed, while at the same time insisting that their different roles in revelation and in human experience must point to ineradicable differences among them. Put at its crudest, they have different "histories." But from the fact that in the INCARNATION (see Article 67) the Son experienced the Father as a Father it does not necessarily follow that this is how for all eternity they relate to one another (except of course in the sense of their both being aware of that history).

Criteria of unity

If relative identity is a defensible notion, then the nature of the divine unity becomes more easily explicable: the Father is the same God as the Son, but not the same person. Peter Geach and more recently Peter van Inwagen (1988) have adopted this approach. However, the objections remain considerable. According to David Wiggins (1980), each of the alleged examples from other spheres resolves into something other than an "is" of identity, such as a different time reference or an "is" of constitution. So, for instance, were I to declare that "the present church is the same church as the old parish church but not the same building," what we would have is not the same thing identified in two different ways (relative identity), but two entirely different things, the church as a building and the church as a continuing congregation. It would therefore seem unwise to rely on such a controversial challenge to strict criteria for identity.

Augustine's strong sense of his own individual identity, as seen in the introspective character of his *Confessions* (up to that date without parallel), may have contributed in part to his hostility toward speaking of the Trinity as three persons. In its place he brings forward as his principal analogy the mind as memory, understanding, and will. David Brown (1985) criticizes him for failing to provide three permanent distinctions within the godhead, since, as Gilbert Ryle observed in *The Concept of Mind* (1949), any faculty analysis of the human mind reduces to no more than a series of dispositional capacities. The most obvious merit in the analogy is the way in which it tries to match "persons" with particular faculties, such as the Son as the Word or Logos of understanding and the Holy Spirit as the will to love. Another advantage is that the model is an interactionist one. What enables the mind to understand is the way in which it can draw on the memory for concepts but it only does so because there is a desire to comprehend what has taken its interest. While the idea that the three persons could literally correspond to these three faculties is incoherent (none of the faculties of itself would possess omniscience since each acts partially in contributing to the mind's overall perspective), Augustine's insistence upon such interaction is surely along the right lines. For once omniscience is conceded to each of the three persons, they will then have immediate access to one another's minds and so such interaction will be inevitable, particularly as their perfect goodness will mean that they also share total identity of purpose (see Article 30, GOODNESS). Under such a scenario it becomes less clear why we should speak of three minds and not one.

The continuing pressure toward the former comes from the fact that there remain experiences that belong uniquely to one or other person. The heretical patripassianism of Noetus and Praxeas was condemned on the grounds that it is the Son alone who suffered, not the Father (or the Holy Spirit). Clearly there is a difference between accessing the experiential knowledge of another divine mind, and being oneself the subject of that experiential knowledge, as God the Son was of Jesus' human suffering. So the instinct of the Cappadocians to preserve some of its usual connotations to the notion of person was right. Gregory of Nyssa's image of a mob or army (*Ad Ablabium*) or Gregory Nazianzen's of the family of Adam, Eve, and Seth (*Theological Oration* 5,11) can, however, easily mislead. Not only does one need to take cognizance of their Platonism, according to which the universal or genus has priority over the particular, also relevant are their assumptions about the relational character of personhood, to which attention was drawn earlier. The point is that, in virtue of their relations, a family or army or even a mob can think and act as one, such that the primary and most appropriate way of identifying them comes to be in the singular form. It is unfortunate that each of the examples suggests hierarchy and forms of leadership, but this is not inherent in the method. Thus individuals in a football crowd may think and act as one, but no leader be present or required.

There is good anthropological evidence to suggest that in some cultures social identity takes priority over individual identity. In the Eskimo language, for instance, it is impossible to differentiate between the second and third person; suffixes merely indicate location – Eskimo here ("I") or Eskimo not here ("you" or "they"). What this odd piece of linguistics reflects is their extraordinarily strong corporate sense of identity, with apparently one person laughing or weeping being sufficient to generate general hilarity or tears. Building on examples such as this, Brown (1989) has suggested that we think of self-consciousness residing in the Trinity as a whole, with consciousness or awareness only in each of the individual persons. That is to say, though logically each of the persons would be an individual entity and aware of itself as such, their identity for them (and thus also for us) would be given by the social whole.

To this it may be objected that without self-reflection the divine persons live at a lesser level of existence than modern human beings. Here we have an evaluative issue, where we may set against the modern view Plotinus' very different account (*Enneads* 1.4.10). According to him we are most committed to an activity when we are least aware of that commitment. For instance, in reading a novel the characters and images of the writer take over, and we wake with a start if attention is drawn to our surroundings. Likewise, there is something wrong with our commitment to the truth if we first have to deliberate whether or not to tell a lie. Similarly, then, with the Trinity, it would seem absurd to suggest that the three persons require any independent reflection before endorsing the "mind" of the social whole.

Bibliography

Bartel, T. W.: "Could there be more than one Lord?", *Faith and Philosophy*, 11 (1994), pp. 357–78.

Brown, D.: *The Divine Trinity* (La Salle: Open Court; London: Duckworth, 1985), pp. 239–44, 272–301.

Brown, D., Kretzmann, N., and Plantinga, C.: "Trinitarian Personhood and Individuality." In *Trinity, Incarnation and Atonement*, ed. R. J. Feenstra and C. Plantinga (Notre Dame: University of Notre Dame Press, 1989), pp. 21–109.

Hegel, G. W. F.: *Lectures on the Philosophy of Religion* (Lectures of 1827), ed. P. C. Hodgson (Berkeley: University of California Press, 1988), Part 3, pp. 389ff.

Stead, C.: *Divine Substance* (Oxford: Clarendon Press, 1977), esp. pp. 157ff.

Swinburne, R.: "Could there be more than one God?" *Faith and Philosophy*, 5 (1988), pp. 225–41.

——: *The Christian God* (Oxford: Clarendon Press, 1994), esp. pp. 170–91.

van Inwagen, P.: "And yet there are not three Gods but one God." In *Philosophy and the Christian Faith*, ed. T. V. Morris (Notre Dame: University of Notre Dame Press, 1988), pp. 241–78.

Wiggins, D.: *Sameness and Substance* (Oxford: Blackwell, 1980), ch. 1, esp. pp. 37–42.

Yandell, K. E.: "The most brutal and inexcusable error in counting?: Trinity and consistency," *Religious Studies*, 30 (1994), pp. 201–17.

67

Incarnation

RONALD J. FEENSTRA

Introduction

The doctrine of the incarnation, which is a central and distinctive Christian doctrine, holds that the eternally divine second person of the Trinity (see Article 66, TRINITY) took on human nature, retaining his full divinity while becoming fully human. This doctrine, which is rooted in biblical affirmations about Jesus Christ, undergirded the faith and worship of the earliest Christians. Still, debates over how to understand Christ's divinity and humanity troubled the early church and led to the councils of Nicaea (325), which affirmed the deity of Christ, and Chalcedon (451), whose affirmation of Christ's true divinity and true humanity set the standard for orthodox teaching on the incarnation.

Since the Enlightenment, some have criticized Chalcedonian Christology as incoherent or self-contradictory, while others have defended its coherence and consistency. At least two contemporary Christologies – the "two-minds" and the kenotic theories – offer plausible accounts of the incarnation.

Biblical roots

The New Testament generates the Christian claim that Jesus Christ is the divine Son of God who took on human flesh, becoming like us in every respect except sin (see Article 68, SIN AND ORIGINAL SIN). In one of the earliest New Testament writings, the apostle Paul, probably quoting an early Christian hymn, says that Christ Jesus, though he was in the form of God, did not consider equality with God something to be clung to, but emptied himself, taking the form of a servant, being born in human likeness (Philippians 2:5–11; Brown 1994, p. 135). The prologue of John (1:1–18) speaks of the Word, who was in the beginning with God and was God, through whom all things came into being, and who became flesh, lived among us, and made God known to us.

Scripture affirms Jesus Christ's divinity in at least five ways. First, despite the biblical affirmation that there is but one God (Deuteronomy 6:4), Jesus Christ is referred to as God (Hebrews 1:8, John 1:1, 18), as Lord (1 Corinthians 8:6, Philippians 2:11), as "our great God and Savior" (Titus 2:13; cf. 2 Peter 1:1), and even as "My Lord and my God" (John 20:28; see Brown 1994, pp. 192–5). In addition, the Gospel of John frequently uses "I am," the Old Testament name of God, to refer to Jesus Christ (6:20; 8:24,28,58; 10:7; 13:19; 18:5–8). Second,

Jesus' equality and unity with God are indicated by his bearing the "exact imprint" of God's being (Hebrews 1:3) and being one with God (John 10:30, 17:22). The "whole fullness of deity" dwells bodily in him (Colossians 2:9). Third, Jesus does the works that God does, as creator (John 1:3, Colossians 1:16, Hebrews 1:10; see Article 39, CREATION AND CONSERVATION), sustainer of all things (Hebrews 1:3), destroyer of death (2 Timothy 1:10), forgiver of sins (Mark 2:5–11 and parallels), ruler (Philippians 2:10, Hebrews 1:8), and judge (Matthew 25:31–46). Fourth, worship and prayer (see Article 73, PETITIONARY PRAYER) are properly directed toward Jesus, thereby acknowledging his divinity (John 18:6, 1 Corinthians 16:22, Hebrews 1:6, Revelation 22:20). Fifth, Jesus' existence prior to creation is adumbrated. Some passages leave the matter unsettled, speaking of Jesus as "the image of the invisible God, the firstborn of all creation" (Colossians 1:15), or as the firstborn, begotten of the Father (Hebrews 1:5–6), or even as having existed before Abraham did (John 8:58). Nevertheless, John 1:1–2 indicates that the Word existed with God prior to creation, and the book of Revelation (1:17, 2:8, 22:13) ascribes to Jesus the divine title of "the first and the last" (Brown 1994, pp. 134–6).

The New Testament also affirms Jesus' humanity and his sharing in our temptations and limitations. Jesus' humanity is evident in his having become flesh, being born in human form (John 1:14; Philippians 2:7), his having eaten with his disciples, his thirst (John 19:28), and his death from crucifixion. Having become like us, he "in every respect has been tempted as we are, yet without sin," so he can sympathize with our weaknesses (Hebrews 2:17–18; 4:15). His having had limited knowledge is implied by statements that he grew in wisdom (Luke 2:52), learned obedience through what he suffered (Hebrews 5:8), wondered who touched him and received healing (Mark 5:30–3), and claimed not to know the day or hour that heaven and earth will pass away (Mark 13:32).

Given the biblical statements regarding Jesus Christ, Christians must affirm both his divinity, despite objections that no divine person could have been human or tempted or non-omniscient (see Article 29, OMNISCIENCE), and his humanity, despite objections that no human being could have pre-existed or been divine (Brown 1994, pp. 25–30).

Historical developments

During Christianity's first four centuries, theologians faced the problem of understanding and articulating Jesus Christ's status in relation to both God and humanity. Although basic outlines of the position were established early on, debates over important issues led to several major councils, including those of Nicaea and Chalcedon.

Already in the second century, Irenaeus of Lyon (ca. 130–ca. 200) saw the soteriological import of affirming both the divinity and the humanity of Jesus Christ: "For if a human person had not conquered humanity's foe, that foe would not have been conquered justly. Conversely, unless it was God who conferred salvation, we should not possess it securely" (*Against Heresies*, 3.18.7, in Norris

1980, p. 54). Still, Christians had no clear and common understanding of what it meant to say that Jesus was both divine and human.

The defining moment arrived when Arius of Alexandria (ca. 250–ca. 336) stated that the Word or Son of God, the firstborn of all creation through whom all other creatures were made, himself came into being at the will of God, had a beginning, and was made out of nothing as God's first creature (Hardy 1954, pp. 332–3). Arius held that the Word, unlike the transcendent God, could be united with human flesh and suffer for our salvation. By proposing that the Son's begottenness entailed his having had a beginning *before* the creation of the world, Arius forced the church to decide whether the Son is as fully divine as the Father.

In response, the Council of Nicaea affirmed what Arius explicitly rejected: the Son is of one essence (*homoousios*) with the Father, begotten but not created, the one through whom all created things were made (Hardy 1954, p. 338). Although its pivotal term, *homoousios*, fails to appear in the New Testament, Nicaea's affirmations grow out of the New Testament's view of Christ (Brown 1994, pp. 142–7).

Later, Apollinaris of Laodicea (ca. 310–ca. 390), thinking it inconceivable that one person should be both God and fully human, proposed that Christ is "not a human being," but rather "uncreated God made manifest in a created garment" (in Norris 1980, pp. 104, 107–8). Given his belief that humanity consists of three parts – spirit, soul, and body – Apollinaris attempted to resolve the problem by asserting that the incarnation involved the divine Son's taking on a human soul and body. In response, Gregory Nazianzen (329–89) stated a principle that became a test of orthodoxy: whatever the Son has not assumed, he has not healed. Since sin had affected humanity's whole nature, Christ must assume the whole nature in order to redeem it (*Letter to Cledonius*, in Hardy 1954, pp. 218–19).

By the end of the fourth century, two schools of thought, one based in Alexandria and the other in Antioch, had developed divergent Christological views. Antiochenes emphasized Christ's full humanity and spoke of the Word's dwelling in the man Jesus Christ and uniting Christ to himself. Alexandrian Christology drew from Athanasius's (ca. 296–ca. 373) claim that Christ was not a human person who became God, but was God and then became human in order to deify us. Alexandrians stressed Christ's deity and power to save, and spoke of the Word's becoming flesh in Jesus Christ. Differences between the two schools erupted into controversy between Nestorius (d. ca. 451), bishop of Constantinople, and Cyril (d. 444), bishop of Alexandria. After becoming bishop in 428, Nestorius challenged important elements of the tradition, including calling the virgin Mary the mother of God (*theotokos*) and predicating human as well as divine attributes of the Word of God (*communicatio idiomatum*) (in Norris 1980, pp. 135–40). In response, Cyril claimed that God the Word did not enter a human being, but, in taking on flesh, so united human nature to himself that all the gospels' statements about him refer to the one incarnate person or *hypostasis* of the Word (Norris 1980, pp. 132–4; Hardy 1954, p. 352).

Attempting to resolve this dispute, the Council of Chalcedon affirmed that Jesus Christ is truly divine and truly human, coessential with the Father as to his deity and coessential with us as to his humanity (like us in all things except sin), with the character of each nature preserved in their coming together in one person or *hypostasis* (Norris 1980, p. 159). The definition of Chalcedon has become the touchstone of Christological orthodoxy, accepted by nearly all Christians.

Objections to Chalcedonian Christology

Modern opponents of Chalcedonian Christology regard it as incoherent or self-contradictory. For example, in *The Myth of God Incarnate*, a collection of essays published in 1977, John Hick asserts that "to say, without explanation, that the historical Jesus of Nazareth was also God is as devoid of meaning as to say that this circle drawn with a pencil on paper is also a square"; furthermore, every explanation thus far suggested for the language of incarnation has had to be repudiated (Hick 1993, p. 3). Even if the concepts of deity and humanity can be adjusted in order to allow a literal understanding of the incarnation, says Hick, it is doubtful that a literal understanding of the incarnation can satisfy "the religious concerns which give point to the doctrine" (Hick 1993, p. 4).

Hick blames the councils of Nicaea and Chalcedon for converting devotional, ecstatic, or liturgical language about Jesus into literal or metaphysical language (Hick 1993, p. 101). By adopting the Greek concept of *ousia*, Nicaea transformed a metaphorical son of God into the metaphysical God the Son; and Chalcedon has led to many unsuccessful efforts over the centuries to formulate incarnation doctrine as a literal assertion by reconciling the incompatible attributes (Hick 1993, pp. 44–5, 102–4). Jesus the eschatological prophet has been changed into "God the Son come down from heaven to live a human life and save us by his atoning death" (Hick 1993, p. 5; see Article 69, ATONEMENT, JUSTIFICATION, AND SANCTIFICATION).

In place of the two-natures doctrine, Hick proposes a metaphorical concept of incarnation that sees Jesus as "a human being extraordinarily open to God's influence and thus living to an extraordinary extent as God's agent on earth, 'incarnating' the divine purpose for human life" (Hick 1993, p. 12). Since an " 'incarnation' of divine love" occurs in anyone who responds to God's loving presence and reflects God's love on earth, and since all great religious figures have " 'incarnated' the ideal of human life lived in response to the divine Reality," Jesus is not intrinsically unique (Hick 1993, pp. 77, 98).

John Macquarrie also rejects traditional Christology: the claim that "Jesus Christ had prior to his birth a conscious, personal pre-existence in 'heaven' " is not only mythological but also "destructive of his true humanity" (Macquarrie 1990, pp. 57, 120–1, 145, 390). Macquarrie finds support from John Knox, who argues that if Jesus Christ pre-existed, then he would have been self-consciously continuous with his pre-incarnate existence, and this would distinguish his humanity from ours, with the result that he would not be truly human (Knox 1967, p. 106). Like Hick, Macquarrie speaks of the incarnation as metaphorical: "God's metaphorical 'sending' of his metaphorical 'son' can be understood in ways that do not imply pre-existence, once we accept that the language is metaphorical and not literal" (Macquarrie 1990, p. 56). Instead of literal or

535

personal pre-existence, Macquarrie proposes, as the only pre-existence that is compatible with Jesus' true humanity, that "from the beginning Jesus too has existed in the mind and purpose of God" (Macquarrie 1990, pp. 390–1). Accordingly, he reinterprets Paul's incarnational hymn (Philippians 2:5–11) to refer to a man "who lays aside any desire to displace God" (Macquarrie 1990, pp. 56–7).

Although it skirts many of the difficulties confronting Chalcedonian Christology, the metaphorical interpretation, with its preconceptions about divine and human nature, inevitably concludes that no literal incarnation could occur, and therefore rejects or reinterprets both Scripture and orthodox Christianity. More interesting is the attempt to develop a coherent position that fits with the statements of Scripture and Chalcedon.

Defending Chalcedonian Christology

Defenders of Chalcedonian Christology have argued that there is no incoherence or contradiction in affirming that Jesus Christ is truly divine and truly human. Although they agree on this basic point, Chalcedon's defenders disagree on the implications of two-natures doctrine for the concepts of divinity and humanity.

Orthodox Christology holds that the Son's divine nature is essential to him, since one who is divine can neither cease to be divine nor ever have become divine, but his human nature is not essential to him, since he could take on human nature while remaining the same person (Swinburne 1994, pp. 192–3). So a person who had all the properties essential to being divine took on in addition all the properties essential to being human, thereby coming to exist in two natures (Morris 1986, p. 40). Defending this claim requires resolving any apparent incompatibilities between Christ's two natures, allowing incarnation doctrine to govern our account of what is essential to divinity and what is essential to humanity.

Resolving apparent incompatibilities between Christ's two natures requires recognizing some important distinctions. First, an "individual-nature," the set of properties essential to an individual's existing and being what it is, is distinct from a "kind-nature," the set of properties any individual must exemplify in order to be a certain kind of being (Morris 1986, pp. 38–9). For example, two human persons share the kind-nature of humanity even though they have distinct individual-natures. Thus, in the incarnation, a person with the kind-nature of deity took on in addition the kind-nature of humanity. Two-natures doctrine also highlights the distinction between *common* and *essential* human properties (Morris 1986, pp. 63–4). Humans may commonly have the properties of being under 9 feet tall, having lived on the surface of the earth, having had a beginning in time, and possibly not having existed. Still, a person could be human who lacks one or more of these properties, since these are common, but not essential, human properties. Finally, incarnation doctrine must distinguish between being *fully* human and being *merely* human (Morris 1986, pp. 65–6). Every merely human person is fully human, but not every fully human person is merely human. Thus, a merely human person could not also be divine, but a person who is fully human – but not merely human – might possess divine as well as human nature. Jesus Christ is fully human if he possesses the essential human properties, even if he does not possess every common human property and even if he possesses divine properties that no other human being possesses.

Chalcedonian Christology also requires holding to the pre-existence of Jesus Christ. Regarding Knox's claim that Jesus Christ's pre-existence implies his self-conscious awareness of his pre-incarnate existence and therefore his lack of genuine humanity, one may observe that Jesus Christ's pre-incarnate existence does not imply his awareness of that pre-existence during his earthly life, since he could have, for all or part of his earthly life, lacked any memory of his pre-existent state (Feenstra 1990, pp. 138–9). Furthermore, even if Jesus was aware of his pre-incarnate existence at some points during his ministry (as John 17:5 seems to suggest), there is no clear argument to show that thinking oneself to have pre-existed means that one cannot be human.

Although Chalcedon's contemporary defenders agree on basic issues in Christology, they differ over some difficult Christological issues. Some defend a "two-minds" theory; others prefer a kenotic approach. The former tend to follow the demands of philosophical theology over against Scripture, while the latter let the statements of Scripture lead to a revision of the concept of God.

The two-minds theory

Largely in response to the tension between the Chalcedonian claim that Jesus Christ was fully divine and the biblical assertions that he was tempted (Hebrews 4:15), grew in wisdom (Luke 2:52), and did not know the time of the end of the world (Mark 13:32), some of Chalcedon's defenders have developed a "two-minds" theory of the incarnation. Thomas V. Morris identifies two distinct ranges of consciousness in God incarnate: the eternal mind encompassing omniscience, and the human mind that came into existence and developed as Jesus grew. There was an "asymmetric accessing relation" between these two minds, with the divine mind having had access to the human mind and its experience, while the human mind had only as much access to the contents of the divine mind as the latter allowed (Morris 1986, pp. 102–3). The relation between these two minds could be like that between a person who is dreaming and the dreamer as a character in the dream, or between two levels of mentality such as the conscious and the unconscious mind (Morris 1986, pp. 104–5). Similarly, Richard Swinburne suggests that a divine person could, in becoming incarnate, retain the "divine knowledge-system" while acquiring a separate "human belief-acquisition system" to guide the actions and statements of this person's human body (Swinburne 1994, pp. 202–3). On this view, biblical statements that Jesus Christ grew in wisdom and did not know the time of the end of the world refer to the human mind, not to the person.

Regarding Christ's temptations, the difficult issue is whether Christ, being divine, was necessarily good (see Article 30, GOODNESS) and therefore unable to yield, or whether he was in fact able to sin. If he was unable to yield, was he genuinely tempted? If he could have yielded to temptation, then could one of the divine persons have ceased to be divine, or at least to be good? On Morris's view, Jesus Christ could be tempted to sin as long as his earthly mind believed that he could sin (Morris 1986, pp. 148–9). Although Jesus' divine nature would have prevented his having chosen to sin, in his earthly consciousness he was unaware that he was necessarily good and therefore freely avoided succumbing to temptation (Morris 1986, pp. 150–3). Swinburne argues that becoming incarnate in such a way that he could do wrong would have been incompatible with God's perfect goodness (Swinburne 1994, p. 204). Still, "God the Son could subject himself to temptation, but only to do a lesser good, not to do wrong" (Swinburne 1994, p. 207).

Although the two-minds theory is promising, its biggest drawback is the difficulty of conceiving of one person's possessing two minds. In addition, the theory results in puzzlement over language about Jesus Christ. If only Christ's human mind lacked knowledge and was liable to temptation, then did only his human mind suffer and die for human sin? The doctrine of communication of attributes allows predicating the suffering and death of the divine Son of God. Yet, on the two-minds theory, one could not say that the divine Son was, even temporarily, non-omniscient.

The kenotic theory

Since the nineteenth century, some theologians have developed kenotic theories of the incarnation in an attempt to adopt Chalcedonian Christology to biblical statements about Christ's humiliation and lack of omniscience during his earthly life. Kenotic Christology (from *ekenosen*, "he emptied himself," in Philippians 2:7) echoes Irenaeus's statement that "the Logos became quiescent so that he could be tempted and dishonored and be crucified and die" (*Against Heresies*, 3.19.3, in Norris 1980, pp. 56–7).

Kenotic Christology attempts to develop a concept of God that allows predicating both divinity and non-omniscience of Jesus Christ, while recognizing that omniscience is, in some sense, an essential divine attribute. If Jesus Christ, the eternal divine second person of the Trinity, became incarnate in such a way that he was divine but not omniscient, then omniscience *simpliciter* must not be an essential divine property, but rather something like the property of being omniscient-unless-kenotically-incarnate, where it is understood that any divine person who possesses this attribute can become kenotically incarnate only temporarily and as a result of that person's free choice (Feenstra 1989, pp. 140–1). Jesus Christ could possess the essential divine property of being omniscient-unless-kenotically-incarnate even during his earthly life, when he is non-omniscient. Moreover, if the kenotically incarnate Christ was unaware of his inability to sin, then he could be tempted in every respect as we are, even though, as divine, he was necessarily good.

Still, if a divine person need not possess omniscience in order to be divine, could any divine person – or even all three divine persons – fail to possess omniscience (Swinburne 1994, p. 232)? Although one could argue that only the divine Son could become kenotically incarnate and therefore temporarily non-omniscient, this might compromise the metaphysical equality of the divine persons. Another suggestion, recognizing that the incarnation is for the purpose of redemption, holds that any divine person could have become kenotically incarnate, but once the Son became incarnate to bring about redemption for people of all time (Hebrews 7:25; 10:14), no other kenotic, redemptive incarnation would be either necessary or possible. The property of being omniscient-unless-kenotically-and-redemptively-incarnate would be the essential property of each divine person, but once the Son became kenotically and redemptively incarnate and accomplished his redemptive purpose, neither the Father nor the Spirit could have become kenotically incarnate (Feenstra 1989, pp. 141–2).

Kenotic Christology requires another distinction, in response to the following problem. If Christ's incarnation required giving up attributes such as omniscience, then his exaltation would have involved either continued non-omniscience or abandoning true humanity. But Christianity typically thinks of the exalted Christ as both omniscient and still human, so Christ's omniscience must be compatible with his possessing human nature. Then why accept the kenotic claim that he emptied himself of omniscience in the incarnation? In response, one must distinguish incarnation and kenosis. The divine Son does not lack attributes such as omniscience because he is incarnate, but rather because he emptied or humbled himself for the redemptive purpose of becoming a high priest who identifies with us and shares our lot or condition (Hebrews 2:17–18). When this redemptive purpose was complete, Christ was exalted to the right hand of the Father even while retaining his human nature. So the kenosis was Christ's temporary sharing of our condition in this life, while the incarnation was his becoming human. Although they began simultaneously, the incarnation continues after the kenosis ceases (Feenstra 1989, pp. 144–9).

In conclusion, the Christian doctrine of incarnation as defined at Chalcedon is based on biblical statements about Jesus Christ. Although scholars have offered criticisms of, and alternatives to, Chalcedonian Christology, no argument has established that Chalcedonian Christology is incoherent or self-contradictory. There are, moreover, at least two promising contemporary theories that attempt to defend Chalcedonian Christology.

Bibliography

Brown, R. E.: *An Introduction to New Testament Christology* (New York: Paulist Press, 1994).

Feenstra, R. J.: "Reconsidering kenotic Christology." In *Trinity, Incarnation, and Atonement: Philosophical and Theological Essays*, ed. R. J. Feenstra and C. Plantinga, Jr (Notre Dame: University of Notre Dame Press, 1989), pp. 128–52.

——: "Pre-existence and personal identity," *Logos: Philosophic Issues in Christian Perspective*, 11 (1990), pp. 127–42.

Hardy, E. R. (ed.): *Christology of the Later Fathers*, Library of Christian Classics (Philadelphia: Westminster Press, 1954).

Hick, J. (ed.): *The Myth of God Incarnate* (London: SCM Press, and Philadelphia: Westminster Press, 1977).

Hick, J.: *The Metaphor of God Incarnate: Christology in a Pluralistic Age* (Louisville: Westminster/John Knox Press, 1993).

Knox, J.: *The Humanity and Divinity of Christ: A Study of Pattern in Christology* (Cambridge: Cambridge University Press, 1967)

Macquarrie, J.: *Jesus Christ in Modern Thought* (London: SCM Press, and Philadelphia: Trinity Press International, 1990).

Morris, T. V.: *The Logic of God Incarnate* (Ithaca and London: Cornell University Press, 1986).

Norris, R. A., Jr (ed.): *The Christological Controversy* (Philadelphia: Fortress Press, 1980).

Swinburne, R.: *The Christian God* (Oxford: Clarendon Press, 1994).

68

Sin and original sin

PHILIP L. QUINN

According to an ancient conception, human faults are transgressions that pollute or defile, that is, produce stains or blemishes which somehow infect the transgressor from without. Because such transgressions need not be morally evil actions, the pollution they produce need not be identified with moral guilt. Hence the remedy for such pollution can be a ritual of purification and need not be a response appropriate to moral guilt. However, when human faults are conceived within the context of a relationship to a personal deity, it is natural to think of them as offenses against the divine will. And when the deity is taken to be morally perfect, it is also natural to think of human faults as morally evil actions that produce guilt. The concept of sin is the concept of a human fault that offends a morally perfect God and brings with it guilt.

The natural home of the concept of sin is in the major theistic religions of Judaism, Christianity, and Islam. They share the idea that personal or actual sins are individual actions that are contrary to the will of a morally perfect deity. In the Hebrew Bible such sins are deviations from the norms of holiness that define the covenantal relationship between Yahweh and the chosen people. According to the Christian New Testament, Jesus teaches that human wrongdoing offends the person whom he addresses as Father. The Qur'an portrays personal sins as acts in opposition to Allah that spring from human pride. The first section of this article discusses personal sins.

The doctrine of original sin is distinctively Christian. Its scriptural warrant is to be found in the Epistles of Paul, and an interpretation of the Pauline texts worked out by Augustine of Hippo in the course of his controversy with the Pelagians has had an enormous influence on Western Christianity. The second section of this article is devoted to the Augustinian conception of original sin and the elaboration of it in the writings of Anselm of Canterbury and Jonathan Edwards. On the Augustinian view, the Fall of Adam and Eve recounted in Genesis 3 had catastrophic consequences for the human race. All the descendants of the first humans, except Jesus and his mother, inherit from Adam and Eve guilt for their first sin and so are born bearing a burden of guilt. Because it attributes innate guilt to humans, this account of original sin is morally problematic. The final section of this article focuses on the alternatives to the Augustinian conception set forth by John Locke, Immanuel Kant, Søren Kierkegaard, and Richard Swinburne.

Personal sins

Personal sins are individual human actions that offend God; they are actions contrary to the will or to the commands of God. Because God is taken to be morally perfect (see Article 30, GOODNESS) by the major theistic religions, all moral wrongdoing will be contrary to the will of God and hence will be sinful. According to divine command ethics, an action is morally wrong just in case and only because it is contrary to a divine command (see Article 57, DIVINE COMMAND ETHICS). On this view, if God did not exist and so there were no divine commands, no actions would be either morally wrong or sinful.

Most theists do not subscribe to such a divine command conception of ethics. According to the majority view, much of morality is independent of the existence and will of God. Divine prohibitions do not make such things as murder, torture, or rape wrong; they serve instead to reinforce an independent morality. Murder is, so to speak, doubly wrong in virtue of being forbidden by God; it is both a wrong against the victim and a wrong against God. But murder would still be morally wrong even if it were not sinful because God did not exist. For actions of this type, moral wrongness is independent of sinfulness.

Not all actions are of this type. It is morally wrong not to express gratitude to benefactors. If God created us and our lives are on the whole good, we have a duty to express gratitude to God for the gift of life. It would be morally wrong and hence sinful to fail to do so. However, if there is no God, life is not a gift and we have no duty to express gratitude to God if we have good lives. In that case it would be neither morally wrong nor sinful to fail to express gratitude to God. So some omissions are such that both their moral wrongness and their sinfulness depend on the existence and actions of God. For such omissions, moral wrongness is not independent of sinfulness.

On the majority view, then, two kinds of personal sin can be distinguished. There are actions or omissions that are morally wrong whether or not God exists and are also personal sins if God exists. And there are actions or omissions that are neither morally wrong nor personal sins if God does not exist but are both morally wrong and personal sins if God exists.

A distinction between objective and subjective personal sin can also be drawn. A human person who does something objectively offensive to God sins objectively and acquires objective guilt. A human person who does something he or she believes to be offensive to God sins subjectively and acquires subjective guilt. Theists who believe that an erring conscience binds will want to allow for cases in which, on account of a mistaken belief about the moral wrongness of an action, a person does what is subjectively but not objectively wrong and so sins subjectively but not objectively. The guilt a personal sin brings with it renders the sinner liable to punishment by God if the sinner satisfies appropriate conditions on responsibility for the deed. A person who sins both objectively and subjectively and whose true beliefs about what offends God are well justified may deserve severe punishment. But a person who sins objectively but not subjectively and whose lack of true beliefs about what offends God does not result from culpable ignorance may deserve little or no punishment.

Christians who hold that hell is a place of everlasting divine retributive punishment for serious personal sins sometimes try to justify belief in such a harsh doctrine of hell by claiming that serious personal sins are infinitely offensive to God. It would seem that only an infinite offense could suffice to justify a punishment that is infinite in virtue of being everlastingly protracted in time. But it is hard to make sense of the idea of a personal sin being infinitely offensive to God, and the supposition that a human sinner could deserve infinite retributive punishment by a morally perfect deity is very problematic. Christians need not adopt this harsh conception of hell, since their traditions allow for alternatives to it (see Article 71, HEAVEN AND HELL). If they opt for a less harsh alternative, they can argue that the relations among personal sin, guilt before God, and desert of punishment are parallel to and no more problematic, morally speaking, than the relations among wrongdoing, moral guilt, and desert of sanctions of various sorts in common morality. This is not the case for Augustinian original sin.

Augustinian original sin

The development of the doctrine of original sin begins with the story of the Fall of Adam and Eve in Genesis 3. When they disobey a divine command not to eat the fruit of a certain tree, God punishes them by subjecting them to toil, suffering, and death. Being subject to such things is part of their legacy to us. But the story does not say that they are punishments in our case, and it does not suggest that we have inherited from the first humans a burden of guilt. That suggestion is made by the Epistles of Paul.

Paul reads the Hebrew Bible as full of anticipations of things that only come to fruition in the life of Jesus Christ. His powerful rhetorical contrast of Adam and Christ begins thus: "Therefore, just as through one man sin entered the world and with sin death, death thus coming to all men in as much as all sinned" (Romans 5:12). It concludes thus: "Just as through one man's disobedience all became sinners, so through one man's obedience all shall become just" (Romans 5:19). The carefully balanced contrasts in the second of these verses suggest that all become guilty as a result of Adam's disobedience. The obedience (good action) of one man (Christ) is that through which all shall (future) become just (positive ethical status), and so, if the set of contrasts is to be complete, the disobedience (bad action) of another man (Adam) must be that through which all became (past) sinners (negative ethical status). But this would imply that all acquired the negative ethical status of being sinners through Adam's sin, which would make sense on the assumption that guilt is somehow transmitted from Adam to his progeny in a way that parallels the transfer of justice from Christ to those who benefit from his atoning work (see Article 69, ATONEMENT, JUSTIFICATION, AND SANCTIFICATION).

Augustine explicitly makes this assumption. He insists that "when the first couple were punished by the judgment of God, the whole human race, which was to become Adam's posterity through the first woman, was present in the first man" (*City of God*, p. 271). All humans were present in Adam, according to Augustine, because human nature itself was present in Adam's semen. And he goes on to claim that "because this nature has been soiled by sin and doomed to death and justly condemned, no man was to be born of man in any other condition" (*City of God*, p. 279). On Augustine's view, then, all of us are born soiled by sin and justly condemned, and this condition is part of what we would today refer to as our genetic endowment, since it is transmitted biologically from Adam to his descendants by means of male semen. When he tries to defend this astonishing doctrine of innate and biologically inherited sin and guilt against his Pelagian opponent, Julian of Eclanum, who rejects it, Augustine frequently appeals to the authority of Pauline texts such as Romans 5:12 and 5:19.

Many contemporary biblical scholars doubt the legitimacy of the appeal to Romans 5:12, arguing that Augustine misunderstood that verse because he read it in Latin translation rather than the original Greek. Apparently he took it to say that through one man sin entered the world and with sin death, death thus coming to all men, *in whom* all sinned (rather than *in as much as* all sinned), and he then mistakenly supposed that the final clause referred back to the one man, Adam, which led him to conclude that Adam's sin brought about not only universal death but also universal sin and guilt. But even if this conclusion is not supported by Romans 5:12, it does seem to be supported by Romans 5:19, and so it has some basis in scriptural texts. The Augustinian view of original sin was accepted by most Western Christian thinkers for more than a millennium. It bears a striking resemblance to the ancient conception of a pollution that infects people from without. Christians often describe the sacrament of baptism, which is a ritual of purification, as cleansing the soul from the stain of original sin.

The Augustinian doctrine of original sin was elaborated in the work of great medieval philosophical theologians such as Anselm. On his view, each human person is a metaphysical composite that includes both a nature, which makes him or her human like others, and a principle of individuation, which makes her or him a particular person, distinct from all others. Original sin is contracted with human nature at the very origin of one's existence as a person; it is therefore innate and unavoidable. It consists of a will that lacks proper orientation because it is not subject to God's will. Anselm is innovative in characterizing the process whereby sin and guilt are transmitted from Adam and Eve to their progeny in terms of a two-way principle that is causal but not specifically biological. It states that "as what is personal passes over to the nature, so what is natural passes over to the person" (*The Virgin Conception and Original Sin*, p. 202). By the first half of this principle, the sin Adam and Eve committed when they ate the forbidden fruit caused human nature itself to become sinful; by its second half, sinful human nature in turn causes their descendants to be sinful and guilty from the first moment they possess it. And Anselm's logical acuity permits him to draw a shocking consequence from his elaboration of the Augustinian doctrine. It is that infants who die unbaptized, before having committed any personal sins of their own and so with only the stain of original sin on their souls, are condemned by God to exclusion from the kingdom of heaven.

Critics of Augustine and Anselm have argued that moral guilt cannot be transmitted from one person to another by biological or other kinds of causal mechanisms. If the critics are correct the Augustinian doctrine of original sin needs revision. Is there a way to understand how all of us could become guilty on account of the first sin of the first humans without assuming that guilt is transmitted causally from them to us? The federal theology of the Reformation proposed that we become guilty in virtue of Adam's sin not by way of causal transmission but by way of divine imputation. According to federalism, Adam was, by covenant with God, the federal head or representative of the entire human race. All of Adam's posterity underwent probation or testing in him, and so guilt for his sin is justly imputed to them by God in consequence of his having fallen while acting by covenant as their representative. Federal theologians allow that a disposition to commit personal sins is causally transmitted from Adam to his progeny, but they insist that guilt for Adam's first sin extends to his descendants because God imputes it to them in accord with the terms of a covenant. Jonathan Edwards uses the ideas of federal theology as one strand in his defense of a traditional doctrine of original sin; he describes Adam in legal terms as a "public person, or common head" (Edwards 1970 [1758], p. 396).

It is, however, far from clear that this revision suffices to render the doctrine of original sin morally unproblematic. Although our legal and moral practices allow for circumstances in which one person can be held liable for the actions of another, they do not allow for circumstances in which one person can become guilty of another's wrongdoing. It seems that one must have performed an act to be guilty of it, and it also seems that one person cannot perform another's act. So the doctrine of original sin remains objectionable even when it is revised along the lines proposed by the federal theologians. Criticism of it abounds in modern philosophy.

Modern philosophical critiques

Christians would have fewer reasons to endorse the harsh Augustinian doctrine of original sin if it could be shown to lack the sort of scriptural support Augustine took it to have. John Locke tried to show this by reinterpreting the Pauline texts cited by Augustine. In his *A Paraphrase and Notes on the Epistles of St Paul*, his procedure is to quote a verse, then to offer his own paraphrase of it, and finally to argue for the paraphrase in an appended note. The paraphrase of Romans 5:12 goes as follows: "Wherefore to give you a state of the whole matter from the beginning. You must know, that as by the act of one man Adam the father of us all, sin enterd into the world, and death, which was the punishment annexed to the offence of eating the forbidden fruit enterd by that sin for that Adams posterity thereby became mortal" (Locke 1987 [1707], p. 523). Having substituted "became mortal" for "sinned" at the end of the verse, Locke has blocked both the inference that sin is inherited and the inference that death is in Adam's posterity a punishment for sin. In the note he tries to justify this substitution by claiming that Paul is here employing metonymy, that is, substituting the cause for the effect, sin in Adam being the cause of his mortality and, through him, the cause also of the mortality of his progeny.

545

Similarly, the paraphrase of Romans 5:19 is this: "For as by one mans disobedience many were brought into a state of mortality which is the state of sinners soe by the obedience of one shall many be made righteous. i e be restord to life again as if they were not sinners" (Locke 1987 [1707], p. 527). The justificatory note is terse: "*Sinners*. Here St Paul uses the same metonymie as above ver. 12 putting *sinners* for *mortal* whereby the Antithesis to righteous is the more lively" (p. 527). If Locke's metonymy gambit were successful across the board, we could always paraphrase away talk of Adam's disobedience making his descendants sinners in favor of talk of Adam's disobedience making his descendants mortal, thereby undercutting the scriptural support for Augustinian original sin. Unfortunately, many biblical scholars would deny that this Lockean stratagem is uniformly successful.

One might have philosophical grounds for rejecting Augustinian original sin even if one were unsure what to make of scriptural passages that seem to support it. In *Religion within the Limits of Reason Alone*, Kant rejects the doctrine of inherited sin and guilt, saying that "however the origin of moral evil in man is constituted, surely of all the explanations of the spread and propagation of this evil through all members and generations of our race, the most inept is that which describes it as descending to us as an *inheritance* from our first parents" (Kant 1960 [1793], p. 35). Yet Kant has a substitute for the doctrine of original sin in his philosophy of religion; it is his doctrine of radical evil in human nature. According to Kant, there is in all humans, as far as we can tell, a morally evil propensity to evil, and he once even calls it *peccatum originarium*.

A propensity, as Kant defines it, is a predisposition to crave a delight which, when once experienced, arouses in its possessor an inclination to it. People with a propensity for whiskey, for example, do not desire whiskey before they first drink it, but once they have tried it they develop a craving for it. Kant regards propensities of this sort as physical because they belong to people considered as determined by laws of nature. Since what is determined by laws of nature is morally indifferent, physical propensities are morally indifferent. Hence if all propensities were physical, a propensity to evil in humans would not itself be morally evil. So there must be non-physical propensities if there is to be a morally evil propensity to evil in humans. According to Kant, nothing is morally evil but libertarian free acts and their products, and so a morally evil propensity to evil has to be a product of an exercise of libertarian freedom. He tells us that, though the propensity to evil can be represented as innate, it should not be represented as merely innate, for it should also be represented as brought by humans upon themselves. It can be represented as innate because, as the underlying ground of all morally evil actions in their lives, it is to be thought of as present in its possessors antecedent to all such actions and so represented temporally as present in them as far back as birth. It should be represented as brought by its possessors upon themselves because, being morally evil, it has to be a product of libertarian freedom for which its possessors can be held morally accountable. And it can be represented as brought by its possessors upon themselves, Kant thinks, because it can be thought of as, and actually is, the product of an atemporal act of noumenal libertarian freedom on the part of each of its possessors.

On Kant's view, therefore, there is radical and innate evil in human nature only in the sense that, as far as we can tell, each and every human has brought upon himself or herself a morally evil propensity to evil by an act of noumenal libertarian freedom. This propensity is not in any way causally transmitted to us from our remote ancestors; in particular, it is no part of the genetic endowment that comes to us through sexual procreation. Nor is it divinely imputed to us. But because it is a product of the exercise of noumenal libertarian freedom, we are morally accountable and so guilty for having brought it upon ourselves. Whether Kantian radical evil makes better philosophical sense than Augustinian original sin depends heavily, of course, on the plausibility of Kant's assumption that there are atemporal acts of noumenal libertarian freedom. Many philosophers do not find this assumption even remotely plausible.

In *The Concept of Anxiety*, Vigilius Haufniensis, Søren Kierkegaard's pseudonym, conducts a simple psychological orienting deliberation on the dogmatic issue of hereditary sin. The result of this deliberation is the conclusion that there is no such thing as inherited sin and guilt. Haufniensis insists that every human is initially innocent. For every human individual, "innocence is always lost only by the qualitative leap of the individual" and "guilt breaks forth in the qualitative leap" (Kierkegaard 1980 [1844], pp. 37, 41). Like Kantian acts of noumenal libertarian freedom, qualitative leaps are not causally determined and so cannot be given deterministic scientific explanations. According to Haufniensis, we are like Adam and Eve in that we all leap directly from innocence into guilt and nothing inherited pushes us over the edge of the precipice. He tells us that "a person can say in profound earnestness that he was born in misery and that his mother conceived him in sin, but he can truly sorrow over this only if he himself brought guilt into the world and brought all this upon himself" (p. 38). So we become guilty only when we commit personal sins, which are free qualitative leaps in the wrong direction and for which we can be held morally accountable.

Although original sin has not been a major issue in the philosophy of religion of the twentieth century, Christian philosophers such as Richard Swinburne have added to the criticism of the Augustinian doctrine (see Swinburne 1989, ch. 9). He acknowledges that a proneness to sin is innate in humans; it stems from strong selfish desires that are part of our evolutionary heritage. But because, like Kant and Kierkegaard, he holds a libertarian view of freedom, he insists that the bad desires in which the proneness to sin consists incline without necessitating and so do not suffice to bring about, or inevitably issue in, actual wrongdoing. And Swinburne emphatically rejects the doctrine of original guilt, according to which all of Adam's descendants are guilty for Adam's first sin. No one, he argues, can be guilty for the sins of another person unless he or she had an obligation to deter that person and failed to do so. Since no one alive today could have had an obligation to deter Adam and Eve from sinning, we cannot be guilty for their first sins. Swinburne notes that there is scriptural support for his view: "The son shall not bear the iniquity of the father, neither shall the father bear the iniquity of the son; the righteousness of the righteous shall be upon him, and the wickedness of the wicked shall be upon him" (Ezekiel 18:20). According to Swinburne, the only

547

exception to the prophet's claim is the guilt we acquire when we violate obligations to deter others from wrongdoing.

In my opinion, the critics of the Augustinian doctrine of original sin are correct in thinking that we are not born bearing a burden of guilt for the first sins of the first humans which comes to us by way of causal transmission or by way of divine imputation (see Quinn 1992). We are guilty only for our own morally evil actions, and so we acquire guilt only by committing personal sins. Christians who share this opinion should also share Locke's concern to interpret biblical verses such as Romans 5:12 and 5:19 in ways that do not support the Augustinian doctrine.

Bibliography

Anselm of Canterbury: *Why God Became Man and the Virgin Conception and Original Sin* (1100), tr. J. M. Colleran (Albany: Magi Books, 1969).

Augustine of Hippo: *City of God* (426), tr. G. G. Walsh, D. B. Zema, G. Monahan, and D. J. Honan (Garden City: Doubleday, 1958).

Edwards, J.: *Original Sin* (1758), ed. C. A. Holbrook (New Haven and London: Yale University Press, 1970).

Kant, I.: *Religion within the Limits of Reason Alone* (1793), tr. T. M. Greene and H. H. Hudson (New York: Harper & Brothers, 1960).

Kierkegaard, S.: *The Concept of Anxiety* (1844), tr. R. Thomte (Princeton: Princeton University Press, 1980).

Locke, J.: *A Paraphrase and Notes on the Epistles of St Paul* (1707), ed. A. W. Wainwright (Oxford: Clarendon Press, 1987).

Quinn, P. L.: "On demythologizing evil," In *Discourse and Practice*, ed. F. Reynolds and D. Tracy (Albany: State University of New York Press, 1992), pp. 111–40.

Swinburne, R.: *Responsibility and Atonement* (Oxford: Clarendon Press, 1989).

69

Atonement, justification, and sanctification

JOHN E. HARE

This article is about the central Christian doctrines about God's work in our salvation, as these doctrines are, or should be, topics in philosophy. The theological labels for these doctrines vary in different traditions within Christianity, but I shall use the terms "atonement," "justification," and "sanctification."

The problem of the moral gap

The problem in philosophy which I shall take to be addressed is the problem about how it is possible for a human being to lead a life pleasing to God, and one which continues appropriately in heaven after physical death. The problem is not about whether we ought to lead such a life; but given the damage that sin has done to our natural capacities (see Article 68, SIN AND ORIGINAL SIN), it might seem that we do not now have the ability to lead such a life, and hence cannot justly be held accountable for the failure to live it. Morality, as we are familiar with it, has a three-part structure. There is, first, the demand on us, interpreted differently by different authors but including centrally, as Jesus put it, the demand to love God with all our heart and mind and strength and to love our neighbors as ourselves. Within the Christian tradition, however, and in many places outside this tradition, there is agreement that this demand is too high for us to meet with our natural capacities, which form the second part of the structure. Aristotle, for example, tells us that the best life "would be superior to the human level," but we ought not to follow the proverb writers, and "think human, since you are human," or "think mortal, since you are mortal"; rather, as far as we can, we ought to be immortal (*Nicomachean Ethics* X, 7,1177b26–34). The third part of the structure is an at least possible being who not only does have the capacity to live a perfect life, but is seen as the source of the demand on us. This being is God, in the Christian tradition. Moral theorists who do not like to talk of God can conform to the structure either by adding to human capacities (R. B. Brandt talked of an ideal observer, and R. M. Hare of an archangel), or subtracting (John Rawls talked of a counterfactual veil of ignorance about our particular place in society). The moral gap presents us with a problem, or antinomy; if it is not the case that we can live by the moral demand, then it is not the case that we ought to live by it. The doctrines that form the subject of this article are doctrines about how the holy being who is the third part of the structure intervenes to forgive our failures and to change our capacities (the second part of the structure), so that we become able to live by the demand (the first part of the structure).

In the way Augustine presents this three-part structure, it might seem that it falls foul of the principle that "ought" implies "can." Augustine says, "God bids us do what we cannot, in order that we might know what we ought to seek from him" (*On Grace and Free Will*, xvi. 32). But the principle is in fact preserved; for what is impossible is not our *doing* what God bids, but our doing it *without his help*. The purpose of the law, Paul says, is to bring us to grace. Martin Luther compares children learning to walk, when their parent tells them to come, "or do this or that, only in order that it may appear how impotent they are, and that they may be compelled to call for the help of the parent's hand" (*Bondage of the Will* 152). Here the objection might be made that God is omnipotent; so that in this expanded sense of "can" (where it encompasses what I can do with God's assistance) I can jump to the moon. Surely this is expanding "can" too far. But in Christian doctrine God offers us the assistance to do what he asks us to do, and he does not ask us to jump to the moon. We have a real possibility of living the kind of life God wants us to live, not merely because he *can* help us to live it, but because he *offers* to help us live it.

Kant

I will start with the treatment of this question in Immanuel Kant, since he raised it clearly and has been central in the discussion ever since he wrote. Kant refers to what he calls Spener's problem (after the famous Lutheran pietist), "How can we become *other* men and not merely better men (as if we were already good but only negligent about the degree of our goodness)?" (Kant 1979, pp. 97, 54; I will put Kant references from the English translation first, and from the Prussian Academy edition second.) We all of us start off, Kant holds, in subjection to what he calls "the evil maxim," which tells us to put our own happiness first and duty second. We are thus corrupt in the very ground of our more specific maxims, all of which take their fundamental moral character from this one. Kant is clear that duty puts us under the good maxim, which reverses the order of incentives, telling us to follow after happiness only so long as the maxims of our actions pass the test of the categorical imperative. A life under the good maxim must, therefore, be possible for us, according to the principle that "ought" implies "can." But how is this revolution in us to be accomplished, since the human propensity to evil is radical, and inextirpable by human powers? Kant says that our extirpation of the propensity could only occur through good maxims, and therefore cannot take place when the ultimate subjective ground of all our maxims is postulated as corrupt. Kant's solution to this impasse is to appeal to "a higher, and for us inscrutable, assistance" (1960, pp. 41, 45).

Kant concedes that Reason cannot, either in her theoretical or practical employment, *use* maxims about God's assistance. But we may be required none the less, he says, to make room in our belief for doctrines from special revelation which do not come to us through Reason, in order to escape what I referred to above as Spener's problem (see 1960, pp. 48, 53). There are also, he thinks, *translations* of the doctrines of atonement, justification, and sanctification available for use by Reason.

First, atonement. Under our initial bondage of the will, Kant says, we enter into all sorts of bad habits which remain with us even after the revolution of the will which takes us under the good maxim. Kant calls the person before this revolution, "the old man," and the person afterwards, "the new man," following Paul's language in his epistles (e.g. Ephesians 4:24, Colossians 3:10). Kant distinguishes between revolution and reform. Revolution is a change of heart, the reversal of the basic ground of all our maxims, and it is seen only by God. What we experience, on this side of the veil of ignorance, is the slow process of reform. The new man, Kant says, is punished on behalf of the old man, and this allows God to reward the sinner justly with eternal life (1960, pp. 67, 73). This is Kant's translation of the view which sees the atonement in terms of penal substitution, where Christ takes on himself as our substitute the just punishment for our sins. Christ's vicarious punishment cannot be used in its historical version by Reason because Reason does not take cognizance of the historical particularities of Golgotha, and also because (Kant thinks) guilt is not a liability that can be transmitted from one person to another. In Kant's translation, Christ is the new man. He undergoes punishment because of the pain involved in remorse and self-discipline and reparation for the failures of the old man, which occurred before and continue after the revolution of the will.

Atonement, on this translation, presupposes that the revolution of the will has taken place. How, then, does Kant translate the logically antecedent doctrine of justification, which in Lutheran theology is God's work of counting us just? Kant says that after the birth of the new man, the heart as it is seen by God is "essentially well-pleasing to him," even though all we can ever experience is gradual improvement, infinitely extended. Kant is not saying here that our experience, and the temporal sequence by which it is informed, are illusory. He is saying, rather, that God, whose intuition is not limited by the temporal sequence, can see the stable disposition of the heart. He judges us as a completed whole "through a purely intellectual intuition" (1960, pp. 60, 67). Intellectual intuition, in Kant's doctrine, is productive or constitutive; when God sees us as "essentially well-pleasing to him," he makes us so. As the Lutheran *Formula of Concord* puts it (III, 2), he "bestows and imputes to us the righteousness of the obedience of Christ; for the sake of that righteousness we are received by God into favor and accounted righteous." When God looks at us, he sees his Son, because he is imputing to us his Son's righteousness. This doctrine would not be usable by Reason if we did not translate God the Son as humanity in its moral perfection, and God the Father as the Idea of holiness. With these translations, we are no longer using "God" as a term with singular reference. The doctrine becomes a way of saying that a human being comes to have a morally good disposition when the Idea of holiness counts the disposition as instantiating humanity in its moral perfection.

The work of God the Spirit is translated for use by Reason in terms of sanctification, or the gradual discipline which leads to a greater conformity of a person's life (both internal and external) to the demands of the moral law. The difficulty that motivates Kant here is that perseverance in the life of duty requires some assurance of "the reality and constancy of a disposition which ever progresses in goodness" (1960, pp. 61, 67). He thinks of this good disposition as a "good spirit" controlling us. But this disposition is not something that Kant thinks I can see directly since I do not have God's ability to see things as they are in themselves. I do have access to it, however, indirectly, by observing my actions (which are, Kant says, its appearances). I can see, if indeed my life is under the good maxim, a fundamental improvement in my way of life, judged by moral standards.

Kierkegaard

These versions of atonement, justification, and sanctification can be seen also in Søren Kierkegaard's description of Judge William, who represents the ethical life in *Either/Or*, volume 2. Judge William does not represent only Kant's account of the ethical life as this is lived within the constraints of the translated doctrines about God's assistance; but he represents at least this account, and gives us a vivid phenomenology of how this life and the transition into it feel from the inside. In the judge's description of the transition from the aesthetic into the ethical life, the self or spirit becomes conscious of itself in the despair caused by the inability of the aesthete to keep his (*sic*) own life interesting. This new subject takes on responsibility for the failures of the old one, and his despair is his own recognition of the failures which are consequently his own. But in choosing this despair, he becomes conscious of his freedom, and is enabled to return to the particular engagements of his life by choosing them in the light of this freedom. It is appropriate to think of this transition in terms of atonement because the judge talks about "losing himself" in order to "find himself." What is required is the suffering of the new man on behalf of the old, a suffering which the judge calls "repentance." "I repent myself out of the whole of existence," he says. "Repentance specifically expresses that evil essentially belongs to me and at the same time expresses that it does not essentially belong to me" (1987, vol. 2, p. 224). In what sense does evil essentially belong to me? The judge's point is that in choosing myself as guilty, as having failed, I collect together all my previous "choices" out of their dispersion within the aesthetic life and accept responsibility for them all; I recognize that none of them were choices for myself as a whole or for myself as free. In what sense does evil not essentially belong to me? Those previous "choices" represent a failure of which I am no longer guilty in my new nature, though I take on responsibility for them from my past nature. If I do take on responsibility for them, in repentance, I am (the judge says) ransoming myself in order to remain in my freedom (1987, vol. 2, p. 232). The structure of repentance, as the judge describes it, is recapitulated (as is much in Kierkegaard) in Martin Heidegger's *Being and Time* (especially pp. 325–48) under the heading of the call of conscience; but there is not space in this article to describe Heidegger's appropriation of the idea.

The language of justification comes in when the judge discusses the problem of the exception, the man who cannot live the ethical life. The judge recognizes himself in this discussion, and tries to use the language of Christian doctrine to get out of the difficulty. Here Kierkegaard is relating his own experience, "I had my thorn in my flesh, and so I did not marry and could take no position. . . . I could have gotten anything I wanted, but in its place I became the exception" (*Journals and Papers* 7 (1): A 126, 5913). The ethical life is the position of the "universally human," which requires, the judge says, marrying and working for a living. Kierkegaard discovered himself to be an "exception," a man who has placed himself outside the universal. Even if the judge is wrong about what the ethical life requires, he is right, according to the structure of the moral gap described at the beginning of this article, in thinking that the moral demand is unreachable by our own devices. The judge tries the expedient, as the aesthete does in volume 1 of *Either/Or*, of thinking that his own suffering can be the occasion for his being justified. "[The exception] will perhaps experience at some time the joy that what caused him pain and made him inferior in his own eyes proves to be an occasion for his being raised up again and in a nobler sense becoming an extraordinary human being" (1987, vol. 2, p. 331).

Alternative solutions to the problem of the gap

There is something unsatisfactory about both the judge's account and Kant's translation of the doctrines for use by Reason. Kierkegaard is conscious of this, and puts the objection (amongst other places) at the very end of *Either/Or*, in the words of a sermon by a pastor who is a friend of the judge. The emphasis of this sermon is that whatever we do, we are in the wrong in relation to God. We can put the point in terms of a dilemma. Either we should reject the notion of extra-human assistance or we should retain it. If we reject it, we are left with the antinomy. If we retain extra-human assistance, we have additional resources to show the possibility of the revolution of the will. But now we cannot stay within the constraints of what Reason can use (at least as Kant understands them).

In general there is a problem for anyone who accepts the existence of a moral gap, as described above, but wants to deny the possibility of divine assistance. Roughly, there are three ways out of this antinomy other than the religious. The first is to keep the demand as high as it is in Kant, and then exaggerate our natural capacities so that they are adequate to the demand. Utilitarianism, though it does not need to be optimistic in this way, has from its beginning exaggerated the powers of moral education to make us fit for the moral demand. The second way is to recognize that our natural capacities are not adequate to such a demand, and to modify the demand so as to fit the capacities. There are, for example, some feminist and communitarian theorists who hold that we do not have universalized moral obligations. This would not necessarily reduce the moral demand; for it might be that the particularist obligations we do have, on these theories, are just as demanding (though different). But there are many non-philosophical examples of theories which do reduce the demand (such as the rational-emotive psychotherapy of Albert Ellis). The third way is to admit the gap, and posit some non-theological or naturalistic mechanism for bridging it. Three types of such mechanism come to mind. First, there is the mechanism of evolution, which (it might be urged) produces under the disguise of moral principles a counterweight to our natural but counteradvantageous tendency to prefer our individual interests. Second, there is rational decision theory, which (it might be suggested) works like an invisible hand to convert self-interest into coordination. Third, there is the possibility that history moves by a Hegelian but non-theistic progress of the spirit through cultural and societal transformation. If we do not have the expectation that any of these mechanisms can bridge the moral gap, we will be left with the antinomy.

The traditional doctrines

There are different ideas within the Christian tradition about how atonement works. I will mention the main alternatives, and attach names (though the views of these authors about the atonement are complex, combining some of the ideas which follow). One idea, suggested by Augustine and many of the early fathers, is that Christ was paying ransom to the forces of evil; our lives were owed to Satan, because of our sin, and Christ's death was the price paid to Satan to secure our release. Another idea, to be found in Anselm, is that Christ's death is compensation or satisfaction paid to God the Father instead of the punishment which properly belongs to sinners; by sinning we fail to give God his due, and so dishonor him, and God's justice requires that this deficit be made good. A third idea, present in Grotius, is that God, by accepting Christ's death, preserves the visible moral order of the world, of which he is governor. A fourth idea, found in Abelard, is that Christ's death is the consequence of his life of perfect obedience, and that this life and death together have the power to transform us as a model of what human life should be. The Bible contains a rich variety of images to describe Christ's death, including centrally the notion that he freely became a sacrifice for us and that we are identified with him in his death and resurrection. It is not necessary to accept only one of these ideas of atonement and reject the others, for they all have roots in biblical language, and any theology of the atonement which wants to be faithful to this language has to reflect this variety.

Justification is the act by which God declares us just or righteous, or pleasing to him. Again there are many alternative ideas within Christianity about how to understand this doctrine. One large question is whether the justification is external and "forensic," and Christ's righteousness is imputed to us without any internal change in us; or whether the declaration of our righteousness recognizes a change in our inner condition, by which Christ's righteousness is imparted to us and not merely imputed.

Different from both justification (if it is seen as external) and regeneration (the birth of the new life within us, if this is seen as happening all at once), will be the gradual process of reform by which our lives become more pleasing to God. There are large theological differences within Christianity about the question of what sort of cooperation there is, if any, between us and God in these various aspects of

554

our salvation, and about the extent of the change in our nature (whether, for example, we become ourselves divine). Finally, there are long-standing disputes about the scope of God's work; whether all human beings, for example, are encompassed in the scope of the atonement, or only those pre-elected by God for such benefit.

These differences in doctrine should all be seen, however, within the constant frame of the structure with which I started this article, the structure of the moral gap. There are important and interesting philosophical issues that reside in the differences, issues for example about divine and human freedom and about the relation between action and character. But the overall philosophical significance of the doctrines about God's work in our salvation lies in the solution they offer to the problem of the moral gap.

Bibliography

Grensted, L. W.: *A Short History of the Doctrine of the Atonement* (Manchester: Manchester University Press, 1920).

Hare, J. E.: *The Moral Gap: Kantian Ethics, Human Limits and God's Assistance* (Oxford: Oxford University Press, 1996).

Heidegger, M.: *Being and Time*, tr. J. Macquarrie and E. Robinson (San Francisco: Harper & Row, 1962).

Kant, I.: *Religion within the Limits of Reason Alone*, tr. T. M. Greene and H. H. Hudson (New York: Harper Torchbooks, 1960).

——: *The Conflict of the Faculties*, tr. M. J. Gregor (New York: Abaris Books, 1979).

Kierkegaard, S.: *Either/Or*, tr. H. and E. Hong (Princeton: Princeton University Press, 1987).

Rossi, P. J., and Wreen, M. (eds): *Kant's Philosophy of Religion Reconsidered* (Bloomington: Indiana University Press, 1991). [Especially articles by Allen W. Wood, Nicholas P. Wolterstorff, and Leslie A. Mulholland.]

Swinburne, R.: *Responsibility and Atonement* (Oxford: Clarendon Press, 1989).

70

Survival of death

STEPHEN T. DAVIS

Introduction

Do human beings survive bodily death? Many answers to this question have been given. Some affirmative answers amount to what might be called weak senses of survival. We survive death, it is said, in that we pass our genes, or our influences, or our accomplishments on to future generations. Or we survive death in that we always remain precious to God in God's memory.

But suppose we ask the question in a more robust sense: do human beings survive death in the sense that they continue to exist after bodily death as conscious persons? Four main answers have been given to this question. First, we do not survive death in any strong sense. Second, we survive death through successive reincarnations. Third, we survive death because our immaterial selves or souls are immortal. Fourth, we survive death because our bodies will be resurrected.

This article is a philosophical reflection on that aspect of Christian theology that concerns survival of death. Of the four possible answers to the question with which we began, it is clearly the last – resurrection of the body – with which Christian theology is most closely associated. As to the first answer, very few Christians have ever held that "death ends all." As to the second, a few avant-garde theologians, especially in the twentieth century, have suggested that reincarnation is compatible with Christianity, but Christian tradition virtually unanimously holds that it is not. With the third answer – immortality of the soul – we encounter a theory that has had a complicated relationship with Christian thought, one that we will discuss. But, as noted, resurrection is the most common Christian answer to our question, so we will talk about it in some detail.

Initial problems

Two problems impede progress on a topic of this sort. The first is the obvious fact that the Christian theological tradition does not speak with one voice on the issue of survival of death. As noted, virtually all Christians affirm that human beings will indeed survive death through some type of resurrection, but Christian teaching about this topic is embedded in larger topics (the nature of God, Christology, sin, justification, eschatology, etc.) about which there is often disagreement. Although this article will attempt to speak from the perspective of what the author perceives to be the center of the Christian theological TRADITION (see Article 75) on this topic, the fact that a significant pluralism exists in Christian circles must be kept in mind.

Second, there are at least two difficult philosophical issues that affect what can be said about survival of death. The first is the so-called mind–body problem, i.e. the problem of explaining the relationship between the mind and the body, or between brain states and mental states, in the human person. The two main sorts of theories that are relevant to our concerns are: (1) materialist or physicalist theories, i.e. those that say that human beings are entirely physical objects, and that there is no such thing as an immaterial mind or soul; and (2) dualist theories, i.e. those that say that human beings consist of both physical bodies and immaterial souls or minds, and that the soul or mind is the essence of the person. Although most Christian thinkers who write about this topic are dualists, a few have defended materialism. It should be noted that a majority of contemporary philosophers who write about the mind–body problem, especially those who are not theists, are materialists of one sort or another (see Article 55, THEISM AND THE SCIENTIFIC UNDERSTANDING OF THE MIND).

The second relevant philosophical issue is the so-called problem of personal identity. This is the problem of establishing the criteria that can be used for identifying and reidentifying persons. On what basis can we say that a certain person who will exist in the afterlife is "the same person" as a person whom we knew on earth? Some emphasize what is called the bodily criterion – the one is the same person as the other if and only if they have the same body. Others emphasize what is called the memory criterion – the one is the same person as the other if and only if they have the same mental characteristics, e.g. memories, beliefs, and personality traits. Obviously, for people who accept the first criterion, bodily resurrection is the only survival of death theory that is available to them. Anybody who believes in immortality of the soul (or reincarnation, for that matter) is committed to the view that the memory criterion by itself can suffice to establish personal identity.

Is survival of death coherent?

Several twentieth century philosophers have argued that the very idea of survival of death, especially incorporeal survival of death, is incoherent (see Flew 1987, and Perry 1978). So it will be important to see whether those arguments can be answered. Let me focus on two of them from John Perry.

Perry first argues that immaterial souls cannot establish personal identity. Since souls, if they exist, are unobservable, we do not know who has what soul or even how many souls a person has. No thesis having to do with the presence or absence of a soul – or of a certain soul – is ever testable; there are no criteria for determining "the same soul." But since we clearly are sometimes able to make secure identity claims (we do successfully recognize and reidentify people), it follows that personal identity cannot consist of sameness of soul.

But surely Perry's argument is based on conflating the notion of *criteria* of personal identity with that of *evidence* for personal identity. He is quite right that souls do not readily count as evidence of personal identity; we cannot, for example,

557

prove that a given person in the afterlife is the same person as a person whom we knew on earth on the grounds that they possess the same soul. This is because, as Perry says, the presence or absence of a soul is not something for which we can successfully test. Still, identity of the soul might be a criterion of personal identity in that the following rule is true: any two temporally separate people are indeed two different temporal episodes of one and the same person if and only if they have the same soul. How we would ever know that at different times they have the same soul – apart, perhaps, from divine revelation – is another matter.

Perry's second argument is that the memory criterion of personal identity, which those who believe in immortality of the soul must rely on, is never sufficient to establish personal identity. This is because memory is fallible: there are past events that we can't remember, and even past events that we misremember. So how do we distinguish – as we must if the memory criterion is to suffice – between genuine memories and only apparent memories? If memory is all we have to go on, no personal identity claims can ever be established. The mere fact that some purported Jones in the afterlife claims to be the Jones we knew on earth – and makes this claim on the grounds that he "remembers" events in Jones's life from Jones's perspective – cannot by itself establish that he is Jones.

Of course if we are talking about bodily resurrection (as Christians normally would), the bodily criterion will presumably be usable too. But even if there is no body, or no knowledge of a body, it still seems that secure identity claims can be made. So far as a *criterion* of personal identity is concerned, all that needs to happen is that God ensure that all Jones's apparent memory claims in the afterlife be genuine memory claims. That, by itself, will solve the criteriological problem. But so far as *evidence* of personal identity is concerned, it seems that secure identity claims can be made quite apart from the bodily criterion in cases where there are many memories, from many people, cohering together and confirming each other. If the purported Jones is recognized by scores of other purported people who knew Jones on earth, and after rigorous testing is accepted by them as Jones, it would be irrational to deny or even doubt that the purported Jones is Jones. Doubt would still be conceivable but irrational.

H. H. Price's classic article "Survival and the idea of 'another world' " (Price 1953), written in 1953 but not widely noted till much later, also supports the conceivability of immortality. Price posited a world of mental images (visual, auditory, telepathic) in which souls are aware of each other's presence, live in a real world (consisting of mental images rather than material objects), communicate with each other telepathically, and have dreamlike (as opposed to bodily) perceptions of their world. Such a world, Price suggests, may have different causal laws than our present world does (e.g. wish-fulfillment may be powerfully efficacious), but it will seem to its denizens just as real and even as "solid" a world as our world does to us.

Price's theory has been criticized. John Hick, for example, argues that it is hard to combine Price's theme of the public, non-solipsistic nature of the world he describes with the theme that the character of the world will be at least in part a function of the wishes of its inhabitants (Hick 1976, pp. 265–77). If it is a public world, sustained by telepathic contact between different individuals, how can wish-fulfillment be as potent a force in shaping it as Price suggests? Hick is doubtless correct in detecting a tension in Price's account, but the problem certainly seems solvable. If there turns out to be no way to reconcile the two themes, the wish-fulfillment one can be jettisoned without damaging the core of Price's argument. In any case, it is widely held by philosophers that Price's article goes a long way toward establishing the coherence of disembodied survival of death.

Immortality and resurrection

Immortality of the soul and resurrection of the body have an interesting and complicated relationship in Christian theology. Traditional Christian theories – e.g. those of Aquinas (*Summa contra Gentiles*, 4.79.11) – combine the two, arguing that after death there is an interim period during which we exist in an attenuated state as mere disembodied souls (with our bodies decaying in the ground), and that only later in the eschaton will our bodies be miraculously raised by God and reunited with our souls, thus making us whole persons again.

This picture was challenged by New Testament scholar Oscar Cullmann, in an influential 1956 essay entitled "Immortality of the soul or resurrection of the dead?" (Cullmann 1973 [1956]). Cullmann radically separated the two theories, arguing that only resurrection is a genuinely Christian notion, and that immortality is an alien theory imported from Greek philosophy. It played no role in primitive Christian conceptions of the afterlife, and ought not to be part of Christian belief today.

Surely Cullmann is correct in distinguishing the two theories. Immortality theory says that souls naturally survive death; resurrection theory says that human persons survive death only if God miraculously intervenes and resurrects them. Immortality theory holds that the body is the intrinsically evil prison-house of the soul; resurrection theory holds that both body and soul were created by God, are now equally corrupt due to sin, and are thus equally in need of redemption. Immortality theory recognizes death as a friend (at least, as Plato says, to the philosopher) precisely because it means escape from the body; resurrection theory sees death as a frightening enemy that must be defeated.

But Cullmann seems too hasty in rejecting any notion of immortality as unchristian. Surely the traditional and Thomistic notion of the bodiless interim state can easily be purged of the problematic aspects that Cullmann correctly sees in some versions of immortality. The survival of death of even the soul can be attributed to a gracious and miraculous act of God; it can be affirmed that souls as well as bodies need to be redeemed; and death can still be seen as an enemy. Furthermore, the traditional notion provides a way of resolving a tension that otherwise can be said to exist in the New Testament concerning the time of entry into eternal life. Pauline thought especially stresses the idea that the general resurrection occurs at the eschaton (2 Thessalonians 2:1–15); yet Jesus said to the "good thief" on the cross, "Today you will be with me in paradise" (Luke 23:43). The solution is that the thief's soul went immediately to paradise (as ours will, when we die), only much later in the eschaton to be reunited with his body (and the same will be true for us).

Resurrection

Resurrection is the doctrine that after death the body disintegrates, but at some point in the future God will miraculously raise it from the ground and reconstitute the whole person. As noted, the traditional Christian notion of resurrection combines with immortality into a doctrine that might be called temporary disembodiment: When I die my body disintegrates, but I continue to exist; for an interim time I exist in the presence of God as a disembodied soul only; then one future day God will raise my body, reunite it with my soul, and constitute me a whole and complete person again.

The resurrection of Jesus, for which I will not argue in this essay (but see Davis 1993), is taken by Christians to be the guarantee or "first fruits" of the general resurrection (Romans 8:11; 1 Corinthians 15:20, 23; Philippians 3:20–1; 1 Thessalonians 4:14; 1 John 3:2). Thus the ability of Christians to defend the coherence and plausibility of the resurrection of all human beings depends in part on their ability to defend the plausibility of the resurrection of Jesus.

Many people today find the very idea of resurrection absurd, and it must be admitted that the physics of resurrection raises some fascinating difficulties. Let me mention the oldest philosophical objection ever raised against resurrection. Virtually all of the church fathers who discussed resurrection tried to answer it. What if a Christian dies at sea and his body is eaten by various sea creatures who then scatter to the oceans of the world? How can God possibly resurrect that body? Or what if another Christian is eaten by cannibals, so that the material of her body becomes the material of their bodies? And suppose God later wants to raise all of them, both the Christian and the cannibals. Who gets which bodily particles? How does God decide?

This objection presupposes something that the church fathers were all willing to assume, but which contemporary defenders of resurrection rarely do, namely, that resurrection entails that God must use the very same matter, the same atoms or "stuff," of which the original body consisted. Indeed, the fathers argued that if God wants to resurrect a given person Jones who lived and then died, God must find and reassemble the same material of which Jones's earthly body consisted. Otherwise the raised "Jones" will not be Jones. Modern defenders of resurrection typically see no need to make this assumption. It could be entirely new matter that God uses – so they insist – but it will still be Jones in the eschaton as long as the new atoms are structured or configured in a completely Jones-like way. I myself agree with this last claim. Still, if the objection to resurrection with which we are dealing can be answered, then God will be able in the eschaton to raise people in the way that the fathers envisioned (if that is what God wants to do). Let us then see if the objection can be answered.

What the fathers typically did in response to this objection was appeal to omnipotence. You or I might not be able to locate and reconstitute the relevant atoms of someone's body, but an all-powerful God can. And as long as (1) the basic constituents of matter (atoms, let's say) endure through time, as of course they normally do, and (2) God's only problem, so to speak, is to locate, collect, and reconstitute the relevant atoms, the church fathers were surely correct. It seems that an omnipotent being could do that.

But with the cannibalism case and other imaginable cases where God must decide which constituent parts shared at different times by two (or even two thousand) separate persons go where, the problem is more serious. God must have some kind of rule or policy. Saint Augustine made the interesting suggestion that atoms will be raised in the human body in which they *first* appeared (see Augustine's *Enchiridion* lxxxviii). Others have suggested that some constituent parts of human bodies are essential to those bodies and others are not. So in raising Jones, for example, God need only locate those atoms that are or were essential to Jones, having already ensured that they have never appeared (or have never appeared as essential atoms) in any other body. Perhaps God will use them as building blocks around which to reconstruct the rest of Jones's body out of entirely new atoms.

Eschatology

As noted, Christian beliefs about resurrection are embedded in larger teachings about eschatology, which is the study of the last days and the end of history. The central Christian claim about history is that it is linear, that it moves in a certain direction, that it aims toward a goal or culmination. For history in general, that goal is the end-time victory of God, which includes the return of Christ, the new heaven and the new earth (Revelation 21:1), and the kingdom of God. For believers, it is (1) the transformation of their earthly bodies into new resurrection bodies that are fit for the kingdom of God, and (2) the beatific vision in which they will see God (Revelation 22:1–4). These experiences will be so transforming that Paul can say, "I consider that the sufferings of this present time are not worth comparing with the glory about to be revealed to us" (Romans 8:18).

Bibliography

Aquinas, Thomas: *Summa contra Gentiles* (Notre Dame: University of Notre Dame Press, 1975).

Augustine, Aurelius: *The Enchiridion on Faith, Hope, and Love* (Chicago: Henry Regnery, 1961).

Cullmann, O.: "Immortality of the soul or resurrection of the dead?" (1956). In Terence Penelhum (ed.): *Immortality* (Belmont, CA: Wadsworth, 1973).

Davis, S. T.: *Risen Indeed: Making Sense of the Resurrection* (Grand Rapids: William B. Eerdmans, 1993).

Flew, A.: *The Logic of Mortality* (Oxford: Basil Blackwell, 1987).

Hick, J.: *Death and Eternal Life* (New York: Harper & Row, 1976).

Perry, J.: *A Dialogue on Personal Identity and Immortality* (Indianapolis: Hackett, 1978).

Price, H. H.: "Survival and the idea of 'another world,' " *Proceedings of the Society for Psychical Research*, 50 (1953), pp. 1–25.

561

71

Heaven and hell

JONATHAN L. KVANVIG

Philosophical reflection concerning heaven and hell has focused on the place of such doctrines in the great monotheistic religions of Judaism, Christianity, and Islam. The philosophical issues that arise concerning these doctrines are not limited to such traditions, however. Any religion promises certain benefits to its adherents, and these benefits require some contrast that befalls, or might befall, those who fail to meet the demands of the religion in question. This contrast to the benefits the religion proffers will raise many, if not all, of the same philosophical concerns raised by the vivid imagery that has come to be associated with the doctrine of hell in Western culture. Here the focus will be on the philosophical issues arising out of such doctrines in Christianity. Such narrowing still preserves in microcosm the general philosophical contours any religion will encounter when it advocates certain patterns of life and rejects others.

In the history of thought about hell, the fundamental issue has always been whether consignment to hell could be fair or just. This problem arises in the context of the *punishment model of hell*, which traditionally is elaborated in terms of four separable theses:

1 the *punishment thesis*: the purpose of hell is to (retributively) punish those whose earthly lives and behavior warrant it;
2 the *no escape thesis*: it is metaphysically impossible to get out of hell once one has been consigned there;
3 the *anti-universalism thesis*: some people will be consigned to hell; and
4 the *eternal existence thesis*: hell is a place of conscious existence.

The *traditional doctrine of hell* in Christianity is just this particular elaboration of the punishment model; this doctrine, or a minor modification of it, has been maintained by most theologians in the history of Christianity. The minor modification arises from the doctrine known as the harrowing of hell, according to which between the time of Jesus' death and resurrection, he preached to the inhabitants of hell, some of whom accepted his message and thereby went to heaven. Those who accept such a doctrine deny the no escape thesis, for they believe that some have escaped hell. The alteration required as a result of this doctrine has no practical effect on us, however, for the event was unique and unrepeatable. Hence, I will ignore this modification here.

Throughout the history of Christianity many have denied both the traditional doctrine and the minor modification just discussed. Annihilationism and the related position called conditional immortalism accept the punishment model, maintaining theses (1) to (3) while denying the eternal existence thesis. On such views hell is understood in terms of non-existence. Second chance theories accept all of the above except the no escape thesis, preferring instead a view of hell on which it is possible to leave hell and enter heaven. Universalists deny only the claim that some people will be consigned to hell, insisting that a God of love either could not or would not allow anyone to suffer the disaster of hell. Worries about the justice of hell have also led to a denial that heaven and hell are exclusive and exhaustive of afterlife possibilities. For example, the need for a doctrine of limbo, the residents of which include children short of the age of accountability and "innocent savages" who have never heard the Christian message, arises from the perceived injustice of the traditional doctrine.

Each of these views accepts the punishment model of hell. One of the strongest arguments for the centrality of the punishment model in the history of Christian thought is that there is no standard alternative to the traditional doctrine of hell that accepts theses (2) to (4) above and denies the punishment thesis. This fact strongly suggests that in the history of Christian thought, the fundamental understanding of hell is in terms of punishment, with other features of hell less central and more easily surrendered in the face of perceived difficulties.

The effectiveness of these alternatives at providing a *mitigation* of the severity of the traditional doctrine is suspect, however, for it is simply false that the alternatives to the traditional doctrine somehow escape the philosophical difficulties perceived in the traditional doctrine. Annihilationism, for example, views the cessation of existence as somehow preferable to unending conscious existence in hell. Our ordinary conceptions of punishment, however, view capital punishment as far more severe than life imprisonment. Annihilationism can only be viewed as a mitigation of the traditional doctrine when the latter is confused with the literary depictions of hell, such as those found in Jesus' parable of the rich man and Lazarus or in Dante's descriptions of hell, central to which is the conscious experience of torturing flames, of fire and brimstone. These literary vehicles make a considerable impression on the psyches of those who hear them, and are thereby superior communicative devices in one respect to the philosophical treatise. The danger, however, is to confuse the packaging with the doctrine itself, which occurs when annihilationism is thought to be a mitigation of the severity of the traditional doctrine. For there is nothing in the traditional doctrine that requires hell to be a place of torture. Such language, as well as the contrasting language of outer darkness, must be treated as the metaphorical language it is, the literal significance of which is to signal an ending for a person that is as bad as anything can be (consistent, of course, with the moral perfection of God). When understood as such, it is clear that annihilationism makes no advance over the traditional doctrine on the issue of the justice of hell; if anything, it appears to raise greater concern about the justice of hell inasmuch as capital punishment is more severe than life in prison.

Universalism is a failure as well. Even if God would secure the presence of everyone in heaven, the problem of the perceived injustice of hell remains. For the

traditional understanding of God not only attributes to him perfect goodness in the actual world, it also portrays God as incapable of being evil in any respect. So if it is merely contingent that all are saved and thus avoid hell, this universalist position only modally masks the problem. If God is incapable of evil and sending a person to hell is always unjust, then there simply cannot be any metaphysically possible world in which anyone goes to hell. That is, it cannot be a merely contingent truth that all are saved; it must instead be a necessary truth. If so, however, presence or absence in heaven or hell has nothing to do with libertarian free will, for if universalism is a necessary truth, then no matter what a person chooses, he or she simply could not choose to go against God. Such a price for avoiding the problem of hell is high, indeed, for it undermines an appeal to free will in attempting to address the problem of evil (see Article 50, THE PROBLEM OF EVIL).

Second chance views fare no better. Some views that go by that name are not alterations of the traditional doctrine at all, but merely insist that because of the severity of hell, consignment to it is postponed after death to give persons a second chance to avoid it. Yet, if such a second chance is deserved, so would be a third chance, launching an infinite sequence of delays. Since an infinitely delayed punishment is no punishment at all, such views are committed to denying the justice of hell altogether. A more appropriate response, in place of such a second chance view, would be to offer an acceptable account of hell, or simply deny the existence of it altogether.

Other second chance views claim that consignment to hell cannot be postponed, but that escape from it is not impossible; all that is needed to get out is the same change of heart, mind, and will required in one's earthly life to be "fit for heaven." Such views face a serious dilemma when they are proposed as a mitigation of the traditional doctrine. On the one hand, if defenders of this type of second chance view hold that the traditional doctrine is not philosophically problematic, it is unclear why one should prefer doctrinal novelty to fully adequate orthodoxy. On the other hand, if the traditional doctrine is deemed problematic because it involves a too severe punishment, a second chance at avoiding such a punishment does not solve the moral problem. Such a second chance doctrine merely substitutes a conditional punishment for an unconditional one, and conditional punishments are subject to the same demands of retributive justice as unconditional ones. For example, if cutting off an arm is an inappropriately harsh retribution for stealing a piece of candy, so is the conditional retribution of cutting off an arm unless an apology is given. Refusing to apologize simply does not make the act of stealing more egregious than it was before. It does show a need for greater character reform, but by hypothesis consequentialist interests are not relevant here, for both the traditional doctrine and second chance theories view hell in terms of retribution for lives and behavior that are unfit for heaven.

The problems listed above are substantive difficulties facing alternatives to the traditional doctrine, but there are also more formal defects that plague such views. Viewed more formally, heaven and hell should be seen as the exclusive and exhaustive eschatological options: one is either with God eternally or one is not, corresponding respectively to heaven and hell. This formal conception raises problems both for the second chance view above and for the doctrine of limbo. Second chance theories are affected because they cannot adequately account for the eschatological dimension of the doctrine of hell. Eschatology is the doctrine of the last things, and one feature of this idea of culmination or consummation is that there is a finality to it. If heaven and hell are mere extensions of an earthly life, where people can pack up and move at will, the doctrines of heaven and hell reduce to doctrines concerning the *next* things, rather than the truly *last* things. Formal difficulties also plague the emendation of the traditional doctrine of hell that results from positing the existence of limbo. Since to be in heaven is to be with God and to be in hell is not to be with God, there can be no third option in the afterlife. The temptation to violate this formal constraint arises when a doctrine of hell appears inadequate, perhaps by punishing too severely some that do not belong in heaven. If the formal constraint above is ignored, it is tempting to posit some third alternative where the harshness of hell can be avoided. The doctrine of limbo arises in precisely this way, from the perceived injustice of the traditional doctrine of hell (and some further claims about what avoiding hell requires). A better approach, however, would be to address the defects of one's conception of hell than to introduce new and indefensible metaphysical dimensions to the afterlife.

The failure of the usual alternatives to the traditional doctrine of hell still leaves that doctrine with its fundamental problem, which is that on it, some people receive an infinite punishment for sins that are not infinitely serious. The standard reply to such a complaint is that it matters not only what the character of your sin is, but also who the sin is against when determining appropriate punishment. Such a response, however, presumes some way of ranking individuals so that sinning against beings higher on the scale is more wrong than sinning against beings lower on the scale. Furthermore, this ranking will have to yield the result that sinning against God deserves infinite punishment. This position is difficult to maintain. Even if it is granted that sin against God is infinitely bad, punishment deserved is not directly correlated with the seriousness of wrong done. Killing is one of the worst things one can do to a human being, but some ways of doing something so seriously bad deserve no punishment at all (accidental killings, for example, or killings in a just war). Punishment deserved must be a function both of the seriousness of wrong done and of some further information about the intentions of the person doing the wrong, and one's basic conception of hell must take into account the possibility that some people never deliberately strike at God (even if it is a contingent truth that all actual persons do so).

This problem motivates positions on the nature of hell that deny the punishment model of hell. On a promising alternative model, hell is conceived in terms of something a person chooses. Hell may be a place where some people are punished, but the fundamental purpose of it is not to punish people, but to honor their choices. There are a variety of conceptions of hell falling within this alternative model, and the fundamental issue facing this choice model of hell is the nature of the choice in question. What exactly is the content of that choice; how must people conceive of their options when deciding in order to choose hell over heaven?

565

My own view is that such a choice requires a clear understanding that the fundamental options are either to be with God and all that being with God requires, or to reject that option. If so, the issue of annihilation is a central issue for the choice model, for there is no possibility of existing without dependence on God. Furthermore, God's perfect goodness constrains him to aim for our perfection always, so a choice to be independent of God, if fully informed, would be logically equivalent to a choice for annihilation.

This discussion of the doctrine of hell reveals how Christian thought on the doctrine has centered around the question of the justice of hell. Reflection on the doctrine of heaven, however, has not focused as much on issues of fairness or justice. Instead, the primary concerns have centered around issues such as whether true happiness or blessedness is possible for those in heaven (perhaps one's memories never fade sufficiently to allow perfect blessedness, or perhaps the suffering of the damned in hell prevents such bliss), why faith or belief in God is a prerequisite for presence in heaven, and whether it is possible to leave heaven once one is there. There are, however, two indications of concern about the justice of heaven in Christian thought. The first is reflected in the central position of the doctrine of justification in Christian theology. This doctrine presents in summary form the entire point of the Christian faith: that through the saving work of Jesus, the broken relationship between God and humans is restored, with the result that those redeemed by God in this way come to share his presence in heaven (see Article 69, ATONEMENT, JUSTIFICATION, AND SANCTIFICATION). The attempt to answer the philosophical issues arising from reflection on the justice of heaven trace to St Paul's argument of the first chapters of Romans that God is both just and a justifier of sinners; that there is no logical conflict inherent in this conjunction, in spite of the fact that a classic example (in the Hebrew Bible and in ordinary intuition) of an unjust judge is one who lets the guilty go free. The doctrine of justification undertakes to show that there is no contradiction between the claims that God is perfectly righteous, just, and holy, that human beings are sinners, and that God justifies such individuals, thereby allowing them a place in heaven. Without an adequate doctrine of justification, Christianity could no longer view heaven as primarily the culmination of God's gracious response to the human condition. Instead of having a doctrine of heaven centering on the concept of grace, one could at most have a concept focusing on reward: heaven would be a reward for those sufficiently responsible in their lives and behavior to God's requirements.

The second aspect of the history of Christian reflection about heaven that signals a concern for the justice or fairness of it is the doctrine of purgatory and the correlative partitioning of heaven so that differential rewards are given to different individuals. The doctrine of purgatory holds a special place in this regard, however, for it is one thing to think that some individuals deserve a greater reward than others, and it is quite another thing to think that some individuals must undergo the inconvenience of purgatory in compensation for failures of the past or for the purpose of character development in preparation for the most blessed experience of (other regions of) heaven. Whereas the point of the doctrine of justification is to relieve Christianity of the charge that its understanding of heaven threatens the righteousness of God, the point of the doctrine of purgatory can be taken to be to rebut the claim that God bestows his grace in a profligate manner. There is both an unfairness involved in granting the same heavenly experience to those redeemed only at the last moment between the saddle and the soil and those whose youthful redemption is followed by lifelong service and faithfulness to God, and an incoherence in maintaining that true blessedness can be experienced by those whose lives and character are still corrupted by sin and evil desires.

Given human nature, it is not surprising that the issues of justice that arise regarding the doctrine of hell have received much more attention than those surrounding the doctrine of heaven. Most of us are much more comfortable with getting undeserved benefits than with shouldering unfair burdens. A point to notice, however, is that the doctrines of heaven and hell are not separable in this way. They are intimately linked, and the account one accepts of one constrains the kind of account one can develop of the other. These points may seem obvious to some, but they have been ignored regularly, especially in discussion of the nature of hell. If we think of hell as a place of punishment, the logical contrast would seem to indicate that heaven is a place of reward. Yet, the Christian conception denies that heaven is fundamentally a reward for faithful service; it is, rather, the free and gracious gift of a loving God, unmerited by anything we have done. Another way to put this tension is to note that explanations of presence in heaven and presence in hell seem to have little in common. On the usual presentation, presence in heaven is explained in terms of God's love, not his justice or fairness, whereas presence in hell is explained in terms of his justice rather than his love. Such explanations are at best incomplete, for love and justice often pull us in different directions regarding how to treat people. Some ways of treating people are just, but unloving; and some ways are caring, but less than fully just. At the very least, some explanation is required concerning the interaction of the motives God has in establishing heaven and hell.

More can be said, however. In the Christian view, God's fundamental motive must be conceived of in terms of love rather than justice. Justice has no hope of explaining the two great actions of God, creation and redemption; only love can account for them. If so, one's account of hell ought also to accord with this hierarchical conception of God's motivational structure. In particular, it will not do to portray God as fundamentally loving until we start discussing the nature of hell, and suddenly portray God as fundamentally a just God.

The most straightforward way to give a unified account of heaven and hell is to portray each as flowing from one and the same divine motivational structure. Whereas the punishment model of hell has difficulty doing so, the choice model can do so easily. If hell is constructed to honor the choices that a free individual might make, it is not hard to see how a fundamentally loving God could so construct it. For in truly loving another, we often must risk losing the other, and part of loving completely requires leaving open the possibility that such love remains unrequited forever. Such a unified conception of heaven and hell has the philosophical capacity to meet the formal and substantive constraints on the doctrine of hell discussed earlier, and as such presents a suitable model for what a philosophically adequate conception of heaven and hell must look like.

Bibliography

Adams, M.: "Hell and the God of justice," *Religious Studies*, 11 (1975), pp. 433–47.

Hick, J.: *Death and Eternal Life* (London: Collins, 1976).

Kvanvig, J. L.: *The Problem of Hell* (New York: Oxford University Press, 1993).

Lewis, C. S.: *The Problem of Pain* (London: Macmillan, 1973).

Stump, E.: "Dante's hell, Aquinas's moral theory, and the love of God," *Canadian Journal of Philosophy*. 16 (1986), pp. 181–96.

Swinburne, R.: "A theodicy of heaven and hell." In *The Existence and Nature of God*, ed. A. J. Freddoso (Notre Dame: University of Notre Dame Press, 1983), pp. 37–54.

Talbott, T. P.: "The doctrine of everlasting punishment," *Faith and Philosophy*, 7 (January 1990), pp. 19–43.

Walls, J.: *Hell: The Logic of Damnation* (Notre Dame: University of Notre Dame Press, 1992).

72

Providence and predestination

THOMAS P. FLINT

Throughout the history of Western monotheism, the belief in divine providence has been a central element of religious faith. The God who has created us, theists insist, has not left us on our own; rather, the events of our world, no matter how chaotic or disturbing they might appear, unfold precisely according to the plan established eternally by our all-knowing and loving sovereign.

In this article, this traditional notion of providence will first be articulated. Two perennial problems raised by the traditional concept, problems concerning freedom and evil, will then be described. Next, four general types of reactions to these problems will be considered, along with the manners in which these four positions tend to explicate a central component of the Christian conception of providence – namely, predestination. The article will conclude with some evaluative remarks concerning these four pictures of providence.

The traditional notion of providence

The traditional idea of providence has both biblical and non-biblical roots. Though the word "providence" is nowhere found in the Bible, Scripture speaks clearly and repeatedly of a God who knowingly and lovingly exercises detailed control over his creation. Nothing, we are told, escapes his gaze (see, e.g., Psalm 33:13–15). Whole nations are in his hands as is clay in the hands of the potter (Jeremiah 18:1–6). Even seemingly chance events are in fact determined by God (Proverbs 16:33), whose plan provides for the needs of all his children (Matthew 6:26–34). While scriptural sources have been predominant in the development of the notion of providence, other factors have also played a role. Chief among these has undoubtedly been the Greek tradition, which includes influential affirmations of at least a rudimentary notion of providence both by philosophers (e.g. Xenophanes, Plato, and many of the Stoics) and by other literary figures (e.g. Herodotus, Aeschylus, and Sophocles).

The traditional notion of providence which grew from these various roots – a notion defended by such varied historical figures as Philo, Justin Martyr, Origen, Augustine, Anselm, Thomas Aquinas, Duns Scotus, William of Ockham, Martin Luther, John Calvin, Francisco Suarez, and Gottfried Leibniz – is in essence a picture óf how a God who is perfect in knowledge, power, and love relates to his creation. Being omniscient (see Article 29, OMNISCIENCE), God has complete and detailed knowledge of his world – its history, its current state, and its future. Being omnipotent (see Article 28, OMNIPOTENCE), God has complete and specific control over that world, a world which has developed and will continue to evolve in accord with his sovereign and never-failing will. Being omnibenevolent (see Article 30, GOODNESS), God has used his knowledge and power to fashion and execute a plan for his world which manifests his own moral perfection and the inexhaustible love he bears for his creation. According to the tradition, then, to see God as provident is to see him as knowingly and lovingly directing each and every event involving each and every creature toward the end he has ordained for them.

Problems with the tradition

Despite the dominance of the traditional notion in Western thought, significant questions have been raised about the coherence and the plausibility of that view. Two general problems with the tradition, those concerning human freedom and evil, have elicited the most discussion.

Freedom has been seen as inconsistent with providence because divine providence implies divine foreknowledge, and such foreknowledge seems to rule out human freedom. For if God knows that I will, say, buy an iguana next year, then this is something he has always known. If it is true that God held, say, ten years ago the relevant belief concerning my future iguana-buying, then the fact that he held this belief is something over which no one now has any control, for no one has power over the past. So I have no control over the fact that God believed ten years ago that I would buy an iguana next year. Since God cannot possibly be mistaken, his believing that something will happen entails that the event in question will occur. Therefore, my buying an iguana is a necessary consequence of a fact over which I have no control. Purchasing the iguana, then, is not something I can avoid doing; but if the action is thus unavoidable, it can hardly be considered free. This *argument from foreknowledge* has long been seen as posing a serious challenge to affirming the traditional concept of providence (see Article 37, FOREKNOWLEDGE AND HUMAN FREEDOM).

Evil also appears to challenge divine providence. According to the tradition, God has a plan for the world and its inhabitants, a plan informed not only by his knowledge and power, but also by his love for his creatures. The existence of evil, especially evil of great intensity, extent, or duration, seems to disconfirm the existence of such a plan. A God of the traditional description, it has been argued, would surely know how to prevent such evils, have the power to prevent them, and desire that they be prevented. This *argument from evil* thus suggests that the traditional picture of a providential deity is misguided (see Article 50, THE PROBLEM OF EVIL).

Reactions to these problems

The ways in which advocates of providence have attempted to respond to these problems are many and varied. Though any attempt to categorize the multiform reactions runs a serious risk of misrepresentation or oversimplification, refusing to categorize them runs perhaps the greater risk of failing to discern the basic choices that the advocate of providence faces. Various systems of categorization might be proposed, but I believe that it is especially illuminating to consider how differing views of freedom lead quite naturally to differing reactions to the two problems with providence we have outlined.

Contemporary philosophers are in basic agreement that there are three general positions open concerning the relationship between freedom and determinism. First, one might endorse both

(1)   all actions are determined ultimately by events external to and not under the causal control of their agents

and

(2)   such determination is incompatible with human freedom.

This position is often referred to as *hard determinism*. Second, one might agree with the existence of the type of determining forces mentioned in (1), yet insist that (2) is false. Only some types of determination, one might contend, render actions unfree. So long as the agent in question is not acting under compulsion, or so long as the agent would have done otherwise had she so chosen, the fact that the action is ultimately externally determined should not be seen as robbing the agent of her freedom. This claim that freedom and determinism are compatible is frequently labeled *compatibilism*. Finally, one might agree with the rejection of compatibilism enunciated by (2), yet repudiate the deterministic claim encapsulated by (1). According to this third position, commonly called *libertarianism*, there are free actions, but no such action can be determined by anything not under the causal control of the agent.

Given these admittedly coarse-grained depictions of positions on freedom, three potential means of reacting to our problems with providence become immediately apparent: one might attempt to defend the traditional view from either a hard determinist, a compatibilist, or a libertarian stance. Call these three positions *determinist traditionalism, compatibilist traditionalism,* and *libertarian traditionalism.* As we shall see, some libertarians have argued that the third of these positions is incoherent, and hence that changes in the traditional account of providence need to be made if libertarianism is to be maintained. Hence, a fourth position, what might be called *libertarian revisionism,* must also be considered.

Though some remarks by Luther and other Reformers could be taken as pointing toward it, determinist traditionalism is a position with few explicit prominent adherents. On this view, human freedom is seen as an illusion, given the all-determining activity of God. Hence, in response to the first of our two problems with providence, the determinist traditionalist would resolve things by accepting the arguments for the incompatibility of freedom and providence, retaining the traditional notion of providence, and rejecting the existence of freedom. Evil on such a view would presumably be seen as in some way an instrumental part of God's good plan.

As noted, determinist traditionalism is not a position which has much support.

Each of the other three pictures of providence, though, has had numerous able proponents. Let us consider each of these pictures separately.

Compatibilist traditionalism

Far more influential than determinist traditionalism has been the second of our four pictures, compatibilist traditionalism. Many of the more ardent defenders of providence, from Reformed thinkers such as Calvin, Leibniz and Jonathan Edwards to Thomists such as Domingo Bañez and Reginald Garrigou-Lagrange, clearly belong in this camp, while many others, including such giants as Augustine and Aquinas, might also (though more controversially) be situated here. Compatibilist traditionalists insist that God, as first cause, is the ultimate causal determiner of all that takes place. As compatibilists, such theists insist that the efficacy of divine decrees is not inconsistent with genuine human freedom, for God determines not only the occurrence of events but also their mode (free or unfree). Many Thomists, for example, have argued that our actions would indeed be unfree were they the deterministic causal consequences of prior events, that is, were the type of physical determinism championed by most contemporary compatibilists true. Yet God, they insist, can still determine free actions, because no action can occur without God's concurrent activity. Hence, *as* the human agent acts freely, God simultaneously determines its act, thereby safeguarding both human freedom and divine control.

Compatibilist traditionalists have various means of dealing with the difficulties which freedom seems to raise with the traditional notion of providence. Some would insist that the argument from foreknowledge shows only that our free acts are ultimately under God's control, a conclusion which such theorists would argue ought not to concern us since, to be free, an act need be under only my proximate control, and such control is fully compatible with God's position as first cause. Other compatibilist traditionalists would base their response to the argument from foreknowledge on the thesis of divine eternity. If God is truly outside of time (see Article 32, ETERNITY), then it makes no sense to speak of him as literally foreknowing what will occur; rather, we need to think of God as having timeless awareness of all that occurs in time. Since the argument from foreknowledge was premised on the supposition that God is in time (and hence believed things ten years ago concerning, e.g., my iguana-buying), that argument dissolves once we see that divine eternity renders that supposition indefensible.

The questions which evil seems to raise for the traditional concept of providence would be addressed in various ways by compatibilist traditionalists. Most would insist that evil be seen as simply part of God's good plan for the world, a part which allows God's nature to be manifested more vividly than would otherwise be possible. Moral evil in particular would be viewed in this way. By seeing to it that some people sin but are still saved, God manifests his mercy and forgiveness; by seeing to it that some sin and are damned, he manifests both his justice and the gratuitousness of salvation. Not all members of this school would agree, though, on precisely how God sees to it that evil takes place. Some, such as Huldreich

Zwingli, suggest that evil can be seen as the direct causal consequence of God's activity. Others, such as Aquinas and many Thomists, insist that God cannot be seen as the actual author of evil. Rather, they suggest, evil occurs not because God causes it, but because he refrains from causing good. Hence, our sinful acts take place not because God causes us to sin, but because he declines to cause us to act virtuously; the evil act which results is thus a product of our own evil nature.

Libertarian traditionalism

By far the most prominent libertarian defenders of the traditional concept of providence have been the followers of Luis Molina (and, among the Reformers, of Jacobus Arminius). Molinists maintain that a libertarian account of freedom is both philosophically attractive and fully compatible with a strong picture of providence. As they see it, the key to this compatibility lies in God's possession of what they call *middle knowledge*. In addition to his natural knowledge (knowledge of necessary truths over which he has no control) and his free knowledge (knowledge of contingent truths over which he does have control), God also knows *counterfactuals of creaturely freedom* – conditionals specifying, for any free creature who might exist and any set of circumstances in which that creature might be placed and left free, what that creature would freely do if placed in those circumstances. Such conditionals would be contingent (since, according to libertarianism, free beings are not necessitated to act in a certain way by the circumstances in effect when they freely act), but would not be under God's control (since it is not up to God how one of his creatures would freely act); hence, God's knowledge of such truths would be neither natural nor free, but lie in the middle between these two. Given his knowledge of counterfactuals of freedom, God could tailor his actions relating to his free creatures so that he achieves his desired goals by putting those creatures into situations in which he sees they will freely act in such a way as to realize those ends. Middle knowledge provides a clear means of explaining how God would possess foreknowledge, since such knowledge would follow immediately upon God's supplementing his middle knowledge with his own volition to create certain individuals in specific circumstances. Similarly, given the infallibility of God's middle knowledge, it provides an ingenious means of combining a strong, risk-free picture of divine control over human affairs with an uncompromisingly libertarian account of freedom.

Though some libertarian traditionalists would respond to the argument from foreknowledge by appealing to divine eternity, more typical responses are to deny the claim that God's past beliefs are fixed elements of the past beyond our control, or (as Molina argued) to deny that the kind of necessity ascribed to God's past beliefs transfers to the future actions whose performance is entailed by those past beliefs. As for evil, though libertarian traditionalists could concur with compatibilist traditionalists on the fittingness of God's including evil in his world, they would insist that more avenues of response are open to them than to their compatibilist colleagues. For example, it follows from God's possessing middle knowledge that certain worlds which are logically possible for God to create are nevertheless such that God cannot create them, because his free creatures would not cooperate in the way necessary for the actuality of those worlds. Hence, certain evils may occur not so much because God preferred that they occur, but because he saw that there was no way to avoid them short of robbing his creatures of their freedom.

Libertarian revisionism

Especially in recent years, libertarian traditionalism has come under attack by libertarians who charge that middle knowledge is impossible because there are no true counterfactuals of creaturely freedom. According to these libertarians, there simply is no fact of the matter about what a free creature would do in a situation in which she is never placed, and hence nothing here to be known by God. Without middle knowledge, though, there is no way for a God who creates beings free in the libertarian sense to possess the type of knowledge and control affirmed by the tradition. Hence, these theorists conclude, the libertarian has no choice but to abandon that tradition and attempt to construct a revised model of providence.

Some libertarian revisionists (such as process theologians) advocate quite radical alterations in the tradition, such as relinquishing the notion that God is a free creator or rejecting his power ever to interfere with the freedom of his creatures. More influential recently among philosophers of religion has been a less extreme brand of revisionism which speaks of the open or risk-taking nature of God. On this view, a God without middle knowledge has at best knowledge of how his free creatures would *probably* act in various situations. Such probabilistic knowledge is insufficient to provide God with complete foreknowledge and severely limits his control over events, since sometimes his free creatures will react in improbable ways. Yet most such theorists look upon these limitations on divine power and knowledge as advantages, not drawbacks, to their position. As they see it, the traditional picture of providence is the unhappy result of an excessive Hellenization of biblical thought, a process which overemphasized the sovereignty and control of God at the expense of the open, responsive, often frustrated but never despairing God of Scripture. According to these libertarian revisionists, a God with only probabilistic knowledge of how his free creatures will react can still have some foreknowledge and an impressive amount of control, but not so much as to turn his creatures into manipulated puppets with whom he can have no genuinely personal relationships.

The manner in which these revisionists can respond to our two problems with providence should be evident. The argument from foreknowledge, they contend, is sound, and its lesson is that the traditional notion of providence is incoherent. And since God has no better course of action open to him than to follow those general strategies in dealing with his creatures which his probabilistic knowledge tells him are likely to work for the best, we have no reason to think that the specific evils which occur were either foreseen or in any sense intended by him. Hence, the claim goes, we are no longer inclined on this revised picture to blame God for evil, and so the argument from evil is at least severely weakened.

Applications to predestination

One way of spotlighting the differences between these four pictures of providence is to note the divergent analyses they would offer of the central Christian doctrine of predestination. According to this doctrine, salvation is ultimately much more a matter of God's choosing us than of our choosing God. Though under no obligation to bring any human infected with original sin to salvation, God gratuitously elects certain people to be saved and decides upon the specific manner in which this salvation will be effected – that is, he decides upon which graces will be bestowed upon which people. The effect of this divine election is that the elect are predestined to glory; their eternal bliss is sure to follow upon the natural and supernatural gifts showered upon them.

Few traditional Christians would disagree with this basic explication of the doctrine, but significant disputes have arisen concerning how precisely this sketch is to be filled out. For example, some Christians (most notably, Calvin) have embraced the thesis that God absolutely wills the salvation of only some people, while the others he unconditionally predestines to damnation. Others have rejected this thesis, and have insisted that the belief in God's universal salvific will must not be sacrificed in our explication of predestination. Similarly, Christians have disagreed concerning whether God's foreknowledge of how a particular individual will respond to an offer of divine grace is to be thought of as explanatorily prior or posterior to his election of that individual.

The existence and significance of these debates ought not to obscure the substantial agreement among traditional Christians concerning the doctrine of predestination. As one might expect, our four pictures of providence lead to predictably different elucidations of the doctrine. Determinist traditionalists would see freedom as having nothing to do with predestination; salvation is the simple causal effect of divine election, an effect in no way mediated by free human responses. Compatibilist traditionalists could, but need not, agree with this assessment. Though God's causal activities provide the ultimate explanation for everything that happens, many compatibilist traditionalists (e.g. most Thomists) will insist that the transformations which make heaven a fitting abode for the just are brought about via the free actions of the just, though these actions are determined by God's intrinsically efficacious grace. Similarly, many (though not all) compatibilist traditionalists will contend that even those not brought by God to salvation are given by him sufficient aid to make them able (in a compatibilist sense) to attain paradise. Libertarian traditionalists typically will reject the claim that God's grace is intrinsically efficacious. Divine assistance sufficient for salvation, most Molinists will insist, is given to all, but whether such grace is efficacious is ultimately up to the agent, not up to God. Of course, since God's middle knowledge informs him prior to any creative decision on his part just how any bestowal of grace would in fact be freely received, his power regarding salvation and reprobation remains quite extensive on the Molinist picture. For libertarian revisionists, though, this power is greatly diminished. Since God lacks middle knowledge, he has no way of knowing how his creatures will react to his gracious intervention,

575

and hence cannot genuinely predestine anyone so long as he respects their freedom. Though revisionists thus generally reject the traditional picture of predestination, they insist that God's probabilistic knowledge still affords him considerable impact on the lives of his creatures, and they suggest that God can have great confidence that many of his people will freely accept his offer of salvation, though his knowledge as to the identity of the saved is inevitably largely conjectural.

Evaluating the four pictures

Of the four pictures of providence discussed here, only one – deterministic traditionalism – lacks significant contemporary support. Each of the other three has been graced with vocal and vociferous proponents, and no sign of consensus is in sight.

As I see it, the case in favor of the libertarian traditionalist picture, though not demonstrative, is by far the strongest. Unlike the compatibilist traditionalist, the libertarian is not faced with attempting to defend a picture of freedom which is implausible philosophically and which can at best offer a convoluted and unsatisfying account of evil and damnation. Unlike the libertarian revisionist, the traditionalist is not forced to view God as having allowed his Church to adopt for virtually two millennia a fundamentally distorted picture of his relationship to his world, nor is the traditionalist left in the unsure hands of a myopic God who is little more than a good-hearted, odds-playing "bookie than which none greater can be conceived." Were the arguments against middle knowledge compelling, the theist would have no choice but to forsake either her libertarian inclinations or her commitment to the traditional notion of providence. Since Molinists have, as I see it, shown that the thesis of divine middle knowledge is resilient in the face of attack, the theist need not and should not embrace either of these unattractive alternatives. Libertarian traditionalism, then, seems the wisest picture of providence for the prudent theist to endorse.

Bibliography

Aquinas, Thomas: *Quaestiones Disputatae de Veritate* (1256–9), V and VI.
———: *Summa Theologiae* (1266–73), I, qs 22 and 23.
Calvin, J.: *Institutes of the Christian Religion* (1536–59), bk I, chs 16–17; bk III, ch. 21.
Flint, T. P.: "Two accounts of providence." In *Divine and Human Action*, ed. T. V. Morris (Ithaca: Cornell University Press, 1988), pp. 147–81.
Hasker, W.: *God, Time, and Knowledge* (Ithaca: Cornell University Press, 1989).
Helm, P.: *The Providence of God* (Downers Grove: InterVarsity Press, 1994).
Molina, L.: *Liberi Arbitrii cum Gratiae Donis, Divina Praescientia, Providentia, Praedestinatione et Reprobatione Concordia* (1595); tr. (of Part IV) A. J. Freddoso, *On Divine Foreknowledge: Part IV of the Concordia* (Ithaca: Cornell University Press, 1988).

73

Petitionary prayer

ELEONORE STUMP

Prayer comes in many varieties, including adoration, propitiation, impetration, and thanksgiving. There are also different forms of prayer. Some prayers are vocal and articulate; others are only mental. So, for example, certain forms of mystical prayer are said to consist just in rest and quietude in the sense of God's presence. In the view of some scholars, "prayer" is also broad enough to include sacrifice, dance, or other attempts to influence the supernatural, but without the use of words. Furthermore, even with regard to vocal prayers, there are distinctions to be drawn. Some vocal prayers are communal and liturgical, and their traditional content is part of the ritual of a religious community. Other vocal prayers are spontaneous or at least composed by the one praying the prayer. In addition, in some religious traditions, vocal prayer does not consist only in the words uttered but may also be a matter of timing, proper clothing, bodily orientation and sequence of bodily actions.

But these distinctions are mentioned here only to be set aside. Impetration or petitionary prayer raises special philosophical problems not raised by other varieties, and these problems arise whatever the form of the prayer. This article is therefore focused on petitionary prayer and takes no notice of the way the petition is expressed.

Petitionary prayer is a request made to a god or other supernatural entity for something specific believed to be good by the one praying the prayer. It is a feature of religion in every culture and period. The earliest written sources in China, for example, dating from the Shang dynasty (ca. 1766–1122 BCE), include inscriptions on bones, the so-called oracle bones, in which petitions are made to the spirits of ancestors regarding such things as success in hunts or wars or a favored royal consort's imminent labor and delivery. From the beginning of philosophy, philosophers, too, have recognized the importance of petitionary prayer for human life. In the *Timaeus* (27 b–c), for example, Plato has Socrates insist that the gods should be invoked before any serious scientific inquiry begins, and Critias, his interlocutor, responds by agreeing that no sensible person would fail to call upon God at the outset of any undertaking whatever. Even earlier, Confucius strongly recommended sacrifice and prayer. In the *Analects* (III.13), he indicates the miserableness of moral wrongdoing by saying "He who sins against Heaven has no one to whom he can pray."

As these examples show, petitionary prayer has been addressed to entities other than the deity of the traditional monotheisms. Even within Christianity, prayer is sometimes made not to the deity but to other supernatural entities, such as the saints, though such cases are often complicated and not straightforward examples of prayer to someone other than God. The official Catholic position regarding prayer to the saints, for example, is that saints are to be petitioned *only* for their prayers to God, who alone is to be petitioned for what is being sought directly in the prayer. In any event, the most challenging philosophical problems regarding petitionary prayer arise because the practice seems incongruent when the recipient of the prayer is supposed to be omniscient, omnipotent, perfectly good, and possessed of the other standard divine attributes (see Article 29, OMNISCIENCE; Article 28, OMNIPOTENCE; and Article 30, GOODNESS). So, what will be at issue here is petitionary prayer offered to God as traditionally conceived by Judaism, Christianity, and Islam.

It has sometimes been held that modern science shows petitionary prayer to be pointless. Some people have supposed, for example, that any answer to petitionary prayer would constitute a miracle (understood as a violation of a natural law) and that science rules out the possibility of MIRACLES (see Article 46). But this is not a particularly effective argument against the practice.

In the first place, science cannot rule out the possibility of miracles. Science is the study of nature and natural law, but nothing in the study of natural law can show that it cannot be violated by something outside nature. Even if we weaken the objection against petitionary prayer to the claim that the *practice* of science requires ruling out the possibility of miracles, the objection is not cogent. Scientific methods commonly rely on a great many simplifying assumptions – that the container is perfectly smooth, that the water is free of impurities – and these are no doubt necessary to the practice of science; but it does not follow that they are true or that they need to be accepted as anything other than pragmatic presuppositions for those engaged in scientific experiments. Furthermore, scientific methods also presuppose certain global or cosmological assumptions, such as that nature is the same everywhere, or that there are no unexplainable events; but the fact that science presupposes such views does not show them to be true, and philosophers of science find it perfectly rational to question them. There are, of course, philosophical arguments (as distinct from arguments from science) against the possibility of miracles, or against the rationality of believing in miracles, but they are not directed against petitionary prayer in particular and so will not be considered further here.

Second, it is not true that every answer to prayer requires a miracle. Just as it is possible without any violation of natural law for one human being to alter the way things happen in the world, either by acting on material objects or by influencing other creatures to do one thing rather than another, so it is possible for God also to exercise providence without engaging in miracles. Answering petitionary prayers does require God's intervention in the world, but divine intervention need not be miraculous. God's guiding the Israelites through the wilderness or instructing his prophets to reprove kings, for example, are interventions that do not obviously require miracles. It is not clear that even divine manipulation of inanimate parts of the world requires violation of natural law. Natural law tells us how one material entity interacts with another, but it says nothing about how an immaterial deity might interact with material things. Of course, if God makes things move in ways that natural law rules out, then God produces a miracle; but it is not clear that whenever God intervenes in the world he moves things contrary to natural law.

There are philosophers who suppose that it is impossible for God to intervene in the world at all, not because such intervention is miraculous and miracles are impossible, but because they think that there is no way in which there can be causal interaction between what is material and what is immaterial. Such philosophers assume that we understand clearly how material substances interact with each other and that we therefore also understand clearly that they could not interact with immaterial substances. But this assumption seems mistaken on both counts. It is not at all clear that we really understand how material substances interact with each other; in fact, quantum physics makes the interaction of elementary particles look distinctly spooky or ghostlike, as Einstein put it. And nothing in what we do know about the interaction of elementary particles demonstrates that they could not be acted upon except by other material entities.

There are also religious grounds on which to reason to the same conclusion – that God does not intervene in the world, so that prayer is pointless. Deism, for example, is a religious position that supposes that it is not consonant with God's dignity or power as creator for him to interfere with the world once it is created (see Article 39, CREATION AND CONSERVATION). On this view, God acts once to create the world. But since he creates it well, he creates it able to run by itself. Consequently, he does not intervene in the created order because there is no need for him to do so. To suppose otherwise, according to deism, is to take the creation to require chronic tinkering on God's part, in a way unsuitable to a transcendent, omnipotent deity.

But deism assumes, mistakenly, that the only reason for God to intervene in creation is some deficiency in creation. It might be the case, however, that God wants to intervene in creation even if he does not need to do so. So, for example, even the most excellent of craftsmen or artists might want to continue to work on something she has made after it is initially finished, just for the joy of continuing the artistry. God might also want to play with his creation, as the book of Job suggests that God plays with the beasts. And, finally, it is difficult to know what the point of God's creating rational persons could be if not to engage in personal relations with them. So there are reasons for an omnipotent deity to want to intervene in his creation, even if he does not need to do so because of some defect in it.

A related objection has to do with the purported difficulty or even impossibility of responding appropriately to all the prayers that are made. Some people pray for rain that the crops might grow, while others are simultaneously praying for dry weather so that the refugee camp might be spared more misery. And in war, people on each side pray for victory. The thought behind this objection is that since no deity could respond appropriately to all these conflicting prayers, the practice of petitionary prayer is pointless.

But the objection supposes that the only way to respond appropriately to a

579

petitionary prayer is to grant it. Because petitions conflict and therefore cannot all be granted, the objection supposes that God cannot respond appropriately to petitionary prayer. But, as politicians know, there are many ways to deal appropriately with conflicting petitions, short of granting them all. Some cases of conflict are only apparent; it is possible, for example, that rain might fall on the crops without falling on the refugee camp. Compromise is also possible when human desires conflict. Jacob wants the blessing of a first-born son to go to Ephraim, and Joseph wants that blessing instead for Ephraim's older brother Manasseh. Jacob prevails, but Manasseh's blessing is not inconsiderable or undesirable: he will be the progenitor of a great people (Genesis 48:19). As far as that goes, a prayer can also be dealt with appropriately by explaining why it is denied, as Jesus explains why he cannot grant the petition that James and John be the greatest in the kingdom of heaven (Matthew 20:20–3), or even by denying the petition without explanation, as when God does not grant Elijah's petition to die (1 Kings 19:4–8).

Finally, some people suppose that empirical evidence can show that even if petitionary prayer is not theoretically pointless, it none the less is routinely inefficacious. It is sometimes suggested, for example, that if there were a point to petitionary prayer, the insurance companies would be the first to know it since the death rate for people prayed for would be lower than for people not prayed for.

But this objection to the practice of petitionary prayer is based on two assumptions, both of which are incompatible with traditional theistic views of God. One is that a good God will invariably withhold some good things, such as health, from some people just because they are not prayed for. The other is that God always gives exactly what he is asked for in petitionary prayer. When we add to this our inability to know for certain which people are being prayed for and which are not, it no longer seems plausible to suppose that empirical evidence of the sort available to insurance companies could establish the inefficacy of petitionary prayer.

More difficult philosophical problems arise when the practice of petitionary prayer is considered in connection with God's omniscience. The practice makes sense only if God at least sometimes does something because of a prayer. This requirement in turn presupposes that there is genuine communication between human beings and God. But if God is omniscient, in what sense can there be such communication? God will know in advance what prayers will be made to him and he will also know in advance what his response to those prayers will be. Therefore, God does not need to wait for the person actually to utter the prayer, and God seems not to be taking part in any real communication between himself and the one praying. Rather, God apparently simply waits for the actual occurrence of what he has foreseen, so that he can proceed with the plan he has had in mind all along. This picture of divine and human interaction in prayer seems to make a mockery of the thought that God responds to human prayers.

Philosophers defending petitionary prayer have proposed two solutions to this objection.

The first is to claim that even if God did determine in advance what to do about a prayer, he would still be doing something in response to that prayer. What is important in divine reactions to prayer is not the relative timing of the prayer and the divine reaction to that prayer, but rather the fact that God does something *because of* the prayer. And God can do what he does as a response to the prayer even if he does not decide on that response *after* the prayer is made.

The second solution is to point out that the objection depends on taking God as temporal although God has traditionally been understood to be eternal, transcending time as he transcends space. If God is outside time, then his responses to prayer will not have been determined at some time earlier than the prayer. Of course, if God is eternal, his responses to prayer are not determined at any time at all; and some philosophers have thought that it is impossible for a deity whose actions are not temporally locatable to have any effects in time (see Article 32, ETERNITY). But there seems to be no reason why God cannot timelessly will that something occur at a certain time, and so it is after all possible for the action of an eternal God to have effects in time. In addition, although an atemporal God does not frame his response to a prayer *after* the prayer, any more than he determines it in advance of the prayer, he can still act *simultaneously* with the prayer (where simultaneity has to be understood in a more sophisticated way than temporal co-occurrence), and nothing in the nature of simultaneity keeps God's action from being a *response* to the prayer, a divine action done because of the petition in the prayer.

This approach also provides a solution to the objection that petitionary prayer is pointless if God is immutable, as he is traditionally said to be (see Article 40, IMMUTABILITY AND IMPASSIBILITY). According to this objection, before a certain petitionary prayer is prayed, it is either the case that God will bring about the state of affairs requested in the prayer or that he will not bring it about. Either way, since he is immutable, the prayer cannot effect any change in what God determines to bring about, and so the prayer is pointless. But if God is eternal as well as immutable, it is possible for him to do something just because a prayer for it was made, without himself undergoing any change, since the prayer and God's determination about his own actions are simultaneous. God can therefore determine to bring about the prayed-for state of affairs *because* it was prayed for, without altering some previous determination of his. It is therefore also clear that prayer can have a point even if it effects no change in God, as long as it is the case that as a result of the prayer God does what he otherwise might not have done.

The most difficult philosophical problem regarding the practice of petitionary prayer, however, is raised by considerations of God's goodness. If he were able to do so, a perfectly good God would always make the world better than it would otherwise be and would never make the world worse than it would otherwise be. But God, who is omnipotent, can do anything unless it is logically impossible for him to do it. So unless making the world worse is somehow logically necessary or making it better is logically impossible, a perfectly good, omnipotent God will always make the world better and never make it worse. Consequently, if what is asked for in a petitionary prayer would make the world worse than it would otherwise be, God would never grant such a prayer (unless it were logically necessary for him to do so). By the same token, if what is requested in a prayer would make the world better than it would otherwise be, God would bring about what is requested in any case (unless doing so is logically impossible). In either event, it seems that the practice of petitionary prayer is pointless.

This problem has received extensive discussion in the history of philosophical theology. Thomas Aquinas, for example, discusses the philosophical problems of prayer at length in various works. In *Summa Theologiae*, he argues that it is appropriate to pray even to an omnipotent, omniscient, perfectly good, immutable God. Divine providence, he says, determines not only what effects there will be in the world but also what causes will give rise to those effects and in what order they will do so (see Article 72, PROVIDENCE AND PREDESTINATION). We pray, then, not in order to change the divine disposition but rather in order to acquire by prayer what God has determined to be achieved by prayer (II–II q.83 a.2).

Even if we bracket the apparent theological determinism of Aquinas's position, it does not seem to constitute a solution to the problem. It is plain enough that, on traditional religious views, God wants human beings to pray to him and has a plan for the world that includes human prayers as partial causes of certain effects. The problem arises because this traditional view seems not to make sense. Why should prayers be included in God's plan as the causes of certain effects? And what sense is there in the notion that God, who disposes and plans everything with omnipotence and perfect goodness, brings about some things because of human prayers?

A different and perhaps more helpful approach is to take seriously the traditional conception of God as a person and to consider what it takes to maintain friendly relations of any sort between persons of very unequal status and conditions (see Article 15, PERSONALISM). If we think about what would be required to establish and maintain friendly relations between, say, the president of the United States and a feckless, ne'er-do-well teenager hired to empty the wastebaskets in the Oval Office, we can begin to see the problem. The personal distance between them is an obvious obstacle to friendship. But it is also possible for an unhealthy kind of closeness to constitute an obstacle, too. Unhealthy closeness can wreck friendship in more than one way. It can turn the person of lower status into a slavish lackey of the other, as anyone allowed to be close to the fierce Mongol Genghis Khan must have been, or, on the other hand, it can make the person of lower status a self-interested manipulator of the other, as the eunuch Chao Kao was with respect to the Ch'in second-generation emperor, whom the eunuch eventually poisoned (ca. 207 BCE). Prayer may bridge the distance between human beings and God, because praying requires some sort of trust, however small, complicated, or double-minded. But what is perhaps more important in this connection is that prayer is also a buffer against the sorts of unhealthy closeness that can develop between two persons when one is vastly superior to the other in some (or all) respects. In petitionary prayer, a person makes an explicit request for help, and he thereby acknowledges his dependence on God for satisfying some need or desire of his own. If he gets what he prayed for, he will be in a position to attribute his good fortune to God's doing and to be grateful to God for what God has given him. Given the undeniable uncertainty of getting what is prayed for, these conditions make the act of asking a safeguard against the sort of self-interested manipulativeness which can wreck the possibility of friendship. On the other hand, because God waits to do some good things until he is asked and does not simply intervene unasked every time he deals with human beings, God helps to safeguard the psychological autonomy of a human person who might otherwise easily lose his sense of identity in his relations with an omnipotent, omniscient, perfectly good God.

So, although on traditional accounts of prayer and God's nature, prayer does not effect a change in God, it can none the less make a difference to God's determination of what to bring about, because prayer effects changes in the person praying. The very fact that a state of affairs is prayed for, then, gives God a reason he otherwise would not have had for bringing about that state of affairs. It is obviously a defeasible reason, and that is why not all prayers are efficacious; but it is a reason none the less, and that is why petitionary prayer is not pointless. There is therefore some good which even an omnipotent God could not bring about without prayer, namely, the good involved in personal relations with his creatures.

Bibliography

Alston, W.: "Divine–human dialogue and the nature of God," *Faith and Philosophy*, 2 (1985), pp. 5–20.

Geach, P.: *God and the Soul* (London: Routledge & Kegan Paul, 1969).

Hoffman, J.: "On petitionary prayer," *Faith and Philosophy*, 2 (1985), pp. 21–9.

Penelhum, T.: *Religion and Rationality* (New York: Random House, 1971).

Phillips, D. Z.: *The Concept of Prayer* (New York: Schocken Books, 1966).

Stump, E.: "Petitionary prayer," *American Philosophical Quarterly*, 16 (1979), pp. 81–91.

Ward, K.: *The Concept of God* (New York: St Martin's Press; Oxford: Blackwell, 1974).

Young, R.: "Petitioning God," *American Philosophical Quarterly*, 11 (1974), pp. 193–201.

74

Revelation and scripture

WILLIAM J. ABRAHAM

Throughout the history of Christian thought, scripture and revelation have been Siamese twins; while they are logically distinct notions, they have been inseparable as actual entities. The crucial debates related to them have invariably centered on how to distinguish and connect them at the same time. The issue has been an epistemic one, for the primary concern has been to develop an account of the place of scripture and revelation in knowledge of God. Thus the very idea of revelation and the very idea of a canon of scripture have been taken to be the equivalent of a criterion of theological truth. From the medieval period until the virtual collapse of both notions in the recent past this has been the conventional construal.

While scripture has been implicated in such epistemological debates, there is nothing remotely epistemic in the bare idea of sacred scripture. Scripture denotes simply a collection of sacred writings. The idea of a canon is more complex. Originally "canon" could mean either a list or a measuring line. Both meanings fit the patristic usage. Yet while the Church over time agreed officially on the books to be used in worship, it never agreed to any particular theory of scripture or of divine revelation. Diverse views on both, represented most clearly by diverse views on divine inspiration, were allowed. Equally, radically diverse views on the epistemology of theology were tolerated; there was no canonical or agreed account of how one knew that one knew God, even though there were very substantial proposals available on this topic in the teachers of the Church.

The matter took a radically new twist in the work of Thomas Aquinas. What had been an informal position in the early Fathers was relocated in a sophisticated account of theology as *scientia* ingeniously derived from Aristotle. In this analysis the propositions of scripture became the premises of a deductive science secured as true by the fact that they were spoken by God. All the teachings of the Church were taken as derivable from scripture, a position exploited brilliantly by the Reformers in their struggle with Rome. The Council of Trent countered the *sola scriptura* of the Reformers by rejecting a two-sources doctrine of authority, yet advocating a doctrine of divine dictation for both scripture and tradition. The nuances of the Tridentine position were often lost in the fierce polemical debates of the period. Underneath these there was amazing consensus at two points. Scripture should be seen primarily in epistemic categories as a norm of truth. The guarantee of this norm was that scripture was spoken or dictated by God.

These claims in turn generated the question of how one knew that scripture rather than, say, the Qur'an was the Word of God. Aquinas dealt with this in terms of miracle and prophecy; John Calvin, while he did not reject arguments concerning the marvelous nature of scripture, appealed to the inner witness of the Holy Spirit. Even then, it was not clear whether this was an appeal to religious experience or to a kind of mystical revelation within. Counter-Reformation polemicists quickly seized on the subjectivism lurking in appeal to the inner witness or happily deployed it themselves. The outcome was a hopeless impasse. Both sides developed an exclusive foundationalism in the epistemology of theology which rested on the same ultimate ground, inner experience of the Spirit, but which led to radically contradictory conclusions. Alternatively, they appealed to competing foundations, scripture or the *magisterium* of the church speaking infallibly through the pope, beyond which one could not proceed. By this time the alternative development of patristic Christianity embodied in the East was not really in on the conversation.

The Cartesian revolution can legitimately be seen as, in part, a brilliant attempt to resolve the impasse created by the clash of foundationalisms in the Church in the West. Through the *cogito ergo sum* René Descartes sought to clear away contested opinion and make room for a foundation which would withstand even the deceptive wiles of the devil. This foundation marked by clarity, distinctness, and universality, became the base for a new foundationalism divorced from all sectarian associations. By this time scripture and revelation had dropped out of the picture and the field of epistemology became more and more a subdiscipline within philosophy.

This trend was continued in John Locke, who replaced Descartes's appeal to reason with an appeal to the "ideas" derived from sense experience. While Locke was in many ways a thoroughly conventional Protestant who believed in scripture and divine revelation, he insisted that reason, now understood as sense experience, was the last rule and guide in everything. Propositions derived from revelation could be above reason but they could not be contrary to reason. Moreover, revelation itself must be secured by the presence of miracles. Belief in the God of miracles was in turn secured by natural theology. The result was a two-stage apologetic strategy. One attained to belief in God by means of natural theology; one arrived at distinctive Christian beliefs, like the immortality of the soul, by means of divine revelation guaranteed by miracle and prophecy. Scripture came into this picture as the medium of divine revelation conceived principally as a form of divine communication.

David Hume demolished this neat and attractive package with his attack on natural theology and miracle. By now the canonical heritage of the Church had been reduced to scripture and interpreted as a criterion of truth, that is, as an item in epistemology. For Protestants Hume's attack precipitated a crisis which has never been satisfactorily resolved. They have oscillated between the search for a new foundation, best represented by Friedrich Schleiermacher's appeal to religious experience, and the reassertion of the rights of divine revelation, best represented by the great Princeton theologians of the nineteenth century and by Karl Barth in the twentieth. In Schleiermacher the concept of revelation did no epistemic work, and scripture became a norm not of truth but of Christian

585

identity. In the Princeton tradition scripture was treated as divine revelation *simpliciter*, while Barth saw it as a unique witness to revelation. The Princeton theologians and Barth interpreted religious experience as a subjective snare; the former were passionately committed to natural theology, while Barth rejected it vehemently on theological grounds. The crucial point to grasp about this tangled journey is that Protestantism found itself constantly beholden to the fortunes of epistemology in the culture. The arrival of feminist and other forms of liberation theology have not altered this situation. Thus feminist theology began with the epistemic slogans of liberal Protestants in its appeal to women's experience but is now drawn into postmodernist construals of rationality, truth, and knowledge.

For those who remained committed to divine revelation as a source of truth, the great problem of the last two centuries has been how to reconcile this move with the application of historical criticism to the content of scripture. Once scripture was construed primarily as spoken and dictated by God, some doctrine of inerrancy was inevitable. The problem then arose of how to square this with contrary observations derived from scientific and historical investigations of reality. Aquinas resolved this dilemma by appeal to God's intentions as the author of scripture. His doctrine of inerrancy, which was pivotal for his account of theology as *scientia*, could be kept intact by positing a divine meaning in the text compatible with the findings of science and history. However, the very idea of a divine meaning behind the text became suspect in all forms of historical investigation which posited merely human meanings in the text. Moreover, Hume's critique of miracles as necessarily devoid of positive evidence was extended by Ernest Troeltsch in his deployment of criticism, correlation, and analogy to mount a devastating attack on the whole idea of divine intervention in history. This cut radically into the whole fabric of scripture and canonical tradition and evoked Rudolf Bultmann's famous plan of demythologizing as a way out of the excruciating problems engendered by the logic of historical inquiry. In this case the content of Christianity was reduced to anthropological proposals related to the doctrine of justification, scripture was effectively reduced to a historically reconstructed *kerygma* which left no room for divine intervention, and the concept of revelation went idling. Recent work on the Jesus of History in the Jesus Seminar has served to raise again disputes about the logic of historical investigation and the problem of relating divine revelation to the historical study of scripture.

In the meantime, philosophers of religion have been exploring new ways of thinking about the whole range of topics related to epistemology in general and the epistemology of Christian theism in particular. The stimulus for these developments has been threefold: the demise of the positivist critique of religious language; the collapse of classical foundationalism; and the exploration of new ways of thinking about perception, rationality, justification, and knowledge. In addition, deep dissatisfaction with the content and confusion of contemporary theology has driven philosophers to explore afresh the topic of divine revelation and the traditional *loci* of Christian theology. Consequently any neat distinction between philosophy and theology has collapsed. As in the case of Aquinas, it is correct to see, for example, the work of Richard Swinburne as simultaneously philosophical and theological. In fact Swinburne is rightly seen as a kind of new Aquinas. This is an extraordinary development which few would have envisaged a generation ago and which has yet to be absorbed into the modern theological curriculum.

The difficulties encountered in medieval and modern construals of scripture coupled with the emergence of new work in epistemology call for a different approach to the construal of scripture and revelation. Scripture and canon, when seen from the point of view of their origins, are not epistemic concepts. In fact scripture was but one element in a complex and rich canonical heritage which was developed by the Church. Over the same time there arose a canon of scripture, a rule of faith or creed, a standard liturgy, a canon of teachers, a normative pattern of iconography, a canon of councils, a standard set of sacraments and other religious rites, a network of flexible regulations related to the daily life of the Church, and an agreed form of episcopal oversight. These were intended to function together to initiate people into the kingdom of God. They constituted means whereby one was granted salvation through humility, repentance, and faith. Equally, they were gifts of the Holy Spirit which could only be received through immersion in the life of the Spirit. Their intention was to create in the believer the mind of Christ, to make one divine, and to bring one into the life of the Triune God. While they indeed mediated genuine knowledge of God, they brought one face to face with an ultimate mystery which could never be expressed in any form of human knowledge or language.

This canonical heritage is best seen in soteriological categories. Through the activity of God, it is a means of healing and restoration. This healing does not take place without knowledge of and about God, but the purpose of the canonical heritage is not to provide an epistemology of theology. At the level of epistemology what we have in the canonical heritage are various epistemic suggestions and proposals about knowledge of God which lie in wait for further analysis and development. These appear most conspicuously in scripture and in the writings of the canonical teachers of the Church. Hence we might say that the church indirectly canonized various epistemic suggestions or ideas, like the importance of divine speaking and the apophatic character of knowledge of God, but it very carefully kept these subordinate to its primary commitments to scripture, creed, sacraments, liturgy, iconography, and the like. Western Christianity injured this delicate balance by epistemizing the canonical life of the Church when it transposed it into such items as scripture, tradition, teaching *magisterium*, and papal infallibility in order to further its epistemic interests. Hence it took what was marginal in the canonical heritage and made it constitutive and central. In so doing it also created the seedbed for the classical foundationalism which became a hallmark of the Enlightenment. The latter was the creation of Christian intellectuals who secularized the working of the Holy Spirit and relocated the foundations of knowledge in reason and experience as opposed to scripture and tradition. Anglicans and United Methodists confusedly tried to develop sophisticated syntheses of reason and experience with scripture and tradition.

Once the original and historic nature of the canonical heritage is acknowledged, we are liberated to pursue the epistemic suggestions of that heritage with

587

freedom and dexterity. Hence we can explore the polymorphous nature of the concept of divine revelation, for revelation can rightly be seen to involve everything from God's action in creation to encounter with the divine mystery in the life to come. In between, we can examine divine revelation in God's speaking to the prophets in various ways, the unique unveiling of God in the INCARNATION (see Article 67), and the ongoing acts of divine speaking in the Church and in the life of the individual. So used, the concept of revelation is the epistemic equivalent of the concept of witness or testimony in jurisprudence. Hence it cannot be used to resolve deeper questions about the reliability of intuition, reason, memory, sense experience, and the like. The latter have to be pursued in their own right. Equally, the concept of revelation cannot dispose of deep questions about how to articulate the meaning and nature of rationality, truth, justification, and knowledge.

An especially interesting issue is that of relating revelation to religious experience and to various arguments for the existence of God. It is relatively easy to assimilate revelation to religious experience, for certain kinds of revelation clearly are given in experience, like the divine promise or warning given to a prophet. Yet not all revelation can be reduced to religious experience, for in many cases of religious experience what is at stake is encounter with the being of God rather than any action or message of God. Moreover, it is possible to move from an appeal to natural theology to an appeal to special revelation in order to support the full contours of Christian theism. In this case we have a kind of natural theology from below completed by a revealed theology from above. However, it is also possible to start with special revelation and then move to the deployment of all sorts of arguments for Christian theism. The latter is a kind of natural theology from above which is not far in logical structure from the thought of Aquinas.

None of these positions would appear to do full justice to the kind of certainty often found among the saints and martyrs of the Christian tradition, nor to the claims of certitude found among a host of ordinary believers. This has led at times to the idea of properly basic beliefs, applied characteristically to the tenets of theism, but also deployed occasionally to belief in special revelation and to the personal status of the individual before God as forgiven and accepted in Christ. It has also led to claims of the inner witness of the Holy Spirit which have removed it from its function of validating the canon of scripture and relocated it in the sphere of perception of the divine or some other favored epistemic context. This constitutes an arena of epistemological investigation which is as yet underdeveloped. Careful exploration of the writings of the canonized theologians of the East, most especially of Simeon the New Theologian, could prove to be exceptionally fruitful when read in the light of the range of epistemic possibilities recently articulated.

Another issue constantly lurking below the surface is the extent to which discernment of divine revelation depends on the healing of our cognitive capacities. Scripture and tradition repeatedly attribute belief and faith to the working of the Holy Spirit. As Paul says, "No one can say that Jesus is Lord except by the Spirit." Because of the obsession with internalist construals of justification, these matters have never been given the epistemic attention they deserve, as they are often dismissed as forms of emotionalism, enthusiasm, and subjectivism. Recent work in

588

reliabilism and virtue theories of knowledge could shed invaluable light on these crucial canonical suggestions related to revelation and epistemology. This work needs to be integrated with the insights of ascetic theology on the role of repentance and purification (see Article 69, ATONEMENT, JUSTIFICATION, AND SANCTIFICATION), of ascent and participation, in coming to a knowledge of God. The notion of spiritual practices as epistemic practices deserves attention, as does the role of God in creating and healing our cognitive abilities. These are precisely the possibilities opened up by the breakdown of classical foundationalism over the last generation.

What is now possible is a fresh appropriation of the canonical clarity and epistemic modesty of the patristic tradition. Scripture is a crucial ingredient in the canonical heritage of the Church, whose purpose along with the whole of that heritage is to redeem and divinize. Revelation is indeed an epistemic concept for it is constituted by an unveiling of the divine nature, actions, and purposes. So formally, it takes us automatically into the field of religious epistemology. At this level, it is entirely appropriate to argue that revelation is a norm of truth. Given God's attributes and his actions in creation and redemption, what God reveals is trustworthy and true. This follows analytically from the concept of God. Yet it is a mistake in logic to conflate revelation and scripture, as has constantly happened. Materially God has spoken and still speaks through the medium of the scriptures. A faithful testimony or record of God's activity in Christ, if Christ is God incarnate, clearly constitutes divine revelation. Hence scripture and revelation, while they are logically distinct notions, are materially inseparable. For this reason alone theological arguments will often take the form of scriptural arguments resting on complex tacit assumptions about the nature of revelation and its availability in scripture.

We return full circle to a platitudinous account of the relation between scripture and revelation. However, we do so unencumbered by a false view of canon and by the predominantly internalist cast of medieval and modern theology. This in no way entails diffidence about the epistemological questions generated by the gospel and the canonical teaching of the Church. Historically, Christian intellectuals have been extraordinarily versatile in exploring epistemic issues. They have also contributed extensively to the development of epistemological theory in their quest to satisfy their own questions and the criticisms of philosophers and theologians. Abandoning the longstanding confusion of ecclesial canons with epistemic norms, of scripture with divine revelation, will enrich rather than inhibit this astounding legacy of epistemic theory and discussion.

Bibliography

Abraham, W. J.: *Divine Revelation and the Limits of Historical Criticism* (Oxford: Oxford University Press, 1982).

Barr, J.: *The Bible in the Modern World* (New York: Harper & Row, 1973).

Fulkerson, M. M.: *Changing the Subject, Women's Discourses and Feminist Theologies* (Minneapolis: Fortress, 1994).

Kelsey, D.: *The Uses of Scripture in Recent Theology* (London: SCM Press, 1975).

Mavrodes, G.: *Revelation in Religious Belief* (Philadelphia: Temple University Press, 1988).

Metzger, B. M.: *The Canon of the New Testament: Its Origin, Development, and Significance* (Oxford: Clarendon Press, 1987).

Popkin, R.: *The History of Scepticism from Erasmus to Spinoza* (Berkeley: University of California Press, 1979).

Swinburne, R.: *Revelation: From Metaphor to Analogy* (Oxford: Clarendon Press, 1992).

75

Tradition

BASIL MITCHELL

The concept of tradition has had a secure place in Christian theology and a controversial status in modern philosophy.

Tradition in Christian theology

A religion such as Judaism or Christianity which is based upon a past revelation requires that the deposit of faith can be transmitted from one generation of believers to another in a reliable form. If the original revelation is enshrined in Scripture it needs to be interpreted and its limits defined. This requirement could be avoided only if the revelation was held to be so clear and specific that it could be recognized and understood by anyone at any period without an intermediary of any kind. Otherwise there is need for a continuing body which would be responsible for maintaining the tradition in its authentic form and would have authority to settle disputes about its interpretation. The individual believer would depend upon this body and the tradition it mediates for his or her understanding of the faith. Hence it would be natural for the Church to take tradition entirely for granted and to regard it as a source of religious truth along with reason and Scripture.

Given the close association of tradition with ecclesiastical authority it is not surprising that it has given rise to a great deal of controversy. The insistence on continuity of doctrine and organization is common to the Roman Catholic, Orthodox, and Anglican communions but they have differed as to where the authority for tradition is located and, to some extent, as to its content. The reformation witnessed a widespread rejection of the hitherto accepted *magisterium* of the Roman Catholic Church, but generated further disagreements as to whether the authority now lay in some other ecclesiastical agency or was vested in the entire community of believers or in the individual conscience. It was also a matter of dispute how far tradition could be a source of new insights. Protestants, including Anglicans, insisted that tradition should be derivable from Scripture, whereas the Roman Catholic Church was prepared to allow "unwritten traditions" which may be authorized by the Church if not inconsistent with Scripture and if supported by a consensus of theologians.

Disputes about tradition have been accentuated by fresh developments in the modern period. The critical study of the Bible made simple reliance on the text of Scripture more problematical. This in itself brought tradition into greater prominence, but the same critical methods applied to Christian origins called in question

591

the processes by which Christian doctrines had been formulated. It was, for example, possible to ask whether the Greek philosophical concepts employed in the formation of the Creeds were appropriate for the God of the Hebrew Bible. Modernists began to question to what extent the hitherto accepted tradition was mandatory upon contemporary Christians who had access to scholarly resources not available in earlier centuries. Scripture and tradition were indeed essential to an adequate understanding of the faith, but they needed to be tested against reason and experience.

Tradition and the philosophers

It is only comparatively recently that questions about tradition have been addressed by philosophers. Modern philosophy, both rationalist and empiricist, began by repudiating ecclesiastical authority and with it the claims of tradition to be a source of knowledge. Even those philosophers who, like René Descartes and John Locke, were themselves religious believers, were convinced that, as philosophers, they must rely on reason and experience alone. The thinkers of the Enlightenment tended to associate theological authority with dogmatic obscurantism and followed Descartes in seeking to construct their philosophy upon a foundation of clear and distinct ideas. Whether these were a priori or derived from experience they possessed a self-evidence which rendered appeal to tradition otiose. Nor was ecclesiastical authority the only kind to be questioned. The rising scientific movement sought to free itself also from the authority of Aristotle.

In these developments Locke was a representative figure. He sought to establish the existence of God by rational argument and appealed to the witness of prophecy and miracle to show that God had revealed himself in propositions which were above reason but not contrary to it. The argument is addressed entirely to the individual and has no place for tradition or the Church as the repository of it. Of the four sources of religious truth – reason, Scripture, tradition, and experience – Locke accepts only the first two, since in his contempt for "enthusiasm" he rejects religious experience as well as tradition.

The emphasis on reason which is common to both the critics and the defenders of religion in the period of the Enlightenment became associated with a powerful concept which militated strongly against any appeal to tradition, namely autonomy, which found its classical expression in the philosophy of Immanuel Kant. The individual bore responsibility for his or her beliefs and it was incompatible with one's integrity as a rational being to defer to any kind of authority. Hence deliberately to align oneself with a tradition was to abdicate from the status of a rational agent. This notion of autonomy is perhaps more definitive of modernity than any other, so that even when, under the influence of the Romantic movement, the claims of reason have been modified or abandoned, the demands of autonomy have been, if anything, reinforced. The typical modern hero is free, independent, and lonely. For him or her to identify with an inherited tradition would be to incur *mauvaise foi*.

Newman's vindication of tradition

The thinker who did most to vindicate the role of tradition against these influences was both philosopher and theologian. John Henry Newman's approach was primarily philosophical. His principal target was Locke (see Locke 1959 [1690]) whom he criticized for his failure to recognize the role in our thinking of antecedent assumptions. Locke assumed, as did all thinkers of the Enlightenment, that if someone's beliefs are to be rationally defensible they must be based on evidence which is presently available to him or her and can be specified and produced on demand. Moreover, the degree of confidence reposed in them must be strictly proportionate to the strength of the evidence. Viewed from this standpoint a historical tradition may indeed be a means of preserving evidence which might otherwise be lost, but it can possess no other claim to rational authority. Newman held that this account was plainly incompatible with the way people actually think. All of us – and not only religious believers – are influenced, and rightly so, by antecedent assumptions which derive from some tradition of thought or practice on whose resources we draw whether we acknowledge it or not. It is simply not the case that we approach the evidence with an entirely open mind. "Antecedent assumptions" cover a whole range of things: theories or systems of thought which are taken for granted, the concepts and attitudes which go with them, and the language in which they are expressed. Newman also insists that when our convictions about matters of importance are at stake, the arguments we use are informal and cumulative so that it is not a straightforward matter to set out the evidence to which we appeal or to articulate and assess the inferences we employ (see Newman 1890, pp. 215, 274).

Newman's arguments, as we shall see, had implications beyond the sphere of theology. But, in theology and in conjunction with his case for the development of doctrine, they provided a defense of the role of tradition in Catholic Christianity against philosophical criticism. They did not, however, resolve the dispute between modernists and traditionalists.

Modernists need not oppose the appeal to tradition in principle, as Newman has interpreted it; their concern was about how to conduct it in the light of current investigations into the Bible and Christian origins. If the Bible was seen to be a collection of writings of different periods and various genres, the need for help in interpreting it became increasingly apparent. Nevertheless, the Church's own traditional interpretation was itself open to criticism when the political and philosophical influences upon it were recognized. Tradition was necessary, but it was not sufficient. It was legitimate to ask how far Christian doctrine, as it was formulated by the Fathers, was derivable from Scripture and what was the continuing authority of the historic Creeds as promulgated by the early Church. Given that modernists were prepared to respect the role of tradition, the way was open to them to seek to modify the accepted teaching of the Church without altogether undermining its foundations. They could even argue that it was traditional to do so – if tradition was properly understood. Attention must be paid to the tradition as an indispensable guide to Christian truth without its being regarded, in its inherited form, as wholly mandatory upon the contemporary believer.

Similarly, Newman's argument made it possible for the *magisterium* to defend its accepted role against Enlightenment critics without incurring the charge of being merely an irrelevant survival.

The most uncompromising form of the appeal to tradition, developed in conscious opposition to the modernists, was to be found in the decisions of the First Vatican Council of 1870. The sole repository of valid tradition was the *magisterium* of the Roman Catholic Church, as indeed the Church has always maintained, but now it was held to be centered in the papacy, so that Pius IX was able to declare "I am tradition." This conclusion was held to follow logically from the premise that God had given human kind a definitive revelation of himself. If this was to be effective it was necessary that it should be transmitted from one generation to another by a body which had authority to determine the canon of Scripture and to interpret it correctly under the guidance of the Holy Spirit which Christ had promised would lead the Church into all truth. Moreover, to ensure that the declarations of this body could be trusted, it must be acknowledged to be infallible.

Such a strong conception of tradition, although logically coherent, had difficulty in responding to criticisms based upon historical and literary research, and thinkers within the tradition of faith, both Catholic and Protestant, set out, not to repudiate the tradition, but to revise it more or less radically. Aware of advances in historical scholarship and of the variety of influences upon the development of doctrine they argued that mistakes had in fact been made and that the tradition had from the start been more fragmented than it had been made to appear. Greek conceptions of a timeless perfection had, for example, been allowed to distort the biblical picture of a God active in history. The job of the contemporary theologian was not to reproduce the formulations of previous ages but to interpret Christian doctrine in a way that best reflected the Christian message in the light of the full tradition of the Church and whatever relevant knowledge was now available which was not possessed by earlier Christians. This "hermeneutic" task was one which was capable of being pursued successfully in the Church under the guidance of the Holy Spirit, but was not guaranteed against error. Reason, Scripture, and experience had all three a part to play in monitoring the tradition.

It is evident that in the continuing debate between more liberal and more conservative adherents of tradition a good deal depends on what the findings of critical study of the Bible and the history of the Church are actually thought to be. Is there sufficient agreement on essentials between Christian thinkers at any given time, and between them and their successors, to justify the claim that there exists and has existed a single coherent tradition of which a defensible contemporary version could be given? Or must we be content to acknowledge an irreducible plurality?

This is not in itself a philosophical issue but, as we shall see, philosophical contentions have been invoked in relation to it.

Philosophical problems about tradition

The idea of tradition has in Western thought been associated primarily with Christian belief and practice. It is only comparatively recently that it has been acknowledged by philosophers as having a role to play in secular as well as religious systems of thought, an acknowledgment which has served to reduce the isolation of theology from the mainstream of Western philosophy.

It is worth noting, to begin with, that Newman's critique of Locke and the Enlightenment is not sufficient in itself to vindicate the role of tradition in revealed religion. He succeeds in refuting the view that judgments must be formed solely on the basis of evidence currently available, and confidence in them strictly proportionate to it, but this serves only to show that the solitary thinker inevitably depends to some extent upon a continuing tradition. It does not have to be unchanging, so long as it does not change too rapidly. T. S. Eliot in his essay on "Tradition and the individual talent" (see Eliot 1932) insists that the writer of genius transforms the tradition to which he belongs and may, presumably, change it radically. Newman's conviction that the tradition of Catholic Christianity is substantially true and that, if properly interpreted, it represents the same truth now as when originally delivered cannot rest solely on his recognition that any system of belief rests on some tradition or other. It requires in addition some defensible account of the identity of a tradition in terms of which the original deposit of faith can be held to retain its meaning through time. Some radical theologians deny the possibility of this on philosophical grounds. In their view the project of restating traditional Christian doctrine in contemporary terms is impossible of achievement, not or not only because of the insufficiency or untrustworthiness of the factual evidence, but because it is logically flawed. It presupposes what is not the case – that it is possible for a twentieth century thinker to understand and assent to the thought-forms of an earlier age. If this view is accepted, the only way of maintaining Christian identity is by reliance on the continuing authority of the Church as an institution, which is held to have the same relationship with God now as in time past, although inevitably conceptualizing it quite differently.

The further question arises how the acceptance of tradition can be reconciled with the ideal of autonomy. So long as the individual's identification with a tradition is only provisional, it may be said, freedom of inquiry is not threatened. It may be necessary to start from some traditional standpoint, but subsequent thought may lead one to modify the tradition or abandon it in favor of another. But this is not possible if the thinker is committed to a Creed which has been formulated once and for all. No doubt, if such commitment is understood weakly as an undertaking to treat traditional beliefs seriously, examine them carefully to see if they provide valuable insights, etc., then reason is not compromised; but if the commitment is wholehearted, it can only be at the expense of that free and impartial review of a case which is a precondition of rational inquiry. To adhere to a tradition in this sense is to have a closed mind.

One way of dealing with this problem is to challenge the underlying assumption that reason is a faculty which can stand aside from a tradition and assess it from a critical standpoint in principle available to all (see MacIntyre 1981, pp. 206–7). If, on the contrary, criteria of meaning and standards of rationality are themselves intelligible only within a tradition, it is not possible to judge the

595

tradition itself in its entirety. Autonomy is exemplified in the act of will by which the individual adheres to a tradition or acquiesces in it.

The question then arises how, if at all, it is possible to make a rational choice between traditions. As it is often put, "there is no neutral ground on which to stand." Reason is no longer able to moderate tradition, because in the last resort it is dependent upon it (see MacIntyre 1988, pp. 393–4).

It remains to consider how far the traditional relationship in Christian theology between Scripture, tradition, reason, and experience can be coherently stated. What conditions would have to be satisfied to enable each to have its due in the face of philosophical criticism?

First, tradition would need to be shown to have preserved truths which can be derived from Scripture or are consistent with it; and Scripture itself must have a sufficient degree of coherence. Inconsistencies and differences of emphasis must not be so great as to rule this out. It would be a matter of judgment how much variety is compatible with essential unity.

Second, it must be possible for a tradition to remain substantially true to its origins. That is to say, it must be possible to rebut the kind of philosophical relativism which challenges any claim to believe what thinkers of some previous age believed.

Third, the aim of keeping the tradition up to date must be realizable. That is to say, it must be open to criticism and capable of being modified in response to it without forfeiting its essential identity. It must be possible, in principle, to decide between rival interpretations of the tradition.

Fourth, criticism must be possible; reason must not be definable solely by reference to the tradition itself.

Finally, it must be possible in principle to assess the claims of the tradition as against rival traditions, however difficult this may be in practice.

Whether these conditions can in fact be satisfied is a controversial issue in theology and the philosophy of religion. The claim that they cannot is characteristic of a radical strain in theology and corresponding positions in the philosophy of science and the philosophy of history. The claim that they can be satisfied makes sense of the disputes which regularly occur between conservative and liberal theologians. Conservative theologians who attach importance to tradition, who are not, that is, Biblical fundamentalists, look for certainty in religious truth and argue that it can be secured only if the Church as *the* repository of tradition is guaranteed against error. The tradition must be safeguarded by a continuing institution whose role is, indeed, supported by reason, but whose deliverances are open to criticism only within rather narrow limits. Liberal theologians maintain that the Christian tradition has always been subject to controversy, which is a condition of growth and by risking error allows fuller understanding. The Church should look not for an unattainable certainty but for a reasoned faith of the sort that is characteristic of the human situation. The guidance of the Holy Spirit is itself a postulate of such a faith.

Bibliography

Eliot, T. S.: *Selected Essays* (London: Faber & Faber, 1932).

Locke, J.: *An Essay Concerning Human Understanding* (1690), ed. A. Campbell Fraser (New York, 1959).

MacIntyre, A.: *After Virtue* (London: Duckworth, 1981).

——: *Whose Justice? Which Rationality?* (London: Duckworth, 1988).

Mitchell, B.: *Faith and Criticism* (Oxford: Oxford University Press, 1994).

Newman, J. H.: *Fifteen Sermons Preached before the University of Oxford* (London: Longman, 1890).

——: *An Essay in Aid of a Grammar of Assent*, ed. I. Ker and A. G. Hill. In *Newman After a Hundred Years* (Oxford: Clarendon Press, 1990).

PART XI

NEW DIRECTIONS IN PHILOSOPHY OF RELIGION

76

Feminism

SARAH COAKLEY

Analytic philosophy of religion has so far shown a marked (if largely silent) resistance to feminist reflection of any sort. Its hostility to feminist *theology* (evidenced in a few scattered articles) is easily comprehensible, granted the initial genesis of that movement in the early 1970s from American "liberal" and "constructivist" theology (to which most analytic philosophers of religion are opposed on other grounds), the biblical and doctrinal conservatism that characterizes analytic philosophy of religion as a whole, and the relative lack of philosophical acuity displayed in much first-wave feminist theology. It will not, however, be the goal of this article to survey types of feminist theology. Rather the focus will be on philosophy of religion's more puzzling avoidance of the sophisticated work done in recent years in feminist *philosophy* (for useful surveys, see Grimshaw 1986, Rooney 1994). If taken seriously by philosophers of religion, this could have far-reaching implications for their fundamental assumptions and preoccupations; and it will be the task here to sketch out these implications in a preliminary form. It will be suggested that the central place accorded in much analytic philosophy of religion to what feminists call the "generic male" (i.e., the privileged male subject posing as a sexless individual of universal instantiation) results in the sidelining not only of issues important to feminism, but also – ironically – of rich spiritual options from the Christian tradition.

The "generic male" and the problem of evil

There is a relative dearth of literature in analytic philosophy of religion on the concept of "self" in *all* its dimensions; attention is more commonly focused on specific issues such as the mind/body problem. The discussion of free will, however, is richly developed on account of the crucial theodicy questions raised by THE PROBLEM OF EVIL (see Article 50). Indeed one could argue that whatever solution the philosopher of religion proposes to this most pressing of contemporary religious questions, this will deeply affect the rest of the accompanying theological and philosophical system. The dominance of an "incompatibilist" view of freedom (in service of a "free will defense" on the problem of evil) is a striking feature of current analytic philosophy of religion – the more surprising, perhaps, when enunciated by those otherwise staunchly committed to the defense of Calvinism. The sovereign, *unconditioned* freedom of the individual to do evil (as well as good), and thereby to effect a temporary evasion even of divine conditioning, is deemed by many contemporary philosophers of religion to be the only acceptable first plank in a convincing solution to the problem of evil.

But it is here that feminist critiques of the "generic male" may be particularly telling, and provide important complements (strange as this may seem) to the theological objections to incompatibilism from the Thomist or Calvinist camps. Feminist philosophers point here, first, to the historical *specificity* of the visions of "autonomy" spawned by the Enlightenment, and the conditionings, relationships, and dependencies – not least those on wife and family – that go unmentioned in these accounts, whilst also being taken for granted in them (see Lloyd 1984). Thus in Enlightenment discussions, woman – the invisible "other" supposedly included under the "generic" autonomous male – turns out, in her occasional moments of explicit recognition, actually to be in need of lengthy education before she can enjoy the fruits of Enlightenment "freedom" (so Immanuel Kant); though she may meanwhile pursue a vocation as "cushion" for her husband against the slings and arrows of free (male) political exchange (so Thomas Carlyle).

One may ask whether these Enlightenment conceptions of "autonomy" continue to infect – albeit unconsciously – the incompatibilist vision of freedom promulgated by many philosophers of religion (including some distinguished women philosophers) in response to the problem of evil. What difference would it make if this were acknowledged? It would, for a start, make it impossible for the promulgators of the "free will defense" to proceed as if incompatibilism were unproblematic in either gender or class terms (quite apart from its more technical philosophical ramifications). When it is said that it is "good that an agent should have . . . power over the universe, the power to determine whether the morally good will prevail," and that "a creator has reason to allow him the opportunity to do so, to allow him through right choices to grow in freedom and morally relevant knowledge until he becomes as the angels" (Swinburne 1991, pp. 158–9), a feminist may appropriately inquire whether this presumes on the part of the (male) agent a particular level of education, political freedom, and financial independence. (And since women only occasionally appear in Richard Swinburne's narrative on the importance of "man's" free will, it is instructive to note what *they* are doing: as minimally necessary for the act of conception (p. 187), as hapless victims of other men's seductive purposes (p. 192), or as desire-inducing distractors from the monogamous path (p. 158).) Philosophers of religion are not accustomed to reading such "subtext"; one implication of an engagement with feminist philosophy would be to raise such gendered material to consciousness.

Furthermore, feminist philosophers of both Anglo-American and continental background have entered into revealing (and critical) debate with Sigmund Freud and his various intellectual descendants. In so doing they have inquired about the childhood development of "autonomous" behavior and its relation to maternal dependence. If this development is in some sense gender-specific (involving a more fundamental repudiation of the mother in the case of male children), then intriguing questions are raised about how philosophical notions of free will relate to this basic familial context, and whether they, too, are covertly "male." In the work of French feminism (strongly influenced by Jacques Lacan) a more radical suggestion is proposed: that even the child's entry into the linguistic realm constitutes a repression of a primal "feminine" creativity associated with the maternal identification of the breast-feeding phase (so Julia Kristeva). This may seem far removed from analytic philosophy of religion's concern with the free will defense: yet a confluence of these debates could have considerable import. If it could be argued that an incompatibilist vision of freedom is unconsciously motivated by rejection of the mother (and everything she symbolizes: dependency, relationship, affectivity, bodiliness, emergent sexuality), then it is hardly surprising that it can also be resistant, in a theological context, to a notion of God as matrix – as sustaining conditioner of all that we are and do (even of acts of compatibilist freedom). As Swinburne puts it in a related context (1991, p. 212), he would want to avoid a circumstance in which "God would be too close for [men] to work things out for themselves." It is left, then, to the staider defenders of Thomas Aquinas and John Calvin to propose a determinism less repudiating of God's "closeness."

The concept of God and feminist critique

It is not so surprising, then, to note in analytic philosophy of religion a striking tendency to image God as a magnified version of the *human* "unmoved mover" (Roderick M. Chisholm) of incompatibilist freedom, an "individual" of unrivaled power and autonomy who takes on the traditional attributes of classical theism, but more revealingly mirrors a (masculinist) vision of self specific to the Enlightenment. Such a predilection becomes evident when – according to some exponents – the traditional attributes (e.g., OMNISCIENCE, see Article 29) have to be modified to accommodate the indeterminism of this privileged vision of human freedom (see Article 37, FOREKNOWLEDGE AND HUMAN FREEDOM); or the alternative view of divine–human relations (some form of determinism) is castigated as mere "puppetry" or "ventriloquism." To a feminist analysis, the dominance of such images of negative control in this debate bespeak a more fundamental failure to conceive of divine–human relations in anything other than competitive terms (where one "individual" either repressively dominates the other or else withdraws to make space for the other's autonomy). What is palpably missing is a sustained or positive reflection on the nurturing and all-encompassing dimensions of divine love – gendered metaphors that have well-known instantiations in the history of Christian theology and spirituality (e.g., Anselm, Julian of Norwich), but do not characteristically leap to the forefront of the analytic philosopher's imagination. In one striking recent counter-instance to this rule, Eleonore Stump (1994) can speak of a solution to the problem of evil in terms of the recognition of the "*mothering* guidance of God" (p. 242) superseding the ostensibly overwhelming presence of evil in the world. That Stump can come to this conclusion without any hint of acknowledgement of feminist influence is, however, itself remarkable.

Other signs of "masculinist" visions of God in analytic philosophy of religion cracking under their own weight may be detected in recent discussions of TRINITY (see Article 66) and INCARNATION (see Article 67). The lack of integration between analytic work on the arguments for the existence of God and more recent defenses of trinitarianism (on rational, not revelatory, grounds) witnesses to this. In the discussion about the arguments, little or nothing is said about the relational and internally complex nature of the Christian God; on the contrary, a great deal of play is made of the principle of simplicity (see again Swinburne 1991). That the divine "individual" established as existent by these arguments is then joined by two other "Gods" (so Swinburne, in more recent work) suggests a covert identification of the former with the "Father" (once again a decidedly non-Thomistic maneuver), and creates strain in dealing with the application of the simplicity principle. A feminist analysis of these developments would point to the failure to write divine *relationship* into the initial case for God's existence. Instead, a whiff of anti-trinitarian deism still tends to hang over the discussion of the arguments, such that the divine monad so established then needs to mount a new foray to the created world (according to one version of the Incarnation) in order to reestablish contact with the human family at all. Is this once more (in subtext) the disassociated "Father" of post-Enlightenment individualism? It is revealing that enormous logical rigor has been applied by analytic philosophers of religion of late to decrying the possibility of a contemporary philosophical defense of Western, "Augustinian" trinitarianism (where priority is given to the unity-in-relationship of the divine triad). The Eastern, "Cappadocian" approach is preferred on account of its (purported) maintenance of "individual" identity for the "persons" and thus its greater coherence. In this, analytic philosophy of religion again displays a predilection for a certain vision of the self spawned long after the fourth century; and in general it reveals a "masculinist" lack of imagination to conceive of inner-trinitarian loving exchange in anything other than extrinsic or contractual terms. There is a notable failure in developing models of *trans*-"individual" identity. None the less, that "relationships" of (divine) "equals" are now on the agenda at all marks a minor advance in the discourse toward feminist ethical and theological concerns.

The "masculinism" that infects discussions of the Incarnation in recent philosophy of religion is more subtly pervasive. It is once again the way that a particular *relationship* is construed that is significant here, in this case the vital "hypostatic" unity of the divinity and humanity of Christ. The favored model for their interaction (tellingly, since the force of the unconscious is so rarely acknowledged in analytic philosophy of religion) is the power of the unconscious over the conscious, as in the Freudian "divided mind." However, this is not a signal that a full range of Freudian themes on sexuality and the unconscious is now entering into discussion (something that feminists would welcome, if not uncritically). On the contrary, one point of the analogy is to demonstrate how one may *maintain* a libertarian view of human freedom in Christ whilst simultaneously promoting a vision of total divine *control* – as if Christ had constraining electrodes implanted in his skull to prevent possible lapses from sinlessness (so Thomas V. Morris, utilizing a thought experiment of Harry Frankfurt). Encoded here is a strange combination of semi-recognition of the potential importance of Freud for philosophical reflection on the divine and the human – the free and the un-free – and a stolid refusal to see in the narrative of Christ's life and death any *upsetting* of stereotypical (gendered) ideas about "power" and "weakness," "control" and "loss of control."

Again, a feminist analysis of these Christological debates can reveal how certain favored (masculinist) "intuition pumps" restricted the range of theological options from the outset (see Coakley 1996).

Feminism and religious epistemology

Arguably the most creative area of development in recent philosophy of religion has been that of epistemology, especially in its relation to "religious experience" (see Article 47, RELIGIOUS EXPERIENCE; and Article 49, REFORMED EPISTEMOLOGY). But the last decade has also seen the emergence of sophisticated work in feminist epistemology (see, e.g., Code 1992, and the essays in Alcoff and Potter 1993) – a development wholly ignored in the debates of analytic philosophy of religion, despite the shared impact on both fields of the collapse of "classical foundationalism." Feminist epistemologists of different schools and philosophical persuasions have presented a range of alternatives, all of them stressing the political, racial, and gendered specificity of the privileged "knower" in mainstream epistemology. To ask "*who* knows" may, first, be the demand to *extend* an empiricist epistemology to include "knowers" previously excluded; as such, this option represents an advance in empirical "objectivity," not its demise. Alternatively, and second, it may involve a turn to "standpoint epistemology," stressing the socially constructed nature of the knowing subject and its partiality of vision (though not necessarily succumbing in all respect to postmodern relativism). Third, and rather differently, as in certain forms of French feminism, it may appeal to an *intrinsically* gendered form of "knowing" that is subversive of "male" rationality *tout court*.

If any of these feminist approaches were to be brought into critical play with analytic philosophy of religion's recent discussions of "religious experience," some interesting insights and new avenues of reflection might emerge. In the first place, it could be suggested that the current intensity of philosophical discussion in this area represents (albeit unconsciously) a heroic attempt to give *cognitive* and *justificatory* significance to an area which has traditionally been sidelined as "private" and "subjective," associated with intensified affectivity and expression in sexual metaphor, and in which women have "starred" as sites of divine intimacy. As such, the argument from religious experience represents a kind of "subjective" surd in the "cumulative case" for theism (see Swinburne 1991, ch. 13), and needs the crucial appeals to "testimony" and "credulity" to give it public cogency. A feminist critic might therefore ask whether this interest in "experiential" intimacy with God is not an intrinsically gendered matter – a move by masculinist philosophy of religion to appropriate the "feminine" power of "mystical" insight and simultaneously to adjust its form to meet the standards of an already-assumed rationality. (Teresa of Avila is the centerpiece of many recent philosophical analyses of "religious experience"; the fact that she was a *woman* mystic confronting male skepticism and disapproval in particular historical and political circumstances is noted by none of them.) Second, the crucial issue of "whose testimony, what credulity?" is a pressing one when once seen through a feminist lens (see Jantzen 1994). If the veracity of appeals to "religious experience" ultimately resides in some primary acceptance of Reidian "credulity," then it is pertinent to ask whether *anyone's* credulity (women's, children's, illiterates'?) will do. Bringing "religious experience" to the bar of rational "justification" may thus appear as the modern counterpart of the male confessor's hold over the medieval female saint's theological status and credibility. In both, the danger is ultimately one of reductive loss: in the case of contemporary philosophy of religion (for all its epistemological finesse) this loss resides in failing to accept the challenge to develop an *expanded* notion of the epistemic subject suggested by the literature of the great "mystics" – one in which affectivity is not subordinated, nor sexual metaphor derided as "smut," nor dark "unknowing" seen as a threat to rationality's stability. The acknowledgement that these latter issues are themselves "gendered" would be the first step in such an advance; the further unraveling of the gendered "standpoints" concealed in the "doxastic practices" (William Alston) of Christian devotion would be another – and very complex – task.

There is much work to be done – both critical and constructive – in feminist philosophy of religion.

Bibliography

Alcoff, L., and Potter, E. (eds): *Feminist Epistemologies* (London: Routledge, 1993).

Coakley, S.: "*Kenōsis* and subversion: On the repression of 'vulnerability' in Christian feminist writing." In *Swallowing a Fishbone? Feminist Theologians Debate Christianity*, ed. D. Hampson (London: SPCK, 1996).

Code, L.: "Feminist epistemology." In *A Companion to Epistemology*, ed. J. Dancy and E. Sosa (Oxford: Blackwell, 1992).

Grimshaw, J.: *Feminist Philosophers: Women's Perspectives on Philosophical Traditions* (London: Harvester Wheatsheaf, 1986).

Jantzen, G. M.: "Feminists, philosophers, and mystics," *Hypatia*, 9 (1994), pp. 186–206.

Lloyd, G.: *The Man of Reason: "Male" and "Female" in Western Philosophy* (Minneapolis: University of Minnesota Press, 1984).

Rooney, P.: "Recent work in feminist discussions of reason," *American Philosophical Quarterly*, 31 (1994), pp. 1–21.

Stump, E.: "The mirror of evil." In *God and the Philosophers*, ed. T. V. Morris (New York: Oxford University Press, 1994).

Swinburne, R.: *The Existence of God*, rev. edn (Oxford: Clarendon Press, 1991).

77

Religious pluralism

JOHN HICK

Until recently the philosophy of religion, as practiced in the West, has meant the philosophy of the Christian religion and has concentrated primarily on the Christian (or the Judeo-Christian) concept of God. However, it is clear that in principle the philosophy of religion has no confessional boundaries and is concerned with religion throughout the world and in its wide variety of forms. Also, during the last decade or so Western philosophers of religion have increasingly felt obliged to take note of the fact that Christianity is only one of the great world faiths and that monotheism is only one of the major types of religion, so that it is now common for new texts on the subject to include a chapter on the problems of religious pluralism. These problems, or areas for research, are of several kinds.

Analysis of religious concepts

There is the philosophical analysis of non-Christian, including non-monotheistic, religious concepts. Some work has been done on Eastern descriptions of unitive mysticism; on Hindu and Buddhist notions of reincarnation, centering on the question of personal identity from life to life; on such Buddhist ideas as *anatta* ("no self"), *sunyata* ("emptiness"); and on a number of other important concepts. But much remains to be done and many other major concepts await attention, both individually and comparatively. Indeed this area of philosophical inquiry has almost unlimited scope for development as Western philosophers of religion take a wider view of their subject and extend their interests to include the Eastern religions (see Article 78, COMPARATIVE PHILOSOPHY OF RELIGION).

The epistemology of religion and conflicting truth-claims

A recent major development in the epistemology of religion has highlighted the problem of the conflicting truth-claims of the different religions. With the widespread consensus that the traditional theistic arguments fail to prove, and that the idea of probability has no useful purchase here – although there are prominent thinkers who resist these conclusions – a different approach to the rationality or otherwise of theistic belief has emerged. This centers upon religious experience as a putative cognition of God. Religious people report a wide range of forms of distinctively religious experience, including mystical experiences of direct awareness of, and even union with, God; a sense of divine presence in moments of worship or of contemplation; an indirect consciousness of God in the feeling of absolute dependence upon a creator, or of a divine presence and activity mediated through the beauties and sublimities of nature, the claims of conscience, the profound significance of human love, the crises of birth and death, and many kinds of personal and historical events. Can such modes of experience count as good grounds for belief in the reality of God?

The older kind of apologetic used religious experience as a phenomenon that points to God as its cause. This is open to the objection that such experiences may have a purely natural origin in the powers of the human imagination. The universe, including human religious experience, thus remains objectively ambiguous. But the new type of apologetic starts at this point. It involves a shift from an external, or third person, use of religious experience to an internal, or first person, use. Instead of asking whether it is rational to infer God from the reported religious experiences of others, it asks whether it is rational for religious experiencers themselves to believe in the reality of God on the basis of their own experience. To take a paradigm case, was it rational for Jesus, continuously conscious of God's presence, so that the heavenly Father was as real to him as his human neighbors, to believe in God's reality? Would it not indeed have been irrational, a kind of cognitive suicide on his part, not so to believe?

At this point the "principle of credulity," or better, the principle of rational credulity, is invoked, according to which it is rational to trust our experience as cognitive of reality except in so far as we have reason to distrust it. We apply this principle in our ordinary experience of our physical environment: we do not need a reason to trust sense experience in general but rather a reason to distrust it on particular occasions. And it is claimed that the same principle should apply, impartially, to religious experience as a form of apparently cognitive experience. Prima facie it is an awareness of a non-physical divine reality; and the critical task is to examine and assess possible overriding considerations.

This approach has been most massively and systematically presented by William Alston (1991). Given the basic principle that religious experience has parity with sense experience as a prima facie ground of rational belief, discussion centers upon reasons to trust one whilst distrusting the other. Such reasons are: first, whereas sense experience is universal and compulsory, religious experience is optional and confined to a limited number of people, so that whilst sensory reports can in principle be confirmed by anyone, religious experience reports cannot; and second, whereas sense experience produces a universally agreed description of the physical world, religious experience within the different traditions produces different and often incompatible descriptions of the divine.

The first objection has met with the reply that whereas our basic freedom as persons is not undermined by a compulsory awareness of the natural world, it would be undermined by a compulsory awareness of an unlimitedly valuable reality whose very existence lays a total claim upon us. Thus the difference on which the objection is based is matched by a corresponding difference between the putative objects of sensory and religious experience respectively. Hence it is appropriate for consciousness of God not to be forced upon us, as is our consciousness of the physical world; and it is accordingly possible for many people, as a result of upbringing or of a conscious or unconscious choice, to shut it out.

The second objection, however, is more formidable. Alston claims (as do many other philosophers who adopt the same kind of apologetic) that because it is rational to base beliefs on religious experience, Christian religious experience entitles those who participate in it to hold distinctively Christian beliefs. But it is obvious that by the same principle Islamic religious experience entitles Muslims to hold distinctively Islamic beliefs, Buddhist religious experience entitles Buddhists to hold distinctively Buddhist beliefs, and so on. Alston acknowledges that and regards it as "the most difficult problem for my position" (Alston 1991, p. 255). It is an equally difficult problem for other related positions, such as the claim that the core Christian beliefs require no justification because they are "properly basic."

Alston's response is based upon the traditional assumption that there can be, at most, only one true religion, in the sense of a religion that teaches the truth. This is David Hume's principle that in matters of religion, whatever is different is contrary. From a religious point of view the question now becomes: which is the true religion? Alston argues that since the beliefs of each major world faith are equally well based in religious experience, and there are no neutral grounds on which to choose between them, I must simply rely on my own form of religious experience and presume that the other forms are (wholly or partly) delusory. On analogy with rival ways of construing the world, "the only rational course for me is to sit tight with the [epistemic] practice of which I am master and which serves me so well in guiding my activity in the world. Hence, by parity of reasoning, the rational thing for a practitioner of CP [Christian epistemic practice] to do is to continue to form Christian M-beliefs [beliefs about divine manifestations], and, more generally, to continue to accept, and operate in accordance with, the system of Christian belief" (Alston 1991, p. 274).

The problem raised by this defense does not lie in the advice to "sit tight" in the situation as Alston defines it, but in the way in which he defines the situation. For the Humean assumption that only one of the competing sets of religious beliefs can be true conflicts with Alston's basic principle that religious experience, like sense experience, gives rise (specific "defeaters" apart) to true beliefs. Indeed it reverses this basic principle by making religious experience within one's own tradition the sole exception to the general rule that religious experience gives rise to *false* beliefs! For the only-one-true-religion premise, together with the fact that the experientially based beliefs of the different religions are often incompatible, entails that religious experience can be a valid basis for belief in the case of only one religion at most. In all other cases beliefs based upon religious experience are false in so far as they conflict with the privileged exception of one's own religion. Thus the fact of religious diversity undermines the entire argument that religious experience has prima facie parity with sense experience in producing true beliefs.

609

The relation between religions

I place this area of discussion third because any solution to the problem just noted must be derived from it.

From a naturalistic point of view, according to which religion in all its forms is a delusory projection upon the universe of our human hopes, fears, and ideals, the truth-claims of the different religions are all false, and the fact that they conflict with one another does not present any problem. However, from a religious point of view, according to which religious experience is not purely human projection but, whilst obviously involving imaginative projection, is at the same time a cognitive response to a transcendent reality, the problem is acute.

A variety of religious, as distinguished from naturalistic, interpretations of religion have been offered, each of which would solve the conflicting truth-claims problem in its own way.

Truth-claims exclusivism

The most widely, if usually implicitly, held view is that there can only be one true religion, and that this is one's own. The others are false, at least in so far as their beliefs are incompatible with those taught by one's own. This is what most of the adherents of each religion, including some but not all of its reflective thinkers, have generally assumed.

However, a "hermeneutic of suspicion" is provoked by the evident fact that in perhaps 99 percent of cases the religion to which one adheres (or against which one reacts) is selected by the accident of birth. Someone born to devout Muslim parents in Iran or Indonesia is very likely to be a Muslim; someone born to devout Buddhist parents in Thailand or Sri Lanka is very likely to be a Buddhist; someone born to devout Christian parents in Italy or Mexico is very likely to be a Catholic Christian; and so on. Thus there is a certain non-rational arbitrariness in the claim that the particular tradition within which one happens to have been born is the one and only true religion. And if the conviction is added that salvation and eternal life depend upon accepting the truths of one's own religion, it may well seem unfair that this saving truth is known only to one group, into which only a minority of the human race have had the good fortune to be born.

This thought has been countered by some Christian philosophers by an appeal to middle knowledge – God's knowledge of what everyone *would* do in all possible circumstances – proposing that God knows of every individual who, because of the circumstances of his or her birth, has not had an opportunity to respond to the Christian gospel, that they *would* have freely rejected it if they had heard it. This suggestion, which could of course be deployed from within each religion, involves an idea that is theologically objectionable to many, namely that God has created vast numbers of people whom God knows will forfeit salvation. There is, however, among contemporary Christian thinkers a strong inclusivist trend which separates knowing the truth from receiving salvation, and holds that some (or all) of those who do not in this life come to know the truth may nevertheless, by divine grace, either be counted now as "anonymous Christians" or may receive Christian salvation in or beyond death. The question here is whether there is not still an arbitrary privileging of one's own religion as the sole channel of salvation.

There are, however, other religious interpretations of religion which do not presuppose that there can only be one religion that knows the truth and is a locus of salvation. These are broadly described as pluralistic.

The transcendent unity of religions

Proponents of the "perennial philosophy" such as Frithjof Schuon (1975), Rene Guenon, Ananda Coomaraswamy, Seyyed Hossein Nasr, and Huston Smith distinguish between the esoteric religion of the mystics and the exoteric religions of the mass of believers. The former is, in its innermost core, identical across the different religions, whereas the latter, consisting of culturally conditioned concepts, doctrines, imagery, lifestyle, and spiritual practices, differ and are indeed at many points mutually incompatible. Each exoteric tradition (historical Christianity, Islam, Hinduism, Buddhism, etc.) should accordingly maintain its own unique individuality, because each is a valid expression of the ultimate reality that is directly known by the mystics in an experience that constitutes the transcendent unity of religion. Mysticism is here seen as the core of religion. A question for this approach is whether it can avoid, as some of its proponents wish to do, a relativizing of the different religious belief-systems and ways of life.

Considerable discussion has centered upon the question whether unitive mysticism constitutes (as is claimed for it) a direct and unmediated awareness of the ultimate divine reality, or whether even this experience is conditioned by the thought-forms of the mystic's tradition (see Katz 1978). For whilst some unitive mystics report union with a divine Person, others report union with a non-personal reality. Are these differences to be attributed to varying theological interpretations of a common ineffable experience, or are the reports to be accepted as accounts of genuinely different experiences? Or should we hold that a pre-conscious interpretative activity enters into the formation of the conscious experience, so that it may be true both that mystics of different traditions are encountering the same reality and yet also that their actual conscious experiences are characteristically different? This latter possibility is developed in the theory next to be discussed.

The Kantian-type "pluralistic hypothesis"

This (Hick 1989, and elsewhere) is based upon a Kantian-type distinction between the Real (or the Divine or the Ultimate) in itself and the Real as variously humanly conceived and experienced. The modern consensus that the perceiver always contributes to the form in which the environment is perceived was most influentially introduced into philosophy by Immanuel Kant, but has been reinforced by work in cognitive psychology, in the sociology of knowledge, and also in quantum physics. It is now a commonplace that we do not perceive the physical world as it is in itself, unobserved, but always and necessarily as it appears to beings with our particular sensory equipment and conceptual resources.

Kant sought to identify the concepts in terms of which we order and give meaning to our experience in the activity of bringing it to consciousness. We can apply the same method to religious experience. The pluralistic hypothesis is that the Real (to select this term from several equally available ones) in itself is present to us, or impinges upon us, all the time and that when this impingement comes to consciousness it takes the form of what we call religious experience. Such experience is, however, very diverse, depending upon the set of religious concepts in terms of which it is constructed. The two basic concepts are deity, or the Real as personal, and the absolute, or the Real as non-personal, the former issuing in the theistic and the latter in the non-theistic forms of religion. We are not, however, aware of deity in general or of the absolute in general. These concepts are (in Kantian language) schematized or made more concrete, not, however, as in Kant's system, in terms of abstract time but in terms of the filled time of history and culture. Thus human beings are specifically aware of the Yahweh who chose and specially treasures the children of Israel; or of the Vishnu or the Siva worshiped within the Hindu traditions; or of the Holy Trinity of Christian devotion; or of the God whose angel revealed to the prophet Muhammad the words of the Qur'an; and so on. These, and the many other God figures, are *personae* of the Real, each jointly formed by its universal presence to humanity and by the particular conceptualities and spiritual practices of the different religious traditions. Again, the non-personal Brahman, Dao, Dharmakaya, Nirvana, Sunyata, are *impersonae* of the Real, formed similarly but by means of very different concepts. A Thomistic principle states that things known are in the knower according to the mode of the knower, and in the case of religion the mode of the knower differs from tradition to tradition.

On this hypothesis the nature of the Real in itself is beyond the range of our (other than purely formal) human concepts. It is in Western terms ineffable, or in Eastern terms formless. In Kantian language, the noumenal Real is humanly experienced as a range of divine phenomena.

The criterion by which religions are judged to be authentic or inauthentic, for this hypothesis, arises within a circular argument which is entered through the acceptance of the religious experience of one's own tradition as not purely imaginative projection but at the same time a cognitive response to a transcendent reality; and through the extension of this principle to other religions whose moral and spiritual fruits seem to be more or less on a par with those of one's own. These fruits thus provide a common criterion by which to recognize the salvific transformation of human existence from natural self-centeredness to a new orientation centered in the Real, a transformation which takes different concrete forms within different religious cultures.

This Kantian-type hypothesis addresses the problem of the conflicting truth-claims of the different religions by the proposal that they do not in fact conflict because they are claims about different manifestations of the Real to different human faith communities, each operating with its own conceptuality, spiritual practices, form of life, treasury of myths and stories, and historical memories. One of the main critical questions about this hypothesis is whether, in reducing the distinctive belief-systems of the different religions from absolute truths to reports of one human perception amongst others of the divine reality, it does not contradict the cherished self-understanding of each. Is it not inherently revisionary rather than purely descriptive?

Other pluralistic theories

Ninian Smart (in Kellenberger 1993, and elsewhere) and Keith Ward (1994, and elsewhere) stress the idea of the complementarity of the world religions. Ward, rejecting the Kantian-type distinction between the Ultimate in itself and the Ultimate as humanly thought and experienced, speaks of "a Supreme Reality which wills all to be consciously related to it" (1994, p. 340), complementary aspects of this Reality being revealed within the different world religions. Thus, for example, "the Semitic and Indian traditions are complementary, emphasizing the active and unchanging poles respectively of the Supreme Spiritual Reality to which they both seek to relate" (p. 331). And through their friendly interactions, each seeking to learn from the others, a "convergent spirituality" may emerge in ways which cannot be known in advance. The question here is whether in the end the conflicting-truth-claims problem has been addressed.

To some (e.g. John Cobb in Kellenberger 1993 and elsewhere) it seems more realistic to recognize a plurality of ultimates, including at least the personal God affirmed by monotheistic religion and the ever-changing interdependent process of the universe (*pratitya-samutpada*) affirmed by Buddhism. Here the critical questions concern the relationship between the different ultimates.

There is already a considerable literature discussing these and the other theories currently in the field (offered, e.g., by such philosophers as David Basinger, William Craig, Paul Griffiths, James Kellenberger, David Krieger, Robert McKim, Sarvepalli Radhakrishnan, Joseph Runzo, etc.; and also by a large number of Christian theologians, most of whom seek to defend in various ways the unique centrality of their own tradition). Each theory brings with it its own problems, and the entire subject is ripe for new approaches and new proposals.

The whole subject of the relation between the religions is so obviously a major problem within the philosophy of religion, and presents so obvious a challenge to a dominant contemporary form of confessional religious apologetic, that it seems inevitable that it will be increasingly widely discussed in the coming decades.

Bibliography

Alston, W.: *Perceiving God* (Ithaca and London: Cornell University Press, 1991).

Christian, W.: *Doctrines of Religious Communities: A Philosophical Study* (New Haven and London: Yale University Press, 1987).

Hick, J.: *An Interpretation of Religion* (London: Macmillan; New Haven: Yale University Press, 1989).

613

Katz, S. (ed.): *Mysticism and Philosophical Analysis* (New York: Oxford University Press; London: Sheldon Press, 1978).

Kellenberger, J. (ed.): *Inter-Religious Models and Criteria* (London: Macmillan; New York: St Martin's Press, 1993). [Contains a variety of viewpoints.]

Schuon, F.: *The Transcendent Unity of Religions* (Paris, 1948) (New York and London: Harper & Row, 1975).

Smith, W. C.: *The Meaning and End of Religion* (New York, 1962) (Minneapolis: Fortress Press, 1991). [Deconstructs the modern Western concept of "a religion."]

Vroom, H. (ed.): *Religions and the Truth: Philosophical Reflections and Perspectives* (Amsterdam: Rodopi; Grand Rapids: Eerdmans, 1989).

Ward, K.: *Religion and Revelation* (Oxford: Clarendon Press, 1994).

78

Comparative philosophy of religion

PAUL J. GRIFFITHS

This article will explore possible understandings of the activity mentioned in its title, and will discuss some examples of it. How comparative philosophy of religion is understood depends in significant measure upon how philosophy of religion is understood, and this is not an uncontroversial question. Some historical remarks are essential, since some of the difficulties in seeing what is denoted by "philosophy of religion" and its derivative "comparative philosophy of religion" are rooted in historical developments specific to Europe since the seventeenth century.

The idea that there is such a thing as philosophy of religion depends in large part upon the idea that there is something called religion which it is reasonable to have a philosophy of; or upon the idea that the phenomenon of religion brings with it, or has involved in it, some philosophical problems. The first way of thinking construes the phrase "philosophy of religion" as containing an objective genitive: it understands religion (or the idea of religion) as the proper object of the philosophy done by philosophers of religion, much as law (or the idea of law) tends to be understood as the proper object of the philosophy done by philosophers of law. The second way of thinking construes the phrase differently, as containing a subjective genitive and therefore as suggesting that the proper scope of the philosophy of religion is those questions that arise out of religion as such, or out of some particular religion. On this construal, "philosophy of religion" indicates the philosophical questions or the philosophical activity that belongs to religion, or to some specific religion. On the first construal a typical question might be: what is the nature of religion? Or: is there only one religion or are there many? Or: are there modes of understanding or judgment peculiar to religion? On the second construal a typical question might be: can one coherently assert both that there are no enduring selves, and that all human persons have had many lives and will have many more? (a question that belongs to or arises out of the Buddhist religion.) Or: does it follow from the existence of abstract objects that God exists? (a question that belongs to or arises out of some theistic religion or other, or out of theistic religion generally).

Both these construals depend upon the assumption that there is something called religion; they mostly also assume that religion is a genus of which there are species: that there is, let us say, the Buddhist religion, the Christian religion, and so forth. On the first construal of philosophy of religion philosophers will focus upon the genus: they will ask about the nature of religion, about the relations that obtain among the phenomena that constitute it, and about the ways in which

615

particular species are related to the genus. On the second construal they will focus upon species-specific questions of the kind mentioned. Both approaches have been widely evident among European and American philosophers since the sixteenth century, though the first is not clearly seen before that time, and the second is not commonly denoted by the phrase "philosophy of religion" until the nineteenth century (though it has of course been practiced by philosophically inclined members of all religious traditions).

The new development in European thought that made it possible to do philosophy of religion in the first sense, and to rename philosophical discussion of questions specific to Judaism or Christianity or Islam "philosophy of religion" (as distinct from "philosophical theology" or "fundamental theology" or some such label), is then precisely the idea that there is a genus religion that has species or particular instantiations. This idea is evident already in thinkers such as Nicholas of Cusa (1401–64) and Lord Herbert of Cherbury (1583–1648), but it becomes a central theme and a standard assumption in the work on religion done by Baruch Spinoza, John Locke, and Gottfried Leibniz in the seventeenth century, and is the very organizing principle of David Hume's writing on religion, and of Immanuel Kant's and G. W. F. Hegel's lectures on the philosophy of religion (Kant usually calls the discipline *philosophische Religionslehre*, and Hegel *Philosophie der Religion*). But this is a new idea. It is not found among Christian thinkers in late antiquity or in medieval Europe, for whom *religio* meant usually the set of institutional arrangements, beliefs, and practices that made possible proper commerce with God, and not a genus of which there are species (Augustine's treatment of the term in his *On True Religion* is typical). Only when this new idea is in play does it begin to make sense to think of philosophy of religion as a discipline distinct from (what Christians call) philosophical theology.

Philosophy of religion as taught in departments of philosophy or religion in anglophone universities today bears the marks of this history (for more see Collins 1967, and Article 13, THE EMERGENCE OF MODERN PHILOSOPHY OF RELIGION). Most of it treats questions that arise out of or are specific to particular religions (usually Christianity, for obvious reasons), and so falls under the second construal of philosophy of religion. Some, following Kant and Hegel, treats questions belonging to the first construal, among which one of pressing contemporary interest (especially for Christians) is that of how to account for the plurality of religions (see Article 77, RELIGIOUS PLURALISM). Given these facts, what might it mean to think of philosophy of religion as comparative? There are three main strategies here, three kinds of intellectual enterprise that have title of some kind to be called comparative philosophy of religion.

Definition and classification

The first approach is typified by Hegel, but is still practiced in various ways. It assumes that there is a genus called religion which has various species, and its main goal is to provide a philosophical account of what is intrinsic to the genus (hence definition), and of the relations among the species (hence classification). In

616

its ideal-typical form, most closely approached by Hegel in the various versions of his lectures on the philosophy of religion delivered between 1821 and 1831 at the University of Berlin, it begins with an a priori definition of religion (Hegel offers several, calling religion, among others things, "spirit that realizes itself in consciousness" and "the relation of human consciousness to God" (Hegel 1984–8 [1821–31], vol. 1, pp. 178, 150), and then uses that definition as a tool for the organization and classification of information about particular religions (which Hegel usually calls "determinate religions").

The classification arrived at may be hierarchical, as it clearly was in Hegel's case. That is, particular religions may be ordered according to the extent to which they approach the ideal type. For Hegel, the particulars of the ordering changed as he became aware of new facts about specific religions that caused him to place them differently in his hierarchy. So, for example, in the lectures of 1824 Buddhism is classified as an example of the religions of magic (1984–8, vol. 2, pp. 303–16), while in 1827 it is reclassified as a religion of being-within-self (vol. 2, pp. 562–79). The change is largely due to Hegel's having discovered new facts about Buddhism that made it seem reasonable to him to alter its place in his hierarchy. And it is this above all that makes it useful to think of Hegel's work as an instance of comparative philosophy of religion: he is responsive to information about particular religions, even though that information is subject to an independent a priori method of classification. Hegel was in fact well informed about the particulars of the determinate religions, better informed than most of his contemporaries, and much better informed, given the limitations on what could have been known about Asian religions by any European in the first half of the nineteenth century, than most anglophone philosophers of religion at the end of the twentieth century.

A similar approach to the philosophy of religion is apparent in the recent work of the English philosopher John Hick. Here too the genus of religion is defined largely in a priori terms, this time as the "transformation of human existence from self-centeredness to Reality-centeredness" (Hick 1984, p. 194; compare Hick 1989 for a more detailed treatment). And here too information about particular religions, especially those that Hick tends to call "post-axial," which means, roughly, Hinduism, Buddhism, Christianity, Judaism, and Islam (Hick 1989, pp. 21–69), is used to show how and to what extent these religions approximate that which is essential to the genus. Hick's goal is different from Hegel's in that his classification is resolutely anti-hierarchical; he wants to show that all particular religions (or at least all the post-axial ones) exhibit the defining characteristics of the genus to a roughly equal degree, and as a result should be considered roughly on a par with one another. This is an important difference, but it should not obscure the more fundamental similarity between Hegel and Hick, which is that both are engaged in the comparative philosophy of religion using the method of definition and classification, and that both are centrally concerned with the kinds of question that arise for those who think of the phrase "philosophy of religion" as containing an objective genitive.

617

Structural analysis

A second strategy that may reasonably be called comparative philosophy of religion interests itself in analyzing one or more of the phenomena that its practitioners take to belong to the genus religion. Such phenomena might include: doctrine (the claims that religious communities make about what is true and right, claims that they feel required to teach to their members, defend against objections, and the like); ritual (the formalized and repeated corporate practices that religious communities require of their members); and exegesis (the methods that religious communities use to interpret and apply the works they think of as being especially authoritative for them). A comparative philosopher of religion concerned with such phenomena under the rubric of structural analysis will treat not so much the truth or desirability or meaning of particular instances of them (particular doctrines, or rituals, or exegetical activities), as the logical or conceptual structure of the phenomena in question and of their possible uses. And in so doing such a philosopher may (but need not) be comparative. since a philosophical treatment of religious doctrine as such, for instance, will often require attention to particular examples of it that are not drawn solely from any one religious tradition.

An example is to hand in the work of the American philosopher William A. Christian, Sr. He has, in works published during the last three decades or so, been mostly concerned with the philosophical questions arising from a structural analysis of religious doctrine. In his *Oppositions of Religious Doctrines* (1972) Christian treats the conditions of the possibility of deep-going disagreement between different religious doctrines, and does so as an instance of what he calls "critical philosophy of religion," by which he means reflection on the concepts, recommendations, and claims distinctive of religious discourse with an eye to showing what constrains this discourse and what structural possibilities it possesses. Similarly, in his *Doctrines of Religious Communities* (1987), he treats in a formal way the relations that might obtain for religious communities between some claim's being a doctrine of the community, on the one hand, and its being true (in the case of a claim about the setting of human life), or right (in the case of a claim about the rightness of some pattern of action), on the other. In both books Christian uses examples from different religions, mostly Judaism, Buddhism, and Christianity, as his principal tools of thought; he is careful to distance himself from making empirical claims as to just what these communities actually do teach, avoiding this by making his claims in this area hypothetical. A philosopher with more historical interests than Christian might turn these hypotheses into descriptive claims about what particular religious communities actually teach, as Hegel and Hick do. But that they are there at all in Christian's work indicates the importance of the comparative dimension in that work.

It is of course possible to treat religious phenomena in this structural fashion without being explicitly comparative about it. Philosophers with special interests in religious language, for example, have been doing so for decades (e.g. Phillips 1976; Ricoeur 1980, pp. 73–154). However, there is rather little work as yet of a philosophically-interested structurally analytical kind that, like Christian's, is also comparative. It is to be hoped that there will soon be more, because the concepts derived from it can be of great use for those wanting to engage less formal and more substantive questions in the comparative philosophy of religion.

Constructive work

Finally, there is work in comparative philosophy of religion that is explicitly constructive. It may depend, like the other two strategies, on the assumption that there is a genus religion, with species. But if it does, this assumption is unlikely to be central, for the main interests of those doing comparative philosophy of religion constructively are in making a contribution of a normative kind to some question that belongs to or arises out of one or more particular religions. So, for instance, one might be constructively interested in the logic of the cosmological argument for the existence of God, but take as one's interlocutors in developing arguments about this philosophers from different traditions – perhaps medieval Indian Srivaisnavas and North African Sunni Muslims. Or, one might want to explore the question of revelation, of whether it is sensible to claim that a particular work is, or contains, words whose origin is not human and that have an especially authoritative claim upon humans – and one might take as one's interlocutors Mimamsakas and Kabbalists, both of which groups have interesting views about this question.

Again, there are relatively few instances of such work. An interesting recent example is Lee Yearley's work on the virtue of courage, drawing upon Mencius and Thomas Aquinas as his main interlocutors (Yearley 1990). Yearley's work is avowedly both descriptive (he wants to be clear as to what Mencius and Aquinas thought about the virtue of courage) and normative (he wants to say how best to think about this virtue). It is carefully exegetical, making use of its sources in the languages in which they were composed. And it pays attention to the complex of theoretical questions raised by bringing together thinkers from such different cultural and linguistic settings. The series in which Yearley's work appears, begun in 1990, has published a number of other studies of this sort, and promises to continue to do so.

The difficulty of such work means that it may often get bogged down in the theoretical and procedural problems it involves (How is comparison possible? Are there not intractable hermeneutical problems raised for any philosopher dealing with works from very different settings?), and fail to contribute to its constructive agenda. Its promise is that it may feed the imagination in ways impossible for and largely unthinkable to those whose constructive work is either mostly done a priori, or on a solidly monotraditional basis (Yearley 1990, pp. 196–203). Constructive philosophical argument is in significant part a matter of the imagination; and if the imagination of philosophers of religion is fed and nurtured by close engagement with works in the history of their own tradition, there seems every reason to think it will be fertilized still more by such engagement with what philosophers from other traditions have thought about the matters that concern them.

619

Of the three strategies discussed here for doing philosophy of religion comparatively – definition and classification, structural analysis, and constructive work – the second and third are likely to prove the most productive in the future, and to attract the most attention. They depend less than the first strategy on the not-unproblematic intuition that there is a genus religion whose definition is a matter of philosophical concern. And they are more likely to engage matters of philosophical substance, and so to make a constructive contribution to questions of pressing current concern in the philosophy of religion. Just as discussion of matters of philosophical interest to Christians was transformed by the recovery of Aristotle and the engagement with Jewish and Islamic philosophical theology in the twelfth and thirteenth centuries (see Article 10, THE ISLAMIC CONTRIBUTION TO MEDIEVAL PHILOSOPHICAL THEOLOGY; and Article 11, THE JEWISH CONTRIBUTION TO MEDIEVAL PHILOSOPHICAL THEOLOGY), so it might now be by serious engagement with the philosophical arguments produced by Buddhists, Hindus, Confucians, and others. Similar claims, *mutatis mutandis*, might be made about discussion of matters of philosophical interest to Jews or Buddhists. Such transformations are the promise of comparative philosophy of religion.

Bibliography

Augustine: *On True Religion* (ca. 390). In *Augustine: Earlier Writings*, tr. and ed., J. H. S. Burleigh, Library of Christian Classics, vol. 6 (Philadelphia: Westminster Press, 1953).

Christian, W. A., Sr: *Oppositions of Religious Doctrines* (London: Macmillan, 1972).

——: *Doctrines of Religious Communities: A Philosophical Study* (New Haven: Yale University Press, 1987).

Collins, J. D.: *The Emergence of Philosophy of Religion* (New Haven: Yale University Press, 1967).

Hegel, G. W. F.: *Lectures on the Philosophy of Religion* (1821–31), tr. R. F. Brown et al., 3 vols. (Berkeley: University of California Press, 1984–8).

Hick, J.: "Religious pluralism and absolute claims." In *Religious Pluralism*, ed. L. Rouner (Notre Dame: University of Notre Dame Press, 1984), pp. 193–213.

——: *An Interpretation of Religion* (New Haven: Yale University Press, 1989).

Phillips, D. Z.: *Religion without Explanation* (Oxford: Blackwell, 1976).

Ricoeur, P.: *Essays on Biblical Interpretation* (Philadelphia: Fortress Press, 1980).

Yearley, L. H.: *Mencius and Aquinas: Theories of Virtue and Conceptions of Courage*, SUNY Series Toward a Comparative Philosophy of Religion (Albany: State University of New York Press, 1990).

Resources for further study

Readers whose interest in philosophy of religion has been stimulated by this book may wish to know where to go to learn more. In addition to the individual books and articles included in the bibliographies of articles in this volume three general kinds of resources are worth noting.

Journals

Philosophy of religion is represented in virtually all the main philosophy journals (*The Journal of Philosophy*, *American Philosophical Quarterly*, and so on), but it is the specific focus of *International Journal for Philosophy of Religion*, *Religious Studies*, *Faith and Philosophy*, *Philosophy and Theology*, *Sophia*, *The Annual of the Society of Christian Ethics*, *American Catholic Philosophical Quarterly* (formerly called *The New Scholasticism*), and *The Thomist*. Theology journals also contain a considerable amount of philosophy of religion, especially *Journal of the American Academy of Religion*, *The Journal of Religion*, *Theological Studies*, *The Journal of Religious Ethics*, *Modern Theology*, *Theology Today*, *Harvard Theological Review*, and *Scottish Journal of Theology*. Philosophy of religion can also be found in cross-disciplinary journals such as *Law and Religion*, *The Journal of Law and Religion*, *Religion and Literature*, *Journal of Literature and Theology*, and *Christian Scholar's Review*.

Books

Several scholarly presses produce series of books in philosophy of religion. Cornell University Press publishes *Cornell Studies in the Philosophy of Religion*, Indiana University Press publishes *The Indiana Series in the Philosophy of Religion*, Kluwer Academic Publishers publishes *Studies in Philosophy and Religion*, and the State University of New York Press publishes *Toward a Comparative Philosophy of Religion*. University presses such as Oxford, Cambridge, Notre Dame, and Temple regularly publish work in philosophy of religion. Prometheus books produces a substantial number of works in philosophy of religion, most of them highly critical of theism.

Organizations

There are regular sessions about philosophy of religion on the programs of the annual meetings of the three divisions of the American Philosophical Association, as well as on the program of the annual meeting of the American Academy of Religion. Societies interested in the philosophy of religion include: the Society for Philosophy of Religion (in the UK), the Society of Christian Philosophers, the Philosophy of Religion Society, the Society for Philosophy of Religion (in the USA), the American Catholic Philosophical Association, the American Humanist Association, the American Maritain Association, the Fellowship of Religious Humanists, the Jesuit Philosophical Association, the Society for Medieval and Renaissance Philosophy, and the Society for Philosophy and Theology. Addresses for many of these organizations are found in the *Directory of American Philosophers*, a publication of the Philosophy Documentation Center, Bowling Green State University.

Index